The Children's Encyclopedia

VOLUME TEN

Printed in Great Britain by
The Amalgamated Press, Ltd., London

THE CRUSADER OF THE COUNTRYSIDE

JOHN WESLEY, RIDING THROUGH ENGLAND, PREACHES AT A LITTLE VILLAGE GREEN

THE CHILDREN'S ENCYCLOPEDIA

FOUNDED

by

ARTHUR MEE

VOLUME TEN

THE EDUCATIONAL BOOK COMPANY LIMITED
LONDON

CONTENTS OF THIS VOLUME

The Story of Immortal Folk Whose Work Will Never Die

Velasquez

Titian

Murillo

Holbein

Tintoretto

Botticelli

THE LIVES OF THE PAINTERS

THE great painters of Europe belong to all time. Their lives come in and out of the story of Europe graciously and beautifully, like their own pictures, giving us a glimpse of humanity both strange and familiar, of hopes and ideals that are as real today as they were five hundred years ago.

English people feel that they have a peculiar claim on Holbein, one of the earliest of these men of genius. He was born in Augsburg in 1497, the favourite son of his father, who was also a painter and also called Hans. It was an ideal family for a genius to be nourished in, the father and uncle and other members engrossed in art, gladly passing on to the young Hans such gifts as they had.

When Hans was about eighteen he went with his brother Ambrose to Basle, looking for work. Very soon after his arrival he had the good fortune to meet the scholar Erasmus, who asked him to do some pen-and-ink drawings for one of his books. Hans, delighted to have a commission, worked hard at the illustrations, and in his spare time painted anything that came handy. He wandered about a good deal, studying people's faces, with never quite enough to do. His wanderings presently took him over the border into Switzerland, where he had a few commissions and stayed a little time. In 1519 he was back in Basle. He married and settled down to work.

At first there were plenty of commissions, and the years slid by. Then came a season of political and religious unrest, and no one wanted any pictures. After a long talk with his friend Erasmus, Holbein took a bold step. He put his brushes and paints and a few garments into a wallet and in 1526 came to England.

Erasmus had given him an introduction to Sir Thomas More. The painter had come at the right moment into a country apparently destitute of artists. He began painting portraits. " The century of Holbein " began. His success was assured. For three years he painted indefatigably, and then returned to Basle with a picture of Sir Thomas More's family for Erasmus, and enough money in his pocket to buy a house for his wife and family in Basle. Unhappy times came then, the flight of Erasmus, and grave religious trouble.

The next year, after a little work in Basle, Holbein was back in England, to make some more money. There also he found changes of a political sort, and Holbein was glad to find patrons among the merchant goldsmiths in the City. Presently chance brought him, in 1534, in contact with Thomas Cromwell, and

EXPLORERS · INVENTORS · WRITERS · ARTISTS · SCIENTISTS

through his influence Holbein was very soon at Court, painting those wonderful pictures which mark out that generation from any other. He drew portraits of Henry the Eighth and his wives, and also went abroad to execute commissions.

During these journeys he managed to visit Basle again, this time in the splendour of silk and satin clothes. Not many more years were left to this painter, who was not the only great artist, as we shall see, to play the part of King's messenger.

In November 1543 one of the recurrent plagues visited London. Holbein died after a couple of days' illness, a young man in his prime, with his work half done.

The next great figure that crosses the stage of northern Europe is Peter Paul Rubens, a descendant of a long line of Antwerp burghers, who was born at Siegen in Westphalia in June 1577. His father died when Peter was ten. A year later the widow brought her children to Antwerp and settled down there. Peter Paul was sent to school, and before he left was able to speak seven languages fluently.

THE DUKE WHO GAVE THE YOUNG RUBENS HIS CHANCE

This lad of many tongues was gifted with a charming personality. "That amiable Rubens" he remained throughout his life. His mother had intended him to become a lawyer, but Peter Paul managed to make her change her mind.

For eight years he laboured in the workshops of the painters of distinction in his day. Then he got the heart's desire of his youth. One fine morning in May, in the year 1600, this handsome young man rode out of Antwerp bound for Italy. His first stay was at Venice, where he painted hard and studied the work of famous men. It happened that he became friendly with a nobleman of Mantua, who presently invited him to Court. The result was that the Duke of Mantua, who loved art and all beautiful things, recognising Rubens's genius, made him Court painter, and was very good to him, sending him here and there to study. He was sent into Spain with presents for Philip the Third and the Duke of Lerma.

Among the gifts were some pictures painted by Rubens, and a gay carriage with seven Neapolitan horses. Unfortunately, the voyage fell in a period of storm, and the Duke's gifts suffered somewhat from twenty days of ceaseless rain.

Rubens's pictures were almost ruined. The audience with the king was delayed while Peter Paul re-painted them.

For some time Rubens stayed in Spain, working for the Duke of Lerma; then he went back to Mantua for two more years, working feverishly. In 1608 he heard that his dear mother was ill, and he set off immediately to Antwerp. The good widow was no longer alive when her son, now a man of thirty, rode back into the city. Grief at her death made a dark place in Rubens's life for several months. Then he was swept into the deep current of his work again, as painter to the Archduke Albert. About this time he married Isabella Brant, whom he painted so often.

WORDS OF WISDOM ON THE ARCHWAY OF THE HOME OF RUBENS

During the years that followed Rubens built himself a house of which only the garden archways remain. On one of the archways are carved some lines from the Roman satirist Juvenal :

A healthy mind in a healthy body is a thing to be prayed for.

The grand house, something like a Renaissance palace, was really a simple home worked on the most regular system. Rubens rose at five o'clock, winter and summer, went to church, and came back straight to work. One simple meal broke the long labours of the day. Sometimes Peter Paul went for a ride on one of his Spanish horses—his only exercise. His evenings were given up to his friends. Rubens's house became a centre of learning and culture in the Flemish city.

The ten years that passed thus were the fullest and richest of his life. The death of the fair Isabella in 1626 broke the charm his home had for Rubens. After that he was glad to divide his time between painting and travelling.

THE GOOD NAME THAT IS BETTER THAN RUBIES

Some important diplomatic missions sent the painter during the next few years up and down the high roads of Europe, the guest first of one Court and then another. He was knighted by both Philip the Fourth of Spain and Charles the First of England, who were at one in this, that they loved art. The University of Cambridge made him an honorary Master of Arts. But better than all honours heaped on him is the testimony of Lord Dorchester: " Rubens is known among

BOTTICELLI, REMBRANDT, AND RUBENS

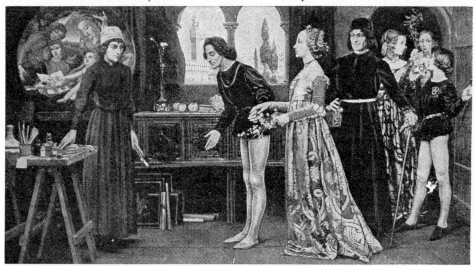

BOTTICELLI RECEIVES VISITORS IN HIS STUDIO—FROM THE PAINTING BY
ELEANOR FORTESCUE-BRICKDALE

AN OLD LADY SITS FOR HER PORTRAIT
BY REMBRANDT

RUBENS'S PORTRAIT OF HIMSELF AND
HIS WIFE ISABELLA

MARIE MEDICI VISITS THE HOUSE OF RUBENS

us as too honourable a man ever to tell an untruth."

In 1630 Rubens married Helena Fourment, and tried to patch up the remnants of his home happiness. Work there was in plenty, and more ambassadorial missions. Rubens now had a large country house as well as a town mansion. To his last years he laboured like a giant, his love for his painting unmarred by the fact that he was now rich enough not to have to do another stroke. His children grew up around him and his old years were happy. He died of heart failure in May 1640.

REMBRANDT'S LIBRARY OF FIFTEEN BOOKS AND AN OLD BIBLE

Rubens, destined throughout his long life to greatness and success, was far removed from humble Rembrandt, whom Europe now delights to honour. This painter's real name was Rembrandt Harmens van Rijn, and he was born in 1606 in Leyden, a town prettily called by one old writer the eye of Holland.

His father was a miller. Rembrandt was sent to school as a preparation for the University, but owing to his dislike for study the idea was abandoned. Rembrandt never became a great scholar, like Rubens. When he was a grown man his library consisted of fifteen books and an old Bible. Whatever else he left unread, Rembrandt loved his old Bible.

The good miller sent his gifted son to various masters, and presently people were declaring that he was ready to set up practice as a portrait painter anywhere. He removed from Leyden to Amsterdam, where he lodged in an art-dealer's house, and met Van Uylenborch, the lawyer, whose daughter Saskia he married.

THE GREAT SORROW THAT CAME INTO THE LIFE OF REMBRANDT

The young portrait painter began very well indeed, with a house of his own and money to spare. It is estimated that he was earning from £5000 to £6000 a year during his early married life. Unfortunately Rembrandt was not a good business man, and although for ten years his success continued almost unbroken, his affairs soon became very disordered. Also he had a passion for buying beautiful things. His house became a small museum.

Eight years after his marriage Saskia was dead, leaving one boy, Titus, a delicate lad, who did not live to reach maturity. After his sad loss Rembrandt's home life broke up miserably. Titus, the child of his golden years, retained his father's love, but the artist's affairs went from bad to worse, ending in 1656 in bankruptcy. His grand house was sold; he was very glad to make a home in a humbler place.

Rembrandt never ceased working, but his art became unfashionable. Prices sank and sank. A mass of troubles fastened themselves like hornets on the artist.

In all these changes his industry never ceased. How much labour he got through it is difficult to say, but of his preserved works we can count about 650 oil paintings, 2000 drawings and studies, and 300 etchings. It is very sad to think that when this man of industry died in 1669 he was what we should term an undischarged bankrupt, with no personal property save his clothes and his painting materials.

Rembrandt was always a humble, quiet, home-loving man, happier with his inferiors than those of higher station. His life is singularly like one of his pictures, with a little golden light backed up by masses of impenetrable shadow.

It seems like coming from a place of storm into the sunlight to think of artists of the south, like Botticelli, Titian, or Tintoretto.

THE NICKNAME BY WHICH A GREAT PAINTER IS KNOWN TO THE WORLD

Botticelli, the earliest of these three great ones, was known by an interesting nickname. His father, a Florentine tanner, was called Alessandro di Mariano dei Filipepi. He had four sons, of whom Sandro, born in 1444, was the youngest. The eldest, Giovanni, became a leather merchant. Outside his shop hung a little barrel, a botticello, the sign of his trade; he was also rather round in figure. From one association or another he came to be known as Il Botticello, and when the younger man rose to eminence he was at once labelled Sandro Botticelli.

Sandro was a delicate, nervous, dreamy lad; he hated his sums and his books, was restless, unhappy. The tanner took him from school and apprenticed him to a goldsmith. But even then he was not content. A chronicler of Italian painters, Vasari, says, "The boy was enamoured of painting, and opened his heart freely to his father who, seeing the force of his inclination, took him to Fra Filippo, a most excellent painter, in order that Sandro might learn from him."

THREE OF THE WORLD'S CHIEF PAINTERS

THE YOUNG MURILLO PAINTING CHILDREN IN
THE MARKET-PLACE OF SEVILLE

SIR THOMAS MORE TAKES THE GREAT ARTIST
HOLBEIN TO HIS HOME IN CHELSEA

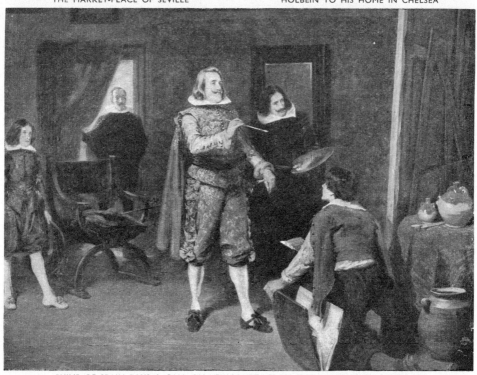

PHILIP OF SPAIN PAYS A CALL ON VELASQUEZ—FROM THE PAINTING BY FRED ROE

The apprenticeship took place when the boy was about sixteen. For several years he worked for the Friar, who loved him dearly. In due course he opened a workshop of his own, and became one of the foremost painters of Florence. He still lived in his father's house. There is something patriarchal in the glimpse we get of the family about 1480. The old tanner, aged 86, is head of a household of twenty souls, the three sons and their children, and Sandro, who "works in the house when he chooses."

HOW BOTTICELLI WAS INFLUENCED BY THE PREACHING OF SAVONAROLA

In 1481 Botticelli's fame had reached Rome, and he was summoned by the Pope to do some work there. For two years the artist stayed in Rome, painting his famous pictures, and the Pope paid him liberally. But Sandro was of a careless, happy-go-lucky disposition, very generous with his friends, and he did not bring much of the Pope's money back to Florence. He stands out in the picture made by the letters and records of his intimate friends as a gentle soul, full of stray sympathies, fond of children, with a boundless enthusiasm for great ideals.

In 1489 a change came over Botticelli. He fell under the influence of Savonarola, the great preacher, whose eloquence shook gay, self-seeking Florence to her foundations. He turned his whole thoughts to religion, meditated more, prayed more.

The next milestone in the painter's life was the death, in 1491, of Lorenzo the Magnificent, who had been friend as well as patron. His son Piero was an unworthy successor; Sandro was glad to have nothing to do with him.

As the painter neared old age sadder years seemed to follow each other. Savonarola's terrible death made a bitter impression on his soul, and religious subjects were more engrossing to him than ever. People gathered in his studio to talk about theology and Savonarola.

THE GENIUS WHO REACHED HIS PRIME AS BOTTICELLI PASSED AWAY

Sandro was now a most important painter, looked up to by all, from his friend Leonardo da Vinci to his favourite pupil Filippino Lippi. Towards the end he became infirm, unable to stand without crutches, a mere shadow of his former self. The death that came in May, 1510, was a release to his gentle spirit, which had never ceased to respond to the beautiful and good impulses of life.

While Florence was mourning Botticelli a man was nearing his prime whose name and fame have since gone to the ends of the earth. This was Tiziano Vecelli, generally known as Titian. He was born about 1477, at Cadore, in the Venetian Alps. When he was only ten years old he left his mountain home to stay with an uncle and learn a trade in Venice. Fortunately for the world the trade chosen was painting.

Titian studied with Gentile and Giovanni Bellini, and with Giorgione. Little is known of him until he suddenly emerges, a master, painting frescoes, and it appears that his fame had already spread over Italy. The death of Giorgione in 1511 left Titian without a rival; the world was at his feet.

It is a pity that the records of Titian's family life should be so scanty. We know that he married a fair girl called Cecilia, and that he had two sons and one daughter. Most of his biographers have been so busy explaining Titian's greatness in art that they have forgotten the little human touches that change a genius into a man. Cecilia died in 1530. To console himself the artist took to travelling.

THE OLD ARTIST WHO HAD NO RIVAL IN ALL ITALY

Presently he was back at Venice, and he began that life, more like that of a prince than a painter, which was natural to one of his temperament. He had a grand house and combined a happy way of living with extreme industry, and appeared to condescend when he took pupils. He could afford to be proud and lofty; he was without a rival; he knew that there was in Italy no prince, or pope, or beautiful woman who did not long to be painted by him.

At sixty Titian was still working, hale, hearty. Life appeared unending for this man favoured of destiny. He went here and there, to Rome at the carefully worded request of the Pope ; and then, at the invitation of the Emperor Charles, he crossed the winter alps to Augsburg to paint some pictures. This journey was made when he was seventy. More honours were heaped on him. He returned to Venice a Count of the Empire. Generations seemed to pass him by. At 88 he was still painting. When at last he laid down his brush it seemed that he might still take it up again. Kings and princes came to visit him; he was Italy's darling. When 99 he died of the plague in Venice; and although a law had been passed to bury plague victims outside the city, a special exception was made in his case. Plague or no plague, even in those terrible hours of anxiety, the city on the sea paid the final tribute to its greatest genius. He was buried with public honours in the church of Santa Maria dei Frari.

Titian it was who introduced to art the famous son of a dyer remembered today as Tintoretto, of whom we read on page 935. We may go on now to read of an immortal Spaniard who came into the world 21 years after Titian left it, a man who was destined to carry the honours of art from Italy to Spain. This was Diego Rodriguez de Silva y Velasquez. He stands apart in the story of European painters, seeming to be free from the artistic rivalries that marred so many lives.

RUBENS'S PORTRAIT OF HIMSELF, IN THE UFFIZI GALLERY FLORENCE

REMBRANDT'S PORTRAIT OF HIMSELF, IN BUCKINGHAM PALACE, LONDON

Velasquez was born in Seville in 1599. He was the child of gentle, cultured people, and neither poverty nor opposition touched his youth. When he was a small boy he announced that he wanted to become a painter; a painter he became. He studied with Herrera and then Pacheco. The five long years spent in the house of Pacheco were very happy.

Velasquez looked back on the peace of those years when he became a powerful presence in the Spanish Court. He married his master's daughter Juana, and but for ambition would have been content to stay in Seville painting, reading, enjoying life in that cultured household. But ambition sent him presently to Madrid with an important picture that is now world-famous, the Water-Seller.

Philip the Fourth had an eye for genius in art and letters. Velasquez was made Court painter, and began that series of the portraits of Philip and his family which have given the world an amazing insight into the character and home of one of the great princes of Europe.

In the summer of 1629 the painter set off on his travels to Italy, and there refreshed himself greatly with the study of other people's work. Four years later he was back in Madrid, more of a favourite with the king than ever. Velasquez settled down to a life that was a mixture of artist and confidant. He saw the king every day, and became his friend.

THE EAGLE IN THE HIGH PLACES AND THE ANGEL IN THE SHADOWS

The years were broken by other journeys to Italy. As the seasons fled it seemed to the painter himself that Velasquez was less and less an artist and more and more a courtier. He could seldom spend an hour alone in his studio. Such was the fate of a man selected to be the favourite of an egotistical and most powerful king. His duties were more arduous than one would think, his health was not good. He died in 1660, at 61.

Murillo and Velasquez follow each other across the stage of Spanish art, contemporaries and yet as divided as the poles. Velasquez has often been called the eagle in art, dwelling in lofty places, Murillo the angel in art, hovering in quiet shadows among little children.

Murillo's real name was Bartolomé Esteban. He was born in Seville on the last day of the year 1617. His parents were humble workpeople and lived in the Jewish quarter. Among these mean, narrow streets, where awnings kept out the fierce glare of the sun, Murillo played and worked till he was ten.

That year a swift and terrible plague carried away both his parents. From these scenes of sordidness and poverty the lad was rescued by an uncle, a doctor who lived in a better part of Seville. The uncle was kind, but poor himself, and could not afford to give the lad a decent education.

THE EARLY YEARS OF STRUGGLE OF A GENIUS IN SPAIN

Murillo had already shown his bent in making drawings on whatever material came handy, and to his intense delight the uncle found him a place in a second-rate artist's studio. The boy had to grind and mix paints, stretch canvases, and act as general odd-job boy in the studio. In his spare hours he drew, and drew incessantly. Here Murillo stayed till he was 23.

Then a change came. His master left Seville and Murillo remained there, facing the uncertain problem of making a living and supporting his younger sister. Murillo had no money, no friends, no influence. There were many days when the two had not enough to eat.

Murillo did everything he could to make a living, painting gay, impressionistic pictures on squares of loosely-woven material called saga-cloth, and selling them himself in the weekly market in the Macarena, the slum district of Seville. He always took his materials with him, and sometimes he would paint one of these pictures while his customer wandered about the fair or dozed in the shade. Here the artist studied to his heart's content the happy, care-free children he painted so beautifully later on.

After a while Murillo was seized by a great desire to see the work of the artists of Europe. He painted a great number of pictures on squares of saga-cloth, and sold them to a man who was going to South America. Then, first taking care that his sister was left in good hands, Murillo took his money, and in 1641 went to Madrid and found Velasquez.

THE HELPING HAND VELASQUEZ GAVE TO HIS FRIEND MURILLO

The great Court painter did not mind associating with a black-haired, shabby-looking tramp. He gave him a room in his own house and arranged for him to see the work of great painters in the Madrid galleries. Three years Murillo spent in Madrid, copying, studying. Then he returned to Seville, and suddenly, miraculously his fortune was made.

He became a favourite, and could not paint pictures fast enough. In 1648 he married a beautiful and highborn lady, and the poor boy of the slums became the head of a grand house. From strength to strength the painter went, gaining more and more favour in the eyes of his generation.

In 1660 Murillo founded the Academy of Seville. The seasons were filled with happy, ceaseless work. Twenty years later he fell from a scaffolding while painting a picture in a church in Cadiz, was brought home to Seville, and died there in April, 1682. He shares with Velasquez the love of the Spanish people and the admiration of the whole world.

The Great Stories of the World That Will Be Told for Ever

THE ENCHANTED KETTLE

MANY think that there is something supernatural about foxes, cats, and badgers. But while foxes and cats are often evil spirits in disguise, badgers are only possessed by Puck-like spirits who love practical jokes.

Often a traveller has been startled at hearing a noise of drums in the wood, and has come upon a badger, standing on his hind-legs and playing a tattoo on himself. The poor man runs away, and hears the badger laughing.

Once upon a time there was a priest who had an old kettle which had made him many fragrant cups of tea. A day came, however, when the head, legs, and tail of a badger sprang from its sides, and it leaped off the fire. Round and round it ran, and then began to fly about the room. At last it settled on the floor, and the badger parts disappeared. The priest, shaking with fright, shut it up in a box.

Next day a poor tinker came to the village where the priest lived.

"Now I can get rid of my useless, horrifying kettle," thought the priest.

The tinker was very glad to buy it cheaply and the priest chuckled at the trick he had played on the man.

That night the tinker was awakened from sleep by a noise in the sack where he carried his poor belongings. No sooner was it opened than out rushed the badger-kettle, and immediately started to gambol joyfully all round him.

The tinker was not frightened, but laughed at the badger's antics. Then he thought, "If I laugh, why shouldn't others?" So he set himself to teach the queer creature tricks.

Soon he became famous as the travelling showman who had a kettle with badger's head and limbs, which walked the tight rope and danced Japanese measures with a fan in his paw. Noblemen and princes bade him perform at their palaces, and soon the tinker had made a modest fortune. Then he said to himself, "I must not be avaricious. The priest who sold me the kettle so cheaply did not know what a wonderful thing it was. I must give it back to him."

This made him sad, for the kettle-badger was a great pet to him, but he did it. Of course the priest had heard all about its adventures long ago, and learned that he need not have feared it. So he was glad to have it back again. But from that day onward it remained quite an ordinary kind of kettle. The badger head, legs, and tail never sprouted again. It was of no use except for boiling water.

IMAGINATION · CHIVALRY · LEGENDS · GOLDEN DEEDS · FAIRY TALES

PRÊTE À MOURIR POUR SON AMIE

This is a French translation of the story told in English on page 3134

Qui était Sydney Carton? La réponse est —Henriette Cannet.

Même ceux qui n'ont pas lu "A Tale of Two Cities" savent ce dont il s'agit; sous la Terreur Sydney Carton change de vêtements avec un condamné à mort. Le condamné retourne à l'amour et à la liberté; Sydney Carton meurt à sa place.

Nous sommes familiarisés avec une partie de l'histoire de Madame Roland, mais non avec le rôle qui concerne Sydney Carton. Nous savons que Madame Roland était une femme de haut mérite, qui, avec son mari, accueillit avec joie la Révolution Française, parce que tous deux haïssaient la tyrannie et les souffrances causées par l'ancien Régime. Mais, lorsque cette belle promesse de fraternité se changea en torture et en carnage, ces deux citoyens courageux protestèrent. Madame Roland fut condamnée à mort par ceux-là même que son influence avait contribué à amener au pouvoir.

Tandis qu'elle était en prison, une amie vint lui dire adieu. Dès que le geôlier fut sorti, cette amie supplia Madame Roland de changer de vêtements avec elle et de s'échapper. Elle lui dit que c'était son devoir de vivre pour son enfant et pour son mari, pour les services qu'elle pourrait rendre à la France avec son intelligence et son influence sur les hommes éminents de l'époque. Sa vie était beaucoup plus précieuse que celle de l'amie inconnue qui l'interpellait.

Or, cette femme qui suppliait Madame Roland de vivre pour la France et pour son foyer était Henriette Cannet, une ancienne amie de pension.

Madame Roland refusa d'accepter ce sacrifice. Regardez-là gravissant les degrés qui mènent à l'échafaud, vêtue de blanc, sa chevelure noire éparse sur ses épaules, ses yeux intrépides fixés sur le peuple ignorant dont elle avait essayé de briser les liens, et qui réclamait son sang à grands cris parce que ses oppresseurs l'incitaient à le faire. Sous ce tableau on devrait toujours graver ces paroles immortelles, qu'elle prononça au moment d'affronter la mort : " O Liberté ! que de crimes sont commis en ton nom ! "

THE QUEEN WHO GAVE UP HER BOY

Near the beginning of the sixteenth century there was born at Fontaine-bleau Jeanne d'Albret, heiress to Navarre and niece to the King of France.

She hardly knew her parents, but was brought up in the country by her governess, and until she was nine she did not realise that she was kept a prisoner by King Francis in a castle on the banks of the Loire. This the king did that when she was quite a child he might compel her to marry a Protestant duke. Little Jeanne was unwilling to marry the duke the king chose, and was glad when the Pope annulled the marriage, and she was free to wed as she chose.

During the peaceful years she spent at Pau Jeanne studied and learned to love the religion of the Huguenots, the persecuted Protestants of France, and she devoted herself to their cause. On the death of her old father she became Queen of Navarre, and while dark clouds were gathering round the Huguenots she helped and encouraged them all she could.

The homeless and persecuted were ever welcome at her Court, which grew to be looked on as a haven of refuge by the sorely-troubled Huguenots. When their leader, the Prince of Condé, fell in the battle of Jarnac, and hope seemed dead, the faithful Queen of Navarre came to their aid. She rode into the camp among the despondent soldiers, bringing with her two fine bright boys—her only son Henry, aged about fifteen, and his cousin, the now fatherless Prince of Condé, a boy of twelve, whom she had adopted.

In stirring words she rallied the little army to defend their religion and to avenge the death of their beloved Condé. Presenting the two boys, she cried : " Soldiers, I offer you everything I have; my kingdom, my treasures, my life, and, more precious than all, my children."

These words were received in breathless silence, and then, as Prince Henry galloped into their midst, the soldiers greeted him with cheers as their leader.

Dark days were before the Huguenots, and to them the sacrifice of the Queen of Navarre seemed vain in the light of after events; yet who shall say that it was so, seeing that her noble deed revived the courage of the Huguenots, and helped to keep alive their beliefs.

STORIES TOLD TO THE CHILDREN OF POLAND

We give here a few more legends told to the children of Poland as they grow up. Other stories, known to every boy and girl in this land of mountain and forest, are given on page 4366.

LEGEND OF THE GOLDFINCH

WHEN God the Father made our World and covered the ground with lovely carpets of flowers, and made trees to grow into the wonderful temples of forests, He wanted those temples to be filled with music, so He made birds.

He made them big and small and gave them different shapes, and when they were all finished He told them to line up to be painted. So all the big birds stood first and all the little ones were at the end.

And there, among the small birds, was one that was very lively—we call him Goldfinch today. He chirped and hopped and moved to and fro, and could not keep in the line. There was such a long row of birds to be painted before his turn came. " I must try my wings for a while: it is so tiring to stand and wait," thought the little bird; and he spread his wings and up he flew, up to the little clouds that looked so white and fluffy against the deep blue background of the sky.

He looked down; how beautiful the world was in its new, fresh loveliness! He flew from tree to tree and meadow to meadow and hill to hill, singing with joy and fluttering in the sunshine. He was so happy in this wonderful world.

Suddenly he remembered his coat had not been painted and that he had been away for a long time. He must hurry back. So he flew as fast as he could, and at last he could see the meadow where the long line of birds had been. But now there were no birds to be seen.

God had finished His work, and He had put away His paints and was washing His brushes.

The little Goldfinch sat on a tree and sobbed. God heard him weeping and asked what was the matter. So the Goldfinch told how he had flown away to see the beautiful world, and how he was too late to have his coat painted.

God saw that he was really sorry, so He said, " Come, and I will see what I can do." So, joyfully, the Goldfinch flew to Him. The colours had all been put away, but there were still many little bits of paint on the palette; so God took all the many little scraps and made of them the wonderful coat of many colours that the Goldfinch wears to this day.

THE VIRGINIA CREEPER

IN the beginning, when God made the plants of the Earth, He first made their stalks and leaves; and when these were finished He went on making their blossoms, painting the petals of their flowers in all the loveliest colours.

The flowers stretched their stalks when He was passing by, so that He might notice those that were not yet painted. But there was one little plant growing at the foot of an old, bare rock. She was so small and humble that she did not dare even to look up when God passed by; so He missed her, and her blossom was not painted; it was just green.

The poor little plant felt very sad at first and wondered what she could do. The bare rock at whose feet she was growing complained of the heat of the sun that burned him. The little plant thought: " I will cover him with my green leaves," and she began to grow, and to climb higher and higher until she had covered all the rock.

One day, when the autumn had come, God sent down an angel to see all the flowers that He had made. The angel went along the fields and meadows, and saw many a beautiful thing. At last he came to the big, bare rock which he knew so well, but there was no rock to be seen; a beautiful green plant had covered its bareness.

" How lovely! " exclaimed the angel.

The little creeper heard and blushed. She blushed the most beautiful crimson, more beautiful than all the flowers.

And every year the little creeper remembers the praise of the angel, and blushes again as she thinks of it.

HOW A HIGHLANDER CHOSE HIS WIFE

ONCE upon a time there lived in the Tatra mountains a young Highlander. He was good-looking, witty, and wealthy, so no wonder many girls were fond of him and would have liked to marry him.

But he wanted a good wife, and he knew that good wives are not easy to find. But he made up his mind to find one, so he dressed himself in rags, covered his face and hands with dirt, and went out to look for a wife.

He knocked at the door of one of his girl friends. "Have mercy, good child, have mercy," begged he when she opened the cottage door. "I am a poor man. I have not touched food since yesterday. Give me some bread or some clothing. Look! I am in rags." The girl was moved to tears; she took some bread and some cheese and gave them to him. He thanked her and went away.

But on the way he said to himself, "That is not a wife for me." He tried another place. Again he knocked at the door, and when a little girl opened it he said in a voice half choked with tears : "Help me, sweet child; I am a poor beggar. I am so weary and weak, for I have not tasted food since yesterday. Look at my rags. Give me some food or some clothing." The girl looked into his eyes, and said in a sad voice : "I cannot give you any food because my mother has locked the larder and she is away; but here is an old coat; take it, it will, at any rate, keep you warm."

Off went the Highland boy, thinking, "This is no wife for me."

He came to another cottage, and when he knocked at the door a beautiful girl opened it. He began the same story, complaining of his misery and hunger, but the girl looked sternly into his face. She looked at his shoulders that were straight and broad, she looked at his hands, that were strong, and she said: "I never help loafers. Go and work, and you will suffer neither hunger nor cold." She banged the door in his face, and was gone.

"This is the wife for me," thought the young boy, full of joy. He went home, washed his face, dressed in his best, and went once again to the girl, and asked her to become his wife.

THE SECRET OF THE FERN BLOSSOM

HAVE you ever seen the white blossom of a fern? People say it grows only in fairyland, but I will tell you how it can be found.

Wait till St. John's Eve, June 23, when the tide of life is at its highest, when all the shrubs and trees are in full blossom and the woods are teeming with wild life. That is the time to start on your quest. Go out into the deepest forest and take no companion. However dark the night may seem, fear not, for it is in loneliness and darkness that you may find the blossom.

You will have to cross many a well-marked path, many smooth roads; but keep away from them: they lead to human dwellings where ferns never bloom.

And when you become tired and weary, and your feet are sore and your heart sad, when thorns and thistles block your way so that you are scarcely able to move, then look out for the blossom; it is nigh. You will come upon it quite suddenly, when you least expect it. There it will be at your feet, white and lovely, shining like a star among the leaves of the ferns.

Take it, and hide it in your bosom. From this moment you are the richest man in the world. All the world is yours, with all its bliss and wonder. There is no sorrow now that can reach you, there is no pain that can hurt you, there is no darkness that cannot be lightened by the shining radiance of the blossom you have hidden on your heart.

DOGS, CATS, AND MICE

IN the old days, when dogs and cats and mice lived in perfect harmony together, the dogs asked the cats to keep certain documents of great importance safely till they came back for them.

The cats looked at the pile of old papers, and they thought, "Why should we be bothered with these old scraps of paper? Let us ask the mice to take care of this queer treasure; it is just what they are fit for." So they did, and the mice promised to keep an eye on the documents.

Meanwhile winter came, and a hard winter too. The poor little mice suffered from hunger and cold. Being in despair, they began to nibble at the old documents. They gnawed and nibbled and ate the best parts, and tore the bad ones into tiny shreds, till there was not one whole piece.

At last one day the dogs wanted their documents back, so they went to the cats. But the cats said, "We thought it would be safer to give your documents to our friends the mice, so they keep them. Now we will go and fetch them for you."

So off they went. But instead of the documents they found only scraps of paper lying on the floor.

The cats were furious. They vowed to kill every mouse they ever met in their way. But the dogs, when they heard the sad news, got angry too, and they began to chase the cats, and they have never stopped doing it since.

THE HERO OF KAVALA

KAVALA, which is a seaport on the coast of the Aegean Sea, had been captured by the Bulgarians. When disaster fell upon the Bulgarians they were afraid their army might be surrounded if they maintained their position, and so withdrew the bulk of it, leaving the fortress in the keeping of two hundred men. These men, before leaving to follow the main army, were to burn the town, so that it might not fall into the hands of the enemy.

News of the decision reached the horrified inhabitants. They learned that the soldiers were collecting stores of petroleum; they heard them sharpening their bayonets, saw them loading their guns. The poor people shut themselves in their houses, expected death, and prayed for life.

Only one man did not give up hope. A Turkish fisherman looked out across the waters and saw the island of Thasos, eighteen miles across the sea. There lay the Greek fleet, and Greece was at war with Bulgaria. So when the sun went down, and only the pale stars lit the way across the waters, the brave boatman, creeping in the shadows past the sentries, stole down to the beach, launched his boat, and stole out of the bay, through the searchlights which lit up the waters round about him. His safe escape seemed miraculous. It was, he said, as if a great hand were stretched above him to hide him from the lights.

With a beating heart and straining muscles he set out to row the eighteen miles to Thasos. Early in the morning he reached the island, glided in among the Greek warships, and cried out to a battleship, " For the love of Allah, and for the love of your God, come quick, for at sunrise the Bulgars sack Kavala."

The answer was immediate. A Greek gunboat got up steam and set out swiftly for Kavala. As the sun climbed up above the horizon the people of the town heard a cry from a watcher on the shore : " The fleet! The Greek fleet! "

Then the inhabitants of Kavala knew that they were saved, for with the Greeks there the Bulgarians would not attempt to sack the town.

Doors and windows were flung open. The people rushed with joy into the streets and down to the shore, and as the captain of the ship that had come to save them stepped ashore they seized him in their arms and carried him shoulder-high at the head of a procession of sailors.

At the back of these stalked a figure in a red fez, stumping stolidly along and nodding contentedly. It was the valiant Turkish fisherman who had rowed to Thasos and brought back the Greek fleet to save the town.

THE BOY WHO SLEPT WELL O' NIGHTS

MANY years ago a farmer needed a trustworthy boy to help him with the work on his farm. In those days there were no Labour Exchanges; men who were out of work used to assemble at the annual fairs, and there the farmers would choose the ones they wanted.

One day the farmer journeyed to a market-place where a fair was being held and began to question the waiting boys.

The first boy said he could plough and reap, the second that he could milk and tend the cattle, the third that he could clip the sheep, the fourth that he could groom the horses, and so on. But the last boy in the line said none of these things. He merely replied quietly that he could " sleep well o' windy nights."

The farmer was so struck by this strange answer and by the steadfast bearing of the boy that he agreed to engage him for a year.

The spring passed and the summer, and the boy worked so well that the farmer was pleased with him and learned to rely on him. Then came the winter.

One night a terrible storm broke over the farm. All night long the lightning flashed and the thunder pealed and the wind howled round the chimneys and the rain poured down in torrents. The farmer shuddered as he lay awake listening to the storm, wondering what damage was being done outside in the fields.

At breakfast he told the boy how he had been kept awake by the fury of the gale. The boy smiled, and replied that he had slept as soundly as ever.

" Why," said the farmer, in amazement, " I could not sleep a wink, thinking of the wind tearing at the tops of the hayricks."

" Oh," replied the boy. " I didn't worry about that. I knew they would be all right. *You see, I put them on.*"

A JAPANESE SPARROW

ONCE upon a time there lived in Japan an old couple who had tamed a sparrow. Every day he came to be fed, and fluttered about their house, sometimes alighting on their shoulders, where, quite at home, he would chirp as though he were on a forest tree.

One day the old woman was in the garden when her bad-tempered neighbour called out: " You won't see your precious sparrow again. He came eating my rice, and I've cut his tongue out." The spiteful woman laughed.

The poor old couple were filled with sorrow. They feared the bird would starve, and they felt sure he would never trust himself near a human being again.

As they could not rest at home they wandered into the woods calling the bird. By and by they came to a clearing. There stood a most beautiful little house, only a few feet high. The sliding door was pushed aside, and out flew their sparrow, followed by his wife and little ones, all twittering a welcome in which the old people could plainly distinguish words.

" How glad I am that my hosts should be my guests! " cried the sparrow. " How happy I am in this enchanted place to be able to tell you how thankful I am for the love you have showed me! "

In and out flew the sparrows, bringing toy-like mats and bowls and cups, which grew quite big as soon as the old couple touched them. They all feasted together in the forest

At last the old couple said they must return. Then the father sparrow brought two little baskets, which he laid at their feet. " One is heavy and one is light," he said; " which will you have? "

The old people chose the light one, as they were not strong enough for great burdens. After tender farewells they set out again. The basket grew from the size of a walnut to that of a trunk, and when they opened it at home they found it filled with brilliant silks, glittering jewels, all the loveliest things fairy hands could have packed into it.

Their neighbour, hearing their cries of excitement, ran in. As soon as she learned their story she hastened away to the woods. She came to the little house and knocked at the door. Out came Father Sparrow, and looked at her sternly.

The woman said she was sorry she had cut his tongue out, but everyone is apt to lose her temper sometimes! She hoped he would overlook it, and give her a present in memory of their having been neighbours.

Without more ado the sparrow brought out two baskets. The greedy woman chose the heavier, and set off for home.

The basket grew and grew, till her arms ached and her back was nearly broken. Only the thought of treasure enabled the exhausted woman to drag it home. With weary hand she lifted the lid. Out sprang two enormous goblins, who carried her off to the dismal place where those who ill-use animals are punished as they deserve.

THE STORY OF EDITH CAVELL

IN the street on the east side of the National Gallery in London stands a stone figure in nurse's uniform. It is of Edith Cavell, an English nurse.

Being in Belgium in the First World War, it mattered not to her whether she was nursing friend or foe. She was the friend of all who needed her, and even Germans she nursed back to health. But one thing this brave woman could not bear: she could not bear to see the German Army forcing Belgians to work against their country. She could not bear to see these men enslaved by German conquerors. And so she sheltered them, and helped them to escape to Holland or to France.

Edith Cavell risked her liberty in doing so, and one day the Germans found her

out, found her guilty of being kind to suffering people; and for this they sentenced her, not to a short imprisonment, not even to penal servitude, but to death.

The ambassadors of other nations appealed in vain against this savage deed, and one night in the dark a German firing party took this woman to a garden. and shot her dead. She died like a daughter of England. Too proud to feel scorn of her enemies, too noble to hate them, she left this message, which will ring for ever down the ages.

Standing as I do in view of God and Eternity, I realise that patriotism is not enough. I must have no hatred or bitterness towards anyone.

With this noble farewell to the world Edith Cavell reached the gate of heaven.

THE DOOM OF THE CHILDREN OF LIR

First of all came a beautiful woman, riding a grey horse with scarlet harness. Her gown and mantle were of green, embroidered with silver and clasped with jewels. There were bracelets on her arms, and a gold circlet on her black hair.

It was Eefa, second wife of Lir, one of the fairy chiefs who ruled Ireland thousands of years ago, before the invasion of mortals caused them to become invisible and hide in the hills. She was going on a visit to King Bov the Red, and with her she took her three step-sons and step-daughter. She was jealous of them, and

Fionuala, the little girl, stood before her three brothers, who clung to her, trembling before Eefa's furious air. Suddenly the Queen's hand dropped; she could not do the terrible thing. Instead she began to recite a magical curse upon the children.

This was the doom she pronounced on the children of Lir: they were to change into white swans. Three hundred years they were to spend on Lake Derryvaragh, three hundred on the Straits of Moyle, and three hundred on the Atlantic by Erris and Inishglory. After that, when " South weds North," the enchantment would end.

THE PRINCE COMMANDS THE PRIEST TO GIVE HIM THE FOUR SINGING SWANS

her visit was but a pretext to get them away from their father and do them harm.

After her came one or two serving women and a group of men armed with swords. Four of them carried each one a child before him, pretty children, royally dressed.

Presently Eefa called a halt in a desolate place near Lake Derryvaragh. Then, as calmly as if she spoke of fowls or swine, she said that the children must be killed, that she would tell a lie to shield the men who obeyed her, and reward them richly.

Though she was their queen, and powerful in witchcraft, a cry of horror rose from her servants. The wicked woman exclaimed that she would do the deed herself, and took a sword from one of the men.

The Queen ceased speaking, and in the blink of an eye there were no children to be seen, but four white swans, who rose in the air with human cries, and beat their way to the waters of the lake.

Eefa and her servants went on in silence. But as Bov stepped forward to welcome his friend's wife her servants cried to him not to touch her guilty hand, and told him what she had done. Then Bov in his wrath cursed Eefa, and she was turned into a bird with a human head, that flew screaming away, never to be seen again.

Bov came to Lir with his bitter news, and the two set off sorrowfully for Lake Derryvaragh. The four white swans came swimming to them, and greeted their father in human words. Fionuala did her best to comfort him, and promised she would always protect the little ones.

The people of their race had two lucky attributes: disease and old age never touched them, and they were great musicians. Fionuala, Conn, Fiachra, and Hugh were even more skilful in melody than their kinsmen, so for three hundred years people flocked to Derryvaragh to hear their singing, and Lir talked with his children daily.

At last the time came when they must accomplish their doom, and fly to the Straits of Moyle. They left their father with heartrending cries, and the wailing of a whole people followed them.

Now, on the straits between Ireland and Scotland, they suffered from tempest and cold, tumult and loneliness, till they would have been glad to exchange their lot for that of some fish with only a few days to live before sea-gull or sea-cannibal put an end to him. But in the icy waters, buffeted against the rocks, their love survived to comfort them. Fionuala, the motherly sister, would spread her wings over the others, would cheer them with stories of the happiness in store at the end of the doom, and would sing to them.

When this period was accomplished they left the half-frozen seas for the western shores of Mayo. One day as they were floating there they saw a young man walking on the sand. He was amazed at seeing them, and still more astonished when they called to him in human voices. But he approached bravely, and answered the poor birds, who were eager to have news of their father, King Lir.

"Alas!" said he, "I never heard of him. I am a poor farmer and have never travelled more than ten miles from the place where I was born."

He was an unlearned man and knew nothing of history, or he could have told them that a new race dwelled in Ireland, and their father's kin now went about invisible, and lived in the hills.

One day the four swans took wing and flew to their old home. With cries of lamentation they circled round and round the hill where their father's palace had once stood, and where there was nothing now to be seen but nettles and thorns. Bewildered, and more unhappy than they had ever been, even in the Straits of Moyle, the poor swans returned to Erris Bay.

The farmer befriended and protected them in many ways, but he grew old, and died. Years passed, and one day the birds were startled by a thin, strange sound coming from the land. At length curiosity overcame fear, and they flew to see what it was.

They found a missionary ringing a bell in a little stone church he had just built. The good man listened pitifully to their story, and then told them the good news he brought to Ireland.

"Brothers," Fionuala said, "my heart tells me this is a true tidings. Let us learn of this gentle-hearted man."

So the swans became friends of the hermit, and sang the holy service, till the news of it spread far and wide.

One day a Princess of Southern Ireland was wooed by a Northern Prince. She said she would marry him if he brought her the four singing swans of Erris Bay.

The chieftain never stopped, except to change horses, till he reached the church. Once there he demanded the swans, and, on being refused, took them by force. In vain were the old missionary's entreaties: they were chained together and dragged off.

The faithful priest followed as fast as he could, in the hope of being able to serve his friends. The chieftain, cumbered by the birds, did not outstrip him by very much.

The last moment of the three hundred years passed as the swans were brought to the Princess's feet. Suddenly the Prince's chains fell from them, and their swan plumage also. There stood four shrivelled, shrunken old people. They looked at each other with amazement.

All fled, but the hermit drew near, and the peasants say that he comforted them. "Friends," he said, "I think you have not long to live here, but in the gardens of Paradise, where you shall live together for eternity, you will find peace to atone for all your sufferings."

So he baptised and blessed them. Then said Fionuala, with the holy water wet on her white hair, and the weakness of death coming upon her:

"Lay us in one grave: lay Conn at my right, and Fiachra at my left, and Hugh before my face; for there they were wont to be when I sheltered them in many a wintry night on the seas of Moyle."

This much was merciful in the doom of the children of Lir: they died all in one hour, and knew not separation.

SON-OF-A-PEACH

THERE was once a poor old Japanese couple who suffered greatly from want, for they had not strength and health enough to do much work.

Often they wished for sons and daughters who would have helped them. One day the old woman was washing clothes in the stream when she saw an immense peach floating towards her. She drew it in, delighted to think what a good meal it would make her husband, for it was nearly as big as a melon. However the fruit burst open, and there lay a lovely little child.

The old woman's joy knew no bounds, for she saw that Heaven had taken pity on them and sent this child to comfort their old age. The old man was equally rejoiced, and called the newcomer Son-of-a-Peach.

He grew ten times faster than other children, and every tree he touched seemed to bear ten times as much fruit. The poor little garden flourished like a king's when he began to tend it. Best of all, he was so sweet-tempered, so cheerful, so unselfish, and so brave, that everyone loved him.

One day he said to his father:

"I have heard of an island not far from the mainland where a band of goblins live. They make raids on the country and carry off children. They plunder and kill. I should like to go and fight these wicked monsters."

The old man's heart sank at the thought of losing his son, but he said to himself:

"He was sent by Heaven, and perhaps it is Heaven's will that he should deliver people from the goblins. I have no right to hold him back."

So he gave Son-of-a-Peach permission to go, and some money for the journey. It was not much; the boy spent it all on provisions, and set off on foot.

At the end of the first day's journey he sat down in a wood to eat his supper. A big dog jumped out of the undergrowth, and said: "If you don't give me food I will tear you to pieces!"

"If you threaten me," replied the boy calmly, "you shan't have a crumb, but if you ask civilly, I shall be pleased to give you half my ration."

"Please, honourable sir," said the dog, with a bow, "give a hungry fellow a cake, and tell him where you are going."

When Son-of-a-Peach told him what he proposed to do the dog said:

"That's an adventure after my own heart. Let me come as your squire."

Son-of-a-Peach agreed, and they slept side by side. At the end of the second day's journey, as they were talking of their plans, a monkey dropped out of the tree above. The dog sprang at him, but Son-of-a-Peach pulled him off, and the monkey cried that he had heard their conversation and wanted to enlist in the expedition. The dog growled jealously that they wanted no mischievous apes, but Son-of-a-Peach said he might come.

Soon after a pheasant flew down to pick up the crumbs of their supper. The dog flew at him and pulled out two tail feathers before the boy could catch him. The pheasant sprang to the boy's shoulder, and said pleadingly:

"Let me come with you too. I shall not eat half so much as your other companions, and I can show you a short cut to the island."

So next day the boy and his three retainers arrived at the shore. Quite close they could see the lovely island and the fortress of the goblins.

First of all Son-of-a-Peach went to the nearest village and asked for the loan of a boat and a sword. Seeing his strange company, the people thought he must be something supernatural, and dared not refuse. They soon rowed off, and landed on the goblin island.

After hiding their boat in a cave they advanced cautiously. Presently they heard weeping, and saw two lovely maidens washing linen in a stream. Son-of-a-Peach did not dare to speak to them in case they should be startled and cry out, so the pheasant fluttered up and whispered gently:

"Why are you weeping, maidens?"

"Once we lived in palaces," one replied, "but now we are slaves to the four demons who live in that fort."

"I and my comrades," said the pheasant importantly, "have come to deliver you. Tell us, how would it be best to attack your wicked masters?"

"Come to the fort at dusk," said the maiden, "when the demons are sleepy with wine and food. We will open the side door to you. Pray Heaven you do not fail, for if you do I shall have to make a pie of you, and it would break my heart to do that ! "

" We are invincible, never fear," said the pheasant, and returned to his friends.

The four lay in hiding till dusk. They saw lights in the fort, and heard music. One of the slaves was playing to the demons. The door was ajar.

In they rushed. The dog sprang at one demon's throat, the ape strangled another, Son-of-a-Peach cut off the head of a third, and the pheasant pecked at another one's eyes so that he was helpless, and the boy soon killed that monster too.

The castle was full of treasure, which Son-of-a-Peach gave to his old parents. He took the maidens home to their royal father, who made the four rescuers noblemen. Then for the rest of their days they wandered about Japan slaying monsters and helping the weak, till every one of them was as famous as Jack the Giant Killer. But the dog never *quite* got over his jealousy.

THE BOY AND THE AMBASSADOR

Dᴜʀɪɴɢ a very wild and dreadful period in French history called the Commune, when cannon were firing all day long in the streets and it was unsafe to stir abroad, Mr. Edward Mallet was acting as British Ambassador in Paris.

One day as he passed the window of his office he glanced down at the courtyard below, and noticed a little shrivelled boy staring pathetically up at the windows. Later on, passing the window again, he saw the little boy still there, and, being struck by his presence in the courtyard of the Embassy, he rang a bell and sent one of his secretaries to inquire what he wanted.

He learned that the boy had asked for the Ambassador and had refused to tell any of the secretaries what he wanted. It seemed an absurd thing to do, but the Ambassador ordered the little urchin to be brought to his room.

The boy was neatly dressed, and his manner was perfectly composed. He seemed to be about eight years old. It amused the Englishman to notice that this tiny French child had all the confidence of a man of the world.

He told his story quite simply. He lived with his mother and two servants in an avenue where there was always fighting, and the dreadful scenes were making his mother very ill. " I take care of my mother," he said. " There are two woman servants, but they are no use; they are more frightened than we are." He wanted to move his mother to a quieter part of the city, but could not do so because they had no money. He needed about twenty pounds. When the postal service was working again properly he would be able to pay back the Ambassador. In the meantime, would the Ambassador kindly lend the twenty pounds?

You can imagine the surprise of the Englishman. He found out that the boy had come to him without telling his mother. After a great many questions, however, he determined to trust the little child. He handed the boy the money.

" Thank you, sir," said the boy, and departed. The Ambassador dismissed the matter from his mind. But when quiet was restored in the city the little boy came to him again.

He told a terrible story. The street into which he had moved his mother turned out to be worse than the other. Blood had been shed all day long in front of their windows. The shells had exploded against their walls. They had been unable to get out to buy food. In the back room of their lodgings they had cowered and starved, expecting every moment to be killed.

" My mother's nerves have been greatly shattered by what she has gone through," said the serious mite. " I think it is better to take her away from Paris, and I have decided to move her to Wiesbaden. I think that rest will bring her round. I shall take her away tomorrow evening."

And then he pulled out a little pocket-book and produced the twenty pounds.

" I have brought you the money as soon as I could, sir, and my mother and I are much obliged to you. Good-bye, sir. Thank you very much."

With that the little fellow held out his hand, and departed.

This is quite a wonderful story for all its shortness. This little boy, living with his invalid mother and two terrified servants, had summoned up the courage of a man, and in a time of bloodshed and panic had made himself the protector of the household.

OEDIPUS AND SAD ANTIGONE

Antigone was the daughter of Oedipus, King of Thebes, but the princess was not as fortunate as the poorest bonds-woman in the palace.

Her grandfather, King Laius, had been told by an oracle that his own son would kill him. Accordingly, as soon as Oedipus was born, Laius ordered a servant to kill the baby. This man carried the poor infant to a lonely place and there tied him to a branch by the heels. But a kindly shepherd found the child, and brought him up without knowing who he was.

When Oedipus grew to be a youth other boys used to taunt him with being a foundling. This made him so wretched that he journeyed to Delphi to ask the oracle there who were his parents. The oracle did not answer his question, but warned him: " Do not go home or you will slay your father."

Oedipus misunderstood the message. He thought that his home was a shepherd's hut, not a palace, and that the father he would slay would be his adopted one. So he wandered on into his true father's dominions. By and by, as he was climbing a narrow mountain path, he met two richly-dressed elderly men. One ordered him out of the way insolently. Oedipus refused to obey and the other drew his sword. The homeless youth was in the mood for a fight. His weapon leaped from the scabbard, and he fought savagely. Both men attacked him, but in the end his youth and hardihood gained the victory. Both the strangers were killed. He could not know that he had slain his father, Laius, and a courtier.

It was a long time before the bodies were discovered and the motive of the murder remained a complete mystery. Creon, the dead king's father-in-law, became regent. Shortly afterwards a terrible monster descended on Thebes, half beast and half human, and colossal in size. It was none other than the Sphinx. It lived on human beings. No weapon could pierce its hide. No bribe that was offered would induce it to leave the realm.

" I will go back to my own land," it cried to the royal messengers, " when a man can answer my riddle: What animal in the morning walks upon four feet, at noon upon two, and in the evening upon three ? Whoever gives a wrong answer I shall devour."

Creon proclaimed that the man who solved the riddle should be given the crown of Thebes. Oedipus heard of the decree. As a beggar's life was not much to lose he decided to risk it.

He confronted the Sphinx in its lair and said : " A man in the morning of life walks on hands and feet; when he has reached manhood he walks on two legs; in the evening of life he supports his aged limbs with a stick."

This was the true answer. The angry Sphinx dashed its head against the rock and killed itself.

Oedipus was made king, without ever suspecting that one of the strangers he had slain long ago in the mountain duel was King Laius. He married, and had a daughter called Antigone and two sons called Polynices and Eteocles. For long years all was happiness, but presently a plague visited Thebes. The oracles were consulted, and said that the plague would go when the murderer of Laius was banished from Thebes.

Oedipus ordered men to search the past till they could discover him. Their investigations at last brought to light not only the whole story of Laius's death, but also the secret of Oedipus's birth. When he learned that he had killed his own father the despair of Oedipus was so great that he put out his eyes, crying, " I am not worthy to see the light! "

Then he consulted the oracle asking: " What is the name of the place where Oedipus will die? "

" It is a sacred grove near Colonus, in Attica," answered the oracle.

" Let me set out for that place now," said the king, " for I do not desire to live."

So he left his palace. With him went faithful Antigone, guiding the sightless man, and weeping as he wept. When they came to the grove Oedipus told her to let go of his hand. He walked forward alone. Suddenly the earth yawned under his feet, and he descended into the Underworld.

Poor Antigone returned broken-hearted to Thebes. Her brothers had decided to reign in turn, for a year at a time. As the months sped by Antigone's grief began to get less. Her chief comforter was her great-uncle Haemon, who loved her dearly. But soon fresh troubles came to her. The brothers fell out. Civil war followed. Both were killed in battle.

Creon was made regent until Eteocles's little son should be old enough to govern. The first thing he decreed was that Polynices, who had done most to cause the bloodshed, should lie unburied. If anyone put his body in a grave, that person should be buried alive.

Terrible as the threat was, Antigone could not bear to think of her brother left a prey to wolf and vulture. She stole out at night and buried him. But she was seen and denounced to Creon next day. In vain did Haemon beg for mercy. Creon could not be induced to break his word. The executioners stepped toward Antigone, but before they could lay hands on her she had stabbed herself.

The tragedy of Oedipus has often made men ask : Why should he have been so heavily punished for a crime committed in ignorance ? But the story is founded on an unshakable law of Nature. Wrongdoing always brings suffering. A man who leads a drunken life ruins his health, and his innocent children may also inherit a tendency to grow up into drunkards. This is not punishment by Heaven, it is simply a law of Nature, like the law of gravity, which makes a dropped thing fall to the ground.

LAOMEDON, BREAKER OF PROMISES

WHEN Troy was a-building under the orders of King Laomedon there was anger in the home of the gods. Neptune and Apollo had disobeyed their king, Jupiter. As a punishment he exiled them to Earth for a year.

Laomedon was startled when the glorious sun god and the weed-clad sea god appeared before him. They told him who they were, and offered to help him to build Troy if he would give all the first-born of his cattle to their temples. Laomedon agreed to this.

For a year the gods worked faithfully, and then they returned to the Heavenly Hills. But Laomedon could not bring himself to part with so much as a lamb or kid in fulfilment of his promise. After a while sickness broke out among his people, and then a great tidal wave came out of the angry sea, destroying the crops. Laomedon was thoroughly frightened, and asked an oracle how to appease the gods.

" Instead of first-born cattle," came the reply, " you shall offer a Trojan maiden to the gods each year. She shall be chained to the rocks at low tide, and at high tide a sea-monster shall come for the sacrifice."

The maidens of Troy were assembled, and cast lots for the honour of dying for their country. Six times a noble maiden perished. Then it happened that the lot fell to Hesione, daughter of Laomedon.

The king loved this girl even more than his warlike son Podarces, or his handsome son Tithonus. She was the dearest thing in his kingdom, and he would have died to save her from the doom. While he was wailing upon his couch a messenger came to say that a stranger was in the town declaring he could deliver the Trojans from the monster if it were made worth his while.

Laomedon sent for him at once. The stranger was no other than the famous hero Hercules, mightiest of men.

" Ask what you will ! " cried the king.

" There are many fine horses pastured near the shore," replied Hercules. " I would rather have them than gold."

" They are mine," said Laomedon. " and they shall be yours if you can kill the sea-monster."

That night Hesione slept in the palace while Hercules took her place on the rock. At dawn he returned, his massive club stained with the monster's life-blood. Great were the rejoicings in every Trojan home. But Laomedon, now that he had nothing to fear, refused to give Hercules the reward he had promised.

The hero was so indignant that he persuaded Telamon, king of Salamis, to besiege Troy with him. Laomedon perished in the war. His children were taken captive, but Hesione was so well treated that she became reconciled to the victors, and consented to marry the ally of the man who had saved her from so terrible a fate.

When she was Queen of Salamis she redeemed her brother Podarces from prison and he took the new name of Priam, which means ransomed. Hercules, who only wanted his horses, not the crown, helped to establish Priam on his father's throne. Priam and Hesione would have given many herds of horses to restore Laomedon to life, but he had sentenced himself to death by his meanness.

THE MEN WHO CHOSE THEIR LIVES

This is the story of Er, told again from the famous Republic of Plato, written 23 centuries ago.

TEN days after the battle in which he had been killed Er was carried home. The colour still lived in his cheeks, as though he only slept, but he was covered with wounds and cold as ice. A funeral pyre was built two days after the sorrowful return. As the mourners gathered round to take a last look at their dear one before the pyre was lighted, his eyelids fluttered and his lips parted in a sigh.

How their hearts leaped! Never was such happiness. Er was carried in to his bed, and nursed back to strength. Then he told an extraordinary story.

After receiving his death stroke, he found himself journeying over a plain with many others. At length he came to a place where judges sat examining all who came. Some were sentenced to take the right-hand road up to Heaven, and the others told to take the left-hand road down to a place of punishment.

Filled with awe, Er awaited his turn. When it came he was told that he had not been summoned for judgment, in order that he might carry back to men an account of the after life. He drew aside, and watched.

Besides the newly-sentenced going up and down he saw those who had finished their punishment coming up, tired and travel-stained, from the under-world, while those who came back from their heavenly reward were shining and tranquil. Greetings passed between many of them, who had known each other on Earth, as they gathered in a large meadow near the place where the judges sat. Many questions were asked. A thousand years had passed since these people died. The sinners had suffered ten times over all the injuries they had done others, while the good had been ten times rewarded for the acts of mercy and charity they had done.

One former sinner told a friend from Heaven that when his time for leaving the under-world was at an end he and his companion were led to the mouth of a hole leading to the upper air. When one of them, King Ardiaeus the Great, approached, the hole bellowed terribly, and the fierce porters of the place declared it was a sign that he had not repented, and dragged him away. "Nothing," he said, " can describe our terror."

For seven days all the spirits rested together in the meadow. Then they set out on a three days' journey till they came to a place of great light, where Necessity sat spinning her magic distaff, which uttered a heavenly tune as it turned. Near her on thrones sat her three daughters, the Fates, clad in white, chanting of the past, the present, and the future.

An interpreter who had conducted the souls thither led them before Lachesis, the Fate who presided over destiny. In her lap lay a number of lots, which the Interpreter sprinkled among the crowd, saying: "Thus saith the maiden Lachesis, the daughter of Necessity. Ye short-lived souls, a new generation of men shall here begin the cycle of its mortal existence. Your destiny shall not be allotted to you, but you shall choose it for yourself. Let him who draws the first lot be the first to choose a life which shall be his irrevocably. He who desires virtue and happiness shall have more of them. The chooser, not Heaven, decides."

When every soul had picked up a lot the Interpreter took from Lachesis a great number of tablets, on each of which was inscribed a plan of life. He spread them out on the ground. Some were human and some were animal, for the spirits of men and beasts were present. Some were high, some were low, some were packed with glory or shadowed with sorrows, but none were wholly joyless, and there were many more to choose from than choosers.

One by one, in the order of their lots, the spirits chose. The first went eagerly forward, and chose the lot of an absolute despot, but so hastily that he did not examine it carefully first, and afterwards saw that the despot was destined to kill his own children.

Er saw that the spirits from heaven often chose foolishly, while the former sinners, schooled by suffering, showed much care and wisdom. He guessed that the foolish spirits from heaven had lived easy, untempted lives on Earth, unlike others who had won their way to Paradise by struggling against great difficulties.

Er saw strange things. Orpheus, who was stoned to death by women, chose to be a swan rather than have a woman for his mother. Brave Ajax chose to be a lion. Agamemnon, rather than taste again the treachery of mankind, chose to be an eagle.

Atalanta, the huntress princess, chose to be an athlete. Odysseus the Wanderer had the last lot. He examined all the plans till he found one of a quiet life, which he picked up gladly, saying, " Had I drawn the first lot this is the life I would have chosen."

Then the souls were led away over a vast dreary plain, till at nightfall they came to the River of Indifference. All drank but Er, and fell asleep. Each soul who drank forgot completely all his former life.

At midnight came a clap of thunder and an earthquake. The souls were carried off this way and that like shooting stars.

Suddenly Er found himself lying on his funeral pyre.

He told his friends that the gods had sent him this vision in order to teach men the great truth that wisdom is necessary not only for goodness, but for welfare. Man must serve Right not only with his heart, but also with his mind. His fate is his own choice entirely.

JOHN MAYNARD, PILOT

In thick darkness the great steamer was creeping through dangerous but smooth waters towards the end of her journey.

The passengers and most of her crew were asleep in their berths. The captain was taking his well-earned rest in his cabin. On the bridge was the pilot, a man named John Maynard, who had left his wife and son to bring this great ship safely into harbour.

It was one of those dark nights at sea when it is impossible to catch a glimpse of the vast ocean through which ships make their way. Not a star shone in the sky. The little discs of light made by the port-holes perished in the wall of darkness enclosing the ship. The only sounds in the darkness were the grinding of the paddles and the deep murmur of the sea.

So smooth, so gentle, was the ocean, that none could dream of disaster. It was a fitting night for the peace and rejoicing of a home-coming.

But suddenly a terrible cry arose above the sea: " Fire! "

Gone now was the darkness. Every face was visible. Every line of terror could be seen in that frightful glare. And another sound was added to the moan of the sea and the noise of the paddles—the rushing, roaring, hissing sound of fire, that leaped in a cloud of sparks to the sky.

The captain cried out in a loud voice: " In ten minutes more we shall have reached land. Our lives may yet be saved. It rests with the pilot. If he can hold on at his post we shall reach the land." He turned round, and called: " John Maynard, are you there? "

A quick answer came from the bridge: " Ay, ay, sir! "

In an instant despair was turned into hope. That answer was so strong, so sure.

The great ship, now a driving shape of flame, cut through the smooth and dangerous water at its highest speed, a race against fire!

Would they reach the land in time? With every turn of the paddles they were nearer to safety; but with every second the flames increased in fierceness.

What of the pilot? Was he still safe at the wheel?

" Are you there, my lad? " cried the captain, anxiety in his voice.

There was no answer.

The passengers felt their hearts sink, and a new terror possessed them. But, just as they began to abandon hope, the answer came.

" Sir, I'll try," said John Maynard.

The thoughts of the passengers at that instant were turned from the faithful pilot. The lights on land suddenly stood out before them in the distance. A loud cheer ascended from the decks. They were saved. Land was near. Boats could be seen putting out to them.

John Maynard, from the bridge, could see mothers clutching their children to their hearts. His own little son, his well-beloved, was asleep at home, far away. The moving mass of roaring flame, which once had been a ship, reached the harbour.

Passengers threw themselves into the waiting boats. Not a thought was given to the pilot. On the sides of the harbour was gathered a dense multitude.

When everyone was saved the boiler exploded with a deafening roar, and John Maynard was hurled into eternity.

Many men who stood on that flaming deck remembered to their dying day, as the most vivid impression of their lives, the look on John Maynard's face as he held to his post in the blinding smoke and the fiercely raging fire.

Nature's Wonderful Living Family in Earth and Air and Sea

Common Sea-Urchin

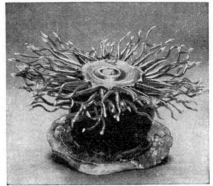

A Beautiful Sea-Anemone

QUEER AND LOWLY CREATURES

ONE of the oddest things that ever was alive is surely the sponge, the Companion of the Bath. Let us examine it with respect and intelligent questioning.

Once, like the child to whose comfort and cleanliness it ministers, it had life, movement, appetite, and, in its early youth, extreme activity.

This curious honeycombed substance, so light and elastic when dry, so soft and collapsible when wet, is simply the skeleton of an animal, and if we catch that animal young enough we may see it scurrying about in the sea with preposterous seriousness, as if it would "sail beyond the sunset and the baths of all the western stars" until it dies.

The lower half of this fussy little navigator is bearded with hair-like processes waving like tiny oars or arms, and so propelling it through the water. There must be something almost like thought in the nervous product of this small organism, for when it desires to progress in a straight line, it does so, approximately, but when it no longer directs its course it stops and its still-waving cilia make it spin like a whirligig beetle in the garden pond.

This consuming activity is of short duration. Like the baby oyster, the youthful sponge thinks better, or worse, of its policy of adventure ; it sinks to the bottom of the sea, attaches itself to rock or weed, or to some shelled animal, and its roamings are at an end.

The oval body with which it set out in life undergoes marked changes. The ciliated part is drawn inwards, and the globe-shaped little creature becomes cup-shaped. Within there is busy reconstruction of parts. The cell masses are converted into canals in which a jelly-like mass of flesh is resident, equipped with more of the vibrating processes to draw water and food into those canals.

The small openings in our bath-sponge are the canals by which water is conveyed to bear life-sustaining oxygen to the sponge and also to feed it. Each draught of water taken in contains organic and vegetable matter which, caught and strained away by a delicate membrane at the junction of the little canals, is digested in the sponge's alimentary system, while the exhausted water, together with waste products of the body, is then forced out of the large openings which we observe, and so all is well.

The sponge grows as it feeds ; it gives rise in due course to eggs which, at the right time, are washed out of the parent body in the flood of water ejected from the main channels, to hatch into free roving little animals which become sedentary.

PREHISTORIC LIFE · MAMMALS · BIRDS · REPTILES · FISHES · INSECTS

Catch a sponge alive, confine it in a sea-pond, and let it have a sufficiency of water for breathing and nutriment, and it will continue its growth. When sponge fishers have little sponges or excess of large sponges in hand, they do keep them in this way, and feed them in the manner indicated, so making it possible for us to have our little joke as to giving the sponge his breakfast.

THE LIMY SPICULES WITH WHICH THE SPONGE DEFENDS ITSELF

Before the sponge can be sent to market its skeleton must be freed from the slimy contents which constitute its vital parts, and from the sand, mud, worms, and other parasites which take up residence within it. A more serious difficulty is the mass of limy spicules which it contains. These are as much part of its fabric as the substance with which we wash. They are a stiffening and a defence. They occur in great numbers in the walls of the canals.

Often we receive a severe scratch or scrape from a new sponge, the reason being that the substance has not been entirely freed from these spicules, and we all know how difficult it is to remove them from the sponge without making ugly rents in it. The paint work of many a good car has been scratched and spoilt because chauffeurs are too indolent or ignorant to look beneath the surface of a coarse sponge for the shell-like mass of limy spines left by the man who prepared the sponge for sale.

The finest sponges for the toilet come from the eastern Mediterranean. These are sponge-fishing grounds of immemorial antiquity, and supplied Aristotle with the specimens which he declared to be animals, 2000 years ago, though men less wise contradicted him down to the middle of the nineteenth century.

THE DIVERS WHO GO DOWN INTO THE SEA TO LOOK FOR SPONGES

Larger sponges come from the waters of Florida and the West Indies, good but not equal in quality to those of the Old World. Contributory sources are the Bahamas and various areas of the Pacific. Methods of collecting the sponges differ, from the enterprise of the fully-clad diver, and the naked native with his foot in a rope tied to a stone sinker, to the longshoreman who, wading into the water, rips off his sponges from the rocks by means of a pronged spear, and so spoils half of them.

So far we have mentioned only the sponges of economic importance, and but one method of reproduction. In most cases multiplication is effected by the budding off of miniature sponges from the parent. We can watch this process for ourselves in the case of one of the fresh-water sponges, the Spongilla. Life passes from the parent sponge with the fading of summer, but from its substance new life takes rise, to drift away with the spring and form new sponges.

As Nature takes more than one means to increase her store of sponges, so she has claimed many situations for this branch of her children, inshore waters, deep-sea abysses, and all the ranges of soundings between. Siliceous spicules enter into the composition of them all, but in the so-called glass sponges the silica is of the thinnest, most brittle texture. Yet this extraordinary substance serves as an anchorage in the Japanese *Hyalonema*, which is attached to the mud by a bundle of strands of " glass rope," which might have been produced by a human glass-blower of unrefined art. In the *Semperella*, the attachment is not a glass rope but an amazing glass-like spicule, as thick as a man's little finger and nine feet long.

HOW THE SPONGES HELP TO MAKE THE WHITE WALLS OF OLD ENGLAND

There are multitudes of sponges with six-rayed spicules in the chalk of our land, and a lovely kind, the *Ventriculites*, shows us how old is exquisite ornamentation in the scheme of things. Our very flints, dug from fields and from the chalk which once had life, have sponges in their composition. A sponge is often the nucleus of these stones, and the siliceous material of which they are fashioned is derived very largely from the spicules of sponges that fed and flourished in ages that are gone.

But if sponges help to form the white walls of Old England, they help to destroy those walls, too. There are forms of these animals which, by some mysterious power, can not only wear their way through the shells of oysters, but tunnel our chalky cliffs.

Most of us who visit Dover have seen chalk there actually toppling or lying where it has fallen from that height to which the blind King Lear was led. If we could see in advance the place from which such falls occur, we should probably find that sponges have been the enemy

NATURE'S LOWLY CHILDREN

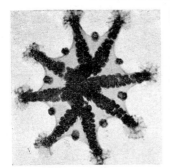

AN UMBRELLA-LIKE JELLY-FISH WITH ITS EGGS

A SEA-ANEMONE IN A ROCK POOL

A STARFISH OPENING AN OYSTER SHELL

A BEADLET SEA-ANEMONE ON A COCKLE SHELL

A SEA-PEN

A LONG-SPINED SEA-URCHIN

A SEA-CUCUMBER

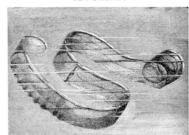

VENUS'S GIRDLE

A SEA-FAN

A DISC JELLY-FISH

BIRD'S-FOOT STARFISH

BEADLET SEA-ANEMONE WITH TENTACLES EXPANDED

RED CORAL

A STARFISH

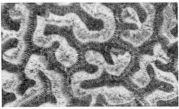

BRAIN CORAL

The pictures on these pages are by Messrs. Berridge, Martin Duncan, Johnson, Ward, and others

within the gates. They bore deep in the yielding chalk, open the way for disrupting water, and make destruction sure, if slow.

Of course, we must not lay the blame for this sort of work to the account of the sponges which we see by the sea between high tide and low; each genus has its station, its own sea-keep, its home in fresh water, its way upon the rock. There is the bread-crumb sponge, a colony of many sponges, living on our shores; there are the Mermaid's Gloves cast up, living, every rough tide; and sponges of all sorts through all seas, till we come to the tremendous Neptune's Cup, a marvellous piece of architecure, three or four feet high, built up by many sponges which act as one, which raise the great stalk, then the vase-shaped cup, and make it lovely as the work of an old Etruscan potter.

A story passing the invention of man's imagination runs through all this. Deep in the fiery crucible of the Earth, mineral boils like water in a kettle, and by volcanic action bursts out to the surface to form granite or other igneous rock, the hardest rocks we have.

THE FASCINATING STUDY OF THE CHEMISTRY OF NATURE

That rock is worn away by the slow file of Time and is washed down into the rivers and so to the sea, to form silica when extracted by diatoms and other microscopic organisms. Such particles are received into the digestive cells of the sponge and form their spicules, their boring tools, their defences, their dwellings, as in the Neptune's Cup, and eventually turn to flint.

Is not the chemistry of Nature inimitable; the study of her works more fascinating than the stories written to fire the minds of adventure-loving boys? If sponges can do such things from this substance that came from a volcano, what can corals do? We shall see presently, but will call by the way on the very converse of the horny sponges, the coral's relatives, those flimsy, transparent discs of life that float in every sea, the jelly-fishes.

These, with the corals and anemones, are called the Coelenterata, and share the common peculiarity of an all-round structure, so to say. That is, they have no " sides," but are circular and symmetrical. Moreover they have no internal divisions of the body, like the higher animals, but are furnished with a digestive system which is not a closed canal, as we should expect to find, but is practically the entire interior of the body. At first sight they appear the most defenceless of creatures, but they have their stings and poisoned barbs most potent.

THE DISCS WITH WHICH THE COMB-JELLIES CATCH THEIR PREY

All our rules have their exceptions, and we must hasten to note some here. For the *Ctenophora*, or comb-jellies, have no stinging cells, but multitudes of tiny adhesive discs, which clutch and secure minute prey. Then, another of the exceptions, the lovely Venus's Girdle, is not circular, like the rest, but exists as a broad ribbon of exquisite life, fringed with cilia which bring food within range. Some of this group have taken to creeping along the sea-bed, and so have assumed a drawn-out two-sided form. All animals are thought to have passed through the Coelenterata stage, and we may guess from the comb-jellies whence the octopus derived his sucker-discs, and, from the crawling species, how two-sided shapes were standardised.

Passing to the *Cnidaria* we have an example of a dazzling contrivance on the part of Nature for distributing her family, in what is called Alternation of Generations. It is not peculiar to this group, but here we may examine the method. Suppose we have a jelly-fish mass which, as with the sponges, comprises many individuals all united into one. If these went on budding and growing, the mass would become inconveniently large. If the component parts all produced eggs, they would overcrowd the sea in their neighbourhood and bring about starvation for themselves and all their kind thereabouts.

HOW THE JELLY-FISH FAMILIES ARE DISTRIBUTED OVER BIG AREAS

Now see what happens. The many-in-one are called a stock. Parts of the stock, charged with eggs, break away, like the gemmules of the sponge, float off and colonise some new area of water, where the eggs are produced. Some of these sink and form new stocks, which will bud off new attached members. Others of the eggs, however, will hatch straightway into free-swimming jelly-fish. The plan is ancient and has been employed in many forms of life by Nature. In the jelly-fishes it has succeeded wonderfully.

The type is represented in all waters,

from the shores of Britain, through the Tropics, and away towards the waters of both the Poles. One would expect the warm-water regions to produce the giants, and mighty forms are there, but probably the chill waters of the far north and south have the Titans, for during an Antarctic expedition there was hauled up from the water, at the foot of the Great Ice Barrier, a jelly-fish which was 29 inches across the upper part, and weighed over ninety pounds.

THE FLOATING UMBRELLAS WITH A MASS OF WAVING ARMS

How much such a monster would weigh after its watery contents had escaped one cannot venture to guess, but we have all heard of farmers carting jelly-fish in loads, a ton and more at a time, as manure for their land, only to find, as children find by the shore, that their sea booty resolved itself into watery films.

Jelly-fish life extends into many species and is complicated and fascinating. In general we know that the body, a mass of glassy jelly enclosed between the upper and lower sides of the bell or umbrella, bears a number of arms or tentacles, and that from these issue the abominable stinging barbs. These can be drawn in and protruded like the action of a glove-finger which is alternately tucked in or pulled out, but when the apparatus is shot forth and touches, its little weapons sting with the rapidity of a nettle, but with infinitely greater virulence.

In the jelly-fish, of which the *Siphonophora* are the highest form, we have the same system of stocks and single individuals as in the former species, but still more remarkably developed. Here, in a single floating mass, we have congregated together a series of individuals united, yet recognisable as many in one.

THE DIVISION OF LABOUR IN THE JELLY-FISH COLONY

Such a jelly-fish colony is more socialistic than a community of ants or bees ; its labours are subdivided yet co-ordinated as in a modern mass-production factory. There are jelly-fish in the united mass which propel the whole colony along, their function being to take in water, contract and squirt it out, and in that way row the living city about. Then there are others which guard the colony from offence, like the huge-jawed soldiers of the warrior ant colonies. In addition there are the members which produce eggs or buds, and finally those which collect the food, digest it and pass the nutritive result from end to end of the entire body of many individuals in one.

Of the *Siphonophora*, the Portuguese man-of-war is the culminating height of jelly-fish perfection, a thing of exquisitely radiant colours, whose body is like a luminous inflated sack, six inches in diameter, with a living nursery attached to its underside, and stinging tentacles, several feet long, streaming like a corrosive battery far in the water.

There are free-swimming jelly-fish, in the *Hydromedusae*, which are solitary and must fight and fend for themselves. Extraordinary facts regarding food supply have been discovered concerning these. Not only do they exhibit instinctive genius in catching food with their tentacles; they are known to collect food which falls on the upper side of the bell, securing this supply partly by the rhythmic movements of the bell, and partly by the action of minute cilia.

The united result is that the prey or organic matter is gathered into little heaps, mixed with mucus, brought to the finely fringed edge of the upper side of the bell, then, by means not yet ascertained, conveyed to the underside and so to the tentacles and thence to the slit-like mouth.

THE TINY ORPHANS WHICH GO TO THE JELLY-FISH FOR PROTECTION

Included in the diet of these jelly-fish it is surprising to find the tiny larvae of oysters, whelks, and the like, eggs of fish, little crustaceans, tiny bristleworms, and multitudes of algae. So the jelly-fish is a free feeder, and takes things that might become food for man. On the other hand, he swallows the enemies of our fishes and molluscs, and is a benevolent nursemaid to many kinds of fishes.

Baby herrings, baby codfish, and a multitude of other friendless orphans which eventually come to table in breadcrumbs or batter, look to the jelly-fish for shelter. But why does it not sting them to death as it stings other fish which do not go to it for aid ?

Certain crustacea, whose hard coats make them indifferent to its stings, play the brigand to the jelly-fish; they attach themselves to it and actually take the food out of its mouth. That is disastrous to the jelly-fish's prospects of long life. Now the little fishes which it shelters are the very ones which need crustacea as the main part of their diet. So, when the robber is pillaging the mouth of the jelly-fish, the welcome fish swim up and devour the intruder.

For that service they are entertained without harm by the master of barbs and stings. But let an enemy of those fish pursue them within range of the jelly-fish, then out go the stings, and the foe is either stunned and caught, or so severely punished that it is glad to escape with bare life.

THE QUAINT ANIMAL WHICH IS LIKE A FLOWER IN APPEARANCE

A similar scheme of mutual aid extends to the relations between the sea-anemones on the one hand and several other types of life, crabs, whelks, fishes, even actual vegetation, on the other hand. For, in spite of the name, the sea-anemone is not a vegetable, like the plant with which it co-operates. It is a true animal, low down in the scale like the sponge, and with decidedly vegetable suggestions in certain of its features. But the most flower-like of all its attributes is its actual appearance.

Anemone it certainly is not, even in outline. We might liken it to some exquisite daisy, chrysanthemum, or dahlia, perhaps, but not accurately to the delicate windflower. No matter, a sea-anemone flourishes as lustily by this name as any other, and it is a thing of rare beauty and wonder to all who have eyes to see and access to its home.

The body, with its leathery covering and strong muscular substance, is always heavily fringed with tentacles about the mouth, and these tentacles are armed with minute thread cells which bear poison, so that the arms not only cling but sting. The strength of a single tentacle may be insignificant, but the drawing power of the entire assembly is astonishing. They cannot pull our finger into the interior of the animal, but the force is noticeable even in the small species which are found round our coasts.

THE ANEMONE WHICH MADE A MEAL OF A PENNY

The anemones are sightless, but the possession in some species of brightly coloured, bead-like prominences at the base of the tentacles around the mouth suggests that they are sensitive to light. These organs might, in course of time, possibly develop into a sort of eyes, though the suggestion is risky considering how ancient a type the anemones form.

Touch and the power to absorb seem the chief assets of the anemone. One has been known to swallow a penny. Another was fed with eleven small crabs in succession. This one was exposed in a rocky pool whence the tide had retreated, and it clung, neatly folded in, looking like a large red jujube.

But it needed only a touch to cause it to thrust out its tentacles and to take in the proffered crab. Again and again it accepted the offering, till it bulged with livestock. Why did not the desperate little crabs eat their way out? The anemone, once it swallows them, is able to paralyse their action and slowly to absorb their fleshy contents.

All the tribe are heavy feeders when the opportunity offers. One swallowed a bivalve as big as a saucer. The meal so distended the anemone that it stretched and divided into two halves, with the result that a second mouth and set of tentacles formed—one set above the prey, the other set below—two anemones in one.

THE NEW ANEMONES WHICH GROW LIKE BUDS ON A STALK

All the anemones are sedentary, attached by a stout foot muscle to rock or sea vegetation, unless they anchor themselves to a moving animal, or, as happens with several species, burrow into the sand.

Sometimes new anemones bud off from that footstalk, but as a rule eggs are laid within the parent body and hatch there, and the larvae swim out when ready, or are ejected in a jet of water which passes out of the adult's mouth.

Great interest attaches to the feeding and general life habits of the anemones, but if one would preserve his poetic conception of their beauty and charm he had better not attend their dinner-table. No syren, no monster of the sea, could ever have been so frightful to ancient human imagination as an anemone must be to the fishes and crustacea which it draws helpless into its insatiable maw.

Nevertheless, there is nothing lovelier in the seas than the anemone, no richer hues in the rainbow. There is no garden in the world more rich and varied in colour and design than sea deeps where tropical and sub-tropical varieties spread their gorgeous filaments and ravenously prey.

It is but a step from an anemone to a

coral polyp, though no anemone ever furnishes itself with a hard skeleton. The coral polyps, on the other hand, are the foremost builders in the realm of Nature. Dead, minute shelled animals have formed mountain ranges, but living, the polyps have changed the bed of many a seaway.

They take mineral matter from the sea, and they take it also from the myriads of microscopic animals with limy coverings which form part of their food; and the whole they convert into coral as hard as rock, which, when brought into human service, takes a polish as fine as marble. Having studied the bee with its waxen cells, the spider and caterpillar with their webs, the molluscs with their shells, and the birds with their lime-coated eggs, we are now prepared to contemplate even these massy marvels of coral with reasoned philosophic belief.

The little animals, flower-like in appearance, grow together in countless profusion in their colonies. Instead of working together to produce wax, like bees or wasps, they build up masses of this lovely limy coral. They are not aware of what they are doing, for they are lowly organisms, in spite of the marvels they achieve.

THE ISLANDS MADE BY TINY CREATURES IN THE SEA

They work together night and day, secreting the material and building it into reefs, into islands, into barriers, into crater-like atolls. They have given us hundreds of islands on which men dwell and make their homes of the material that these minute animals have created. They alter the depths of seas by changing the levels of sea-beds. They nearly cost us the lives of Captain Cook and all his crew, when a piece of coral from the Great Barrier Reef off the east coast of Australia penetrated the hull of his ship, and then, by remaining fast in the hole thus caused, saved him from the wreck which must have resulted had the mass become dislodged before he gained harbour and the chance to careen and repair his ship.

Age after age these great structures rise beneath warm seas. Coral polyps are born and die. They are eaten by fishes which, like sheep on the downs, browse where the polyps thrust out their bodies with waving tentacles to gather food from the water. But their work goes on, century after century, epoch after epoch. Coral polyps are growing at the bottom of

the Red Sea today whose ancestors were at work there when Moses led the Israelites from Egypt.

Many illustrious names are associated with the problem of coral structure. Everybody believed the substance to be sea vegetation, that the polyps were the blooms, and that the mineral, covered with a sort of skin, was the trunk of the plant or shrub.

But how were they to account for the rocklike consistency of a living shrub? " Ah," said the wise ones, " the coral is soft and flexible, like plants of the Earth, till it reaches the air, then it instantly hardens into this rock-like substance."

THE GREAT BARRIER REEF WHICH IS 1250 MILES LONG

Eventually a French scientist conducted experiments with professional coral fishers. He made them dive and feel at the coral. They came up reporting that the undersea coral was as hard as that out of the sea. He could not, dared not, believe it, so, slipping off his clothes, he, too, dived, groped among the coral, and found the report to be true.

The amount of coral created by these puny animals is beyond human calculation. The animals are in every area, and even in fresh water, though it is in warm seas that they attain their greatest luxuriance. On some coasts they appear merely as scattered groups or mounds of coral rock, but west of the Fiji Islands is an area of coral reef 3000 square miles in extent, and the Great Barrier Reef of Australia attains a length of 1250 miles, all the work of these minute animals.

Engineering so terrific as this naturally spells jeopardy to navigation, and the menace grows from age to age as the unflagging builders toil. But they have fashioned many a sweet sanctuary for ships by their atolls, many a home for man in the midst of blue and sunny seas. On and on, up and up they build.

THE TIDE-BORNE LIFE WHICH COMES TO THE NEW ISLANDS

Fish tear and rive at the coral, worms tunnel, waves break and crumble the rock, wrench off boulders of it and use these as battering rams to demolish still more. At last there is a fine deposit to which one day a voyaging coconut comes and takes root, rises into a tree from which new nuts fall and create a grove. Birds, weary of sea flight, arrive and make their nests; tide-born seeds and drift-carried animals, reach the island.

Finally, one day a man in a boat casts anchor in the bay. Crusoe has come to his kingdom, but not through shipwreck.

None of us forgets that not all corals build reefs or barriers and islands. Some lovely isolated forms exist, marvellous in beauty of design, dainty as flowers in colour. There are the extraordinary star coral, the brain coral, the branching *Dendrophyllia*, the massive *Astroides*, the exquisite sea-pen, the sea-fan, and hundreds more, an inexhaustible study.

THE HUNDREDS OF SUCKERS IN EACH FINGER OF THE STARFISH

Another important group of sea animals turn the mineral properties of sea water to account in a different way. They have put on a lime-charged mail, which is either prickly or of a gritty, leathery texture. The prickly ones give the name to the sub-kingdom. That name is *Echinoderm*, which is derived from two words meaning hedgehog-skin. The whole class is jointless and limbless, though the starfish would seem to be five-limbed.

These are not legs in the ordinary way, but fingers. Yet it is by their aid that the creature moves and gains its livelihood; not by walking, however, but by suction. In each of those fingers are some hundreds of suckers, which, withdrawn when the starfish is at rest, can be protruded to grip the ground and pull the whole body forward. The starfish does not walk, then ; it glides, following every inequality of the surface by fitting itself over it, and slithering forward.

THE MIGHTY PULL WITH WHICH THE STARFISH OPENS THE OYSTER

Some children have a horror of starfish, thinking that the creatures sting. We have no reason to fear them; they do not hurt us, except commercially. Molluscs should fear them—the mussels, oysters, and cockles. The starfish can do what a man cannot; it can open an oyster with its fingers. Raising itself on the tips of its fingers, it grips the shells of the oyster firmly and pulls. The oyster is very strong, as we all know, but that steady pull wearies it. The shells are forced apart, and the starfish eats the oyster.

Enormous damage is done to our shell-fishes in some years by starfishes. In 1918 they attacked the East Coast shellfish beds in such swarms that one small trawl alone dredged up 37 tons of the five-rayed foes, but not till the latter had devoured every mussel and cockle in the channels of the low-lying areas on which they had advanced. And that followed the destruction, two years earlier, of 75 tons of starfish in the same area. Fishermen hate these little creatures, and were wont to tear them to pieces. This was fatally mischievous, as well as cruel, for sundered pieces of starfish grow into new starfishes!

There is no such charge of damage to urge against the starfish's cousins, the sea-urchins and the sea-cucumbers. It is generally possible to find a sea-urchin without going to the sea. One has only to gain access to a chalky formation and dig, and fossil urchins are practically certain to be there. These are the creatures which, in addition to a limy shell, possess the prickles, like a hedgehog, which give the name to the whole group.

THE STRANGE CREATURE WHICH SHEDS ITS INSIDE WHEN FRIGHTENED

The sea-cucumbers lack the prickles, but lime enters largely into the composition of their covering. The proportion of this mineral in the sea-cucumber determines its value in countries where these animals are eaten. The sea-cucumber has the faculty of dismembering itself. A lizard can snap off its tail, a brittlestar can shiver its fingers to pieces, a lobster or a crab can shed its shell and the lining of its digestive system while preserving its soft body-form; but the sea-cucumber, if it is frightened, or angry, or unwell, can discard its entire interior, stomach, intestines, tentacles; everything, one would think, which makes life either tolerable or possible.

Away go all its physical possessions save the mere empty skin. There lies this apparently lifeless husk, for weeks, perhaps months; a husk in which the life principle alone remains, the tendency to grow and regenerate. The creature cannot eat or drink or in any perceptible way take nourishment. Yet, as the lobster regrows its claws, the lizard its tail, the starfish its fingers, so this lowly marvel develops a new body, which the external covering alone remains to house.

Animal life, one would think, could hardly go deeper into primitive characters than these we have been considering, but the profoundest deeps of life have not yet been reached.

The Story of the Things We See About us Every Day

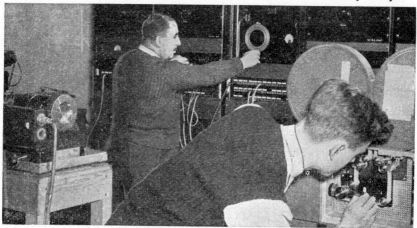

In the sound-recording room of a film studio

HOW THE CINEMA CAME

WHEN the men of the Stone Age painted pictures of running horses on the walls of their caves they drew the legs of the animals in very queer positions. The attitudes of the horses, indeed, seemed so unnatural that when modern explorers found the pictures they laughed at them.

But the men of the Stone Age were accurate after all. Horses do run like that, and it was the Cinema that proved the ancient artists to be right, for the instantaneous photographs taken for a film show the galloping horse's legs in exactly the same positions as they were drawn by the Cave Men. Those early artists might indeed call the moving-picture maker of the twentieth century as a witness to their accuracy of observation.

The cinema is undoubtedly one of the most wonderful of the many wonderful inventions of modern times. It makes a picture live, and by its aid we can reconstruct the past, we can bring the whole world of the present with its varied and magic life into a room, and we can see not only the actions and hear the voices of men, but we can witness the processes of Nature herself in operation.

Unlike the telephone, the gramophone, and many other wonders of the day, the cinema cannot be said to have been invented by any one man. Rather is it the product of the discoveries and inventions of many men, all working toward the same end. The moving picture is, in fact, not so much an invention as an evolution. The inventors of the ordinary photograph were, of course, the pioneers, though even without them we could have had moving pictures of a kind. But such would have been drawings, and might or might not have been true to life according to the skill or otherwise of the artist. It was photography that opened up the vast possibilities which have come, and are still coming, to fruition in the splendid moving picture of today.

It is a matter of great satisfaction that Englishmen should have played the leading part in the development of the cinema. So far back as 1833 an apparatus called the Zoetrope, or wheel of life, was invented or described by an English mathematician, W. G. Horner, and gave to pictures an appearance of vivid movement. It consisted of a hollow cylinder with a number of slots cut round its upper part, and round its lower part inside was arranged a series of drawn pictures showing successive stages in the movements of a galloping horse, a walking man, or other moving objects. When the cylinder was rotated, and one peeped through the slots which came in rapid succession as though they were one slot, the horse seemed to be galloping, or the man walking. This was due to each picture of the series impressing the eye for only a moment, and the whole set becoming merged into what seemed to be one picture combining the successive positions of the legs and body, with the illusion of motion.

HOW THE FIRST MOVING PICTURE OF A HORSE WAS TAKEN

The zoetrope was soon improved upon, and was succeeded by a number of later and better appliances with long and difficult names, like praxinoscope; but we must remember that the old zoetrope was really the parent of the modern cinema, the same principle, the illusion of motion, being used in both instruments.

A great advance was made in 1872 when the idea of adapting photography to the zoetrope was first thought of. In that year Edward Muybridge, a native of Kingston-upon-Thames living in San Francisco, conceived a novel way of obtaining a series of snapshot photographs of a galloping horse. He arranged 24 cameras side by side along a track, and on the opposite side of the track he erected a high fence painted white, while across the track at intervals he stretched 24 threads, each of which was connected with a spring holding in position the shutter of a camera. A horse was then set galloping along the track, and, as it passed each thread, it snapped it, opening the shutter, and taking a photograph of itself.

THE MEN WHO GAVE US THE FILM AND THE MOVING PICTURE CAMERA

The result was a series of 24 instantaneous photographs, more or less in silhouette, showing successive movements of a horse galloping.

But before the moving photograph could become a practical proposition the film had to be invented, for without it a thousand cameras would have been needed to take sufficient photographs to show a moving picture for one minute on a screen. Several attempts were made to devise a suitable film, but it was not until 1884 that the first real photographic film was invented by George Eastman of Kodak fame.

The next thing needed was a camera that would take a series of pictures on a film, and the first moving-picture camera to use perforated celluloid film as we know it was patented by William Friese-Greene, a native of Bristol, in 1889. His claim to be the true inventor of the moving-picture camera was decided in the United States Circuit Court of New York. As early as 1885 he had produced a moving-picture camera in which glass plates were used, and in other cameras of his he used strips of sensitised paper and celluloid strips which had no perforations.

Another cinema man of this time to whom great credit is due is Louis Aimé Augustin Le Prince, a Frenchman who had settled in Leeds. While in America in 1886 he invented a multiple-lens camera for taking moving pictures, and after further experiments he produced a single-lens camera with which he photographed scenes on Leeds Bridge in 1888. On this occasion he used a strip of sensitised paper; though he, too, thought of the idea of having perforated edges for his films.

Friese-Greene and Le Prince were thus working along the same lines although entirely independent of each other.

Later, Edison invented the kinetoscope, into which we looked to see the moving picture, turning a handle to rotate the photographs; this he patented in 1893, showing it at the World's Fair at Chicago.

THE IMMENSE MULTITUDE OF PEOPLE WATCHING MOVING PICTURES

Both Friese-Greene and Le Prince succeeded in projecting their pictures on to screens, but the first really satisfactory projector was invented by Robert W. Paul, another Englishman, in 1895.

From that time to this the story of the cinema has been one of constant progress and improvement. The most important development was the introduction of talking films in 1929, which made the cinema a greater rival to the legitimate theatre than ever before. Films in full colours are an attractive but more recent development.

The chief appeal of the cinema is as an entertainment, but it also plays a very great part in education. The moving-picture industry, which has grown up during this century, is one of the greatest in the world. In the United Kingdom alone every year over 1600 million seats are occupied by people watching the films. It is a record without parallel.

No longer is the film producer entirely dependent on the weather for his outdoor scenes. With wonderful cameras and with batteries of powerful lamps to provide extra lighting, outdoor photography of excellent quality is sometimes possible even on dull days, and night scenes are often taken out of doors. Here we see cameramen photographing an out-door scene for a film from a travelling camera-crane, with a battery of lamps in the background.

SYNCHRONISING SOUND TRACK AND PICTURE

The scenes in a film are photographed in any convenient sequence, and so at the beginning of each scene a board giving the scene number and other details is held in front of the camera. On top it has a " clapper " which is shut with a sharp rap to assist subsequent synchronisation of sound track and picture.

In the finished picture this appeared as a scene in eighteenth-century Germany, but if we had walked into the studio we should also have seen all the paraphernalia of a twentieth-century film studio. The lamps and other apparatus above the scene are of course outside the range of the moving-picture camera.

LOOKING DOWN ON THE SCENE IN THE STUDIO

It is sometimes necessary to photograph scenes from unusual angles. For this purpose a camera crane is used. Fixed on to the platform at the end of the crane arm, the camera, with the camera crew and director, can be moved in any direction.

The camera photographs the scene which is to be part of the film, but if it were turned in other directions in the studio this is typical of what it would reveal—a maze of cables and lamps.

MAKE-BELIEVE IN THE FILM WORLD

It does not require a very vivid imagination to feel that we are inside one of the large rooms in a hotel situated high up in the Alps, when looking at this picture. Yet the scene was built up in a London studio with a huge photograph of an actual scene in the Alps used as a background.

The carpenter's shop is an important department, for here are built, under the direction of experts, not only the great variety of scenery used, but also many objects required in the films. Here we see some boats being made.

BELGIUM IN THE ENGLISH COUNTRYSIDE

On the double score of expense and convenience it is often better to construct a large outdoor scene than to go to the actual place which it is desired to represent in the film. On the left of this picture we see a square in a Belgian town, while on the right we see the flimsy framework on which the apparently substantial buildings were constructed. This scene was taken in the Hertfordshire countryside, while an interested crowd looked on.

Even where the place to be portrayed is quite near, it is often more convenient to construct the scene in the studio; and this though the scene may show for only a few seconds in the film. Here a scene at a railway station is being filmed

PALESTINE AND LONDON IN THE STUDIO

A popular technical device for reducing the cost of expensive sets is back projection. A previously-filmed background is projected on to a screen in the studio and blends in with the foreground constructed on the stage, as can be seen in this filming of an episode in the Biblical story of Ruth and Naomi.

There is nothing in the picture on the right to suggest that it is not a London street scene, but the figures in the picture on the left, showing the scene being photographed, reveal that a model was used. A realistic accident in which the crane and the bus were involved on a stormy night was staged with the aid of this model.

TWO KINDS OF FILM IN THE MAKING

The travellers we see departing on a long-distance continental train, or on a ship, need not have gone farther than the studio. Here are two such scenes in course of production in a film studio in London.

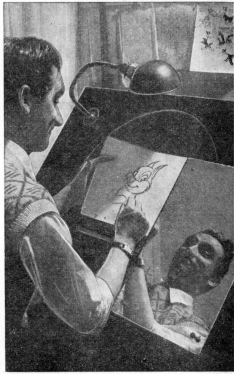

An animated cartoon is built up from a number of successive pictures thrown on to the screen at the rate of 24 a second. A film lasting ten minutes would thus be built up of 14,400 separate drawings. These pictures show artists at work on two of the characters in a series of British-made coloured cartoons. The man on the right uses a mirror so that his own reflection may suggest expressions for the character he is sketching.

MAKING A STORY FROM PIECES OF FILM

The sound and picture films taken during the previous day's work, having been developed and printed, are then synchronised, the girl operator being helped by the picture and sound of the clapper striking, as described on page 6706.

The film, approved by the director, is passed on to the editor, who gradually builds up the complete story, cutting out any surplus material. He uses a special machine with which he can stop or reverse the film at will.

When the editor has prepared his complete story the many pieces of positive film are welded together in this splicing machine. An identical version has then to be cut out and assembled from the original negative.

By means of a mixing panel a sound engineer can re-record the various sounds used in a film, such as dialogue, music, and sound effects, on to one strip of film. The panel enables him to vary the volume of each type of sound.

When editing is complete, the film is shown on a special projector, which can show separate sound and picture tracks simultaneously. Thus, any necessary alterations can be made to one without affecting the other.

Here is a peep at a film vault, where numerous strips of sound and picture film are stored. Thus, almost any sound effects that may be needed can quickly be found, as well as extra "takes" of various scenes.

SPORTING AND INSTRUCTIONAL FILMS

The cine-camera is a familiar sight at all big sporting events. In the picture on the left we see a camera being erected on the roof of a van for the filming of equestrian events, and in that on the right a cameraman on a 24-foot high steel tower is taking shots during an athletic meeting at Wembley Stadium in London.

Films are being widely used for educational purposes in all kinds of schools, and instructive pictures have for many years found a place in the programmes of cinemas. Here we see a camera at work in the High Tension Room of the famous Cavendish Laboratory, Cambridge, while making a film on Atomic Physics.

DEVELOPING AND PRINTING THE FILMS

This picture shows one of the principal methods of developing films today. The developing solutions are sprayed on to the films instead of immersing the films in tanks.

Here we see a film printing-machine which is used for all types of optical trick work. It can deal with 16-mm. as well as the standard 35-mm. films.

The modern developing machine seen in this picture is used for colour film. The film has to pass through a large number of tanks for this process. In course of time black-and-white films will probably become as obsolete as silent films.

WORKERS BEHIND THE CINEMA SCENES

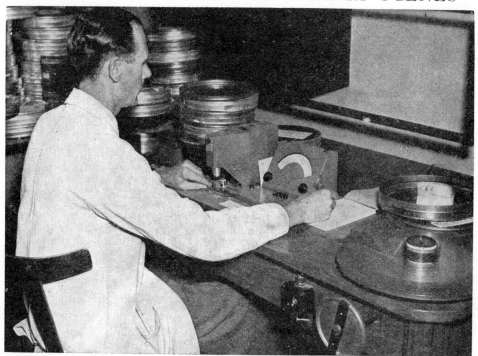

This picture shows a modern densitometer in use. This electrical instrument is used to measure density of image on the film in order that the picture on the screen shall be neither too light nor too dark.

In this picture we see film negatives being cut and joined. The girl wears gloves at her work and handles the film with the utmost care to avoid any risk of scratching the tiny pictures.

RECORDING THE SOUND FOR A FILM

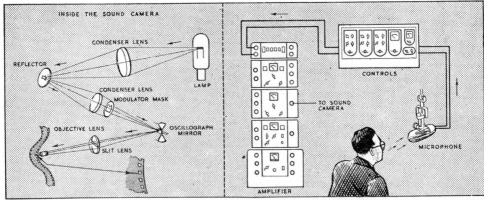

In producing talking films the sound is usually photographed on to the film simultaneously with the picture record of the action. The talker speaks into a microphone, which converts the sound waves into electrical impulses, as in the telephone. These are amplified, and cause a mirror to vibrate according to the variations of the electrical impulses. Light rays are directed through a lens on to the mirror, which is a part of the oscillograph, or modulating device. This mirror reflects the light on to another lens through which it passes to the moving film on which the photographic record is made.

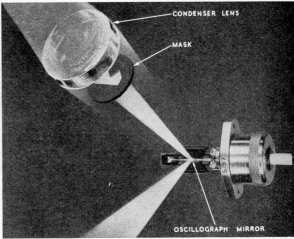

The pictures and sound are photographed on separate films and mounted side by side, the sound film 14½ inches ahead of the pictures. They are then developed as one film. Here we see the sound section on the left as two bands of light which are varied in area to make a picture of the sound waves, exactly as the electrical impulses were photographed.

Here is the oscillograph, which is a form of vibrator. A loop of wire is stretched into a kind of narrow hairpin with the two parallel sides very close together. Attached across the centre of the loop is a tiny oblong mirror. The ends of the loop are connected to the amplifiers, which strengthen the sound impulses, and the loop itself is suspended between the poles of a magnet. When the sound impulses arrive, the loop vibrates, and of course the mirror with it, so causing the reflected beam of light to dance up and down and thus produce sound-wave pictures on the film.

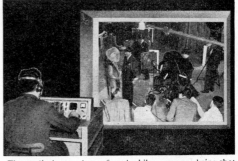

Here we see the sound camera which photographs the sound waves. The film placed in the right-hand magazine unwinds and passes before the lens, where the sound waves are photographed, and then into the left-hand magazine. The film moves constantly at a speed of 90 feet a minute.

The studio is sound proof, and while scenes are being shot a man sits inside a sound-proof compartment, watching the action and listening carefully to the sounds picked up by the microphone. The control panel which he has before him is connected to the microphone, and he controls the volume and the quality of the sound.

HOW THE PICTURE IS PROJECTED

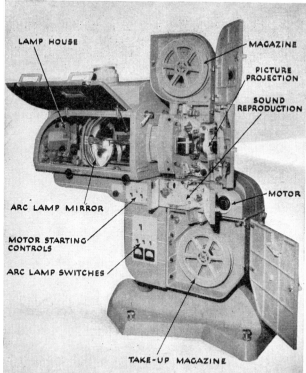

LAMP HOUSE

MAGAZINE

PICTURE PROJECTION

SOUND REPRODUCTION

ARC LAMP MIRROR

MOTOR STARTING CONTROLS

ARC LAMP SWITCHES

MOTOR

TAKE-UP MAGAZINE

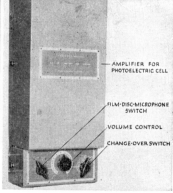

AMPLIFIER FOR PHOTOELECTRIC CELL

FILM-DISC-MICROPHONE SWITCH

VOLUME CONTROL

CHANGE-OVER SWITCH

The switch marked Volume Control allows the projectionist to keep the sound at a constant pitch. The changeover switch enables him to change to another projector when he has reached the end of one reel. The left-hand switch is for playing records and making announcements.

EXCITER LAMP

LENS

PHOTO-ELECTRIC CELL

FILM DRIVING SPROCKETS

This is the projector which presents the film in the cinema. The film is loaded into the magazine, the lights are switched on, and the film is set in motion. While the pictures are passing before the lens at the rate of 24 a second, the corresponding portion of sound-film is passing steadily before the sound projector below. As the soundhead is below the picture lens we see why the sound film has to be placed 14½ inches ahead of the pictures.

When the sound film is reproduced, light passing through lenses is focused on to the film. The light rays passing through the film are modulated by the area of the sound track and directed on to a photo-electric cell, where the light waves are converted into electrical impulses and then amplified.

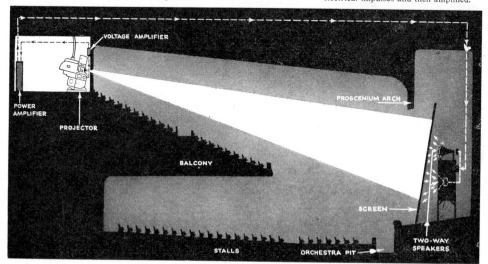

VOLTAGE AMPLIFIER

POWER AMPLIFIER

PROJECTOR

BALCONY

PROSCENIUM ARCH

SCREEN

STALLS

ORCHESTRA PIT

TWO-WAY SPEAKERS

This elevation gives an impression of the arrangements in a cinema. The sound waves amplified in the projector cabin are passed by wiring through the theatre to loud speakers behind the screen. The screen is perforated to allow the sound waves to pass through and be heard without muffling by the audience. Two-way speakers give correct rendering to the upper register (such as consonants in speech), and to the lower register (for example, bass instruments in orchestras), and so render a truer balance of sound.

Pictures on these pages are by courtesy of companies within the J. Arthur Rank Organisation.

A DIAMOND AND ITS STORY

For thousands of years men and women have sought after diamonds and have paid fortunes to obtain them. At one time all diamonds came from India, and when these gems were found in Brazil they had to be sent to India and sold from there as Indian diamonds, because people did not believe that Brazilian

| A million years ago a mass of iron and carbon lay mixed together in the earth's crust, with enormous pressure upon it. | By some means the substances became molten at a great depth, and a drop of carbon floated in the liquid iron. | Gradually the mass cooled, and the drop of carbon became a crystal, which we now know to be a diamond. | An explosion forced a channel to the surface of the earth, and volcanic mud containing the diamond was forced up. |

| Water passed over the place later and gradually washed away the earth, carrying the diamond with the mud. | Other mud was deposited on top of the diamond, and centuries later this had become hard rock beneath dry land. | One day men came and dug out the earth, including a piece of rock which contained the diamond. | The rock was spread out in the sun and left for months, till it had become less hard and more easy for crushing. |

| It was then taken to a factory, where the piece of rock containing the diamond was crushed with similar pieces. | Next the crushed rock was washed round and round till all the heavier fragments, including the diamond, had sunk | The fragments were then passed with water over a series of greased tables, the diamond sticking to the grease. | The diamond, with others, was sorted out, washed, weighed, and valued, and then packed and sent to Europe or America. |

| It was next handed to a diamond-cutter, who cut away the flaws and gave it facets so that it would scintillate. | After being cut it was polished on flat metal discs, fed with diamond-dust and oil, and revolved at great speed. | It was then mounted, with other diamonds, by a jeweller, who made it the chief stone in a beautiful necklace. | And when a lady wore it the diamond was admired by all, though how many who saw it could guess its ancient history? |

diamonds were genuine. The biggest find of diamonds has been in South Africa, where stones worth more than 16 million pounds have been taken out in a single year, although production for many years has been considerably less than this. The Cullinan diamond, biggest ever found, came from a mine in the Transvaal.

Plain Answers to the Questions of the Children of the World

How Far We See When Our Eyes are at Various Heights

1....1¼	14....5	60....10¼	130....15	600....32½
2....1¾	16....5¼	65....10½	140....15½	650....33¾
3....2¼	18....5½	70....11	150....16¼	700....35
4....2½	20....6	75....11½	200....18¾	800....37½
5....3	25....6½	80....12	250....21	900....40
6....3¼	30....7¼	85....12¼	300....23	1000....42
7....3½	35....8	90....12½	350....24¾	2000....59¼
8....3¾	40....8½	95....13	400....25½	3000....72½
9....4	45....9	100....13¼	450....28	4000....83¾
10....4¼	50....9½	110....14	500....29½	5000....93½
12....4½	55....10	120....14½	550....31	5280....96

The first figure is the height in feet, up to a mile; the second is the rough distance seen in miles (not exact to small fractions).

HOW FAR CAN WE SEE?

When we say that our eyes see, all we really mean is that light has entered them, and has affected them. If that happens, we see. It does not matter whether the light has been produced by a match that someone has held in front of our eye, or whether the light has come from a star so distant that its light took ten thousand years to reach us. In either case, if light enters our eye in sufficient quantity to affect it, we see. The answer to our question, therefore, is that our eyes can see to any distance from which light can reach them. The question whether the light has travelled billions and billions of miles, or only half an inch, makes not the slightest difference to our eyes.

It is quite a distinct question at what distance our eyes can distinguish the details of a particular thing. This depends on many things, but it can be reckoned to some extent, and it is very important to do this for the case of different telescopes. We know that, if there were any building on the Moon as large as St. Paul's, it could be recognised in our best telescopes.

Standing at any given point, we can usually see what is called the horizon, from the Greek word *horos*, which means a boundary, and in this case means the boundary between the Earth and the sky. We understand, of course, that the line we see on the horizon is not really the boundary between Earth and sky, but merely the boundary between them as they appear to our eyes.

As we stand by the seashore, the sky and the sea seem to meet. We can see a line which seems to be the end of the sea and the bottom of the sky. That is the horizon. Similarly, if we stand on a plain of land we can, if there are no trees or houses, see where the end of the land seems to touch the bottom rim of the dome we call the sky. That also is the horizon.

Its distance depends on how high our eyes are from the level of the sea if we are looking across the sea, or from the level of the land across which we are looking if we are looking over a plain. A boy standing on the shore looks out on the sea from a distance about four feet higher than the level of the sea—the height of his eyes from sea-level. He can see just a little more than two and a half miles in front of him, and his horizon is just this distance away. The eyes of a boy on the edge of the cliff, on the other hand, are 100 feet above sea-level, and he can see about 13¼ miles off, and that is where the horizon is. Again, the top of a lighthouse is 150 feet above sea-level, and a boy looking out on the sea from this point would see about 16¼ miles, his horizon being 16¼ miles away.

The scientific explanation of all this would be that "range of vision is determined by the altitude of the observer." In simple language, this means that the higher up we are the farther we can see. That is because our world is a globe. Perhaps we can understand better how this is if we stand in front of a row of houses forming a bulging crescent. Stand close to one of the houses, and turn your head first to the right, and then to the left. You cannot see much of the row of houses, perhaps only a little bit of the house on each side of the one of which you stand in front. Step back into the middle of the road, and look again. Now you can see a good many more of the houses, but still not all if the row is long. Then cross to the far side of the road, and many more will be found to have come within range.

To look for the horizon is much the same thing. The Earth is round, and the farther we are above the ground along which we are looking, the farther we can see. The table on page 6719 shows how far anyone can see at various distances from the Earth's surface. At one mile high we can see 96 miles. The figures are generally correct, but not quite exact, as the table is drawn up for simplicity, and so avoids small fractions.

Why Does it Rain so Much in Scotland?

This is one of those difficult questions about the weather which no one can fully answer. One of the great causes of rain is the existence of much water for the Sun to draw up, and so any island is far more rainy than the interior of a continent, such as the Sahara Desert. That applies to the whole of the British Isles. But the rain that falls in our islands is principally brought from the greatest expanse of water near them, which is the Atlantic Ocean. So it is chiefly the " warm, wet western wind " that brings the rain. It deposits the rain most where it is most cooled, and as Scotland is farther north than England it is colder; and so its climate condenses more rain than the climate of England does. Scotland also has a very broken west coast, so that the water of the sea comes far up into the land, as in the case of the Clyde, round which there is more rain than anywhere else in Scotland. The west coast of Ireland is very rainy, too, and Ireland catches part of the rain which would otherwise fall on England. Scotland, again, is very hilly and mountainous, and air is cooled in rising over hills, and so

deposits much of its moisture as rain. Of course, the east coast of Scotland is far drier than the west, for when the west wind reaches it, it has already spent most of its moisture farther west.

Why is it Easier to Swim in Salt Water Than in Fresh?

The answer depends wholly on the heaviness of our bodies as compared with the heaviness of the water. Our bodies are more than three-fourths water, but most of the rest is heavier than water. The fat of our bodies is lighter than water, and so helps us to float. Now, fresh water is less heavy than salt water, and so our bodies, though only a little heavier than it, tend to sink in it. Ordinary sea water is heavier than fresh water, because it contains a lot of salts melted in it, just as the water of our own bodies does ; so we find it easier to float and swim in sea water. But in some parts of the world there is water that is much salter than even sea water; this is the case, for instance, in the Dead Sea, and we have all heard of the Great Salt Lake in America. There is so much salt in the water of the Dead Sea that it is actually heavier, on the whole, than our bodies are, and you cannot sink in the Dead Sea! On the other hand, there are some liquids much lighter than water, and if a man were to fall into a lake of one of them he could not swim at all, however good a swimmer he was, for his body would sink like a stone.

Who Founded the Boys' Brigade?

The Boys' Brigade, which is the oldest of our national organisations for boys, was founded in Glasgow, in 1883, by Sir William Smith.

Religion and discipline are the foundations of the movement, whose object is : " The advancement of Christ's Kingdom among Boys, and the promotion of habits of Obedience, Reverence, Discipline, Self-Respect, and all that tends towards a true Christian manliness."

Sir William and two colleagues banded together thirty boys to start the Boys' Brigade; today there are some 3,200 companies throughout the world, with a membership of about 110,000 officers and boys. The boys' ages range from 12 to 18, and in the junior branch—the Life Boys with a membership of some 60,000 boys—between 9 and 12.

WHAT DO THE WORDS ON A WEATHER MAP MEAN ?

There are many strange-looking words on a weather map, and if we are to understand the weather report we must know their meanings.

Perhaps the most familiar are the words beginning with *iso*. This prefix means equal, and the words are used of certain irregular curved lines appearing on the map. Some of these are called *isobars*, and join up places of equal barometric pressure, that is to say, places where the reading of the barometer is the same. *Isotherms* are the lines joining places of the same temperature, the word meaning equal heat. *Isohels* are lines showing equal duration of sunshine, *hels* being from the Greek word helios, meaning the Sun. *Isohyets* are lines showing equal amounts of rain, *hyets* being from heutos, meaning rain. *Isodynamics*, a word meaning equal power or force, is used in two senses. It may mean lines connecting places where the intensity of the Earth's magnetism is equal, or lines joining places where the winds are of a specified force.

A *cyclone* in a weather chart does not mean a raging tornado; it is simply the name given to a region of low barometric pressure, that is, a region where the pressure of the air is less than that round about. The result is that air from the surrounding regions of high pressure pours in and so there is a movement of the atmosphere in which the wind blows spirally round and in toward a centre. This movement may be gentle or rapid, and general or local. When it is gentle, it is quite as truly a cyclone as when it is dangerously rapid. A cyclone in this sense is also called a *depression* (or a low).

An *anti-cyclone* is a region in which the barometric pressure is high, or greater than that of surrounding districts ; and it is generally shown on a weather chart by roughly circular or oval curves representing the isobars. The wind blows spirally outwards, the region of highest pressure being the central region of the anti-cyclone. The word anti-cyclone, of course, means the opposite of a cyclone, and sometimes the word high is used instead of anti-cyclone.

A *V-shaped depression* is the expression used to describe isobars having the shape of the letter V, which enclose an area of low pressure. The point of the V is always to the south or the east. A *barogram* is the continuous record of atmospheric pressure made by a barograph, or a self-recording barometer. In the same way an *anemogram* is the record of an anemograph, an instrument recording the speed or force of the wind, the Greek word *anemos* meaning the wind. *Katabatic* (made up of two Greek words meaning going down) is a word used in weather reports to describe the downward motion of the air. A local cold wind is called katabatic when it is caused by cold air descending from high ground by gravitation.

Veering is the changing of the wind in the direction of the motion of the hands of a watch; the opposite is called *backing*.

Aerology is a word which has come into use in recent times to indicate that part of meteorology which is concerned with the study of the upper air, a study carried on by means of small free balloons filled with hydrogen gas. They are released, and by following their progress with the help of a specially designed theodolite, knowledge is gained of the wind currents at great heights.

Humidity, a familiar word for dampness, is used in meteorology to describe the amount of water vapour in a measured volume of air. The term *saturation*, when applied to the air, means that the air contains as vapour all the moisture it can possibly hold at that temperature.

Phenology is a term used to describe the study of the natural changes taking place from season to season, and it includes all natural phenomena, such as seed-times, harvests, flowering, ripening, migration, and so on ; but in practice it is often limited to the times on which certain trees and plants come into leaf and flower each year, and to the dates of the first and last appearance of birds and insects.

Insolation is a word used to describe the solar radiation received by the Earth and other planets. A *pentad* (Greek for five) is a period of five days. Five-day averages are used in meteorology because five divides into 365, the number of days in our year.

Serein is fine rain falling from an apparently clear sky; a *line-squall* is a squall of wind accompanied by rain or hail, associated with a sudden drop of temperature and the passing of a long line of dark cloud.

TEMPERATURE MAPS OF THE BRITISH ISLES

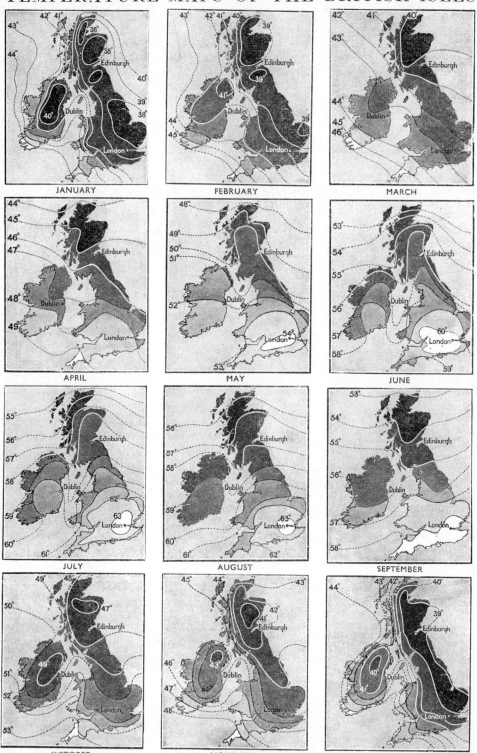

JANUARY   FEBRUARY   MARCH

APRIL   MAY   JUNE

JULY   AUGUST   SEPTEMBER

OCTOBER   NOVEMBER   DECEMBER

In these maps the figures show the average temperatures and the lines enclose areas of equal warmth

RAINFALL MAPS OF THE BRITISH ISLES

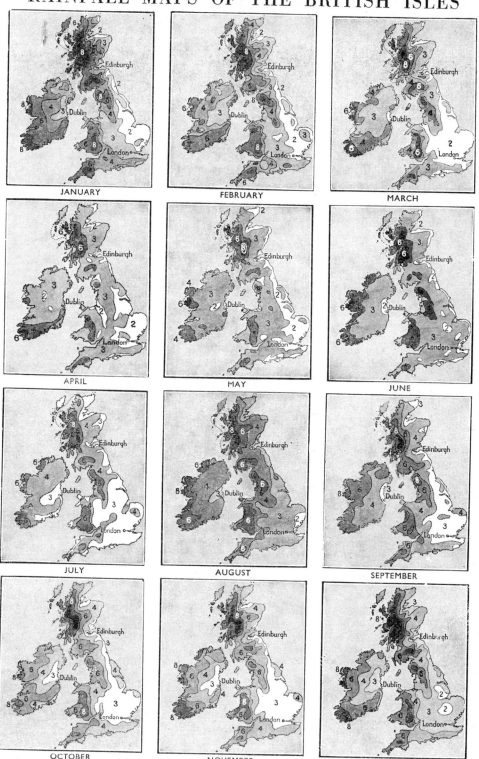

In these maps the figures show the average rainfall in inches for the areas marked

6723

Can the Planting of Grass add Acres to England ?

It has been found that the cultivation of rice grass enables derelict mud banks to be reclaimed in a way which is not otherwise possible. Acres of marshy land on our East Coast have been planted with this strong-growing plant, which holds the sediment deposited on it through floods and binds this newly-acquired material so that the level of the mud flats is gradually raised. The grass, too, forms good food for grazing animals, both as fresh grass and as cut hay.

Could a Wireless Wave Go Round the Universe ?

A wireless wave, whether regarded as a vibration or an assemblage of electric particles, would, when once started on its journey, continue its path without ceasing unless impeded on its way. A wireless wave will go round the world because it is continually reflected back from a kind of electric layer miles above the Earth's surface. But if we ask whether it can similarly go round the Universe we have to consider whether it is true, as some 20th-century mathematicians have declared, that the Universe is a sphere.

Some doubt on this idea has been cast by Professor Einstein, who lent his support to it, but declared later that it was impossible to determine mathematically the curvature of such a sphere. Consequently it is quite as likely that space is boundless and our wireless wave could go on for ever, never returning on itself as it would if it were travelling round a spherical universe.

It may be worth while to consider what would be the radius of a spherical universe if we allow ourselves to believe that such is its shape and to ask also why we should think that it may be. The width of the great galaxy of a thousand million stars to which we belong is 100,000 light-years. Multiply that figure by six billions and we have its diameter in miles. If our wireless wave had only to travel round that spiral it would return on itself in something over 300,000 years.

But beyond our spiral are other spiral universes, the nearest 850,000 light-years away. There are many beyond them. Does this distribution also come to an end, or are there other super-systems beyond? There is one ray of light on this dark prob-

lem. These spiral universes seem to be hurrying away from us at speeds sometimes approaching 1000 miles a second. Why do they appear to do so ? A possible answer is that the vibrations of light coming from them deceive us and have really travelled round a large portion of a spherical universe before reaching us instead of coming in a direct line.

On that theory the radius of space, or let us say the Universe, can be calculated as 20 times the average distance of the nebulae, or say 100 million light-years. A ray of light or a wireless wave would take something more than six times that number of years to travel round.

How Did the Great Silence Begin ?

The keeping of a two-minute silence on Remembrance Day was an application of an old idea to a very solemn occasion. The idea of the Angelus bell with its call for a brief respite for silent prayer, is but one of the examples of the spiritual values of silence. Two-minute silences were observed at all the meetings of the Anglican Conference in London in 1906, and before then the Society of Friends had always stressed the value of silence for meditation. The originator of the Silence on Remembrance Day was Edward Honey, an Australian reporter working in Fleet Street, who wrote an article about it. This was read by the South African statesman Sir Percy Fitzpatrick, who asked Lord Milner to convey the proposal to King George the Fifth, who authorised its adoption.

Who Suggested the Idea of the Unknown Warrior ?

The man who first realised the consolation to the bereaved which would result from the burial of an unknown victim of the First World War in Westminster Abbey was David Railton. He was a curate at Folkestone who had served in France as a chaplain. Later he became Vicar of Margate and of Bolton, near Bradford. Mr. Railton took his suggestion to the Dean of Westminster, who placed it before the Cabinet. The Union Jack which hangs above the grave in the Abbey is the very flag which David Railton used in France as a pall for the bodies of the soldiers he buried. It is one of the very few British flags which were taken to France during the First World War.

WHAT IS A SALMON-LADDER?

To continue its species, the salmon must leave the open sea and find its way up the rivers to the source-stream where it was born. Nothing but death will prevent it from doing so. It will battle its way against the strongest currents, swim through the fiercest rapids, and leap the waterfalls until it reaches the head waters and tributaries where the current flows gently through quiet pools. Here the salmon finds its spawning bed, the very bed where it began its own life. To reach this spot it has fought the river for

native stream for two years after hatching, and acquire the homing instinct.

To reduce casualties, " salmon ladders " have been devised to help them past the worst waterfalls. Alongside the steep cataracts, less difficult leaps are provided. Part of the down-flow is diverted over a series of stairs, or ledges, so that the salmon can mount by stages.

Such ladders become the more necessary when salmon-rivers are dammed to provide hydro-electric power and the waterfalls are channelled through generators. This makes impossible obstacles for the fish. A spill-over by-passes the dam, over the terraces of the salmon-ladder. The leaps are still considerable because the struggle for survival is part of the nature of the salmon.

There are also freshwater fish with a similar urge, among them being the little *pla soi* of Thailand which battle up the mountain rivers. For them, similar ladders have been devised. The fish are about the size of a sardine. To surmount one cataract, a twelve-stage ladder has been made, with the first and last steps a metre high. This means that the fish jump ten times as high as their own length—like a man jumping an obstacle 6o feet high—against the strong current and with the certainty, if they fail, of being devoured by the carnivorous fish waiting in the pool below.

The salmon-ladder by the power-station at Pitlochry, Perthshire. Right: a salmon makes a great leap.

days, and sometimes even up to several weeks.

The cock salmon uses its body to dig a hole about a foot deep in gravel, into which the hen fish lays some hundreds of eggs. These are fertilised by the cock fish, then covered with stones and gravel, and left to hatch out.

Its task fulfilled, the salmon, now changed by its exertions from the silvery king of the river to a dirty, tarnished, flabby *kelt*, drifts and tumbles listlessly down the river to the sea—there to regain its strength and colour to repeat the hazardous performance a year later. The young salmon usually remain in their

WHAT IS THE MEANING OF AUTOMATION?

THE word " automation " was originally coined in America to describe the automatic handling of manufactured parts during progressive stages of production. Its use has since been extended to the whole range of automatic control in industry.

In the more advanced countries, human effort for pulling, lifting, and carrying heavy loads has been largely replaced by machines—machines driven by steam, petrol, oil, or electricity, but controlled by men.

Where machine-power takes the place of man-power we speak of mechanisation. Where automatic control is added to machine power, then we have automation.

Automation became possible with the development of machines able to control and supervise their own operations. But it is not a new discovery. Its principles have been known to engineers for many years. One example is the thermostat which automatically maintains heat at a constant temperature ; yet another is the automatic telephone exchange.

These machines use a principle known as " feedback," which is inseparable from true automation. They have self-operating control mechanisms capable of " feeding back " a signal or impulse to the main component, causing it to modify its function, or perform a new one. Engineers are now able to construct machines in which a whole series of different feedback controls can be linked. One such machine, making cylinder blocks for car engines, automatically controls and supervises no fewer than 555 successive and continuous operations.

The great progress in automation in recent years is due to the introduction of electronics. As long ago as 1904 Sir Ambrose Fleming patented the thermionic valve, and from this have sprung radio, television, and radar, as well as the more recent application of electronics to office and factory machines.

The Second World War brought many urgent scientific problems. Among them were those relating to the science of ballistics, which deals with the motion of projectiles—shells, bombs, and guided missiles. Scientists and mathematicians were seriously hampered by the overwhelming number of calculations needed before they could arrive at the results of their experiments. The answer was to build a machine—the so-called " electronic brain " which could automatically make all these calculations.

The first purely electronic calculating machine was completed in the United States in 1946. It is still operating and will probably remain the largest electronic computer or calculator ever to be built—it has 18,000 valves. Engineers have since found it possible to design computers with greater capacity but needing less equipment, and small machines are being constructed for ordinary commercial and industrial use.

These electronic machines work at lightning speed. They are equipped with storage units or " memories," which enable them not only to absorb the data on which calculations are being made, but also detailed instructions telling them exactly what arithmetical formulae they are to follow, and the required sequence of each computing step.

Apart from their ability to add, subtract, divide, and multiply, these electronic machines can exercise judgment in comparing the sizes of different pairs of numbers, and discrimination in choosing alternative procedures according to the conditions met with during their operations. They are therefore able, in a matter of minutes (or, at the most, in a few hours) to do complex sums which normally would take weeks or months.

For any calculating or accounting procedure the electronic computer is first provided with a programme. Nothing must be omitted from the programme because, contrary to popular belief, the computer is not an " electronic brain." All the thinking necessary must be done for it—and done beforehand. After this " the machine takes charge."

The same principles are involved in the automation of manufacturing processes and control systems. The machine will see that all instructions are faithfully performed, so long as those instructions are clear and definite. It will plan and machine complicated aeroplane parts a hundred times faster than skilled operators. An aircraft turbine blade takes three weeks to plan and manufacture by normal methods ; but computer-controlled machine tools can produce it in four hours.

WHAT IS AN AQUALUNG?

A<small>N</small> aqualung, as the name suggests, is a device which enables a diver to breathe under water. It consists of a cylinder of compressed air held by harness on the diver's back, and a breathing tube which leads to a face mask, the front of which is a one-piece lens. The mask traps a layer of air between the eyes and the water, thus compensating for the difference in light refraction in air and water and providing almost normal vision when submerged. A single-cylinder apparatus enables a diver to stay submerged for 30 to 40 minutes and a double cylinder for about an hour.

An essential part of the equipment are which automatically supplied compressed air to the diver at the same pressure as that of the surrounding water. This was incorporated into the aqualung, giving Man the " freedom of the ocean."

This very freedom is, in fact, the diver's biggest danger. Nitrogen is ever present in the air we breathe and is normally quite harmless, but under great pressure, in other words, at great depths, the nitrogen taken into the lungs affects the brain. It causes the diver to lose all sense of judgment, so that he is quite likely to feel that he does not need his air pipe, and even to offer it to some passing fish. " The rapture of the deep " was the name

AN UNDERWATER SWIMMER USING AN AQUALUNG

the flippers, worn on the feet to propel the diver, thus leaving his hands free to carry tools or a camera. In cold waters, too, most divers wear a rubber suit for warmth ; and because the body is buoyant—in other words, tends to float on the surface—weights are worn in a belt round the diver's waist.

Underwater swimming is not new. For hundreds of years the South Sea Islanders have dived to great depths to catch fish ; and the Indian and Japanese pearl divers long ago learned to explore the sea bed. The aqualung, however, which enables Man to swim almost as easily as a fish, is a comparatively new invention.

In 1936 Jacques-Yves Cousteau, an officer in the French Navy, started diving while wearing underwater goggles. In the next few years he made many experiments, but it was not until 1943 that French engineer, Emile Cagnan, designed a valve given by Cousteau to this strange feeling of elation.

There are, of course, other dangers. The dreaded diver's bends, for example, caused by a diver ascending from a great depth too quickly without allowing the nitrogen in the blood to be eliminated. There is also air embolism, caused by rising to the surface with the lungs full of air which has been supplied at great pressure. But experienced divers know how to avoid these dangers.

Great developments in this new form of underwater exploration took place in the latter stages of the Second World War, when divers used the aqualung for a variety of purposes. In peacetime, too, the aqualung enables divers to carry out many jobs virtually impossible to anyone else, as well as providing a thrilling sport for enthusiasts who want to explore the strange, silent world under the waves.

Why Does a Straight Stick Seem Bent in Water?

We see a stick, as we see anything else, by the rays of light which come from it. These rays have certain laws as to how they travel. If they possibly can, they travel in straight lines; and so, if the stick is straight, and we see it from end to end through one substance (air or water) it appears to be straight. But we never see it straight if it is half in water and half out.

We can see for ourselves with a pencil in a glass of water. The bend always occurs at the surface of the water. If we raise the glass and look at it sideways we then see half the stick through air and half the stick through water.

Now, the rule is that whenever light passes from one thing to another, it gets bent ; and so, though the part of the stick under water appears straight enough, it is bent at an angle at the part above the water. This sharp bending of rays is called refraction.

Why are a Man's Fingerprints Photographed?

We often see in the newspapers that the police have taken a photograph of finger-prints left by a burglar on a window-pane or a piece of furniture. The reason for this is that the police hope to catch the burglar by means of these finger-prints. If we look at our hand closely we shall see that the skin is in little ridges, and it is these ridges that have come to the aid of justice. The pattern of the ridges on the tip of our finger never changes while we live, and this pattern is different from the pattern on any other finger in the world. Those who study finger-tips tell us that there are four main types, which they name according to the loops, arches, and other patterns of the ridges, but no two are the same.

We see, therefore, that if we take a print of a man's finger-tip we have a certain means of identifying him, and the police take the finger-prints of all the criminals who fall into their hands, and file them away according to a certain organised system, so that when the impression of a finger-print is found anywhere they can turn up the records and see whose it is.

As far back as 1858 Sir William Herschel, a distinguished Indian Civil servant, became interested in this idea, and fought hard to introduce the system into a British Court of Justice. But the actual public origin of the method was a letter sent to Nature in 1880 by Dr Henry Faulds, an Englishman, who shares with Sir William Herschel the credit for devising one of the most valuable instruments of justice known to man. Scotland Yard has more than a million finger-prints filed away.

Some day the finger-tip impression of every child will probably be taken at its birth as a means of identification. Mark Twain once wrote a clever novel showing how valuable such a universal system would be in settling cases of disputed identity, but he can hardly have believed that the system would actually one day be seriously proposed. If it is ever done, a country will have an absolute means of identity for every one of its citizens.

Why is a Staff Sometimes Given to an Engine Driver?

There are many sections of railway where both up and down trains use the same set of rails, and a very simple system of avoiding collisions is adopted without relying on the ordinary signals.

Before an engine-driver may take his train along a single line he must have in his possession a visible sign of his authority to enter that section of line, and so a staff with a loop at the end is handed to him. When he reaches the other end of the single line the staff is given up and passed on to another driver, who is waiting to take another train back over the same line. Until this staff is actually in the possession of the driver he must not enter the single line section.

It sometimes happens that two or more trains are to proceed in the same direction before another train comes the opposite way. In this case the staff is shown to the driver of the first train and a ticket or disc is handed to him before he enters the single line section. This ticket is given up at the other end of the single line, and the official there knows that another train is to follow because the staff has not been produced. When the last train is about to enter the section the staff is given to the driver, and the official at the other end, on receiving the staff from the driver, knows that the line is clear.

Why Does a Train not Run off the Lines when Rounding Curves ?

Newton's first law of motion says that a moving thing tends to go on moving in the same direction, and, indeed, must do so, unless something alters it. It follows from this law that the train going round a curve must run off the lines unless some forces are brought to bear on it that will tend to alter its direction.

As we know, trains can be made to run round curves. We simply have to find out what the arrangements are which interfere with the tendency to move straight. We first think of the flanges on the wheels, but these are of small importance. If there were nothing else, the

These pictures show why a train keeps on the rails. The tyres are slanting, as seen on the right, and not flat, as on the left; this causes the wheels to press outwards and the flanges keep them in position on the rails.

train would ride off the rails in a moment. The next point is the way in which the tyres are cut, as we can see on this page; and, finally, there is a most important arrangement by which the outer rail on a curve is raised. When the railway is made, men have to calculate how sharp the curve is, at what rate trains are permitted to go round it, and then they have to raise the outer rail in proportion. The resistance offered by the outer wheels having to go uphill, so to speak, keeps the train in the path we desire.

What is the Acropolis ?

Acropolis was the name given to the highest part of cities in Ancient Greece, the part surrounded with fortifications, sheltering temples, statues of gods, and all that was precious to the people. Most of the towns of Greece, of Asia Minor, of Ancient Italy, had their Acropolis, and important ruins still remain for our admiration.

The most famous, the richest in buildings, and also the best preserved, is at Athens, and is generally known as *the* Acropolis.

The buildings cover the top of a hill 900 feet long and 450 feet wide, spread with temples, masterpieces of the celebrated artists of the great time of Pericles. There was the Parthenon, erected to Minerva, patron goddess of Athens (it was from here that the famous Elgin Marbles, now in the British Museum, were brought to England in 1812) ; the Erechtheum, with its beautiful Porch of the Caryatides ; the Propylaea, a monumental vestibule of columns leading to all the shrines ; and many other treasures.

No other place in Ancient Greece had such sacred and glorious memories. The Acropolis was almost entirely spared until the seventeenth century, but in 1656 the explosion of a Turkish powder-store destroyed a part of it. Most of it is now in ruin, destroyed by war and centuries of neglect.

Are the Stars Round ?

The reason why stars do not look round is simply that they are so far away. The planets are smaller than the stars, but are so near that when we look at them through a telescope we can easily see that they are round. They have a *disc*, as we call it. But, however powerful the telescope through which we look at the brightest or nearest stars, we never see even the smallest disc, but only a *point* of light. Though the star that shines as a point through the largest telescope may be a million times larger than a little planet like Venus or Mars, which shows a disc through even a small glass, it is so far away that its disc cannot be seen, and it seems probable that no improvement in the telescope, and no increase of its size, will ever enable us to see the disc of a star. But we have no doubt that the stars *are* really round like the Sun.

Why are There so Many Meteors in November?

Meteors are fragments of shattered comets, and the fragments revolve in orbits as the planets do. It happens that in November the Earth, as it revolves in its orbit, crosses the path of a great meteor swarm. Every thirty-three years the Earth during November passed through the centre of the swarm of revolving fragments, and then there were tremendous showers of meteors. In the November of 1833 hundreds of thousands of meteors were seen, and also in the same month in 1866. Since then the expected heavy displays at 33-year intervals have been disappointing and there seems little doubt that the stream has been diverted. It is unlikely that there will ever again be such a fine display as was seen in 1833.

These November meteors are known as the Leonids, because they appear to us to start from the constellation of Leo (the Lion), and they are believed to be fragments of a vanished comet.

What is the Great Pitch Lake of Trinidad?

More than three centuries ago Sir Walter Raleigh found excellent pitch to caulk the seams of his ship in the wonderful Trinidad lake of La Brea, an immense deposit of bitumen in the crater of an old volcano. Today La Brea lake is one of the most wonderful natural sources of wealth in the world, as it is well over a hundred acres in extent and 285 feet deep in the centre. Although some nine million tons of bitumen (or asphalt) have been taken from the lake its level has subsided only 30 feet.

The surface of the lake—grey, creased, and with pools of water filling the depressions—seems quite solid and motionless except for a patch in the centre where the asphalt heaves and rises as gas bubbles escape. But although apparently still, the lake is nevertheless always slowly on the move. Gangs of up to 250 men can work on the surface at the same time, but the pits they dig disappear in two or three days. The surface can support two light railway tracks, but these have to be re-laid daily, or they would gradually sink.

An example of the lake's slow but irresistible movement occurred in 1928 when a tree suddenly appeared in an upright position and continued to rise until it was six feet above the surface. (A log then cut from the tree showed it to be some 5000 years old.) The tree rose until it was ten feet above the surface, then gradually tilted over and began to sink, disappearing in a few days.

Trinidad Lake asphalt is invaluable for the surfacing of roads and is exported all over the world for that purpose. It is also much used for roofing shingles, floors of industrial plants, cable insulation, and for waterproofing tunnels, dams, and reservoirs.

What Holds a Stone Up when we Throw It?

It would be more reasonable to ask: Why does the stone ever return? We shall understand the case by seeing what actually happens when the stone is thrown, and we must be careful to remember Newton's first law of motion, that a moving thing must go on moving in the same straight line at the same speed for ever, *unless something stops it.*

When the stone is thrown, motion, or power, is put into it, and Newton's law, the law that all power has to be accounted for, teaches us not to wonder what keeps the stone up in the air, but to expect that it will go on moving until it leaves the Earth altogether. It is held up by the force we put into it; part of the energy of our arm is behind it.

Two causes, one much more powerful than the other, bring it back. One is the resistance of the air, which the stone pushes against as it rises; the other is the Earth's gravitation, against which the force in the stone has to fight until it is exhausted. Then the stone returns, but the power that was in it has not gone, as we soon discover if it happens to fall on our head.

Who Invented the Kaleidoscope?

The kaleidoscope, which was very popular at the beginning of last century, was perfected in 1816 by Sir David Brewster, though a man named Bradley is said to have invented it about 100 years before. It consists really of a tube in which symmetrical and multi-coloured designs are produced by an arrangement of mirrors, and is familiar chiefly as an optical toy. Designers formerly used Brewster's kaleidoscope for inventing new patterns of carpets and such things.

The Story of the Beautiful Things in the Treasure-House of the World

The Orchard, a piece of beautiful English tapestry designed by William Morris

THE CRAFTSMEN AND THEIR WORK

THE art of making stained glass grew to its perfection in the medieval years of Europe. The earliest kind of coloured windows appeared very different from the large sheets of stained glass that we see here and there today: they looked like windows made of jewels; the glass, of exquisite tints, was used in small fragments of various shapes.

At first the stained glass windows were made by glaziers, and they relied on pieces of coloured glass to make a pattern. After a time the art of the painter was called in to supply the artistic quality that the glazier lacked. Stained windows ceased to be patterns in colour; they became pictures of saints and Bible figures, with all sorts of setting and backgrounds.

Some of the greatest painters of Europe have at one time or another lent their skill to this beautiful craft. Schools and centres of glass painting grew up all over Europe. Very often a whole family concentrated on this work, like the Van Linges of Holland, who worked in the seventeenth century. Sometimes it happened that famous artists designed the window and a glass painter carried out the work. This was the case in France, where men like Jean Cousin, Jean Ingres, Delacroix, and Horace Vernet found time to design coloured glass.

Generally speaking, until comparatively recent times few names of the men who created stained glass windows have been preserved. The best work occurred in the thirteenth to the fifteenth centuries, and is found in the cathedrals and churches of that period.

A great number of coloured windows were made during the Gothic revival in the nineteenth century. In spite of the unnatural stiffness that was produced during that period, some of the stained glass is good—as, for instance, that by John Clayton in Truro Cathedral and King's College Chapel, Cambridge, the work of Charles Winston in Glasgow Cathedral. A. C. Pugin is worthily remembered, and John Powell, who followed in his steps.

When the pre-Raphaelite movement came, Burne-Jones, Ford Madox Brown, and Dante Gabriel Rossetti made some beautiful glass work, which was fine in design and lacked the peculiar stiffness of the imitation Gothic.

Stained glass work, mosaic, and woodcarving are associated in our minds with religious architecture. The best work in all these crafts was done in the Italian Renaissance and the Golden Years of Europe, when men worked simply and slowly and were not trying to be clever.

PICTURES · STATUES · CARVINGS · BUILDINGS · IVORIES · CRAFTS

Mosaic work, the setting together of small cubes of variously coloured marble and glass, is a very ancient craft The Egyptians, Babylonians, Persians, Greeks, and Romans knew all about it long before the Byzantine builders made the interior of their churches one glowing mass of coloured mosaics. We read of this in our chapters on Byzantine art and architecture.

THE FINE MOSAIC PAVING THE ROMANS LAID IN BRITAIN

Sometimes entire walls were covered with mosaic work. In other cases marble mosaics of varying sizes were used for floors and pavements. In St. Mark's, Venice, is some of the finest mosaic pavement in the world. It was done in the twelfth century.

An Italian artist called Odericus laid the mosaics in the Confessor's Chapel in Westminster Abbey, about 1268. There are remains of Roman mosaic at York, Woodchester, Cirencester. The Romans were the greatest mosaic pavers in history, wedging their minute squares of marble into a cement bed in such a way as to defy the destructive hand of time for many centuries.

In the Confessor's Chapel and on the tomb of Henry the Third in Westminster Abbey is also seen some of the glass mosaic work that was common in Italy during the medieval period. It was used to adorn tombs, pulpits, and bishops' thrones. The most famous masters of this craft were the Cosmati family, in Italy.

Mosaic work is common in Mohammedan architecture. Here and there, as in the Taj Mahal at Agra, are fine specimens of marble mosaic, but for the most part Mohammedan mosaic in buildings set up from the fourteenth to the seventeenth centuries was in wood, with ivory and mother-of-pearl added.

THE ANCIENT ART THAT GOES BACK TO THE CHILDHOOD OF THE WORLD

The use of wood in any way goes back to the childhood of the world. Just as boys whittle a piece of stick today, so did untaught savages carve their mysterious shapes and emblems thousands of years ago. The Maoris brought woodcarving up to a national art. In India and the East native carving in wood and ivory is of a great delicacy and beauty.

When the Gothic genius overswept Europe, woodcarving came, with stained glass window work, iron and metal work, goldsmith's and silversmith's work, to supplement the bare edifice and make the cathedrals a miracle of the craftsman's labour as well as the builder's skill.

The woodcarving of medieval Europe was extremely beautiful. It exists today in domestic objects like bride chests, benches, door panels, and door heads, apart from monumental things like the great cathedral doors and pulpits, altar pieces, and rood screens.

Among many other lovely treasures in England there is the fourteenth-century woodcarving of Bishop Stapleton's throne in Exeter Cathedral, to show us what kind of work this was. One of the most wonderful altar pieces in the world was carved in wood for Schleswig Cathedral by Hans Brüggemann. It has several panels set with carved figures.

Woodcarving was a beautiful craft in Europe until the nineteenth century, when the introduction of machine-made work killed it for ever, it would seem. After the Gothic years it is marked by certain developments. The fifteenth and sixteenth centuries saw the wealth of carving in private houses, the beautiful " linen fold " and other kinds of panelling; house fronts, nearly all wood, gave excellent opportunity to the craftsmen.

THE MASTER CRAFTSMAN WHOSE WORK DOMINATED ALL EUROPE

In Elizabethan times beds, cabinets, benches, were richly carved; but the most important object in the room was the mantel piece, or shelf, and this was carved very ornately. This work was interesting, but not to be compared with that of the seventeenth and eighteenth centuries, when the school of Grinling Gibbons dominated Europe.

Grinling Gibbons was an Englishman who lived from 1648 to 1721. He was a sculptor and woodcarver, one of the greatest craftsmen in European history. His work is mainly shown in the Renaissance buildings of England—St. Paul's Cathedral, Trinity College Oxford, Trinity College Cambridge, Hampton Court Palace, Chatsworth, and many other places.

Gibbons's work was rich, heavy, and marked by a peculiar minuteness and delicacy of finish. It passed the test of all great carving : the work was suitable to the material and the purpose.

Presently, after the simple benches, settles, stools, and other domestic fittings

THE ART OF THE CRAFTSMEN

A BOXWOOD MEDALLION WITH
A PORTRAIT OF JOHN OF LEYDEN

GRINLING GIBBONS'S WOODWORK
IN ST. PAUL'S CATHEDRAL

A BOXWOOD MEDALLION OF
THE WIFE OF MAXIMILIAN II

THE EIGHTEENTH-CENTURY BRONZE GATES OF THE CAMPANILE OF ST. MARKS, VENICE

A BRONZE LAMP IN NAPLES

A TWELFTH-CENTURY SILVER PYX

A SHERATON CHAIR

A THIRTEENTH-CENTURY
ENAMEL OF ST. JOHN

AN ITALIAN NECKLACE OF THE
SIXTEENTH CENTURY

A SILVER EWER OF THE
SIXTEENTH CENTURY

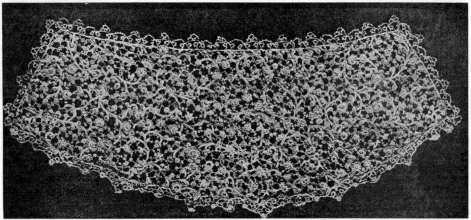

A PIECE OF BEAUTIFUL CLUNY LACE

A SECRETAIRE OF THE
EIGHTEENTH CENTURY

A CLOCK IN SÈVRES
PORCELAIN

STAINED GLASS IN THE CHURCH
OF ST. DOMENICO, PERUGIA

A CHIPPENDALE CHAIR
IN MAHOGANY

A HANDSOME FRENCH CABINET
OF THE EIGHTEENTH CENTURY

A HEPPLEWHITE CHAIR
IN WALNUT

A BRONZE PLAQUE OF THE
EIGHTEENTH CENTURY

A SILVER SALVER OF THE
SIXTEENTH CENTURY

A WOODEN CANDLESTICK IN
A CHURCH IN VERONA

PETER VISCHER'S BRONZE
STATUE OF KING ARTHUR

A SÈVRES PORCELAIN VASE
IN THE WATTEAU STYLE

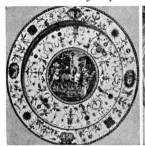

AN ITALIAN PLATE OF THE
SIXTEENTH CENTURY

A FINE MOSAIC IN PISA CATHEDRAL
DESIGNED BY CIMABUE

A SIXTEENTH-CENTURY
MAJOLICA PLATE

MAGNIFICENT CARVED WOODWORK IN THE CHURCH OF SAINT GIUSTINA IN PADUA

A THOUSAND-YEAR-OLD IVORY IN THE
NATIONAL MUSEUM, FLORENCE

SHEEP-SHEARING—A GOBELINS TAPESTRY OF
THE EIGHTEENTH CENTURY

Pictures reproduced by courtesy of Messrs. Alinari, Anderson, Brogi, Gray, the Victoria and Albert Museum, and others

of early times, furniture as we understand it appeared in Europe, giving opportunity for a great deal of bad work. Craftsmen's fancies ran riot. It seemed not to be necessary to make furniture for strength and durability and suitability to a house; it was made in order to give the cabinet-maker a chance of being clever.

THE LOVELY FURNITURE OF CHIPPENDALE, SHERATON, AND HEPPLEWHITE

Out of the mass of various domestic styles some fine things appeared; furniture made by men like Thomas Chippendale, Ince and Mayhew, Sheraton, Johnson, and Hepplewhite. This furniture was good in that it was suited to the material and the purpose. Also it revealed an excellent taste, which, so far, we have not been able to improve upon.

With the era of domestic furniture came the days of marquetery and inlay. Things like long-case clocks, chests of drawers, cabinets, were embellished by patterns made of ivory, bone, brass, tortoiseshell, and mother-of-pearl inlaid into the wood. The seventeenth-century Dutch workers were the finest " marqueteurs." A famous French marquetery artist, André Charles Boule, worked for Louis the Fourteenth.

Side by side with the development of domestic furniture came that of the craft of pottery, or ceramics as it is generally called. This craft, like that of wood-carving, is one of the most ancient in the world. Each nation has developed its own pottery, some to a fine art, like the Greeks, Etruscans, Persians, and the Chinese, some keeping a beautiful simplicity, as in the case of the Italian, Breton, and Dutch peasant ware. It is only since the era of cheap machine-made pottery that villages and provinces all over the civilised world have ceased to have their own little potteries.

WHAT CHINA TAUGHT THE WESTERN WORLD IN THE ART OF POTTERY

To the Chinese belongs the honour of being the greatest race of potters ever known. While other countries were content with clay and terracotta vessels of various kinds, some very beautifully shaped and coloured, like the Moorish pottery, the Chinese were slowly perfecting their art. In the fulness of time they developed the kind of ware known as porcelain, and during the fifteenth century this beautiful white and translucent pottery began to find its way to Europe.

It became the foundation of the ceramic art of the Western world.

Florentine potters turned their attention to the Chinese ware and began to imitate it. Hundreds of years passed while first one European country and then another developed artistic porcelain pottery on its own lines. During the course of this long development certain famous centres arose. In Italy there was the famous Majolica ware, a richly-coloured, finely-glazed pottery that got its name from the island of Majorca, a port of call for trading ships. A great deal of beautiful pottery was made in France, some of it distinguished by names of towns, like Nevers and Rouen, and some by names of makers like Bernard Palissy, the famous potter of the sixteenth century. Later there came the St. Cloud porcelain and the famous Sèvres ware. In the eighteenth century Sèvres became the most important porcelain factory in Europe. Some of the greatest artists of the day helped to make the wonderful figures and groups of the famous Sèvres "biscuit" ware.

THE DELFT WARE OF HOLLAND AND THE PORCELAIN POTTERY OF GERMANY

Pottery of a very different kind was evolved at Haarlem in the beginning of the seventeenth century. This is the famous Delft ware—a curiously enamelled earthenware. Germany was the home of stoneware made at various towns on the Rhine, and presently evolved a fine and beautiful porcelain pottery which is known by the names of the towns where the industry centred, such as Meissen, Vienna, Berlin. Meissen was the most important of these, and branches sprang up in places as distant as St. Petersburg.

In about the middle of the eighteenth century porcelain manufacture started in England. Factories producing dainty and exquisite bowls, figure groups, arose at Chelsea, Bow, Worcester, and Derby. The Chelsea porcelain is the most famous of these wares and is very rare. It was only made for about a generation, and by 1784 the factory had moved to Derby. By this time Josiah Wedgwood had won renown through his skilful handling of the cream-coloured Staffordshire pottery. In comparatively modern times the Doultons of Lambeth and Villeroy and Boch of Germany revived the old stone ware.

The art of enamelling is in some ways kindred to the art of finely glazed pottery. Here again we are touching on a very old handiwork of artistic peoples. This baking of a beautifully-coloured and designed glassy substance on a hard material like metal or brick was a favourite device of the races of the old world.

The Egyptians, Assyrians, Greeks and Etruscans, Chinese and Japanese, were great enamellers, and satisfied their love of shining colour in this way, bringing the enamel in conjunction with gold and silver-smith's work wherever possible. The early Celts of the British Islands had this art. Exquisite enamels made in Ireland long ago are in Dublin Museum.

THE BEAUTIFUL FORMS THE ART OF ENAMELLING MAY TAKE

Enamel played a great part in Byzantine art, and naturally had its place in the art of the Romanesque period, the craft thus spreading all over Europe. There were centres of enamelling in many European towns. As the Renaissance years passed, enamel developed into a very fine art indeed. In a way it is still developing.

There are several kinds of enamelling, according to the method in which the enamel is applied to the metal base. Sometimes, as in the plique à jour enamel, the base is taken away after the enamel has been fixed, and the result is a kind of beautiful translucent coloured stone. The cloisonné enamel was made by soldering little metal strips, the shape of the design, on the metal base, and setting the pulverised enamel in these compartments. Another variety is painted enamel, which involves very intricate and absorbing labour indeed.

The most famous painter of enamels in Europe was Léonard Limosin, which meant Leonard of Limoges, who lived in the sixteenth century. Limoges enamel is famous all the world over. Jean Pénicaud was another great enameller who worked in a different way.

AN ANCIENT GREEK VASE AND ITS TAPESTRY-WEAVING FRAME

From painting pictures on glass or pottery we come to the weaving of pictures—tapestry. Once more we are in the presence of an ancient, beautiful, and homely craft. Tapestry has been used from ancient times for the covering of floors, walls, furniture. Penelope's tapestry-weaving frame is shown on a Greek vase of the fifth century B.C. The Romans too were great makers of tapestry. Presently, by way of monasteries, where

much weaving was done, the craft spread into Europe and became incorporated with the labours of the guild of weavers. Tapestry weaving is associated with certain towns, and rare names like Jean Duval of Flanders. In the fourteenth and fifteenth centuries Arras was the great place for tapestry; then Brussels, a hundred years later, followed by Middelburg and Delft. Some men from Arras came over to work in England; hence the name arras for a woven wall hanging. In the sixteenth century Paris became a centre of the craft, and still is. In the seventeenth century Mortlake was famous for its tapestries.

Artists of great renown have made designs for tapestries—the Van Eycks, Roger van der Weyden, Raphael, Da Vinci, and many others. The princes of Europe who were great patrons of art, like the Medici, the Stuarts, the Hapsburgs, took intense interest in the tapestries they ordered to be made. In the sixteenth century William Sheldon founded tapestry factories in Warwickshire, and they did beautiful work, some of which is still preserved. A little later some good tapestry weaving was done in Ireland.

THE FAMOUS FACTORY FOUNDED BY A KING OF FRANCE

Here again, machine-made goods have done away with the world-value of hand-woven tapestries. William Morris, Burne-Jones, and others made valiant efforts to revive the craft in the late nineteenth century; but tapestry has become a luxury for the few. It is still made at the famous Gobelins and Beauvais manufactories in France. The Gobelins factory was founded by Louis the Fourteenth in 1661, and was under the personal supervision of his art directors.

While this " picture cloth " was being woven in various places in the old Europe, a great deal of attention was being paid to its sister-craft, embroidery. Work of this kind covers a very wide field, for it includes both embroidery for religious purposes, for the robes of great and royal persons, and the decorations of a house.

Embroideries were made in great quantities, of a beautiful and exquisite kind, by the princesses, housewives, and nuns of medieval and later Europe. For about a thousand years a great and minute art has been spent on the embroidery for church fittings and vestments. The ladies of Europe, both inside convents and out, gave their best years to triumphs of needle-work for both secular and sacred houses, which are as far from the competence of the young girl of today as one of Raphael's composition would be from the average art student. An infinite patience and an

Mohammedan and Hindu temples, treasure pieces of needlework; lovely specimens are to be found in most of the museums of Europe.

Probably the most famous piece of embroidery in the world is the so-called

THE FOUR MARTYRS OF TREBIZOND—A RELIQUARY IN ST. MARK'S, VENICE

FIFTEENTH-CENTURY GOTHIC CARVING IN SANTA MARIA GLORIOSA DEI FRARI, VENICE

intense love went to this labour; the kinds of stitches used seem countless.

In China, Japan, India, Egypt, Palestine, and wherever olden civilisations took root, we find beautiful embroideries. Nearly all Christian churches and cathedrals,

Bayeux Tapestry. This is a strip of linen about 230 feet long, and on it is embroidered, in coloured wools, the tale of the Norman Conquest. It is said to have been the work of Queen Matilda and her ladies. It is reproduced on pages 709 to 716.

Lace work is equally diversified and historic, and often makes part of an embroidery. Here again is an amazing variety of stitches and styles, from the various points and crochets to the old pillow-lace of Flanders.

THE BEAUTIFUL THINGS MADE FROM GOLD AND SILVER IN BIBLE DAYS

Side by side with these various minor crafts, whose object was to supplement the larger arts, the work of the silversmith, goldsmith, and iron-worker was being not so much developed as continued. We are accustomed to thinking of gold and silver merely in connection with jewellery. We forget these metals were used in enormous quantities by the ancients. The Eastern nations, long before the dawn of Christianity, had brought the art of gold and silver work up to a very high pitch. We remember the silver and gold cups of Bible story, and here is a description of a palace in ancient Greece that makes us feel we live in days of mean achievements:

There was a gleam as it were of sun or moon through the high-roofed hall of great-hearted Alcinous. Brazen were the walls . . . and round them was a frieze of blue, and golden were the doors that closed in the good house. Silver were the door posts that were set on the brazen threshold, and silver the lintel thereupon, and the hook of the door was of gold. And on either side stood golden hounds and silver . . . to guard the palace of the great-hearted Alcinous, being free from death and age all their days . . . Yea, and there were youths fashioned in gold, standing on firm-set bases, with flaming torches in their hands, giving light through the night.

So wrote Homer of a Greece that was already old. In the days of the rich art of Europe, this craft work was carried on by gifted men.

THE ADVENTUROUS LIFE OF ONE OF ITALY'S MASTER CRAFTSMEN

In sixteenth-century Italy there was among many others, Benvenuto Cellini, who worked in gold and bronze. This man is one of the most interesting characters in the history of art. He lived from 1500 to 1571, was sculptor, goldsmith, engraver, and the author of an autobiography which tells us a great deal about his times apart from its bearing on his own riotous life. He swung a sword as readily as he wielded his tools, could never hear of a quarrel, big or small, without flinging himself into it. Exile and imprisonment were more than once his lot. He seemed to bear a charmed life, and in the intervals of his escapades produced some of the finest craft work of Italy. His best known statue is the Victorious Perseus. A great many lovely little boxes, coffers, cups, plates, were chased and embossed by Italian artists like Cellini. They can be seen in all museums, and were so much a matter of ordinary work that very often the maker's name or sign is not engraved on the work. One such example is a most beautiful thirteenth-century golden cup which has underneath, " Nicholas of Hereford made me."

In Germany, in the sixteenth century, there was a fine school of bronze workers headed by Peter Vischer. His tomb of St. Sebald, in the church of St. Sebald, Nuremberg, is an exquisite piece of metal work. Vischer also made the fine King Arthur statue which stands among the twenty-four bronze figures that guard the tomb of the Emperor Maximilian I, in the Hofkirche at Innsbruck in Austria.

THE UNKNOWN WORKERS IN METAL WHO ENRICHED THE GOTHIC CATHEDRALS

In France there were numbers of " imagiers " in gold, silver, and bronze, whose names have been forgotten. They helped to make the Gothic cathedrals unforgettably beautiful. Notable among them was Biscornette, who wrought the iron doors of Notre Dame. In the seventeenth century a famous craftsman, called Caffieri, an Italian, was working in France for the " Sun King." He superintended the metal work that was carried out at the Gobelins factory.

A great deal of labour in bronze and metalwork is taken for granted. It is only when we see fine gates and grilles, whose lines are strong and beautiful, that we realise how much poorer the world would be without this very old craft. We think of beaten work, like the great gates of Shalmaneser, in the Assyrian Hall of the British Museum; the Eleanor Grille and Henry the Seventh's bronze screen in Westminster Abbey; the gates of Hampton Court Palace; and then we wonder at their complete and satisfying union of beauty and strength.

All the examples of craftsmanship of which we have written in these pages have come to us from the past. This century, too, has its master craftsmen whose work will live and be admired by future generations.

The Story of the Peoples of All Nations and Their Homelands

The ship of the desert in the great Sahara

THE AFRICAN CONTINENT

AFRICA is an exciting continent. It was said of old: *Ex Africa semper aliquid novi* (From Africa there is always something new). The same has remained true all through the centuries, partly because there is much to learn about Africa, and partly because we have been so slow in learning it.

Until the Suez Canal was opened in 1869, Africa was linked with Asia by land, and traders passed backwards and forwards across the isthmus. The Bible story of Joseph and his brethren shows that this traffic was going on between 3000 and 4000 years ago, and even then Egypt was a land of ancient renown. In later days, on the African coast south of Italy, the rise of Carthage under the Phoenicians, and Hannibal's early successes against the Romans, brought further renown to North Africa. In the end, Carthage was destroyed and the Roman power spread along both sides of the Mediterranean.

Many and famous as were these happenings, they did little to make Africa known as a whole. Except along the Nile, the habitable lands of North Africa are only a narrow strip. Beyond them lies the great desert barrier of the Sahara. Rumours reached the north about the wonders that lay beyond the desert. There is a story that 600 years before Christ a Phoenician ship sailed from the Red Sea round the coast of Africa to the Mediterranean. It is less in doubt that a Carthaginian admiral named Hanno, in charge of a colonising expedition about 500 B.C., sailed along the West African coast as far as the Gulf of Guinea. Another story tells of some youths who journeyed to a far country inland and were captured by pygmies.

It is difficult to tell truth from fiction in these stories. What is certain is that knowledge of Africa south of the Sahara remained vague during the decline and fall of the Roman Empire; also during the later centuries when Arab rule spread through North Africa and the Moors overran Spain, right up to the time when Spain and Portugal rose to power in the Middle Ages. Then, under the influence of Prince Henry the Navigator, hardy Portuguese sailors made their way farther and farther along the west coast of Africa till at last Vasco da Gama, on his great voyage in 1498, sailed beyond the Cape of Good Hope, round the south coast of Africa and up the east coast, and finally crossed the Indian ocean to India.

The Portuguese soon made settlements in both West and East Africa. At a later

THE FIVE CONTINENTS & 100 NATIONS & RACES THAT INHABIT THEM

date, English and Dutch and other European trading stations were set up in West Africa, and the terrible slave trade began. South Africa, too, was being opened up. But still knowledge was mostly confined to the coastal lands; and it needed the explorations of James Bruce in Ethiopia and Mungo Park along the Niger in the 18th century, followed by the great journeys of Livingstone and other explorers of many nationalities in the 19th century, to fill in the map of the interior.

THE VAST CONTINENT THREE TIMES THE SIZE OF EUROPE

As we know it today, Africa has an area of 11,500,000 square miles; only Asia is larger among the continents, and it is over three times the size of Europe. From north to south it extends over a distance of 5000 miles, and its greatest width from east to west is nearly the same. For the most part it has a narrow coastal plain, from which the land rises more or less steeply towards the interior, either as a mountain range or a giant staircase leading up to wide plateaus. In the heart of the continent the level may drop again, forming enclosed basins like those of Lake Chad, south of the Sahara, and Lake Ngami, north of the Kalahari; or nearly enclosed basins like that of the Congo, which was once an inland sea. In eastern Africa the plateau is cleft by the Great Rift Valley, the result of some old convulsion of nature, extending from the Zambesi as far north as Palestine. Scattered along the Rift Valley and on the neighbouring plateau are many lakes, comparable with the North American Great Lakes; the largest, Lake Victoria, is second only to Lake Superior; they are the largest two lakes in the world, unless the Caspian Sea be counted as a lake.

AFRICA'S LOFTY VOLCANOES AND MANY GREAT MOUNTAIN RANGES

Lofty volcanoes, mostly extinct, but some still active, tower above the general level in various parts of Africa. The highest are in East Africa—Kilimanjaro (19,340 feet), on the Kenya border of Tanganyika Territory; Mount Kenya (17,040 feet), in the heart of Kenya Colony; and Ruwenzori (16,794 feet), the once fabled " Mountains of the Moon," on the borders of Uganda and the Belgian Congo. On the west coast the Cameroon Mountain rises to 13,500 feet. Apart from these and other volcanic peaks, Africa has many mountain ranges, including the Great Atlas (14,800 feet) in Morocco, and the Drakensberg (Dragon Mountains, 12,000 feet), known as the " Switzerland " of South Africa.

Most of the rivers of Africa are broken by rapids and falls where they descend the giant "staircase" round the coast or force their way through the mountains. Many of them are comparatively short, but some rise beyond the coastal ranges and either lose themselves in the interior, like the Shari River, which flows into Lake Chad, or follow long roundabout courses before they break through to the sea.

The " Big Four " among the rivers of Africa are the Nile (estimated length 4160 miles), the longest river in the world, draining north-east Africa from the Great Lakes to Egypt and the Mediterranean ; the Congo (2720 miles), draining western equatorial Africa and flowing into the Atlantic Ocean; the Niger (2600 miles), the great river of West Africa, draining into the Gulf of Guinea; and the Zambesi (1600 miles), rising near the Congo but flowing south and east instead of north and west, and finally discharging into the Indian Ocean.

NATURAL BARRIERS TO NAVIGATION ON AFRICA'S FOUR GREAT RIVERS

The Congo becomes unnavigable within a hundred miles of the open sea. The three other rivers can be ascended for longer distances, but sandbanks and shifting channels make them difficult of navigation by large vessels, and all are broken by rapids and falls in their upper reaches. Most famous of these barriers are the Victoria Falls of the Zambesi, on the borders of Southern and Northern Rhodesia, where the course of the river is crossed by a chasm about 100 yards wide, and the whole volume of the Zambesi—which is here a mile wide—plunges down a sheer cliff nearly 360 feet deep.

Africa has been described as the " Continent of Contrasts." Most of North Africa is a great desert, the Sahara, in parts of which travellers may scorch by day and freeze by night. The name comes from the Arabic *Sahra*, an uninhabitable wilderness, and it has been calculated that this desert covers nearly 3,500,000 square miles, nearly a third of the continent. Despite tree plantation schemes to stop the drifting sands, the area of desert is still growing.

In Equatorial Africa are vast areas clothed with dense jungle, and off the West Coast are islands which are a picture of luxuriant beauty, with tropical flowers, plants, and trees flourishing in a climate of perpetual steamy heat. Almost on the Equator are mountains crowned with snow and glaciers, while at intermediate levels, from 5000 feet to 8000 feet, are wide stretches of open woodlands and grassy plains where Europeans have settled with their families in permanent homes.

The animal life presents almost as many contrasts as the Zoo. Quadrupeds include dainty little gazelles, the ugly, clumsy-looking hippopotamus and rhino-

numbers of Indians and Arabs who have migrated there through the centuries.

As time went on, the Europeans who had formed settlements along the shores of tropical and South Africa gradually extended their influence over the scattered tribes inland. There were traders and missionaries and government officials, and rivalries grew up among the different nationalities. War in Europe often meant war in Africa, with outposts of empire changing hands. In the second half of last century, rivalry between the European powers to stake out their claims led to what was known as the " Scramble for Africa." Today, it is the declared aim of

A NATIVE MARKET-PLACE IN PARATAU, DAHOMEY

ceros, the lofty giraffe and mammoth elephant, the haughty camel and lordly lion—but not the tiger. There are hosts of chattering little monkeys, big baboons, and fierce gorillas the size of men.

The people differ greatly. There are the light-coloured, regular-featured, historic peoples of North Africa—Egyptians, Arabs, Berbers, Moors. There are the Negro people of tropical Africa—black, with flat noses, thick lips, woolly hair. There are giants and there are pygmies, and, in South Africa, yellowish-brown Hottentots and Bushmen, who make curious clicking sounds when they speak. In many territories there are also large

the Colonial Powers not to take advantage of the African peoples but to work in partnership with them.

Africa has made wonderful strides in the past hundred years, and if wisely developed it should have a still greater future. But the drawbacks should not be forgotten. The Sahara is not the only desert tract ; other regions lack water, and West Africa has large areas of laterite, a reddish clay baked by the sun into very hard masses. Unskilled farming has exhausted vast areas of good land; unprotected and uncultivated, the soil of old clearings has been washed away by the tropical downpours, and the result is

" eroded " country, barren and desolate. So widespread are these conditions that soil erosion has become one of the main problems of agricultural development in Africa.

Before the First World War there were seven Powers in control of African territory : Britain, France, Germany, Portugal, Belgium, Italy, and Spain. After that war, Germany's possessions were divided among the neighbouring territories, under mandates from the League of Nations. In the Second World War, the Italian territories were occupied by the Allies and put at the disposal of the United Nations.

The parts of the British Commonwealth which fall within Africa are described elsewhere in these pages, and so is Egypt. Here we will glance at the rest of the African continent, in its political divisions.

TERRITORY UNDER FRENCH INFLUENCE

THE French sphere of influence in Africa extends over 4,280,000 square miles. This is half-a-million square miles larger than the British Commonwealth and Empire in Africa, and more than a third of the whole continent. But the value of this vast territory is lessened by the fact that a large part of it consists of the Sahara. All but a small fraction forms a continuous stretch of territory, filling most of the broad north-west shoulder of Africa. This great area falls into three divisions : North Africa, West Africa, and Equatorial Africa.

NORTH AFRICA

FRENCH influence spreads over an area in the north-west corner of the continent, with coasts on both the Mediterranean and the Atlantic. It is made up of Algeria, which is a French possession fronting the Mediterranean, and two former protectorates—Tunisia on the east, Morocco on the west. Behind the coast, the Atlas Mountains run roughly east and west through all three countries. These mountains are not a single range, but a series of mountain chains, with fertile valleys whose crops and flocks and herds are a main asset of French North Africa. Between the chains are plateaus some 3500-4000 feet above sea level, where it can be very cold in winter (North Africa is outside the tropics). Much of this upland country has poor soil, and scattered through it are great salt marshes. South of the Atlas Mountains the three territories merge into the Sahara.

In the fertile valleys of the north, cereals are widely grown, and fruits and vegetables, especially grapes for wine (chiefly in Algeria), and olives for olive oil (chiefly in Tunisia). Sheep number nearly 20 million, half of them in Morocco. There is also considerable mineral production, chiefly phosphates and iron ore. Nearly 5000 miles of railway link up the principal towns in the north and, in Algeria, reach out into the desert on the side of both Morocco and Tunisia.

ALGERIA is the largest of the three North African territories and has been longest under French control. It was conquered in 1830, and more lately has been extended far into the Sahara. Now its area is 848,000 square miles— about four times the size of France—and it supports about 9,500,000 people, mostly in the northern valleys and along the coast. Algiers, the capital and chief port, has nearly 355,000 inhabitants. It was infamous in earlier days under the rule of the " Deys " of Algiers as a nest of pirates. Other large towns are Oran, Constantine, and Bône.

Until recently the Arab Moslems, who outnumber the European settlers by 9 to 1, seemed to accept the French policy of treating Algeria as a part of France. But following the trend of events in neighbouring Morocco and Tunisia, where Moslems had fought for and obtained independence from the French, there have been uprisings in Algeria, too; and it seems likely that Algeria also will eventually be separated from France.

TUNISIA, whose " Bey " placed his country under French protection in 1881, covers 48,300 square miles, and has a population of some 3,500,000. It takes its name from its capital, Tunis, a city with nearly 365,000 inhabitants. Not far from the capital are the ruins of Carthage, the rival of Ancient Rome. Tunisia is more advanced than Algeria

THE NATIVE PEOPLES OF AFRICA

FOUR SAKALAVA GIRLS OF MADAGASCAR

A JEWISH SINGING-
GIRL OF ALGERIA

A GIRL OF TUNISIA PREPARING COUSCOUS,
A PREPARATION OF RICE

A LADY
OF MOROCCO

A MOSLEM BOYS' SCHOOL AT BISKRA, IN ALGERIA

28 c 10*

A LADY
OF MOROCCO

A YOUNG URCHIN
OF BISKRA

DAUGHTER OF A WEALTHY
BEDOUIN OF TUNISIA

ARAB MERCHANTS TAKING COFFEE AT A MOORISH CAFÉ

ARAB GIRLS OF BISKRA

ARAB OF ALGERIA

YOUNG MUSICIANS OF BISKRA

A NATIVE OF ANGOLA, OR
PORTUGUESE WEST AFRICA

A BEAUTIFUL LITTLE GIRL
OF TUNISIA

A NEGRO BOY
OF FRENCH SUDAN

AN OLD ARAB VEGETABLE SELLER IN TUNIS

BEDOUIN BEGGARS OF TUNIS

A GIRL OF ALGERIA

GIRLS OF TUNIS

A WOMAN OF FRENCH GUINEA
AND HER BABY

A MOTHER AND CHILD
OF MADAGASCAR

A MOTHER AND CHILD
OF DAKAR, IN SENEGAL

WOMEN OF MADAGASCAR MAKING MATS

AN ARAB WOMAN OF
ALGERIA AND HER CHILD

A HAPPY HOME
IN MOROCCO

A YOUNG FAMILY
OF TRIPOLITANIA

or Morocco, for many Moslem Tunisians have studied at French schools and universities. After the Second World War, Tunisians hoped to be allowed to govern themselves, but negotiations with the French authorities broke down. The Tunisian nationalists then resorted to force. In June 1955 conventions were signed between France and Tunisia giving the Tunisians some control over the running of their country, and in March 1956 the French Government recognised the independence of Tunisia.

MOROCCO

THE area under French influence covers about 153,850 square miles with a population of about 8,500,000. The port of Rabat (156,000) is the official capital. The commercial capital is the port of Casablanca (682,000), fourth biggest city in Africa. Inland are the old Moorish capitals: Fez (179,000), Marrakesh (245,000), and Meknes (140,000).

The Sultan accepted a French protectorate in 1912, but after the Second World War the Moroccan Moslems followed the Tunisians in agitating for independence. The Sultan was sent into exile by the French Government, but two years later (in October 1955), he was allowed to return. In March 1956, after 44 years of French protection, Morocco regained full independence.

A few weeks later Spain, who controlled a much smaller area than France, acknowledged the Sultan's right to rule over the whole of Morocco. This includes an area of 225 square miles around Tangier city, near the entrance to the Strait of Gibraltar, which is at present under an international administration.

FRENCH WEST AFRICA

FRENCH WEST AFRICA is the largest administrative unit in the continent. It covers 1,920,000 square miles—more than half the size of Europe—and has a population of some 18 million. It is a federation of eight colonies, with a Governor-General over all.

The colonies fall into two groups—five of them scattered along the coast, to which they reach out from the interior like the fingers and thumb of a giant hand, separated by British and other non-French territories; and three inland colonies,

linking the others together and stretching back to French North Africa. All the colonies are engaged in exports, chiefly groundnuts and groundnut oil—which accounts for between a third and a half of the total—coffee, bananas, cocoa, palm kernels and palm oil, and oil-cake.

SENEGAL, the senior colony, lies in the extreme west of Africa, and is nearly as big as England and Scotland together. It takes its name from the Senegal River, 1000 miles long, which in its lower course is the colony's northern boundary. St. Louis (62,000), the capital, founded in 1658, is at the mouth of the Senegal. But it is inferior both as a commercial centre and as a port to Dakar (150,000), which has one of the best harbours in West Africa and an important airport. Dakar is the capital of the federation, and is the seat of the Governor-General.

Going south and east we come to FRENCH GUINEA, which is bigger than the United Kingdom. It not only grows many crops, but has a flourishing livestock industry in the Futa Jallon highlands, where the Senegal, the Gambia, and the Niger rivers rise.

Round the bend of the coast is the IVORY COAST, half as big again as Britain. Its capital is Abidjan, a port with a magnificent harbour. The country supplies most of the coffee and cocoa exported from French West Africa.

Still farther east is DAHOMEY, the smallest of the colonies, especially noted for its oil palms, estimated to number some 30 million. The chief town is Porto Novo (29,000).

MAURITANIA, French West Africa's fifth colony with a seaboard, lies to the north of Senegal and merges into the Sahara. In an area of 323,000 square miles it has a population of less than two to the square mile—mostly nomad tribes with their flocks and herds. It is administered from St. Louis, capital of Senegal.

Of the three inland territories, the FRENCH SUDAN and the NIGER COLONY are each far bigger than Mauritania, and though not so thinly populated, they too merge into the Sahara. The French Sudan includes the Upper Senegal and Niger basins, with that famous old city, Timbuctoo. As a contrast, the last of the territories of French West Africa, the Upper Volta, is the best populated of all—28 to the square mile. Nearly twice as big as England and Wales, it lies north of the Gold Coast and is watered by the headstreams of the Volta.

France is the United Nations Trustee for the greater part of Germany's former West African possessions, namely, EASTERN TOGOLAND, adjoining Dahomey, and all the Cameroons except a narrow strip attached to Nigeria. French Togoland is three times the size of Wales, but has fewer than a million inhabitants.

THE FRENCH CAMEROONS, extending from the angle of the Gulf of Guinea to Lake Chad, covers 167,000 square miles and has three million people. Much of it is dense primeval forest. The name comes from the Portuguese Camaraos, meaning shrimps or prawns; these were found in vast numbers by early navigators on the shores of the deep estuary now known as the Cameroons River.

FRENCH EQUATORIAL AFRICA

FRENCH EQUATORIAL AFRICA, which is crossed by the Equator, combines four colonies under a Governor-General. There are two coastal territories, the Gabun and Middle Congo, together bigger than France, and two inland territories, Ubangi-Shari, itself bigger than France, and Chad, more than twice the size of France. Though so different in size, they are alike in being thinly populated, each averaging between four and five persons to the square mile. The total area is nearly a million square miles.

The Gabun, like the Cameroons, takes its name from a so-called " river " which is really the estuary of several rivers. It is covered with tropical forest and is especially noted for a rose-tinted, scented timber called okumé, used for plywood. Libreville, the capital, owes its name to its having been founded as a home for freed slaves in 1849.

The Middle Congo is the only one of the four territories with a railway. The line runs from north of the mouth of the Congo, around the Congo rapids, to Brazzaville, on Stanley Pool. Brazzaville is the capital of French Equatorial Africa, and facing it across the Pool is Leopold-ville, capital of the Belgian Congo. Beyond Stanley Pool the Middle Congo boundary follows the right bank of the Congo river up to the in-flow of its great right-bank tributary, the Ubangi, and then follows the right bank of that river to the boundary of the Ubangi-Shari territory. This takes its name from the rivers Ubangi and Shari, the latter flowing north to Lake Chad. Cotton and coffee are largely cultivated.

The Chad territory includes the lower Shari basin, where cotton and groundnuts are widely grown. North of Lake Chad it extends into the Sahara to the Libyan frontier, rising in the Tibesti Highlands to 13,000 feet. There is a big pastoral industry.

Other French Territory

IN East Africa is FRENCH SOMALILAND (9070 square miles; population 65,000). Its position at the southern end of the Red Sea is important, and commercially it is the Gateway to Ethiopia, with which it is connected by rail from Jibuti, the capital and chief port.

Out in the Indian Ocean, 250 miles from Portuguese East Africa, is the large island of MADAGASCAR (228,642 square miles), with a population of over four million. It became a French protectorate in 1895 during the reign of the Madagascan queen Rànavàlona III. From north to south it measures a thousand miles, and along the west coast are wide plains leading up to a coastal plateau, which drops abruptly on the east to a coast lined with lagoons. Peaks of over 9000 feet rise from the plateau, on a ridge of which, over 4000 feet above the sea, stands the capital, Tananarive (187,000).

A railway 229 miles long links it with the chief port, Tamatave, on the east coast, and other lines bring the railway mileage to 534. Rice (for local consumption), coffee, vanilla, sugar and other export crops are grown, but the chief industry is cattle-raising; there are more than six million head of cattle, and the chief export is frozen and preserved meat.

Between the northern end of Madagascar and the mainland are the volcanic Comoro Islands, almost as large as the Orkneys and Shetlands, with nearly 180,000 people. They produce vanilla, sugar, cocoa, and essential oils for perfumery. Eastward from Madagascar is the French colony of RÉUNION, a volcanic island of 970 square miles, rising to over 10,000 feet, mainly dependent on sugar.

TWO TRADING CITIES OF AFRICA

MUD HUTS IN THE TRADING CENTRE OF SOKOTA, CAPITAL OF A PROVINCE OF NORTHERN ETHIOPIA

TIMBUCTOO IN THE FRENCH SUDAN, ON THE CARAVAN ROUTES BETWEEN WEST AFRICA AND TRIPOLI

PORTUGUESE AFRICA

SOME 350 miles west of Morocco is the Portuguese island of Madeira. It is nearly twice the size of the Isle of Wight, with grand mountainous scenery, rising to 6000 feet in extinct volcanic peaks. Vegetation is luxuriant, the climate mild and sunny. Funchal, the capital, is a favourite health resort, and Madeira wine is famous.

Farther south, 300 to 400 miles west of the great bulging shoulder of West Africa, are the volcanic CAPE VERDE ISLANDS (1550 square miles). Dry, dust-laden winds from the Sahara limit cultivation, and every year the young men go to South America for harvest work. A fuelling station on St. Vincent is much used by ships trading with South America.

On the mainland, between Senegal and French Guinea, is Portuguese Guinea (14,000 square miles ; 520,000 people). This is as far north as the oil palm flourishes in West Africa. The country is little developed, but usually over 12,000 tons of palm kernels, and 1000 tons of palm oil are exported, and 30,000 tons of unshelled groundnuts.

SÃO THOMÉ (St. Thomas) and PRINCIPE (Prince's) are volcanic islands in the bend of the Gulf of Guinea. São Thomé, half as large again as the Isle of Man, rises to 7000 feet ; Principe, as large as Jersey, to 3000 feet. So lovely are they that the Portuguese call them " The Pearls of the Ocean." With slave labour they produced large crops, first of coffee, later of cocoa. Output has since dwindled.

ANGOLA, as the Portuguese call their main West African possession, has an area of nearly half-a-million square miles and a population of over four million. The coast stretches from the mouth of the Congo southward for over 1000 miles to the borders of South-West Africa. Much of it is arid. Scanty rainfall in the north serves the needs of park-like country, and richer vegetation clusters round the river mouths ; but the south is practically rainless.

There are some historic towns with grim memories of slave-trading days. Chief of these is the capital, Loanda, a town of about 140,000 people, with a deep-water harbour protected by an outlying island. Benguela and Mossamedes have some fine old buildings, but have lost much of their importance ; their ports are merely open roadsteads.

From these towns, and from little Porto Amboina, railways climb inland to high plateau country. The rainfall is heavier where the westerly winds strike the steep escarpments and mountains behind the coast, and settlers on the plateau are able to carry on mixed farming.

The chief railway, the Benguela Railway, starts from the modern town and port of Lobito Bay, runs along the coast for 22 miles to Benguela, then turns inland, crosses Angola, and continues to the Katanga copper fields, as described in the section on the Belgian Congo. British enterprise had a lot to do with the building of this railway, and one of the towns on the plateau is named Robert Williams after Sir Robert Williams, who played a leading part in the arrangements. A few miles farther on is Nova Lisboa (New Lisbon), an important business centre, including the railway repair shops.

Angola's exports are chiefly coffee, diamonds, palm oil and palm kernels, cotton, sisal, maize, sugar, and dried and salted fish.

MOZAMBIQUE, or Portuguese East Africa, is smaller than Angola but has more people—nearly six million in 298,000 square miles: 20 to the square mile. It is very irregular in shape. With a coastline of 1400 miles, it extends inland for 50 miles in the south, 400 miles in the north, and 700 miles in the centre, along the Zambesi river. For the most part the territory does not rise above the coastal lowlands—1500 feet. It takes in a strip of plateau country both south and north of the Zambesi, especially in the north, where Mozambique stretches back to Lake Nyasa. Here and there are mountains up to 6000 feet high, and even to 8000 feet. But in general, Portuguese East Africa may be described as the first step of the staircase leading up to the high plateaus of South Central Africa. As such, it is very much interested in the traffic up and down—to and from the Transvaal in the south, Southern and Northern Rhodesia in the centre, and Nyasaland in the north.

The Gateway to the Transvaal is Lourenço Marques, the capital of Mozambique, a town of 93,000 people on Delagoa

Bay. Founded over 400 years ago, it was unhealthy and making little progress till growing trade and sanitary reforms turned it into a busy port and pleasure resort, following the construction of a railway to the Transvaal. Under the Mozambique Convention between Portugal and the Union of South Africa, Lourenço Marques is guaranteed a proportion of the Transvaal's trade, and the Transvaal is guaranteed labour for the Rand mines.

Beira, farther north, is the Gateway to both Southern Rhodesia and Nyasaland: the terminus of railways by which both countries have access to the sea. The line to Nyasaland crosses the Zambesi by a bridge over two miles long, the longest in the world. From this point a line is being built up the Zambesi valley to a coalfield near Tete. A railway is also being built to Lake Nyasa from the coast opposite to the island of Mozambique, on which stands the city of the same name; it was long the Portuguese capital and still has a fine old fort. Another railway line from Lourenço Marques runs northwards to the border at Pafuri, where it will join the new Southern Rhodesian Railways line to Bannockburn.

Mozambique Territory has large plantation crops, principally cotton, copra, sugar, and sisal.

BELGIAN AFRICA

KING LEOPOLD II of Belgium took a great personal interest in Sir Henry Stanley's exploration of the Congo and in an association formed to take over the government of the Congo Basin. The Berlin Conference of the Powers in 1885 recognised King Leopold as the personal sovereign of the Congo Free State, which was to be governed on ideal lines. In practice, the Free State excited a great deal of criticism, and by a treaty approved in 1908 it was taken over by Belgium. Many reforms were introduced, and the BELGIAN CONGO, as the country is now called, has since made steady progress.

It is a big country (nearly 80 times as big as Belgium) forming a rough quadrilateral in the heart of Africa, with no outlet to the sea except at the mouth of the Congo. It is well watered by the Congo, which flows through the country in a great arc (going north, then east, then

south), and by the many other rivers of the Congo basin. The Equator runs through the northern half of the country, which is covered with primeval forest, thinning to open woodlands as the country rises southward and eastward. There is mountainous country on the eastern border, in the region of the Great Lakes, reaching nearly 17,000 feet in the peaks of Ruwenzori. There are mountains,

A SWIMMING POOL IN THE RUANDA-URUNDI REGION OF THE BELGIAN CONGO

too, on the western side, and where the Congo breaks through these its course is obstructed by rapids for over 200 miles between Leopoldville (300,000), the capital, and the port of Matadi.

Such interruptions are not uncommon on the Congo and its tributaries; but they are navigable for long stretches—in the case of the Congo itself for over 1000 miles above Stanley Pool, before Stanleyville and Stanley Falls bring more obstructions. River steamers ply on these navigable stretches for a total distance of over 7000 miles, and, on the main river, railways make a detour of the rapids. From Matadi to Leopoldville there are two pipelines through which oil is pumped for the use of the river steamers.

The principal railways are in the far south, where the " Copper Belt " of Northern Rhodesia is continued in the copper fields of Katanga. The mineral wealth of this region has been a magnet for communications with the outside world. The Rhodesian railways have been extended through Elizabethville, the chief town of Katanga, to Bukama, on the Lualaba (Upper Congo), and thence north-east to Port Francqui, at the head of navigation on the Kasai, 3288 miles from Cape Town. From Tenke, 176 miles beyond Elizabethville, a line branches off to the west and runs for 1158 miles through the Belgian Congo and Portuguese West Africa to Lobito Bay, on the Atlantic. This is the shortest route to Katanga, and as Katanga is connected by the Rhodesian railways with the port of Beira, in Portuguese East Africa, it is possible to cross the continent by rail.

Minerals—copper, gold, tin, and precious stones—provide half the value of exports. The Congo is the world's second largest supplier of uranium and produces 75 per cent of the world's cobalt. Palm kernels and palm oil, cotton and coffee are other valuable exports. About a million acres are under cotton.

Livestock thrives in the Trustee Territory of Ruanda-Urundi (north of Lake Tanganyika) which was formerly part of German East Africa and is now attached to the Belgian Congo.

SPANISH AFRICA

UNTIL recently, Spain controlled an area of 18,000 square miles of Morocco, mostly along the Mediterranean coast—except around the international zone of Tangier (100,000)—but some facing the Atlantic. This mountainous area, rich in minerals and exporting large quantities of iron ore, was returned to Morocco after 44 years of Spanish guardianship by an agreement signed in April 1956.

Spain still holds the Mediterranean ports of Ceuta (60,000) and Melilla (80,000), which have been Spanish possessions since the sixteenth century, and the country around the Atlantic port of Ifni which was ceded to her as a fishing settlement. Beyond this extends the Spanish Sahara, with an estimated area of 105,500 square miles, supporting a small nomad population. Westward are the volcanic CANARY ISLANDS, known of old as the Fortunate Isles, and still a favourite health resort. Scattered over 250 miles of sea, they include seven inhabited islands. The total area is 2800 square miles, and the population 800,000, mostly living in Grand Canary and Tenerife, including their respective capitals, Las Palmas and Santa Cruz. Fruit and vegetables are grown for export.

SPANISH GUINEA includes a mainland territory, Rio Muni, of 11,000 square miles, still mostly undeveloped, and several outlying volcanic islands. The Governor lives in the largest island, Fernando Po, which rises to 9000 feet and is noted for its loveliness. Santa Isabel, the capital, stands on a cliff above a deep-water harbour, part of an old crater. Cocoa and coffee are largely grown.

LIBERIA

LIBERIA is a negro republic on the Guinea Coast of West Africa; it has an area of 43,000 square miles and a population approaching three million. It was founded by Americans as a home for freed slaves, and constituted as a free independent republic in 1847. In recent years the Americans have done much to develop the country, constructing a railway, roads, and airfields, and enlarging ports. Monrovia (20,000), the capital, is a fine port, one of nine along Liberia's 350-mile coastline. The biggest export is rubber.

ETHIOPIA

ETHIOPIA, which owes its name to a Greek word meaning " burnt " because the Ethiopians appeared so dark to the Mediterranean peoples, was formerly known as Abyssinia. In Biblical times the Ethiopian Queen of Sheba visited King Solomon and in the fourth century Christianity became the country's religion.

The Italians claimed a protectorate at the end of the nineteenth century but were defeated at the battle of Adowa. Trouble broke out again in 1936 when Mussolini invaded Ethiopia despite condemnation by the League of Nations. The Italians ruled the country until 1941, when with British help they were defeated and the Emperor Haile Selassie was restored to his throne. He rules through a Council of Ministers and a Parliament.

Ethiopia, which has an estimated population of 20 million, ranges from stifling lowlands to bracing highlands. Addis Ababa (400,000), the capital, lies at over 8000 feet, and there are mountains as high as 14,000 feet. Lake Tana (6000 feet) is the source of the Blue Nile. From Addis Ababa a railway descends to the coast at Jibuti (486 miles), in French Somaliland. The Italians have left a legacy of good roads, but more are being built. There are air services to many parts of Africa.

A wide range of crops is grown at different levels, there are valuable forests, and millions of cattle and sheep range the high plateaus.

ERITREA, formerly a colony of Italy—and her first—is today a self-governing State, federated to Ethiopia. It has an area of 48,350 square miles and a population of more than a million. Asmara, the capital, 75 miles from the coast, lies 7700 feet above sea level. A railway climbs to it from Massawa, the chief port, and then continues inland. Livestock is numerous, and there is considerable export of hides and skins.

SOMALIA

AFTER the First World War, territories on the right bank of the Juba river were ceded by Britain to Italy and became the Italian colony of Somaliland. During the Second World War British Forces occupied the area and for several years Britain remained in charge. In 1950 the United Nations placed the territory under Italian trusteeship with a promise that the Somalis should be granted independence in 1960. The first Somali parliament was inaugurated on April 30, 1956 ; it replaced the territorial council—a consultative non-elected body which helped the trusteeship administration.

Somalia is a low-lying, semi-desert area of 194,000 square miles south-east of Ethiopia. It has over one-and-a-quarter million inhabitants, cattle-rearing and camel-breeding being among their chief occupations. Cultivated areas border the Webi Shebeli and Juba rivers. From Mogadishu (78,000), the chief port and capital, a railway of 70 miles runs through a fertile district.

LIBYA

LIBYA, in North Africa, became an independent kingdom under the Amir Mohammed Idris el Senussi on December 24, 1951, in accordance with decisions made by the United Nations. Its main province, Tripolitania, came under Turkish domination in the sixteenth century and remained under Turkish rule until shortly before the First World War when Turkey recognized Italian sovereignty over the area. Tripoli, its chief city and port, is now the capital of the kingdom.

After the expulsion of the Germans and Italians from North Africa during the

A POLICEMAN IN BENGHAZI

Second World War, Tripolitania and the province of Cyrenaica east of it (chief city Benghazi, 62,300) were placed under British military administration. The southern desert area of the Fezzan was administered by the French military authorities. Having achieved independence, Libya concluded treaties with Britain, the United States, and France. She now receives financial and military assistance from Britain and the U.S. in exchange for permitting them to have bases on Libyan soil.

Libya covers about 700,000 square miles but has little more than a million people. There being few natural resources which the country could exploit, they are almost entirely dependent on farming. The coastal zone alone is properly suited for growing cereals and fruits and raising livestock. Farther south stretch desert or near-desert lands.

THE REPUBLIC OF THE SUDAN

THIS vast country is one of the youngest sovereign States in Africa, a new and proud Republic. Its name comes from the Arabic *Belad es-Sudan* meaning " country of the blacks." It was the name given by the Arab invaders of North Africa to the whole stretch of country south of the Sahara desert from the Atlantic Ocean to the Red Sea. (See also the French Sudan in the section on French West Africa.)

Throughout the later Middle Ages and down to the beginning of the nineteenth century relations between Egypt and the Sudan were limited to commerce. Every year two large caravans travelled from the Sudan to Egypt with Negro slaves and various products—ivory, gum, ostrich feathers, gold dust—and returned with manufactured goods.

During the nineteenth century the Egyptians increased their hold on the northern Sudan, and later penetrated into the Southern Provinces, where Sir Samuel Baker and General Charles Gordon, as governors of Equatoria province, were making efforts to stamp out the slave trade.

Discontent in the country led to a Sudanese revolt under the direction of the Mahdi, a religious leader of a Moslem sect. In 1885 they took Khartoum by storm and assassinated General Gordon, who had been sent there to evacuate the Egyptian garrison. It was not until 1898 that Kitchener reconquered the country, winning the decisive battle at Omdurman, the Mahdist capital.

In the following year Britain and Egypt agreed to set up a Condominium in the Sudan ; that is they decided to rule the country jointly. The British and Egyptian flags flew side by side on Government buildings. The Governor-General, who was the chief administrator, was appointed by the Egyptian Government on the recommendation of Britain. From that time—and for half a century—the Sudan developed along the lines of a British colony.

After the Second World War rapid progress was made, leading to the signing of an Anglo-Egyptian agreement in February 1953. In 1954 the first all-Sudanese government was formed and by the end of the year control over the administration, the police, and the armed forces had passed out of the hands of the Condominium Powers : the " Sudanisation " of the Sudan was complete. In December 1955 the Sudanese parliament unanimously passed a resolution declaring that the Sudan was to become " a fully independent sovereign State," and asking the Condominium Powers to recognise the declaration. This was done on January 1, 1956. On that day the Sudanese flag was hoisted and the Sudan achieved complete independence.

Covering nearly 970,000 square miles, the Sudan is a quarter the size of Europe, but its population numbers little more than eight million. The White Nile flows through the country from south to north, and on the way is joined by the Blue Nile, coming from Ethiopia.

At the meeting place of these waterways, facing each other across the White Nile, stand the new capital, Khartoum (380,000) and the old Mahdist capital, Omdurman (125,000). North of Ethiopia the Sudan extends eastward to the Red Sea, where the modern Port Sudan is the coastal terminus of the Sudan Railways.

The country may be divided into two regions. There is the northern half of deserts and steppelands—a south-eastern continuation of the Sahara—which is the home of Arabic-speaking Moslems. And there is the southern half, consisting largely of tropical forests and swamps, which is inhabited by primitive tribes leading a nomadic or semi-nomadic existence. In former days the northern Arabs descended on the South and captured their slaves, and for this reason the Southerners are still suspicious of the intentions of the Northerners sent to administer Southern provinces, there being as yet insufficient Southerners trained for administrative duties.

The chief agricultural industry is cotton-growing in the Gezira, a plain of five million acres in the angle between the White and Blue Niles. A great dam has been built at Sennar on the Blue Nile, 220 miles above Khartoum, and nearly a million acres have been brought under cultivation by irrigation. Exports from the Sudan include gum arabic—of which the Sudan is the world's chief source of supply—cotton, oil seeds, nuts and kernels, cattle and sheep, and hides and skins.

MAPS AND PICTURES OF AFRICA

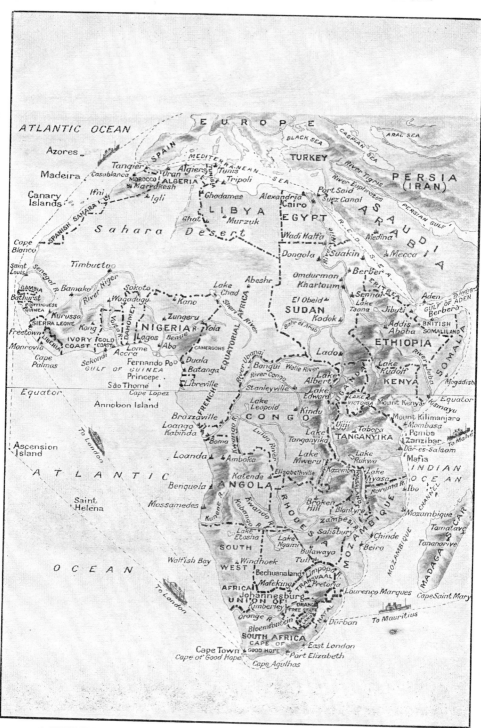

A BIRD'S-EYE VIEW OF AFRICA, SHOWING ITS CHIEF RIVERS AND MOUNTAINS, AND THE
GREAT SAHARA DESERT COVERING ONE-FIFTH OF ITS SURFACE

THE INTERESTING PHYSICAL FEATURES OF THE AFRICAN CONTINENT

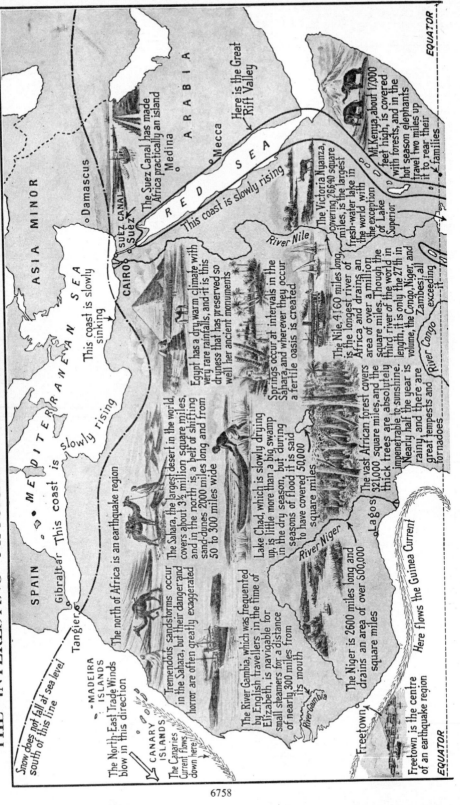

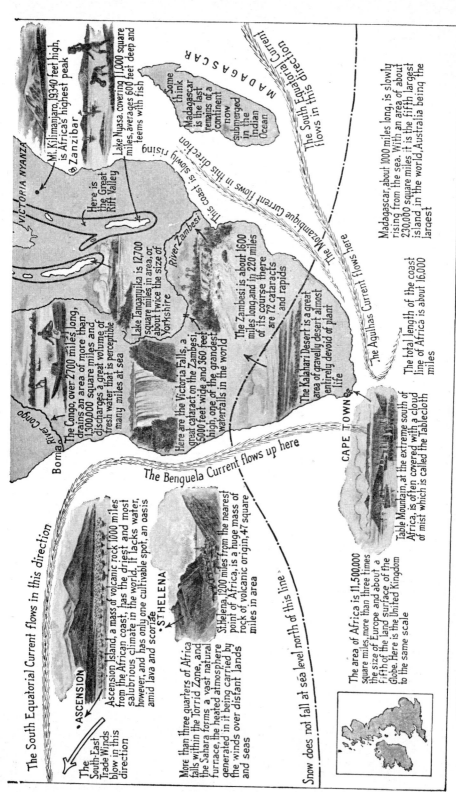

Mt.Kilimanjaro, 19,340 feet high, is Africa's highest peak

Zanzibar

VICTORIA NYANZA

Some think Madagascar is the last remains of a continent now submerged in the Indian Ocean

MADAGASCAR

Lake Nyasa, covering 11,000 square miles, averages 600 feet deep and teems with fish

The South Equatorial Current flows in this direction

Here is the Great Rift Valley

This coast is slowly rising

The Mozambique Current flows in this direction

The Congo, over 2700 miles long, drains an area of more than 1,300,000 square miles and discharges a great volume of fresh water that is perceptible many miles at sea

River Zambesi

Lake Tanganyika is 12,700 square miles in area, or about twice the size of Yorkshire

Madagascar, about 1000 miles long, is slowly rising from the sea. With an area of about 230,000 square miles it is the fifth largest island in the world, Australia being the largest

Boma

River Congo

Here are the Victoria Falls, a great cataract on the Zambesi, 5000 feet wide and 360 feet high, one of the grandest waterfalls in the world

The Zambesi is about 1600 miles long, and in 220 miles of its course there are 72 cataracts and rapids

The Kalahari Desert is a great area of gravelly desert almost entirely devoid of plant life

The Agulhas Current flows here

The total length of the coast line of Africa is about 16,000 miles

The Benguela Current flows up here

CAPE TOWN

Table Mountain, at the extreme south of Africa, is often covered with a cloud of mist which is called the Tablecloth

The South Equatorial Current flows in this direction

Ascension Island, a mass of volcanic rock 1000 miles from the African coast, has the driest and most salubrious climate in the world. It lacks water, however, and has only one cultivable spot, an oasis amid lava and scoriae

ASCENSION

The South-East Trade Winds blow in this direction

ST.HELENA

St.Helena, 1200 miles from the nearest point of Africa, is a huge mass of rock of volcanic origin, 47 square miles in area

More than three quarters of Africa falls within the Torrid Zone, and the Sahara forms a vast natural furnace, the heated atmosphere generated in it being carried by the winds over distant lands and seas

Snow does not fall at sea level north of this line

The area of Africa is 11,500,000 square miles, more than three times the size of Europe and about a fifth of the land surface of the Globe. Here is the United Kingdom to the same scale

BESIDES THE BIGGEST DESERT, AFRICA HAS ONE OF THE BIGGEST FORESTS AND THE SECOND LARGEST FRESH-WATER LAKE IN THE WORLD

AFRICA AND THE AMAZING WEALTH OF HER PLANT LIFE

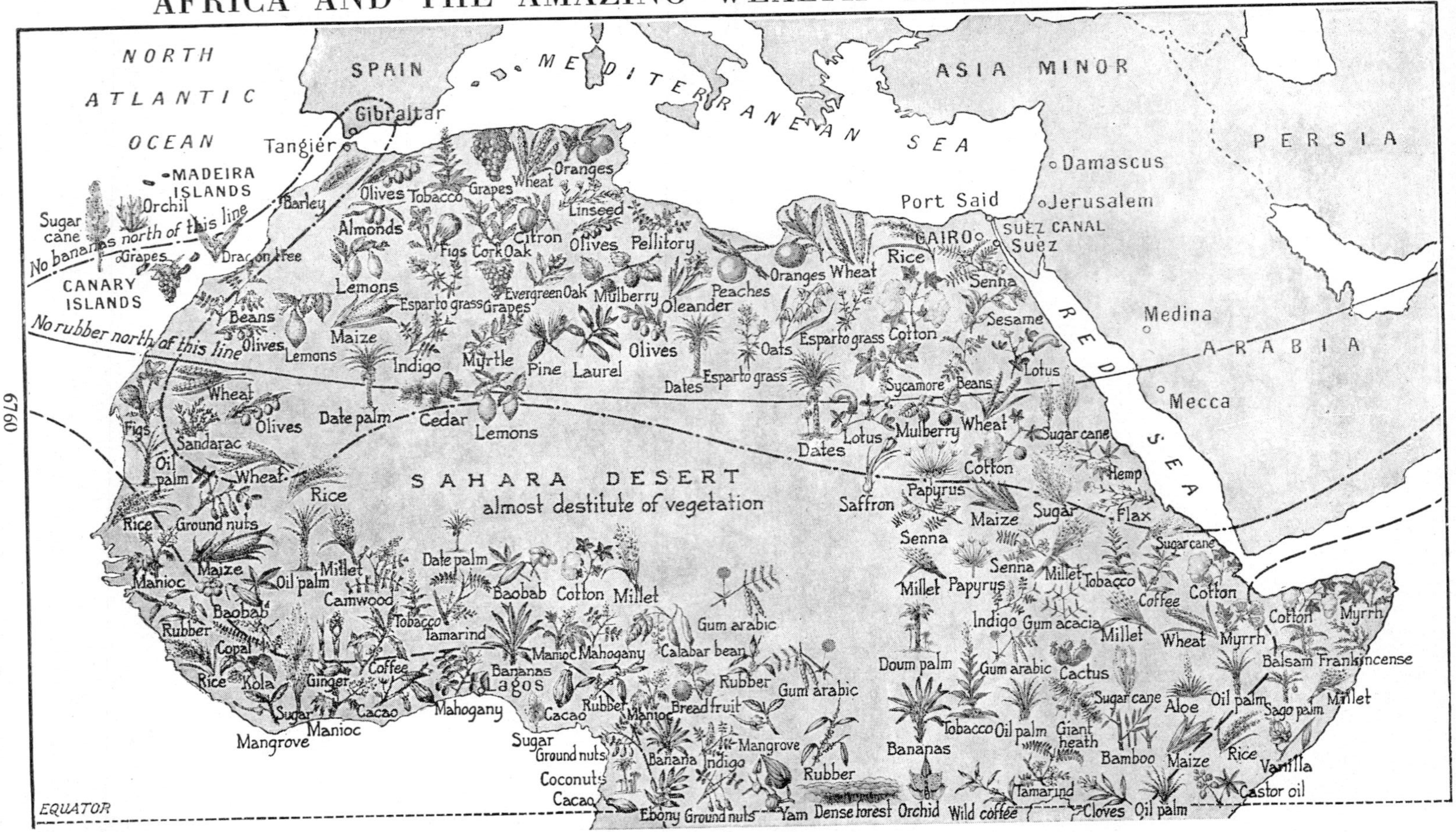

NORTH ATLANTIC OCEAN

SPAIN

PERSIA

ASIA MINOR

MEDITERRANEAN SEA

Gibraltar
Tangier
Damascus
Jerusalem
Port Said
Suez Canal
Suez
Cairo
Medina
Mecca

ARABIA

RED SEA

MADEIRA ISLANDS
CANARY ISLANDS

Sugar cane north of this line
No bananas north of this line
No rubber north of this line

SAHARA DESERT
almost destitute of vegetation

EQUATOR

6760

AS MAY BE SEEN FROM THIS PICTURE-MAP, MANY FOOD PLANTS, AND PLANTS OF GREAT COMMERCIAL VALUE, ARE GROWN IN AFRICA

ALGIERS, CAPITAL OF ALGERIA, BUILT ON A HILLSIDE OVERLOOKING THE MEDITERRANEAN

A MARKET-PLACE
IN TUNIS

THE GREAT MOSQUE OF
ALGIERS

A MOSQUE IN FEZ, A CAPITAL
OF MOROCCO

MARINE AVENUE IN TUNIS

A MOSQUE IN TUNIS

AN OLD SUDANESE MOSQUE DUG OUT OF THE SAND AT DJENNE, IN FRENCH SUDAN

A GATEWAY IN
TRIPOLI

THE SOUTH GATE
OF TANGIER

THE ROMAN CATHOLIC
CATHEDRAL IN TUNIS

THE HOTEL DE VILLE AT BISKRA IN ALGERIA

THE MOSQUE OF SIDI-EL-RAMAN IN ALGIERS

THE STATE PALACE IN TRIPOLI, LIBYA

THE BEY'S PALACE IN TUNIS

THE BEAUTIFUL SWEEP OF THE LUNGAMARE, OR ESPLANADE, AT TRIPOLI, LIBYA

RAILWAY STATION AT LEOPOLDVILLE, IN THE
BELGIAN CONGO

A BLOCK OF FLATS AT DAKAR,
IN SENEGAL

GOVERNMENT HOUSE AT LOANDA, ANGOLA

A STREET IN MONROVIA, LIBERIA

A CORNER OF MAKALE, ETHIOPIA

COMMERCIAL CENTRE OF HARAR, ETHIOPIA

THE VILLAGE OF EDD, ON THE COAST OF ERITREA

MODERN BUILDINGS IN ASMARA, ERITREA

GENERAL VIEW OF MASSAWA, ERITREA

THE GOVERNOR'S CASTLE IN GONDAR, ETHIOPIA

CROWDED MARKET-PLACE OF HARAR, ETHIOPIA

THE YACHTING HARBOUR AT ALGIERS

THE PORT OF BÔNE IN ALGERIA

A NATIVE VILLAGE
IN SENEGAL

THE BERDAIN GATE OF
MEKNES, MOROCCO

A WELL NEAR JIBUTI IN
FRENCH SOMALILAND

THE RAMPARTS OF MARRAKESH IN MOROCCO

THE SULTAN'S PALACE AT RABAT, MOROCCO

A BOULEVARD IN CASABLANCA

RUE DE COMMERCE, AT TAMATAVE, MADAGASCAR

MOUNTED ON CAMELS, A POLICE DESERT PATROL LEAVES THE MUD-BUILT BARRACKS IN THE SUDAN

MARKET IN THE GEZIRA DISTRICT OF THE SUDAN

RIDING ON A TRAM IN KHARTOUM

THE UNIVERSITY COLLEGE AT KHARTOUM, CAPITAL OF THE SUDAN

THREE TYPES OF SUDANESE—A STUDENT, A NUBA HIGH PRIEST, AND A POLICE SERGEANT

A CLASS FOR MEDICAL STUDENTS IN THE UNIVERSITY COLLEGE AT KHARTOUM

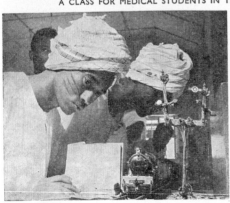 

PROUD YOUNG WORKERS OF THE PROUD YOUNG REPUBLIC OF THE SUDAN.   ON THE LEFT ARE RAILWAY
ENGINEERING APPRENTICES ; ON THE RIGHT ARE TYPISTS IN THE RAILWAY OFFICES

One Thousand Poems of All Times and All Countries

Shelley's Lament for Keats

THE poet Shelley had some acquaintance, though not very intimate, with John Keats, and when Keats died he lamented him, under the poetical name of Adonais, in one of the great elegies of English literature. The poem is too long to be given here, but below is a selection from its 55 stanzas. Shelley calls on the Muse Urania to join him in his grief. He compares the old misused poet John Milton and the young misused poet John Keats ; but Keats has passed beyond man's disdain and neglect to a loftier destiny. A description of the last resting-place of the poet in Rome follows, and then, in a great finale, Shelley imagines his own spirit, " borne darkly, fearfully, afar," joining the soul of Adonais in the realms of the Eternal.

ADONAIS

I WEEP for Adonais—he is dead!
    O, weep for Adonais! though our tears
Thaw not the frost which binds so dear a head!
And thou, sad Hour, selected from all years
To mourn our loss, rouse thy obscure compeers,
And teach them thine own sorrow, say:
" With me
Died Adonais; till the Future dares
Forget the Past his fate and fame shall be
An echo and a light unto eternity! "

O WEEP for Adonais—he is dead!
    Wake, melancholy Mother, wake and weep!
Yet wherefore?   Quench within their burning bed
Thy fiery tears, and let thy loud heart keep,
Like his, a mute and uncomplaining sleep;
For he is gone where all things wise and fair
Descend; oh, dream not that the amorous Deep
Will yet restore him to the vital air;
Death feeds on his mute voice, and laughs at our despair.

Wishing to make the contrast between old and young poets who had been scorned and ill-used in their day, Shelley now turns to Milton, and from him leads again up to Keats, the last and youngest sufferer.

MOST musical of mourners, weep again!
    Lament anew, Urania! He died,
Who was the Sire of an immortal strain,
Blind old and lonely, when his country's pride,
The priest, the slave, and the liberticide,
Trampled and mocked with many a loathèd rite
Of lust and blood; he went, unterrified,
Into the gulf of death; but his clear Sprite
Yet reigns o'er earth; the third among the sons of light.

MOST musical of mourners, weep anew!
    Not all to that bright station dared to climb;
And happier they their happiness who knew,
Whose tapers yet burn through that night of time
In which suns perished; others more sublime,
Struck by the envious wrath of man or god,
Have sunk, extinct in their refulgent prime;
And yet some live, treading the thorny road
Which leads, through toil and hate, to Fame's serene abode.

BUT now thy youngest, dearest one, has perished,
The nursling of thy widowhood, who grew
Like a pale flower by some sad maiden cherished,
And fed with true-love tears instead of dew;
Most musical of mourners, weep anew!
Thy extreme hope, the loveliest and the last,
The bloom, whose petals, nipped before they blew,
Died on the promise of the fruit, is waste;
The broken lily lies—the storm is overpast.

After an outburst against the harsh critics in the Press for their treatment of Keats, the poet regains his calm, and, rebuking himself for the violence he has shown, says:

PEACE, peace! he is not dead, he doth not sleep;
He hath awakened from the dream of life.

POEMS · SONGS · BALLADS · VERSES AND RHYMES WITH MUSIC

He passes on into the most tender and lovely part of the poem, in which he develops the idea that the poet has escaped all human woes and has been re-absorbed into the Creative Power from whence he came.

HE has outsoared the shadow of our night;
    Envy and calumny and hate and pain,
And that unrest which men miscall delight,
Can touch him not and torture not again;
From the contagion of the world's slow
    stain
He is secure, and now can never mourn
A heart grown cold, a head grown grey in
    vain;
Nor, when the spirit's self has ceased to
    burn,
With sparkless ashes load an unlamented
    urn.

He is made one with Nature; there is heard
His voice in all her music, from the moan
Of thunder to the song of night's sweet
    bird;
He is a presence to be felt and known
In darkness and in light, from herb and
    stone,
Spreading itself where'er that Power may
    move
Which has withdrawn his being to its own;
Which wields the world with never-
    wearied love,
Sustains it from beneath, and kindles it
    above.

He is a portion of the loveliness
Which once he made more lovely: he doth
    bear
His part, while the one Spirit's plastic
    stress
Sweeps through the dull, dense world,
    compelling there
All new successions to the forms they wear;
Torturing th' unwilling dross that checks
    its flight
To its own likeness, as each mass may bear;
And bursting in its beauty and its might
From trees and beasts and men into the
    Heaven's light.

After a vision of the poet joining the dead poets who are " inheritors of unfulfilled renown," but yet are " robed in dazzling immortality," Shelley leaves these empyrean heights and leads us to the grave in Rome—the grave of which he said " it might make one in love with death to think that one should be buried in so sweet a place."

OR go to Rome, which is the sepulchre,
    Oh, not of him, but of our joy; 'tis
    nought
That ages, empires, and religions there
Lie buried in the ravage they have
    wrought;
For such as he can lend; they borrow not

Glory from those who made the world
    their prey;
And he is gathered to the kings of thought
Who waged contention with their time's
    decay,
And of the past are all that cannot pass
    away.

Go thou to Rome—at once the paradise,
The grave, the city, and the wilderness;
And where its wrecks like shattered
    mountains rise,
And flowering weeds, and fragrant copses
    dress
The bones of Desolation's nakedness,
Pass, till the spirit of the spot shall lead
Thy footsteps to a slope of green access
Where, like an infant's smile, over the dead
A light of laughing flowers along the grass
    is spread;

And grey walls moulder round, on which
    dull Time
Feeds, like slow fire upon a hoary brand;
And one keen pyramid with wedge
    sublime,
Pavilioning the dust of him who planned
This refuge for his memory, doth stand
Like flame transformed to marble; and
    beneath
A field is spread, on which a newer band
Have pitched in Heaven's smile their camp
    of death,
Welcoming him we lose with scarce ex-
    tinguished breath.

Here pause: these graves are all too young
    as yet
To have outgrown the sorrow which con-
    signed
Its charge to each; and if the seal is set
Here, on one fountain of a mourning mind,
Break it not thou! too surely shalt thou
    find
Thine own well full, if thou returnest home,
Of tears and gall.   From the world's bitter
    wind
Seek shelter in the shadow of the tomb.
What Adonais is, why fear we to become?

And now begins the great finale of the poem. The poet sees all life as a temporary vision, and the human spirit as an emanation from God going back to God, and, freed from earthly restraints, he rises on the wings of imagination to join the soul of Adonais in the realms of the Eternal.

THE One remains, the many change and
    pass;
Heaven's light for ever shines, Earth's
    shadows fly;

Life, like a dome of many-coloured glass,
Stains the white radiance of Eternity,
Until Death tramples it to fragments.
Die,
If thou wouldst be with that which thou
dost seek!
Follow where all is fled! Rome's azure
sky,
Flowers, ruins, statues, music, words, are
weak
The glory they transfuse with fitting
truth to speak.

That Light whose smile kindles the
Universe,
That Beauty in which all things work and
move,
That Benediction which the eclipsing
Curse
Of birth can quench not, that sustaining
Love
Which, through the web of being blindly
wove
By man and beast and earth and air and
sea,
Burns bright or dim, as each are mirrors of
The fire for which all thirst, now beams
on me,
Consuming the last clouds of cold mor-
tality.

The breath whose might I have invoked
in song
Descends on me; my spirit's bark is driven
Far from the shore, far from the trembling
throng
Whose sails were never to the tempest
given;
The massy earth and spherèd skies are
riven!
I am borne darkly, fearfully, afar;
Whilst, burning through the inmost veil
of Heaven,
The soul of Adonais, like a star,
Beacons from the abode where the
Eternal are.

CHERRY-RIPE

This little lyric in praise of Julia's smiling lips was written
by Robert Herrick, who was born in 1591 and died in 1674.
He was a master of the art of writing lyrical poetry.

CHERRY-ripe, ripe, ripe, I cry,
    Full and fair ones; come and buy.
If so be you ask me where
They do grow, I answer: There
Where my Julia's lips do smile;
There's the land, or cherry-isle,
Whose plantations fully show
All the year where cherries grow.

TILL WE HAVE BUILT JERUSALEM

William Blake, the mystical poet and painter, who was
born in 1757 and died in 1827, wrote in visions, which must
always have a poetical interpretation. He speaks through
spiritual suggestions that have a moving but indefinite
beauty, which characteristic is illustrated in these much-
quoted yet evasive lines. They are really an appeal for
the reign of the Christ-like spirit in the life of England.

AND did those feet in ancient time
    Walk upon England's mountains
    green?
And was the holy Lamb of God
    On England's pleasant pastures seen?

And did the Countenance Divine
    Shine forth upon our clouded hills?
And was Jerusalem builded here
    Among these dark Satanic Mills?

Bring me my bow of burning gold!
    Bring me my arrows of desire!
Bring me my spear: O clouds, unfold!
    Bring me my chariot of fire!

I will not cease from mental fight,
    Nor shall my sword sleep in my hand,
Till we have built Jerusalem
    In England's green and pleasant land.

AE FOND KISS

This parting love song by Robert Burns was a real parting
that actually took place and lasted. The lady concerned
was the friend with whom the poet carried on a corre-
spondence under her pen-name of Clarinda. Sir Walter
Scott once said that the last four lines of the second verse
" contain the essence of a thousand love tales."

AE fond kiss, and then we sever!
    Ae fareweel, alas, for ever!
Deep in heart-wrung tears I'll pledge thee,
Warring sighs and groans I'll wage thee.
Who shall say that fortune grieves him
While the star of hope she leaves him?
Me, nae cheerfu' twinkle lights me,
Dark despair around benights me.

I'll ne'er blame my partial fancy,
Naething could resist my Nancy;
But to see her was to love her,
Love but her, and love for ever.
Had we never loved sae kindly,
Had we never loved sae blindly,
Never met, or never parted,
We had ne'er been broken-hearted.

Fare thee weel, thou first and fairest!
Fare thee weel, thou best and dearest!
Thine be ilka joy and treasure,
Peace, enjoyment, love, and pleasure.
Ae fond kiss, and then we sever;
Ae fareweel, alas, for ever!
Deep in heart-wrung tears I'll pledge thee,
Warring sighs and groans I'll wage thee.

LOUD IS THE VALE

This poem tells the story of Wordsworth's mind as he took an evening walk in the Lake District, in September 1806, after he had read in the newspaper that the popular statesman of that day, Charles James Fox, lay dying. A heavy storm had passed, and all the mountain streams were rushing into the valley. The poet was calmed by the thought that the passing from Earth of men's leaders is but an incident in the universal drama of God's great design.

LOUD is the vale! the voice is up
  With which she speaks when storms
  are gone,
A mighty unison of streams!
Of all her voices, one!

Loud is the vale; this inland depth
In peace is roaring like the sea;
Yon star upon the mountain-top
Is listening quietly.

Sad was I, even to pain deprest,
Importunate and heavy load!
The Comforter hath found me here
Upon this lonely road;

And many thousands now are sad,
Wait the fulfilment of their fear;
For he must die who is their stay,
Their glory disappear.

A power is passing from the earth
To breathless Nature's dark abyss;
But when the great and good depart
What is it more than this:

That Man, who is from God sent forth,
Doth yet again to God return?
Such ebb and flow must ever be,
Then wherefore should we mourn?

HOME NO MORE HOME TO ME

When Robert Louis Stevenson left his homeland, in 1887, to nourish his failing strength in high, dry parts of America and farther afield, he seemed to have a feeling that he would not return. Not long before his death in the Samoan Islands he sent home Songs of Travel, written during the seven years of his wanderings, and into them came farewell strains which afterwards seemed prophetic. This poem, written after the break up of the Scottish family household, shows how pathetic memories haunted his exile.

HOME, no more home to me, whither
  must I wander?
  Hunger my driver, I go where I must.
Cold blows the winter wind over hill and
  heather;
  Thick drives the rain, and my roof is
  in the dust.
Loved of wise men was the shade of my
  roof-tree.
  The true word of welcome was spoken
  in the door:
Dear days of old, with the faces in the
  firelight,
  Kind folks of old, you come again no
  more.

Home was home then, my dear, full of
  kindly faces;
  Home was home then, my dear, happy
  for the child.
Fire and the windows bright glittered on
  the moorland;
  Song, tuneful song, built a palace in the
  wild.
Now, when day dawns on the brow of the
  moorland,
  Lone stands the house, and the chimney-
  stone is cold.
Lone let it stand now the friends are all
  departed,
  The kind hearts, the true hearts, that
  loved the place of old.

Spring shall come, come again, calling up
  the moor-fowl;
  Spring shall bring the sun and rain,
  bring the bees and flowers;
Red shall the heather bloom over hill
  and valley,
  Soft flow the stream through the even-
  flowing hours;
Fair the day shine as it shone on my
  childhood,
  Fair the day shine on the house with
  open door;
Birds come and cry there and twitter
  in the chimney,
  But I go for ever and come again no
  more.

LEISURE

These lines are perhaps the best example of the natural simple poetry of W. H. Davies (1871–1940), who won attention by his descriptions of experiences as a tramp. He saw the worlds of outdoor life and of human character with a poet's eye and had a rare intuition for romance as universally felt. He had, too, a fine gift of selective criticism. This poem is given by permission of Messrs. Jonathan Cape, publishers of his works.

WHAT is this life if, full of care,
  We have no time to stand and stare?
No time to stand beneath the boughs
And stare as long as sheep or cows.

No time to see, when woods we pass,
Where squirrels hide their nuts in grass.

No time to see, in broad daylight,
Streams full of stars, like skies at night.

No time to turn at Beauty's glance,
And watch her feet, how they can dance.

No time to wait till her mouth can
Enrich that smile her eyes began.

A poor life this if, full of care,
We have no time to stand and stare.

SONG

Shelley had a keen poetic appreciation of the unhappiness he caused himself. He turned the edge of his troubles by putting them into poetry. In this song he is so conscious of doing it that he almost smiles at himself. And then how charmingly he enumerates the delightful things he loves that contradict his own despondency!

Rarely, rarely, comest thou,
　Spirit of Delight!
Wherefore hast thou left me now
　Many a day and night?
Many a weary night and day
'Tis since thou art fled away.

How shall ever one like me
　Win thee back again?
With the joyous and the free
　Thou wilt scoff at pain.
Spirit false! thou hast forgot
All but those who need thee not.

As a lizard with the shade
　Of a trembling leaf,
Thou with sorrow art dismayed;
　Even the sighs of grief
Reproach thee, that thou art not near,
And reproach thou wilt not hear.

Let me set my mournful ditty
　To a merry measure;
Thou wilt never come for pity,
　Thou wilt come for pleasure;
Pity then will cut away
Those cruel wings, and thou wilt stay.

I love all that thou lovest,
　Spirit of Delight!
The fresh Earth in new leaves dressed,
　And the starry night;
Autumn evening, and the morn
When the golden mists are born.

I love snow, and all the forms
　Of the radiant frost;
I love waves, and winds, and storms,
　Everything almost
Which is Nature's, and may be
Untainted by man's misery.

I love tranquil solitude,
　And such society
As is quiet, wise, and good;
　Between thee and me
What difference? but thou dost possess
The things I seek, not love them less.

I love Love—though he has wings,
　And like light can flee;
But, above all other things,
　Spirit, I love thee.
Thou art love and life! Oh, come,
Make once more my heart thy home.

AFTERWARDS

Of all the poetry with which Thomas Hardy (1840-1927) surprised the world in his later years this suggestion of what his neighbours might say of him when he was gone is the most tender. It brought a new friendship for him into every heart. Two verses of the poem are here omitted.

When the Present has latched its
　postern behind my tremulous stay,
And the May month flaps its glad green
　leaves like wings,
Delicate-filmed as new-spun silk, will the
　neighbours say,
　"He was a man who used to notice
　　such things?"

If it be in the dusk when, like an eyelid's
　soundless blink,
The dewfall-hawk comes crossing the
　shades to alight
Upon the wind-warped upland thorn, a
　gazer may think,
　"To him this must have been a familiar
　　sight."

And will any say when my bell of quittance
　is heard in the gloom,
　And a crossing breeze cuts a pause in
　　its out-rollings,
Till they rise again, as they were a new
　bell's boom,
　"He hears it not now, but used to notice
　　such things?"

WE MUST BE FREE OR DIE

The year 1802 was one of terrible danger to England. She had made a hampering and insincere peace with Napoleon, which he was obviously using to prepare for her complete overthrow. Every action of his showed that he was preparing for deadly war, and that England was the enemy. This was the time when Wordsworth penned the proud claims for British freedom and manhood in this rousing sonnet.

It is not to be thought of that the flood
　Of British freedom, which, to the
　　open sea
Of the world's praise, from dark antiquity
Hath flowed, "with pomp of waters,
　unwithstood,"
Roused though it be full often to a mood
Which spurns the check of salutary bands,
That this most famous stream in bogs
　and sands
Should perish; and to evil and to good
Be lost for ever. In our halls is hung
Armoury of the invincible knights of old:
We must be free or die who speak the
　tongue
That Shakespeare spake; the faith and
　morals hold
Which Milton held. In everything we are
　sprung
Of Earth's first blood, have titles manifold.

ODE TO DUTY

This ode to Duty shows Wordsworth writing in his more massive style. The determined simplicity of his earlier poems is laid aside, and he takes the formal measure of Gray's Ode to Adversity as his model, and personifies duty in the eighteenth-century manner. He is using the idea to strengthen his own character. If that were all, the poem would be mainly useful. But, as in the second, third, and especially the sixth stanzas, the poet's exhortations pass into glorious, me odious poetry, ethereal in thought.

STERN Daughter of the Voice of God!
  O Duty! if that name thou love,
Who art a light to guide, a rod
To check the erring, and reprove;
Thou, who art victory and law
When empty terrors overawe;
From vain temptations dost set free;
And calm'st the weary strife of frail
  humanity!

There are who ask not if thine eye
Be on them; who, in love and truth,
Where no misgiving is, rely
Upon the genial sense of youth;
Glad hearts! without reproach or blot;
Who do thy work, and know it not:
Oh! if through confidence misplaced
They fail, thy saving arms, dread Power,
  around them cast.

Serene will be our days and bright,
And happy will our nature be,
When love is an unerring light,
And joy its own security.
And they a blissful course may hold,
Even now, who, not unwisely bold,
Live in the spirit of this creed,
Yet seek thy firm support, according to
  their need.

I, loving freedom, and untried;
No sport of every random gust,
Yet being to myself a guide,
Too blindly have reposed my trust:
And oft, when in my heart was heard
Thy timely mandate, I deferred
The task, in smoother walks to stray;
But thee I now would serve more strictly,
  if I may.

Through no disturbance of my soul,
Or strong compunction in me wrought,
I supplicate for thy control;
But in the quietness of thought:
Me this unchartered freedom tires;
I feel the weight of chance-desires:
My hopes no more must change their name,
I long for a repose that ever is the same.

Stern Lawgiver! yet thou dost wear
The Godhead's most benignant grace:

Nor know we anything so fair
As is the smile upon thy face:
Flowers laugh before thee on their beds,
And fragrance in thy footing treads;
Thou dost preserve the stars from wrong;
And the most ancient heavens, through
  Thee, are fresh and strong.

To humbler functions, awful Power!
I call thee: I myself commend
Unto thy guidance from this hour;
Oh, let my weakness have an end!
Give unto me, made lowly wise,
The spirit of self-sacrifice;
The confidence of reason give;
And in the light of truth thy bondman let
  me live!

THE ISOLATION OF GENIUS

" Uneasy lies the head that wears a crown " has its counterpart in all forms of success. Envy, detraction, ambitious rivalry, challenge those who reach life's summits. In these lines, which are taken from the third canto of Childe Harold, Lord Byron sets forth that truth in poetic imagery.

HE who ascends to mountain-tops shall
  find
The loftiest peaks most wrapt in clouds
  and snow;
He who surpasses or subdues mankind
Must look down on the hate of those
  below;
Though high above the sun of glory
  glow,
And far beneath the earth and ocean
  spread,
Round him are icy rocks, and loudly blow
Contending tempests on his naked head,
And thus reward the toils which to those
  summits led.

IN TIME OF THE BREAKING OF NATIONS

The great sensations of history come and go, but the homely toil and simple lives of men and women continue, almost unnoticed, that the Earth may bring forth her increase; and they make up in the truest sense the life of mankind. This thought is here expressed with a noble simplicity by Thomas Hardy, the great English novelist and poet.

ONLY a man harrowing clods
  In a slow, silent walk
With an old horse that stumbles and nods
  Half asleep as they stalk.

Only thin smoke without flame
  From the heaps of couch grass;
Yet this will go onward the same
  Though dynasties pass.

Yonder a maid and her wight
  Come whispering by;
War's annals will cloud into night
  Ere their story die.

FAIR DAFFODILS

Robert Herrick, the writer of this charming song about the daffodils, was a clergyman who lived from 1591 to 1674, and wrote an immense amount of poetry, many of his poems taking rank among the most beautiful in our language.

Fair daffodils, we weep to see
   You haste away so soon;
As yet the early-rising sun
   Has not attained his noon.
      Stay, stay
   Until the hasting day
      Has run
   But to the evensong;
And, having prayed together, we
   Will go with you along.

We have short time to stay, as you,
   We have as short a spring;
As quick a growth to meet decay
   As you, or anything.
      We die,
   As your hours do, and dry
      Away
Like to the summer's rain;
Or as the pearls of morning's dew,
   Ne'er to be found again.

BEFORE ACTION

Here is one of the finest of the many fine poems written by soldiers during the First World War. William Noel Hodgson, the writer, was the son of the Bishop of Ipswich. He was a fine soldier and athlete at school and college. This prayer-poem, with its love of the beauty of Earth, resigned with only a sigh, was written four days before the writer fell in the advance on the Somme.

By all the glories of the day
   And the cool evening's benison,
By that last sunset touch that lay
   Upon the hills when day was done,
By beauty lavishly outpoured
   And blessings carelessly received,
   By all the days that I have lived,
Make me a soldier, Lord.

By all of all man's hopes and fears,
   And all the wonders poets sing,
The laughter of unclouded years,
   And every sad and lovely thing;
By the romantic ages stored
   With high endeavour that was his,
   By all his mad catastrophes,
Make me a man, O Lord.

I, that on my familiar hill
   Saw with uncomprehending eyes
A hundred of Thy sunsets spill
   Their fresh and sanguine sacrifice,
Ere the sun swings his noonday sword
   Must say goodbye to all of this;
   By all delights that I shall miss,
Help me to die, O Lord.

BEYOND THE LAST LAMP

The poet's power of fixing for ever in the minds of men a picture stamped on his own mind is illustrated wonderfully in this poem by Thomas Hardy. Walking near Tooting Common, in suburban London, he twice passed a man and woman in long, earnest, and sad talk. He did not know, and we do not know, who they were, or what was their trouble, but the tragedy of their looks is passed on by his poetic art to all the world to be a lasting problem.

While rain, with eve in partnership,
   Descended darkly, drip, drip, drip,
Beyond the last lone lamp I passed
   Walking slowly, whispering sadly,
   Two linked loiterers, wan, downcast:
Some heavy thought constrained each face
And blinded them to time and place.

The pair seemed lovers, yet absorbed
In mental scenes no longer orbed
   By love's young rays. Each countenance,
     As it slowly, as it sadly,
   Caught the lamplight's yellow glance,
Held in suspense a misery
At things which had been or might be.

When I retrod that watery way
Some hours beyond the droop of day,
   Still I found pacing there the twain
     Just as slowly, just as sadly,
   Heedless of the night and rain.
One could but wonder who they were,
And what wild woe detained them there.

Though thirty years of blur and blot
Have slid since I beheld that spot,
   And saw in curious converse there
     Moving slowly, moving sadly,
   That mysterious tragic pair,
Its olden look may linger on—
All but the couple; they have gone.

Whither ? Who knows, indeed . . And yet
To me, when nights are weird and wet,
   Without those comrades there at tryst
     Creeping slowly, creeping sadly,
   That lone lane does not exist.
There they seem brooding on their pain,
And will, while such a lane remain.

FAITH

These verses by Fanny Kemble, the famous actress who died in 1893, are a warning against allowing deceitful people to make us feel that everybody is deceitful.

Better trust all, and be deceived,
   And weep that trust and that deceiving,
Than doubt one heart that if believed,
   Had blessed one's life with true believing.

O, in this mocking world too fast
   The doubting fiend o'ertakes our youth!
Better be cheated to the last
   Than lose the blessèd hope of truth.

SHUFFLE-SHOON AND AMBER-LOCKS

That sweet-minded writer of verses for children, the American Eugene Field, here combines the charm of childhood with the gentle pathos of old age, the forward dreams of youth and the backward dreams of gracious memory.

SHUFFLE-SHOON and Amber-Locks
  Sit together, building blocks ;
Shuffle-Shoon is old and grey,
Amber-Locks a little child ;
But together at their play
Age and youth are reconciled,
And with sympathetic glee
Build their castles fair to see.

" When I grow to be a man,"
So the wee one's prattle ran,
" I shall build a castle so,
With a gateway broad and grand ;
Here a pretty vine shall grow,
There a soldier guard shall stand ;
And the tower shall be so high
Folks will wonder, by-and-by !"

Shuffle-Shoon quoth : " Yes, I know ;
Thus I builded long ago !
Here a gate, and there a wall,
Here a window, there a door ;
Here a steeple wondrous tall
Riseth ever more and more !
But the years have levelled low
What I builded long ago !"

So they gossip at their play,
Heedless of the fleeting day ;
One speaks of the Long Ago,
Where his dead hopes buried lie ;
One with chubby cheeks aglow
Prattleth of the By-and-by ;
Side by side they build their blocks,
Shuffle-Shoon and Amber-Locks.

WYNKEN, BLYNKEN, AND NOD

Eugene Field is among the choicest of the poets who have written for children, and this is often considered the best of all his poems. The explanation of it comes in the last verse, which tells us plainly who Wynken, Blynken, and Nod are, and how they went off together into the delightful land of childish dreams.

WYNKEN, Blynken, and Nod one night
  Sailed off in a wooden shoe,
Sailed on a river of crystal light
  Into a sea of dew.
" Where are you going, and what do you
  wish ?"
  The old Moon asked the three.
" We have come to fish for the herring fish
  That live in this beautiful sea ;
Nets of silver and gold have we,"
    Said Wynken,
    Blynken, and Nod.

The old Moon laughed and sang a song
  As they rocked in the wooden shoe ;
And the wind that sped them all night long
  Ruffled the waves of dew ;
The little stars were the herring fish
  That lived in that beautiful sea.
" Now cast your nets wherever you wish,
  But never afeared are we ! "
So cried the stars to the fishermen three,
    Wynken,
    Blynken, and Nod.

All night long their nets they threw
  For the fish in the twinkling foam,
Then down from the sky came the wooden
  shoe,
  Bringing the fishermen home ;
Twas all so pretty a sail, it seemed
  As if it could not be ;
And some folk thought twas a dream
  they'd dreamed
Of sailing that beautiful sea ;
But I shall name you the fishermen three,
    Wynken,
    Blynken, and Nod.

Wynken and Blynken are two little eyes,
  And Nod is a little head ;
And the wooden shoe that sailed the skies
  Is a wee one's trundle-bed.
So shut your eyes while Mother sings
  Of wonderful sights that be,
And you shall see the beautiful things
  As you rock in the misty sea
  Where the old shoe rocked the fisher-
  men three,
    Wynken,
    Blynken, and Nod.

THE SINGER

This is how John Addington Symonds sees the poet—not necessarily the individual man, but the poet who reappears in mankind and, in age after age, interprets afresh to the race the truths that purify life and make it beautiful.

HE fills the world with his singing,
  High notes of the heavenly morn,
For ever and ever ringing
  As age after age is born.

And then he is still, and we know not
  Whither his thoughts have fled ;
Only the clear notes flow not,
  And we say the singer is dead.

But the nightingales that he cherished,
  They carol and cannot die ;
Though the man whom we loved hath
  perished,
  His melody throbs for aye.

PIGGY WIGGY WEE

Bil-ly Prin-gle had a lit-tle pig, When it was young it wasn't ve-ry big,

When it was old it lived in clo-ver, Now it's dead and that's all o-ver. Bil-ly Prin-gle

he lay down & died, Bet-ty Prin-gle she lay down & cried. So there was an end of

one, two, three: Bil-ly Prin-gle he, Bet-ty Prin-gle she, and the pig-gy wig-gy wee.

A'S FOR THE ANTE-
LOPE
ALWAYS ON VIEW,
WHICH ALGERNON
SAW
WHEN HE WENT
TO THE ZOO

B WAS THE BEAR
THAT
CAME UP AT A
RUN
WHEN BENJAMIN
THREW HIM
A VERY NICE BUN

C'S FOR THE CAMEL;
"POOR THING,
WHAT A LUMP!"
WAS WHAT CARO-
LINE SAID
WHEN SHE LOOKED
AT HIS HUMP

D'S FOR THE DEER
WITH THE SOFT,
PRETTY EYES;
DORIS FOUND THEM
SO TAME
SHE HAD QUITE A
SURPRISE

E WAS THE ELE-
PHANT;
SIXPENCE A RIDE,
BUT ERIC SOON
FOUND
THAT YOU CAN'T
SIT ASTRIDE!

F WAS THE FOX,
VERY CRAFTY
AND SLY,
WATCHING FRANK
FROM HIS DEN
WITH A CUNNING
OLD EYE

G'S THE GIRAFFE
WHICH MADE
GERALDINE SMILE;
SHE WAS SURE WITH
HIS NECK
SHE COULD SEE
QUITE A MILE

H WAS THE HIPPO
ASLEEP IN HIS
POOL.
HARRY THOUGHT IT
AN EXCELLENT
WAY TO KEEP
COOL

I WAS THE IBEX,
A KIND OF WILD
GOAT.
IDA THOUGHT HIS
HORNS NASTY,
BUT LIKED HIS FINE
COAT

J WAS THE JAGUAR,
LIKE A BIG
CAT,
BUT JANE DIDN'T
THINK
SHE WOULD LIKE
HIM TO PAT!

K WAS THE KAN-
GAROO
OFF WITH A BOUND;
A FINE WAY,
THOUGHT KEN,
TO GET OVER THE
GROUND

L'S FOR THE LIONS;
THEY MADE SUCH
A FIERCE NOISE
LAURA WISHED SHE
WERE SAFELY
AT HOME WITH THE
BOYS

M'S FOR THE MON-
KEYS,
ALL PATTER AND
CHATTER,
BUT MILES COULDN'T
TELL
WHAT ON EARTH
WAS THE MATTER

N'S FOR THE NILGAI
WHICH JUMPED
OFF A ROCK;
HE TOOK SUCH A LEAP
THAT
NELL HAD QUITE A
SHOCK

WE SAW AT THE ZOO

O'S FOR THE OSTRICH, A WISE-LOOKING BIRD, BUT OLGA REMEMBERED THE TALES SHE HAD HEARD

P'S FOR THE PARROT THAT HAD LOTS TO SAY; AND TRIED TO PECK PAUL AS HE PASSED BY THAT WAY

Q'S FOR THE QUAGGA, WHICH QUENTIN FOUND TAME; HE IS QUITE LIKE A ZEBRA, WITH STRIPES AND A MANE

R IS THE RHINO, A FIERCE-LOOKING BEAST; ROSE WATCHED HIM WITH AWE IN THE MIDST OF A FEAST

S IS THE SNAKE WHICH SUZANNE FOUND ASLEEP; HE WAS SHINY AND SLIMY AND MADE HER FLESH CREEP

T'S FOR THE TIGERS THAT GAVE TIM A FRIGHT; HE WAS HORRIBLY SCARED LEST THEY GOT OUT AT NIGHT

FOR U (THAT'S THE UNICORN) NOBODY LOOKS; AS UNA CAN TELL YOU, HE'S ONLY IN BOOKS

V'S FOR THE VULTURE, A BIG BIRD OF PREY; VERONICA SAW HIM— AND SOON RAN AWAY!

W'S FOR THE WOLF LYING FLAT ON THE GROUND, THOUGH WHEN WALTER CAME NEAR HE WAS UP WITH A BOUND

X JUST LOOKS ON AND HAS NOTHING TO DO; THERE'S NO CREATURE THAT CLAIMS HIM THROUGHOUT THE WHOLE ZOO

Y IS THE YAK; HE'S WORTHY OF NOTE; YVONNE WAS AMAZED AT HIS LONG SHAGGY COAT

Z'S FOR THE ZEBRA THAT KEPT ZOE BUSY; SHE COUNTED HIS STRIPES TILL SHE FELT SHE WAS DIZZY

LITTLE BLACKEY-TOPS

Oh, all you lit-tle black-ey-tops Pray do not eat my fath-er's crops, While I lie down to take a nap. Shu-a . . . . O! Shu-a . . . . O!

LITTLE MISTRESS MINE

The poet's title for these verses is Villanelle. A villanelle is an artificial form of French poetry with only two rhymes. It consists of nineteen lines, five three-line verses and one four-line verse. One line of the first verse must be repeated in each of the next four verses, and the last verse must repeat two lines of the first verse. Its form is here illustrated perfectly by Sir Edmund Gosse in this villanelle from a dying sparrow to its mistress, who is asked to dig its grave.

LITTLE mistress mine, good-bye !
   I have been your sparrow true;
Dig my grave, for I must die.

Waste no tear and heave no sigh;
   Life should still be blithe for you;
Little mistress mine, good-bye!

In your garden let me lie,
   Underneath the pointed yew
Dig my grave, for I must die.

We have loved the quiet sky
   With its tender arch of blue;
Little mistress mine, good-bye !

That I still may feel you nigh,
   In your virgin bosom, too,
Dig my grave, for I must die.

Let our garden friends that fly,
   Be the mourners, fit and few.
Little mistress mine, good-bye!
Dig my grave, for I must die.

THE THOUGHT

Here is one of the deeper poems of William Brighty Rands. The Thought of Day is what we think of this life. The Thought of Night is what we think of the life beyond.

INTO the skies one summer's day
   I sent a little Thought away,
Up to where, in the blue round,
The sun sat shining without sound.

Then my Thought came back to me:
Little Thought, what did you see
In the regions whence you come?
And when I spoke my Thought was dumb.

But she breathed of what was there
In the pure, bright upper air;
And, because my Thought so shone,
I knew she had been shone upon.

Next by night a Thought I sent
Up into the firmament,
When the eager stars were out,
And the still moon shone about.

And my Thought went past the moon,
In between the stars, but soon
Held her breath and durst not stir
For the fear that covered her;
Then she thought, in this demur:

" Dare I look beneath the shade,
Into where the worlds are made;
Where the suns and stars are wrought?
Shall I meet another Thought?

" Will that other Thought have wings?
Shall I meet strange, heavenly things?
Thought of Thoughts, and Light of
   Lights,
Breath of Breaths, and Night of Nights?"

Then my Thought began to hark
In the illuminated dark,
Till the silence, over, under,
Made her heart beat more than thunder.

And my Thought came trembling back,
But with something on her track,
And with something at her side;
Nor till she has lived and died,
Lived and died, and lived again,
Will that awful thing seem plain.

THE VOICELESS

Thomas Gray surmised, in his immortal poem on Stoke Poges churchyard, that some mute, inglorious Milton might perchance rest there. In this poem Oliver Wendell Holmes develops this thought by supposing that many have the experiences that poets express in song. The common failure in expression saddens him. But is there not all the poetry in the world available for those who are themselves voiceless? All the poetry in the world is ours.

WE count the broken lyres that rest
   Where the sweet, wailing singers
     slumber,
But o'er their silent sister's breast
   The wild flowers who will stoop to
     number?
A few can touch the magic string,
   And noisy Fame is proud to win them:
Alas for those that never sing,
   But die with all their music in them !

Nay, grieve not for the dead alone
   Whose song has told their hearts' sad
     story,
Weep for the voiceless, who have known
   The cross without the crown of glory!
Not where Leucadian breezes sweep
   O'er Sappho's memory-haunted billow,
But where the glistening night-dews weep
   On nameless sorrow's churchyard pillow.

O hearts that break and give no sign,
   Save whitening lip and fading tresses,
Till Death pours out his cordial wine
   Slow-dropped from Misery's crushing
     presses;
If singing breath or echoing chord
   To every hidden pang were given,
What endless melodies were poured,
   As sad as earth, as sweet as heaven!

BOG LOVE

This grimly realistic picture of love on the commonest level is by Sir Shane Leslie, the Irish author and journalist.

WEE Shemus was a misdropt man
  Without a shoulder to his back;
He had the way to lift a rann
  And throttled rabbits in a sack.

And red-haired Mary whom he wed
  Brought him but thirty shillings told;
She had but one eye in her head,
  But Shemus counted it for gold.

The two went singing in the hay
  Or kissing underneath the sloes,
And where they chanced to pass the day
  There was no need to scare the crows.

But now with Mary waked and laid
  As decent as she lived and died,
Poor Shemus went to buy a spade
  To dig himself a place beside.

TO EXILES

Perhaps no country has sent out so large a proportion of its population to colonise the world as Scotland has, and no country calls her children back at last with a more appealing mutual love. In this poem Neil Munro pictures vividly the Scotland which rears hardy men for the world's work, and calls them home to her strength and beauty when they have succeeded. Known most widely as a novelist, Neil Munro (1864–1930), was also a true poet.

ARE you not weary in your distant places,
  Far, far from Scotland of the mist
    and storm,
In drowsy airs, the sun-smite on your
    faces,
  The days so long and warm?
When all around you lie the strange fields
    sleeping,
  The dreary woods where no fond
    memories roam,
Do not your sad hearts over seas come
    leaping
  To the highlands and the lowlands of
    your Home?

Wild cries the Winter, loud through all
    our valleys
  The midnights roar, the grey noons
    echo back;
About the scalloped coasts the eager
    galleys
  Beat for kind harbours from horizons
    black;
We tread the miry roads, the rain-
    drenched heather,
  We are the men, we battle, we endure!
God's pity for you people in your weather
  Of swooning winds, calm seas, and skies
    demure!

Wild cries the Winter, and we walk song-
    haunted
  Over the hills and by the thundering
    falls,
Or where the dirge of a brave past is
    chaunted
  In dolorous dusk by immemorial walls.
Though rain may beat us and the great
    mists blind us,
  And lightning rend the pine tree on the
    hill,
Yet are we strong, yet shall the morning
    find us
  Children of tempest all unshaken still.

We wander where the little grey towns
    cluster
  Deep in the hills, or selvedging the sea,
By farm lands lone, by woods where wild-
    fowl muster
  To shelter from the day's inclemency;
And night will come, and then far through
    the darkling
  A light will shine out in the sounding
    glen,
And it will mind us of some fond eye's
    sparkling
  And we'll be happy then.

Let torrents pour then, let the great winds
    rally,
  Snow-silence fall or lightning blast the
    pine;
That light of Home shines warmly in the
    valley,
  And, exiled son of Scotland, it is thine.
Far have you wandered over seas of
    longing,
  And now you drowse, and now you well
    may weep,
When all the recollections come a-thronging
  Of this old country where your fathers
    sleep.

They sleep, but still the hearth is warmly
    glowing
  While the wild Winter blusters round
    their land;
That light of Home, the wind so bitter
    blowing—
  Look, look and listen, do you under-
    stand?
Love, strength, and tempest—oh, come
    back and share them!
  Here is the cottage, here the open door;
Fond are our hearts although we do not
    bare them;
  They're yours, and you are ours for
    evermore.

RAIN IN SUMMER

Though Longfellow, the most widely-read American poet, was not specially a poet who interpreted Nature, he could write a striking description when his eye was attracted directly by a scene or an object, and in this poem we see him picturing sympathetically the relief that comes to the parched earth with a summer downpour of rain. We can really feel the coolness and the pleasant stir of the scene.

How beautiful is the rain!
    After the dust and heat,
In the broad and fiery street,
    In the narrow lane,
How beautiful is the rain!

How it clatters along the roofs,
Like the tramp of hoofs!
How it gushes and struggles out
From the throat of the overflowing spout!
Across the window-pane
It pours and pours;
And swift and wide,
With a muddy tide,
Like a river down the gutter roars
The rain, the welcome rain!

The sick man from his chamber looks
At the twisted brooks;
He can feel the cool
Breath of each little pool;
His fevered brain
Grows calm again,
And he breathes a blessing on the rain.

From the neighbouring school
Come the boys,
With more than their wonted noise
And commotion;
And down the wet streets
Sail their mimic fleets,
Till the treacherous pool
Engulfs them in its whirling
And turbulent ocean.
In the country on every side,
Where far and wide,
Like a leopard's tawny and spotted hide,
Stretches the plain,
To the dry grass and the drier grain
How welcome is the rain!

In the furrowed land
The toilsome and patient oxen stand;
Lifting the yoke-encumbered head,
With their dilated nostrils spread,
They silently inhale
The clover-scented gale
And the vapours that arise
From the well-watered and smoking soil.
For this rest in the furrow after toil
Their large and lustrous eyes
Seem to thank the Lord
More than man's spoken word.

Near at hand,
From under the sheltering trees,
The farmer sees
His pastures and his fields of grain
As they bend their tops
To the numberless beating drops
Of the incessant rain.
He counts it as no sin
That he sees therein
Only his own thrift and gain.

BETTER THINGS

We always find George MacDonald praising the virtue of humility, the delight in simple things. In the following verses he celebrates those " better things " which we are apt foolishly to despise in our search after the vanities of life.

Better to smell the violet cool than sip
    the glowing wine;
Better to hark a hidden brook than watch
    a diamond shine.

Better the love of a gentle heart than
    beauty's favour proud;
Better the rose's living seed than roses
    in a crowd.

Better to love in loneliness than to bask
    in love all day;
Better the fountain in the heart than the
    fountain by the way.

Better be fed by a mother's hand than eat
    alone at will;
Better to trust in God than say: " My
    goods my storehouse fill."

Better to be a little wise than in know-
    ledge to abound;
Better to teach a child than toil to fill
    perfection's round.

Better to sit at a master's feet than thrill
    a listening State;
Better suspect that thou art proud than
    be sure that thou art great.

Better to walk the real unseen than watch
    the hour's event;
Better the " Well done! " at the last than
    the air with shouting rent.

Better to have a quiet grief than a hurrying
    delight;
Better the twilight of the dawn than the
    noonday burning bright.

Better a death when work is done than
    earth's most favoured birth;
Better a child in God's great house than
    the king of all the earth.

PEGGY

The " wawking of the fauld " means the watching of the fold, and this tender love-song for youth and maid takes us into the quiet of the evening. Allan Ramsay (1686-1758), the writer, was one of the masters of the Scottish vernacular. " A' the lave " means all the rest.

My Peggy is a young thing,
  Just entered in her teens,
Fair as the day, and sweet as May,
Fair as the day, and always gay;
My Peggy is a young thing,
  And I'm not very auld,
Yet well I like to meet her at
  The wawking of the fauld.

My Peggy speaks sae sweetly
  Whene'er we meet alane,
I wish nae mair to lay my care,
I wish nae mair of a' that's rare ;
My Peggy speaks sae sweetly,
  To a' the lave I'm cauld,
But she gars a' my spirits glow
  At wawking of the fauld.

My Peggy smiles sae kindly
  Whene'er I whisper love,
That I look down on a' the town,
That I look down upon a crown;
My Peggy smiles sae kindly,
  It makes me blyth and bauld,
And naething gives me sic delight
  As wawking of the fauld.

My Peggy sings sae saftly
  When on my pipe I play,
By a' the rest it is confest,
By a' the rest, that she sings best;
My Peggy sings sae saftly,
  And in her sangs are tauld
With innocence the wale of sense,
  At wawking of the fauld.

THE GREEN FIELDS OF ENGLAND

Arthur Hugh Clough, the poet friend of Matthew Arnold, had to leave England in search of health, and in these verses he seeks to express his love and longing for her.

Green fields of England! wheresoe'er
  Across this watery waste we fare,
One image at our hearts we bear,
Green fields of England, everywhere.

Sweet eyes in England, I must flee
Past where the waves' last confines be
Ere your loved smile I cease to see,
Sweet eyes in England, dear to me.

Dear home in England, safe and fast,
If but in thee my lot lie cast,
The past shall seem a nothing past
To thee, dear home, if won at last ;
Dear home in England, won at last.

A PIPER

The naturalness of joy is one of the big things we are liable to forget, but poets are licensed to believe that a merry piper can bring it alive again. The poet who writes these lines is Seumas O'Sullivan, an Irishman, and the Irish are always fluctuating between sadness and mirth.

A piper in the streets today
  Set up, and tuned, and started to
  play,
And away, away, away on the tide
Of his music we started; on every side
Doors and windows were opened wide,
And men left down their work and came,
And women with petticoats coloured like
  flame.
And little bare feet that were blue with
  cold
Went dancing back to the age of gold,
And all the world went gay, went gay,
For half an hour in the street today.

YE LITTLE BIRDS THAT SIT AND SING

The poets of the early Stuart days were adepts in love poetry. Here is an example from that most prolific of dramatists, Thomas Heywood, who in these lines commissions the birds to plead his cause with his lady-love.

Ye little birds that sit and sing
  Amidst the shady valleys,
And see how Phillis sweetly walks
  Within her garden alleys ;
Go, pretty birds, about her bower ;
Sing, pretty birds, she may not lower :
Ah me ! methinks I see her frown !
  Ye pretty wantons, warble.

Go, tell her through your chirping bills,
  As you by me are bidden,
To her is only known my love,
  Which from the world is hidden.
Go, pretty birds, and tell her so ;
See that your notes strain not too low,
For still methinks I see her frown ;
  Ye pretty wantons, warble.

Go tune your voices' harmony
  And sing, I am her lover ;
Strain loud and sweet, that every note
  With sweet content may move her ;
And she that hath the sweetest voice,
Tell her I will not change my choice ;
Yet still methinks I see her frown !
  Ye pretty wantons, warble.

O fly ! make haste ! see, see, she falls
  Into a pretty slumber !
Sing round about her rosy bed
  That, waking, she may wonder ;
Say to her, 'tis her lover true
That sendeth love to you, to you !
And when you hear her kind reply,
  Return with pleasant warblings.

POETRY

THE FULL SEA ROLLS

W. E. Henley's was the restless soul that conceived these striking verses, when under the stress of physical pain.

The full sea rolls and thunders
  In glory and in glee,
O bury me not in the senseless earth,
  But in the living sea!

Ay, bury me where it surges
  A thousand miles from shore,
And in its brotherly unrest
  I'll range for evermore.

THINGS THAT NEVER DIE

Miss Sarah Doudney was an English writer well known for her many excellent stories for grown-ups as well as her books for girls. Here we give an illustration of her pleasing verse.

The pure, the bright, the beautiful,
  That stirred our hearts in youth,
The impulse to a wordless prayer,
  The dreams of love and truth,
The longings after something lost,
  The spirit's yearning cry,
The strivings after better hopes:
  These things can never die.

The timid hand stretched forth to aid
  A brother in his need,
The kindly word in grief's dark hour
  That proves a friend indeed,
The plea for mercy gently breathed
  When justice threatens high,
The sorrow of a contrite heart:
  These things shall never die.

The memory of a clasping hand,
  The pressure of a kiss,
And all the trifles, sweet and frail,
  That make up love's first bliss;
If with a firm, unchanging faith,
  And holy trust on high,
Those hands have clasped, those lips have met:
  These things shall never die.

The cruel and the bitter word
  That wounded as it fell;
The chilling want of sympathy
  We feel but never tell;
The hard repulse that grieves the heart
  Whose hopes were bounding high;
In an unfading record kept
  These things will never die.

Let nothing pass, for every hand
  Must find some work to do;
Lose not a chance to waken love:
  Be firm and just and true:
So shall a light that cannot fade
  Beam on thee from on high,
And angel voices say to thee
  " These things shall never die."

FOR THOSE WHO FAIL

To the thought in these verses every heart will respond, for the world has had new reasons for honouring men who die before victory. The writer, Joaquin Miller (1841-1913), who was born in Indiana, published many volumes of verse. mostly on the life of the Western States.

All honour to him who shall win the prize,
  The world has cried for a thousand years,
But to him who tries and who fails and dies
  I give great honour and glory and tears.

Give glory and honour and pitiful tears
  To all who fail in their deeds sublime;
Their ghosts are many in the van of years,
  They were born with Time in advance of Time.

Oh, great is the hero who wins a name,
  But greater many and many a time
Some pale-faced fellow who dies in shame
  And lets God finish the thought sublime.

And great is the man with a sword undrawn,
  And good is the man who refrains from wine;
But the man who fails and yet still fights on,
  Lo, he is the twin-brother of mine.

LULLABY

Exquisite alike in feeling and expression is this lullaby by William Barnes, the Dorsetshire parson, one of the few poets who have been able to touch the heart equally in ordinary and in dialect verse. The memory of this good clergyman, who died in 1886, remains as fragrant in Dorsetshire as his verse is fragrant wherever it is known.

The rook's nest do rock on the tree-top,
  Where few foes can stand;
The martin's is high and is deep
  In the steep cliff of sand;
But thou, love, a-sleeping where footsteps
  Might come to thy bed,
Hast father and mother to watch thee
  And shelter thy head.
    Lullaby, Lilybrow, lie asleep;
    Blest be thy rest.

And some birds do keep under roofing
  Their young from the storm;
And some wi' nest-hoodings o' moss
  And o' wool do lie warm.
And we will look well to the house-roof
  That o'er thee might leak,
And the beast that might beat on thy window
  Shall not smite thy cheek.
    Lullaby, Lilybrow, lie asleep;
    Blest be thy rest.

THE DAY IS DONE

Few of the shorter poems written by Longfellow are more deservedly popular than the following, which has hardly a verse that does not contain some rare beauty of poetic thought and expression. The longing for quiet and peace at the end of a strenuous day has never been better conveyed in poetic form, and the pure pleasures of a good man's domestic life are here celebrated in the worthiest verse. The last stanza of the poem is a favourite quotation.

THE day is done, and the darkness
    Falls from the wings of Night,
As a feather is wafted downward
    From an eagle in his flight.

I see the lights of the village
    Gleam through the rain and the mist,
And a feeling of sadness comes o'er me
    That my soul cannot resist:

A feeling of sadness and longing
    That is not akin to pain,
And resembles sorrow only
    As the mist resembles the rain.

Come, read to me some poem,
    Some simple and heart-felt lay,
That shall soothe this restless feeling
    And banish the thoughts of day.

Not from the grand old masters,
    Not from the bards sublime,
Whose distant footsteps echo
    Through the corridors of Time.

For, like strains of martial music,
    Their mighty thoughts suggest
Life's endless toil and endeavour;
    And tonight I long for rest.

Read from some humbler poet,
    Whose songs gushed from his heart
As showers from the clouds of summer,
    Or tears from the eyelids start;

Who, through long days of labour
    And nights devoid of ease,
Still heard in his soul the music
    Of wonderful melodies.

Such songs have power to quiet
    The restless pulse of care,
And come like the benediction
    That follows after prayer.

Then read from the treasured volume
    The poem of thy choice,
And lend to the rhyme of the poet
    The beauty of thy voice.

And the night shall be filled with music,
    And the cares that infest the day
Shall fold their tents, like the Arabs,
    And as silently steal away.

THE CHARACTER OF A HAPPY LIFE

Sir Henry Wotton was a famous Englishman who lived from 1568 to 1639, and was eminent in the service of his country, being for many years ambassador at Venice. He became a clergyman, and wrote essays of a religious character. Like most of the scholars of his age, he also wrote poetry, and the following is the most remarkable of his few poems.

How happy is he born and taught
    That serveth not another's will;
Whose armour is his honest thought,
    And simple truth his utmost skill!

Whose passions not his masters are;
    Whose soul is still prepared for death,
Untied unto the world by care
    Of public fame or private breath;

Who envies none that chance doth raise,
    Nor vice; who never understood
How deepest wounds are given by praise,
    Nor rules of state, but rules of good;

Who hath his life from rumours freed;
    Whose conscience is his strong retreat;
Whose state can neither flatterers feed,
    Nor ruin make oppressors great;

Who God doth late and early pray
    More of His grace than gifts to lend,
And entertains the harmless day
    With a well-chosen book or friend:

This man is freed from servile bands
    Of hope to rise or fear to fall;
Lord of himself, though not of lands,
    And, having nothing, yet hath all.

THE USEFUL PLOUGH

This is a charming old English song whose writer is unknown, but who must have known and loved rural life.

A COUNTRY life is sweet!
    In moderate cold and heat
To walk in the air how pleasant and fair
In every field of wheat;
    The fairest of flowers adorning the
        bowers,
And every meadow's brow;
    So that I say no courtier may
Compare with them who clothe in grey
And follow the useful plough.

They rise with the morning lark,
And labour till almost dark;
    Then, folding their sheep, they hasten to
        sleep;
While every pleasant park
    Next morning is ringing with birds that
        are singing
On each green, tender bough.
    With what content and merriment
    Their days are spent whose minds are
        bent
To follow the useful plough!

ENGLAND'S DEAD

Never since the world began has any race of men strewed its dead so widely as the men of our Little Treasure Island. The frontier lines of our British dead, fallen in discovery, travel, business enterprise, and war, have been finely commemorated by modern poets, particularly by Rudyard Kipling. But in a plain, open way Mrs. Hemans set the example in this poem, and not unworthily, for it is picturesque and vigorous as well as true.

Son of the ocean isle !
  Where sleep your mighty dead ?
Show me what high and stately pile
  Is reared o'er Glory's bed.

Go, stranger ! Track the deep,
  Free, free, the white sail spread !
Wave may not foam, nor wild wind sweep,
  Where rest not England's dead.

On Egypt's burning plains,
  By the pyramid o'erswayed,
With fearful power the noonday reigns,
  And the palm trees yield no shade;

But let the angry sun
  From heaven look fiercely red,
Unfelt by those whose task is done !
  There slumber England's dead.

The hurricane hath might,
  Along the Indian shore,
And far by Ganges' banks at night
  Is heard the tiger's roar;

But let the sound roll on !
  It hath no tone of dread
For those that from their toils are gone;
  There slumber England's dead.

Loud rush the torrent-floods
  The western wilds among,
And free, in green Columbia's woods,
  The hunter's bow is strung;

But let the floods rush on !
  Let the arrow's flight be sped !
Why should *they* reck whose task is done ?
  There slumber England's dead.

The mountain-storms rise high
  In the snowy Pyrenees,
And toss the pine-boughs through the sky
  Like rose-leaves on the breeze.

But let the storm rage on !
  Let the forest-wreaths be shed:
For the Roncesvalles' field is won;
  There slumber England's dead.

On the frozen deep's repose,
  'Tis a dark and dreadful hour,
When round the ship the ice-fields close,
  To chain her with their power.

But let the ice drift on !
  Let the cold-blue desert spread !
Their course with mast and flag is done;
  Even there sleep England's dead.

The warlike of the isles,
  The men of field and wave !
Are not the rocks their funeral piles,
  The seas and shores their grave ?

Go, stranger! track the deep,
  Free, free, the white sails spread !
Wave may not foam, nor wild wind sweep,
  Where rest not England's dead.

THE HEAVENS IN LONDON TOWN

This poem by Edward Shillito (1872–1948), a Congregational minister, takes us back to the nights when under the terrors of war from the skies the lights of London were dimmed. Then the stars reappeared in London's midnight sky, and the poet felt he was seeing London canopied by night as Alfred, Raleigh, Shakespeare, Wesley, and Keats had seen it. So he treasured the memory of their companionship in the gloom against the coming nights when once more London's glare of lights would shine forth and obscure the deep peace of the stars.

Before the winter's haunted nights are o'er
  I thankfully rejoice that stars look down
Above the darkened streets, and I adore
  The Heavens in London Town.

The Heavens beneath which Alfred stood when he
  Built ramparts by the tide against his foes,
The skies men loved when in eternity
  The dream-like Abbey rose.

The Heavens whose glory has not known increase
  Since Raleigh swaggered home by lantern-light,
And Shakespeare, looking upwards, knew the peace,
  The cool, deep peace of night.

Under those Heavens brave Wesley rose betimes
  To preach ere daybreak to the tender soul;
And in the heart of Keats the starry rhymes
  Rolled, and for ever roll.

I, too, have walked with them the heavenly ways,
  Tracing the sweet embroideries of the sky,
And I shall not forget when arcs shall blaze,
  And all the lights are high.

MY LAND

Irish poets have been very faithful to their Motherland. This is the tribute paid to her by Thomas Davis, a poet and patriot who died in 1845, when only thirty years old. It has in it an echo of a song by Robert Burns.

SHE is a rich and rare land;
    O, she's a fresh and fair land;
She is a dear and rare land,
    This native land of mine.

No men than hers are braver,
Her women's hearts ne'er waver;
I'd freely die to save her,
    And think my lot divine.

She's not a dull or cold land;
No ! she's a warm and bold land;
O ! she's a true and old land,
    This native land of mine.

Could beauty ever guard her,
And virtue still reward her,
No foe would cross her border,
    No friend within it pine.

O, she's a fresh and fair land,
O, she's a rare and true land !
Yes, she's a rare and fair land,
    This native land of mine.

MY WILL

This delightful picture of a country life by choice for settling down in, good unto the end, is from the charming pen of Dr. Arthur Christopher Benson, son of an Archbishop of Canterbury and sometime Master of Magdalene College, Cambridge. Instead of living as he would according to this poem, the writer spent a bachelor life in the comparative seclusion of college buildings. But his dream makes a pleasing and enviable picture none the less.

I WOULD live, if I had my will,
    In an old stone grange on a York-
shire hill,
Ivy-encircled, lichen-streaked,
Low and mullioned, gable-peaked,
With a velvet lawn, and a hedge of yew,
An apple orchard to saunter through,
Hyacinth-scented in spring's clear prime,
And rich with roses in summer-time,
And a waft of heather over the hill,
    Had I my will.

Over the tree-tops, grave and brown,
Slants the back of a breezy down;
Through my fields, by the covert edge,
A swift stream splashes from ledge to
ledge.
On to the hamlet, scattered, gray,
Where folk live leisurely day by day;
The same old faces about my walks;
Smiling welcomes and simple talks;
Innocent stories of Jack and Jill;
    Had I my will.

How my thrushes should pipe ere noon,
Young birds learning the old birds' tune !
Casements wide, when the eve is fair,
To drink the scents of the moonlit air.
Over the valley I'd see the lights
Of the lone-hill farms, on the upland
heights;
And hear, when the night is alert with rain,
The steady pulse of the labouring train,
With the measured gush of the merry rill,
    Had I my will.

Then in the winter, when gusts pipe thin,
By a clear fire would I sit within,
Warm and dry in the ingle nook,
Reading at ease in a good, grave book;
Under the lamp, as I sideways bend,
I'd scan the face of my well-loved friend;
Writing my verses with careless speed,
One, at least, would be pleased to read:
Thus sweet leisure my days should fill,
    Had I my will.

Then when the last guest steps to my side—
May it be summer, the windows wide—
I would smile as the parson prayed,
Smile to think I was once afraid;
Death should beckon me, take my hand,
Smile at the door of the silent land;
Then the slumber, how good to sleep
Under the grass where the shadows creep,
Where the headstones slant on the wind-
swept hill !
    I shall have my will !

REMEMBER

This tender sonnet, written by Christina Rossetti, is in the tone of gentle sadness felt in many of her writings. Miss Rossetti was a sister of Dante Gabriel Rossetti, who was known as a poet and painter in mid-Victorian days.

REMEMBER me when I am gone away,
    Gone far away into the silent land;
When you can no more hold me by the
    hand,
    Nor I half turn to go, yet turning stay.
Remember me when no more day by day
    You tell me of our future that you
    planned:
    Only remember me; you understand
It will be late to counsel then or pray.
Yet if you should forget me for a while
    And afterwards remember, do not
    grieve:
    For if the darkness and corruption leave
A vestige of the thoughts that once I
    had,
Better by far you should forget and smile
    Than that you should remember and
    be sad.

LITTLE VERSES FOR VERY LITTLE PEOPLE

Hey diddle, dinkety, poppety, pet,
　The merchants of London they wear scarlet;
Silk in the collar and gold in the hem,
So merrily march the merchantmen.

Little Robin Redbreast
　Sat upon a rail;
Niddle naddle went his head
Wiggle waggle went his tail.

Once I saw a little bird
　Come hop, hop, hop;
And I cried, Little bird,
Will you stop, stop, stop?
I was going to the window
To say How do you do?
But he shook his little tail,
And away he flew.

Cuckoo, cuckoo, cherry tree,
　Catch a bird and give it me;
Let the tree be high or low,
Let it hail or rain or snow.

Oats and beans and barley grow
　For you and me, as all of us know.
Thus the farmer sows his seeds,
Thus he stands and takes his ease;
Stamps his foot and slaps his hand,
And turns him round to view his land.

O rare Harry Parry,
　When will you marry?
When apples and pears are ripe.
I'll come to your wedding
Without any bidding,
And dance and sing all night.

Pit, pat, well-a-day,
　Little Robin flew away;
Where can little Robin be?
Gone into the cherry tree.

Tommy Trot, a man of law,
　Sold his bed and lay upon straw;
Sold the straw and slept on grass,
To buy his wife a looking-glass.

If I had money I'd buy a clown;
　If I had a horse I'd ride to town;
If I had a ship I'd Westward Ho,
And if I was sick I wouldn't go.

If Candlemas Day be bright and fair
　Winter will have another flight;
If on Candlemas Day be shower and rain
Winter is gone and will not come again.

A, B, C, and D,
　Pray, playmates, agree.
E, F, and G,
Well, so it shall be.
J, K, and L,
In peace we will dwell.
M, N, and O,
To play let us go.
P, Q, R, and S,
Love may we possess.
W, X, and Y
Will not quarrel or die.
Z and Ampersand
Go to school at command.

Little Betty Blue
　Lost a holiday shoe;
What can little Betty do?
Give her another
To match the other,
And then she may walk out in two.

Ride, baby, ride!
　Pretty baby shall ride,
And have a little puppy-dog tied to her side,
And a little pussy-cat tied to the other,
And away she shall ride to see her grandmother.

There was an old woman sat spinning,
　And that's the first beginning;
She had a calf,
And that's half;
She took it by the tail
And threw it over a wall,
And that's all.

One, two, three,
　I love coffee,
Billy loves tea,
How good you be.
One, two, three,
I love coffee
And Billy loves tea.

Elizabeth, Elspeth, Betsy and Bess
　They all went together to seek a bird's nest;
They found a bird's nest with five eggs in;
They all took one and left four in.

When I was a bachelor
    I lived by myself;
And all the bread and cheese I got
    I put upon the shelf.

The rats and the mice
    They made such a strife
I was forced to go to
        London
    To buy me a wife.

The streets were so bad,
    And the lanes were so narrow,
I was forced to bring my wife home
    In a wheelbarrow.

The wheelbarrow broke,
    And my wife had a fall.
Down came wheelbarrow,
    Little wife, and all.

Awake, arise, and rub your eyes,
    And hear what time of day;
And when you've done just move your
        tongue,
And see what you can say.

Snail, snail, come out of your hole,
    Or else I will make you as black as
a coal.

To make your candles last for aye
    You maids and wives give ear-o,
To put them out's the only way,
Says honest John Boldero.

Our saucy boy Dick
    Had a nice little stick,
Cut from a hawthorn tree;
And with this pretty stick
He thought he could beat
A boy much bigger than he.

But the boy turned round
And hit him right sound,
Which did so frighten poor Dick
That without more delay
He ran quite away,
And over a hedge he jumped quick.

I had a little boy, and his name was
    Blue Bell,
I gave him some work and he did it very
    well;
I sent him upstairs to pick up a pin,
He stepped in the coal scuttle up to the
    chin;
I sent him to the garden to pick some sage,
He tumbled down and fell in a rage.

There was a little man, and he had
        nought,
    And robbers came to rob him;
He crept up to the chimney top,
    And then they thought they had him.

But he got down on t'other side,
    And then they could not find him;
He ran fourteen miles in fifteen days,
    And never looked behind him.

Good little boys should never say
    ' I will ' and ' Give me these ';
Oh, no ! that never is the way,
    But ' Mother, if you please.'

And ' If you please ' to Sister Anne
    Good boys to say are ready;
And ' Yes, sir,' to a gentleman,
    And ' Yes, ma'am ' to a lady.

I have a little hen, the prettiest ever
    seen,
She washed me the dishes and kept the
    house clean;
She went to the mill to fetch me some
    flour,
She brought it home in less than an hour;
She baked me some bread, brought milk in
    a pail,
And sat by the fire and told me a tale.

As Tommy Snooks and Bessy Brooks
    Were walking out one Sunday,
Said Tommy Snooks to Bessy Brooks,
Tomorrow will be Monday.

Imperishable Thoughts of Men Enshrined in the Books of the World

Bunyan's Masterpiece

NO book except the Bible has had greater influence for good on the minds of men than The Pilgrim's Progress. Written in simple, straightforward English, by a plain, straightforward man, who, from being a poor tinker, became a powerful preacher of God's message to mankind, this immortal story is likely to be read as long as our literature endures. The story is told as an allegory, illustrating the trials that beset a Christian on his way through life, but is better than most allegories, because the characters are so human that we are instantly interested in each for his own sake, as well as anxious to know what happened to them all. John Bunyan, the author, was born at Elstow, near Bedford, in 1628, and died in London in 1688. He was imprisoned for twelve years for preaching without the sanction of the Church, and while in Bedford prison he wrote the first part of his immortal story. Here we take from it certain passages which tell the story in Bunyan's own words.

THE PILGRIM'S PROGRESS

As I walked through the wilderness of this world I lighted on a certain place where was a Den, and I laid me down in that place to sleep, and as I slept I dreamed a dream.

I dreamed, and behold I saw a man clothed with rags, standing in a certain place, with his face from his own house, a book in his hand, and a great burden upon his back. I looked, and saw him open the book and read therein; and as he read he wept and trembled, and at length brake out with a lamentable cry, saying: "What shall I do?"

In this plight he went home and told his wife that he was informed that their city would be burned with fire from heaven, in which fearful overthrow himself, his wife, and his sweet babes, would miserably come to ruin, except some way of escape could be found. His relations tried, without avail, to rid him of his fears.

Now, I saw upon a time when Christian (for this was the man's name) was walking in the fields that he was reading in his book; and as he read he burst out as before, crying: "What shall I do to be saved?" I looked then and saw a man named Evangelist coming to him, who asked : "Wherefore dost thou cry?"

When he had answered, Evangelist said: "If this be thy condition, why standest thou still?"

"Because I know not whither to go," he answered.

Then Evangelist gave him a parchment roll, and there was written thereon: "Flee from the wrath to come." The man read it, and, looking upon Evangelist carefully, said: "Whither must I fly?"

Then said Evangelist, pointing with his finger over a very wide field: "Do you see yonder wicket-gate?" The man said: "No." Then said the other: "Do you see yonder shining light?" He said "I think I do." Then said Evangelist: "Keep that light in your eye and go up directly thereto, so shalt thou see the gate, at which, when thou knockest, it shall be told thee what thou shalt do."

So I saw in my dream that the man began to run. Now, he had not run far from his own door, but his wife and children and neighbours, perceiving it, cried after him to return. But the man ran towards the middle of the plain.

Two of his neighbours, Obstinate and Pliable, resolved to fetch him back by force. When they came up with him he told them that if they died in the City of Destruction, where he and they were born, they would sink lower than the grave.

They talked together, and Christian asked them to read in his book. Obstinate cried: "Away with your book! Will you go back with us or no?"

ROMANCE　·　HISTORIES　·　DRAMAS　·　ESSAYS　·　WORLD CLASSICS

"No, not I," said Christian, "because I have laid my hand to the plough."

Obstinate then went back, but Pliable offered to go with Christian, and even urged him to mend his pace. But Christian had a burden on his back, and Pliable was unencumbered.

Now, I saw in my dream that, just as they had ended this talk, they drew very near to a very miry slough, and, being heedless, they did both fall suddenly into the bog. The name of the slough was Despond. And Christian, because of the burden that was on his back, began to sink in the mire. Then said Pliable: "Ah, neighbour Christian, where are you now?"

"Truly," said Christian, "I do not know."

At this Pliable began to be offended, and angrily said to his fellow: "Is this the happiness of which you have told me all this while? May I get out again with my life, you shall possess the brave country alone for me."

And with that he gave a desperate struggle and got out of the mire on that side of the slough which was next to his own house, and Christian saw him no more.

Christian, left to tumble in the Slough of Despond alone, endeavoured to struggle to that side that was next to the wicket-gate; which he did, but could not get out because of the burden that was upon his back. But I beheld in my dream that a man came to him whose name was Help, and set him upon sound ground.

Now, as Christian was walking solitarily by himself, he was met by Mr. Worldly Wiseman, who advised him that he could get rid of his burden much more easily by applying to one Legality, whose house was on a high hill he pointed out. So Christian turned out of his way to go to Mr. Legality's. But the hill seemed so high, and that side of it which was next to the wayside did hang so much over, that Christian was afraid to venture farther. His burden seemed heavier, and flashes of fire came out of the hill that made him afraid that he should be burned.

In this way he was found by Evangelist, and once more set on the right path; and so, in process of time, he got up to the wicket-gate. The gate was opened to him by Goodwill, who, after hearing his story, asked him to look before him at a narrow way. "That," said Goodwill, "is the way thou must go."

"But," said Christian, "are there no turnings or windings by which a stranger may lose his way?"

"Yes," said the other, "there are many ways butt down on this, and they are crooked and wide. But thus thou mayest know the right from the wrong, the right only being straight and narrow."

Then Christian went on till he came to the house of the Interpreter. After he had knocked and the door had been opened, I saw in my dream that the Interpreter showed him a picture of the man whom the Lord of the place whither he was going had authorised to be his guide, and other things such as would help him in his journey. When the Interpreter had shown him many strange and wonderful sights and expounded their meaning, and offered him good counsel, he gave him his blessing, and Christian went on his way.

Now, I saw that the highway up which he had to go was fenced on either side with a wall, called Salvation. Up this way, therefore, did burdened Christian run, but not without great difficulty, because of the load on his back. He ran till he came to a place somewhat ascending, and upon that place stood a cross, and a little below, in the bottom, a sepulchre. So I saw in my dream, just as Christian came up with the cross, his burden loosed from off his shoulders, and fell from off his back, and began to tumble, and so continued to do till it came to the mouth of the sepulchre, where it fell in and Christian saw it no more.

Then was Christian glad and lightsome, and stood awhile to look and wonder, till the springs that were in his head sent the waters down his cheeks. As he stood looking and weeping for gladness, behold three Shining Ones came to him and saluted him with: "Peace be to thee." The first said to him: "Thy sins be forgiven thee"; the second stripped him of his rags, and clothed him with change of raiment; the third also set a mark on his forehead, and gave him a roll with a seal upon it, bidding him look on it as he ran, and that he should give it in at the Celestial Gate. So they went their way, and Christian gave three leaps for joy and went on, singing.

CHRISTIAN ARRAYED FOR THE COMBAT WITH APOLLYON

CHRISTIAN'S FIGHT WITH APOLLYON

While resting on the hill called Difficulty, Christian fell into a deep sleep. And as he slept his roll dropped from his hand. At the summit of the hill he met two men, named Timorous and Mistrust. They said they were returning, because the farther they went the more dangers they met with.

This caused Christian to feel in his bosom for his roll, that he might read therein and be comforted. But, finding it not, he went down the hill again to the arbour, where he had slept. Who can tell how joyful this man was when he had gotten his roll again, which was to be his pass into the Celestial City? How nimbly did he now go up the hill!

But before he got up, the sun went down upon him and he thought of the lions in the way, of which Timorous and Mistrust had told him. But while he was blaming himself for sleeping, he lifted up his eyes and saw before him a stately palace, the name of which was Beautiful. So he made haste that, if possible, he might get lodging there.

Before he had gone far he entered a very narrow passage, about a furlong off the porter's lodge, and espied two lions in the way. The lions were chained, but he saw not the chains, and was afraid. But the porter, whose name was Watchful, called out to him to keep in the midst of the path, if his faith was strong enough. This Christian did, and so entered the Palace Beautiful, which was built for the relief and security of pilgrims.

There came forth to meet him a beautiful damsel called Discretion, who, on learning his story, called out Piety, Prudence, and Charity. Thus was Christian welcomed into the house.

Here he had much profitable discourse, such as he had had at the Interpreter's house. After supper, Christian was given a large upper chamber, and here he slept.

Before he left this place, the rarities of which were shown to him, he was taken up on to the roof, whence he beheld at a great distance a most pleasant mountainous country. The mountains were the Delectable Mountains, and the country was Emmanuel's Land, from which he was told he would be able to see the gate of the Celestial City.

Christian was now anxious to be setting forward, but before letting him go his hosts took him into the armoury, where they harnessed him from head to foot, except upon his back, with what was proof against attack, lest perhaps he should meet with assaults on the way. At the gate he learned from the porter that one Faithful, a fellow-townsman, had passed that way. Oh! said Christian, I know him; he is my near neighbour. How far do you think he may be before? The porter answered that he must have got by this time below the hill.

Then he began to go forward, but Discretion, Piety, Charity, and Prudence accompanied him to the foot of the hill, which led to the Valley of Humiliation. Christian went down very warily, for the hill was dangerous, yet he had a slip or two. When all were at the foot of the hill, his good companions gave Christian a loaf of bread, a bottle of wine, and a cluster of raisins; and then he went on his way. But poor Christian had gone only a little way in the valley before he espied a foul fiend, hideous to behold, coming to meet him, and dispute his passage.

The name of the fiend was Apollyon. Christian was at first afraid, and began to cast in his mind whether to go back or stand his ground. But as he had no armour on his back, he thought that to turn might give the enemy the greater advantage to pierce him with his darts. So he went on, and Apollyon, when he refused to go back, straddled quite across the path and hurled a flaming dart at Christian's breast. Thus began a sore combat that lasted for over half a day.

When Christian had been wounded in head, hand, and foot, and was almost spent, Apollyon came to close quarters, and, wrestling with him, gave him a dreadful fall, so that his sword flew out of his hand. Then said Apollyon: "I am sure of thee now." And with that he almost pressed him to death. But while Apollyon was fetching of his last blow, Christian nimbly stretched out his hand and, regaining his sword, gave the fiend such a thrust that he spread his dragon's wings and sped him away. Then there came to Christian a hand with some of the leaves of the Tree of Life, which Christian took, and applied to his wounds, and was healed immediately. He also sat down, and, after being refreshed, resumed his journey, with his sword drawn in his hand, but he saw no more of Apollyon.

THE FATE OF FAITHFUL

Now, at the end of the Valley of Humiliation was another, called the Valley of the Shadow of Death. And Christian must needs go through it, because the way to the Celestial City lay through the midst of it. The pathway was extremely narrow. On the right hand was a very deep ditch. On the left hand was a very dangerous quag. Besides, the darkness was so great that Christian could hardly tell where, or on what, in going forward he should next set his foot.

About the midst of this valley, and near the wayside, was the mouth of the Underworld. Ever and anon flame and smoke would come forth with hideous noises. Christian heard doleful voices, and fiends came towards him. Near the burning pit one of the fiends came up softly to him, and whisperingly suggested many bad thoughts which he verily believed proceeded from his own mind.

When Christian had travelled in this disconsolate condition some considerable time, he thought he heard the voice of a man, as going before him, saying: " Though I walk through the Valley of the Shadow of Death, I will fear no evil, for Thou art with me." Then he was glad, because he gathered that some who feared God were in this valley as well as himself.

Now, as Christian went on his way he came to a little ascent, which was cast up on purpose that pilgrims might see before them. Up there Christian, looking forward, saw before him Faithful, his fellow townsman, of whom he had heard from the porter at the Palace Beautiful. Then said Christian aloud : " Ho, ho, soho! stay, and I will be thy companion!"

Then I saw in my dream that they went very lovingly on together, and had sweet discourse of all the things that had befallen them in their pilgrimage, and of what had happened in the City of Destruction after Christian had left.

When they were got out of the wilderness, they presently saw a town before them, and the name of that town is Vanity. And at the town there is a fair kept, called Vanity Fair; it is kept all the year long. Almost five thousand years ago there were pilgrims walking to the Celestial City, and Beelzebub, Apollyon, and Legion, with their companions in evil, perceiving that the pilgrim's way to that city lay through this town of Vanity, contrived here to set up a fair, wherein should be sold all sorts of vanity.

As Christian and Faithful entered into Vanity Fair, the people wondered at their apparel and at their speech. The town itself was in a hubbub about them. That which did not a little amuse the merchandisers was that these pilgrims set very light by all their wares. They cared not so much as to look upon them, and when asked what they would buy answered gravely: " We buy the truth."

The behaviour of Christian and Faithful so little suited the people of Vanity Fair that the pilgrims were taken and examined, and those that examined them did not believe them to be any other than mad, or else such as came to put all things into a confusion in the fair. Therefore they took them and beat them, and besmeared them with dirt, and then put them into the cage, that they might be a spectacle to all.

Then some of the men in the Fair, that were more observing than the rest, seeing the patience of Christian and Faithful, began to check and blame the baser sort for their treatment of the pilgrims. Thus, after words had passed on both sides, the disputants fell to blows.

Then were these two poor men brought before their examiners again, charged with causing the hubbub, beaten, loaded with irons, led in chains up and down the Fair as an example and terror to others, and with threats remanded again to the cage.

A convenient time being appointed, they were next brought before Lord Hategood for trial. They were charged with injuring the trade of the town, and with causing commotions by winning a party to their most dangerous opinions. Evidence against Faithful was given by Mr. Envy, Mr. Superstition, and Mr. Pickthank, and, the jury finding him guilty, he was sentenced to the most cruel death that could be invented. They therefore brought him out, scourged him, buffeted him, stoned him, pricked him with their swords, and finally burned him to ashes at the stake. But a chariot and horses waited for him, and took him up through the clouds to the celestial gate.

As for Christian, he was taken back to prison, where he remained for a space, but He that overrules all things so wrought it about that Christian escaped them and went his way.

CAPTIVES IN DOUBTING CASTLE

Now, I saw in my dream that Christian went not forth from Vanity Fair alone, for there was one whose name was Hopeful—being made so by the beholding of Christian and Faithful in their words and behaviour in their sufferings at the Fair. This man joined himself unto him and, entering into a brotherly covenant, told him that he would be his companion.

Having passed over the little plain called Ease, and refused the invitation of one Demas that they should leave the narrow way to look at the silver-mine on the hill called Lucre, they came to a stile leading into Bypath Meadow.

The road that they had come by was very rough, and Christian, looking over the stile, saw that a path led along by the way on the other side of the fence.

"Here is the easiest going," said Christian. "Come, good Hopeful, and let us go over!"

"But how if this path should lead us out of the way?" said Hopeful.

Christian remarking that it went along by the wayside, Hopeful was persuaded, and the two went over the stile, and found the path very easy for their feet. Presently the night came on, and it grew very dark; then it began to rain and thunder and lighten in a very dreadful manner. They saw they had lost their way, and Christian began to blame himself for bringing his companion out of the way.

But Hopeful comforted him and forgave him, and presently they were at rivalry as to who should go first, and so meet any danger that might lie in wait for them on the way back to the stile. By this time the waters were greatly risen, and the way was perilous. At last, lighting under a little shelter, after having been nearly drowned nine or ten times, they decided to rest there till daybreak. But, being weary, they fell asleep.

Now, near where they lay was a castle called Doubting Castle, the owner whereof was Giant Despair; and it was in his grounds that they were sleeping. And he, getting up early, saw them, bade them awake, and, driving them before him, put them into a dark and stinking dungeon of his castle, where they lay from Wednesday morning till Saturday night.

On the Thursday, acting on the counsel of his wife Diffidence, Giant Despair got a crab-tree cudgel, wherewith he beat them fearfully. On the next morning, again on the advice of his wife, he came to them and advised them to make away with themselves. And when they prayed him to let them go, he rushed upon them, and had doubtless made an end of them himself, but that he fell into one of his fits—for he sometimes, in sunshiny weather, fell into fits—and lost for a time the use of his hand.

Towards evening the Giant went down into the dungeon again, and finding that they were still alive, fell into a rage and threatened them so dreadfully that Christian's courage began to fail. But Hopeful comforted him by reminding him of the victory he had had over Apollyon, and how he had come through the Valley of the Shadow of Death.

On Saturday morning, the Giant, having had further counsel with his wife, had the prisoners into the castle yard, and, after showing them the bones and skulls of those he had already despatched, told them he would tear them into pieces within ten days. With that he beat them all the way back to the dungeon.

That night the Giant and his wife began to renew their talk about their prisoners; and the Giant wondered that he could neither by his blows nor his counsel bring them to an end. His wife replied that she feared they lived in hope that someone would come and release them, or that they had picklocks about them. The Giant at this resolved to search them in the morning. But about midnight on the Saturday, Christian and Hopeful began to pray, and a little before day Christian exclaimed:

"What a fool am I thus to lie in a stinking dungeon when I might as well walk at liberty! I have a key in my bosom, called Promise, that will, I am persuaded, open any lock in Doubting Castle."

And he pulled it out. It opened the dungeon door, the outward door, and the iron gate.

The gate as it opened made such a creaking that it waked Giant Despair, who, hastily rising to pursue his prisoners, felt his limbs fail; for his fits took him again, so that he could by no means go after them. Then they went on, and came to the King's highway, and so were safe at last.

HOPEFUL SUPPORTS CHRISTIAN AS THEY CROSS THE RIVER

THE END OF THE PILGRIM'S JOURNEY

Christian and Hopeful afterwards came to the Delectable Mountains. Here they were welcomed by the shepherds. The shepherds, whose names were Knowledge, Experience, Watchful, and Sincere, had them to their tents and gave them good counsel as to their way, and showed them through their perspective glass the gates of the Celestial City.

So they went on, and behold a man, black of flesh but covered with a very light robe, came to them, and, learning that they were bound to the Celestial City, bade them follow him, for it was thither, he said, that he was going.

Now, the name of this man was Flatterer, and by-and-by, before they were aware, he led them both within the compass of a net. Taken in their distress they remembered the shepherds had warned them of the man.

At last they espied a Shining One coming towards them, with a whip of small cords in his hand. When the Shining One was told that they were poor pilgrims going to Zion, he rent the net, put them in the way again, and, having chastised them, bade them go on and remember the other warnings of the shepherds.

They went on till they came into a certain country, whose air tended to make one drowsy if he came a stranger into it. Hopeful was for falling asleep, but Christian remembered that this must be the Enchanted Ground, of which they had been warned. And so, to prevent themselves from falling into a sleep from which there was no awakening, they fell to good discourse.

In time they were got over the Enchanted Ground, and entered into the country of Beulah, whose air was very sweet and pleasant. The way lying directly through this country, they solaced themselves there for a season. Here they heard continually the singing of birds, and saw every day the flowers appear in the earth, and heard the voice of the turtle-dove in the land. In this country the sun shineth night and day; wherefore this was beyond the Valley of the Shadow of Death, and also out of the reach of Giant Despair, neither from this place could they so much as see Doubting Castle. Here they were within sight of the city they were going to, also here the pilgrims were met by some of the inhabitants thereof.

As they went they were met by two men in raiment that shone like gold, also their faces shone as the light. These men asked the pilgrims whence they came; and they told them. Then said the men: " You have but two difficulties more to meet with, and then you are in the city." Christian, then, and his companion asked the men to go along with them; and they said they would. So they went on together until they came within sight of the gate. But betwixt them and the gate was a river, and there was no bridge to go over. The river was very deep.

The men that were with them, in answer to their questions, told them that they must go through the river, which they would find deeper or shallower as they believed in the King of the place. They then entered the water, and Christian began to sink, crying out to his good friend Hopeful: " I sink in deep waters; the billows go over my head."

Then Hopeful bade him be of good cheer, and had much ado to keep his brother's head above water. But after a while they both took courage, and Christian presently found ground to stand upon, and so it followed that the rest of the river was but shallow. Thus, they got over.

Now, upon the bank of the river, on the other side, they saw the two Shining Ones, who there waited for them. Wherefore, being come out of the river, they saluted them, saying: " We are ministering spirits, sent forth to minister for those that shall be heirs of salvation."

Now, you must note that the city stood upon a mighty hill, but the pilgrims went up that hill with ease, because they had these two men to lead them up by the arms. They had likewise left their mortal garments behind them in the river.

And I saw in my dream that Christian and Hopeful, after giving in their certificates, went in at the gate; and lo, as they entered, they were transfigured, and they had raiment put on that shone like gold. There were also those that met them with harps and crowns, and gave these to them. Then I heard in my dream that all the bells in the city rang again for joy, and that it was said to them: " Enter ye into the joy of our Lord."

The Story of the Most Beautiful Book in the World

Matthew　　Bartholomew　　James　　John　　Philip　　Thomas

Peter　　James the Less　　Simon　　Andrew　　Judas　　Thaddeus

THE TWELVE

THE twelve humble men who walked with Jesus in Palestine would have been astounded if someone had prophesied to them that they would change the history of the world, and for thousands of years would remain the most interesting group of men in the books and languages of all nations.

They did not realise how near they were to the supreme mystery of life. At the arrest of their Master they forsook him and fled. It was not until after his death that they realised the divine majesty of him with whom they had lived.

And even then they did not see the whole truth of their destiny. They thought the end of the world was at hand. They believed that Christ would appear in the heavens before their generation had passed away. They remained in Jerusalem waiting for his coming. It was beyond their imagination to realise that out of their simple lives, out of their own simple story of the Master, would come the great revolution of Chritianity. How interested we are to look back on these men! They actually lived, day after day, in the society of Jesus. They heard his voice, they looked into his eyes, they walked at his side, they sat with him at meals, they touched him with their hands, they knew his ways, his every habit.

Ah, if they had only realised, as we know by experience, the long road that Christ's religion had to travel, would they not have told us more of the Master, and filled whole books with their memories of his life on Earth? Not one of them, it seems, considered how it would be when they were dead, and there was left on Earth no one alive who knew Jesus.

Among this little group of men none is so interesting to us as that disciple whom Jesus loved—the beloved disciple, as he has ever since been called—the fisherman's son, John. He was the disciple who was nearest to Jesus.

The father of the beloved disciple was a well-to-do Galilean fisherman named Zebedee, able to hire servants and to live in some ease. James and John, his two sons, probably received some education in their boyhood, and certainly from their mother, the pious Salome, they must early and all through life have gained the chiefest impulse of all education, a desire to live closely with God.

They were strong, healthy, thoughtful youths; they understood the seamanship of their day and country; they could face hardship, and were inured to danger; they earned their living as fishermen, but did not think that living ended there; they were conscious of God and the mystery of Life.

So far as we can gather, John was sufficiently reflective to feel that the priests of his religion were far from the secret mystery of the human heart. It

GREAT FIGURES OF THE OLD TESTAMENT · THE LIFE OF JESUS

seems that early in his life he went to hear the extraordinary preaching of the hermit of Jordan, who cried aloud for repentance, and who baptised his converts into a new and deeper form of life. It is easy to imagine how James and John talked together in their ship about the mystery of life and the problems of their nation.

We can see how the preaching of John the Baptist, with its reality, its fierce passion, and its splendid vigour, must have appealed to these young men. Perhaps the refined disposition of John felt that there was some difficulty about following the Baptist; but his hunger and thirst after reality in the spiritual life made him at last a disciple of this new prophet. Many follow a leader in whom they do not see all they desire to see, because they can find no higher, and are themselves incapable of leading men.

JESUS CALLS JOHN TO HIMSELF AND TEACHES HIM THE SECRET OF LIFE

It was while the fisherman John was listening to John the Baptist at Bethany that Jesus found him, and called this son of Zebedee to follow him. The first step had been made when John sought the Baptist rather than the rabbis; the second step was when he left the thunders of the Baptist for the love of Jesus.

Henceforth the road was clear before his eyes. The secret of life was discovered. Instead of thinking about sin and wrath and judgment, he thought of love. He saw that the heart is at rest when it answers the Father's love with a son's yearning. Intimately, then, he was able to enter into the idea of Jesus, destined to shake the world and transform the whole orb of human life. If we open our Bible at the First Epistle of John, and read it over quietly by ourselves, we shall see how wonderfully this Galilean fisherman entered into the true spirit of Jesus.

When we read these immortal simplicities, so tender, so overflowing with solicitude, do we not realise how close and how dear a companion to the Master must have been the man who wrote them?

It is the spirit of the whole Bible that has given light and joy and freedom to mankind; and it is the spirit of the Gospel according to John which shows us how intimately, and with what perfect insight, the beloved disciple understood the heart of his Master.

Mark was a man who observed; John was a man who perceived. In the Gospel according to Mark—the earliest, the simplest, the most picturesque, and in some ways the most useful of all our documents—we have a wonderful *narrative*, written by a man who saw the value of details, had an eye for the picturesque, and stated all the essential things he said and saw.

THE WRITINGS OF JOHN THAT REVEAL TO US THE SECRET OF THE MASTER

In the Gospel according to John we have the document of a man who perceived the meaning, the inner significance, the spiritual mystery of all he saw and heard.

If we read the good tidings according to John, we shall see how the writer had entered into the secret of his Master. It is the Gospel of love.

These things have I spoken unto you (he heard Jesus say) that my joy might remain in you, and that your joy might be full. This is my commandment, That ye love one another, as I have loved you. Greater love hath no man than this, that a man lay down his life for his friends. Ye are my friends, if ye do whatsoever I command you.

And again:

A new commandment I give unto you, That ye love one another; as I have loved you, that ye also love one another. By this shall all men know that ye are my disciples, if ye have love one to another.

JOHN'S VISION OF JESUS AS THE LIGHT OF THE WORLD

And how wonderful and illuminating is this record by John of our Saviour's words:

I am come a light into the world, that whosoever believeth in me should not abide in darkness. And if any man hear my words, and believe not, I judge him not; for I came not to judge the world, but to save the world.

No other disciple perceived so surely as John that without the idea of Jesus, that is to say, the Fatherhood of God, the Brotherhood of Man, and Love as the laws of the universe, life was a darkness. John saw, as no other saw, that Christ was a Light; John felt, as no other felt, that this Light was warm and gladdening, and full of comfort. Among the friends who walked with Jesus in Galilee almost every character of humanity is represented, and through them every conceivable idea of Jesus has been presented to the world. But it is to the beloved disciple that we owe chiefly the true, and therefore the most victorious, idea of Jesus, namely, the

Jesus of Love—the Love given to make men happy, the Light shining that men might no longer walk in the darkness.

Because John loved he was beloved, and because he loved he understood. We can never understand any person deeply and satisfactorily unless we love. John loved Jesus, and he understood the spiritual mystery of his Master's teaching. Through him has shone down the ages the pure light of the love and mercy of the Master.

THE LAST MAN ON EARTH WHO HAD SEEN AND KNOWN JESUS

We know little of his long life. It is certain that he remained at Jerusalem for some time after the Resurrection. We also know that he was put in prison, and that he was sent as a missionary.

It is thought that he presently retired to Ephesus, and it seems that many people flocked to him for instruction. There was some idea, apparently, that he would never die, that Jesus would come again with power and great glory before death touched the disciple of love, and therefore John must have been eagerly sought by those who believed in Jesus.

He lived to be a very old man, outliving, we imagine, all his companions, and he remained for many years on Earth, the last man who had known Jesus.

Legends of many kinds sprang up around his memory, but we are not interested in them. If he was miraculously delivered from torture and death, it makes no difference to our ideas concerning him. What interests us, and holds all our wonder and affection, is that this fisherman alone among the Twelve penetrated to the secret of Jesus, and that through him we have received the idea of Love. He was beloved by Jesus; he has been beloved by men and women all over the world for nearly two thousand years; he will always be loved by those who have the great secret of Love in their lives.

THE LITTLE BAND OF TWELVE WHO WALKED WITH JESUS

When we look back into the documents of the past there is little, all too little, to be learned of this little band of men who walked with Jesus and revolutionised the world. We have looked at John; let us see what we can learn of the others.

On that day when Jesus came to John the Baptist, there was listening to the preacher of the wilderness a young fisherman named Andrew.

He was born in Bethsaida, in Galilee, and he earned his living with a brother named Simon Peter, sharing a house with him at Capernaum. It seems that his disposition was religious, that he was discontented with the formal religion of the priests, that he felt a desire for some deeper and more spiritual communion with the great God who had created Heaven and Earth. As he stood listening to John he saw Jesus approach, saw him present himself for baptism, and heard the Baptist pronounce words of special blessing on the Young Carpenter. When he went home he narrated the incident to his brother, and Simon Peter heard the tale with interest. Perhaps they discussed the matter as they mended their nets, or as they fished together under the stars on the Sea of Galilee. Their partners, James and John, must have shared these interesting conferences.

THE FISHERMEN WHO LEFT THEIR NETS TO BECOME FISHERS OF MEN

Some time passed, and one day, when they were fishing from the shore, Jesus approached and said: " Follow me, and I will make you fishers of men."

In this one sentence, so quiet and so simple, he flashed upon their conscience the light of eternity. They saw the immense comparison—fishing to earn their own bread, toiling to save others. Their old longing for a fuller life took complete possession of them. " And they straightway left their nets and followed him."

Of the rest of St. Andrew's life we know little, except that he was ever on the fringe of that little inner brotherhood which was so close to Jesus. Peter and James and John were the nearest to Jesus—James and John were brothers—and occasionally Andrew, the brother of Peter, was called into this inner circle. It is said that Andrew went as an apostle to many foreign countries; legend ascribes to him the working of extraordinary miracles. There was a gospel called *The Acts of Andrew*, but it was not accepted by the Church, and now it has vanished. Tradition declares that he died a martyr's death by crucifixion, on a cross shaped like an X. This is the origin of the St. Andrew's Cross with which we are familiar in the Union Jack.

Among the four fishing partners, the brothers Simon Peter and Andrew, and the brothers James and John, Simon

Peter, by the very force of his character, was the chief. He was marked out during his discipleship for special favour. It was to his home in Capernaum that Jesus resorted, and that humble home came to be spoken of among the brotherhood as " the house," as if it were the very home and centre of the Master's life. Then it was to Peter that Jesus confided the care of the Brotherhood after the Crucifixion.

THE FAILURE OF PETER AND ITS LESSON FOR US ALL

To follow the story of Peter's life as an apostle is to convince oneself of the truth of the Christian religion; nothing could be more human, more real, more honest. If our documents were false, the great struggle between Peter and Paul—on which the history of Christendom depended—would have been hidden or denied. And from Peter's failure—for Peter failed to realise the immensity of the Idea of Jesus—we learn a lesson of great value. We all remember how Peter, when our Lord called him to walk over the water, suddenly doubted and began to sink. Yet, despite Peter's doubts on this occasion, and on the occasion of the casting of the nets, and on that other terrible occasion when he denied his Master, our Lord loved and trusted him. In after life Peter was always true to this trust, and was called a pillar of the Church.

It was said that all his later life Peter spent in repentance of his early faults, and that when he died, each cheek was furrowed deep with the shedding of tears.

IMPULSIVE PETER, THE MOST HUMAN OF ALL THE DISCIPLES

All through the history of Christianity Peter has been dearly loved by the faithful, perhaps because he was so human. His temper was hasty, but he was swift to make amends, and as he grew older the nobility of his character seemed to shine out more and more. He was a great leader among the apostles, and one of his finest characteristics was his humility. There is a legend that at his death he begged his executors not to crucify him in the position in which our Lord had been crucified, and that he was therefore put to death head downward.

Peter, impulsive Peter, was the kind of man we often meet in life, the man who is all courage one moment and all fear the next; always wanting to go forward and always drawing back.

For the rest of his life he was a bold and quite a beautiful preacher of the Fatherhood of God and the Brotherhood of Man. He died gloriously in defence of his faith, perishing on the cross, a willing martyr in the service of the Master whom he adored in his heart, and whose truths he nobly upheld. A more interesting, a more human, a more lovable man was not to be found among the Twelve. We admire the genius of Paul; we give our love to Simon Peter. Of John we read on another page; now we will see what we can learn of the other apostles of Christianity.

James, the brother of John, is one of the interesting group of four who were always close to the heart and counsels of the Master. His devotion is unquestionable. The one unhappy incident in his life is that of the ambitious request that he might sit with his brother John, one on either side of Christ, in the Kingdom of heaven. But who will judge him for such a plea? Surely, in a moment of deep affection, he may have uttered his soul's longing. Love is often responsible for mistakes of judgment. But we know that James was a devoted apostle.

A BEAUTIFUL STORY OF JAMES THE SON OF THUNDER

Jesus named him, with John, " a son of thunder," as if to signify the passionate impetuosity of his nature; and, after the Crucifixion, James occupied a chief place among the Twelve. And when Agrippa determined to punish the followers of Jesus, it was upon James that his vengeance fastened. There is a legend that when the man who accused James heard the apostle's answer before the judges he was filled with remorse, and cried out that he, too, would follow Jesus; and the story tells that, on the way to the place of execution, this accuser, doomed to die with James, pleaded to the apostle for forgiveness; and James, looking earnestly upon him, answered: " Peace be with thee," and kissed him. Thus, says the old legend, died the Son of Thunder, one of the earliest martyrs, one of the most beautiful of all those who loved and followed Jesus.

There is another James among the apostles about whom we cannot be sure of many important facts. Who was James, the son of Alpheus? We cannot say. Nothing is known of him. According to certain people he is one and the same with James, " the brother of the Lord," about whom information is scant. After the Crucifixion Jesus appeared to James, and then James afterwards became a pillar of the brotherhood in Jerusalem. One of the stories tells that James the Less was of such dignity and power that the Pharisees hoped to persuade him to denounce Jesus. Instead of denouncing Jesus he confessed himself the servant and apostle of the Lord. So furious were the priests that they seized James then and there, and flung him down, killing him.

Philip lived at Bethsaida, and was one of those who listened to the teaching of John the Baptist. He brought Nathanael to Jesus, and was ever an eager seeker after God. It was Philip who said to the Master: " Lord, show us the Father, and it sufficeth us "; it was Philip to whom Jesus made the great answer: " Have I been so long time with you, and yet hast thou not known me, Philip? He that hath seen me hath seen the Father."

THE MYSTERY OF THE LIFE AND DEATH OF THE APOSTLE WHO DOUBTED

Philip's life as an apostle is utterly unknown. Some say he died without confessing Jesus. Another story tells that he was crucified head downward. Jesus is said to have appeared to him and to have rebuked him for want of meekness. But all these are legends.

Bartholomew was brought to Jesus by Philip, and it is probable that he is the same man as Nathanael. It seems that he became a missionary, and legend says that he was crucified with his head downward in Armenia. All we can be more or less certain about concerning this companion of Philip is that he lived the devoted life of a missionary.

Thomas was a carpenter and builder. He lives for ever as the man who would not believe in Jesus without material proof. He had known Jesus intimately, had served him, questioned him, listened to his teaching; but we read that when he saw the risen Jesus he could not and would not believe that his Master had truly risen. And then the doubting disciple, covered with amazement, exclaimed: " My Lord, and my God! "

Then answered Jesus: " Thomas, because thou hast seen me thou hast believed; blessed are they that have not seen and yet have believed."

After this Thomas carried the good news of Jesus into Parthia and India, and we lose sight of him altogether, going out into the great darkness of the outer world preaching the religion of Jesus.

MATTHEW, THE ONE RICH MAN AMONG THE DISCIPLES

Matthew interests us as, perhaps, the one rich man among the twelve apostles. Matthew the apostle is the same as Levi the publican, and he must have known comfort and luxury, and must have been a hard and avaricious man before the magic of Christ's personality called him to the life of a wandering disciple. Although the Greek and Roman churches call him a martyr, it would seem that he died a natural death.

Simon the Canaanite is supposed to have spread the knowledge of Jesus through Egypt, and to have died the death of a martyr. Some writers believed he preached Christianity in many countries, and even carried it as far as Britain; but this is evidently a confusion of Simon with Simon Peter, the great head of the Brotherhood having been credited with missionary labours all over the Earth.

Thaddeus has left behind no memory of his work. He is merely a name on the page of Holy Writ. We know more of Mary and Martha than we do of this companion of Jesus, chosen, we may be sure, for some good reason, and destined for work of immense importance. It is said that he became a missionary in Edessa, and we may be certain that by his influence the Light of the World streamed through the darkness of paganism.

THE MEN WHO LOST THEMSELVES IN A GREAT LOVE FOR THE MASTER

Nothing is more remarkable in the lives of the apostles than the way in which they all completely submerged themselves in the work of their divine Master. They had one thought only, in which they lost themselves, and this thought was to spread abroad the good news of Jesus.

Matthias, who took the place of Judas Iscariot, has been supposed by many to be the same as Zaccheus and Barnabas.

The apostles have left us no definite record of themselves. They lost themselves utterly and gladly in the mystery and joy and triumph of their Master.

(Next chapter in this group, page 6931)

THE OLD DANCES OF OLD ENGLAND

1. The Morris Dance called Leap-Frog. Each man does a caper as he comes to the top.

2. Another Morris Dance, The Gallant Hussar, showing the galley, a favourite step, in which the dancer jumps on one foot, and twirls the other.

3. This is a Sword Dance called Ampleforth. The leader is holding up the lock, and the victim in the middle is kneeling down, before being " killed."

4. The Running Set, from Kentucky, showing the promenade, which comes between every figure.

The Interests and Pleasures of Life for All Indoors and Out

The Morris Men of Bampton dancing on the lawn of a country mansion on Whit Monday

THE STORY OF OUR ENGLISH DANCES

IN the early 1900's there began a revival of country dancing, and a great many children learned how to dance the old English country dances which had died out in Britain about a hundred years previously, and had been almost forgotten.

Now in every part of England, at schools, at Girl Guide meetings, and at special classes, we can see children, and grown-ups also, dancing Hey Boys, Goddesses, Gathering Peascods, and many other dances which everybody knew and loved when Shakespeare was a boy. From the days of Henry the Eighth, for two hundred years at least, these country dances were the chief amusement at all times of merry-making, not merely in the country among the common people, but at the King's court too.

But there are other kinds of old English dances as well as the country dances, and, like the country dances, they are called folk dances. This is because they were invented by the peasants themselves, by ploughmen who could not even write their own names, and not by professional musicians or dancers.

Some of these dances have been altogether forgotten, but two kinds, the morris dance and the English sword dance—which is quite different from the Scottish sword dance—were discovered just before they too died out.

These dances are meant to be for men only, though women and boys dance some of them; and they are much more difficult and complicated than the country dances. But although the country dances are for partners, boys and girls dancing together, and morris and sword dances are not, there are many ways in which they are alike; and they all started in the same way.

People who study old customs and the rites of savages tell us that dances of this kind are to be found in the history of every nation in the world. They were danced in the early times when almost everybody lived by tilling the soil; the success of the crops each year was the most important and necessary thing in their lives.

Before anyone had heard of Christianity, men had strange customs and beliefs, many of which were about the ways of making the gods of the weather send rain and sun at the best times for the corn. They thought it pleased these cruel gods if they killed a man or an animal in their honour; and in the middle of winter, when all the earth seems dead, or in the spring, when the green corn begins to sprout, they had a great ceremony of sacrifice.

Before they killed the victim they always danced, partly to do honour to the gods, partly to excite themselves enough to do the killing—for it was not easy even for a savage to kill a helpless man whom he did not hate or even know. And if it was an animal that they killed, it was a sacred animal that no one must hurt at any other time, for they thought that the gods would be best pleased if they sacrificed something very precious.

CRAFTS · GAMES · NEEDLEWORK · PUZZLES · SCIENCE EXPERIMENTS

When the dancers had killed the animal, they ate part of it, thinking that it would make them specially strong and healthy, because it belonged to the gods.

With the same idea, all the people would make a ring round a sacred tree, in the spring, and would run forward and touch it with their hands, thinking that the hidden strength which made the leaves come out on the tree would thus be given to them.

Now, all this may seem to have very little to do with our English folk dances, and, of course, we no longer believe in these strange customs, and no one remembers what they used to mean. But the maypole, which children dance round on May Day, is only that old sacred tree; and some country dances—Gathering Peascods, for instance—are maypole dances. When the dancers now run into the centre and clap their hands, they would have touched the tree in the days of old. But the survival of these rites can be seen far more easily in the morris and sword dances. In the first place, these dances are still performed only on special occasions, once in a year—on Boxing Day, or May Day, or Whit Monday. They are danced only by a single team of men, specially dressed up.

Above all, in some of the sword dances the " killing " is still done. The dancers each hold a sword in one hand, and grasp another dancer's sword by its point. Then they make complicated figures by following a leader over or under the swords, and finally, running in a ring, they plait the swords into a shape like a star with a hole in the middle of it. This shape, which is called the lock, or rose, is held up by the " captain " of the dancers, and a man runs into the middle of the ring and kneels down. Then the lock is dropped over his head, round his neck; the dancers each take hold of a sword, and run round the victim, faster and faster, till at the end of the music they all draw their swords out of the lock, and the " victim " falls down and pretends to be dead.

The morris dances are shorter, more violent, and more difficult in the steps than the sword dances. The men wear bells on their legs, and hold handkerchiefs, or, less often, sticks in their hands. The pictures on page 6804 are of men who have learned to dance morris dances from teachers who have discovered the old dances ; but the picture on page 6805 is a photograph of the village dancers of Bampton, in Oxfordshire. These men learned the dances from their fathers, and their fathers in turn from their fathers, and so on back to a time which nobody knows; and every Whit Monday, for about five hundred years, there have been morris dances at Bampton. You can go to see them.

Very few country dances have been danced like this without a break for many years. But there is one country dance, called the Running Set, which has a strange story.

In the middle of North America, in the mountains of Kentucky, many of the people are descendants of English men and women who sailed over to America over three hundred years ago, and they still dance this group of country dances which had quite died out in England. Picture 4 shows a figure in the Running Set being danced by English people who learned from the man who found it in America. So that dance has travelled a good deal, first from England to Kentucky, and then back again across the Atlantic.

THE PUZZLE OF THE BROKEN PLATE

A WEALTHY collector of antiques was horrified one day to hear a terrific crash in the room where the maid was dusting some very valuable china.

Hurrying to see what had happened, she found that the girl had dropped a large and costly plate. It was a piece of perfect porcelain of the richest blue, with no design at all on it, and it had been broken into eleven bits.

The pieces were gathered up and placed on a table, and the owner tried to fit them together   But in gathering them from the floor their order had become mixed, and there was no pattern to act as a guide. For an hour she tried to get them into the right order, but without success.

THE PLATE AS GIVEN TO THE REPAIRER

She therefore decided to stick the pieces in this order on a sheet of cardboard, thus preventing any of them being lost, and to hand them to a dealer in old china, so that he might have the fragments properly arranged and stuck together.

The dealer engaged an expert to do the work, and the plate was restored so that the joins could hardly be seen. How did the expert arrange the pieces to form a perfect plate?

If we put a piece of thin paper over the picture of the fragments given here, trace them off, and then cut them out with scissors, we shall be able to experiment, and arrange them as we wish. The solution is given on page 6940.

THE RIGHT WAY TO SLIDE AND SKATE

SLIDING is, after walking and running, probably the most natural of all physical exercises for a boy, and by teaching the laws of balance, it greatly helps him to learn to skate.

The best place for a slide is a small pond covered with ice stout enough to bear, with a good run on land at each end of the slide. The slide should be across the pond from one side to the other, from sixty to a hundred feet long, and not far off should be a return slide so that players can go over one way and then, leaving the pond, turning round, and taking a short run, slide back over the ice to the starting point.

There is little instruction needed for sliding; experience is the best teacher. The feet should be kept close together and parallel with the line of the slide, the necessary speed and momentum being given by the preliminary run.

Skating cannot, of course, be learned from books, though useful hints may be obtained in this way, and put into practice at home. For strange as it may seem, all skating can be practised in the house with or without skates. (If skates are worn, the floor must be protected, of course.) By practice at home, it is not meant that we should glide round a room on a rink, but that we should perform the various skating movements and learn to balance correctly while standing in one spot.

The art of skating successfully and gracefully consists in knowing thoroughly the rules of gravity, or balance. The greatest danger is a fall backwards through the feet slipping away in front, and this is avoided by throwing the weight of the body forward. But as tumbles are bound to come, especially at first, it is wise to learn the right way to fall.

It is a mistake to struggle to regain the balance. This only results in a general tensing-up and the fall becomes a good hard one, causing bad bruises. If we just let ourselves go, relaxing every muscle, we will soon discover that a tumble on the ice is all in the day's fun.

In learning to skate we must dismiss from our minds all notion of walking; we place our feet flat on the ice; there is no toe to heel bending of the foot, and no rising on the toe.

To advance the skates we stand with the heel of the right foot a few inches away from the hollow of the left, and then with the left skate press out against the ice, with the blade gripping along its length, to thrust the right foot forward. This gives the necessary impetus, and bringing up the left foot parallel with the right we go forward till the force is exhausted. Then we repeat the motion, but with the left foot in front, the push off being given with the right skate.

As we get on we must remember that the great principle of successful skating is to keep only one foot on the ice at a time in a gliding motion.

The weight must be on this gliding foot, and at each stroke is transferred from one foot to the other at the moment when they are side by side. The ankle of the gliding foot should be pushed forward and the knee bent at the beginning of the stroke, there being a gradual straightening up as the other foot comes up for the next stroke.

The stroking foot should leave the ice with an action to the side and back, and should be stretched above and behind the gliding foot, with knee out. This is something we can quite well practise at home, in front of a long mirror, pushing off with one foot

PRACTICE MAKES SKATING PERFECTION

and balancing on the other as if gliding.

All the time our aim should be to keep our skating even. A long stroke with one foot and a short one with the other is bad style and not at all graceful. The stroke should be as long as possible, too. When we have gained confidence and have command over our feet, we may then increase the length of our stroke. For a beginner three to five yards is enough space to cover at each stroke, but good skaters do four times that distance.

The skater should never look at his feet, and his face should always be turned in the direction in which he is going. All movements should be done gracefully without spasmodic effort.

All this time we have been skating on the inside of the skate. The outside edge is used in skating curves, and good practice for this is to place something on the ice, such as a stone, to act as centre to a circle, and then, standing three or four yards away, with our right side toward the stone, and looking over our right shoulder at the stone, to press the outside edge of the right skate firmly into the ice, and with our left skate propel ourselves round the stone, leaning well inward.

After a time we shall be able to lift the left foot off the ice; and we should practise doing this as long as possible, supporting ourselves on the outside edge of the right skate. Then we should practise the same movements the other way round, pressing the outside edge of the left skate into the ice, and propelling ourselves round with the right.

When skating in the open, we must never attempt to go on ice that is not absolutely safe. If there is the slightest doubt about it, we must keep away.

Many beginners will find the most difficult part of skating is learning to stop, especially if it is necessary to do so suddenly to avoid another skater. We do this by bringing both feet together and turning the whole body with a quick twist to the side, finishing a right turn on the outside edge of the right skate and the inside edge of the left (in the left turn the positions would be reversed).

In the ordinary way, to slow down we make the skates act as a brake by turning the feet in to the centre in pigeon-toed fashion, at the same time pushing the blades outwards against the ice.

SCENERY FOR YOUR MODEL RAILWAY

WHETHER your train is a clockwork one or a working model you have made yourself, you will get a great deal more pleasure from it if it is set in natural surroundings.

It is worth taking a lot of trouble to get this background right, and before starting to build bridges, banks, tunnels, and platforms, be sure you know the correct scale of your railway, and make everything to that same scale.

Make buildings in cardboard. Cut the four walls in one straight strip, then mark where the corners will come, and with a sharp knife or a razor blade, score down these lines on the *outside* of the building, cutting only part way through the cardboard, which will then bend neatly to shape without breaking. For a small gauge railway, matchboxes stuck together will make houses, sheds, signal boxes, and suchlike.

The larger cardboard models can be covered with dolls'-house papers of brick and slate, which can be bought cheaply at model shops and at some which sell wallpaper. But do not get the kind in which every brick or every slate is exactly alike, or if you do, " weather " it down with a touch of paint here and there. Corrugated cardboard, suitably painted, makes excellent roofs for sheds and farm buildings.

Slate paper on cardboard can well be used for a stone bridge, and a strip of sandpaper will make the road across the bridge.

For an embankment, use slightly crumpled brown paper stuck to a cardboard foundation. It can be painted green or wiped over with glue and, while still wet, sprinkled with sand or fine gravel. Small stones stuck here and there break it up and look like rocks.

For trees, bushes, and small hedges cut up a cheap sponge or a loofah, and dye the pieces green. Hedges along a road, or between large fields, can be cut from a piece of wood of square section, shaped and dented with a chisel to look as natural as possible, before being painted. Along the top stick a narrow strip of green sponge or loofah, with a few flowers or berries painted on, or better still, made of minute scraps of coloured felt and stuck on. Felt or green baize can be used for a lawn, but should be made rough with a teasel or a wire brush to break up the surface.

Gates and fences can be constructed from used matches stuck together, or pieces of wire soldered. A short length of wooden rod makes a good post. A number of these, spaced a little apart and with small screw-eyes in the top, can be connected by corded string or wire threaded through these screw-eyes, to make fences for large models.

Then you should have, on your stations and beside your track, some advertisements and hoardings, which are such a feature of our main-line railways. Small coloured pictures and reproductions of large advertisements often appear in magazines, on the paper coverings of tins, and on food cartons, and these make good miniature posters.

If you are lucky enough to have a permanent raised track around the walls of a room, a country background can be painted, or be cut out of posters and pasted to the walls, the foreground being matched up to this. A winding stream gives a rural touch, but remember it must be lower than its banks. Paint streaky lines of bluey green on its bed and cover this with plain glass. Then here and there against the banks and in mid-stream, stick a few small stones, and paint white streaks for the eddying waters.

ANSWERS TO PUZZLES ON PAGE 6672

1. America. 2. 54 and 45 miles. 3. Let every man skin his own skunk. 4. Beautify, beatify. 5. A-corn. 6. The young man was the second woman's son. 7. Peace. 8. Bath, Bedford, Dover, Ely, Paris. 9. Peace. 10. *a* Because he cannot get a living without somersaults (some assaults). *b* Bacon. *c* When it is scaled. *d* When it is Browning. *e* Because he should never sleep on his watch. *f* One gives milk and the other gives way (whey). 11. Chocolate. 12. Few, fewer. 13. Danes, Andes. 14. Grope, rope, ope. 15. Nameless. 16. Bar-net. 17. A Shadow. 18. Idea. 19. Rhine. 20. Fifty.

The Story of Immortal Folk Whose Work Will Never Die

Archimedes   Mencius   Akhnaton

GREAT MEN OF ANTIQUITY

EACH generation is inclined to think it is wiser than all that have gone before, and in some respects the claim can be made good. But the more we know of the earliest ages of civilisation, the more surprised we are at the wisdom, energy, mental power, and elevation of spirit displayed in them. No age has lacked great men.

Some periods are but dimly known, and their greatest figures only appear mistily, but we know from the effects they produced that these men must have been great in mind and soul. They so impressed their fellow men that they survive in memory as legendary heroes.

Here we are about to notice some of these varied figures from a past that lies close to the horizon of history. They cover a wide range of time—more than two thousand years—and they belong to many centuries. Their thought and activity leave a deep impression that powerful human personality has always been appearing, and will always appear. That is one of the world's great sustaining hopes.

The Chinese, the most numerous race, until recently regarded as fixed in a somewhat backward state, brought forth at least two great men comparatively early. They had such influence that they have moulded Chinese character for more than

two thousand years. The mental power they wielded was used for good purposes. Perhaps it was too successful. It was so great that it was not modified, as time went on, to suit the changes that naturally come in the world.

These two fine men of early China were Confucius, of whom we have read elsewhere, and Mencius. Confucius had died 106 years before Mencius was born, in the province of Shan-tung, in 372 B.C. Mencius made the extension of the work of Confucius his life's ideal. We do not hear of him till he was forty years old. Almost all we know of his early life is that he attributed his views and his character to the teachings of his mother in boyhood; and there is a tradition that he was also trained in wisdom by a grandson of Confucius. When he was about 45 he became the confidential adviser of one of the Chinese kings, with whom he remained five years. But no king would carry out the reforms which he recommended, for he insisted that the welfare of the people should be the sole aim of any king, and not wealth, or power, or glory.

Finding he was resisted by the king, who was his friend, he went to other Chinese kingdoms, for China was then much divided, and he was followed wherever he

EXPLORERS · INVENTORS · WRITERS · ARTISTS · SCIENTISTS

went by a band of admiring disciples. Later he returned to the kingdom of Chi for eight years, and then went wandering again, scattering his wisdom in the Courts of small kings, where he was treated with respect as a man who taught noble ways of living, particularly to kings and governors, who, however, excused themselves from putting his precepts into practice. When he died at 83, he had a band of faithful followers who had treasured his sayings, and by writing them down preserved them so that now China has the works of Meng-tse in seven books. Meng-tse is the name which we write as Mencius, that being the Latin form of it.

The teaching of Mencius was that men are naturally good rather than bad, and ought to take great pains to develop the good side of their nature through kindness, wisdom, and right conduct. He advocated freedom in trade, low taxes, sound work, near-at-hand markets, and good roads. Kings should so act that they will be welcomed with joy wherever they go in their kingdom, for popular happiness and prosperity are the real tests of kingship. Till they are attained a true king will not rest or be satisfied.

A MAN OF OLD CHINA WHOSE VIEWS ARE RESPECTED TODAY

Mencius also argued strongly against war, and was an advocate of benevolence towards the poor; but he did not believe in popular wisdom. He thought the mass of the people needed guidance from those who are wiser than themselves. Their interests should come first, before the interests of the king or the wealthy, but that should be brought about by the free will of the powerful and prosperous. His views have always had great influence in China, and, indeed, are still regarded as of a semi-sacred character.

Moses, the leader and law-giver, who welded the Israelites into a tribe of people, and gave them some measure of national feeling, is unquestionably one of the greatest figures of antiquity. When allowance has been made for the fact that much writing and much religious direction has been attributed to Moses which come from an age far later than his, there is a lofty sense of dignity, power, and organising ability in him, as the Bible story develops.

Moses, it is clear, apart from his curiously contrasted meekness, had enormous power over his fellow-tribesmen. The date of his entry into the field of history is somewhere about 1300 B.C. That he had sufficient influence over the men of his race to gather them from Egypt, the land of forced labour, and from the neighbouring deserts of northern Arabia, and to change and hearten them till they rallied round a new religious ideal, and became a people with a common aim, proclaims him a man strong in human magnetism and spiritual force.

MOSES AS THE FOUNDER OF MORALITY FOR THE WORLD

His was the formative genius round which the wonderful Jewish race gathered for its strange march through the ages. From him came the very core of its tenacious religion. Around that core a later highly developed priestly system elaborated a minute ritual, but at the centre of it all are the Ten Commandments that he made the foundations of morality, first for his race and then for all the world.

Stripped of trivial formalities the Mosaic ideal, from the first, united a lofty spiritual conception of God with most practical rules of life for a people living under Oriental conditions. The broad lines of human justice were laid down, boldly and firmly, by this great pioneer. It may be said that the statutes of Moses, spiritual and practical, were not new. Most of them were in existence long before the days of Moses, but if that was so there was selection and adoption on a higher level than heretofore.

Though the story of Moses is indefinite in parts, and ends in mystery, the impressions produced are those of power, dignity, and elevation unsurpassed.

Hammurabi (or Khammurabi), king of Babylon, the sixth king in the first dynasty of that empire, according to the records, reigned about the year 2100 B.C., more than 4000 years ago, and is the most famous monarch of those early times.

THE KING WHOSE NAME FIGURES IN THE BOOK OF GENESIS

In the Book of Genesis we read of a war when Abraham was alive. Amraphel, king of Shinar, and Chedorlaomer, king of the Elamites, with three other kings, were fighting against four kings in the neighbourhood of the Dead Sea, and Abraham's nephew Lot was captured, but Abraham managed to rescue him. The land of Shinar was Babylon, in the Mesopotamian Plain, and Amraphel was

XERXES, CYRUS, AND HAMMURABI

XERXES AT THE HEAD OF HIS TROOPS CROSSING THE HELLESPONT ON HIS WONDERFUL BRIDGE

CROESUS APPEALS TO THE
CONQUERING CYRUS

KING HAMMURABI DICTATING
HIS CODE OF LAWS

another name for King Hammurabi. The Elamites lived in the hilly country to the east of the River Tigris, where the land rises into Persia, and their king, called Chedorlaomer in the Bible, and Kudar-Lagamar in the Babylonian records, was at first the most powerful monarch in the East But Hammurabi drove the Elamites out of the Plain of Babylon into their native hills, and then, extending his conquests northward into Assyria, and westward into Asia Minor, federated all the minor kings under his own rule, and reigned from the Persian Gulf to the Mediterranean Sea, with Babylon as his capital. The special god of Babylon was Bel Merodach, or Marduk, and Samas, the sun-god, had a wider sway.

THE MESSAGE OF HAMMURABI WHICH HAS ENDURED THROUGHOUT THE CENTURIES

Here is a proclamation by Hammurabi written in two languages on clay cylinders, now in the British Museum.

Hammurabi, the mighty king, king of Babylon, king of the four quarters, the founder of the land, the king whose deeds unto the heart of Samas and Marduk are well-pleasing, am I.

The summit of the wall of Sippar, like a great mountain, with earth I raised. With a moat I surrounded it. The canal of Sippar I dug out, and a wall of safety I erected for it.

Sippar and Babylon in a peaceful habitation I caused to dwell continuously.

Hammurabi, the darling of Samas, the beloved of Marduk, am I.

That which from days of old no king had built, for Samas my lord gloriously have I accomplished.

We might suppose from reading this memorial inscription that Hammurabi was somewhat of a braggart, but if we look closer at what he says we shall see that, besides serving his gods faithfully, he was doing sound and useful work. It is not because of his conquests in war, though they were great, but because of his substantial work for the good of his people that he has lived long and honourably in history.

THE SPLENDID CODE OF LAWS OF AN EARLY CIVILISATION

Through him we know more about the remarkable civilisation that existed for thousands of years in the Plain of Mesopotamia than from any other source. The lands that he won by war, during his reign of 43 years, he held in a large degree in peace, because be brought them under the rule of law and justice. His great Code of Laws exists to this day, and had a lasting influence in the East down to the times of the Greek conquests under Alexander the Great, and later. From those early laws many of the laws of the Jews were derived. Abraham, the founder of the Jewish race, we must remember, was a native of Ur, one of the cities under Hammurabi's rule. Not from Egypt, but from Babylon, the Jewish people derived laws in existence a thousand years before Moses was born.

The laws of Hammurabi covered every department of life. There was a system of trial by judges, with the elders of the people in attendance, and right of appeal to higher courts and to the king. The tenure of land, the honesty of trade, the soundness of work done, the wages to be paid, housing and rent—subjects which we regard as specially belonging to our own times—were all regulated by law in Hammurabi's reign. Religion had its own endowments in land, but also its own duties. It was expected to relieve poverty, to provide seed for those whose harvest had failed, and to ransom prisoners who were too poor to buy their freedom.

CONDITIONS OF LIFE IN THE DAYS OF HAMMURABI

All the legal doings under this enlightened king were recorded for reference, and we have today, in the Babylonian writing, many sample judgments, many charters giving wider liberties than had existed, many legal contracts to ensure fair dealing in business, many despatches recording public occurrences.

As regards practical affairs, Hammurabi's reign was conspicuous for its enlightenment. There was a police system in full working order. A regular postal delivery helped business. Irrigation was scientific, and a public duty. Waterways were carefully preserved and new canals were cut. Corn was stored to guard against the effects of bad harvests. Trade by caravan passed freely along safe and well-supervised roads.

The worst feature of the laws was the severity of the punishments. Fines were the commonest punishment, but death was the penalty for many faults if they were wilful. A man who lied might have his tongue cut out; a forger might have his writing hand cut off; a bad wife might be drowned. Any serious wrong-doing was a serious danger to the guilty person. But law and safety were there for the well-doer in the reign of the great law-making King Hammurabi.

Akhnaton, the most interesting king of the eighteenth Egyptian dynasty, was a son of Amenhotep the Third, one of the most luxurious and magnificent of the kings who ruled Egypt when she was at the height of her power, wealth, and glory. Egypt under Amenhotep was held in deep respect from the Euphrates to the Black Sea and the Levant, most of this wide region being formed of tributary States. The religion of the country was then a worship of many gods, mostly in animal forms, though the chief centres of worship were Thebes, in the temples of Ammon or Amen, and Heliopolis, in the temples of Ra, or Aton. Between the priesthoods of these two shrines keen rivalry prevailed. The reigning kings absorbed Ammon into their own names, and Akhnaton succeeded Amenhotep the Third, under the name of Amenhotep the Fourth, when he was a boy of eleven.

THE KING OF OLD EGYPT WHO BELIEVED IN ONE GOD

But the mother of the boyish king was a confirmed worshipper at Heliopolis of the Sun-god Ra, or Aton, and when he was seventeen and felt he could assert his preferences as a king, he changed his name from Amenhotep, which means The Peace of Ammon, to Akhnaton, which means The Glory of Aton. Henceforward his great aim in life was to spread the worship of Aton the Sun-god, and to discountenance the worship of any other gods. In short, living in the midst of the worship of innumerable gods, each of them supported by a clique of priests, and specially believed in by some section of the people as their favourite deity and fortune bringer, Akhnaton was bold enough to conceive of one God as the originator and sustainer of life, and to conceive of Him as the father and mother of all beings He had made.

He carried out his conviction by leaving Thebes, the city of Amen-worship, and by building a new capital, El Amarna, and dedicating a large site in it to Aton. Also he systematically defaced the inscriptions to other gods, and included in the obliteration the names of his own ancestors, and his own name where Ammon formed a part.

Akhnaton was not only absorbed in his religious reforms, but he was opposed to war. His interest in the outlying parts of his dominions slackened, and towards the end of his reign he was threatened by revolt from many quarters, and opposed at home by the adherents of the gods he had dispossessed. When he died at the age of 28, in the year 1350 B.C., and was succeeded by his son-in-law Tutankhamen, who reverted to that name from Tutankhaton, the nation quickly returned to Amen worship, and a multiplicity of gods. The temples Akhnaton had built to Aton as the one God were defaced, and the city he had founded was deserted.

AKHNATON'S BOLD EFFORT TO STAMP OUT THE WORSHIP OF IDOLS

Akhnaton, though his plans of spiritual reform failed, has the distinction of being a king who, in the midst of surroundings altogether unfavourable to independent thought or change, cared enough, and was bold enough, to cast aside the idea that mixed idolatry can be helpful to the soul of man. He worshipped the all-reviving Sun as the symbol of an eternally creative Deity, and though, may be, his views were crude, they were a long step in advance of the views held in the days before Moses had begun to present to men a purer faith.

The years of Persia's glory in history, from the rise of Cyrus the Great to the conquest of Darius the Third by Alexander the Great, were only 208. In that period Persia produced three great conquerors, Cyrus, Cambyses, and Artaxerxes the Third, and two great rulers, Cyrus and Darius the First; and in Xerxes the First she had a king who made a mighty show in the world.

HOW CYRUS OVERCAME HIS MASTER THE KING OF THE MEDES

Of Cyrus legendary stories abounded, and were included in Greek histories, but the plain truth seems to be that he was a Persian king of a small State in the country of the Elamites, and paid tribute to the King of the Medes, who at that time (550 B.C.) was the most active Eastern monarch. The Median King, Astyages, for some unknown reason, attempted to chastise his vassal, but was defeated and captured, and soon Cyrus was accepted as King of the Medes and the Persians.

Cyrus was a gentleman, large-minded and tolerant, and many of the surrounding States were only too glad to be ruled by such a king. The largest rival State was

Babylon, which was then ruled by the antiquarian King Nabonidus, who did much to preserve Eastern history, but was a dreamer rather than a man of action, and had lost grip of the outlying parts of Babylon. The Jews, who were then captives in Babylon, were looking eagerly to Cyrus as a possible deliverer, and no doubt many subject peoples hailed his growing power with delight. So, when he approached Babylon with his army, the city welcomed him, and he preserved it and gave it freedom and safety.

THE GREAT SOLDIER WHO WAS ALSO A GREAT STATESMAN

The Jews were released and sent back to Palestine. With the possession of Babylon, Cyrus succeeded to the Syrian and Hebrew possessions of the Babylonian kings. Where opposition was offered to him, as by King Croesus and certain allies in Asia Minor, he crushed it by force of arms, and soon he reigned from Kashmir to the Black Sea.

Cyrus was a great statesman as well as a soldier. He gave peoples and towns subject to him reasonable independence as long as they were loyal and fulfilled imperial obligations. In religion a follower of Zoroaster as a Sun-worshipper, he was singularly free from fanatical prejudices. As an organiser of Government he had method and firmness and kept in close touch with all parts of his wide dominions. By his rise from obscurity, his energy in war and government, and the impression he produced on men's minds through his character, Cyrus the Persian has a right to be called great. He fell in an obscure war on the northern frontier of his Empire.

THE STORY OF KING DARIUS WRITTEN ON THE ROCKS

After the death of Cambyses, the son of Cyrus, who succeeded him, and who added Egypt to the Persian Empire, there was a period of confusion when usurpers were seeking to gain the kingship. Out of this confusion emerged Darius, a man of the royal blood, who surprised and slew the usurper who had been temporarily successful. This occurred in 521 B.C., and Darius, called the Great, ruled for 36 years.

He is the one ancient monarch who has helped history by graving on the rocks a summary of his doings as king, which reads as if it were quite frank and true. His inscription on the great rock of Behistun is famous, and has already been referred to on page 6387; and there are other instances of this useful habit by which Darius left useful messages to posterity about himself.

Darius was not a conqueror of set purpose. He knew that the Empire he ruled was quite as large as the resources of the Persians and Medes and their federated races could manage, so he set himself to govern well that which he already had. But he was obliged to go to war, now here, now there, with the wild tribes that fringed his empire round, and to establish order in their midst as a means of defence for his own country. So whether he desired extension of territory or not his possessions increased. In this way he crossed the Bosphorus to chastise the aggressive Scythians, and passed the Danube in pursuit of them, and so came into that close touch with Europe, and the European Greeks, that was to cost Persia dear. Many Greeks lived in Asia along the coasts, and were under the government of Darius and knew its value.

THE HAPPY REIGN OF ONE OF THE GREATEST KINGS IN HISTORY

They advised the Greeks in Greece to leave the Persians alone; but the advice was not taken, and, as they had done before, many of the Greeks on the mainland gave help to the enemies of the Persians, and so drew Darius into sending expeditions against Greece itself. Two such expeditions were defeated, one at Mount Athos and the other at Marathon, and when Darius died he was planning a final attack on Greece.

It is not by his successes or failures in war that Darius should be judged. He left throughout his dominions a feeling that he had promoted their welfare with foresight and fairness. In Egypt, which had only just been conquered when he came to the throne, he was rated as one of its most appreciated kings. He made a canal from the Nile to the Red Sea so that small ships could sail from the Persian Gulf into the Mediterranean Sea. He developed the trade of his lands, and gave them a common coinage. On the most sensitive of all points—religion—he conciliated races with widely divergent views. The Jew, the Greek, the Babylonian, and the Egyptian, all acknowledged the advantages of his rule. We should have to look far through the pages of history to find a greater king or ruler of men.

FOUR GREAT MEN OF OTHER DAYS

THE TERRIBLE HAROUN-AL-RASCHID SENDS HIS
BEST FRIEND TO HIS DEATH

HANNIBAL WATCHES HIS ARMY CROSSING
THE ALPS ON THE WAY TO ROME

ARCHIMEDES DIRECTS THE WORKING OF ONE OF
HIS MACHINES AT THE DEFENCE OF SYRACUSE

MOSES, ANGERED BY THE PEOPLE'S SIN, BREAKS
THE TABLES OF THE COVENANT

Xerxes, the successor of Darius, had the double claim to the Persian throne of being descended from both Darius and Cyrus. Darius was his father, and Cyrus his grandfather, through his mother, Atossa. Xerxes had to suppress rebellions in both Egypt and Babylon before he set out on the expedition by which he is best known in history—the attempt to conquer Greece by the biggest army that the world had ever seen. All the resources of the Persian Empire were used to collect men and material for the campaign. The Hellespont was bridged in two places. Alliances were sought with the Greek States which were hostile to Athens. A huge fleet was concentrated in Levantine waters. At first the armies of Xerxes swept the Greeks away after defeating their fleet, and Athens was taken. When all seemed lost, the Greek fleet again engaged the Persian fleet and, in the bay of Salamis, won a decisive naval victory which gave them the command of the sea and cut off the army of Xerxes from the Asiatic shore.

THE DRAMATIC END OF THE GREAT EXPEDITION OF XERXES

Realising that his campaign had failed, Xerxes himself returned to Persia, leaving his army in Greece under the command of his general, Mardonius. The Greeks were now as encouraged as the Persians were discouraged, and attacking the invaders at Plataea, in 479 B.C., they utterly routed them. The Persians were quite unable to resist the solid masses of Greek infantry armed with long spears, and advancing in the formation known as the phalanx.

Xerxes, who is the king known in the Book of Esther as Ahasuerus, tried in vain to infuse a confident spirit into the Persians. They were beaten and knew it. The king himself, as time went on, became demoralised, and finally was murdered by his prime minister. After Xerxes had been dead 110 years the Persian King Artaxerxes the Third attacked and conquered Greece, but seven years after his death Persia was prostrate before the victorious invasion of the Greek King Alexander the Great.

Naturally, perhaps, the eyes of posterity are turned most frequently on men who did sensational deeds in the past that arrested general attention—on kings who fought great battles and annexed foreign countries, or on men who wrote books that

stir for ever the minds or the hearts of their fellow men; but the past is also adorned by quiet, inconspicuous men of science who passed on through the ages learning or inventions that have proved inconceivably useful in later times. One of the greatest of such men was Archimedes, a Greek mathematician, who sought knowledge for its own sake.

THE GREAT IDEA THAT CAME TO ARCHIMEDES IN HIS BATH

Archimedes was born about 287 B.C. in the Greek city of Syracuse in Italy. He studied, when young, in Alexandria, then the most famous centre of the world's learning. Nearly all his later life was spent in his native city, where he was the intimate friend of its king.

His studies in mathematics are much too difficult to explain here. Suffice it to say they have been of great use to men of the highest learning, particularly many forms of measurement.

Three things he did are practical enough to be understood by anyone. The king asked him to find out if his crown was of pure gold. This he did by putting the crown in a vessel full of water, and observing exactly how much water is caused to run over the sides of the vessel. Then he put an equal weight of gold in the same full vessel of water, and observed exactly how much water that displaced, any difference being occasioned by metal in the crown which was not gold. It was this experiment that he thought of while he was in his bath, and in his excitement sprang out of the bath and ran home without his clothes shouting, " Eureka ! " which means " I have found it."

HOW THE INVENTIONS OF ARCHIMEDES KEPT THE ROMANS AT BAY

The Archimedean screw for raising water was his invention. During his later years Syracuse was besieged by the Romans under Marcellus, and at the request of his friend the king, the philosopher invented mechanical engines of defence which lifted the prows of the Roman ships out of the water and then dropped them and sank them. He is also said to have set the ships on fire by burning mirrors. His inventions delayed the capture of the city for three years. When it was stormed he was killed by a Roman soldier while he was working out a mathematical problem in the sand of the seashore. The Romans buried him with great honour, for they fully realised he was a man of genius.

Of all the kings of the ancient world Minos is probably the one which the modern world would be most interested in hearing about in a definite manner. He reigned in the island of Crete when it was the centre of a civilisation that is now called Minoan after him, and that for thousands of years was forgotten.

Such knowledge as we have comes to us in three ways. First, some of the Greek historians wrote of him as one of the wisest and best kings who had lived before Greece became famous. His laws were said to have been those on which the oldest laws of Greece were based. He kept order, by land and sea, in the Eastern Mediterranean, and his country was magnificent and prosperous, great in art and in commerce.

KING MINOS

Then, around his name sprang up many legends, transmitted through Greek poetry, as in later times legends were woven round the names of King Arthur of Britain, and Charlemagne, King of the Franks. It was said that in his palace was an underground labyrinth or maze, in which any stranger was lost; and there was kept a strange monster, half man and half bull, known as the Minotaur. Every ninth year the tyrant king demanded as tribute from Greece seven young men and seven maidens, who were devoured by the monster. So strange were these mythological stories about Minos that some who read them thought there had not been any king Minos, but that he was only a figure in poetical fable.

HAMMURABI'S CODE OF LAWS INSCRIBED ON A STONE

In recent years, however, the traditional site of the palace of Minos, at

Knossos in Crete, has been carefully and thoroughly excavated, with remarkable results. The palace, a most labyrinthine building, has been disclosed, and a great deal of knowledge has been gained about the people who lived in Crete in the days of Minos, as we read on page 322. We still know practically nothing about the personal life of Minos, but it is clear that he lived in the midst of a civilisation of an advanced kind, in great magnificence, and that his country played a leading part in the eastern Mediterranean, exchanging the products of its industry and art with ancient Egypt, and influencing powerfully the life of the world.

His people seem to have been the precursors of the Phoenician mariner race who later dominated the sea-borne trade of the world; and it is now believed that the invention of the alphabet and writing which had been attributed to the Phoenicians, was not by rights theirs, but that they only changed in style the writing of the Minoans. In short, it may be said that a stage in human development that lies beyond the thought and art of the Greeks had been lost to men's knowledge when Knossos and other Cretan towns were destroyed. Indeed, the one personality in that forgotten period that impressed itself on men's minds was a real and great king, Minos by name;

A PICTURE OF DARIUS, FROM PERSEPOLIS

and his greatness is shown by the fact that when all his works were buried in the earth, vague memories of him, dressed up in fanciful forms, were transmitted from generation to generation. So Minos comes to us as a great, though shadowy, king.

There are many students of war who believe that the greatest general who ever lived was not Alexander the Great, or Julius Caesar, or Napoleon Bonaparte, but Hannibal of Carthage. That leading commercial city was founded in northern Africa, about 822 B.C., near the present site of the city of Tunis, by the Phoenicians. It succeeded Tyre as the mistress of the Mediterranean. As time went on it captured Sicily, Sardinia, and the Balearic Islands, and founded settlements in Madeira, the Canary Islands, and on the west coast of Africa. Then frequent wars followed with Rome, which ended in the conquest of Sicily by the Roman army.

THE PASSAGE OF THE ALPS WHICH COST HANNIBAL HALF HIS ARMY

As a balance to this loss Carthage invaded Spain with Hamilcar as the general. When he was killed he was succeeded by his son-in-law Hasdrubal, and, on his death, the Carthaginian army elected young Hannibal, son of Hamilcar, as their general. As soon as he was appointed commander-in-chief he completed the conquest of Spain as far as the Ebro, and then planned an attack on Rome.

He could not hope to cross the Mediterranean Sea with an army large enough to capture Rome, so he determined to march from Spain through France, then called Gaul, and cross the Alps into Italy. This wonderful feat he safely accomplished. Carthage itself provided him with comparatively few soldiers, but he recruited his army in Spain, and in Gaul, where Rome had many enemies. The passage of the Alps cost him nearly half his army, but when he reached the plain of northern Italy he repeatedly defeated the Roman armies through superb generalship, and reached the neighbourhood of Rome. He had not, however, with him the means wherewith to besiege the city, and so had to wait for supplies from Carthage. Those supplies never reached him in sufficient amounts to enable him to take Rome ; but for fifteen years he remained in Italy.

THE TERRIBLE YEARS AT THE CLOSE OF HANNIBAL'S LIFE

Meantime the Romans had crossed to Africa, and were attacking an untrained army, and opposed to him were the victorious veterans of the Roman general Scipio. In that unequal fight Hannibal was defeated, and Carthage was obliged to submit to Rome and pay tribute to her. The Carthaginians, however, made him their chief magistrate, and so well did he

rule that the country began to revive, and Rome began to fear her old enemy afresh, and demanded that he should be surrendered to her. The remainder of his life was spent in passing from country to country, chased by the Roman power, and finally, when he was about to be betrayed by a servile king in Asia Minor, he took poison to escape capture.

The greatness of Hannibal's skill as a soldier is shown by what he achieved with the most slender resources. His life was spent far from home, in enemy lands, without adequate support from his own countrymen. In all probability he would have taken Rome if his brother Hasdrubal had been able to join him in Italy with reinforcements. But the Romans intercepted Hasdrubal and defeated him, and Hannibal only heard of his brother's failure through his head being thrown into the Carthaginian camp.

One of the most remarkable kingly figures that has ever dazzled the eyes of men was the Caliph Haroun-al-Raschid, chief of the Moslem world between A.D. 786 and 809. He now lives in men's minds chiefly through The Arabian Nights, into which he is introduced.

THE AIR OF SPLENDOUR SURROUNDING A KINGLY TYRANT

Both as ruler and as religious leader he was acknowledged as absolute from India through Asia and northern Africa to the Atlantic Ocean. Early in his life he had showed an aptitude for war, and throughout his reign he was one of the most active of governors, frequently visiting many parts of his dominions; but his wealth and magnificence, his patronage of learning, and his will to do whatever he pleased, have most impressed the world.

Haroun was the completest example of a kingly tyrant. No consideration weighed with him if his vanity was hurt. He rose to worldly greatness through the faithfulness of his friends when he was young, and the more loyal they were to him the more certain was a cruel fate to overtake them if he saw any reason to regard them with jealousy. His wise Vizier Yahya and his dearest friend Jaffar were among them.

All the world knew Haroun-al-Raschid as the world's supreme example of human power and magnificence in his own day. Now he is its greatest proof of the impossibility of uniting unchecked power with justice and true greatness.

The Great Stories of the World That Will Be Told for Ever

HOW THE MOON CAME TO HAWAII

THERE was once a King in Hawaii who sent for his court wizard, and said: "Every time my fishermen let down their lines in a certain part of the sea the hooks are cut off. They feel no tug as though a fish were biting, but when they draw up the line it is cut through."

The wizard replied: "They must have been fishing over the country of Lalo-Nana, which lies at the bottom of the sea. A sister and two brothers live there, all far more beautiful than mortals."

"I must see them," cried the King.

The wizard said that the brothers were on a journey, but he would try to entice the woman ashore.

A few nights afterwards a trumpet was blown, and the sound awoke the sea-maiden in Lalo-Nana. She left her coral house and her garden of sea-flowers and her luminous fishes to see what it was. To her surprise she saw something like a man hanging midway between the surface and the bottom. She drew near, and found it was only an image suspended by a cord, but it was beautifully carved and richly dressed. Cautiously the sea-maid swam to the surface to see what kind of fishermen were angling with such strange bait. She saw a row of canoes anchored at intervals all the way to the shore, and in each of them was an image.

The sea-maid swam from one to another, admiring their ornaments and clothes in the starlight, for there was no Moon in those days. Perhaps she thought a magician had turned all the islanders to wood. Now it would be safe to explore the forbidden upper world. So she stepped ashore, and followed a line of images through the flowery forest of Hawaii till she came to a little house. Weary with long swimming and walking, the sea-maid sank down to sleep.

She was wakened by the King, who had fallen in love with her and who begged her to be Queen of Hawaii. She consented, and for a long time she was delighted with the wonders of the island. Then she wished to give her husband a present in return for the necklaces and bracelets he had given her.

"Send a diver to my coral house under the sea," she said. "There he will find a casket, which he must bring ashore unopened. In it is a treasure which my brothers and I have guarded for years."

The diver brought the casket to the palace safely, but as soon as the Queen opened it a great shining thing flew out and sailed through the door up to the skies. It was the Moon. There it shone among the stars, but, to the Queen's terror, its reflection shone in the sea as well!

IMAGINATION · CHIVALRY · LEGENDS · GOLDEN DEEDS · FAIRY TALES

"My brothers will know I have lost the treasure," she cried. "They will return to the coral house and find me gone. They will come ashore in a great flood to find me."

"Fear not, Hina," said the King (for Hina was the sea-maid's name). "We will all go up to the mountains with our cattle and treasure. The sea cannot reach us there."

So the Hawaiians fled to the mountain-tops. Soon after a storm arose, and presently a huge tidal wave rushed ashore. Hina saw her two brothers riding on the foam, and heard them calling her. When the flood subsided all the crops were ruined, and the whole island lay desert.

Everyone was far poorer now, even the King, and from thinking that Hina was the cause of his misfortunes he came to hate her. He made her toil from morn to dusk at the hardest work till her life was slavery, and often as the poor woman laboured she thought, "Ah! If I could only find some place to rest in!"

She dared not go back to the sea for fear of her brothers. She could not escape from her husband on the island. One day,

as she was fishing, she saw a rainbow bridge stretching to Earth. She understood that the Sun had pity on her, and was showing her this way to escape.

Hina began to climb the rainbow, but as she got nearer to the Sun the great heat scorched her till she could bear no more. She swooned, and slipped from the bridge to the ground.

When she recovered from her fall it was night. She could hear her husband calling her angrily, and knew he would ill-use her for the work left undone. At that moment a wonderful thing happened. A Moon rainbow appeared.

"Ah, it is very quiet in the Moon!" said Hina. "There I shall be able to rest."

She began to climb the silver bridge. The King came out of the trees and ran up to stop her. He was afraid to climb the magic bridge, but he seized her foot. She wrenched it free, breaking it, and crawled on. At length she reached the cool, silvery Moon country.

There she still lives, lame but happy, and the fairy-like clouds you see drifting round the Moon are of Hina's spinning.

THE HEROINE OF NOTTINGHAM CASTLE

ONE of the brightest stories from the Civil War is that of the defence of Nottingham Castle by Colonel and Mrs. Lucy Hutchinson.

The king set up his standard on August 22, 1642, at Nottingham, near which town the Hutchinsons lived. The whole country was in a ferment, and Henry Ireton, their neighbour and relative, urged them to support the Parliamentarians, which they did. Mr. Hutchinson received a commission as lieutenant-colonel, and the family removed to Nottingham. Soon, as Governor of Nottingham Castle, Colonel Hutchinson had to defend it.

For four years Mrs. Hutchinson was shut up in the castle, acting as surgeon during the siege, tending the sick, supplying food for the big household, and ever cheerful and wise in her counsels.

She shared all her husband's plans, approved his stern refusal of the many attempts to bribe him into submission, and showed in the notes she wrote down at the time that she must have witnessed scenes and undergone anxiety enough to quell the stoutest heart.

There were her little children, too, who needed her constant care.

Newark, a neighbouring town, was on the Royalist side, and many of the citizens of Nottingham were also Royalists. One of them during the night secretly let the Governor of Newark and six hundred soldiers into the town. Next morning the colonel found himself besieged in his little fortress with eighty men. Enemies were all around, but messengers got through and sent for succour to the garrisons at Derby and Leicester.

On the third day Colonel Hutchinson was invited to parley with the Royalists, and his answer was to hoist a red flag on the tower of the castle. Two more days passed, and then, to their relief, the watchers on the tower saw a party of horse-men galloping to their assistance. As these men drew near the Royalists retreated, but not without a sally from the besieged.

When the war was over Mrs. Hutchinson acted as peacemaker between a band of soldiers preparing to attack the town and the citizens arming for its defence; and later, when the Stuarts came back to power after Cromwell's death, she worked to secure her husband's pardon. It was denied, and the brave wife comforted her imprisoned husband until his death.

STORIES OF THE SAINTS

In early times, in every land, there grew up round the memory of men and women who had been greatly admired stories which made their fame lasting, though the details might be changed. The impression remained, if sometimes it became more legendary than historical. We see it in the rude, fierce heroes of the Northern races, who admired force and bravery ; in the poetical imagery of Greece ; in the dreamy tales of the religious heroes of the gentler East ; in the legends of the great figures of the Age of Chivalry. And as goodness spread, as the gentle power of the Christ-like life was seen in the men and women whom we now call Saints, there grew up many legends around the memory of these saintly characters. Many of them are both beautiful and true, but all are worth knowing. Such lives, founded on fact, but sometimes cast in story form, are the foundation of much of the art of the early painters, and by the beauty of their teaching they have influenced a vast multitude of lives.

THE PATRON SAINT OF SHOEMAKERS

THE patron saint of shoemakers is St. Crispin, and the reason is this. In the third century there lived at Soissons two brothers who were called Crispin and Crispinianus.

They were teachers of Christianity; but they thought it right to earn their own living, and this they did by making shoes. They took money from the well-to-do, but charged the poor nothing.

Their fame spread so that many of the people in Gaul visited them, and learned from them the story of Christ's love. At last there came to Soissons the heathen emperor, and he commanded that these shoemakers should be arrested. They were tried, tortured, and afterwards beheaded.

Whenever you see the picture of a saint with the palm of victory in one hand and an awl in the other, you may know it is either Crispin or Crispinianus, the patron saint of shoemakers.

SANTA CLAUS

A YOUNG and rich man was walking one day through the streets of his native town when he heard sounds of lamentation from the house of a nobleman whose money was all lost, and who was now living on the verge of starvation with his three daughters. The young man listened, and he heard a girl's voice say : " Father, let us go into the streets and beg, for it is hard to starve."

Then he heard the father answer: " Not just yet. Not tonight. Let us wait one more night. I will pray God again to save my children from such disgrace."

Nicholas hurried home. Among the treasures he had inherited from his father were three bars of solid gold. He took one of these bars at night to the house of the poor man, and, finding an open window, which he could just reach by standing on tiptoe, he thrust in the bar of gold. He came a second night,

and left the second bar; and the third night, and left the third bar. But the third night he was discovered, and the poor father, who believed the gold had come from Heaven, knelt at his feet. Nicholas lifted him up, and said:

" Give thanks to God, for it was He who sent me to you."

This and many another splendid gift of love did Nicholas in the name of God, and always in secret, so that he is called St. Nicholas, and children believe that at Christmas he fills their stockings with gifts. They know him as Santa Claus.

THE LITTLE POOR MAN OF ASSISI

THERE lived in the town of Assisi, in Italy, in the thirteenth century, the son of a very wealthy merchant, and his name was Francis.

He was a handsome, bright-eyed, merry-hearted boy, and as he grew up to manhood he lived only for pleasure and excitement.

But in the midst of his wild and selfish life there came to him a voice from heaven, and he saw all at once how foolish he had been.

Francis gave up his mad ways and set himself to serve God. He tore off his rich clothes and lived like a beggar. His father was angry. His old companions pelted him with mud. Nearly everybody thought he was mad. But some people began to perceive that a great change for good had indeed come over Francis. For he did not rave, he did not shout; he was the same cheerful, bright-eyed, happy-minded man, but with this difference—that all his cheerfulness came from the love of God.

And this was the secret of St. Francis. He adored poverty. If, said he, Christ became a poor carpenter's son for us, surely we ought to make ourselves poor for Him. He spoke of poverty as a lady, and said he had married this beautiful lady of poverty. He wore a rough brown dress, ate simple food, and spent all his time in teaching people to desire poverty; that is to say, to love God so much that everything rich and grand and magnificent appears silly and trivial and unworthy.

He loved everything that God has made. He hated cruelty. He told people to love " our sisters the birds "; he spoke of the wind as " our brother," and of the rain as " our sister." He felt that all things are related, and that God is the Father of all.

For six hundred years men have loved St. Francis, whom we call the Little Poor Man of Assisi. He is dear to us for many reasons; but perhaps we are most grateful to him for just this simple teaching: that we should never be unkind to bird or beast, but should spread the love of God among every living thing.

CECILIA THE SWEET SINGER

THERE was a strange scene one day in Rome in the early days of Christians. A handsome young Roman soldier, Valerian, had just brought home his bride, a beautiful Roman girl, Cecilia. The festivities were over. The guests had all gone. Valerian was alone with his bride. Then Cecilia said to him:

" I am your wife, but I do not belong to you. I belong to Christ. All my life I have given myself to Christ, and I have an angel who will guard me from evil."

Valerian was much surprised, for he had no idea that the noble parents of Cecilia were among the despised Christians. To be a Christian in Rome meant death.

" Show me this angel," he said; " then I shall know if what you say is true."

She told him that he could not see the angel until he had learned to love Christ; and she bade him go along the Appian Way, outside the walls of Rome, and ask the people there to direct him to Urban the Good. This Valerian did, and he found Urban underground in the Catacombs. Urban told him the story of Jesus, and Valerian believed and was baptised. So happy was he in his new faith that he persuaded his brother also, and these two, with the beautiful Cecilia, spent their lives in doing good. The home was very happy, for Cecilia had a lovely voice, and she sang songs of praise which thrilled the hearts of the two brothers, and they knew that after death they would all meet in a happier world.

Soon it became known that Valerian and his brother were Christians, and they were put to death. But Cecilia became bolder in preaching, and was brought before the governor.

" What sort of a woman are you? " he asked roughly. " And what is your name?"

" I am a Roman lady," she replied proudly. " Among men I am known as Cecilia, but my name is Christian." And for her faith, so courageously confessed, she was condemned to a cruel death.

THE STRONG MAN WHO CARRIED THE POOR

AN old hermit was sitting in his cell one day when there appeared before him a mighty man, who said his name was Offero, and told him a strange story.

" I was strong from my youth up," he said, " and beat every comer at games. But I wearied of these idle things. A voice within me drove me forth, and would not let me be satisfied.

" So I put on my armour and took my sword, and journeyed till I came to the palace of the greatest king on Earth. Him I served till one day I saw him make a sign on his forehead whenever the minstrel who sang before him made mention of the Evil One. I would not serve him longer because he feared the Evil One, and was not a brave man.

" So I journeyed on, till in the centre of a black forest I found Satan keeping his court. ' Art thou the bravest king on Earth? ' I asked, and as he said that he feared nothing I took service with him.

" But one day I saw him cower from a little wooden cross set up on the highway, and I challenged him, saying: ' What! are you the bravest man on Earth, and fear a piece of wood? ' ' It is not the cross I fear,' said he, ' but Him who once hung there.'

" So I left him, and have ever since striven to discover who is this Christ that hung upon the cross. And now the voice within me has brought me to you. Tell me, I pray you, the story of Christ."

The hermit told him, and the giant swore that he would serve only Christ henceforth. The hermit said that Christ did not wish men to fight for Him, but to fight against evil by gentle living.

Offero said that might well be true; but God had not given him great muscular strength for nothing, and that strength he would devote to Christ.

So the hermit took him to the banks of a wide and angry river, and bade him dwell there and help poor people to cross. This pleased Offero well, and he built a hut, and tore up a pine tree for a staff; and when poor people wanted to cross the angry flood he carried them over, and said he did it for the love of God.

One wild night a child came to him to be carried across, and Offero set him on his shoulder and waded into the stream.

But as he went the child grew heavier and heavier, so that Offero's knees bent under him. Yet he got across, and when he set the child down he said:

" How is it that you are the heaviest burden I ever carried ? "

Then the child became glorious with a wondrous light, and said to Offero:

" Heavy did I seem because I bear the sins and sorrows of the world. I am Christ. And because thou hast been kind to the weak, and borne Christ on thy shoulders, I will call thee Christopher."

Then the Child vanished, and Christopher kneeled in the darkness.

THE GIRL WHO DEFIED AN EMPEROR

ONE of the commonest sights on the Fifth of November is the catherine-wheel. It is named after Saint Catherine, who was bound to a wheel. Catherine of Alexandria was the cleverest girl of her day in Egypt. She lived in the fourth century, when most of the people about her were heathen. One day she heard that the Emperor Maximinus had ordered that many poor people should be slain as a sacrifice to the idols the emperor worshipped, and Catherine went to his palace and condemned his cruelty.

It was in vain that he tried to argue with her. She was too clever for him. So the emperor sent for his wise men to argue with her; but she defeated them all in a great debate, and many people became Christians on hearing her wonder-ful words. This made the emperor angry, and he ordered that she should be put to death—tortured on a wheel.

What this wheel was like we do not know. One account says that it was shaped like an ordinary wheel but armed with spikes. Another account says that it was not one wheel, but four wheels joined. Whatever the nature of the wheel, poor Catherine was bound to it.

But a wonderful thing happened. No sooner had she been tied to the wheel than an angel appeared and set her free. He broke the wheel in pieces.

But the emperor was not content. He had Catherine beaten with scourges, and cast her into a dungeon without food; and at the end of twelve days she was led forth and beheaded.

JOHN OF THE GOLDEN VOICE

FROM out the dimness of the far distant past there comes to us the fame of two very wonderful orators who impressed men so deeply that the echo of their voices seems to reach us still. Those orators were Demosthenes, a heathen but highly civilised Greek, and John of Antioch, who was welcomed into the list of Christian saints, and who is for ever known as Chrysostom, meaning the golden-mouthed.

John Chrysostom's life falls into about five chapters, and all of them are honour-able. First he was a good boy, taught by a pious mother, and so had the pure joy of growing up sweet in spirit. Then he was educated in oratory that he might be a lawyer. But his mind turned naturally towards religion, and he went into solitude to think and pray and pre-pare himself for Christian work.

Returning presently to the crowds of men, he became a preacher who charmed all ears, and at last he was made arch-bishop of Constantinople.

And now, having power, he became a great reformer and a generous helper of the poor and suffering. He lived a pure life himself and demanded it from others, especially from those who were in posi-tions of influence, like kings and priests. If the lives of such people were on a low level he made them uncomfortable by very plain speech.

For this he was at last banished into the wilderness of Asia Minor; but that did not trouble him, for there he found people who needed his preaching. And every-where were people who wished to hear him preach, and demanded that he should be restored to the world. His persecutors gave way and pretended to bring him back to freedom, but they treated him so badly that he died on the way.

Yet still Constantinople, which knew him best, asked for him, and in 438 his persecuted body was taken to the city, and his name was enrolled among the saints.

Chrysostom wrote much as well as spoke much. His character was of great loveliness all through his life. Here is a deep and wise saying of his that deserves to be written in letters of gold, for it bears thinking about for a lifetime: *No man can hurt him who will not hurt himself.*

THE MARTYR GIRL OF SICILY

QUINTIANUS, the Governor of Sicily, was in love with a very beautiful Catanian girl named Agatha.

She was proudly bred and of rich parentage; so that when she avoided him he thought she was moved to do so by her pride. But presently he discovered the truth. Agatha was a Christian.

The governor had her brought before him. For a long time he pleaded with her to give up her religion; but she would not. Then the love of Quintianus turned to a hideous hatred. He had this beautiful girl cast into a dungeon. Then she was stretched on the rack; but she clung to Christ and would not deny her faith.

Then the monster who had once loved her attacked her with his sword, and she was thrown back into her prison terribly wounded. No doctor was allowed to see her, no nurse to tend her. As she lay on the ground of her cell, no cry or moan escaped her lips; and she sighed out her soul in a great peace.

THE BOY WHO FLED FROM ROME

MANY years ago there was a wealthy family in Italy, and the only son was the hero of the house. His parents wished him to become a judge, and they sent him to Rome to study law.

But the boy, whose name was Benedict, was shocked by the luxury that met his eyes in Rome, and at last he ran away and hid in the hills, determined to serve God in loneliness. But his old nurse followed Benedict, and waited on him.

For a long time he lived in this manner, until it seemed to him wrong that he should let this old nurse fetch him food, and once more he ran away.

This time he travelled far into the mountains, and lived in a wild cave.

Many years passed, and people heard of the holy man living alone in a cave and visited him. A company of monks were so impressed by his preaching that they asked him to come and rule over them, and this he agreed to do. But Benedict found that the monks lived too easily, and he introduced a greater sternness into their lives. Then the monks repented that they had ever asked him to be their superior, and Benedict returned to his cave. Many holy men came to live near him, and he built houses for them to live in.

St. Benedict caught a fever in nursing the poor. He was borne into the chapel, and died before the altar he loved.

URSULA AND THE TEN THOUSAND MAIDENS

A WONDERFUL sight was seen one day in Brittany. In a great meadow were gathered together ten thousand maidens from Britain, and on a throne was seated the Princess Ursula of Brittany, telling the story of Jesus.

Ursula was the only daughter of the King of Brittany, and so lovely that the story of her beauty had passed into all lands. Prince Conan of Britain desired her for his wife, and she told him to send her ten of his great ladies, each escorted by a thousand maidens, and to wait for her three years. Then she taught these maidens Christianity, and set out with them to visit foreign lands.

Ursula and her company of ladies made a wonderful impression wherever they went, and many people became Christians because of them. And Prince Conan followed her, with many bishops and clergy, including even the Pope of Rome.

But in her pilgrimage Ursula came to a place where the people rose against her, and slew the bishops and clergy, and Prince Conan and his knights, and all the women except herself.

So Ursula was brought before the king, who declared that he would marry her; but she spoke to him so truly of the wicked things he had done that he seized an arrow and with it pierced her heart.

ALTHAEA AND THE BURNING BRAND

ALTHAEA, Queen of Calydon, lay with her new-born babe at her side. It was night, and the room was lit only by a wood fire. The nurse slumbered, but the mother lay awake thinking of the little son, who was to be called Meleager.

All at once she saw three misty shapes in the room. As they grew clearer she saw that they were old women, crowned with narcissus, and guessed that they must be the three Fates who preside over man's birth and death.

" He shall be valorous and great," whispered one of the old women.

" He shall be stronger than mortal men," said another.

" He shall live as long as that firebrand is unconsumed," prophesied the last.

Then they faded away.

Althaea rose with all haste, drew the stick from the fire, and put out the flames with water. Then she locked it away as the most precious treasure in the whole kingdom, for it was her son's life.

Meleager grew up as the Fates had foretold, a famous hero. He was one of the Argonauts. He defeated his father's enemies when they invaded Calydon. He finally slew the monster boar, whose hunting is one of the great events in mythological history.

All the chieftains of Greece were at the hunting, including Althaea's dearly-loved brothers Toxeus and Plexippus. There was also in the party Princess Atalanta, the huntress and swift athlete, whom Meleager loved. She was the first to wound the Calydonian boar, and when Meleager finally slew it he gave her the head and hide for trophies.

Toxeus and Plexippus were angry at such honour being shown a woman. They had as much right as she to the monster's relics, they thought. Together they went to Atalanta's tent, and tried to take the trophies by force. Atalanta defended her prize with the sword, and called on Meleager for help. He ran up and, seeing his beloved attacked, became beside himself with rage. In the scuffle that followed he killed both his uncles.

News of the boar's death had reached Calydon already, and Althaea went to the temple to give thanks. On her way she met two biers.

" Who are the dead? " she asked.

" Your brothers Toxeus and Plexippus," answered an old servant of the princes, " slain by your son Meleager."

At this such grief and wrath seized Althaea that she forgot all else. She hastened home, unlocked the chest where she kept the firebrand, and flung it on the fire. The stick was dry, and burned in a few seconds. As it fell to ashes Meleager, returning to Calydon in triumph, fell dead on his horse's neck.

When Althaea's fury had passed a great terror seized her. She clung to the hope that perhaps after all the firebrand was only ordinary wood. But soon messengers came with the news that Meleager was dead.

Now Althaea knew that she had loved her son above everything in life. In utter despair she slew herself, so that her ghost might seek his and crave its pardon.

THE CHILDREN OF THE SKY

IN the morning of the world an angel was sent on a message to a holy man dwelling in a desert in Persia. But as the angel was flying through the air he saw a beautiful Persian girl sitting by the side of a well and braiding her hair with blue forget-me-nots. He came down and made love to her, and for a while they lived very happily together.

Suddenly the angel remembered that he had not delivered the message with which he had been entrusted. He flew back to Heaven to ask pardon for his forgetfulness, but he found that the gate was closed to him. For a long time he stood by the shut gate weeping, and then the Archangel Gabriel appeared, and said,

" You must people the Earth with the Children of the Sky before you can bring a daughter of the Earth into Heaven."

The angel did not understand what this meant, and asked his beautiful bride if she could explain it.

" Yes," she replied, taking some of the flowers from her hair. " These lovely little blue forget-me-nots, which reflect the exquisite colour of Heaven, are the Children of the Sky."

So the angel and his bride wandered hand in hand over the Earth, and planted forget-me-nots in every country. Then, when their task was ended, the angel took his bride in his arms and carried her up to the gate of Heaven.

DAMON ET PYTHIAS

This is a French translation of the story told in English on page 4365

Denys était un célèbre tyran qui régnait à Syracuse, ville de Sicile. Quiconque avait le malheur de lui déplaire était mis à mort.

La colère du tyran s'abattit un jour sur un jeune homme nommé Pythias, qui s'était plaint de la cruauté de Denys, et qui fut condamné à mort. Il demanda la permission d'aller voir sa femme et ses enfants, mais Denys se moqua de lui, pensant : " Une fois que tu seras hors de ma portée, tu ne reviendras sûrement pas."

Pythias dit qu'il avait un ami qui se porterait garant de son retour, et son ami Damon s'offrit comme otage pour Pythias. Si Pythias ne revenait pas, disait-il, il mourrait à la place de son ami.

Le tyran fut surpris qu'un homme aimât son ami à un tel degré, et il accorda à Pythias six heures pour aller voir sa femme et ses enfants.

Pythias s'attendait à être de retour au bout de quatre heures, mais les quatre heures s'écoulèrent et Pythias ne revenait pas. Cinq heures, presque six passèrent, et toujours aucun signe de lui. L'homme le plus heureux de toute la prison était Damon, qui espérait positivement que Pythias ne reviendrait pas, car il désirait vivement souffrir à sa place, et sauver son ami, par égard pour sa femme et ses enfants. Enfin l'aube du jour fatal parut, l'heure approcha, et Denys vint voir mourir son prisonnier.

Tranquillement, courageusement, Damon se prépara au supplice. Son ami, disait-il, avait eu quelque accident, peut-être était-il malade. Cependant, presque au moment même de l'exécution, Pythias arriva et embrassa son ami.

Il était fatigué, ses vêtements étaient poudreux. Son cheval avait été tué, il lui avait fallu s'en procurer un autre ; mais, en allant grand train, il était arrivé juste à temps pour empêcher Damon de mourir à sa place. Mais Damon ne l'entendait pas ainsi. Il supplia Pythias, il supplia Denys, de lui permettre de subir le supplice au lieu de son ami.

Jamais Denys n'avait été témoin de pareille amitié. C'était quelque chose de grandiose, dont il ne soupçonnait pas l'existence, que cette amitié qui accueillait la mort avec joie, si la mort devait venir en aide à son ami. Son cœur s'émut ; il voulut que de tels hommes devinssent ses amis à lui.

Il s'approcha de Damon et de Pythias, occupés à se disputer, chacun avide de donner sa vie pour l'autre. Denys les prit par la main, les mit en liberté, et les supplia de lui permettre de partager leur amitié.

THE BABY WHO COULD NOT BE LOST

One of the interesting little stories of the First World War is this tale of a baby who could not be lost, a princeling, passed from hand to hand through a series of golden deeds, till he found himself at home once more.

Prince Vladzis Geodric was but a babe in arms when his Galician father, a connection of the then Royal House of Austria, left his home to fight for Austria against Russia.

But the Russian army in its advance swept over Galicia, beyond the castle where the baby was born, and his mother fled with him towards safety, as she hoped. When the flight grew into panic the babe was left behind, and, as he lay wailing in a ditch, was picked up by a kind-hearted Russian officer, and by him handed over to a Russian lady, who adopted the tiny waif and took him to her distant home at Tiflis, in Georgia.

There the little fellow, as well became such a lucky baby, had his photograph taken, and, as photographs will, it found its way into a Russian illustrated paper.

Presently the tide of war changed, and it was the Russians who were falling back and being taken prisoners. One of the prisoners had in his pocket the picture paper with the child's portrait when he was taken before an Austrian officer to be searched. That officer was Prince Cyril Geodric, the father of the little lost Vladzis.

Even in war there are pleasant ways of being friendly when hearts are touched, and the end of this story is happy. Through the Swedish Court the Austrian prince managed to send a message to the Georgian lady who was rearing the lucky lad so kindly, and presently the little boy was on his way home along the war-crowded railways, under the charge of a special courier, and with two attentive nurses to care for him.

All along, it will be seen, hearts were softened by the sight of a little child.

KING ARTHUR'S RIDDLE

ONE Christmastide, when King Arthur's Court was at the height of its glory, a lady came into the banquet hall crying for vengeance.

Kneeling before the King, she told how she and her betrothed were riding over the moor when they came to a great castle by a lake. A tall knight came out, and challenged the new-comer to combat; but the place was enchanted ground, and the lady's sweetheart could not draw his sword. The knight of the castle dragged him from the saddle like a child, and carried him into the castle, a prisoner. When the lady ran to her lover's aid she was knocked down by a buffet on the face.

"Go," cried the churlish knight, "go to Carlisle and ask vengeance from King Arthur. Tell him many of his knights are rotting in my dungeon now, and if he dare venture in the shade of my castle he shall join them."

King Arthur leaped to his feet, and swore he would not taste food or drink again till he had fought this insolent knave.

At dawn next day he set off alone. The poor lady had told him how to find the castle, which stood on the heath by Tarn Wathelan. When King Arthur reached the place there was no sign of life. He drew his sword Excalibur and blew his bugle three times. Then he shouted:

"Come forth and fight, Knight of the Castle! King Arthur has come to punish you for your crimes."

Instantly the door of the castle opened, and the enchantment fell on the King. Excalibur clattered to the ground from his helpless hand, the reins dropped on his horse's neck. The knight of the castle came out, swinging his great club.

"You are my prisoner, King," he said, "but I will give you one chance of ransoming yourself. Swear by the Rood to return in a year's time and tell me *what thing it is that all women most desire*, and I will let you go now."

King Arthur, his head bowed in shame, vowed to return. The knight went in, and strength again returned to the King.

Mournfully he rode away, but not to Carlisle. He gave a shepherd some gold, and bade him take a message to Queen Guinevere to say that he was going on a long journey. Then he rode north and south, east and west, asking every woman he met the knight's riddle.

Nearly every one made a different answer, according to whether they were religious or worldly, proud or loving, covetous or charitable. The King wrote down all the answers, but he did not know which of them was right, and he grew more miserable every day as the seasons sped, and Christmas drew near.

It was a sad man who rode through the snow-clad woods toward the enchanted castle. All at once he saw a patch of crimson through the trees. A woman sat between an oak and a holly. The King drew near to ask his riddle, but when he saw the face of the woman in the red gown his heart turned cold, fearing she was a witch. She had one blear eye, ragged grey hair, a crooked nose, a long mouth which showed stumps of teeth, a nutcracker chin, and withered cheeks.

"All hail, King Arthur!" che cried. "Would you like to know what thing it is that all women most desire?"

The King was quite certain now that she was a witch.

"I will tell you and save your life" said the old hag, "if you promise to find me a brave, courteous, and handsome husband from the knights of your Court."

King Arthur promised, for he was fain to live on in the light of the Sun and to see his wife and home again. The old woman gave him the answer. Then he rode on to the castle by Tarn Wathelan, and sounded his bugle. The knight came out, swinging the keys of his dungeon.

"Well!" he asked, "what is it that all women most desire in the world?"

"Their own way," replied the King.

At this the knight gave a cry of wrath. "You are ransomed," he cried, "but some witch has helped you to find the answer, and she shall burn for it."

King Arthur hastened back to Carlisle, where he was met with great rejoicings. But he would not speak of his absence, and was heavy at heart. At last his nephew Sir Gawain drew him to one side and begged to know the cause of the King's sorrow. When he had heard the story he said: "But why are you mournful, Uncle?"

"Because I cannot keep my promise to the old woman," said the King. "No one would marry her."

"I will if no one else will," said Gawain; "you shall not be dishonoured."

6827

The King thanked him heartily. Next day he called for a hunting party, and led them to the wood near Tarn Wathelan. As uncle and nephew rode through the woods they suddenly heard shouts of laughter from some knights were were on ahead. They hastened up, and found Sir Kaye and a few others jeering at the old woman in the crimson robe sitting between the holly and the oak.

" By my fay," cried Sir Kaye, " here is a pretty wood nymph! Here is a damsel to set all the shepherds' hearts aching! "

" Do not mock this woman," said the King; " she saved my life, and I am pledged to grant her a boon. Which of my knights will redeem my promise and marry her? "

One and all drew back muttering, " She is eighty years old," " She is lame," " She is humpbacked." The old woman began to weep at their scorn and loathing. Then Gawain knelt and asked her to be his bride. She smiled at him with her dreadful mouth, and said, " Noblest of knights, heaven will reward your chivalry."

The company rode back to Carlisle, Gawain bearing the old hag in front of him on his horse.

Guinevere was her lady-in-waiting at the bridal, and Arthur was the groomsman. There was a great feast, and afterwards the bridal pair led the dance. Gawain's grace and courtesy made men sigh as he guided the limping old crone through the stately measure. At length the bridesmaids led her away to rest. Gawain sat mournfully among the revellers, who dared not mock his wife aloud, but whispered many a cruel jest about her behind his back.

Presently Gawain went to his wife's room. She was sitting by the fire. As Gawain entered a log fell, the flame blazed up, and he saw a beautiful young maiden. As he gazed, speechless, she said: " You are silent, husband, at the sight of your own work. My stepmother, who is a witch, cast an enchantment upon me, which by your chivalry is half broken. Henceforth I may be myself, either by day or by night, and an old hag the rest of the time. Choose which it shall be."

Gawain thought at first that he would like her to be beautiful in the daytime, at tournments and hawking parties; afterwards he thought he would like her to be beautiful by torchlight, when the minstrels sang, and kinsmen gathered round the fire. But at last he said: " Choose thyself; thou hast the right, and thou art wiser than I."

At this she clapped her hands and cried: " Now is the enchantment quite broken, and I shall be myself for evermore! "

So King Arthur was ransomed, Sir Gawain won a lovely wife, and the lady had her own way.

HERO AND LEANDER

WHEN Hero was a little golden-haired girl her parents dedicated her to be a priestess in the temple of Venus at Sestus. There she grew up, very lovely, and content with her solemn duties.

But one day she noticed among the worshippers a dark and handsome youth who looked a king among athletes. She learned that his name was Leander, and that he dwelled across the strait, in Abydus. After that Leander often came with offerings for the shrine, and they fell in love. Then, for the first time, Hero understood how her parents had wronged her in childhood. She was bound to her service in the temple. She could not marry. If she were suspected of loving Leander she would suffer a terrible death.

Yet the young lovers could not live without even speaking to each other. At nightfall Leander would swim the Hellespont, while Hero held a torch on the shore to guide him. Every night they would sit in the lee of the rocks, talking of their separate lives. None knew of these secret meetings save one friend of Leander's.

A stormy night came. The sea ran high. No other man would have attempted the crossing, but Hero saw a lantern waved three times on the opposite shore and she knew Leander was coming to her. She lit her torch, and in the hours that followed she had to relight it often, for the tempest grew more and more boisterous. Drenched to the skin and agonised with suspense, she watched the white foam tops of that black sea all through the night. Leander never came.

She tried to think that, finding the sea too rough, he had wisely turned back to Abydus, but soon news was brought that his dead body had been washed up. Then Hero ran to the highest cliff near Sestus and flung herself into the sea.

THE LEGENDS OF CHARLEMAGNE

A great number of legends grew up in the Middle Ages around the mighty figure of Charlemagne, the famous emperor whose fame spread to all parts of the known world about the end of the ninth century. We read of him on page 2521. Here we give a few of these stories which were once so well known.

HOW ROLAND GOT HIS COAT-OF-ARMS

THE most famous of all the paladins, the knightly champions of Charlemagne, was Roland, Shakespeare's Child Roland, who to the dark tower came.

He was the son of a very great knight related to the Emperor, but, having married Charlemagne's sister secretly, the knight was banished from France, and wandered as a beggar, with his wife, until he came to Sutri, in Italy, There the couple were too poor to have a home, so they took refuge in a cave, and it was in this cave that Roland was born.

He was a fine boy, stronger than any of the other boys in the district, and he had many knightly graces; but his parents were so poor that he never had enough clothes and was often hungry.

He was a great favourite with all the boys around, and though he had thrashed Oliver, the son of the governor of the town, in a boyish quarrel, they became close companions, and their friendship lasted through life.

One day four boys, knowing how ill-clad poor Roland was, took pity on him and brought him some cloth. Two brought white cloth and two red, and when Roland became a famous knight, and acquired a coat-of-arms, he remembered the kindness of his boy friends, and had his coat made with quarterings of red and white as a reminder of their kind act.

THE EMPEROR'S DINNER

ROLAND, when a boy, was very distressed when he saw his parents hungry, and one day when his mother had had nothing to eat, he heard that Charlemagne, who was on his way to Rome, was dining in public at Sutri.

He went to the place of banqueting, and there saw a right royal feast, with more food than the party could ever consume.

"Why should not my mother have some of this?" he thought; "she is of royal birth;" and without any further hesitation he rushed upon the party, and, quickly seizing as much food as he could carry, ran off with it to the cave.

Charlemagne ordered three knights to follow the boy, who, when they were about to enter the cave, would have cudgelled them had not his mother restrained him.

The knights, learning who she was, promised to obtain her pardon from the Emperor, and this they speedily did.

Roland was received into favour and returned with Charlemagne to France, where he very soon became the most powerful supporter of the throne and one of the greatest champions of Christendom.

ROLAND DEFEATS THE GIANT

THE giant Ferragus was of enormous strength, with a skin so tough that no sword could penetrate it. That was why the Christian knights feared him, for he used to seize his adversaries and bear them off in his arms; and, no matter how true their steel, they could never manage to wound him.

Roland, for all his skill, could only just keep out of the giant's clutches, and when after long fighting Ferragus grew weary, and offered a truce, it was agreed to.

The giant lay down on the ground and fell asleep, and, of course, no Christian knight would take advantage of him then, for the laws of chivalry were very strict. Roland saw how uncomfortably the giant lay for lack of a pillow, so, taking pity on him, he found a smooth stone and placed it under the sleeper's head.

After a time Ferragus woke up, greatly refreshed by his sleep. Then, seeing what Roland had done for him, he became sociable, though still very boastful, and told how every part of his body was invulnerable except the middle of the breast.

Soon the truce was up, and the fighting was resumed, when Roland, remembering what he had learned, pierced the giant in his vulnerable spot.

Great was the joy of the Christian warriors when they saw that their powerful foe was dead.

A ROLAND FOR AN OLIVER

GUÉRIN DE MONTGLAVE, the lord of Vienne, quarrelled with Charlemagne, and war broke out between them. But as Marsilius, the King of Spain, was advancing to invade France, Charlemagne agreed to decide the quarrel with Guérin by means of single combat between two knights, one being selected by each side.

Guérin was an old man, but when a knight was to be chosen by lot to champion his cause he had his name put with those of his sons and grandsons into a helmet. The name drawn was that of Oliver, and on Charlemagne's side Roland was chosen.

Fully armed, the two men met on an island in the Rhone, and neither knew who the other was. At the first onset both lances were broken, so the warriors dismounted and fought with swords. Never had such a fight been seen. For two hours or more the knights battled fiercely, neither showing any signs of weariness, but at last Roland struck Oliver's shield so furiously that his trusty sword Durindana was buried in it, and could not be withdrawn. At the same moment Oliver thrust with so much vigour at Roland's breastplate that the blade snapped off short at the handle.

Then, weaponless, the two brave men rushed together, and each tore off the other's helmet. Their amazement was great when they recognised one another, and for some moments neither could move. The next moment they ran into one another's arms, Roland crying, " I am conquered," and Oliver at the same moment crying out, " I yield."

The other knights crowded round and acclaimed them equals in bravery and glory, and ever since to give a Roland for an Oliver has meant a contest in which the give and take is equal.

Soon after Charlemagne's quarrel with Guérin was settled, and the Emperor was then at liberty to march against Marsilius.

HOW RINALDO CONQUERED BAYARD

RINALDO, or Renaud, was the cousin of Roland, whose exploits he longed to rival. On the day that his uncle, the Emperor, gave him the honour of knighthood, he vowed that he would never wear a sword till he had wrested one from some famous knight.

But first of all he must have a horse, and he determined that he would conquer the famous steed Bayard, which was formerly owned by Amadis of Gaul, but was now running at large in the Forest of Arden, wild and untamed.

To attack this horse men said meant certain death, but Rinaldo plunged bravely into the forest, where he met and fought a Saracen knight named Isolier. Rinaldo proved the better man, but when they were about to renew the combat a peasant ran forward to say that Bayard was near.

The two knights became friends, and determined to meet the fierce horse together. Bayard came rushing through the forest, and first attacked Isolier, who received him on his lance; but the spear snapped in two. Then the knight drew his sword and struck at the horse. But he did not know that the animal's skin was too tough for the keenest sword to make any impression upon. At last the terrible horse ran at the Saracen knight, who fell to the ground lifeless.

Rinaldo's turn had now come, and for a long time a fierce fight went on between knight and horse, neither gaining any advantage. But by chance Bayard's hoof was caught between the branches of an oak and, seizing his opportunity, Rinaldo sprang forward, put forth all his strength, and hurled the horse to the ground.

Directly Bayard touched the ground his rage subsided, and he became gentle and quiet. Then Rinaldo stroked him, and, putting a saddle upon his back, rode back on him to Charlemagne's Court, where he became a great and famous paladin.

THE WATERS OF OBLIVION

ROLAND, having fallen in love with Angelica, the beautiful daughter of the King of Cathay, whom he had once found sleeping in a field of lilies and roses, went to her father's Court in search of her. Leaving Charlemagne's camp, he travelled long in the direction of the East, making inquiries everywhere, but all in vain.

One day he arrived at a bridge under which flowed a foaming river, and there a maiden met him and offered him a goblet of the sparkling water. She told him it was the custom for all travellers to drink of the waters of the river, and Roland thereupon tossed off the cup. But no sooner had he done so than he became dizzy, and, forgetting the object of his journey, followed the maiden into a magnificent palace, where there were many other knights gathered together.

These, like Roland, had all drunk of the Cup of Oblivion which had been offered them by the maiden at the bridge, and had completely forgotten their quests.

Roland might have remained in the palace for ever had not Angelica found her way thither, and, by means of a magic ring, disenchanted him and the other knights, so that they all regained their memories and continued their journeys.

THE WASPS

This is the story of one of the plays of Aristophanes, the famous dramatist of ancient Greece.

BDELYCLEON was a fashionable youth whose father was a great trial to him. Instead of leading a life of dignified ease, devoted to art and learning, as he should have done, Philocleon spent all day and every day in the law courts.

He was one of the dicasts whose votes, in the shape of shells, were cast either into the death urn or the mercy urn, and decided the defendant's fate.

For their services the dicasts were paid three obols each. They loved their importance, the prayers of relatives who thronged the gates begging for mercy, and the fear they inspired. Most of them were of a vindictive nature, and The Wasps was no bad name for them.

At length Philocleon's love of law suits became a mania. He was shabby in his dress, restless in his sleep, and never at home from one year's end to another. To save him from becoming a laughing-stock his son locked him up, for argument was of no avail whatever. But Philocleon would jump out of windows and climb up chimneys to escape, and then run back immediately to the law courts.

At length Bdelycleon hit upon the idea of turning his house into a court, and making his father judge. Two jars did duty for the urns of death and of mercy. A hurdle did for the judgment bar. Slaves were employed in getting up cases.

The first case Philocleon tried was one of stealing. Labes the mastiff was accused of eating a Sicilian cheese. His puppies were brought into court to move the judge to pity. A plate, a porringer, and a cheese-scraper were called for the defence. Labes's counsel described how faithfully he kept wolves and robbers from the door. He also pleaded youth, saying that Labes did not know the first rules of music, with which Greek education always began. All in vain; Philocleon would have him hanged. But he dropped his cockle-shell into the urn of mercy by mistake.

When the malicious old man discovered what a royal chance he had lost with his solitary supreme vote he fell into such a passion of rage that he was never known to speak of a law suit again.

TRIPTOLEMUS

ONE day the daughters of King Celeus saw an old woman weeping by the roadside. Their father had taught them to have compassionate hearts, so they asked her kindly what ailed her.

" My daughter has been stolen from me! " cried the old woman. " I have wandered far and wide to find her, and I think I shall never see her again."

" You are worn out with travelling," said the princesses. " Come back with us to Eleusis. After you have rested you will be stronger to continue your search. Besides, you may hear tidings of your daughter, for all tidings are sure to come to our father's house."

The old woman was touched by their kindness, and returned with them. Her sad story moved the queen to say. " She shall be my baby's nurse. In caring for him she will forget her own sorrow."

Triptolemus was the name of the little baby, who was a sickly weakling. His fretful wails ceased as soon as the old woman took him in her arms and kissed the little yellow face.

That night the queen lay awake. She began to upbraid herself for letting a stranger have charge of her baby. She rose and stole quietly to the nursery.

There she saw a dreadful thing. The old woman was muttering charms over the baby, who lay on a brazier of burning coals. The queen shrieked and snatched up her child, who was unharmed. When she looked from him to the nurse she saw a stately, golden-haired woman.

" I am a goddess," she said. " My name is Ceres. My daughter Proserpine has been stolen from me, and I seek her in disguise. For your kindness I would have made your son immortal. You have prevented me. But I shall not forget him."

Before the queen had recovered from her astonishment the tall stranger had gone.

Many years passed. Triptolemus grew up. Ceres discovered her daughter in King Pluto's underground kingdom. Then she returned to Eleusis, in her own guise, and said to the young prince: " Nursling, I will make you a blessing to the whole world if you will follow me to the plains."

There she taught him to plough, to sow, and to reap corn. She gave him a great store of the precious grain, and lent him her magic chariot, so that he might travel round the world teaching all people how to grow and use corn.

Imagine the difference this knowledge made to mankind. Instead of living by hunting alone, it was now possible to lay in a store against the winter days when there were no fruits, rivers were frozen, and beasts were curled up for their winter sleep. No wonder that there is a corn legend in every mythology, describing its discovery as a gift from the gods.

Triptolemus was honoured and blessed everywhere; but the King of Scythia was jealous of his renown, and determined to murder him. Accordingly he invited Triptolemus to stay in his palace and tell him more about this wonderful corn.

When everyone was asleep Lyncus, the king, stole toward his guest's room, sword in hand. He knew no slave would consent to strike the benefactor. But suddenly Lyncus dropped the sword and fell on hands and knees. A queer anguish seized him. Fur sprang on his limbs. He was turned into a lynx. Terrified of being killed by his own guards, the traitor king fled into the wilderness. A lynx has typified treachery ever since.

When Triptolemus had travelled all over the world he gave back the chariot, and settled down at Eleusis. He inaugurated festivals there in honour of Ceres, the goddess of harvests, and her daughter Proserpine, the spring.

The Eleusinian festivals became famous, and continued to be celebrated for hundreds of years, long after the age of dim legends had given place to the age of history.

HOW THE TRAIN WAS SAVED

In a wild part of Western Virginia lived a poor old widow in a roughly-made log hut on the edge of a chasm, miles away from any neighbours.

The Baltimore and Ohio Railway had its track close by, and ran across a wooden bridge over the yawning chasm.

One windy day in March the snows were melting on the mountain heights, and the river that flowed through the gorge was filled with an icy flood of melted snow. As the day lengthened the waters grew noisier, and their ceaseless roar made the old woman and her daughter uneasy. They went to bed at last in fear and trembling.

About midnight a crash caused them to start up in terror. Clinging to each other, they crept down to the edge of the gorge, and found the bridge broken to pieces.

No sooner had the old woman realised what had happened than the awful thought came to her that the night mail would be due in half an hour. There was no one, no signal-box, no telegraph, to warn the approaching train of the terrible danger that lay before it.

Was there nothing she could do? There was one thing—a light! The driver would see a light, though shouts would seem no more than a faint whisper in the roar of the raging wind. But where was she to get a light? In the hut she had but half a candle, and if she took that on to the line the rain and wind would put out the light directly. In her poverty she had neither lamp nor lantern.

Searching anxiously round the little hut, her eyes rested on the wooden bedstead and two wooden chairs, dry and old.

With trembling and eager hands the women chopped and cut at the bedstead until it lay on the floor in pieces; then, carrying these in their arms, they climbed on to the line, and piled up the wood in the middle of the track.

Shielding a match from the wind, the old woman struck it and put it to the pile of furniture. To her joy, this caught light; just in time, for as it began to blaze up the rumble of the train could be heard.

How eagerly mother and daughter watched that burning pile, hoping and praying that the engine-driver would see it in time to stop the train! The mother took off the red skirt she wore, tied it to a stick, and hurried up the line, waving it about in the light from the fire, while the daughter flourished a burning post.

Nearer and nearer came the roar of the train; it was rounding the curve; they could see the light in front of the engine. Then gradually the train slowed down, and came to a stop close to the blazing pile.

The driver's keen eyes, accustomed to see far ahead, discovered the dangerous chasm and the empty space where there should have been a bridge; and as his eyes travelled to the burning furniture and the figures of the old woman and her daughter he recognised the act of courageous self-sacrifice that had come from a brave heart.

BELLEROPHON AND THE WINGED HORSE

BELLEROPHON came to the Court of King Iobates of Lycia with a letter from the king's kinsman Proetus. The youth thought that it was a letter of recommendation, but Proetus was jealous of Bellerophon, and had written asking Iobates to have him killed for a crime which, in truth, he had never committed.

Iobates looked up from the letter at the stranger's frank face and fearless bearing. The king thought: " He does not look a scoundrel. If he must die it shall not be by the rope or the assassin's dagger. He shall die in open fight."

He made Bellerophon welcome as though the letter had indeed been one of friendly praise from Proetus. But that night he began to talk of courage.

" There are no heroes today," said the king; " all men are cowards, in spite of their fine armour and strutting airs."

Bellerophon flushed, and said, " My lord, I am no hero, but no one has the right to call me a coward."

" But you would not fight the Chimera, for all your brave words," said the king.

" I will fight him, whoever he may be," cried the youth.

" You have promised," said Iobates, " but you will break your promise when I tell you that the Chimera is a horrible monster who lives on a burning mountain, and has killed every warrior I have sent to destroy him."

" I will go to his lair tomorrow, even if there should be twenty of the brood ! " declared Bellerophon.

Iobates knew that Bellerophon would be killed, and that Proetus would have his desire; but the king was sorry, for Bellerophon seemed to him a modest, brave man, such as he would have had for a son.

Next day Bellerophon set off with a little store of provisions and his armour. He had a short journey to make before he reached the burning mountain. As he went along he thought of the stories that he had been told about the Chimera. It seemed an invincible monster, but Bellerophon would rather have perished than have let Iobates mock at his courage.

At length he came to a place where he could see the burning mountain sending up rosy smoke above the trees which clothed its sides. He put on his armour, and bent to drink at a brook, perhaps for the last time. When he lifted his eyes he saw a tall and glorious woman standing on the opposite bank, holding a great winged horse by the bridle. From her helmet and spear he knew she was the goddess Minerva.

" Brave youth," she said, " you shall not perish in an unequal contest. The gods lend you this horse, whose name is Pegasus. He will bear you to victory."

She put the reins into Bellerophon's hands, and vanished. He leaped on to his winged steed, who sailed into the air, and bore him to the Chimera's cave.

This monster had the fore-parts of a gigantic lion, and ended like a scaly dragon. Its swift pounces, terrible talons, and fiery breath would soon have destroyed Bellerophon if Pegasus had not wheeled and darted just out of the creature's reach, returning to let his master thrust his sword at its tough hide. After a struggle it was slain. Bellerophon urged Pegasus into the air, and flew to Lycia.

Everyone ran out to behold the winged horse flying over the house-tops, and when Iobates saw who rode it he cried : " Bellerophon was innocent. Proetus lied. The gods have aided him."

Bellerophon dismounted at the palace steps, but he kept a firm hold of the reins. After he had told Iobates that the Chimera was dead, he took Pegasus to the stables and tied up the horse.

There was a feast at the palace that night, and Iobates bade his courtiers drink to Bellerophon, the betrothed of the Princess, and heir to the crown of Lycia.

The youth ought to have been contented with such wonderful fortune, but Bellerophon dreamed of a greater achievement. Mounted on Pegasus he would fly to heaven and see the gods face to face.

One day he led the steed from its stall, mounted, and turned its head skyward.

But the gods were displeased with Bellerophon for having kept Pegasus after the Chimera was slain, and for dreaming of invading the sky. They sent a fly to sting Pegasus. He plunged violently at the pain, and flung his rider.

Bellerophon was not killed by the fall, but stunned. When he recovered consciousness he found he was in a dreary country which was almost a desert. There, among savages, he spent the rest of his life, unable to return to Lycia.

When heaven lends us wings (poetry, music, painting, and sculpture are gifts like that) we must use them reverently.

MY LORD BAG-OF-RICE

HIDESATO, a Japanese hero, as brave as any knight of King Arthur's Court, was one day wandering about in search of adventure when he came to a lovely lake at the foot of a mountain.

It was crossed by a bridge, but on that bridge a hideous dragon lay asleep. Hidesato feared nothing, so he clambered over the dragon's scaly coils, and was going on when he heard a voice calling: " My lord! My lord! "

Hidesato looked round. The dragon had vanished from the bridge, and in its place there stood a handsomely-dressed man with red hair, who wore a flashing crown.

" I have just proved that you are a brave man," said he, " now I beseech you to help me against my enemy."

" If your enemy be an evil person I will fight him," said Hidesato, " for that is the duty of a knight. But who are you? "

" I am the King of the Lake," said the stranger. " My enemy is a monstrous centipede, half a mile long, and as thick as the biggest tree in the world. His skin is as tough as steel. Every night he comes down into the lake and carries off one of my people. Yesterday he took away my favourite child."

" If he does not slay me I will slay him," said Hidesato.

The King of the Lake thanked him joyfully, and bade him come to the palace beneath the water. Hidesato followed his host boldly. He found a beautiful flowery country under the lake. The palace was of crystal, furnished with gold and ebony. While they feasted, ten goldfish played the lute and ten carp danced to amuse the guests. But all at once the merriment was interrupted by a rumbling like thunder. Everyone except Hidesato grew silent and trembled. With white lips the King of the Lake whispered: " My enemy is coming! "

" Take me to the bridge," said Hidesato.

As soon as they reached the surface he saw a dreadful sight. Down the mountain came the monster, lighting up the whole scene with its fiery eyes.

Hidesato had three arrows. He drew his bow. The first arrow struck the centipede's head and glanced off. The same thing happened with the second. Then he remembered that his grandmother had told him human saliva was as deadly to dragons as a snake's venom is to mortals. Hidesato moistened the tip of the last arrow in his mouth, and drew the bow again. It pierced the monster's brain. Over and over it rolled, down into the lake, which was churned into a storm as the creature thrashed about in its death agony.

No words can describe the joy and gratitude of the Lake people. They drew Hidesato down to their palace, and begged him to stay for ever; but he vowed that a knight must not sit feasting while the world is full of wrongs that need righting.

When they saw he would not stay they let him go, but sent a retinue of servants to escort him to the nearest town. They were goldfish till they rose to the surface of the lake. When Hidesato reached the town they laid three parcels before him, bowed, and vanished.

In the first parcel was a roll of silk which never grew less, however much was cut off. In the second there was a cooking pot which boiled without fire. In the third there was a bag of rice which could not be emptied. Hidesato was thus enabled to clothe the naked and feed the hungry wherever he went.

Because of the magical bag the poor folks called him " My Lord Bag-of-Rice."

THE MAN IN THE ENGINE-ROOM

ONE of our poets began his first book of verse by saying that he would write of the great deeds of nameless men:

Not the be-medalled commander, beloved of the throne,
But the lads who carried the koppie and cannot be known.

Of such is an unnamed chief petty officer of the light cruiser Calliope. The warship had left behind the lights of the Cornish coast on her way to the Azores when, in the black midnight, a pipe burst in the engine-room and escaping oil set the ship ablaze. The danger of the boiler and magazines exploding was extreme.

But the Calliope has a name honoured in the history of the Navy, and well was it sustained by the chief petty officer on that day. Alone he went down into the engine-room and turned on a steam-pipe that averted the danger; and presently the Calliope, flooded and crippled, crept back to Plymouth, the fire extinguished, and a new laurel in her crown of fame.

THE STOLEN BELL

BENKEI was not only the strongest man in Japan but, except for Hercules, the strongest in the whole world.

He was at first a monk, though he was not much suited for a religious life. Indeed, he used to go to a narrow gorge, put on black armour, and challenge all comers to fight. He kept the swords of those he vanquished, and had nearly a thousand when one day the hero Yoshitsune came and defeated him.

After that Benkei became the hero's faithful squire, and followed him round the land doing knightly deeds. But let us go back to Benkei's early days, when he was a young monk.

Not far away stood the temple of Miidera, which possessed a very fine and large bronze bell. One night Benkei set off over hill and dale to Miidera, broke into the belfry unobserved, and lifted down the bell. He next took down the crossbeam, hung the huge bell on one end and his paper lantern on the other, and marched back to his own monastery.

When he had hung up the bell he woke his fellow monks, and proudly showed them the new possession. They were delighted. One of them pulled the bell-rope and the bell moaned:

" I want to go back to Miidera ! "

Benkei's jaw dropped. However, the other monks were as dishonest as he was, and even when they knew the bell was stolen they determined to keep it.

" Soon it will get used to its new home," they said hopefully.

They used to praise it loudly, and only pull the rope gently; but it always sobbed out: " I want to go back to Miidera ! "

At last Benkei lost patience. He seized a bar of iron and dealt the bell a huge blow, meaning to shatter it. The bell only roared out, so that it could be heard for miles: "I want to go back to Miidera!"

Then Benkei unhooked the bell and carried it to the door of the monastery, which stood on a hill. There Benkei gave it a tremendous kick. Off it bounded, chattering and ringing, bounding up hill and rolling down dale, till at last it reached the temple gates of Miidera.

There it was warmly welcomed, and hung in its own belfry, where it never spoke anything but bell-language for the rest of its days.

ECHO AND NARCISSUS

EARTH and Air once had a daughter who was called Echo.

She was a beautiful, gay, talkative nymph, and was one of Juno's hand-maidens in the skyey palace of the gods. Soon, however, Juno found that her pretty favourite was such a gosssip that she babbled out the most important and secret matters. Jupiter was angry and sent her away to live on Earth. Lest her tongue should do harm there, as it had done in the Cloud Court, he decreed that she should only be able to repeat what others said.

At first Echo was happy enough in the lovely woods of Greece. She found beings like herself there, tree-spirits called Dryads, and the great Pan, with shaggy legs and cloven hoofs, but a sweet voice and music-making hands. He was the lord of all wild birds and beasts. He cared for straying lambs or kids. He blessed the poor man's garden and byre.

This wood god loved Echo, but she turned from his ugliness in scorn. His sad piping, as he sat apart from the dancing rout, could not touch her heart. She was gay, though her tongue was tied.

One day, however, Echo was stricken by the same sorrow as Pan. She heard a horn in the woods, and peeped through the bushes. A young huntsman called Narcissus was calling his dogs. He was as beautiful as a girl, though he did not know it, for he had never seen a mirror.

Echo fell in love with him. She came out of the bushes, but she could not speak, except to echo his words, and he would not speak to her. He turned from the stranger to seek his dog. She followed, through bog and thicket. The huntsman grew angry, and said: " What do you want ? "

Echo repeated his words.

" I have no money, beggar-woman. Do not follow me," cried Narcissus.

Echo, who longed to ask to be a servant in his house, could only say, " Do not follow me ! "

" You are mad. Go away ! "

" Go away ! " echoed the nymph.

At last the bewildered huntsman grew so harsh and threatening that she fled away into a cavern, where she mourned till nothing was left of her but a voice.

Venus was sorry for the nymph, and determined to avenge her.

One hot summer day Narcissus was led by a flying hart to the very cavern where Echo had died. It had been a long chase, and when the huntsman had slain his quarry he was glad to notice a still pool of water near by. As he bent to drink he saw a lovely face in the pool. He did not know it was his own reflection, but thought he had seen a water-nymph. Straightway he loved her, and tried to drag her from the depths. But she disappeared at once in the troubled water.

Narcissus withdrew, hoping that when all was still she might conquer her fear and leave the pool. After a time he tip-toed back. The image smiled up at him. He began to woo her gently.

"Timid spirit," he said, "do not fear me. I love you!"

A faint voice echoed "I love you!"

"Then leave your pool, and be my wife," said the huntsman. "My father has flocks and herds and a fine house. You should have soft apparel and gold ornaments. You should have all you desire. I will love no other."

"I will love no other!" sighed Echo.

"Then come!" coaxed Narcissus.

"Come!" mocked Echo.

But when Narcissus again tried to seize the lovely face, once more it disappeared.

By sunlight and moonlight he watched and pleaded, while the image smiled and answered his love vows. Yet she would not come to him.

Narcissus thought she was imprisoned by some enchantment, and at length, worn out by fasting and despair, he died.

When Venus saw his body she turned him into the flower we call Narcissus. Every spring it stands by the pool, gazing at its own reflection till it pines to death. But next year it will rise to love and sorrow all over again. Echo haunts the cave to this day.

SISTER DORA AND THE TOILERS OF WALSALL

In the little village of Hauxwell, in Yorkshire, was born in 1832 a girl named Dorothy Pattison, who in later life, when working as a nurse in Walsall, became known as Sister Dora.

She was a bonnie, merry girl who much liked to get her own way, and, growing restless in the little country village where her home was, longed to go with Florence Nightingale to the Crimea.

She was not then trained for nursing, and her father would not consent to her going, so she stayed at home and taught the village children. But she soon found her life-work in nursing and caring for sick people. She seemed to bear a charmed life, to have strength more than human, and her courage, self-sacrifice, and devotion to all who needed her help made her life one long golden deed.

In 1864 Sister Dora joined the Sisterhood of the Good Samaritan at Coatham, in Yorkshire, and the experience she thus gained in nursing poor people and taking interest in their needs was very helpful to her in her future hospital work.

Where pain and misery were, there was Sister Dora to help and cheer. When a worker in a coal-mine met with an accident, and the surgeon at her hospital wanted to cut off his right arm, it was Sister Dora who pleaded to be allowed to try to save it. She did save it, too, and the grateful man used afterwards to walk eleven miles every Sunday to ring the hospital bell with that arm, and inquire about Sister Dora when she was lying ill herself.

When smallpox broke out in the town, Sister Dora spent her hours of rest in nursing in their own homes those who had none to care for them. For six months she battled with disease and death almost single-handed, herself putting sufferers into the ambulances and taking them away to be nursed, struggling with delirious patients and mothering tenderly every sick child.

And with all her ceaseless work and untiring energy she was so strong, merry, and full of fun, that she *made* her patients want to get well; as one of them said, "She'd make you laugh if you were dying." No one could be gloomy or hopeless when looking on her face.

But when only 56 Sister Dora died, all her strength spent for others : yet, true to her noble nature, she worked to the end, keeping her own suffering hidden from those around, and passing from one bed to another with her soothing touch, her cheery word, and her loving smile.

Nature's Wonderful Living Family in Earth and Air and Sea

Earthworms and their casts

THE WONDERFUL WORK OF A WORM

WE are all on the side of Cowper and Darwin now; of Cowper the worm's poet-friend, of Darwin the worm's historian.

Says our gentle poet:

I would not enter on my list of friends
(Though graced with polished manners and
    fine sense,
Yet wanting sensibility) the man
Who needlessly sets foot upon a worm.

That gives the worm a title to respectability in poetry where, throughout the ages, he has been a much abused, much misunderstood little fellow. To Darwin, and to the followers he inspired, the worm owes its vindication as the first of husbandmen, who ploughed before Adam, and long before man tilled the soil prepared it for his coming.

What an unmerited reputation for evil the worm has had to live down ! If any creature were evil, men called it a worm, and posterity asked for no further evidence of its villainy.

Forty times and more Shakespeare slanders this poor tenant of the earth, as the worker of mischief, or as the symbol of misdoing and fatal melancholy. Vile worm, poor worm, viperous worm, gnawing worm, eyeless venomed worm, worm of the Nile (which means a snake), there is no goodness in the worm, the worm is not to be trusted—so runs the master's pen.

Shakespeare was clear-eyed and accurate in all things he observed at first hand, but he took the worm's character at second hand, and lo, it was very bad. The standard books on natural history available to him asserted that worms " be full evil and malicious; some be footless, and some have six feet and be enemies to mankind."

Yet out of the very wickedness of worms men were to distil anti-toxins against " shrinking of sinews and biting of serpents and scorpions." Also, if the armourer stamped upon worms, strained them through cloth, then added an equal quantity of oil of radish-roots, and used the mixture in the making of swords or daggers, " the same shall cut through iron after, as though it were lead."

The Church was equally emphatic about worms. There still survives the charge, drawn up by the martyr Trypho of Lampsacus, wherein, addressing worms and various insects he says:

O ye worms, and all other creatures that cling to and wither the fruit of the grape and all other herbs, I charge you by the many-eyed Cherubim and by the six-winged Seraphim, which fly round the Throne, and by the holy Angel and all the Powers, hurt not the vines, nor the land, nor the fruit trees, nor the vegetables of——————, the servant of the Lord, but

depart into the wild mountains, into the unfruit-
ful woods, in which God hath given you your
daily food.

Truly the harmless, necessary worm
needed a Cowper and deserved a Darwin,
the one to bespeak its life, the other to
trumpet forth its manifold virtues.

" If I but *see* a worm, I have no appetite
for the next three days," said a lady once,
not realising that but for worms there
would be little food to satisfy her appetite.
How does this boneless, limbless creature
discharge its great service to the Earth, to
vegetation, and so to all animals and to
ourselves who depend on them? It is a
living mill, grinding up soil day and night,
reducing the mountains of other eras, with
the verdure and carrion of yesterday, to
the fine compost from which all plant life
springs and grows.

THE ASTONISHING DIGESTIVE SYSTEM
OF A WORM IN THE EARTH

Its body is segmented, ringed throughout, and through the interior of that long
body runs the astonishing digestive system.
The thin, pointed end of the worm is the
head, bearing the mouth, which has neither
jaws nor teeth, but a lip for grasping. A
muscular sac, called the pharynx, leading
to the gullet, or food-canal, is responsible
for suction to aid in taking in food. The
matter eaten, as it passes down the gullet,
comes in contact with glands, not found in
any other animal, which secrete a large
quantity of carbonate of lime and aid in
the breaking-down process by which the
food is reduced to digestibility.

From the crop to the gizzard the meal
progresses, and, arrived in this powerful
mill, it undergoes a grinding similar to that
to which the food of a bird is subject. In
the gizzard, as we should expect, are
numerous small stones, varying between
one-twentieth and one-tenth of an inch in
diameter. Many small stones must be
swallowed with the earthy material
absorbed in the ordinary act of feeding,
but a battery of stones is maintained here
for the purpose of grinding; they are, in
fact, the millstones of the miller of the soil.

Having been revolved and ground in the
gizzard, the food passes on into the long
food canal beyond. This organ is richly
supplied with mechanism for the absorption of nutriment. When all goodness
which can be extracted has been obtained,
the residue passes on and is expelled from
the worm's body, and issues from the

opening of its burrow in what we all
know as wormcasts. These casts, if lightly
swept over the dry lawn, form the best
dressing the turf can have.

The worm has no eyes, but it has quick-
acting sense-organs. It can detect the
difference between light and dark. It never
shows itself in bright daylight unless it is
frightened from its hole, or unless it is sick
and ailing, or threatened by the flooding
of its dwelling.

HOW THE WORM PREPARES FOR
ITS FUTURE GENERATIONS

With no nose, it can smell; with no
ears, it can detect vibrations. It breathes
through its skin; it feels heat and cold, it
is keenly sensitive to contact; it displays
a decided sense of taste in the selection of
its food, showing preferences for various
types of vegetation over other kinds,
choosing the fat of flesh before the lean,
and liking fresh meat better than foul,
though not disdaining to eat the bodies
of its dead kind when they are left to
cumber the ground about its burrow and
so to threaten corruption and danger.

The thickened ring of lighter colour
than the rest of the body near the head is
not, as may be supposed, the scar of an
injury; it marks the presence of a gland
from which is poured out the fluid com-
posing the cocoon in which the eggs of
the worm are laid. For even the lowly
worm has, implanted within it, the sense of
duty to its posterity.

Eggs so laid produce little worms resembling their parents in all but size;
there is none of the wonderful changes of
form such as mark the career of the
insects. It is not true that if a worm be
cut in halves and we apply the head to
the tail the two parts will unite, though
this belief is widespread. It is true,
however, that if a worm is halved, the tail
portion will produce a new head, the
head portion a new tail, and so two worms
will appear where one lived before.

THE REMARKABLE BODY OF A WORM
AND ITS POWER OF BURROWING

It is the nature of a worm to writhe
and wriggle in order to escape, but seeing
that a mere touch or even a puff of air is
terrifying to them, we should give them
the benefit of the doubt, respect their
possible pains, and remember the words
of Cowper. So much, then, for the worm
itself; let us proceed from this point to
the work which made Darwin declare the

worm to be the most important animal in all the world.

The powerful cylindrical body of the worm is ideally fitted for burrowing. Its muscles endow it with thrust, and bristly appendages springing from the segments, like microscopic claws, increase its power excavated while burrowing through the soil. The ordinary burrow runs a foot to a foot and a half in depth, though to escape frost or flood the worm goes far deeper, and exceptional burrows for normal life have been found between five and six feet in depth. In many directions it

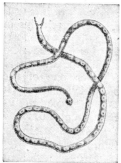
Polygordius, a segmented worm

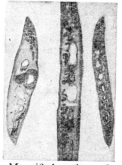
Magnified sections of Liver flukes

Tomopteris Marine Worm

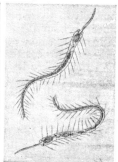
The beaked Nais

A Bristleworm and its eggs

The Sea-Mouse, a marine worm common round the coasts of Britain

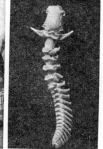
Chaetopterus, a marine phosphorescent worm

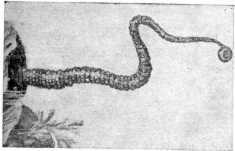
The Rock Leech

Myrianida, a sea worm

RELATIONS OF OUR FRIEND THE COMMON EARTHWORM

of locomotion. But the worm does not butt its way through the soil. It eats as it goes, and the head, obstructed by a stone, finds a way round; and there are few obstacles too difficult for its passage.

By absorbing the soil, the worm has a less difficult task than many animals whose ways we have followed, which have to throw out the matter which they have tunnels, but, let us remember, it cannot do this without eating the soil. The soil itself is heavily charged with vegetable and mineral débris, and it is this which the worm extracts during the complicated process of digestion.

Doubtless there are properties in the soil which this little wonder of the underworld finds of value to it, notably for the production of the carbonate of lime with which the acid of its food is attacked. The lug worm, which teems below high tide mark on our sandy coasts, eats sand in order to obtain organic remains washed down into it, and so helps materially to keep our beaches sweet and clean when the tide is out. The earthworm must sweeten our soil in the same manner, but that is not its primary value to us.

No matter how deep the worm goes, the process is always the same—the soil must be eaten before it can be cast out of the burrow. So the medium in which it works is continually being brought up to the surface, exposed to the air, freshened, fertilised by the absorption of atmospheric gases, and receiving new deposits of organic matter to enhance its fertility.

Now, as the earth which has been eaten is expelled from the end of the worm's body, and the wormcast is always brought to the surface, how can the worm manage to turn round in its almost straight cylindrical shaft? Turn it must, for we know that the normal attitude of the animal is head uppermost. We have but to go out on to the lawn with a lantern on a warm, dark evening to see the grass covered with worms, like an intricate lacework of life.

THE SWIFT RETREAT OF THE WORMS ON THE APPROACH OF DANGER

Rarely, however, do we find a worm free of its burrow. The tail end remains within the shaft, and a flash of direct light or the vibration caused by a footstep sends the worms down into their holes with amazing swiftness. Their retreat is like that of the startlingly sudden withdrawal of a tortoise's head into its shell.

Worms do roam about the surface; their tracks can be followed in many directions, but they are mostly found in the position indicated—heads out, tails at home. How, then, do they perform this marvellous somersault which enables them to bring the soil to the surface—how do they turn upside down in their tube?

The probability is that at the lower end of their perpendicular or obliquely descending shafts they nearly always have a more open chamber in the earth in which to perform this mystifying evolution. Such chambers have repeatedly been found, lined with stones of minute size, with seeds and other smooth substances. They have been regarded as the retreats

of the worm from great cold and equally deadly drought, but they must, one would think, serve this other necessary purpose of affording room to turn.

Whatever the method, the turn is performed, and out into the open comes the eaten soil, as fine as these living grinding mills can make it, the ideal potting mould. Not quite all of it is thus thrown out, however; a little remains in the shafts. The worm is a comfort-loving creature. Like the princess who wept with discomfort because there was a crumpled roseleaf under one of the many feather beds on which she lay, it must have ease and elegance in its lodging. It cannot bear a rough surface to its tunnel-lining.

THE LITTLE UNDERGROUND TUNNEL WITH ITS LINING OF CEMENT

To avoid this it lines the burrow with a cement of fluid mud, adding here and there smooth particles of stone and glass or whatever may be found on the surface, with particles of leaves and other vegetation, and smoothing all with a connecting clothing of moistened soil. As this hardens it becomes quite polished by the movement of the worm up and down, and so facilitates that swift withdrawal into the hole which we have noted.

In addition to eating earth and its contents, the worm banquets on dead leaves, fallen blossoms, seeds, and other vegetable substances lying near the mouth of its burrow. With instinctive genius it draws the leaves down its hole in such a manner that the small end always goes first, so taking the line of least resistance.

Many of these leaves and other substances it eats; many, or parts of many, it leaves to decay and form new material for the regeneration of the soil.

THE LOWLY WORM AND THE SPLENDID WORK IT HAS DONE FOR MAN

There we have two valuable processes, the bringing-up of old soil to the surface, and the addition of leaves and other substances to the soil. In addition to this, the worm is constantly opening out channels in the earth which allow air and moisture to enter, preventing it from caking and becoming non-porous.

Moisture is received in these little canals; it penetrates through their walls and so affords a wide distribution of the dampness indispensable to plant life. All these perforations and dampings of the soil open up ways for the germination of seeds, for the spread of the tender root-hairs of plants which, in hard, unbroken soil, would with difficulty make their way about to find nourishment for the growth of which they are feeders.

Up above, the wormcasts are blown by the wind or in other ways broken down, and so are carried through cracks and little channels down into the soil again as rain falls and makes its way into the earth. The worm's quest for food and homes has the effect of mixing soil and vegetation and animal remains into an ever-increasing mass of vegetable mould which is the seed-bed of the richest plant life.

It is computed that there are about fifty thousand worms to an acre of land, and that they raise from 14 to 18 tons of soil to the surface every year, adding an inch a year in this way to the depth of the vegetable mould.

In climates like that of Britain they burrow deep to escape frost and drought, as we have seen, and such contingencies must send fifty thousand worms an acre burrowing down three, four, and five feet deep, three or four times a year, each descent being achieved only by eating and bringing up the soil excavated.

THE RICH BLACK SOIL WHICH PRODUCES THE WORLD'S BEST WHEAT

The consequence is that air and moisture reach down far deeper than plough or spade, and wherever air and moisture go, the soil is enriched and fertilised. How many worms must have worked for ages to give Manitoba her matchless land of rich black mould which produces such magnificent wheat! No other agency but worms can have done it, and Manitoba should give its worms a monument.

We see how the worms plough and till the fields for us, preparing the way for human cultivation. They have given us all the agricultural land we have, and all the land which lies awaiting cultivation.

For it is not only in temperate Britain and America that worms are at work. They are scattered all over the world. Some of the earthworms of tropical countries are quite alarming in their dimensions, five feet long and of prodigious girth. If our little worker worms bring up their 20 ounces of soil per annum, how much more will these giants pass through their bodies for the ultimate benefit of agriculture, or even of natural wild growth?

We have concrete examples of the husbandry of worms before our eyes in England and on the Continent. Where the Wash has receded in three English counties, the worms have re-colonised. They are bringing back every yard of that land into cultivation where, but for them it must have remained sour and unproductive for an age. During the First World War certain parts of Belgium were so long flooded and other parts so ravaged that many doubted if these parts would be of service again for the purpose of agriculture within our own lifetimes.

HOW THE WORMS HAVE RECLAIMED THE WAR-RAVAGED LAND

But great areas of the land have again yielded crops, thanks to the work of the worms which returned to their old haunts, burrowed and tunnelled, sweetened and fertilised, and prepared the way once more for the arts of scornful man.

Worms have made the soil of the world. They eat the fallen vegetation. They eat mineral fragments and reduce it to powder. They pass through their bodies the tiny mineral débris which once formed part of mountains, and add these to the soil. They tunnel and let in acid and moisture which erode the rocks lying beneath the covering of soil, and so cause these to become friable and slowly resolve into soil.

Vast tracts of land have been left derelict in the United States where careless farmers took out of the land more than they put in; they reaped and harvested, without manuring the land, till it became sterile. Then they moved on to fresh land. The worms will have to restore that exhausted soil, and they will, in time.

THE LITTLE ALLIES THAT GUIDE THE AFRICAN NATIVES TO PASTURES NEW

Meanwhile they are at their good work in advance of civilisation, and are not unrecognised where conditions of savagery prevail. It has been noted that in certain districts of Africa the natives look for wormcasts as the Red Indians used to look for the trail of men and animals. Where wormcasts are plentiful, these skilled sons of the wilds settle for brief cultivation, knowing that they will secure a harvest for their labours. Where wormcasts are few, they do not attempt to grow crops, realising that their efforts would be useless.

There is another important part played by worms of which no mention has yet been made. If they make ready the land for the coming of civilisation, they are the great undertakers where civilisation has passed. They are the preservers of the sites of ancient buildings.

They gradually bury with their casts the buildings of old time, whose upper walls have fallen or been destroyed. Darwin, who gave over thirty years to the study of earthworms before writing his delightful book on them, has recorded how a field which in his boyhood was covered with stones gradually lost all trace of these stones, so that the field became a soft grassy place, and its stones a memory.

THE CHANGING FACE OF THE LAND THROUGHOUT THE CENTURIES

What worms can do in a generation with a stony field, they can do in the course of centuries with buildings, perhaps with cities. Beneath the deep foundations of great pillars and columns they may not be able to penetrate, but beneath the floors, where cement and concrete decay and crack, they can work. And it is there that they dwell, devouring the soil, and casting it up between the cracks so that, in course of time, the dried and scattered casts cover the floors, rise and cover the broken remains of walls, and bury all feet deep in soil, safe yet secret.

The very site and existence of such buildings passes from human knowledge. The plough does not go very deep, and harvests ripen over the site where beauty, wealth, and power once reigned. Accident at last takes pick and shovel deeper than the plough, and there comes to light a fragment of wall, a stretch of an old tessellated pavement, and there, when careful search is made, is some fine old Roman villa, whose sides and upper parts are gone, its floors and foundations preserved by the labours of generation after generation of worms.

SOME HARMFUL COUSINS OF OUR LOWLY FRIEND

But the earthworm is not the sole representative of its great class. There are worms in the sea, worms in still waters, worms on the shore, worms with almost unbelievable life-histories which live as parasites on animals and human beings. There are worms which, called flukes, arise from eggs in water, creep as larvae into snails, and pass from these to vegetation eaten by sheep, in which the larvae complete their course.

These creatures sometimes become a plague among sheep, and periodically cause enormous losses among our flocks. Other forms infest the minnows, frogs, and birds. They are not harmful to adult birds, in whose crops they are killed, but if they are transferred unhurt by the old birds to baby birds they develop in the nestlings and kill them.

The tiny worms which develop under the skin of human beings in hot countries; worms which penetrate human muscles and cause the disease known as trichinosis; the extraordinary U-shaped worms, formidable with bristles; all the leeches which suck human and animal blood—these are members of the great group to which the earthworm belongs.

The earthworm is perhaps the least picturesque of them all, yet it is our only friend among them. We can all watch these for ourselves, for they thrive well in a bucket of good garden soil. They can be observed at night by the aid of a shaded light, where we may see them collecting little stones, feathers, and leaves with which to bar the entrance to their burrows. Not all the things they collect are taken below and devoured. They line their shafts with leaves, they make barriers to their front doors. Behind the barrier they lie with the head near the entrance, a habit which so often makes them prey to thrushes, blackbirds, and starlings, for the head is easily reached and the body pulled out.

THE WORK OF THE MASTER GARDENER OF THE EARTH

This fatal position which they assume in the burrow is supposed to arise from a desire to be near the open air, perhaps to snuggle up to the warmth which, in such a position, exceeds that of the damp earth below. When we see dozens of birds foraging on the lawn, tearing up worm after worm, we wonder how the stock of worms can be maintained, but it is constant. The numbers born equal the numbers eaten, and so the world goes on.

The heavy soil overlying the clay which is the foundation of the lawn is gradually worked over and over, the drainage is improved, sour soil sweetens, the advance of moss is checked, the rich green grass grows stronger, and we have turf soft, thick, and velvety, and a joy to tread.

It is the worm, our master gardener, who does the work. Out of sight and out of mind, he makes soil fruitful, fine, and rich for the whole of our habitable Earth.

The Story of the Things We See About Us Every Day

Cleaning one of the clock faces of Big Ben and replacing one of the giant bell's rubber buffers

THE STORY OF THE CLOCK

ALFRED THE GREAT, one of the noblest kings who ever ruled over England, never saw a clock. He used to allow himself eight hours for work, eight hours for pleasure, and eight hours for sleep. In order to divide the time like this he had candles made which took a certain time to burn away, and so told him how the hours were passing.

Even that was better than many men were able to do. They knew how long a year was, because it takes the Earth a year to go round the Sun. They knew how long a month was, because it takes a month for the Moon to go round the Earth. They knew how long the day and the night were, because it takes just a day and a night, all but a few odd minutes, for the Earth to turn round once. But all sorts of things had to be invented before clocks were made to tell how an hour passed, and some of these ways of telling time are shown on page 2297.

But there is nothing so simple and so good as a clock, which tells us the time at a glance as soon as we have learned to understand it.

There are many different sorts of clocks. Some will go for years, once they have been wound up. Others will go for eight days; others need winding every day. Electric clocks need no winding at all; once they are connected to the electric mains they work on without gaining or losing time. In all clocks, however, wheels have to be made to go round so regularly that it will always take them a certain time to do their work. When you wind up what is called a grandfather's clock you wind strings on to a sort of barrel. At the end of the strings heavy weights are fixed. These weights hang down and are always pulling. The pulling makes the wheels go round, as the pulling of a horse makes the cart go. The wheels have cogs, or teeth, which fit into the cogs of other wheels, and all have to go round at the same time, though not all as fast as one another. Some wheels have a lot of teeth, others have not so many. So while one wheel turns round in sixty seconds, or one minute, another wheel takes sixty minutes, or one hour in which to turn round. All this turning is to make the hands move round and round the face.

There are many parts always at work. There is the pendulum swinging, and there is the part which prevents the clock from doing its work too quickly or too slowly. If the clock goes too quickly, or gains time, as we say, we unwind a little screw at the bottom of the pendulum. This lets the weight at the end of the pendulum

INDUSTRIES · HOW THINGS ARE MADE · WHERE THEY COME FROM

slip down a little, and causes the pendulum to swing more slowly. If the clock loses time we wind the screw up a little. This makes the pendulum shorter, and causes it to swing a little faster. Some clocks have no pendulum. They work with a spring. Then, instead of altering the pendulum, we have to move a little pointer. If we push it to the right we make the spring tighter, and the clock goes a little faster. If we push the pointer to the left we make the spring looser, and the clock goes more slowly.

THE WATCH THAT RINGS A BELL TO TELL TIME IN THE DARK

Some clocks not only tell the time with their hands, but strike the hour. When the long minute-hand points to the figure twelve, and the short hour-hand points to one, a little hammer at the back of the clock gives one blow on a bell or gong fixed in or on the clock. This tells us that it is one o'clock, without our having to look. Some clocks strike as each quarter of an hour passes; others play a tune at the end of each hour.

Clocks and watches can be made to do very wonderful things. One watch, called the repeater watch, can be made to tell us what time it is even when we are in the dark. We have simply to press a knob and a little bell rings out the number of the hour, and the number of the quarter-hours that have passed since that hour was reached. Then there is the alarm clock, which rings a bell at the hour for which we have set it.

So through day and night, week after week, year after year, the faithful clock goes on telling us the time. Some clocks last hundreds of years. The editor has heard a tune played in Holland by a clock which was ticking when Napoleon was alive, and another in an old church in England which has lasted more than three hundred years. Both these clocks still tell the time as correctly as if they had been made only a year ago.

THE CLOCK THAT SAVED A MAN'S LIFE BY MAKING A MISTAKE

But nothing is perfect in this world. There is a story that once a man's life was saved by a mistake made by a clock. A sentinel, who was supposed to keep awake all night at Windsor Castle, was said to have fallen asleep while on duty at midnight. If they had been able to prove that he had been asleep he would have

been shot, so he was very anxious to show that he was awake. "I can prove that I was not asleep," the man said. "I heard Great Tom of Westminster strike thirteen." At first they thought this a stupid story, because clocks do not strike more than twelve; but when inquiries were made it was found that what the man said was true. The clock had something wrong with it that night, and struck thirteen instead of twelve. That mistake of the clock saved the soldier's life. It is curious that many people may have heard Big Ben strike thirteen since, for as wireless carries Big Ben's notes round the world those who live in Westminster may, by going quickly to the window, catch the last note once again, because wireless waves travel quicker than sound waves.

THE GREAT BELL WHICH IS RUNG ON SOLEMN STATE OCCASIONS

Great Tom of Westminster was the name of a great bell cast in the reign of Edward the First. It was hung at Westminster Hall, where the judges used to sit, and tolled the time of day. At last William the Third, in whose reign the incident recorded above is said to have occurred, presented the old bell to St Paul's Cathedral where it was hung and became the striking bell of the old clock. Westminster Tom still hangs in the clock tower of the cathedral, but is silent except when struck on certain solemn State occasions. But for about five months in 1956 Great Tom became almost as famous as Big Ben. His chimes echoed round the world while the great clock above Parliament was being overhauled.

Big Ben at Westminster has had a chequered history. As originally cast it was hung for testing purposes at the foot of the Clock Tower and soon cracked. It was recast and hoisted into position. Once again, however, it cracked. After some time a lighter hammer was employed and, the striking-point being altered, the tone was considered satisfactory. For about a century now, Big Ben has been ringing old days out and new days in, little the worse for the crack in his side. The clock and its bells cost £22,000.

It is lovely to think of Big Ben's song ringing round the world, saying:

> So hour by hour
>   Be Thou my guide ;
> That by Thy power
>   No step may slide.

THE GREAT FACE OF BIG BEN

At the top of 360 steps in the Clock Tower at Westminster Big Ben has marked time for a century. It is not possible to understand the size of the clock as we stand on the ground. It has four faces, each 23 feet across : nine or ten times as wide as a door. The minute hands are 14 feet long : they would reach higher than an ordinary room. The pendulum weighs nearly 450 lb. The figures on the face are each two feet long, and the minute spaces are a foot square. The minute hand of Big Ben jumps half a foot every time

it moves. It is not easy to believe these figures, but the two photographs on the left, taken at close quarters while the clock was being restored in 1956, give a very good impression of the size of the great dial of Parliament's world-famous clock. Big Ben is not the biggest clock in Great Britain, for it has a neighbour on the Thames Embankment with a face 25 feet across. Liverpool, also, has a clock with a face 25 feet across, and the face of the Singer clock at Clydebank is 26 feet across.

FIXING THE TIME FOR THE WHOLE WORLD

On the left is the pendulum clock at Greenwich from which for over a century the world has set its time. By means of electrical contacts on the pendulum each second is relayed to the electrical monitoring apparatus on the right, which checks the accuracy of the time to the fourth decimal point.

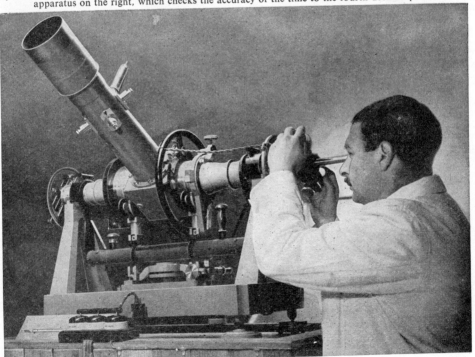

This is the instrument through which readings of the stars are made to fix Greenwich Mean Time. Of the ten stars selected for observations examples which are not too bright are preferred, as these give a clear image on the instrument. As they travel across the sky from east to west the stars are seen through a prism.

TURNING OUT CLOCKS IN THOUSANDS

Mass-production is the keynote in this clock factory. This is a press for turning out chassis.

Here we see a multiple small-parts press. A supervisor on a mobile chair inspects the machinery.

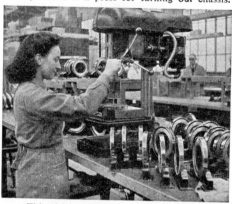

This girl is drilling holes in the clock faces ready for the hands to be fitted in.

Finished clocks move along a conveyor belt while workers assemble hands and faces of other clocks.

Here marine lever clocks are being assembled. For greater precision, these clocks are hand-made.

This picture shows rows of new marine lever clocks being timed with the aid of a chronometer.

HOW A WATCH WORKS

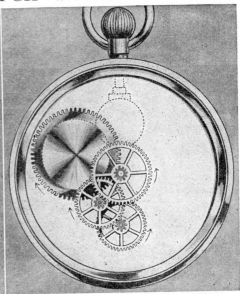

When we turn the knob we are putting into the watch the power that will make it go. By means of a series of gear wheels the mainspring, on the left, is coiled up tightly, power being thus stored-up in it. The spring is enclosed in a barrel, to the side of which one end of the spring is hooked, the other end being attached to the barrel axle.

When the mainspring begins to unwind it pulls the barrel round, still in the same direction, cogs engaging and causing a series of toothed wheels to revolve at various speeds, so giving motion to the mechanism. We are looking at the back of the watch, and although for the sake of clearness complete wheels are shown, parts of two are really hidden.

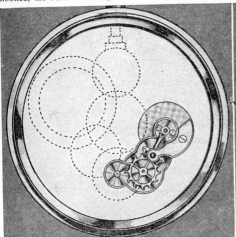

The fourth wheel of the series drives what is known as an escape wheel, which is connected by an ingenious mechanism (known as the pallets and lever) with a roller turning on the same axle as the balance-wheel and hairspring.

The balance-wheel and hairspring of a watch act in the same way as the pendulum of a clock : they regulate the movements of the escapement, the part of the watch which prevents the mainspring from running down rapidly.

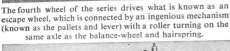

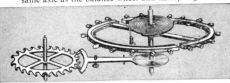

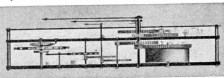

On the left is an enlarged view of the lever escapement. The teeth of the escape wheel are locked and unlocked in turn by the pallets projecting from the lever, thus moving the lever on its pivot and giving a partial turn to the balance-wheel. The hairspring is slightly wound up but immediately unwinds, turning the balance-wheel in the opposite direction. The lever is pushed back, the escape-wheel again moves on, and the whole action is repeated again and again. The picture on the right gives a side view of the mechanism; the hands are seen attached to their respective wheels.

Plain Answers to the Questions of the Children of the World

A model traffic roundabout for children in a London park

WHAT ARE THE RULES OF THE ROAD?

THE highways are for the use of all: people, animals, and vehicles. We cannot use them as if they were ours alone.

Traffic has grown so much that the quiet roads of our grandfather's day have become crowded with vehicles, some moving slowly and some fast, and the roads are full of surprise. Unless we are careful we may plunge into injury or death, for the road has become the most dangerous place in the country. It is made more dangerous because so many people use it without thinking, running into it suddenly, crossing without looking, forgetting how fast a car goes.

If we are all careful the road is quite safe.

It is easy to cross if we are wise and take our time. But even on the best of roads there will be dangers, for among so many drivers there are always some who are selfish, some who are incompetent, and some who get suddenly excited and do not know what to do.

The Ministry of Transport has been doing its best to make the roads easy for all—for those who walk and those who cycle and those who drive—and it has issued a Highway Code which sets a standard of conduct for all who use the roads. For pedestrians, crossing the road is often a hazardous business and in busy streets there are special crossing-places which we may call the Safeways.

There is the Safeway controlled by lights; and here we should watch the traffic as well as the lights and cross the road when we can see it is safe.

There is the Safeway controlled by a policeman; and here we must do as the policeman directs.

There is the Safeway without a policeman and without lights—a Zebra crossing; and here we ourselves may signal to stop the traffic.

We should make a habit of crossing by the Safeway in busy streets ; but before we cross any road we should *Stop, Look Right, Look Left, Look Right again,* and then, if the road is clear, cross at right-angles, keeping a sharp look-out.

In all cases when we cross in traffic we should *look toward the traffic coming to us* and let the drivers know that we see them. A driver who knows that we see him knows what to do; it is good to give him a signal. Never loiter in the roadway. Evil is wrought by want of thought. Often a driver does not know what a walker will do, and many accidents are

FIRE · WIND · WATER · LIFE · MIND · SLEEP · HOW · WHY · WHERE caused by careless walkers. A driver may turn suddenly to save a walker and may kill someone else.

It is not only on the roads but on the footpaths that we must be careful. We should always walk on the left, so that we are facing the traffic coming on. Walk left and drive left is the universal rule of safety, except in roads where there is no footpath; then we walk right to face the danger.

The rule is very simple: walk right if we have to walk on a road, so that we see what is coming, but walk left on the footpath.

We should give ourselves time and not dash across; a new situation may develop any moment (a car may skid or we may slip), and we should give ourselves time for surprises. We should remember that all the people on the roads are doing their best, and should not add to their difficulties. If we are with young people or old people we should guide them.

Remember that the most dangerous places are the corners, where anything may be coming along four ways. Another great danger is in getting out of vehicles. Never step off a vehicle till it is stopped, and look carefully where you go. Never get out of a car on the traffic side. Never run across behind a standing vehicle or a slow one; something fast may be coming that you cannot see. Never hang on to a vehicle, and never run out of a gateway into the road. Remember to take your time and look where you go. It is carelessness that makes the danger. Perhaps we may learn such rules as these by heart :

> Cross by the Safeway
> Look before you cross
> Let a driver know you see him
> Guide the young and old
> Walk left on the footpath
> Walk right on pathless roads
> Do not loiter in the road
> Beware of fast cars hid by slow ones
> Never play in busy streets
> Be careful in leaving a bus
> Never step off a moving vehicle
> Never hang on a vehicle
> Do not run into the roadway

The roads are not for selfish or careless people; they are for people who remember others and care enough about their lives to give a little thought for them.

The road is generally safe for the wise and always dangerous for the foolish.

Who Was Romulus Momyllus ?

Romulus Momyllus was the last emperor of the Roman western Empire. He was the son of Orestes, who was killed after the sack of Rome in 455. Romulus called himself Augustus, after the first Roman Emperor, but the Romans nicknamed him Augustulus, meaning little Augustus. The name Momyllus is a Greek mistranslation of his first name Romulus. Romulus resigned in 476, and nothing was known of him until this century when Professor Flinders Petrie found his jade seal in a tomb in Egypt. On this jade seal is the portrait of Romulus, the last of the rulers of a city which was founded by one who bore the same name.

What is the Great Hole in the Kalahari Desert ?

The Kalahari Desert of South Africa is an almost waterless waste west of Rhodesia and stretching to Namaqualand which has little water or vegetation and supports only the native Bushmen. It has been and is traversed notably by a trekking community which established itself on the farther side of it in fertile country, but one of its curiosities is so well hidden and off the beaten track that few have ever seen it. It is a mighty hole half a square mile in area with nearly perpendicular walls and more than 160 feet deep.

So cunningly concealed are the edges of this pit that the wild beasts of the Kalahari sometimes miss their footing and fall to the rocky bottom, and once a man was trapped within it for three years.

He was Erlanger, a German who was trekking across the desert with a Boer friend Oosthuizen, and they outspanned near the brink of the great pit. During the night Erlanger's wagon slid down a slope near the edge, burst through the slender barrier of bushes at the edge of the pit, and shot down into it. By a miracle he escaped death, though stunned and bruised. But Oosthuizen, believing that he must have perished, moved away from the terrifying place without taking any steps to find him.

Erlanger was in the most dreadful situation that can be imagined. When he found strength enough to look about him he found there was a small stream beginning on the north wall of the pit and running along the bottom to disappear in a cavern. So at any rate he had water, and for weeks he lived on the carefully hoarded provisions in his shattered wagon.

One night a crash woke him and he found that six hartebeestes had fallen into the pit and had been killed. He secured the meat, dried it, and lived on it for many days. But there were many days to come, for he lived in this prison more than three years. He would have died if it had not been that from time to time other animals fell into the crater: eland, giraffe, even elephant and rhinoceros. The end of this tale of courage in privation is not a happy one.

Erlanger found it impossible to climb the steep sides of the pit, and he then attempted to make a ladder of pegs out of the ruins of the wagon. Many were the failures, but at last, after nearly three years of his solitary confinement, he reached the lip of the hole, only to find himself still alone in a desert that had not even the water which had sustained him in the pit. He was almost perishing of thirst when five Bushmen found him and got him back to civilisation. He died two months later, living long enough only to tell his strange and almost incredible tale.

Who is John Bull ?

Many countries have nicknames and are represented in pictures by an animal. The British lion is the animal which stands for England, and John Bull is its owner and master. The lion is the country; John Bull is the nation. The name of John Bull comes from a work written by John Arbuthnot, a witty Scottish doctor and writer, a great friend of Swift and Pope. He was born in 1667 and died in 1735. The sketch he wrote dealt with the political affairs of Europe at the time, and the countries were made to appear as if they were men and women. England was John Bull, and Queen Anne was Mrs. Bull. The Church was Mr. Bull's mother. Scotland was John Bull's sister Peg. England was made to appear a man of very good nature, but not without faults. John was shown to be an honest, plain-dealing man, courageous, and rather hot-tempered. He was supposed to be always ready to meet the French king with any sort of weapon, in earnest or in play. He was very difficult to deal with, especially if anyone tried to master him ; but, treated with kindness and a little flattery, he could be easily led.

Why Do We See Ourselves in a Mirror ?

A mirror is made with a layer of quicksilver behind it. If that were not there we could see through the glass as we see through the window; but the quicksilver prevents the light going through and sends it back again. The glass and the quicksilver are both perfectly smooth and flat, and we can see ourselves in anything that is perfectly smooth and flat and that is able to throw the light back to us. We cannot see ourselves in what we call dull surfaces, because they keep the light; nor can we see ourselves in things with rough surfaces, because they do not throw the light back fairly, but scatter it in all directions. If we throw a ball against a perfectly smooth wall it will come straight back to us. If we throw it sideways it will come off the wall in a certain way. We could easily throw it to the wall so that it would bounce off it at an angle to a friend standing farther along the wall. But if, instead of a smooth wall, we had a heap of loose stones to bounce the ball against, we could never tell where the ball would go.

When we stand opposite a good mirror the light from our face hits the glass and comes straight back; but if we stand opposite something rough the light comes back this way, and that, and the other, as if we threw a handful of marbles against a heap of stones. In that way, of course, we cannot see ourselves.

Why is Lancashire the Cotton County ?

Nature fashioned Lancashire to be the greatest cotton manufacturing county in the world. It is sheltered on the east by lofty hills, which, to a great extent, keep off dry land winds. From the south and west come winds which are moist and mild through passing over the Gulf Stream. The effect of this is that Lancashire has a very heavy rainfall, sometimes twice as heavy as that on the east coast. Naturally, then, the air of Lancashire is moist. This favourable air makes the cotton fibre soft and easy to handle.

Do People Rise to the Surface Three Times Before They Drown ?

The answer to the question is no, and the old story that drowning men rise three times is entirely wrong. Sometimes people who drown do not rise at all—for instance, sometimes they strike their heads against something hard at the bottom. Usually they do rise, for our bodies are only very slightly heavier than water, and the movements of arms and legs, even of a person who is not a swimmer, will raise his body to the surface until he takes in so much water into his stomach and lungs that his body gets heavier and can rise no more.

It is a matter of chance how often, if at all, a drowning person rises. A diver in London once hit the water flat so that he was winded. He simply lay at the bottom, for he was unconscious and could make no movements. If everyone had waited for him to come up even once, he would have been drowned, but a swimmer dived in and brought him up, and he was soon all right.

This case shows that it is not safe to believe in old-world traditions, however old or popular or pleasant they may be, without confirmation, though it does not follow from this that all tradition is untrustworthy. Indeed, many so-called superstitions have a basis of fact.

Why Does Chloroform Send Us to Sleep ?

All our consciousness depends on work done by the brain. A person who has breathed a sufficient quantity of chloroform or ether, or has had a large enough dose of alcohol, cannot feel pain even when the skin is cut, because pain is really felt in the brain, and the brain of such a person is prevented from working.

The question, then, is: How do anaesthetics, as these things are called, stop the working of the brain ? We do not know much about it yet, but we know that such an anaesthetic as chloroform is made up of certain chemical molecules; we can prove that when chloroform is breathed, these molecules pass into the blood as it circulates through the lungs, and so are carried by it to the brain. We know, too, that chloroform is a very volatile thing, and readily passes through the walls of the blood-vessels in the brain into the substance of the brain itself. There the chloroform molecules combine with the molecules of the brain, probably with the result that the brain can no longer use up the oxygen in the blood, and stops working.

Who Was the Maid of Saragossa ?

Probably the fiercest resistance Napoleon ever met with came from the people of the old Spanish city of Saragossa, the capital of the ancient kingdom of Aragon. Early in 1808 French troops swarmed across the Pyrenees to make Napoleon's brother Joseph king of Spain, but though disorganised, the whole country rose as one man against the invaders. When the French laid siege to Saragossa, the people defended their city so desperately that the attackers had to draw off after suffering terrific losses.

But in the winter of the same year another French army appeared before the city, and it was in this second siege that Augustina, known as the Maid of Saragossa, won a heroine's fame. Her lover having fallen at his battery, she took his place, and her deeds of bravery were such that the whole garrison was heartened by them. Though Saragossa was eventually taken, Augustina and the gallant Spanish commander Palafox won a place for themselves in history by their stubborn defence against tremendous odds.

Who Made the First Adding Machine ?

In Ancient Greece and Rome there was an adding machine in general use, and it flourished almost unchanged down to the Middle Ages. It was called an abacus, and consisted of a smooth board with a narrow rim, on which were arranged rows of pebbles or pieces of bone or ivory. Later it took the form of beads or balls strung on wires, and this kind of adding machine is still in everyday use in many eastern countries.

In Europe attempts were made to improve on the abacus, and in the seventeenth century Blaise Pascal made a calculating machine with trains of wheels, which worked somewhat on the principle of the cyclometer. The greatest advance, however, was made by Charles Babbage, an Englishman who died in 1871. He invented a very elaborate calculating machine, the drawings for which covered 400 square feet of surface. The Royal Society examined a small model of it, and reported so favourably that the Government voted Babbage £1500 to help him to perfect the apparatus. He worked hard at it, but after seven years the machine was still unfinished, although the Government had spent £7200 on it, and Babbage an additional £7000 of his own money. It was completed to work sums only up to five figures, and was shown at the Great Exhibition of 1862. A little later two Swedish scientists were so sure that Babbage's idea was practicable for were so complicated as to be useless for ordinary office work, owing to their cost, but several really clever and ingenious adding and calculating machines were at last evolved, working almost any kind of sum with unerring accuracy. In the

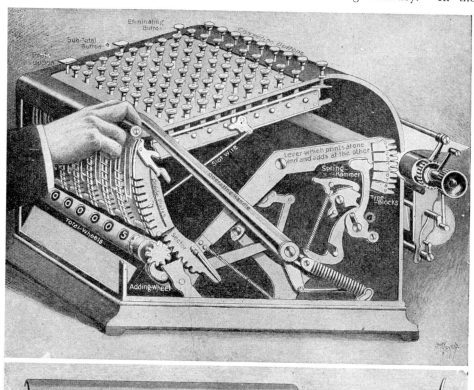

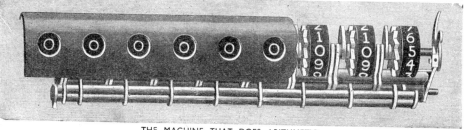

THE MACHINE THAT DOES ARITHMETIC

This wonderful machine prints a column of figures, adds them together automatically, and prints the total. The upper picture shows the work of a lever, of which there is one for each column. When a key is depressed—say, 5, as in the drawing—the sector drops five points, being regulated by a slot wire attached to the key. At the same time the other end of the lever is raised 5 points, bringing an attached type figure 5 opposite the spring hammer. This hammer, actuated by the operating handle, strikes the type figure and prints it. As the handle returns, the rack on the sector engages with the cogs of the adding wheel, turning the wheel five figures forward. Other figures are added to the wheel in the same way, up to 999,999,999 on the machine illustrated. The total is printed by pressing down a key and drawing down the operating handle. The lower picture shows the front of the adding wheels, three being shown uncovered.

large numbers, that they worked at it, and after twenty years they completed a new machine. The English Government paid £1200 for a copy of the apparatus, and this was set up in the Registrar-General's department at Somerset House, London, and was long used there. Such machines service of science today there are electronic computing machines which, by adding and subtracting electrical impulses, can multiply numbers and return the answer in a thousandth of a second. There is a picture of one of these giant machines on page 2717.

How Does a Sailor Know His Way in the Middle of the Ocean ?

For centuries the sailor who ventured out of sight of land had only the Sun or the stars to guide him.

The position of the Sun and most of the stars changes from hour to hour, however, and until an accurate clock could be carried by the ship the best means of finding direction in the Northern Hemisphere was by the North or Pole Star, whose apparent position does not vary. Nowadays, in addition to using the sextant, by which he can fix his position in terms of latitude and longitude, a navigator steers his ship by either a gyro-compass, such as is described on page 3575, or more generally by the magnetic compass.

The Earth is itself a huge magnet, having a north magnetic pole and a south magnetic pole. What we call the north pole of a magnetic needle always points to the north magnetic pole, and thus the sailor can steer his course with the help of the compass more accurately than if he went by the North Star.

What is Selenium ?

Selenium is an element discovered in 1817, and named after the Greek word for the Moon, Selene. When it was discovered that the electrical resistance of selenium varied with the amount of light shining on it, experiments were made, and it soon became possible to utilise this property. From these experiments the selenium cell was developed. In appearance a selenium cell is rather like a wireless valve or electric lamp. Inside the glass globe is a flat ground-glass surface which is coated with a film of metallic selenium, the edges of which are in contact with the electrodes. Selenium cells were used in the early television and talking film apparatus, but have now given place to a more sensitive type of cell which uses a potassium or caesium element. The selenium type of cell is cheaper than these photo-cells, as they are called, and is still widely used for light-actuated apparatus where sensitivity to small changes of light is not important. An example of this use is the invisible-ray burglar alarm. Here a beam of infra-red light is focused, across a doorway or window or across the front of a safe, on to a selenium cell. If this beam of light is interrupted the resistance of the selenium changes, and, operating a switch, starts an alarm bell. The selenium cell is also used for automatic door opening, smoke detection, counting articles on conveyors or people or vehicles passing by, and for turning on street lamps or advertising signs at dusk and turning them off again at dawn.

Why is a Train so Noisy in a Tunnel ?

What do we mean by making a noise? Noise is produced by a large number of waves of sound so mixed up and combined that, though no musical note is formed, a mere impression of sound is conveyed to the brain. We all know how sound is made up of vibrations in the air. These vibrations travel through the air and gradually disappear. Noise, however, as well as musical sounds, can be intensified by interfering with the sound-waves.

Thus a sound in a room is apparently much louder than the same sound in an open space, although actually the volume of sound is no greater, the difference being that in one case the sound is concentrated instead of being dissipated in space. In the room the sound-waves are caught by the walls and thrown back upon our ears again and again, so producing the sensation of loudness. So with the train in a tunnel. As the walls of the tunnel are quite close to the wheels of the train, the sound produced is thrown backward and forward with great rapidity, instead of the sound-waves easily escaping as in the open, and the result is that an almost deafening noise reaches our ears.

What was Fortuna's Wheel ?

In the ancient world one of the most powerful gods after the dwellers on Olympus was Fortuna. She was the goddess of chance and dealt at will with riches and poverty, with happiness and sorrow. All human blessings or pains were supposed to be dependent on her, so that everyone worshipped her.

Asiatics, Greeks, Romans, adored Fortuna and built temples to her; Rome had two of them, crowded with rich offerings. On ancient buildings the goddess was sometimes figured as a blindfolded woman carrying a horn of plenty and standing on a wheel, a symbol of the inconstancy of fortune. Modern sculptors have often represented her with a rudder, meaning that she steers the course of Fate.

What is the Aurora Borealis ?

The Aurora Borealis, or Northern Lights, seen in the Arctic regions of the northern hemisphere and sometimes farther south, are, like the Aurora Australis and the Auroral curtains of the Antarctic, caused by collisions between electric particles arriving from the Sun and the particles of rarefied gases on the outskirts of the Earth's atmosphere. Many of these beautiful curtains were painted in delicate colours by Dr. Edward Adrian Wilson when accompanying Captain Scott on his expeditions to the Antarctic.

the other. If this cage of force is bombarded by a countless number of electric messengers arriving in streams from the Sun, its balance and order are upset. The result is a serious disturbance of the magnetic field.

But why do these phenomena appear at some times and not at others; and why are they seen at some places more than at others? The answer to the first part of the question is that they seem to be provoked by special kinds of activity on the Sun, and more particularly by those which are associated with sun-spots.

THE WONDERFUL FORM SOMETIMES TAKEN BY THE AURORA BOREALIS, OR NORTHERN LIGHTS, DURING THE ARCTIC NIGHT

In the British Isles the display of the Aurora Borealis is most common in the late evenings about the period of the equinoxes, March and September. It may occur, however, at any time of the year. It usually lasts for a few hours, and may be visible on successive evenings.

The Earth as it spins on its axis is like a revolving magnet or dynamo, surrounding itself with a field of magnetic force, which might be pictured in a diagram as a sphere (the Earth) in a wire cage, of which the wires, representing the lines of force, curve outwards from one Pole to

When sun-spots (which are electrical storms on the Sun) are in progress, there are emitted from the disturbed solar areas streams of charged electric particles *which travel in straight lines*. As they travel in straight lines from a given area on the Sun the streams may sometimes miss the Earth altogether. If, however, the Earth in its journey becomes immersed in one of these enormous beams or streams of particles, these particles are deflected towards the Poles by the Earth's magnetic field. As they enter the Earth's atmosphere at a mean height of 70 miles, though a height of over 160 miles has actually been measured, these particles collide with the atoms and molecules of the oxygen and nitrogen gases and cause them to become luminous. Changes in the relative strengths of the red and green lines of the spectrum of oxygen in particular cause the different colours seen in the auroral displays at different times.

The effect is of something the same character as when an electric discharge is sent through a tube of highly rarefied gas, such as is sometimes called a Crookes tube. In these tubes a glow appears, of a colour which depends on the thin gas which is there. The aurorae show glows which are like these vacuum tube glows.

The Earth as it revolves carries the charged outer gases with it, away from the Sun and its electric battery; and on the dark side of the Earth a discharge takes place into the shadow; and so it continues until the stream of electric charges is cut off.

Who are the Bluecoat Boys ?

The boys of Christ's Hospital are usually called Bluecoat Boys owing to their quaint dress, which is a survival from that worn when Edward the Sixth founded the school in 1553. Originally the boys wore a blue woollen gown with a narrow red belt, knee-breeches, yellow petticoat and stockings, a clergyman's bands at the neck, and a blue worsted cap; but the cap and the petticoat were discontinued about the middle of last century. The school itself stood in Newgate Street, London, for 350 years, but was removed in 1902 to its present site at Horsham in Sussex.

Who Invented Shorthand ?

There is no historical record of the actual invention of any system of shorthand in any ancient country.

Probably shorthand was written in Greece, and certainly in Rome, though the ancient methods were forgotten and brief examples that remain cannot be deciphered. Many systems have been practised in this country, since rapid writing was needed. England has indeed led the way in the attempt to make writing keep pace with speech. The earliest teachers, in Queen Elizabeth's day, were a Dr. Timothy Bright, who secured a monopoly for his books for fifteen years, and Peter Bales, who was a contemporary; but their systems demanded a prodigious memory.

Shelton's system (1620) was the one used by Pepys in his diary. Many systems that followed were simply based on the alphabet; but some were phonetic, like Pitman's modern system. The best of the alphabetic systems was Taylor's, which used the vowel dot. Taylor's system was introduced, with variations, into France, Germany, Italy, Sweden, and Spain. Mason's system, modified by Gurney, became the official shorthand of the British Parliament in the nineteenth century. Byrom's system gained the protection of an Act of Parliament. Pitman's Stenographic Sound-Hand, now called Phonography, or sound-writing, was first published in 1837. It has been developed and made known with such care and skill that it has won the obvious advantage of almost universal use. Its special feature has been its insistence on a distinctly phonetic basis.

Why are Some People Colour Blind ?

Consider first how we see. Light is reflected from an object into the eye in a train of vibrations. Think of a rope extending from an electric light to the eye, and imagine that the rope is being shaken violently from side to side so that waves of movement pass down it, becoming reduced to quite small ripples if the rope is thin enough, and is shaken fast enough. That is how light reaches the eye. The ripples of light go through various eye lenses, passing finally through the retina and coming up against a structure in the eye from which they are reflected through the retina again. On their return passage they influence another most important part of the eye, the rods and cones. The rods are like microscopic pencils, the cones like tiny flasks, the smaller end pointing outwards; and these two together form the outer end of the nerve which joins the brain, and which, when affected, gives the sensation of light. In the outer part of the rods is a substance named visual purple, which is sensitive to light, and is in fact altered when light falls on it, as the chemicals of a photographic plate are changed by light that falls on them. The change brought about in the visual purple is much the same as if an instantaneous photograph were printed on the cones and despatched to the brain. The visual purple will alter with any kind of light. But among the one-coloured lights some affect it faster than others. It bleaches (and recovers) fastest when greenish - yellow rays fall on it. The blues are next most effective as bleachers; the reds come last. We may here remember that, so far as numbers of vibrations go, red light vibrates 395 billion times a second, and violet 763 billions. It is easy to understand that these great differences in number of vibrations would affect the rate of bleaching process in varying degrees, and most eyes would be able to recognise the difference. But if the visual purple is badly distributed, or is insufficient in quantity, the less marked differences in its bleaching (by different colours falling on it in vibrations) will not be recognised by the brain, and the person will be colour blind.

What is a Stalactite ?

A stalactite is like an icicle, and is formed in something of the same way by water, which trickles down and hardens into a solid. In an icicle, however, it is cold which is hardening the water into

WONDERFUL SHAWL-LIKE STALACTITES IN YALLINGUP CAVE, WESTERN AUSTRALIA

GREAT STALAGMITES AND LITTLE STALACTITES IN THE JENOLAN CAVES IN NEW SOUTH WALES

solid ice, while in the water forming a stalactite the hardening matter is contained in the water itself, being in fact some mineral substance dissolved in it. Just as the mineral dissolved in water is left behind as a deposit on the inside of a kettle, so this mineral remains behind when the water drips from the stalactite. In a stalactite the mineral gradually grows downwards from the place where the drops begin to fall. A stalagmite is merely a stalactite pointing upwards from the floor, usually of a cave, on to which the water is dripping and is formed in much the same way, climbing upwards instead of downwards. Frequently these things meet, and when this happens they make a wondrous natural spectacle in the gloom of a cave.

As the illustrations show, there are fine examples of stalactites and stalagmites in Australia; and the stalactite caves in the Cheddar Gorge in Somerset, England, attract visitors from all over the world.

WHAT ARE THE HIGHEST MOUNTAINS?

The top of the world—mighty Mount Everest

The highest mountain in Europe is Mont Blanc, in the Alps (15,781 feet high); in North America, Mount McKinley in Alaska (20,269 feet); in South America, Mount Aconcagua in the Andes (23,081 feet); in Africa, Mount Kilimanjaro in Tanganyika (19,340 feet); and in Australia, Mount Kosciusko in New South Wales (7305 feet). In Antarctica the highest named peak is Mount Markham (15,100 feet). But Asia has many peaks far higher than any in the other continents, and the highest of all is Mount Everest (29,028 feet) in the Himalayas.

To scale Mount Everest and thus be the first to stand on the highest point on the world's surface, had long been a challenge to man. But not until 1922 was the first attempt made. In that year a party of explorers led by General Charles Bruce worked their way across glaciers and snowfields up towards that forbidding white head of the " Goddess Mother of the World," as the Tibetans called it. Two of the climbers reached a height of 27,300 feet, but the summit defied them.

The next attempt, in 1924, resulted in the death of two gallant British spirits, George Leigh Mallory and Andrew Irvine, after another pair, Norton and Somervell, had been beaten by exhaustion at 28,000 feet. George Mallory was a 37-year-old schoolmaster ; Andrew Irvine was only 22. They established a camp still higher than the one from which Norton and Somervell had set out, and it was from this eyrie, on June 8, that they made their final heroic attempt to reach the top of the world.

Below, another of their comrades, N. E. Odell, saw them reach a point, " going strong," where all the world was below

them save its highest peak. Then the clouds closed in on them. They were never seen again.

Their tragic disappearance only whetted the appetite of adventurers to make new attacks on the merciless mountain. Three more expeditions tried again—in 1933, 1936, and 1938. All of them were unsuccessful, but each added to the sum of knowledge which was to benefit later expeditions.

Meanwhile, climbers had been pondering the question of approaching the peak from a different direction—from the southwest, and in 1951 a British mountaineer, Eric Shipton, led a party to reconnoitre the possibilities of this route.

In 1952 two Swiss expeditions, following this approach, failed to reach the summit, but a year later a British expedition made history by conquering Everest. It was commanded by Sir John Hunt, and its success was to an extent due to experience gained by previous climbers on the new approach.

Sir John planned his attack on the top of Everest like an operation in war. He made a careful plan and camps were established up the Arctic-like slopes until the last, consisting of only one tent, was rigged only some 1100 feet below the summit. From here on May 29, 1953, the dauntless New Zealander, Sir Edmund Hillary, and the tough Himalayan native mountaineer, Sherpa Tenzing, grimly hacked their way up to the highest place on the Earth's surface.

Almost exactly three years later the summit of Mount Everest was reached again, on two successive days, by members of a Swiss expedition led by Dr. Albert Eggler.

WHAT IS THE WORLD LIKE AT THE POLES?

The question can be answered quickly if we mean what could we see when looking around if we were standing at the North Pole or the South Pole.

At the North Pole we should be standing on a flooring of ice, perhaps flat, perhaps ridged and hummocky; and there would be no sign that anyone had ever been there before us. Around us, as far as we could see, would be ice—a world of white; and under the ice on which we stand would be a deep sea, probably three times as deep as Ben Nevis is high.

There would not be any American flag there, nor any inscription to show that Robert Edwin Peary, of America, was the first white man to reach the locality known as the North Pole. Whatever Peary left would long ago have drifted with the moving ice, and probably have sunk into the deep, cold sea that fills the hollow in the Earth's surface which exists at its extreme northerly point and far around.

For the Arctic Ocean, which fills the space within the Arctic Circle between Iceland, northern Norway, northern Russia, Siberia, Alaska, northern Canada, and the island of Greenland round to Iceland again, is always being slowly crossed by its floating burden of ice, drifted by currents and winds, and never long stationary over any part of its chilly depths. Sometimes open stretches of sea are left, but by and by the icefields close again on each other and grind and thrust their edges into hummocky ridges. So the North Pole may be where there is open sea, or it may be on a vast icefield.

If we were stationed at the South Pole the surroundings would be widely different from those at the North Pole. We should of course be surrounded by a white world of snow; but we should be standing with land underneath us and far around, on a lofty plateau twice as high as Ben Nevis, and with land stretching in all directions about us, probably to an extent almost equal to that of Australia. Instead of a great sea, as at the North Pole, the South Pole is in the centre of what may be called a continent. Another great difference is that while the Polar sea of the North is closed in by masses of land on all its shores—by Asia, America, and Europe, the Polar continent of the South is surrounded by wide oceans. It is not companioned by any other land of considerable extent. The southern tip of South America is the nearest land mass, and next to that, except some scattered islands, is New Zealand.

In consequence of its distance from other lands, and its bleak loftiness, the Antarctic continent is much more inhospitable than even the Polar ocean of the North. It is fringed round for wide distances, often hundreds of miles, by ice-floes through which ships approaching it have to break their way, and when the land is seen it is found to be fenced off from the sea by lofty cliffs of ice. On landing, voyagers find very few traces of life. No men normally live there. There are no land animals. The birds are of few species—chiefly penguins—and plant life scarcely exists. But the seas that wash its icy shores have a good deal of animal life—walruses, seals, whales, and dangerous forms of predatory fish.

This absence of life on the land within the Antarctic Circle is in striking contrast with what is found in the lands that surround the Arctic ocean. On the large islands that extend from the north of the Canadian mainland into the Polar sea, and are separated from each other by straits and sounds, a very considerable amount of both animal and plant life exists, right up to the edge of the ice-covered sea in the midst of which is the North Pole. In the brief summer, when the sun circles round the sky in one continuous day, and never sets, the snow melts to a large extent on those low-lying islands, and plant life springs up—though not in the form of trees—and affords pasturage for animals that have crossed the ice in winter. The ground is gay with flowers.

The Arctic fox and the wolf are there, and prey on hares and lemmings, which often are numerous. Ermine and other fur-clad animals migrate backward and forward with the changes of the season. Wild reindeer roam without much molestation, and herds of musk-oxen live on even the most northerly islands. On the shores, the Polar bear, stalking the abundant seals, is the animal king. A clever hunter can find animal food, ashore and in the waters.

This, however, is not true of Greenland, except around its coasts, for central Greenland is a lofty plateau capped deeply by ice—as lofty as the Antarctic continent—and bitterly cold. Central Greenland is colder than the North Pole.

Explorers are continually adding to our knowledge of what conditions are like at the Poles, and here it is fitting to mention something which happened in Antarctica, in March 1958—something which meant that the Antarctic would never, in a special sense, be quite the same place again, for it had been conquered by man.

Early on the second day of that month, Dr. (later Sir) Vivian Fuchs, leader of the Commonwealth Trans-Antarctic Expedition, completed the first overland crossing of the Antarctic continent, covering the 2150 miles in 99 days.

The crossing of the great Antarctic continent has always been a dream of South Polar explorers; Shackleton had tried it in 1914-16 and failed. The idea of another attempt occurred to Dr. Fuchs, an experienced geologist, in 1949 when leader of the Falkland Islands Dependencies Survey. After years of preparation an expedition set out under his leadership as part of the programme of the International Geophysical Year. Part of America's contribution to this programme was the setting up of a well-equipped base at the South Pole itself; this meant that when Dr. Fuchs arrived at this halfway point across the frozen continent, having set out from Shackleton Base on the Weddell Sea, he found people already there to welcome him !

He travelled on to Scott Base on McMurdo Sound, being assisted on the last lap of the journey from the base known as Depot 700 by Sir Edmund Hillary, the famous conqueror of Mount Everest.

Who Were the Seven Wise Men of Greece ?

The seven men the Greeks chose to consider as the wisest in their world were all renowned for their practical wisdom and wit, but the fame of only two of them has come down to modern times. The list of seven names usually given are Thales, Solon, Bias, Chilon, Cleobulus, Periander, and Pittacus, all of whom lived in the sixth century B.C., so that it is clear the number was drawn up long before the days of Socrates and Aristotle. Thales was, of course, the great geometrician and astronomer of Miletus, and Solon is famous

as the law-giver of the Athenians; Periander was a severe and crafty tyrant of Corinth, but of the others little more survives than their names.

Are the Rivers Always Growing Longer ?

A river and its basin are not fixed and unchanging features of the Earth's surface, for rivers are constantly changing their beds, some more, some less, and they become longer or shorter according to whether they are cutting out straighter or more winding channels. It is on this account, and because of the many twists and turns, that it is so difficult to measure the length of a river. Even the length of a familiar and comparatively short river like the Thames varies in the various reference books between 215 and 250 miles, owing to differences in measuring the windings. In atlases a shorter river will often appear, on this account, as long as a river which may be hundreds of miles longer.

There is no apparent law governing the distribution of rivers except the position of slopes and the amount of rainfall. The Amazon and the Congo are both within the belt of almost constant rains. A big river must, however, lie in a large area of land, as Columbus knew, for when he entered the mouth of the Orinoco he at once declared that the country lying southward was a continent.

How Do We Get the Word Dunce ?

The learned doctors of the Middle Ages were fond of holding long arguments, often on points of no importance, and sometimes on subjects which seem to us ridiculous. Among the great doctors of those days, Thomas Aquinas was the most famous, and he had many admirers who did no original thinking for themselves, but followed him in everything he said and wrote. At last rose a Scottish scholar who did think for himself, and would not follow Thomas Aquinas. This greatly annoyed the disciples of Thomas, and they hurled all kinds of ridicule and abuse at the new doctor and his followers. The Scottish doctor was born at Dunse, in Berwickshire, and he was called Duns Scotus. His disciples were called in ridicule, by the followers of Thomas Aquinas, " dunse men," and then " dunces," and even now, if we want to say a man has no real knowledge, we call him a dunce.

Why is British Money Called Sterling?

We often come across the word *sterling*, used to denote our British money. Other countries have no special name for their money. United States money is referred to as dollars, that of France as francs, Italy's as lire, India's as rupees, and so on. But all over the world our money is called sterling.

The origin of the word sterling is not certain, but it is generally thought to have come from Easterlings, the medieval name for the merchants of north-east Germany, some of whom settled in London in the 14th century and founded a Hansa, or guild. The coins they minted and issued came to be considered as the most reliable sort of money one could have, for they were always of the same weight and quality of metal. In those days a " sterling " was a silver penny, 240 of which went to a " pound sterling."

The word sterling, however, was used for certain coins before the German merchants came to London, and it has been suggested that it is derived from the old English word starling, meaning " a little star," which was a device on some coins of the time of William II. It is also thought by some to have come from the birds on the coins of Edward the Confessor.

What is a Jubilee?

The term Jubilee has come to mean the fiftieth anniversary of any famous event, the sixtieth anniversary being known as the Diamond Jubilee, and the twenty-fifth as the Silver Jubilee.

The word Jubilee is derived from the Hebrew name for a ram's-horn trumpet, yobel, because this instrument was blown to announce the beginning of every fiftieth year in Jewish history. There is a full account of this Year of Jubilee in the twenty-fifth chapter of Leviticus. It began on the Day of Atonement after harvest, and during this period the land was allowed to lie fallow, all slaves were set free, everyone returned to his family, and all property, except that within a walled city, was returned to its original owners or their descendants. It was instituted to celebrate the release of the Hebrews from their bondage in Egypt, and probably was intended to check the growth of a land-owning class and to preserve the family as a unit.

Years of Jubilee from Christmas to Christmas were instituted by the Popes; during them full pardon was granted to all who repented, confessed, and visited the churches of St. Peter and St. Paul at Rome. At first the Jubilee was for each hundredth year, but from 1470 it has been held every twenty-fifth year.

Who Wrote the National Anthem?

It is not actually known who wrote the original words or the music. At the beginning of last century a Richard Clark stated that an Elizabethan named John Bull composed the tune. This may or not be so. The writer of the words was possibly Henry Carey.

The National Anthem was originally in Latin and was sung in the time of the Stuarts. An English version appeared after the exile of James the Second, and our modern English version was written in opposition, hence the reference to " knavish tricks " and " politics." The first line ran " God save our Lord the King," but it was altered to " God save our Gracious Queen " when Victoria ascended the throne. The words of the Anthem are given on page 6903.

What Character in Shakespeare has the biggest Speaking Part?

Hamlet, Prince of Denmark, has many more lines than any other character in the plays. He speaks 1569 lines, but few actors recite them all on the stage today. Richard Crouchback, a man of action and therefore a contrast to the philosophic prince, comes next with 1161 lines. Here is a list of characters and the number of lines Shakespeare wrote for them:

Hamlet	1569	Touchstone	516
Richard III	1161	Imogen	541
Iago	1117	Helen (All's Well)	479
Othello	888	Isabella	426
Coriolanus	886	Desdemona	389
Timon	863	Mistress Page	361
Lear	770	Viola	353
Richard II	755	Volumnia	315
Brutus	727	Beatrice	309
Macbeth	705	Lady Macbeth	261
Cleopatra	670	Katherine (Shrew)	220
Prospero	665	Miranda (Tempest)	142
Romeo	618	Perdita	128
Petruchio	585	Cordelia	115

It will be seen that Shakespeare's women characters are not so talkative as his men. Cleopatra heads the list with 670, but Cordelia's 115 are enough to endear her to every reader of King Lear.

HOW DOES TRAFFIC WORK ITS OWN SIGNALS?

Many automatic traffic signals are actually controlled by the traffic itself. If there is a pause in the flow of traffic on the road which has the right of way the signal lights automatically change to give the right of way to the other road *if traffic is waiting to cross over.*

In each road is a movable section, or detector, as seen in the first picture on this page. The weight of a vehicle passing over the detector closes a contact and completes an electrical circuit, sending an impulse of current to the control-box, which is seen in the next picture. In the control-box are a number of relays and switches which control the lights.

In a relay a current passing through a coil of wire wound round a core of soft iron magnetises the iron and attracts the hinged metal armature on the right of the relay. This forces together the contact springs mounted above, and so makes a circuit for a current to flow in another path. Immediately the current ceases to flow in the coil the coil ceases to be a magnet, and the springs open and force the armature to its normal position.

In the solenoid are a similar coil of wire and a core of soft iron. But the core slides in and out of the coil, being pulled into it when the current is flowing and pulled out

A car passing over the detector, a rubber-covered movable strip in the road. Each time it is depressed an electric contact is made.

The control-box containing the electrical apparatus which operates the coloured signal lights seen on the right of the picture.

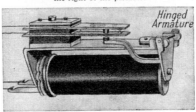

One of the relays employed in the circuit. It is a kind of electro-magnetic switch.

The solenoid, another form of electro-magnetic switch that operates the lights.

of its normal position by a spring when the current ceases. These in-and-out movements operate a switch.

The picture on the opposite page shows how the system operates.

The signal at green shows that traffic may pass. Condenser 1 is fully charged with electricity from the main supply, and each time a vehicle crosses a detector and operates Relay 1 a certain amount of current is allowed to run to earth through the resistance. This loss is slowly made good again from the main supply, and until it is made good the right of way cannot go to the other road.

This happens if there is a seven-seconds pause in the flow of traffic, which means that no impulses have been received from the detector for that period. At the end of the pause the condenser is fully charged. If a vehicle crosses a detector on the other road it operates Relay 4, and the current is allowed to run to earth by way of the neon valve and the coil of Relay 2. The relay makes a circuit which causes the solenoid to operate and change the lamp signals, so giving the right of way to the waiting traffic.

The other neon valve, Condenser 2, and Relay 3 form a limiting circuit which prevents one road from holding the right of way to the exclusion of the other; but if

HOW TRAFFIC CONTROLS ITSELF

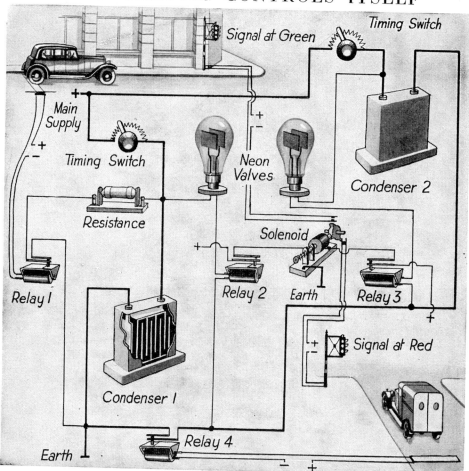

A simplified picture-diagram showing what happens in the control-box of the robot traffic signals described on the opposite page. To avoid complication only two sections of the crossing are shown.

The automatic traffic-control system at a cross-roads, with the buildings cut away to show all four detectors and the white lines beyond which waiting vehicles may not pass. These pictures have been prepared with the help of the Automatic Electric Company of Liverpool, makers of the Electromatic traffic control equipment.

there is a seven-second pause in the flow of traffic on one road, waiting traffic on the other is given the right of way.

Should a vehicle cross a detector while the right of way is on the other road, and before the expiry of the maximum limiting interval, the relay is prevented from being released by a locking circuit. The limiting interval may be fixed as needed by means of a timing switch.

In the last picture the broken lines indicate the wires from the detectors to the controller and the dotted lines wires from the control box to the lanterns.

How Fast Do Animals Travel ?

Though man has copied the shapes into which Nature has moulded her creatures to give them speed over the land, in the air, and under the water, man himself unaided is no match for the fastest members of the Animal Kingdom. He can run a hundred yards at a speed of about 22 miles an hour, but an angry elephant can cover a hundred yards at 20 miles an hour, and a lion can charge nearly as far at 60 miles an hour. A lion has actually been timed at 62 miles an hour for three seconds. An antelope has maintained this speed for three miles. The cheetah could catch the antelope in a course of a few hundred yards, for this Indian cat has kept up with a car at 80 miles an hour. The racehorse at 35 and the greyhound at 37 miles an hour seem slow movers in contrast.

The mammal of the sea, the whale, swims at 24 miles an hour, but his foe, the swordfish, is much faster. The average cruising speed of the pike is nine miles and of the salmon seven miles an hour. The speeds of wild mammals and fishes have not been so carefully measured as those of the birds. There are a few birds capable of flying over 100 miles an hour, which, of course, is exceeded when gravity aids them in a swoop. Birds have two speeds, the normal used in migration, and the rapid used in attack or escape. Thus a swift normally flies at 70 miles, but can attain a velocity of 106 miles an hour. Dr Fraser Darling once timed a golden eagle chased by falcons for three miles at 120 miles an hour on an ascending course, the eagle eventually escaping by a terrific swoop. Even stay-at-home birds like starlings travel fast, both Miss Frances Pitt and Colonel Richard Meinertzhagen

estimating their speed at over 45 miles an hour. For speed over a long distance the lapwing probably holds the record. Lapwings marked and liberated in England were found in Canada a little over 24 hours later. With a following wind they had flown at 100 miles an hour.

Colonel Meinertzhagen, a famous ornithologist, has used anti-aircraft instruments in compiling a table of the speeds at which birds can fly. Here are some of his results, the figures indicating miles per hour.

Lammergeier	110	Kestrel	43
Swallow	106	Partridge	40
Lapwing	80	Rook	40
Duck	59	Raven	39
Goose	55	Pigeon	36
Stork	48	Finch	33
Sandgrouse	47	Pheasant	33

Even that gawky flightless bird the ostrich, can attain a remarkable speed. It is faster than a horse, and has reached 40 miles an hour when timed on a track.

What is the Wateler Peace Prize ?

This is an annual prize of about £2500 awarded by the Carnegie Foundation to the person who has rendered the most valuable services to the cause of peace or who has contributed to finding means for the combating of war. The money is the interest from property left to the Trustees of the Foundation by M. Wateler, a Dutchman.

What Is Conditioned Air ?

Most big factories, public buildings, theatres, and so on, have an air-conditioning plant which ensures a continuous supply of pure air which may be heated or cooled as desired. Certain manufactures demand an atmosphere of a particular degree of humidity which Nature does not always supply; so the air-conditioning plant is made to supply throughout the factory air of the desired humidity. With the aid of this apparatus we can, in other words, make our own weather, and the pictures on the opposite page explain how this is done.

The Underground Railways are given a supply of conditioned air and so are the holds of vessels which carry fruit from the far corners of the world. Gramophone, broadcasting, and film studios, too, require a control of the temperature and humidity of their atmosphere. In fact, the use of conditioned air is ever-increasing in modern times.

MAKING WEATHER FOR A FACTORY

A scene in a silk factory, with a row of diffusers above.

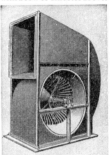

Here is a factory of three floors which is supplied with conditioned air by the plant shown below. Air is drawn down the shaft on the left, through the apparatus, and is pumped up the shaft on the right, entering the rooms through the diffusers.

The fan which draws the fresh and used air through the apparatus.

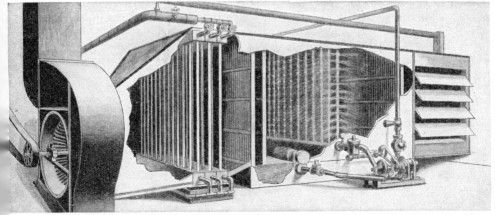

This plant, known as the Carrier Humidifying System, is usually in the basement of the building. The suction fan on the left, shown uncovered, draws air through the openings on the right, sucks it through the humidifier, where sprays of water saturate it, and then through the steam heater, and finally drives it up the shafts to the rooms. By regulating the apparatus, air of any temperature, hotter or cooler than that outside, or of any desired humidity, can be obtained.

Why, from a Train, do the Telegraph Wires Seem to Go Up and Down ?

The telegraph wires stretching from pole to pole do not hang perfectly straight even when tightly drawn, but sag in the middle, as a tow-rope stretched from tug to ship will do. They are so nearly horizontal, nevertheless, that the eye of anyone standing still and looking at them from a distance cannot readily detect the looping effect. But when the eye is taken very quickly along by the side of the wire the falling away from the horizontal straightness is detected and exaggerated, so that the apparent up-and-down motion of the wire is optically increased in such a way that it can almost be called an optical illusion, though actually it is founded on fact. In the same sense, if not quite the same way, raindrops falling straight down seem, when the eye looks at them from a moving train, to be slanting towards the onlooker. That is also an optical illusion arising from the train's motion.

How Can a Bird Fly Though it is Heavier Than Air ?

It is a fact well known to everybody that when a bird in flight is killed by a shot it falls to the ground. In other words a dead bird obeys the force of gravitation exactly as a hailstone, or a raindrop, or a meteorite must do. The force of gravitation is always acting, even on the living bird. It is therefore plain that some force is produced which acts against gravitation, balances it when the bird maintains its level in the air, or more than balances it when the bird rises in the air. This force is produced by the life of the bird. It can be produced in things that are not alive, as in an aeroplane that we cause to fly. In any case, there is produced a force which acts in the opposite direction to the force of gravitation, and is, for the time being, superior to it.

In the case of the bird the necessary force is produced by burning the sugar in its muscles; in the case of the aeroplane it is produced by burning fuel in the engine. Foolish people sometimes speak as if these were cases of defying one of Nature's laws, but they are nothing of the sort. Gravitation goes on acting on the bird whether the bird rises or falls; but when the bird rises into the air a greater force is being successfully opposed to the force of gravitation.

Can Chemistry Build Up Life ?

No; chemistry certainly cannot build up living matter. But we ought to know how far chemistry can go in this direction. It was long believed that none of the things made by life, such as sugar or alcohol, could possibly be made in any other way; but nearly a hundred years ago a compound called urea, which is one of those made inside our bodies, was made by a chemist *outside* his body; and now chemistry can build up thousands of compounds which are made by living things; and can build them up from their separate elements. This teaches us that chemistry inside living things cannot be so very different from chemistry outside them.

No doubt chemists will some day be able to make all the compounds that compose living matter, or protoplasm, and then call the mixture protoplasm; but it will be only *dead* protoplasm, we may be sure. Living protoplasm is far more than a mixture of proteids and sugar and salts and water. It has an architecture, and is as much more than a mixture of these things as a cathedral is more than a heap of bricks. The bricks need a builder to make them into a cathedral, and the compounds that compose living matter need a builder to make them into living protoplasm. Otherwise it will be only protoplasm, without the property which all living protoplasm has, and which is the power of growth.

What is Caste ?

Caste is a term for the division of society into clearly marked grades. It is most complete in India, but has existed in a less degree in other lands, as between Patricians and Plebeians in Rome. From remotest history India has had four chief castes—the Brahmin, or priestly caste; the Kshattriya, or warrior caste; the Vaisya, or mercantile and agricultural caste; and the Sudra, or artisan and labouring caste. Sudras represent, historically, the black natives who were conquered by the Aryan invasion and became enslaved to the other three castes.

These chief castes branch into secondary castes, which represent often special professions or occupations. Outside all castes are the pariahs, or outcastes. The system of caste delays social improvement, but to the unambitious and contented it gives a certain degree of easy security.

ARE BIRDS FRIENDS OF THE FARMER?

A GREAT deal of controversy has raged about this subject since the end of the 19th century, and it has often been indulged in by people already biased either in favour of the birds or against them. In recent years, unbiased ornithologists have realised that although we know quite well the *variety* of foods eaten by the majority of our British wild birds, we know extremely little about the *quantities* of the various types of food they eat.

It is folly, therefore, simply to brand birds as harmful, beneficial, or neutral to man's interests (except in one or two cases) until we know exactly what they eat, how much they eat, and where they get their food. Moreover, such grouping is complicated by the difficulty of deciding the place of a bird with a mixed diet— a bird which may eat insect pests as well as valuable grain.

To attempt to reach a decision by balancing the proportions of a diet of pests against a diet of grain is meaningless, because we cannot easily assess their value. How can we honestly say that 20 wireworms are balanced by an equal volume of barley grains? The 20 wireworms, if allowed to live and breed, might ultimately have caused the loss of an even greater amount of barley. On the other hand, birds may actually increase the number of harmful insects by destroying mainly those which are diseased, or plagued by parasites, and so easier to catch, thus strengthening the stock.

Although it is true that many of our wild birds (especially warblers, titmice, and flycatchers) feed largely on pests of agriculture and forestry, there is as yet little evidence that they significantly keep down the numbers of these pests. Climatic conditions and other insects, such as ichneumon flies, may be more important, although it is possible that birds are a valuable link in a chain of controls.

But if all the birds vanished we might find that these other controls would be insufficient to keep the pests in check. Certainly birds help to keep down the numbers of caterpillars which ravage the woodland trees in late Spring. In woods where there are few birds the trees are almost completely stripped of foliage by plagues of hungry caterpillars.

With these facts in mind it can be seen that the food of each wild bird needs to be studied in careful detail before we can decide which species should be reduced in numbers and which should be encouraged. It is extremely difficult to make an accurate study of the food of birds, particularly the small insect-eating ones, but new ways have been found, and are still being found.

Ornithologists have already studied several species—notably the Starling, Jackdaw, Jay, Magpie, Rook, Heron, Swift, Pied Flycatcher, and the Titmice —and have obtained most interesting results. It has been found that the Jackdaw, Jay, and Magpie feed their nestlings almost entirely on caterpillars of the various moths which defoliate the woodland trees in May and early June. It has been found, too, that Rooks feed almost entirely on earthworms, except in summer months, when they eat a great many leatherjackets—all collected from grassland. Outside the breeding season, the Jackdaw also obtains much of its animal food from grassland. Such factors suggest that these particular birds are not nearly as harmful to agriculture as has often been alleged.

On the other hand, all enquiries into the Wood-pigeon's diet have shown this bird to be a great destroyer of the farmer's crops; certainly it cannot be claimed as his friend. But it is true to say that birds like the Rook and Wood-pigeon might never have become pests had it not been for man felling the primeval forest and changing the appearance of the countryside, thus providing more abundant food for them and allowing more to survive.

Rooks were probably rare before the countryside was cultivated. It seems to be another case of man cutting a stick to beat his own back. And now that they *are* pests, it is difficult to decide which is the more expensive process: to give them a free hand (or beak) to eat their fill; or to attempt to control their numbers.

Clearly, until our knowledge grows, the farmer is well advised to take action against wild birds only when he has definite evidence that his crops are suffering badly from raiding by a certain species. Even then, the raiding may only be local in extent and does not necessarily mean that war should be declared on that bird everywhere else.

Why Have Foreign Parliaments Such Strange Names ?

We frequently read in the news from foreign countries that a law has been passed by an institution with a curious name such as Riksdag, Storthing, or Cortes. These are the names by which their Parliaments are known in their respective countries, and they often have an interesting history. Even our own word Parliament has an interesting origin, meaning a speaking together, from the Latin *parlare* which comes from two Greek words meaning *to cast side by side*, which is essentially what is done with points of view in discussion.

The word for *day* enters into many names of Parliaments because their meetings are called for a set day. The word Diet, used for Japan's old Imperial Diet and for many historical assemblies, means this. Thus we have the Danish Rigsdag, the Swedish Riksdag, and the Dutch Rijksdag, in which the first syllable means the realm. The Anglo-Saxon word *thing* in its meaning of council comes into the name of Iceland's Althing, the council or assembly of all, and of Norway's Parliament, the Storthing, in which the first syllable means great.

The name of the former Parliament of Russia, the Duma, means council or court, our word doom or judgment coming from the same source. Spain's Cortes is allied to our court. The rat which we find in the Swiss names for their two Houses of Parliament, Standerat and Nationalrat, also implies court or council; we find it again in the Rathaus, the council-house or town hall, of Germany.

Why Does a Steel Ship Float ?

Wood floats, as we know, and steel does not. But if we imagine the steel ship turned into a closed box full of air it is easy to imagine it floating. It is then the steel and air in it that are floating. So long as the ship and the air contained in it do not weigh more than a body of water of the same size it will float. That is an important principle, called displacement, which was discovered by an ancient Greek called Archimedes.

If we have a basin full of water and put in it a toy boat some of the water flows over the side of the basin; that water is displaced.

Suppose it were possible to put a closed-up ship under water without letting any water get in. The ship would push aside, that is, displace, a certain quantity of water. Then, if we could weigh that displaced water we should find it was so many tons heavier than the ship. Therefore the ship, whether of wood, iron, or steel, floats because its weight is less than that of the water it displaces.

Who Was Parson Thwackum ?

Parson Thwackum is a character in Henry Fielding's famous novel Tom Jones, which was published in 1749. Thwackum was a precise cleric, honest and learned but very selfish and bad-tempered.

He has become proverbial for a clergyman with a very narrow outlook. For instance, to Parson Thwackum religion meant the Christian religion, which meant Protestant religion, that is to say the religion of the Church of England excluding all others.

What is a Wind Scale ?

The speed and pressure of the wind are important for the calculations of both mariners and engineers. A recognised name for a wind blowing at a certain speed was found necessary many years ago, and Admiral Beaufort in 1809 drew up a scale which today is still recognised as one of the bases of meteorological work. His descriptions of the wind have a meaning much more exact than the loosely used words zephyr, breeze, gale, or cyclone. The Beaufort scale ranges from 0 to 12, and gives the name for the wind blowing at a given number of miles an hour.

Beaufort number	Speed of wind	Name of wind
0	under 2	calm
1	2–4	light air
2	4–8	slight breeze
3	8–12	gentle breeze
4	12–17	moderate wind
5	17–22	fresh wind
6	22–28	strong wind
7	28–34	high wind
8	34–41	fresh gale
9	41–49	strong gale
10	49–57	whole gale
11	57–65	storm
12	over 65	hurricane

When blowing at 24 miles an hour wind has a pressure of one and three-quarter pounds a square foot, but at 68 miles an hour this pressure amounts to 14 pounds.

What are the Apocrypha ?

The Apocrypha are books written in very early times and put forward for acceptance as Scriptures, either in the Old Testament or the New Testament, but not accepted by the whole, or in many cases by any part, of the Christian Church. The most generally known of these books are the Old Testament Apocrypha, as formerly printed in Protestant Bibles between the Old and New Testaments.

These Hebrew books were translated into Greek in what is called the Septuagint version, but were not accepted by the Jews of Palestine as sacred Scriptures. They are accepted as Old Testament books by the Roman Catholic Church, if they are included in Jerome's Latin translation from the Septuagint known as the Vulgate. Thus, 1 Maccabees and 2 Maccabees are included, and 3 Maccabees and 4 Maccabees are not. The Eastern (Greek) Church also accepts them. There is a great deal of other apocryphal Jewish literature of the Old Testament period which is neither accepted as authoritative by the Jewish religion nor by any branch of the Christian Church. Furthermore, many apocryphal gospels, histories, epistles, and visions, written in Christian times and claiming to come from apostles and others mentioned in the New Testament, are rejected as Scriptures by the Church, though some have a historical value.

A great deal of apocryphal literature produced by the Jews in the centuries just before Christ, and by Christians in the centuries immediately after, was of the kind called apocalyptic, or visionary. Examples of writing of this kind included in the Bible are the prophecies of Ezekiel in the Old Testament, and Revelation in the New Testament.

What is a Ghetto ?

In the Middle Ages the Jews in Europe were compelled to live separately from the Christians, and practically every city of note had its Jewish quarter, called the ghetto. These were first started in Italy about the middle of the eleventh century, the name being from the Italian borghetto; but how it arose is not certain. Medieval ghettos were enclosed by walls, with the gates locked at night; Jews were forbidden to leave their own quarter after dark, and on Sundays and holy days. Within the walls, however, they were allowed comparative freedom. The ghetto system endured into the middle of the nineteenth century, but nowadays a ghetto means merely a quarter where many Jews live.

Where Did the Alphabet Come From ?

There are many alphabets in which each character, or letter, is a symbol for a sound or a combination of sounds. New alphabets have to be made to indicate sounds in languages that have not been written before. Where our own alphabet came from is as yet a question to be settled by learned men when they understand more about the languages in use in very early times around the eastern shores of the Mediterranean Sea. There is little doubt that the Greeks borrowed their alphabet from the Phoenicians, the people who chiefly carried on the sea trade of the Mediterranean. Did the Phoenicians invent our letters ? Some have held that they received them in part from the Egyptians. Others say that the probability is that the people called in the Bible the Philistines found our alphabet, or something resembling it, in use in the island of Crete during the Minoan period, and that the Phoenicians, who were akin to the Philistines, borrowed it from them, and circulated it along all the Mediterranean coasts. It is necessary to have more examples of the writing of ancient peoples round the Eastern Mediterranean, and to compare them, before we can say with confidence how far the Minoans, the Egyptians, and the Phoenicians were concerned in forming it.

Which are the Smallest Countries in Europe ?

There are three independent European countries each with an area of less than 100 square miles—Liechtenstein, San Marino, and Monaco.

Liechtenstein is an ancient Principality formerly associated with the Holy Roman Empire, lying on the eastern side of the Rhine valley as it approaches Lake Constance. Here reigns Prince Franz Joseph the Second, the hereditary ruler of about 65 square miles of Alpine pasture land, in his castle of Liechtenstein in the picturesque little town of Vaduz. When the German Confederation was dissolved in 1866 Liechtenstein became independent and since 1868 it has had no army. It is mainly agricultural, and is commercially joined with Switzerland. The population numbers about 13,500. Its popular governing body, the Diet, has 15 members.

San Marino, a little Republic of 38 square miles and some 12,100 people, inland of Rimini on the Adriatic Sea, claims to be older, as a State, than any other country. Admittedly it has existed since the ninth century. It is governed by a Council of 60, elected every four years by popular vote. The sixty meet twice a year, in April and October, and choose two of their number to be Regents, or Reigning Captains, for six months. When their six months of office is over they cannot be elected again for three years. The town of San Marino has about 2000 inhabitants The little Republic has a citizen army of 900 men.

Monaco, a principality on the French Riviera coast, with an area of about 370 acres, consists of three adjoining towns with a total population of about 20,200. The towns are Monaco-Ville, La Condamine, and Monte Carlo.

Another of these pocket states is the Republic of Andorra, in the Pyrenees, which although far larger (191 square miles) has a population of only about 5200. Although it is self-governed, Andorra is under the joint suzerainty of the head of the French Republic and of the Spanish bishop of Urgel.

What is the Revised Version of The Bible ?

All people in the world today, except the few who can read ancient Hebrew and ancient Greek, must read the Old and New Testaments in translations. At first the Hebrew of the Old Testament was translated into Greek. Then the Greek and the Hebrew were translated into Latin, and the first complete English translation was made from Latin into English. But as time went on other translations were made direct from the original Hebrew and Greek, and greater correctness was secured. More ancient copies of the Scriptures in the original languages were found and studied until, at last, at the beginning of the seventeenth century, it was felt that the best scholarship of Britain should be brought together to make a translation as correct, and as fitly worded, as was possible. So 47 scholars revised the whole Bible afresh,

and it was published in 1611 as the Authorised Version. This translation was based on earlier English translations. A Bible called the Bishops' Bible was taken as the foundation. It had been published in 1568. But that was a revision of another Bible, the Great Bible, published in 1539, and the Great Bible had been a revision of an earlier Bible known as Matthew's Bible. That, again, had been made up from translations by William Tyndale and Miles Coverdale. Really, Tyndale's Bible, supplemented by a Bible by Coverdale, was the far-off translation which, revised again and again, made the broad foundation for the Authorised Version. But the 47 translators went back, in all their work, to comparisons with the Hebrew and Greek in which the Scriptures had originally been written. Also, they had by them the Roman Catholic translation known as the Rheims Version.

The Authorised Version of 1611 was almost universally used by British Protestants for 270 years; but toward the close of this period it was felt that men had now much more knowledge of Hebrew and Greek than the 47 translators who produced the fine Authorised Version. They also had many more ancient manuscripts from which to secure the best forms of the original text by comparisons. Translations of parts of the Bible were appearing from time to time showing that the Authorised Version did not always express the true meaning of the ancient languages. In short, knowledge had increased, and another revision was necessary to free the old version from errors. So, in 1870, preparations began for forming two companies of learned men, one to revise the Old Testament of the Authorised Version, and the other the New Testament, and a Revised Version was published, the New Testament in 1881, the whole Bible in 1885, and the Apocrypha in 1895.

The Revised Version is obviously the more correct, but the music of the language is less sustained. Many lovers of the Bible feel that the revisers made too many small unnecessary changes, and shirked greater necessary changes by putting them in the margin as alternatives. While the British Revised Version was being produced an American Protestant Revision Committee was doing parallel work in the United States.

What is the Sound Barrier ?

When missiles or aircraft travel at the speed of sound they encounter a barrier through which they have to crash with explosive force. This is heard on the ground as " supersonic bangs " and the noise can break glass or damage property.

The speed of sound varies according to height. At sea level it is 761 miles an hour, but between 40,000 and 100,000 feet it is only 663 miles an hour. This difference is due to temperature. Under cold or freezing conditions the ripples which sound makes in the air are shorter and therefore more easily compressed. Therefore the sound barrier is more quickly reached in high, cold altitudes than it is near the ground. At the speed of sound, objects create a wall through which they have to crash.

This means that objects flying at the speed of sound themselves create this barrier ; and this is why :

A moving body sends out sound waves in the direction in which it is travelling. A ball, when thrown, creates advance waves to blaze a trail—giving the air ahead warning to arrange itself in a proper flow pattern. Those waves are like the policemen on motor-cycles who go ahead of a State procession. At their warning the atmosphere divides like crowds getting on the pavement and making way for the official cars behind.

When those outriders are well ahead the crowds have time to arrange themselves in an orderly way ; but if the speed of the processional cars is almost as fast as the outriders, the crowd have to stumble and hustle out of the way. If the procession were to outstrip the motor-cyclists, then the crowds would have no advance warning. Instead of dividing and making way, they would jam tighter in a panicking mass with which the procession would disastrously collide.

Similarly with sound waves. Suppose an aircraft is travelling at 200 miles an hour, a thousand feet above the ground. The advance waves which it sends out travel at 761 miles an hour and so are 561 miles ahead, providing ample warning and clearing a passage through the atmosphere.

But when the aircraft speed approaches that of sound and is almost overtaking its own sound waves, the air is thrown into confusion. It no longer flows evenly over the shape of the machine. It stumbles and tries to get out of the way ; it jostles and clutches at the aircraft, pulls and drags, wrestles with the structure of the machine and with the pilot at the controls. In this way aircraft have been torn to pieces and pilots hurled to their deaths.

Then at the speed of sound, the waves are compressed into a formidable physical obstacle, an invisible wall. Tearing through it produces the bangs, but, once beyond it, the aircraft has wrenched clear of its own sound waves and is ahead of them so that they no longer encumber it. Sound Barrier pilots have described the sensation as like crossing stormy shoals and finding a quiet lagoon beyond.

What is the Heat Barrier ?

The heat barrier is a problem which confronts the designers of high-speed, high-flying machines, rockets, or missiles. It can take one or both of two forms. The first is the friction of the atmosphere, and the second is a " heat-belt " about 150 miles above the Earth. A rocket going up 200 miles would encounter both.

The friction of the atmosphere can best be understood in terms of a meteor, or shooting star, which can be seen glowing in a clear sky. It is debris from space— perhaps the fragment of an exploded star. The fragment may be no bigger than a pebble, but, as it hits the atmosphere surrounding the Earth, the speed at which it is travelling causes so much friction that it glows like a star and is " burned up " in a few minutes or seconds.

Rockets intended for space travel would develop friction which might melt metals, or at least overheat them, because they would have a speed of at least 18,600 miles an hour. This speed is necessary to offset the forces of gravity. Just as a bullet is pulled back to earth when its speed slackens, so a rocket is pulled back if its speed cannot drag it clear of the attraction of the earth.

This speed of 18,600 miles an hour is called the " escape velocity." To produce this speed, designers have to design rockets in several sections. The first section is like a high-speed shunting engine. It takes the rocket so far and then drops off. The second section rocket takes over. It is already travelling with the initial speed of the first, but it adds its own speed—and so on in as many sections as are needed to attain the ultimate speed. The production of metals to withstand the high temperatures of jet engines shows that the friction problem is not insuperable. In 1956 an American aeroplane which flew at 1900 miles an hour when nearly 13 miles up was made of stainless steel and nickel alloy. Designers may turn to other materials, such as plastics.

Apart from friction, however, there is the " heat-belt." Although progressively colder up to heights of about 70 miles, the temperature beyond this rises until at 150 miles height it is hot enough to melt iron. But above this the temperature again declines.

What is a Cyclotron?

A cyclotron is one of the " atom-smashers." It is a machine which turns atomic particles—neutrons, protons, and beta particles—into projectiles and fires them into other atoms in order to split them.

The first atom-smashing machine was made by Cockcroft and Walton at Cambridge in 1932. It was a " high-voltage accelerator," a device which increased ordinary current to millions of volts and passed this through hydrogen, giving protons (atoms of hydrogen, without the electrons) the force to hit a target and split its atoms.

Professor Ernest Lawrence, of Berkeley University, California, then devised the cyclotron. This depends on the fact that if a charged particle is introduced between the poles of a magnet and given a push it will go round and round in circles; it will describe wider and wider circles, and given an occasional " kick " will travel faster and faster.

If a round carton in which wrapped cheeses are sold is cut in two, and the parts then separated, one gets an idea of what a cyclotron looks like. The two half-circles are called " Dees," because they look like the letter D. Each half has a different electric charge but each switches rapidly from having a positive charge to having a negative (oscillates).

The source of the particles is between the " Dees " and is immediately attracted to the " Dee " of opposite charge and enters it. Magnets make it travel in a circle, and while this is happening the other " Dee " changes its charge so that the

particle is drawn across the gap into it. The particle is thus kicked from behind by one " Dee " while it is pulled by the other.

All this is happening in fractions of a millionth of a second and the particles in an incredibly short time are travelling at millions of volts energy, emerging as a jet, or beam, of tremendous force, capable of smashing atoms.

What is a Coelacanth?

Pronounced *Seelakanth*, which means "hollow spine", the coelacanth is the oldest kind of fish in the world. Its ancestors swam in the oceans 300 million years ago, long before any of the giant dinosaurs roamed the earth, before even the Alps or the Himalayas took shape. Fossil remains of the coelacanth led scientists to believe that it had become extinct 60 million years ago. Then, in 1938, came the exciting news that a living

THE COELACANTH CAUGHT OFF SOUTH AFRICA
IN 1938

specimen had been caught off the South African coast. Unluckily, its internal organs and flesh were thrown away before they could be scientifically examined, but another, caught off Madagascar in 1952, was carefully preserved.

This one was indeed an odd-looking fish. About five feet long, and weighing 100 lb., it was steely-blue in colour and had long fins that looked something like legs.

This ancient species of living creature is of great importance to students of evolution. It is an offshoot of the group of fish that gave rise to land vertebrates (amphibians, reptiles, mammals, birds), and it has preserved many of the features of the fish that first began leaving the water. But unlike those distant ancestors which went ashore to develop new shapes and characteristics, the coelacanth evolved leggy fins, but never left the ocean.

Thus has the species lived on for millions of years, unchanged in form but growing rarer and rarer until it has become almost extinct.

The Story of the Beautiful Things in the Treasure-House of the World

The Art of Ages Past

WE have looked in these pages at the story of Art in its various phases. We have looked at the work of the painters whose pictures have become familiar to the world, some of them for centuries. We have looked at the work of the sculptors, who have taken the marble from the rocks and have fashioned it into wonderful and beautiful shapes. We have glanced at the work of the craftsmen who made beautiful things in metal and ivory and glass and wood. We have been able only to suggest the marvellous work that men have done in all these ways ; but we have been able, we hope, to make it clear that the history of Art is one of the most enthralling stories in the world. Here we look at another chapter in this history, the story of the digging up of the buried remains of the ancient world and of the light it throws upon the arts and crafts of those days of long ago.

DIGGING UP THE ANCIENT WORLD—1

FOR the disclosure of buried civilisations and the lost peoples who created them only one thing can be done: it is to dig hopefully and diligently where their suspected localities once were, so as to come on evidence of them. But if and when they are found there is the harder task of interpreting their meanings.

We are certain to come on vast quantities of broken pots and shards, yet there is danger in this profusion, for they were thrown into the refuse pit because they had so little value. It is safer to pin our faith to objects which were most valuable or most precious to those who preserved them, and to what we must believe was the genius or craft of those who made them. Thus, in the Tomb of the Sumerian Queen at Ur of the Chaldees we learn from her gold-leaved coronet, her jewels, her many stringed golden harps, nearly all that can be told of the Queen she was and the beliefs of her people who created the treasure about her to go with her to that silent land from which no traveller returns.

The same tradition re-appears a thousand years later, carried no doubt from Mesopotamia to Egypt, in the Tomb of Tutankhamen, where everything the Pharaoh could need on his last long journey, his golden coffin, his golden crown, his weapons, and his furnishings, would be at hand if he wanted them. It is visible even two thousand years

later, strangely enough, in the Sutton Hoo Ship burial in Suffolk, where a Scandinavian king's equipment, to the last detail, is buried with him in his sailing ship by the river. But yet another significance attaches to this burial. It is the only one in England, though Norway has others. It is the recognition that the Valhalla of the old gods has gone, to admit the coming of the Christian faith into our island.

Sir W. Flinders Petrie believed that the first great people were those of Elam in Mesopotamia, a land now known as Iraq. That may be considered likely, because this region was settled and fertile before almost any other, and it afforded room for a large and peaceful population. The Elamites were making beautiful carvings of ivory when Egypt was populated by a people who belonged to the Older Stone Age.

The next great civilisation was that of Egypt, to which, before it was established, the carvings and pottery of Elam were coming by way of Palestine. Professor Petrie exhibited, at University College in London, dishes, bowls, beads, and pottery figures made by a people who came, perhaps, from the north through Palestine 9000 or 10,000 B.C. He called their civilisation the Badarian culture.

We may suppose that there were several places where civilisations sprang up and flourished independently, and that many

PICTURES   ·   STATUES   ·   CARVINGS   ·   BUILDINGS   ·   IVORIES   ·   CRAFTS centuries after such beginnings the civilisations mingled. Thus, after the Egyptian world was developing, Crete appears as an independent civilisation which can be traced back to 4000 B.C., when the Egyptians were building Pyramids, but it may have been older than that. Crete waxed and waned with the Egyptians; it was great in 3000 B.C. and at its greatest in 1500 B.C. After this China appears with a civilisation of its own which it may have taken from Persia or Babylon, but which has always had a character of its own. Next after that was the North Syrian, which the Egyptians, to their surprise, found well established when in 1500 B.C. they invaded the country by way of Palestine and met the Hittites.

WHAT HAS BEEN FOUND IN EGYPT

The three stages of the disclosure of an ancient civilisation are the exploration of the country where it flourished, the excavation of the sites of its greatness, and the reading of the meaning of the relics unearthed.

Egypt drew the explorers from very early times, and some, like Herodotus, described remains, such as the great irrigation lake of Moeris, which nobody else was able to find afterwards. But the first systematic exploration of Egypt began with a military expedition. Napoleon in 1798 took to Egypt with his Army of Conquest a number of draughtsmen and engineers whose work endured when Napoleon's dream had faded. The work was well done; the descriptions of Egypt continued to appear from 1809 to 1813. A second survey by the great French archaeologist Champollion, aided by Rossellini, was made by 1828. This made known all the country below Aswan to Alexandria. Later in the century Lepsius surveyed the other part of Egypt from Nubia to Khartoum, as well as Memphis and the Egyptian mines in the Sinai Peninsula.

The deciphering of the inscriptions on the antiquities laid bare went on even while the country was being explored. The great discovery of the Rosetta Stone described on page 6596, thanks to the labours of De Sacy, Akerblad, Dr. Thomas Young, and especially to the work of Champollion, provided the key to the hieroglyphic alphabet, so that all the written history of old Egypt as inscribed on its monuments could be read.

Mariette, another Frenchman, was the pioneer excavator in Egypt. He disclosed the Temple of the Sphinx at Gizeh and the great cemeteries at Sakkara; the temples at Abydos, at Dêr-el-Bahari, and at Edfu. He laid bare the vista of the columns of Karnak.

Gaston Maspero succeeded Mariette, and in 1881 he discovered the hiding-place of royal mummies which thousands of years before the priests had secretly removed from the Valley of the Tombs of the Kings to preserve them from the sacrilege of robbers. But though the plan saved them for many hundreds of years the robbers found the burial place at last, and slowly rifled it, selling the relics cautiously to travellers. One day some pages of an illuminated papyrus were shown to Maspero, who knew at once that they could have come only from a royal tomb and learned that they had been bought at Thebes. Suspicion pointed to four Arab brothers who lived in some deserted tombs. Maspero offered a heavy reward, and the Arabs agreed to lead the way to the hidden tomb near Dêr-el-Bahari, where Queen Hatshepset built her famous valley temple. It was a perilous and mysterious way, too, a black shaft forty feet deep leading to a tunnel where the explorers had sometimes to go on hands and knees. A corner was turned, another passage, a flight of steps in the rock, and at last they found a chamber piled and lined with mummy cases.

Another black tunnel sloped downwards to a chamber filled with such an assemblage of royal mummies as no Egyptologist had ever set eyes on before: Rameses the Second, Thothmes the Third, Seti the First, eleven kings in all and nine queens. All, wrapped in sail cloth, were transported to Cairo.

That was one of the strangest adventures in Egyptian discovery; but in importance it was not greater than Maspero's opening of the pyramid of Unas at Sakkara about the same time. On the walls of this Fifth Dynasty chamber were found inscriptions of texts, rites, and incantations which were of inestimable

RELICS OF EARLY CIVILISATIONS

A TEMPLE OF ISIS IN EGYPT

THE GREAT STATUE OF RAMESES THE SECOND NEAR BEDRASHEIN

 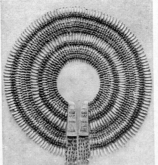 

AN ANIMAL WHICH ADORNED THE KING'S COUCH, A COLLARETTE, AND A HEAD FROM THE
CORONATION CHAIR, FOUND IN TUTANKHAMEN'S TOMB

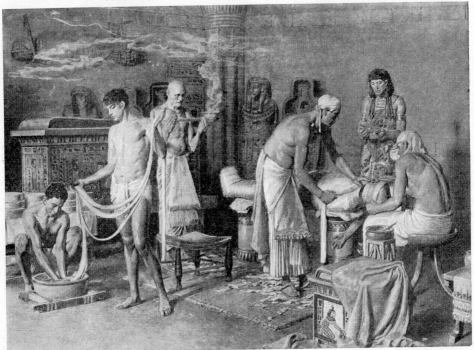

A SCENE IN ANCIENT EGYPT—THE MASTER OF CEREMONIES SUPERINTENDING THE WRAPPING
OF A ROYAL MUMMY

A PANEL OF TUTANKHAMEN'S
CORONATION THRONE

THE CHAIR OF
QUEEN TIYI

THE UPPER FRONT PANEL OF ONE
OF TUTANKHAMEN'S CHARIOTS

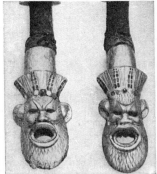

THE CORONATION THRONE, A WOODEN EFFIGY OF THE KING, AND PARTS OF THE HARNESS
OF A ROYAL CHARIOT, FROM TUTANKHAMEN'S TOMB

A SCENE IN ANCIENT EGYPT—REMOVING THE ROYAL MUMMY FROM THE PALACE TO THE TOMB

A SILVER BRACELET OF QUEEN
TAUSRET OF EGYPT

THE DELUGE TABLET,
FROM NINEVEH

A COPPER LION DISCOVERED
AT UR

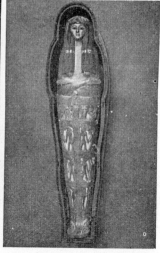

THE MUMMY OF THENT-
MUTES-KEBTI

A CYLINDER OF SENNACHERIB,
KING OF ASSYRIA

THE MUMMY OF AN
EGYPTIAN PRINCESS

THE GENEALOGICAL TREE OF RAMESES AT KARNAK

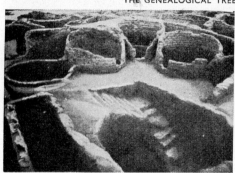

SPIRAL STEPS LEADING TO A WELL IN A
HOUSE AT TEL-EL-AMARNA

AN INLAID GOLD PECTORAL OF A KING OF EGYPT
OF THE TWELFTH DYNASTY

A WOODEN FIGURE FROM AN
EGYPTIAN TOMB

A WALL PAINTING
FROM THEBES

A LION-HEADED FIGURE FROM
THE TEMPLE OF MUT AT KARNAK

A PORTION OF THE WONDERFUL BRONZE GATES AT BALAWAT

RUINED WALLS OF OLD BABYLON

THE ENTRANCE TO THE SERAPEUM AT MEMPHIS

*The pictures on these pages of objects from Tutankhamen's tomb are from The Times World Copyright Photographs by
Mr. Harry Burton ; other pictures are reproduced by courtesy of the E.N.A., Dr. Hall, and others*

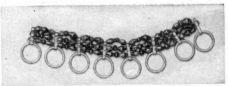

ONE OF THE MANY BEAUTIFUL NECKLACES FOUND
DURING THE EXCAVATIONS AT UR

GOLD VANITY CASE AND
ITS CONTENTS FROM UR

A TOILET-BOX OF
STONE FROM UR

THE GOLD WIG OF A
PRINCE FROM UR

A HAND ON A SILVER PIN
FOUND AT UR

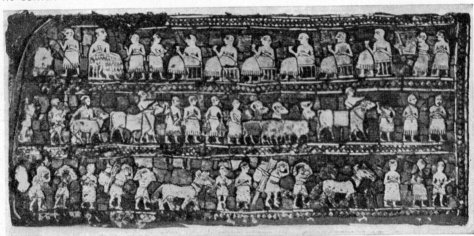

A MOSAIC PLAQUE SHOWING THE ROYAL FAMILY AT A FEAST, DISCOVERED AT UR

A LAMP IN THE FORM OF A DUCK
DISCOVERED AT UR

A DAIRY FARM FOUND ON A FRIEZE
NEAR UR

DAGGERS MADE OF SILVER,
GOLD, AND COPPER FROM UR

AN ADZE MADE OF GOLD
FOUND AT UR

Photographs taken for the British Museum and Pennsylvania University Museum by the staff of Sir Leonard Woolley

value for the study of the Egyptian language and of the early religious ideas of the priesthood.

Although today, and indeed for over half a century, the Cairo Museum has reserved the right to keep in Egypt anything that is found there, other countries, Great Britain, the United States, and Switzerland, have been allowed to excavate; and the work of the English Egypt Exploration Fund and Society, begun in 1883, is a witness to the value to knowledge of this permission.

THE ANCIENT GREEK CITY FOUND IN THE DESERT OF EGYPT

The efforts of the various nations have produced an extraordinary amount of knowledge as well as of wonderful objects.

The discoveries include the finding by Professor Petrie of the sites of Tanis and the early Greek city of Naukratis in 1884–85, to which the clue was given by an Arab who offered Petrie part of an alabaster statuette which the professor recognised as Greek work. The Arab said where he had found it, and Petrie, after a journey of twenty miles from the railway into the desert, found many mounds scattered with Greek pottery. When next year he came back to excavate, almost the first stones he turned over were part of a tablet with a proclamation of the city of Naukratis, a place so long lost that its existence was doubted. The discovery by Petrie at Hawara of the sarcophagus containing the mummy of the noble Horuta, wrapped in a network of beryl, lapis lazuli, and silver, with its amulets and ring, and birds of gold, is a romance in itself, but a romance of immense labour and determination, for the sarcophagus was in a flooded chamber at the bottom of a shaft forty feet deep.

HOW THE KING OF BABYLON SENT LETTERS TO THE KING OF EGYPT

But far more important as revealing the forgotten past were the discoveries at Tel-el-Amarna, which began in 1887 with the clay tablets on which were inscribed letters sent by the king of Babylon to the king of Egypt. They were accidentally picked out by an Arab woman who was searching for trifles to sell to tourists. In them is mentioned a present of some couches which may be the very objects afterwards found in Tutankhamen's tomb. Found at Tel-el-Amarna in the ensuing years of excavation were the relics and tablets of Akhnaton, who was called the Heretic King because he renounced the old gods of Thebes and commanded men to worship one god, the Sun.

From Tel-el-Amarna the Germans carried off to Berlin the contents of the tomb of the sculptor Thuthmose, and with them the lovely head of Nefertiti, of which everyone can now buy a copy, and some heads of her husband King Akhnaton. After a brief reign of faithful failure Akhnaton was succeeded by Tutankhamen, who after an equally brief reign had his name erased from the official list of Egyptian kings. But time brought for him its revenges, for the sensational discovery of his tomb by Howard Carter and Lord Carnavon carried his name all over the world. Its wealth of gold and jewels made it one of the largest and richest collections that ever had been found.

THE PRICELESS COFFIN IN THE TOMB OF TUTANKHAMEN

Some of the treasures are of exquisite workmanship and beauty ; some not so fine. But the coffin in which the mummy of the king was found ranks as the strangest. The outer stone coffin, the sarcophagus, was enclosed in four shrines, and in the sarcophagus were three coffins, the outer two in wood plated with gold, the innermost of solid gold. As bullion it is worth many thousands of pounds, as a work of art it is beyond price. The diadem of the king is also a supreme example of the goldsmith's art. But these illustrious gems of ancient culture were surrounded by many miscellaneous objects, why and how heaped together is a mystery.

There are magnificent examples of funerary furniture heavily gilded and carved in low relief with gods and beasts; boxes of wood inlaid with precious stones; drinking cups of glass and finely cut faience, and even silver trumpets which can be and have on ceremonial occasions been blown. Some of the innumerable other things are, it must be confessed, not of the highest taste or ornament, but they may not have been so considered by those who heaped them here in rude plenty. It is rather saddening to contemplate that this is all the glory left to the king, yet his name will not be forgotten.

Between these discoveries came that by E. H. Naville in 1887–89 of the site of Bubastis, a place known to Herodotus and rich in statuettes; and Petrie's excavations in the Fayoum which at last showed where the fabled Labyrinth of Herodotus and Lake Moeris must have been. Many remarkable Greco-Roman mummy portraits were found here and the first great collection of papyri in Greek and Roman characters. De Morgan found the treasures of the Pyramids of Dahshur, a mass of pectorals, rings, bracelets, necklaces, chains, pendants, and diadems that belonged to the wives of three of the pharaohs of the Twelfth Dynasty. One of these that belonged to the wife of Senusert the Third is marvellous in its taste and dexterity of workmanship, a miracle of gold threads and jewelled flowers so fine that it could never have been worn, but must have been made to lie on a tomb.

Then came the tombs of the kings of the early Dynasties at Abydos, which Amélineau first opened, to be followed by Petrie and Naville in later years. To Petrie in 1896 fell the discovery of the inscriptions of the King Meneptah which referred to Israel. Then followed discoveries which put back the Egyptian clock thousands of years to the race that possessed Egypt before the Dynastic kings. The relics of this pre-dynastic people were first found by Petrie at Nakadah in 1895–96. They were a race which buried their people crouching in graves surrounded by black-topped ware and hand-made pottery going back to the Stone Age. This opened up a new vista of the origins of Egypt quite distinct from those who cut in the rock the tombs of the kings near Thebes. Later came Petrie's discoveries at Badaria in 1924 of the oldest civilisation known,

11,000 B.C. The Badarians were the very first agriculturalists to settle in Egypt. Their implements were flint and polished stone; their garments, tanned hides; and their metalwork, copper. Another triumph was Mr. Firth's identification near the Step Pyramid of Sakkara of the oldest stone building in the world.

Other excavations were those of the tomb of Osiris at Abydos, which Naville found, and those due to the same archaeologist at the Temple of Dêr-el-Bahari where the diggers almost stumbled on the hidden chamber where stood the Goddess Hathor in the shape of a cow, one of the most beautiful and impressive pieces of sculpture of the ancient world.

Among more recent discoveries are the treasures found at Kawa with the shrine of Tirhakah, the king of Ethiopia who reigned over Egypt in the days of Hezekiah, and who warned him as we may read in the Bible against Sennacherib, the king of the Assyrians—the "wolf that came down on the fold." The shrine of Tirhakah now stands in the Ashmolean Museum at Oxford.

We conclude this necessarily very brief account of Egyptian discovery with a note on Egypt's well-known monument, the Sphinx. This great block of rock near Cairo was carved into the likeness of the Sphinx in the time of Chephren of the Fourth Dynasty nearly 5000 years ago. The sand which long obscured its riddle has been cleared away—to reveal that this great god, for it was not a goddess, had feet of clay, for the great paws are partly made up of brickwork.

WHAT HAS BEEN FOUND IN IRAQ

As in Egypt so in Iraq (formerly known as Mesopotamia) the history of its peoples remained a sealed book till the nineteenth century. The tradition of the site of Nineveh near Mosul and Babylon near Baghdad remained, and many travellers, including Niebuhr, had gazed on the heaps that covered them. The first to survey them carefully was C. J. Rich, who lived as the agent of the East India Company in Baghdad, where he died aged 33 in 1820. Rich prepared the field for later explorers by careful statement of the gigantic remains of the lost cities and civilisations of the Assyrians, Babylonians, and their predecessors. Niebuhr had surveyed

Persepolis in 1765; but it was not till (as in Egypt) a military expedition was in the country that exact knowledge of the sites was placed before the world. General Chesney's mission in 1835 was peaceful, but it carefully surveyed the courses of the Tigris and the Euphrates, and all later explorers used Chesney's maps. The surveys of Assyria by J. F. Jones and of the site of Babylon under Selby which were made later were also of great value and interest to archaeologists.

Excavation had not yet begun, but the extensive rubbish heaps of the ruins yielded clay tablets and bricks inscribed with unknown characters. There seemed something like a parallel between these characters and the threefold characters of the Rosetta Stone of Egypt, but they presented a far more difficult problem than faced the interpreters of the Egyptian hieroglyphics. The three Babylonian writings were made out to be Old Persian with perhaps 40 symbols or letters; a more difficult writing which should be that of the early Mesopotamians, the Susians, or Elamites; and a still more elaborate writing distinguished as Babylonian. All the help for deciphering them in 1802 lay in the fact that the three writings were often found side by side.

In that year Grotefend, by picking out three royal names in the simplest of these forms of writing, took the first step, and he ascertained about one-third of the old Persian letters. But his essay on the

Others were now following: Dr. Hincks, an Irish clergyman of immense scholarship, who stands first as the examiner of the second and third script characters, Oppert, De Saulcy, and Talbot. So strange seemed the reading of these ancient characters, that there were doubters. These were silenced when, in 1857, a newly found clay cylinder inscribed with the characters was brought home from Mesopotamia and submitted to Rawlinson, Hincks, Talbot, and Oppert for independent translation. When their translations were unsealed they all gave the same version.

Only one step more in the unravelling of the dead languages need be recorded here. Hincks saw that these cuneiform writings of Babylon had come from some other source. So it seemed that this early Babylonian civilisation had been borrowed

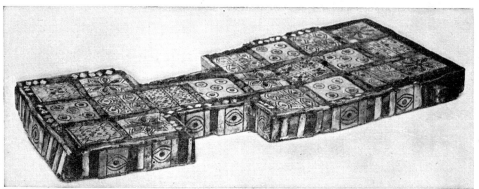

INLAID DRAUGHTBOARD OF 3500 B.C., FROM UR OF THE CHALDEES

subject was not published till ninety years later, when others had had all the credit as well as the work to do over again.

In those years much progress was made by De Sacy in reading the Old Persian; and then in 1835 came Sir Henry Rawlinson, who was aided by a knowledge of the ancient tongue of Zend, just as Champollion had known Coptic. Rawlinson, like Chesney, a soldier, was in Persia on diplomatic duty, and he had the true intelligent curiosity of the man of science. He found the key to the cuneiform inscriptions on the Rock of Behistun in 1846 through fitting together two inscriptions in different scripts, identifying the names of Hystaspes, Darius, and Xerxes, and thence deducing the alphabets of Old Persian. He first got 14 letters, and the deciphering of this, the simplest cuneiform, was a matter of time. A picture of him copying the inscription is on page 6272.

from another, the people of Sumer, or Akkad. The second group of cuneiform characters is now recognised as a late form of the old language of Susa or Elam. But whether the oldest language is that of the Sumerians or Semites is not known.

Naturally a tide of excavation followed in Mesopotamia the deciphering of the inscriptions, though it had begun with Paul Botta, the French Consul at Mosul, who in 1842 had turned an inquiring eye on the great mounds of Kouyunjik and Khorsabad. At Kouyunjik, the reputed site of Nineveh, he had no fortune, but one day a good-natured Arab looking inquisitively at Botta's men at work asked what they sought, and, being shown a brick with the cuneiform characters on it, remarked laughingly that there were thousands of them at his village of Khorsabad. Botta was doubtful, but he sent workmen to sink a shaft there.

They had not gone far before they came on a wall.

Botta hastened to the spot and digging was resumed furiously; and as the upshot of these labours they unearthed a crumbling building with slabs on which were sculptured fighting men. There were the ruins of the great palace of Sargon which crumbled as it was disclosed, for it had been destroyed long ages ago by fire.

LAYARD'S AMAZING ADVENTURES ON HIS JOURNEY TO THE EAST

Among the friends of Botta was a young Englishman, Austen Henry Layard, whose mind wandered from the study of the law to the fabled East.

After his father's death, Layard was asked by his uncle, a coffee planter in Ceylon, to join him there, and the young man jumped at the chance, but resolved on seeing as much as he could of the East by travelling overland. While he was still on the east of the Jordan the Bedouins captured him and he was a slave for six months. He escaped, and at last reached Damascus in rags and half-starving. The British Consul sent him on with a little money and some clothes, and he tramped his way to Constantinople.

Layard eventually reached Mosul, near Khorsabad, where Botta was excavating the Palace of Sargon. Layard sent to London an account, with drawings, of the discoveries, and asked for funds to make excavations of his own. James Fergusson, the writer on architecture, and John Murray, the publisher, talked them over, and were the first to start a small private subscription which brought old Assyria to light.

THE UNEXAMPLED TREASURES FOUND BY LAYARD ON THE SITE OF NINEVEH

Provided thus with funds, Layard set out on the dangerous road to Mosul again, and in a fortnight had set diggers to work at the mounds of Kouyunjik that had been given up by Botta as a bad job. Here Layard found the unexampled treasures which are now in the Assyrian halls of the British Museum—remains of the palaces built by Shalmaneser the Second and Garhaddin Ashurnasirpal the Second; the huge winged bulls which guarded the gateway; the sculptured lions of the Throne Rooms; the black obelisk of Shalmaneser. Layard went on yet another expedition, and searching anew Botta's site of Kouyunjik, found the Palace of Sennacherib.

His work was followed up by one of his native companions, Hormuzd Rassam, a cultured and able man who found the palace of Ashurbanipal, more familiar perhaps under the Greek name of Sardanapalus, with sculptures and the library. Years later he found the bronze gates of Balawat and partially disclosed the site of Sippar.

Layard had meanwhile transferred his attention to Babylonia. There was nothing quite so immediately startling here as at Nineveh; but knowledge of language and religion was piled up, and apart from the excavation of the temple of the Moon God at Ur of the Chaldees, the most striking thing for a number of years was Rawlinson's examination of the tower temple of Nebuchadnezzar.

De Sarzec excavated the mound of Telloh, where the Babylonian city of Lagash had been. There had been kings in Lagash before Babylon. De Sarzec found the sculptures and relics of Gudea and the mighty ones who had ruled in Sumer. His work pushed back farther the beginnings of the history of the world of cities, of rulers, of laws, of civilisation.

THE ANCIENT CIVILISATION DISCOVERED AT UR OF THE CHALDEES

The identification of the beginnings of civilisation, in fact, has shifted during this century from Egypt and the Nile Valley to Asia and the fertile plains of the Euphrates and the Tigris. Whereas it was believed in the nineteenth century that Egypt was the centre from which culture, or civilisation, had radiated over all lands, the excavations at Ur of the Chaldees, twelve miles from Baghdad, set up an imperious question mark. It referred the question back to the Sumerians, an ancient gifted people, or to the unknown hill country from which these immigrants descended into the great Mesopotamian plain. They were town-makers and town-dwellers who proceeded to civilise the shepherds and farmers they found there and survived the disastrous flood arising probably from insufficient drainage as the rivers overflowed, and mentioned in the Babylonian records and in the Book of Genesis. The Sumerians were not the only town-makers of their age, but they left an indelible mark of their work centuries later at Ur of the Chaldees, from which

Abraham led his flocks to the Promised Land of Palestine.

The earliest royal cemetery discovered at Ur is at least as old as the First Dynasty of Egypt, whose civilisation was less advanced, for the Sumerians had invented not only the potter's wheel but were experts in metals. As confirmation of their antiquity was the finding at Kish of the inscriptions of A-An-Hi-Pad-Da, King of Ur about 3100 B.C.

The excavations in Ur of the Chaldees began in 1922 and were undertaken by the joint expedition of the British Museum and the University of Pennsylvania Museum, with a grant from the Carnegie Corporation. Dr. H. R. Hall had already excavated a royal palace at Kish and a temple at Tell-el-Obeid, both of the first dynasty of the kings of Ur, when Ur itself, the capital of King Ur-Engur of the Third Dynasty, was uncovered. The most remarkable building at Ur is the Temple of the Moon God Nannar, patron of the city. Sir Leonard Woolley succeeded Dr. Hall, and it is to him we owe most of our knowledge of the ancient Sumerians.

Two months after the digging had begun in the Royal Cemetery area at Ur a gold dagger appeared as an indication of the treasures to come. This was followed by the discovery of a royal tomb, which had been robbed in antiquity; but afterwards in a nearby wide trench appeared bodies of men and women elaborately clothed and wearing headdresses of gold and lapis-lazuli. Then came a second tomb, which revealed the unaltered burial of a queen—complete with all her richest possessions. She was Queen Shubad. On her head was the regal crown, with wreaths of gold and flowers, with a comb of gold and heavy gold earrings. Beside her were a toilet box ; a gaming board ; her gold lyre ; a harp with a golden bull's head ; a mosaic standard ; and a vast collection of golden vessels and ceremonial weapons of gold. A procession on the mosaic standard reveals much of the dress and ceremonies of the Court at Ur.

A catalogue of all that was found was completed by Sir Leonard Woolley in two magnificent volumes. They contain coloured reproductions of a kingly gold helmet, gold goblets and bowls ; and, strangest of all, of a life-size ram caught in a thicket, a relic which passed into Jewish tradition centuries later.

THE LOST EMPIRE OF THE HITTITES

In north Syria the perseverance of nineteenth-century excavators and scholars resuscitated the lost empire of the Hittites and Amorites, who so troubled Jehoram. Uriah, the servant of David, was a Hittite. Hebrew merchants were the middlemen of the trade between the Hittites and the Egyptians, but the Egyptians had fought them before the time of Elijah, and the Hittites were a great people long before the days of the Exodus.

The first notice of this lost empire was due to Otter, in 1736, and nearly 80 years later, when the Rosetta stone of Egypt and the cuneiform inscriptions of Babylonia were being scrutinised, the writings on the famous Hamath stones, casts of which are in the British Museum, invited attention to an unknown script. Richard Burton had copied them. Dr. Wright, an Irish missionary at Damascus, sent the casts home and was the first to suggest that these were writings of the Hittites; and Professor Sayce was the first to attempt to decipher them.

Sayce has told us more of this lost people than any other writer. Their sway stretched far over Asia Minor. The Hittite Empire was to the north, its northern capital at Boghaz-Keui (Khatti), where Dr. Winckler excavated in 1906, and its southern capital was Carchemish, the modern Jarabis.

At the mountain fortress of Boghaz-Keui thousands of tablets inscribed in script have been found, and revealed as Hittite political records. They frequently mention a people, identified with the Achaeans of Homer, who were Greek seagoing raiders who served the Hittite kings.

French excavations on the North Syrian coast have carried the tale farther, for at Ras Shamra was a Greek settlement in which Achaeans mingled with Semites, perhaps Phoenicians, and to which were brought things from Cyprus, Babylonia, and Crete. There was a library with tablets in eight languages and dictionaries for the use of scribes. It was the meeting-place of East and West. At Shamra also were found relics in gold and ivory of Mycenean art.

The Hittite Empire was at its height just before Tutankhamen, and from tablets of Tel-el-Amarna we learn that the Hittites were then pressing southward and causing much apprehension in Egypt. The two Empires fought and the Hittites were not worsted. But the long wars of a century exhausted them and so prepared the way for the entry of the Israelites into the promised land of Canaan.

All these things are written in the book of knowledge which first Wright and then Sayce compiled from the references to the Hittites in Egyptian hieroglyphs, and to a lesser extent in Assyrian cuneiform writings, where the first clear account of the Hittites appears in the annals of Tiglath-Pileser the First, who besieged Carchemish. The Hittite Empire only went down before that of Sargon of Nineveh some seven centuries B.C.

In 1879 Professor Sayce went with an escort of Turkish soldiers to see two figures carved on a rock in the Pass of Karabel, near Smyrna, so ancient that Herodotus knew of them and said that Sesostris of Egypt had left them there. These warriors with bows and spears Sayce declared to be Hittite, and the inscription Hittite also. He had been led to this conclusion by an examination of those strange-looking hieroglyphics cut on a stone of black basalt and built into the corner of a house at Hamath. There were other stones as venerable. Dr Wright persuaded the Turkish Governor to remove the stones under a guard of soldiers to Constantinople, and plaster casts were made of them.

A HITTITE GOD AT CARCHEMISH

The casts or photographs were seen by Dr. Hayes Ward, of New York, who perceived in them a resemblance to seal writings found in Nineveh by Layard, which were neither Assyrian nor Phoenician nor Egyptian. To Sayce it seemed most reasonable that they were the writing of the Hittites. His supposition was confirmed by the excavations at Carchemish.

The truth flashed on Sayce. The figures in the Pass at Karabel were not Egyptian, but Hittite. He spent three hours in the niche between the rocks, taking impressions of the writing, and with joy was able to confirm his belief. The Sesostris of Herodotus turned out to be not the pharaoh who fought the Hittites, but a symbol of the far-reaching power of his opponents. Hittite art and Hittite writing, if not the name of Hittite, were proved to have been known from the banks of the Euphrates to the Aegean Sea.

Herodotus must have described the figures from hearsay, for he said they were three feet high. They are more than life size; and the one that has suffered least from usage and time stands high above the path marching toward Ephesus and the Maeander. Not far away another sculpture has been found, a strange figure of a woman carved on the cliffs of Sipylos near Magnesia, seated on a throne with a lotus-flower on her head and hair streaming down her shoulders. She is the goddess of Asia Minor, the great Cybele. Sayce found one word on the inscription meaning king. The artist who graved it on Mount Sipylos must have learned his art on the banks of the River Nile.

The Amazons were the priestesses of this goddess, whose religion spread from Carchemish with the Hittites. It was a powerful religion, and the priestesses, in places numbering thousands, were armed. Ephesus was dedicated to her, though when it passed into Greek hands the goddess became the Greek Artemis. Sculptures found at Boghaz-Keui depict her in a chariot drawn by lions. Near Boghaz-Keui is Euyuk, where are the remains of a vast palace of stone, its entrance flanked by monoliths of granite carved with Sphinx-like figures and a double-headed eagle, the way being carved with bas-reliefs as in Assyria.

Carchemish was first identified as the site of the Hittite capital by W. Skene, the English consul at Aleppo; it was visited by George Smith, famous as the reader of the Assyrian Deluge tablet; and the site was bought by Mr. Henderson, a later Aleppo consul, for the price of a cow! The Hittite Empire subsidised the Greek colonies; moreover, the sculptured lions at Mycenae, at the Lion Gate behind which Schliemann excavated, were inspired by Hittite art.

The Story of the Peoples of All Nations and Their Homelands

The minarets that rise above Cairo

EGYPT AND ITS LONG, LONG STORY

For over ten thousand years men have lived and thrived on the banks of the River Nile.

In spring and early summer the mountains of Ethiopia and Central Africa send down their waters to flood and make fertile the narrow valley and the delta of the Nile. Egypt, as this enriched area is called, is therefore a long oasis through the desert belt which crosses the world from Morocco to China. It has been felt to be a favoured land almost as far back as human records go. Long before Britain had even a name Egypt was rich and powerful, and the ruins of her ancient glory remain one of Earth's wonders.

Egypt is today a rich land, with abundant, oft-recurring harvests. Yet the area of its productive part is very small, merely alongside the Nile. Though Egypt, including its outlying deserts, occupies 386,000 square miles, the Nile valley and delta, where the Nile broadens out through canals towards the sea, is only 13,574 square miles, nearly twice the size of Wales. Yet it has a population of about 23 million. The country is, therefore, very thickly peopled in some parts, and sparsely in others.

Its great ancient cities are populous. Cairo, the capital, has nearly 4,000,000

inhabitants; Alexandria (once the most learned city in the world) has over 1,000,000 ; and Port Said, at the northern entrance to the Suez Canal, has over 178,000.

The products of Egypt are mainly agricultural (cotton, sugar, rice, tobacco, maize, wheat, barley, and millet), and so helpful is the climate that it allows three crops yearly. The area farmed by each worker is small, for out of 23 million people there are about 2,600,000 landowners.

The crops are almost entirely dependent on irrigation schemes based upon the River Nile which flows for 960 miles through Egypt without receiving any tributaries. The Nile now irrigates over five million acres, its flow being held up by huge dams such as that of the Gebel Awlia reservoir which is over 5400 yards long and holds up to 2000 million cubic metres of water. The famous Aswan reservoir can hold over twice that quantity.

Cotton is the backbone of Egypt's industrial wealth; petroleum and phosphates are her chief mineral products.

The life of the ordinary people remains, in spite of modern inventions and the spread of education, much the same as it was in the distant past, and may be imagined from many of the features in

THE FIVE CONTINENTS & 100 NATIONS & RACES THAT INHABIT THEM

the history of this ancient land that must now be recalled.

When we glance at Egypt as it is today we are reminded at every turn of a great and wonderful past. Its true glory lies in distant times. Grand and immense buildings, such as those we see by the banks of the Nile, exist only as the result of the movement of material—hard and laborious work, indeed—by thousands of human beings. We must realise that a pyramid is solid, except for the passages and the funeral chambers to which they lead.

THE PYRAMID SET UP IN THE SANDS BY A HUNDRED THOUSAND SLAVES

The base of the Great Pyramid is almost exactly the same size and shape as Lincoln's Inn Fields. What a scene must have been the building of such a mass, with such a base and such a height!

The huge granite facing-stones of the pyramid had to be quarried in the neighbourhood of Aswan, and brought down the river for hundreds of miles, and then, with enormous toil, men had to drag, push, and roll them over the burning sands.

Let us think of the stupendous work of getting it all into place. It is said that a hundred thousand slaves took part in this huge piece of work.

We may well wonder what was the object of building the Pyramids at such immense cost and labour. As far as we know it was not merely for the glory of the King and to provide a secure resting-place for his remains ; it was because the prosperity of the whole land was thought to depend on the King's survival after death.

The Egyptians therefore did all that they possibly could to preserve the body, as long as possible, whole and entire. This they did by making mummies of the bodies and putting them in decorated coffins hidden away in great rock tombs, and in the Pyramids, where it was hoped that no one would ever be able to find or disturb them.

THE TREASURES OF THE TOMBS THAT TEMPTED THE ROBBERS

Alas, for the last 3000 years at least, robbers have broken into the tombs from time to time, attracted not by the mummies but by the treasure that was buried with them. For the Egyptians believed that, in some mysterious way, in the new life to which he had gone, the departed person would need the things he had owned in his earthly life. So, with the mummies of royal and rich people were put their valuable ornaments and their possessions, besides furniture, clothes, and food for the use of the spirit of the departed, and the quaint little figures that were supposed to do the work that would be required in the fields of the land of peace.

It is in the Valley of the Kings, among the limestone hills behind the plain of Thebes, that the most richly equipped tombs of the Pharaohs have been found.

It is the sight of these personal belongings that brings us into such close touch with the Egypt of 3000 or 4000 years ago. For we have in the British Museum cases full of such treasures as the dolls with clay beads for hair, and the toys and little worn shoes and sandals of the children; the dressing cabinet of the fine lady, containing ointments for the eyes, elbow-cushions, and dainty pink kid slippers. We have, too, the palette and paints of the scribe, the musical instruments of the musician—in short, hundreds of articles of everyday use that bring us face to face with the people to whom they belonged centuries ago.

THE SPLENDID AND GIGANTIC TEMPLES BUILT BY THE OLD EGYPTIANS

The attention of the whole world has been drawn in our time to the intense personal interest of the Egyptian tombs by the discovery of the tomb of King Tutankhamen of which we can read on page 6881.

And, besides these interesting personal belongings and thousands of little figures, with nets and field implements painted on them, there were always put beside the mummy representations of the numberless gods to whom the Egyptians prayed, and to whom they erected wonderful temples, whose ruins still form one of the sights of Egypt. There is a great group of these temples on the Nile, where the magnificent city of Thebes once stood, far on the way to Aswan. The great halls, imposing gateways, and rows of pillars form a beautiful sight in brilliant sunshine and deep purple shadow, and, as we gaze at them, we fancy them once more in their first beauty, with long processions of chanting priests and priestesses, and gorgeous display of kingly magnificence when the king came to pay his worship, amidst the stately monuments of gold and silver, adorned with ivory and precious stones.

If we look at the walls and columns of the temples, at the solid vaults, at the coffin-cases, at the sculptures and the wall-paintings, we shall find most of them covered with picture-writing. Until the nineteenth century no one could guess what it meant. In 1799 an engraved stone was found at Rosetta, near Alexandria, now at the British Museum, which has served as a sort of key to unlock the mystery. There is a picture of this stone on page 685.

This discovery also opened up to us the how they expected to be judged, and how they believed they would live and work on their way through the underworld. Besides this and other religious books, there are many other papyri of great age, and they include fairy tales, war poems, medical and astronomical books, and lengthy instructions as to behaviour.

The first historical king of all Egypt is put by some in the thirty-fifth century before Christ. Some think that he, Menes, who is said to have turned the course of the Nile, lived much earlier. Before him there are legends of god-kings and heroes, and kings of small States. Specimens of very old pottery, with pictures on it of

CHILDREN AT A KINDERGARTEN IN CAIRO

old books and chapters of books constantly found in the tombs. These were in long rolls, or *papyri*, so called from the material on which they are written, the inner part of the papyrus reed growing on the Nile banks. We get our word paper from it.

The work of the scribes was to make copies of these papyri. The one most copied is called the Book of the Dead, parts of which are believed to be older than the pyramids themselves. Certain chapters of this book were always laid beside the mummies, to instruct them what to say and how to behave in the underworld. There is no end to the interest of the Book of the Dead, not only on account of its entrancing illustrations, but also for the teaching it gives about the religion of Egypt, how men tried to fit themselves in life for a happy hereafter; soldiers and boats, very like children's drawings of today, give an idea of the first known life on the Nile long before Menes.

For the sake of convenience, in dealing with the great number of kings who followed Menes, we group them into thirty or more dynasties, or families, and the names are gleaned from the various lists of kings on tablets and papyrus, made from time to time through the centuries, which have come down to us. When looking at inscriptions we can always distinguish royal names because they are surrounded by an oval line supposed to be a cord tied in a knot to preserve the name from contact with common ones. This oval is called a *cartouche*.

Before the king's name will generally be found some Egyptian words composed of a sign like an umbrella and an insect over two half-circles. These signs mean King of the North and South, for Egypt was long divided into two parts, and so we hear of the double crown, which is made up of the red crown of North Egypt and the white crown of South Egypt.

Each king also called himself Son of Ra, or the Sun, which is shown by a goose and a sun with a dot in the middle.

Very little is known of the kings of the first three dynasties. It was under the rule of the fourth that the three great pyramids near Cairo are believed to have been built by Khufu, by Khafra, and by Menkaura.

If we would see the speaking features of Khafra, and note how he sat to give audience to the overseers and officers of his great building works, we can find a cast of his wonderful lifelike portrait in the British Museum. There he sits on his throne, surrounded by memorials of the officials who superintended the building of the second pyramid.

Of Menkaura the museum possesses part of his skeleton and the fragments of his coffin, taken from the third pyramid, with the inscription saying he was just and merciful.

Not far from the Pyramids of Gizeh is an enormous monster, hewn out of the living rock, with a human head and the body of an animal, called the Sphinx, so large that it could scarcely be got into the drum below the dome of St. Paul's. Between the front paws is a little temple in which the Ancient Egyptians worshipped.

THE FAMILY FROM A FAR LAND WHICH CAME IN SEARCH OF FOOD

Many interesting tombs belong to this period, perhaps 2400 years before Christ. One of them has wall-paintings representing the arrival in the country of a family, such as that of Abraham, the great founder of the Jewish race. The story of his visit to Egypt in search of food, when there was a famine in his own country beyond the Isthmus of Suez, is familiar to us in the pages of the Bible. What a change it must have been to the patriarch, for many years used to a wandering tent life and the silence of wide spaces, to enter into the busy life of the Nile valley, with its great cities and huge buildings, and to see the luxury and splendour of the king's Court! It must have carried him back to his boyhood, to his native land, where there were also great cities and much wealth, a country, as we read in another part of this book, as old as Egypt itself.

We can well imagine that Abraham would tell stories of this visit to Egypt to his son Isaac, who would tell them to his son Jacob, and Jacob to Joseph. We read the story of Joseph elsewhere; let us follow him again on his sad journey to slavery in Egypt, fitting in all we can to make real his daily life.

THE BASKETS IN THE BRITISH MUSEUM WHICH JOSEPH MAY HAVE SEEN

The baskets in the upper Egyptian rooms at the British Museum might well have been those which the chief baker carried on his head; the models of the granaries show how corn was stored, and bring to mind Joseph's great work in fighting the famine that lasted so long.

Fashions changed so little in Egypt for centuries that we can well borrow those seats and other furniture and paintings in the cases around to put in the palace of the king to whom Joseph became as a son, and we may fancy them together discussing earnestly affairs of state—the king on his throne, in a black wig of little curls and plaits, like the one found in a reed box; and Joseph with his reed pens and paints, reading his report from a papyrus roll.

Little is known of the history of Egypt at this time, for the kings who ruled then destroyed monuments rather than set them up. But when these Shepherd Kings passed away many famous names of builders and soldiers rose up during the years Israel lived in bondage. Among them was Thothmes III, who inscribed and set up the great obelisk we call Cleopatra's Needle, though the famous queen lived several centuries after it was built. This pillar now stands on the Thames Embankment.

A GREAT QUEEN AND A KING WHO PERSECUTED THE ISRAELITES

Then there was the great Queen Hatshepset, often called the Elizabeth of Egyptian history. She sent most interesting expeditions to discover unknown countries, and had an account of them, with fine illustrations, engraved on the walls of a magnificent temple she built near Thebes. Rameses II is believed to have been the great oppressor of the Israelites, and we can see his face in the huge stone monuments he set up. More wonderful still is his mummy, which has been found, together with the mummies of many of his race, and put into the museum in Cairo. Thus, the features upon which so many looked with awe, perhaps the little Moses among them, are shown again to the world more than 3000 years after the great king's death.

THE SUFFERING OF EGYPT AT THE HANDS OF THE ASSYRIANS AND PERSIANS

For about a thousand years after this brilliant line of the Rameses dynasty, the history of Egypt, on the whole, was one of gradual decline and gathering trouble. It was during this time that the priests of the splendid temples became richer and richer and even more powerful, till at last they made themselves kings.

Dynasties of foreigners followed the priest-kings, and the country was breaking up and everything going down, when the kings of Assyria saw their chance, and began to attack Egypt on her own frontier. They overran the whole of the country, spoiling the harvests, so that the people starved, and the fine temples and monuments began to fall into decay. Egypt revived for a little while, only to be again devastated from end to end by the Assyrians, till Assyria, too, fell under the great power of the Persians.

The Egyptians took every opportunity to revolt against the Persians. Between the second and third revolts, in the fifth century before Christ, a traveller came to Egypt, notebook in hand, for he was an author, anxious to collect material for his History of the Persian Wars. This was the Greek Herodotus, the Father of History, who set down in a pleasant, chatty way his impressions of the wonderful country, of the Nile in flood, of the pyramids, and other great buildings.

THE GREEK SOLDIER WHO FOUNDED THE GREAT CITY OF ALEXANDRIA

The Persians, in their turn, were driven out by Alexander the Great, of Greece. His stay was but short in Egypt; but his passage has left marks for all time. He flashed across the desert to worship at the shrine of the god Jupiter Ammon, whom he claimed as an ancestor, and he planned and founded the great city of Alexandria, called after him, which, under his successors, became one of the most important cities in the world.

Three centuries before Alexander, an Egyptian king had employed Greek soldiers and allowed Greek traders to settle in the delta. Before this Egypt had been closed to foreigners; but these Greeks found their way into the country, and, little by little, their cleverness in trade, their wonderful power in art and in learning spread Greek influence ever farther along the Nile. Naukratis became a famous Greek city during this time, and today explorers find much Greek treasure of all kinds buried in various parts of the Nile delta.

The kings succeeding Alexander were the Ptolemys, the first of the name being one of Alexander's generals. They were great builders and restorers, and to them we owe the temple of Edfu. The Ptolemys also favoured the city of Alexandria, and started in it the immense library, afterwards unhappily burned, also the university to which were attracted some of the most famous Greek scholars.

Another Ptolemy built the tall lighthouse, said to be three times as high as the Monument in London, and, like the Pyramids, one of the wonders of the ancient world. The flare from its top guided the shipping of Alexandria safely into its double harbour for long years, but not a trace of it now remains.

HOW THE OLD TESTAMENT WAS TRANSLATED INTO GREEK

The same Ptolemy caused the Old Testament, originally written in the Hebrew language, and understood only by comparatively few people, to be translated at Alexandria into Greek, the beautiful language which was soon to be carried over the known world. Another good work of this same king was to cause an Egyptian scribe named Manetho, who knew Greek well, to write in that language a history of Egypt and its religion, and though his actual records have been lost, other writers have copied from Manetho, and thus his work has been of very great use.

Egypt became part of the Roman Empire in 31 B.C. on the defeat of Cleopatra, who was the last of the Ptolemys.

The country's prosperity now declined still further, and after Constantinople had become the capital of the eastern half of the Roman Empire, the burden of taxation caused the Egyptians to rebel. The result was that the Egyptian national or Coptic church broke with Constantinople, and the unsettled state of the country made it an easy prey to the invading Arabs (about A.D. 640).

The Arab conquest started a new phase in Egyptian history—a phase which indeed has lasted down to the present time. In 1517 Egypt was conquered by the Ottoman Turks who ruled from Constantinople, and for over 200 years Egypt was a province of Turkey, and when Napoleon came to Egypt in 1798 he found only the ruins of a great civilisation.

After the withdrawal of Napoleon's army, which was defeated by the British and the Turks, a Turkish officer named Mohammed Ali became governor of Egypt and built up a military force which made him almost independent of his master, the Ottoman Sultan.

Mohammed Ali's son Sa'id, after whom Port Said is named, granted the French financier de Lesseps a concession for the cutting of the Suez Canal. By the time it was completed (1869) Ismail, a grandson of Mohammed Ali, had come to the throne. He determined to press on with making Egypt an up-to-date country, but his ideas failed and the country fell into economic and financial chaos.

WHEN BRITAIN WAS INVITED TO HELP EGYPT

Then Britain was invited to take on the task of putting Egypt on its feet again. Lord Cromer was appointed British Consul-General in Egypt and his British advisers became the real rulers of the country.

In 1922 the British recognised King Fuad, a great-grandson of Mohammed Ali, as monarch of an independent Egypt, but Britain continued to maintain forces in the country for the protection of her own imperial communications.

In the Second World War the British Commonwealth forces in the Middle East continued to be based on Egypt. King Farouk, son of Fuad, had succeeded his father in 1936, but in July 1952 a group of young army and air-force officers forced Farouk to abdicate, abolished the political parties, and established a military dictatorship.

The young revolutionaries felt they needed an older man as the figure-head of their movement, and chose General Mohammed Neguib as President, Egypt being proclaimed a republic in June 1953. But the next year Neguib was dismissed. Colonel Abdul Nasser became President, and the British Government was persuaded to withdraw its garrisons from the Canal Zone and from the Sudan, which chose to become independent of both Britain and Egypt. .

EGYPT'S BID FOR LEADERSHIP OF THE ARAB WORLD

By the end of 1954 foreign observers agreed that President Nasser's group was the best government Egypt had had for many years, though the President himself was unpopular with some extremists who made an attempt on his life. Now began an attempt by Egypt's rulers to secure leadership of the Arab world, and an agreement to obtain armaments from the Communist countries of Eastern Europe in exchange for cotton was highly popular with the majority of Arabs, who saw in it a means for a war of revenge against Israel.

But Egypt's continued dealings with the Soviet Union led the American and British Governments in July 1956 to withdraw their offer of financial aid, to which Nasser replied by confiscating the property of the Suez Canal Company, which still had a right to operate in Egypt for another twelve years. Nasser had already been giving material help to the Muslim rebels against the French in Algeria, and had encouraged rebellion against British authority in southern Arabia and elsewhere.

So the British and French Governments, as the two countries most interested in the Suez Canal Company, decided that the time had come to check the Egyptian dictator, and when the United States Government refused to give practical support, the two European nations acted alone, invading the Canal Zone at the end of October 1956.

THE DIFFICULTIES THAT FACE THE PRESENT EGYPTIAN REGIME

This armed intervention was unanimously condemned by the United Nations, the United States and Russia voting together, and the British and French troops were withdrawn in December. President Nasser claimed that he had won a big diplomatic victory, but as the months passed his military dictatorship appeared to become less confident.

Meanwhile the country's economic development is faced with difficulties, and the hungry population continues to multiply. It would seem at the time of writing as if Egypt stands at an important cross-roads in her long history.

EGYPT, ANCIENT AND MODERN

THREE SYMBOLS OF OLD EGYPT—CAMEL, PYRAMID, AND SPHINX

HOUSES OF WORKERS AT MEHALA EL KUBRA, CENTRE OF THE TEXTILE INDUSTRY

THE PORT AUTHORITY AND CUSTOMS HOUSE AT PORT SAID

THE PALACE HOTEL, A SPLENDID BUILDING IN HELIOPOLIS, A SUBURB OF CAIRO

THE COMMITTEE HOUSE OF THE
UNIVERSITY OF CAIRO

OPERA HOUSE AND STATUE OF
IBRAHIM PASHA AT CAIRO

CAIRO, THE CAPITAL OF EGYPT—THE CITADEL WITH ITS GREAT MOSQUE

A BUSY STREET IN THE
NATIVE QUARTER

MOSQUES IN THE STREET OF
THE WEZIR GATE

THE MOSQUE AND STREET
OF EL BENAT

A STREET OF MODERN BUILDINGS
IN CAIRO

THE NILOMETER ON THE ISLAND
OF RODA NEAR CAIRO

THE OLD, OLD STORY OF EGYPT

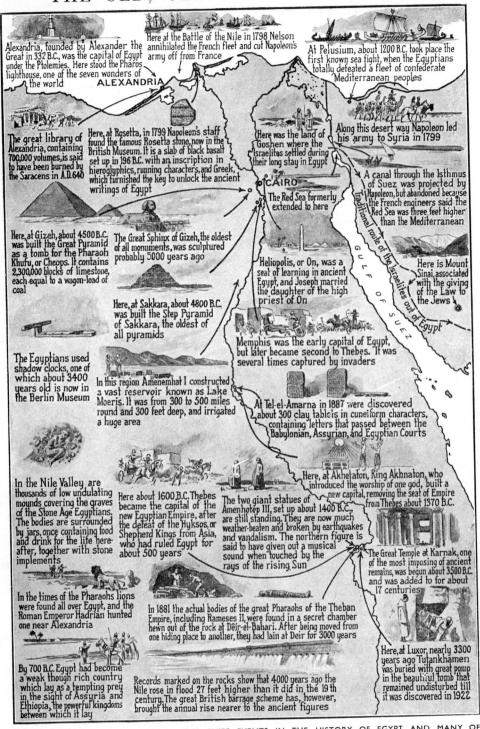

Alexandria, founded by Alexander the Great in 332 B.C., was the capital of Egypt under the Ptolemies. Here stood the Pharos lighthouse, one of the seven wonders of the world
ALEXANDRIA

Here at the Battle of the Nile in 1798 Nelson annihilated the French fleet and cut Napoleon's army off from France

At Pelusium, about 1200 B.C. took place the first known sea fight, when the Egyptians totally defeated a fleet of confederate Mediterranean peoples

The great library of Alexandria, containing 700,000 volumes, is said to have been burned by the Saracens in A.D.640

Here, at Rosetta, in 1799 Napoleon's staff found the famous Rosetta stone, now in the British Museum. It is a slab of black basalt set up in 196 B.C. with an inscription in hieroglyphics, running characters, and Greek, which furnished the key to unlock the ancient writings of Egypt

Here was the land of Goshen where the Israelites settled during their long stay in Egypt

Along this desert way Napoleon led his army to Syria in 1799

CAIRO

The Red Sea formerly extended to here

A canal through the Isthmus of Suez was projected by Napoleon, but abandoned because the French engineers said the Red Sea was three feet higher than the Mediterranean

Here, at Gizeh, about 4500 B.C. was built the Great Pyramid as a tomb for the Pharaoh Khufu, or Cheops. It contains 2,300,000 blocks of limestone, each equal to a wagon-load of coal

The Great Sphinx of Gizeh, the oldest of all monuments, was sculptured probably 5000 years ago

Heliopolis, or On, was a seat of learning in ancient Egypt, and Joseph married the daughter of the high priest of On

Here is Mount Sinai, associated with the giving of the Law to the Jews

Here, at Sakkara, about 4800 B.C. was built the Step Pyramid of Sakkara, the oldest of all pyramids

The Egyptians used shadow clocks, one of which about 3400 years old is now in the Berlin Museum

In this region Amenemhat I constructed a vast reservoir known as Lake Moeris. It was from 300 to 500 miles round and 300 feet deep, and irrigated a huge area

Memphis was the early capital of Egypt, but later became second to Thebes. It was several times captured by invaders

At Tel-el-Amarna in 1887 were discovered about 300 clay tablets in cuneiform characters, containing letters that passed between the Babylonian, Assyrian, and Egyptian Courts

In the Nile Valley are thousands of low undulating mounds covering the graves of the Stone Age Egyptians. The bodies are surrounded by jars, once containing food and drink for the life hereafter, together with stone implements

Here about 1600 B.C. Thebes became the capital of the new Egyptian Empire, after the defeat of the Hyksos, or Shepherd Kings from Asia, who had ruled Egypt for about 500 years

The two giant statues of Amenhotep III, set up about 1400 B.C., are still standing. They are now much weather-beaten and broken by earthquakes and vandalism. The northern figure is said to have given out a musical sound when touched by the rays of the rising Sun

Here, at Akhetaton, King Akhnaton, who introduced the worship of one god, built a new capital, removing the seat of Empire from Thebes about 1370 B.C.

The Great Temple at Karnak, one of the most imposing of ancient remains, was begun about 3500 B.C. and was added to for about 17 centuries

In the times of the Pharaohs lions were found all over Egypt, and the Roman Emperor Hadrian hunted one near Alexandria

In 1881 the actual bodies of the great Pharaohs of the Theban Empire, including Rameses II, were found in a secret chamber hewn out of the rock at Dêir-el-Bahari. After being moved from one hiding place to another, they had lain at Deir for 3000 years

Here, at Luxor, nearly 3300 years ago Tutankhamen was buried with great pomp in the beautiful tomb that remained undisturbed till it was discovered in 1922

By 700 B.C. Egypt had become a weak though rich country which lay as a tempting prey in the sight of Assyria and Ethiopia, the powerful kingdoms between which it lay

Records marked on the rocks show that 4000 years ago the Nile rose in flood 27 feet higher than it did in the 19th century. The great British barrage scheme has, however, brought the annual rise nearer to the ancient figures

THIS PICTURE-MAP SHOWS SOME OF THE CHIEF EVENTS IN THE HISTORY OF EGYPT AND MANY OF THE ANCIENT MONUMENTS WHICH HAVE STOOD FOR THOUSANDS OF YEARS

See Main Index for other pictures of Egypt's ancient monuments

One Thousand Poems of All Times and All Countries

The Most Famous Poem of Macaulay

LORD MACAULAY, the brilliant historian, was also famous in his day as a poet, and though his poems are not now in the fashion, we ought to be large-minded enough to admire their vigour and fire. He lived in his mind in days historical. Old happenings were real to him. Even the legendary days of old Rome, before regular history was written, were as alive to him as the days he lived in. We see it in this poetical account of a famous incident in traditional Roman times, soon after the Republic was formed. It does not matter a bit to us who were the people he introduces into the poem. The scene is stirring and romantic, and the story is finely told. The poet has the power of making mere names of men and places sound heroic and noble, and the spirit of patriotism shown throughout, and especially towards the close of the Lay, is thrilling. The poem is not quite complete here.

HOW HORATIUS KEPT THE BRIDGE

LARS PORSENA of Clusium
    By the Nine Gods he swore
That the great house of Tarquin
    Should suffer wrong no more.
By the Nine Gods he swore it,
    And named a trysting day,
And bade his messengers ride forth,
East and west and south and north,
    To summon his array.

AND now hath every city
    Sent up her tale of men;
The foot are fourscore thousand,
    The horse are thousands ten:
Before the gates of Sutrium
    Is met the great array.
A proud man was Lars Porsena
    Upon the trysting day.

BUT by the yellow Tiber
    Was tumult and affright:
From all the spacious champaign
    To Rome men took their flight.
A mile around the city,
    The throng stopped up the ways;
A fearful sight it was to see
    Through two long nights and days.

TO eastward and to westward
    Have spread the Tuscan bands;
Nor house, nor fence, nor dovecote
    In Crustumerium stands.
Verbenna down to Ostia
    Hath wasted all the plain;
Astur hath stormed Janiculum,
    And the stout guards are slain.

I WIS, in all the Senate,
    There was no heart so bold
But sore it ached and fast it beat
    When that ill news was told.

Forthwith up rose the Consul,
    Up rose the Fathers all;
In haste they girded up their gowns,
    And hied them to the wall.

THEY held a council standing
    Before the river-gate;
Short time was there, ye well may guess,
    For musing or debate.
Out spake the Consul roundly:
    " The bridge must straight go down;
For, since Janiculum is lost,
    Nought else can save the town."

JUST then a scout came flying,
    All wild with haste and fear:
" To arms! to arms! Sir Consul;
    Lars Porsena is here."
On the low hills to the westward
    The Consul fixed his eye,
And saw the swarthy storm of dust
    Rise fast along the sky.

AND nearer fast and nearer
    Doth the red whirlwind come;
And louder still and still more loud,
From underneath that rolling cloud,
Is heard the trumpet's war-note proud,
    The trampling, and the hum.
And plainly and more plainly
    Now through the gloom appears,
Far to left and far to right,
In broken gleams of dark-blue light,
The long array of helmets bright,
    The long array of spears.

AND plainly and more plainly,
    Above that glimmering line,
Now might ye see the banners
    Of twelve fair cities shine;
But the banner of proud Clusium
    Was highest of them all,
The terror of the Umbrian,
    The terror of the Gaul.

POEMS · SONGS · BALLADS · VERSES AND RHYMES WITH MUSIC

And plainly and more plainly
  Now might the burghers know,
By port and vest, by horse and crest,
  Each warlike Lucumo.
There Clinius of Arretium
  On his fleet roan was seen;
And Astur of the fourfold shield,
Girt with the brand none else may wield,
Tolumnius with the belt of gold,
And dark Verbenna from the hold
  By reedy Thrasymene.

Fast by the royal standard,
  O'erlooking all the war,
Lars Porsena of Clusium
  Sat in his ivory car.
By the right wheel rode Mamilius,
  Prince of the Latian name;
And by the left false Sextus,
  That wrought the deed of shame.

But when the face of Sextus
  Was seen among the foes,
A yell that rent the firmament
  From all the town arose.
On the house-tops was no woman
  But spat towards him and hissed;
No child but screamed out curses,
  And shook its little fist.

But the Consul's brow was sad,
  And the Consul's speech was low,
And darkly looked he at the wall,
  And darkly at the foe.
" Their van will be upon us
  Before the bridge goes down;
And if they once may win the bridge
  What hope to save the town? "

Then out spake brave Horatius,
  The Captain of the Gate:
" To every man upon this earth
  Death cometh soon or late;
And how can man die better
  Than facing fearful odds
For the ashes of his fathers
  And the temples of his gods?

    .   .   .   .   .

" Hew down the bridge, Sir Consul,
  With all the speed ye may;
I, with two more to help me,
  Will hold the foe in play.
In yon strait path a thousand
  May well be stopped by three.
Now, who will stand on either hand,
  And keep the bridge with me? "

Then out spake Spurius Lartius,
  A Ramnian proud was he:
" Lo, I will stand at thy right hand,
  And keep the bridge with thee."
And out spake strong Herminius,

Of Titian blood was he:
" I will abide on thy left side,
  And keep the bridge with thee."

" Horatius," quoth the Consul,
  " As thou sayest, so let it be."
And straight against that great array
  Forth went the dauntless Three;
For Romans in Rome's quarrel
  Spared neither land nor gold,
Nor son nor wife, nor limb nor life,
  In the brave days of old.

Then none was for a party,
  Then all were for the State;
Then the great man helped the poor,
  And the poor man loved the great;
Then lands were fairly portioned;
  Then spoils were fairly sold;
The Romans were like brothers
  In the brave days of old.

Now Roman is to Roman
  More hateful than a foe,
And the Tribunes beard the high,
  And the Fathers grind the low.
As we wax hot in faction,
  In battle we wax cold;
Wherefore men fight not as they fought
  In the brave days of old.

Now while the Three were tightening
  Their harness on their backs,
The Consul was the foremost man
  To take in hand an axe;
And Fathers mixed with Commons
  Seized hatchet, bar, and crow,
And smote upon the planks above,
  And loosed the props below.

Meanwhile the Tuscan army,
  Right glorious to behold,
Came flashing back the noonday light,
Rank behind rank, like surges bright
  Of a broad sea of gold;
Four hundred trumpets sounded
  A peal of warlike glee,
As that great host, with measured tread,
And spears advanced, and ensigns spread,
Rolled slowly towards the bridge's head,
  Where stood the dauntless Three.

The Three stood calm and silent,
  And looked upon the foes,
And a great shout of laughter
  From all the vanguard rose;
And forth three chiefs came spurring
  Before that deep array;
To earth they sprang, their swords they
    drew,
And lifted high their shields and flew
  To win the narrow way:

Aunus from green Tifernum,
  Lord of the Hill of Vines;
And Seius, whose eight hundred slaves
  Sicken in Ilva's mines;
And Picus, long to Clusium
  Vassal in peace and war,
Who led to fight his Umbrian powers
From that grey crag where, girt with
    towers,
The fortress of Nequinum lowers
  O'er the pale waves of Nar.

Stout Lartius hurled down Aunus
  Into the stream beneath;
Herminius struck at Seius,
  And clove him to the teeth;
At Picus brave Horatius
  Darted one fiery thrust;
And the proud Umbrian's gilded arms
  Clashed in the bloody dust.

Then Ocnus of Falerii
  Rushed on the Roman Three;
And Lausulus of Urgo,
  The rover of the sea;
And Arnus of Volsinium,
  Who slew the great wild boar,
The great wild boar that had his den
Amidst the reeds of Cosa's fen,
And wasted fields and slaughtered men
  Along Albinia's shore.

Herminius smote down Arnus;
  Lartius laid Ocnus low;
Right to the heart of Lausulus
  Horatius sent a blow.
" Lie there," he cried, " fell pirate!
  No more, aghast and pale,
From Ostia's walls the crowd shall mark
The track of thy destroying bark.
No more Campania's hinds shall fly
To woods and caverns when they spy
  Thy thrice accursed sail."

And now no sound of laughter
  Was heard among the foes.
A wild and wrathful clamour
From all the vanguard rose.
Six spears' length from the entrance
  Halted that deep array,
And for a space no man came forth
  To win the narrow way.

But hark! the cry is Astur:
  And lo! the ranks divide;
And the great Lord of Luna
  Comes with his stately stride.
Upon his ample shoulders
  Clangs loud the fourfold shield,
And in his hand he shakes the brand
  Which none but he can wield.

He smiled on those bold Romans
  A smile serene and high;
He eyed the flinching Tuscans,
  And scorn was in his eye.
Quoth he, " The she-wolf's litter
  Stand savagely at bay;
But will ye dare to follow
  If Astur clears the way? "

Then, whirling up his broadsword
  With both hands to the height,
He rushed against Horatius,
  And smote with all his might.
With shield and blade Horatius
  Right deftly turned the blow.
The blow, though turned, came yet too
    nigh;
It missed his helm, but gashed his thigh;
The Tuscans raised a joyful cry
  To see the red blood flow.

He reeled, and on Herminius
  He leaned one breathing-space;
Then, like a wild cat mad with wounds,
  Sprang right at Astur's face;
Through teeth, and skull, and helmet
  So fierce a thrust he sped,
The good sword stood a hand-breadth out
  Behind the Tuscan's head.

.   .   .   .   .

On Astur's throat Horatius
  Right firmly pressed his heel,
And thrice and four times tugged amain
  Ere he wrenched out the steel.
" And see," he cried, " the welcome,
  Fair guests, that waits you here!
What noble Lucumo comes next
  To taste our Roman cheer? "

.   .   .   .   .

But meanwhile axe and lever
  Have manfully been plied;
And now the bridge hangs tottering
  Above the boiling tide.
" Come back, come back, Horatius! "
  Loud cried the Fathers all.
" Back, Lartius! Back, Herminius!
  Back, ere the ruin fall! "

Back darted Spurius Lartius;
  Herminius darted back;
And, as they passed, beneath their feet
  They felt the timbers crack.
But when they turned their faces,
  And on the farther shore
Saw brave Horatius stand alone,
  They would have crossed once more.

But with a crash like thunder
  Fell every loosened beam,

And, like a dam, the mighty wreck
  Lay right athwart the stream.
And a long shout of triumph
  Rose from the walls of Rome,
As to the highest turret-tops
  Was splashed the yellow foam.

And, like a horse unbroken
  When first he feels the rein,
The furious river struggled hard,
  And tossed his tawny mane,
And burst the curb, and bounded,
  Rejoicing to be free,
And whirling down, in fierce career,
Battlement, and plank, and pier,
  Rushed headlong to the sea.

Alone stood brave Horatius,
  But constant still in mind;
Thrice thirty thousand foes before,
  And the broad flood behind.
" Down with him! " cried false Sextus,
  With a smile on his pale face.
" Now yield thee," cried Lars Porsena,
  " Now yield thee to our grace."

Round turned he, as not deigning
  Those craven ranks to see;
Nought spake he to Lars Porsena,
  To Sextus nought spake he;
But he saw on Palatinus
  The white porch of his home;
And he spake to the noble river
  That rolls by the towers of Rome.

" Oh, Tiber! Father Tiber!
  To whom the Romans pray,
A Roman's life, a Roman's arms,
  Take thou in charge this day! "
So he spake, and speaking sheathed
  The good sword by his side,
And with the harness on his back
  Plunged headlong in the tide.
   .   .   .   .

Never, I ween, did swimmer,
  In such an evil case,
Struggle through such a raging flood
  Safe to the landing-place;
But his limbs were borne up bravely
  By the brave heart within,
And our good Father Tiber
  Bore bravely up his chin.
   .   .   .   .

And now he feels the bottom,
  Now on dry earth he stands;
Now round him throng the Fathers
  To press his gory hands;

And now, with shouts and clapping,
  And noise of weeping loud,
He enters through the River Gate,
  Borne by the joyous crowd.

They gave him of the corn-land,
  That was of public right,
As much as two strong oxen
  Could plough from morn till night;
And they made a molten image,
  And set it up on high,
And there it stands unto this day
  To witness if I lie.

It stands in the Comitium,
  Plain for all folk to see;
Horatius in his harness,
  Halting upon one knee:
And underneath is written,
  In letters all of gold,
How valiantly he kept the bridge
  In the brave days of old.

And still his name sounds stirring
  Unto the men of Rome,
As the trumpet-blast that cries to them
  To charge the Volscian home:
And wives still pray to Juno
  For boys with hearts as bold
As his who kept the bridge so well
  In the brave days of old.

And in the nights of winter,
  When the cold north winds blow,
And the long howling of the wolves
  Is heard amidst the snow;
When round the lonely cottage
  Roars loud the tempest's din,
And the good logs of Algidus
  Roar louder yet within;

When the oldest cask is opened,
  And the largest lamp is lit;
When the chestnuts glow in the embers,
  And the kid turns on the spit;
When young and old in circle
  Around the firebrands close;
When the girls are weaving baskets,
  And the lads are shaping bows;

When the goodman mends his armour,
  And trims his helmet's plume;
When the goodwife's shuttle merrily
  Goes flashing through the loom;
With weeping and with laughter
  Still is the story told,
How well Horatius kept the bridge
  In the brave days of old.

THE DONKEY

In these famous verses G. K. Chesterton begins, as so many do, by belabouring the patient ass sorely; but he makes a liberal recompense in his reminder of the glorious time when an ass carried Jesus into Jerusalem in the hour of His triumphal entry into that city, when the people acclaimed Him with Hosannas and strewed palms in His path.

WHEN fishes flew and forests walked
  And figs grew upon thorn,
Some moments when the moon was blood,
  Then surely I was born.

With monstrous head and sickening cry
  And ears like errant wings,
The devil's walking parody
  On all four-footed things.

The tattered outlaw of the earth,
  Of ancient crooked will;
Starve, scourge, deride me: I am dumb,
  I keep my secret still.

Fools! For I also had my hour;
  One far fierce hour and sweet:
There was a shout about my ears,
  And palms before my feet.

THE HEATHER

Scotland has appropriated the heather. There is plenty of it in England, here and there, and wherever it grows it captures the fancy and the heart; but Scotland reserves it as really hers. Neil Munro, novelist and poet, was a Scot of Scots, and here he gives us a fine poetic glimpse of the national feeling for the national garniture.

IF I were King of France, that noble fine land,
  And the gold was elbow deep within my chests,
And my castles lay in scores along the wine-land
  With towers as high as where the eagle nests;
If harpers sweet, and swordsmen stout and vaunting,
  My history sang, my stainless tartan wore,
Was not my fortune poor, with one thing wanting,
  The heather at my door?

My galleys might be sailing every ocean,
  Robbing the isles, and sacking hold and keep,
My chevaliers go prancing at my notion,
  To bring me back of cattle, horse, and sheep;
Fond arms be round my neck, the young heart's tether,
  And true love-kisses all the night might fill,
But oh! *mochree*, if I had not the heather
  Before me on the hill!

A hunter's fare is all I would be craving,
  A shepherd's plaiding and a beggar's pay,
If I might earn them where the heather, waving,
  Gave fragrance to the day.
The stars might see me, homeless one and weary,
  Without a roof to fend me from the dew,
And still content, I'd find a bedding cheery
  Where'er the heather grew!

THE DAFFODILS

No poet has felt a kinship with Nature more intensely and intimately than Wordsworth. This fine illustration of the appeal of natural beauty to the heart of man was written in 1804, when Wordsworth's poetic genius was at its height. The dancing daffodils carpeted a meadow skirting the lovely lake of Ullswater, and remained to him an unfading memory.

I WANDERED lonely as a cloud
  That floats on high o'er vales and hills,
When all at once I saw a crowd,
  A host of golden daffodils;
Beside the lake, beneath the trees,
Fluttering and dancing in the breeze.

Continuous as the stars that shine
  And twinkle on the Milky Way,
They stretched in never-ending line
  Along the margin of a bay:
Ten thousand saw I at a glance,
Tossing their heads in sprightly dance.

The waves beside them danced; but they
  Out-did the sparkling waves in glee:
A poet could not but be gay
  In such a jocund company;
I gazed, and gazed, but little thought
What wealth the show to me had brought:

For oft when on my couch I lie,
  In vacant or in pensive mood,
They flash upon that inward eye
  Which is the bliss of solitude;
And then my heart with pleasure fills,
And dances with the daffodils.

THE LAW THE LAWYERS KNOW ABOUT

The narrow limits of classified knowledge that is proud of itself are here happily exposed by H. D. C. Pepler, who realises that the simple things we do not know are more numerous than the things we do know and understand.

THE law the lawyers know about
  Is property and land;
But why the leaves are on the trees,
And why the winds disturb the seas,
Why honey is the food of bees,
Why horses have such tender knees,
Why winters come and rivers freeze,
Why Faith is more than what one sees,
And Hope survives the worst disease,
And Charity is more than these,
  They do not understand.

IF I FALL

These eight lines, which contain a noteworthy thought for everyone, are from the graceful pen of Janet Begbie.

IF I fall
　　I hinder all;
If I rise
To the skies
I shall help to drag the load
One step farther on the road,
On the common road we climb,
Dead and living for all time.

THE BUGLE

The hope of the world has its perennial spring in the heart of youth. This cheering thought is here given the music of rhyme and the ring of faith by Harold Begbie. The poem was specially written for the Children's Newspaper.

WHO stands upon the mountain's crest,
　　Heir of the burning sun,
And with a trumpet at his lips
　　Blows every call save one?
'Tis Youth, whom none can overthrow,
　　And nothing shall defeat;
Hark how his lifted trumpet sounds
　　All calls except Retreat.

The terrors of black night descend
　　Upon that steadfast form;
Fierce flash the lightnings, thunders roll,
　　The chariot of the storm;
But firmer still on that wild crag
　　Youth plants his golden feet,
And lifts his trumpet to his lips,
　　And never sounds Retreat.

The night shall pass, the dawn will come;
　　Fear not, ye trembling old,
Man's path lies upward through the stars,
　　And heaven is for the bold!
Youth's trumpet rings from height to
　　　height.
　　On to the Judgment Seat!
Only the coward soul would sound
　　The traitor call Retreat!

Youth faces always to the Light,
　　Great courage fills his heart.
Ever for him the sun will shine,
　　Ever the night depart:
His faith is in the power of Right,
　　His Truth no shame can cheat;
Ten thousand times he'd rather die
　　Than sound a base Retreat.

His trumpet rings wherever Right
　　Goes up to conquer Wrong:
Old Science hears it at his toil,
　　The Poet through his song;
In garrets where brave Genius starves,
　　And on through street to street,
The trumpet of the mountain calls:
　　" On, Pilgrim!　No retreat! "

ENGLAND AND AMERICA IN 1782

In these verses Tennyson expresses the feeling of all thoughtful men of the British Isles towards the Americans in their struggle for liberty near the end of the eighteenth century. British people should be proud that their American descendants inherited a love of freedom strong enough to defy the Motherland when she was tyrannous. John Hampden will be regarded as the whole world's champion of freedom to the very end of time.

O THOU, that sendest out the man
　　To rule by land and sea,
Strong mother of a Lion-line,
Be proud of those strong sons of thine
　　Who wrenched their rights from thee!

What wonder if in noble heat
　　Those men thine arms withstood,
Retaught the lesson thou hadst taught,
And in thy spirit with thee fought,
　　Who sprang from English blood!

But thou rejoice with liberal joy,
　　Lift up thy rocky face,
And shatter, when the storms are black,
In many a streaming torrent back.
　　The seas that shock thy base!

Whatever harmonies of law
　　The growing world assume,
Thy work is thine—The single note
From that deep chord which Hampden
　　　smote
Will vibrate to the doom.

WILLIAM BLAKE

This poem by James Thomson represents in some measure, but not with completeness, the isolation of William Blake. Blake was not unknown, nor was he unappreciated. His aloofness from men arose from the mystical character of his mind. His ideas and his art were not readily understood even by his friends, but he was far from friendless. Unlike the writer of these verses, " the poet of despair," Blake was happy in his mental isolation.

HE came to the desert of London town
　　Grey miles long;
He wandered up and he wandered down,
　　Singing a quiet song.

He came to the desert of London town,
　　Mirk miles broad;
He wandered up and he wandered down,
　　Ever alone with God.

There were thousands and thousands of
　　　human kind
In this desert of brick and stone;
But some were deaf and some were blind,
　　And he was there alone.

At length the good hour came; he died
　　As he had lived, alone:
He was not missed from the desert wide;
　　Perhaps he was found at the Throne.

TO A SKYLARK

Wordsworth wrote two poems to the lark, one To the Skylark (or the whole species) and the other To a Skylark (or a particular bird that influenced his mind as he listened to it). He was downhearted, but the happiness of the bird roused his spirit, and enabled him to feel contented. The poem To the Skylark (see page 6150) is the better known, but this address to the one cheering bird is a happy example of the poet's power of refreshing his soul from Nature.

UP with me! up with me into the clouds!
   For thy song, Lark, is strong;
Up with me! up with me into the clouds!
   Singing, singing,
With clouds and sky about thee ringing,
   Lift me, guide me, till I find
That spot which seems so to thy mind!

I have walked through wildernesses
   dreary,
And today my heart is weary;
Had I now the wings of a fairy,
   Up to thee would I fly.
There is madness about thee, and joy divine
In that song of thine;
Lift me, guide me, high and high,
To thy banqueting-place in the sky.

     Joyous as morning,
Thou art laughing and scorning;
Thou hast a nest of thy love and thy
   rest,
And, though little troubled with sloth,
Drunken Lark! thou wouldst be loth
To be such a traveller as I.
Happy, happy Liver,
With a soul as strong as a mountain river
Pouring out praise to the Almighty Giver,
Joy and jollity be with us both!

Alas! My journey, rugged and uneven,
Through prickly moors or dusty ways
   must wind;
But hearing thee, or others of thy kind,
As full of gladness and as free of heaven,
I, with my fate contented, will plod on
And hope for higher raptures when life's
   day is done.

THE TWELVE-FORTY-FIVE

Joyce Kilmer, an American poet who was one of the saddest losses in the First World War, was a newspaper man who regularly caught a homeward train after midnight, and was one of the few who found poetry in a familiar railway ride. These lines are from a poem showing vividly how the 12.45 train in the dead of night appealed to him.

WITHIN the Jersey City shed
   The engine coughs and shakes its
   head.
The smoke, a plume of red and white,
Waves madly in the face of night.
And now the grave, incurious stars
Gleam on the groaning, hurrying cars.

Against the kind and awful reign
Of darkness, this our angry train,
A noisy little rebel, pouts
Its brief defiance, flames and shouts;
And passes on, and leaves no trace,
For darkness holds its ancient place,
Serene and absolute, the king,
Unchanged, of every living thing.

The houses lie obscure and still
In Rutherford and Carlton Hill.
Our lamps intensify the dark
Of slumbering Passaic Park.
And quiet holds the weary feet
That daily tramp through Prospect Street
What though we clang and clank and roar
Through all Passaic's streets? No door
Will open, not an eye will see
Who this loud vagabond may be.
Upon my crimson-cushioned seat,
In manufactured light and heat,

I feel unnatural and mean.
Outside the towns are cool and clean;
Curtained awhile from sound and sight,
They take God's gracious gift of night.

But of it let this thing be told,
To its high honour be it said,
It carries people home to bed.
My cottage lamp shines white and clear;
God bless the train that brought me here!

GOD SAVE THE QUEEN

The second verse of our National Anthem is rarely sung today, and was, in fact, omitted from Queen Elizabeth the Second's Coronation ceremony. We discuss its origin on page 6861.

GOD save our Gracious Queen,
   Long live our noble Queen,
   God save the Queen!
Send her victorious,
Happy and glorious,
Long to reign over us,
   God save the Queen!

O Lord our God, arise,
Scatter our enemies,
   And make them fall;
Confound their politics,
Frustrate their knavish tricks;
On Thee our hopes we fix;
   God save us all.

Thy choicest gifts in store
On her be pleased to pour,
   Long may she reign.
May she defend our laws,
And ever give us cause
To sing with heart and voice,
   God save the Queen!

SHE WALKS IN BEAUTY

That Byron could write with all the charm of the Elizabethan masters of song may be seen in this sketch.

SHE walks in beauty, like the night
　　Of cloudless climes and starry skies;
And all that's best of dark and bright
　　Meet in her aspect and her eyes:
Thus mellowed to that tender light
　　Which heaven to gaudy day denies.

One shade the more, one ray the less,
　　Had half impaired the nameless grace
Which waves in every raven tress,
　　Or softly lightens o'er her face;
Where thoughts serenely sweet express
　　How pure, how dear, their dwelling-
　　　　place.

And on that cheek, and o'er that brow,
　　So soft, so calm, yet eloquent,
The smiles that win, the tints that glow,
　　But tell of days in goodness spent,
A mind at peace with all below,
　　A heart whose love is innocent!

GLORY TO THEE, MY GOD, THIS NIGHT

The writer of this oldest and best of evening hymns, Bishop Thomas Ken, was such a man as the writer of such a hymn ought to have been. He was honest to the core, and fearless in support of what he felt to be right. Ken's morning and evening hymns were written in 1674, for the boys of Winchester school, where he had been educated. Ken was one of the bishops who were sent to the Tower by the wretched James the Second; yet he would not take the oath to William the Third when he superseded James. The respect he commanded during his life has never waned.

GLORY to Thee, my God, this night
　　For all the blessings of the light;
Keep me, O keep me, King of kings,
Beneath Thy own almighty wings.

Forgive me, Lord, for Thy dear Son,
The ill that I this day have done,
That with the world, myself, and Thee
I, ere I sleep, at peace may be.

Teach me to live, that I may dread
The grave as little as my bed;
Teach me to die, that so I may
Rise glorious at the awful day.

O may my soul on Thee repose,
And may sweet sleep mine eyelids close,
Sleep that may me more vigorous make
To serve my God when I awake.

When in the night I sleepless lie
My soul with heavenly thoughts supply;
Let no ill dreams disturb my rest,
No powers of darkness me molest.

Praise God, from whom all blessings flow,
Praise Him, all creatures here below:
Praise Him above, Angelic host;
Praise Father, Son, and Holy Ghost.

AT THE GATE

The writer of these lines, Colwyn Philipps (1888–1915), expresses here the feeling, which must come to us all at times, that we can never completely know each other, however much we may wish to do so.

A WALL and gulf for ever lie between.
　　Not all that we may do through love
　　or wit
Can quite avail to pull away the screen,
　　Nor yet succeed in bridging o'er the pit.
He knows the reason, He that ordered it,
　　Who made us love but never understand.
He fixed the barrier as He saw fit,
　　And bade us yearn and still stretch forth
　　the hand
　　Across the very sea He said should ne'er
　　be spanned.
Be sure this great and aching love of mine,
　　That ever yearns to know and to be
　　known,
Can tear the veil that sometimes seems so
fine
As though 'twere cobweb waiting but the
blow
To fall asunder and for ever go.
　　E'en as I rise to strike it is too late,
The cobwebs billow, thicken, seem to grow
　　To a thick wall with buttress tall and
　　great.
　　I stand alone, a stranger at a city gate.

A MILE WITH ME

This sketch of the qualities that are most helpful in a friend is from the pen of Dr. Henry Van Dyke (1852–1933), one of America's best known poets. He was United States Minister to the Netherlands and Luxemburg from 1913 to 1917.

O WHO will walk a mile with me
　　Along life's merry way?
A comrade blithe and full of glee,
Who dares to laugh out loud and free,
　　And let his frolic fancy play,
　　Like a happy child, through the flowers
　　gay
　　That fill the field and fringe the way
Where he walks a mile with me.

And who will walk a mile with me
　　Along life's weary way?
A friend whose heart has eyes to see
The stars shine out o'er the darkening lea,
　　And the quiet rest at the end o' the day—
　　A friend who knows, and dares to say
　　The brave, sweet words that cheer the
　　way
Where he walks a mile with me.
With such a comrade, such a friend,
I fain would walk till journey's end,
Through summer sunshine, winter rain,
And then? Farewell, we shall meet again!

FAREWELL

This graceful yet sad farewell to the Sun is from the pen of John Addington Symonds, a poet and able prose writer whose work took a minor tone owing to ill-health.

THOU goest; to what distant place
  Wilt thou thy sunlight carry?
I stay with cold and clouded face;
  How long am I to tarry?
Where'er thou goest morn will be;
Thou leavest night and gloom to me.

The night and gloom I can but take;
  I do not grudge thy splendour.
Bid souls of eager men awake;
  Be kind and bright and tender.
Give day to other worlds ; for me
It must suffice to dream of thee.

THE CHORUS OF THE PITIES

This is taken from the close of Thomas Hardy's great poetic drama The Dynasts, which pictures the last ten years of the life of Napoleon. Spirits are portrayed as watching the scenes of the drama and the terrible deeds and sufferings of men in Napoleon's wars. Why does God allow such sufferings? The Chorus of Spirits representing the feeling of Pity here give the final reply, which is that the Divine Controller of the Universe is fulfilling a great plan we cannot comprehend, but which will bring all men at last into eternal joy, for the good that is in men shows that their Creator cannot be lacking in tender mercy.

TO Thee whose eye all Nature owns,
  Who hurlest Dynasts from their
    thrones,
And liftest those of low estat
We sing, with her men consecrate!

Yea, Great and Good, Thee, Thee we hail,
Who shak'st the strong, Who shield'st the
    frail,
Who hadst not shaped such souls as we
If tender mercy lacked in Thee!

Though times be when the mortal moan
Seems unascending to Thy throne,
Though seers do not as yet explain
Why Suffering sobs to Thee in vain;

We hold that Thy unscanted scope
Affords a food for final Hope,
That mild-eyed Prescience ponders nigh
Life's loom, to lull it by and by.

Therefore we quire to highest height
The Wellwiller, the kindly Might,
That balances the Vast for weal,
That purges as by wounds to heal.

The systemed suns the skies enscroll
Obey Thee in their rhythmic roll,
Ride radiantly at Thy command,
Are darkened by Thy master hand!

And these pale, panting multitudes
Seen surging here, their moils, their moods,

All shall " fulfil their joy " in Thee,
In Thee abide eternally!

Exultant adoration give
The Alone, through Whom all living live,
The Alone, in Whom all dying die,
Whose means the End shall justify!

DRAKE'S DRUM

This heart-stirring poem by Sir Henry Newbolt, one of the most soundly famous of our modern patriotic poets, is based on the legendary supposition that if the great sea captain should ever be needed by England, in a time of dire extremity, he will be there to help. We take these verses from Poems New and Old, published by John Murray.

DRAKE he's in his hammock an' a
    thousand mile away
  (*Capten, art tha sleepin' there below ?*),
Slung atween the round shot in Nombre
    Dios Bay,
  An' dreamin' arl the time o' Plymouth
    Hoe.
Yarnder lumes the Island, yarnder lie the
    ships,
  Wi' sailor lads a dancin' heel-an'-toe,
An' the shore-lights flashin', an' the night-
    tide dashin',
  He sees et arl so plainly as he saw et
    long ago.

Drake he was a Devon man, an' ruled the
    Devon seas
  (*Capten, art tha sleepin' there below ?*)
Rovin' tho' his death fell, he went wi'
    heart at ease,
  An' dreamin' arl the time o' Plymouth
    Hoe.
" Take my drum to England, hang et by
    the shore,
  Strike et when your powder's runnin'
    low;
If the Dons sight Devon, I'll quit the port
    o' Heaven,
  An' drum them up the Channel as we
    drummed them long ago."

Drake he's in his hammock till the great
    Armadas come
  (*Capten, art tha sleepin' there below ?*),
Slung atween the round shot, listenin' for
    the drum,
  An' dreamin' arl the time o' Plymouth
    Hoe.
Call him on the deep sea, call him up the
    Sound,
  Call him when ye sail to meet the foe;
Where the old trade's plyin' an' the old
    flag flyin'
  They shall find him ware an' wakin', as
    they found him long ago!

TO MEADOWS

The lovely side of Robert Herrick's country muse, when he delights in flowers and in village customs, is most prettily illustrated in these verses. They tell how the meadows, but lately besprinkled with cowslips, have been despoiled doubtless for the making of old-fashioned cowslip wine. The poet brings before us a charming scene of long ago.

YE have been fresh and green,
　　Ye have been filled with flowers,
And ye the walks have been
　　Where maids have spent their hours.

You have beheld how they
　　With wicker arks did come
To kiss and bear away
　　The richer cowslips home.

You've heard them sweetly sing,
　　And seen them in a round;
Each virgin, like a spring,
　　With honeysuckles crowned.

But now we see none here
　　Whose silv'ry feet did tread,
And with dishevelled hair
　　Adorned this smoother mead.

Like unthrifts, having spent
　　Your stock, and needy grown,
You're left here to lament
　　Your poor estates, alone.

THE COMING OF SPRING

This charming description of the coming of Spring is from White Rose and Red, a story in verse by Robert Buchanan, who made his mark as poet, novelist, and dramatist.

THE swift is wheeling and gleaming,
　　The brook is brown in its bed,
Rain from the cloud is streaming,
And the Bow bends overhead;
The charm of the winter is broken!
The last of the spell is said!

The eel in the pond is quickening,
The grayling leaps in the stream;
What if the clouds are thickening?
See how the meadows gleam!
The spell of the winter is shaken;
The world awakes from a dream.

The fir puts out green fingers,
The pear tree softly blows,
The rose in her dark bower lingers,
But her curtains will soon unclose,
And the lilac will shake her ringlets
Over the blush of the rose.

The swift is wheeling and gleaming,
The woods are beginning to ring,
Rain from the cloud is streaming;
There, where the Bow doth cling,
Summer is smiling afar off,
Over the shoulder of Spring.

VENICE

Every intelligent visitor to Venice must be thrilled by this sonnet, with the noble-sounding opening line. It was written in 1802, the year when Wordsworth wrote the greatest of his sonnets. The occasion was the handing over of Venice to Austria by Napoleon, and the suppression of the Venetian Republic. Already Venice had fallen from her high estate as mistress of the trade of the East, and Wordsworth evidently thought of her last change as bringing final ruin. But after his victory at Austerlitz, in 1805, Napoleon brought back Venice from Austria into Italy.

ONCE did she hold the gorgeous East in fee,
And was the safeguard of the West: the worth
Of Venice did not fall below her birth,
Venice, the eldest Child of Liberty,
She was a maiden city, bright and free;
No guile seduced, no force could violate;
And, when she took unto herself a mate,
She must espouse the everlasting sea.
And what if she had seen those glories fade,
Those titles vanish, and that strength decay;
Yet shall some tribute of regret be paid
When her long life hath reached its final day:
Men are we, and must grieve when even the shade
Of that which once was great is passed away.

HOME, SWEET HOME

This song, expressing the love of home, is first favourite wherever the English language is spoken; but its writer, who was an American, never had a real home. John Howard Payne was an actor, born in 1792. In 1823 he produced in London an opera in which this song was first sung. But afterwards he lived a wandering life, and died in 1852.

MID pleasures and palaces though we may roam,
Be it ever so humble, there's no place like home!
A charm from the skies seems to hallow us there,
Which, seek through the world, is ne'er met with elsewhere.

Home, home, sweet, sweet home!
There's no place like home!

An exile from home, splendour dazzles in vain!
Oh, give me my lowly thatched cottage again!
The birds singing gaily that came at my call—
Give me them! and the peace of mind dearer than all!

Home, home, sweet, sweet home!
There's no place like home!

THE EARTH AND MAN

This charming comparison of the life-producing power of the earth with the joy-producing power of the human heart is from Stopford Brooke, whose reputation as a preacher and a literary critic of the nineteenth century somewhat obscured his merits as a poet. He lived from 1832 to 1916.

A LITTLE sun, a little rain,
　A soft wind blowing from the west,
And woods and fields are sweet again,
　And warmth within the mountain's
　　breast.

So simple is the earth we tread,
　So quick with love and life her frame,
Ten thousand years have dawned and fled,
　And still her magic is the same.

A little love, a little trust,
　A soft impulse, a sudden dream,
And life as dry as desert dust
　Is fresher than a mountain stream.

So simple is the heart of man,
　So ready for new hope and joy;
Ten thousand years since it began
　Have left it younger than a boy.

A CONSECRATION

This powerful poem was the introduction to Salt Sea Ballads, the first book of verse published by John Masefield. Not only is it remarkable for the intensity of the spirit of humanity which permeates it, but also as a prophecy of the later work of that boldly masculine poet. Mr. Masefield has been true to the ideal he pledged himself to pursue.

NOT of the princes and prelates with
　periwigged charioteers
Riding triumphantly laurelled to lap the
　fat of the years,
Rather the scorned, the rejected, the men
　hemmed in with the spears;

The men of the tattered battalion which
　fights till it dies,
Dazed with the dust of the battle, the din
　and the cries,
The men with the broken heads and the
　blood running into their eyes.

Not the be-medalled Commander, beloved
　of the throne,
Riding cock-horse to parade when the
　bugles are blown,
But the lads who carried the koppie and
　cannot be known.

Not the ruler for me, but the ranker, the
　tramp of the road,
The slave with the sack on his shoulders
　pricked on with the goad,
The man with too weighty a burden, too
　weary a load.

The sailor, the stoker of steamers, the man
　with the clout,
The chantyman bent at the halliards
　putting a tune to the shout,
The drowsy man at the wheel and the
　tired look-out.

Others may sing of the wine and the wealth
　and the mirth,
The portly presence of potentates goodly
　in girth ;
Mine be the dirt and the dross, the dust
　and scum of the earth!

Theirs be the music, the colour, the glory,
　the gold;
Mine be a handful of ashes, a mouthful of
　mould.
Of the maimed, of the halt, and the blind
　in the rain and the cold,

Of these shall my songs be fashioned, my
　tale be told.　Amen.

WHEN YOU ARE OLD

W. B. Yeats (1865–1939), most famous of modern poets of Ireland, was a master of musical words with mystical meanings that do not readily disclose themselves to the average reader. This is one of the best-known of his shorter poems. We quote it from his volume of collected works.

WHEN you are old and grey and full of
　sleep,
　And nodding by the fire, take down this
　　book,
　And slowly read and dream of the soft
　　look
Your eyes had once, and of their shadows
　deep;

How many loved your moments of glad
　grace,
　And loved your beauty with love false
　　or true;
　But one man loved the pilgrim soul in
　　you,
And loved the sorrows of your changing
　face.

And bending down beside the glowing bars
　Murmur, a little sadly, how love fled,
　And paced upon the mountains over-
　　head,
And hid his face amid a crown of stars.

ON A PEOPLE'S POET

The idea that men may love a song till they spoil it is the burden of this clever couplet by Sir William Watson. But all true songs will live again and yet again.

YES, threadbare seem his songs, to
　lettered ken.
They were worn threadbare next the
　hearts of men.

BLOSSOMS

The graceful flow of Robert Herrick's fancy is charmingly seen in this brief song on the fragility of much that is beautiful. He pleads with the blossoms to stay a little while.

FAIR pledges of a fruitful tree,
   Why do ye fall so fast?
Your date is not so past,
But you may stay yet here awhile
To blush and gently smile,
   And go at last.

What! were ye born to be
   An hour or half's delight,
   And so to bid good-night?
'Twas pity Nature brought ye forth
Merely to show your worth,
   And lose you quite.

But you are lovely leaves, where we
   May read how soon things have
   Their end, though ne'er so brave:
And after they have shown their pride
Like you awhile they glide
   Into the grave.

THE MINISTRY OF ANGELS

This lovely poetical setting of the idea of angelic guardianship of human creatures occupies the first two stanzas of the eighth canto of the second book of Edmund Spenser's great poem The Faerie Queene, published in 1590.

AND is there care in Heaven? And is
   there love
In heavenly spirits to these creatures base
That may compassion of their evils move?
There is—else much more wretched were
   the case
Of men than beasts. But O! th' exceeding
   grace
Of highest God, that loves His creatures so,
And all His works with mercy doth em-
   brace,
That blessed angels He sends to and fro
To serve to wicked man, to serve his
   wicked foe!

How oft do they their silver bowers leave
To come to succour us, that succour want?
How oft do they with golden pinions
   cleave
The flitting skies, like flying pursuivant,
Against foul fiends to aid us militant?
They for us fight, they watch and duly
   ward,
And their bright squadrons round about
   us plant :
And all for love, and nothing for reward:
O why should heavenly God to men have
   such regard?

LITTLE BOY BLUE

Among the tender poems about childhood that have touched the heart of the world none takes a dearer place than this, by Eugene Field, on the toys of Little Boy Blue.

THE little toy dog is covered with dust,
   But sturdy and staunch he stands;
The little toy soldier is red with rust,
   And his musket moulds in his hands.
Time was when the little toy dog was new,
   And the soldier was passing fair;
And that was the time our Little Boy
   Blue
   Kissed them and put them there.

"Now, don't you go till I come," he said,
   "And don't you make any noise!"
So, toddling off to his trundle-bed,
   He dreamt of the pretty toys.
And as he was dreaming an angel song
   Awakened our Little Boy Blue:
Oh, the years are many, the years are long,
   But the little toy friends are true!

Aye, faithful to Little Boy Blue they stand,
   Each in the same old place,
Awaiting the touch of a little hand,
   The smile of a little face;
And they wonder, as waiting the long
   years through
   In the dust of that little chair,
What has become of our Little Boy Blue
   Since he kissed them and put them there.

LAKE ISLE OF INNISFREE

This call of the life of simplicity and rural beauty to man in a city's throng, expressed in the choicest melody of words by W. B. Yeats, has found its way into almost every selection of poems in the English tongue. We take these verses from his collected works.

I WILL arise and go now, and go to
   Innisfree,
   And a small cabin build there, of clay
     and wattles made;
Nine bean rows will I have there, a hive
   for the honey bee,
   And live alone in the bee-loud glade.

And I shall have some peace there, for
   peace comes dropping slow,
   Dropping from the veils of the morning
     to where the cricket sings.
There midnight's all a glimmer, and noon
   a purple glow,
   And evening full of the linnet's wings.

I will arise and go now, for always night
   and day
   I hear lake water lapping with low
     sounds by the shore:
While I stand on the roadway, or on the
   pavements gray,
   I hear it in the deep heart's core.

TWEEDLEDUM AND TWEEDLEDEE

TWEEDLEDUM AND TWEEDLEDEE
RESOLVED TO HAVE A BATTLE.

FOR TWEEDLEDUM SAID TWEEDLEDEE

HAD SPOILED HIS NICE NEW RATTLE.

JUST THEN FLEW BY A MONSTROUS CROW.
AS BIG AS A TAR BARREL,
WHICH FRIGHTENED BOTH THOSE HEROES SO
THEY QUITE FORGOT THEIR QUARREL.

WONDROUS WISE

THERE WAS AN OLD MAN OF OUR TOWN
AND HE WAS WONDROUS WISE.

HE JUMPED INTO A BRAMBLE BUSH
AND SCRATCHED OUT BOTH HIS EYES.

AND WHEN HE FOUND HIS EYES WERE OUT,
WITH ALL HIS MIGHT AND MAIN,

HE JUMPED INTO ANOTHER BUSH
AND SCRATCHED THEM IN AGAIN.

THE LITTLE CROOKED MAN

THERE WAS A CROOKED MAN,

WHO WALKED A CROOKED MILE,

HE FOUND A CROOKED SIXPENCE

UPON A CROOKED STILE,

HE BOUGHT A CROOKED CAT

WHO CAUGHT A CROOKED MOUSE,

AND THEY ALL LIVED TOGETHER
IN A CROOKED LITTLE HOUSE.

RING OUT THE OLD, RING IN THE NEW

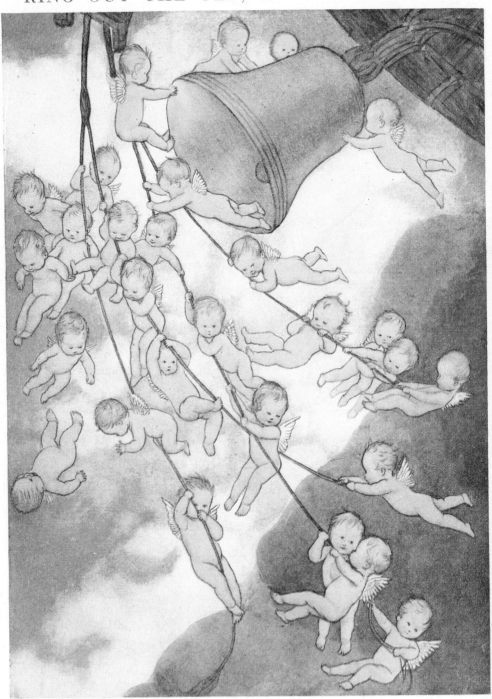

RING OUT, WILD BELLS TO THE WILD SKY,
THE FLYING CLOUD, THE FROSTY LIGHT :
THE YEAR IS DYING IN THE NIGHT ;
RING OUT WILD BELLS, AND LET HIM DIE

RING OUT THE OLD, RING IN THE NEW,
RING, HAPPY BELLS, ACROSS THE SNOW :
THE YEAR IS GOING, LET HIM GO ;
RING OUT THE FALSE, RING IN THE TRUE

CUCKOO SONG

This is the oldest song in the English language. It was written by John of Fornsete, a monk at Reading Abbey, in the thirteenth century, and shows how men's hearts responded then, as now, to the influences of Spring. Noo, or nu, is an ancient form of our word now, which still keeps its old sound in the Scottish tongue.

Sumer is icumen in,
  Lhude sing cuccu!
Groweth sed, and bloweth med,
And springth the wude nu:
        Sing cuccu!

Awe bleteth after lomb,
  Lhouth after calve cu;
Bulluc sterteth, bucke verteth,
Murie sing cuccu!

Cuccu, cuccu, well singes thu, cuccu;
  Ne swike thu naver nu;
Sing cuccu, nu, sing cuccu,
Sing cuccu, sing cuccu, nu!

Summer is a-coming in,
  Loud sing cuckoo!
Groweth seed, and bloweth mead,
  And springeth the wood new:
        Sing cuckoo!

Ewe bleateth after lamb,
Loweth after calf cow;
Bullock starteth, buck verteth,
  Merry sing cuckoo!

Cuckoo, cuckoo, well singest thou, cuckoo;
  Nor cease thou ever noo;
Sing cuckoo, noo, sing cuckoo,
Sing cuckoo, sing cuckoo, noo!

THE ROCK-A-BY LADY

Eugene Field, the American poet of childhood, had the rare gift of giving sweet singing words to the daintiest fancies of little children. Here we see how he could give a personal form to the influences which soothe the tired child into slumber. The poetry of a child going to sleep after the toy-born dreams of the day has never been caught more tenderly and sweetly than in these four verses.

The Rock-a-by Lady from Hush-a-by
    Street
  Comes stealing, comes creeping;
The poppies they hang from her head to
    her feet,
And each hath a dream that is tiny and
    fleet;
She bringeth her poppies to you, my sweet,
  When she findeth you sleeping!

There is one little dream of a beautiful
    drum,
  " Rub-a-dub! " it goeth;
There is one little dream of a big sugar-
    plum,
And lo! thick and fast the other dreams
    come

Of pop-guns that bang and tin tops that
    hum,
  And the trumpet that bloweth !

And dollies peep out of those wee little
    dreams
  With laughter and singing;
And boats go a-floating on silvery streams,
And the stars peek-a-boo with their own
    misty gleams.
And up, up, and up, where the Mother
    Moon beams,
  The fairies go winging!

Would you dream all these dreams that
    are tiny and fleet?
  They'll come to you sleeping;
So shut the two eyes that are weary, my
    sweet,
For the Rock-a-by Lady from Hush-a-by
    Street,
With poppies that hang from her head to
    her feet,
  Comes stealing, comes creeping.

A LITTLE LIFE

This tender little picture of human life was written by George du Maurier (1834–1896), famed both as artist and author, Trilby being his best-known work.

A little work, a little play—
    To keep us going—and so—
        Good-day.

A little warmth, a little light
Of love's bestowing—and so—
        Good-night.

A little fun to match the sorrow
Of each day's growing—and so—
        Good-morrow.

A little trust that when we die
We reap our sowing—and so—
        Goodbye!

TREES

A young poet of great promise whose life was cut short by the First World War was Joyce Kilmer, who was becoming widely known in America by his love of Nature and the freshness and simplicity of his style. He died when he was only thirty-one years old. Had he written nothing except this poem on a tree he would be long remembered.

I think that I shall never see
    A poem lovely as a tree,
A tree whose hungry mouth is prest
Against the Earth's sweet, flowing breast;
A tree that looks at God all day,
And lifts her leafy arms to pray;
A tree that may in summer wear
A nest of robins in her hair;
Upon whose bosom snow has lain;
Who intimately lives with rain.
Poems are made by fools like me,
But only God can make a tree.

THE LAY OF THE LAST MINSTREL

Sir Walter Scott's Lay of the Last Minstrel, his first ambitious poem and one which attracted general attention, pictures an aged minstrel, the last of the wandering bards, arriving at a stately castle and receiving a friendly welcome from its mistress. In return he offers to play a long forgotten melody, and after a halting start bursts into the lay that makes the substance of the poetic romance. So well does he perform that the lady of the castle retains him there for the rest of his life. Here we give the opening and close of the poem—the reception and reward of the aged harper.

THE way was long, the wind was cold;
　The Minstrel was infirm and old;
His withered cheek and tresses gray
Seemed to have known a better day;
The harp, his sole remaining joy,
Was carried by an orphan boy.
The last of all the Bards was he,
Who sung of Border chivalry;
For, well-a-day! their date was fled,
His tuneful brethren all were dead;
And he, neglected and oppressed,
Wished to be with them, and at rest.
No more on prancing palfrey borne,
He carolled, light as lark at morn;
No longer courted and caressed,
High placed in hall, a welcome guest,
He poured to lord and lady gay
The unpremeditated lay.
Old times were changed, old manners gone;
A stranger filled the Stuarts' throne;
The bigots of the iron time
Had called his harmless art a crime.
A wandering harper, scorned and poor,
He begged his bread from door to door,
And turned, to please a peasant's ear,
The harp a king had loved to hear.

He passed where Newark's stately tower
Looks out from Yarrow's birchen bower;
The Minstrel gazed with wistful eye,
No humbler resting-place was nigh.
With hesitating step at last
The embattled portal arch he passed,
Whose ponderous grate and massy bar
Had oft rolled back the tide of war,
But never closed the iron door
Against the desolate and poor.
The Duchess marked his weary pace,
His timid mien, and reverend face,
And bade her page the menials tell
That they should tend the old man well;
For she had known adversity,
Though born in such a high degree;
In pride of power, in beauty's bloom,
Had wept o'er Monmouth's bloody tomb!

When kindness had his wants supplied,
And the old man was gratified,
Began to rise his minstrel pride:
And he began to talk anon
Of good Earl Francis, dead and gone,

And of Earl Walter, rest him, God!
A braver ne'er to battle rode:
And how full many a tale he knew
Of the old warriors of Buccleuch;
And would the noble Duchess deign
To listen to an old man's strain,
Though stiff his hand, his voice though weak,
He thought even yet the sooth to speak,
That, if she loved the harp to hear,
He could make music to her ear.

The humble boon was soon obtained:
The agèd Minstrel audience gained.
But, when he reached the room of state,
Where she with all her ladies sate,
Perchance he wished his boon denied;
For, when to tune his harp he tried,
His trembling hand had lost the ease
Which marks security to please;
And scenes long past, of joy and pain,
Came wildering o'er his agèd brain;
He tried to tune his harp in vain!
The pitying Duchess praised its chime,
And gave him heart, and gave him time,
Till every string's according glee
Was blended into harmony.
And then, he said, he would full fain
He could recall an ancient strain
He never thought to sing again.
It was not framed for village churls,
But for high dames and mighty earls;
He had played it to King Charles the Good
When he kept court in Holyrood;
And much he wished, yet feared, to try
The long-forgotten melody.
Amid the strings his fingers strayed,
And an uncertain warbling made,
And oft he shook his hoary head.
But when he caught the measure wild
The old man raised his face and smiled;
And lightened up his faded eye
With all a poet's ecstasy.
In varying cadence, soft or strong,
He swept the sounding chords along;
The present scene, the future lot,
His toils, his wants, were all forgot;
Cold diffidence and age's frost
In the full tide of song were lost;
Each blank, in faithless memory void,
The poet's glowing thought supplied;
And, while his harp responsive rung,
'Twas thus the Latest Minstrel sung.

. 　 . 　 . 　 . 　 .

Hushed is the harp—the Minstrel gone.
And did he wander forth alone?
Alone, in indigence and age,
To linger out his pilgrimage?

No; close beneath proud Newark's tower
Arose the Minstrel's lowly bower;
A simple hut; but there was seen
The little garden hedged with green,
The cheerful hearth, and lattice clean.

. . . . .

So passed the winter's day, but still,
When summer smiled on sweet Bow hill,
And July's eve, with balmy breath,
Waved the bluebells on Newark heath;
When throstles sung in Harehead shaw,
And corn was green on Carterhaugh,
And flourish broad, Blackandro's oak,
The aged harper's soul awoke!
Then would he sing achievements high,
And circumstance of chivalry,
Till the rapt traveller would stay,
Forgetful of the closing day;
And noble youths, the strain to hear,
Forsook the hunting of the deer;
And Yarrow, as he rolled along,
Bore burden to the Minstrel's song.

TO A MOUSE

In none of his poems is the intense sympathy of Robert Burns with animal life seen more clearly than in these tender verses, written after he had turned up a nest of mice with his plough. The poem comes straight from the heart, and goes straight to every heart that is naturally kind. It was written in 1785, the year before Burns published his first volume of poems. The meanings of the Scottish words are: brattle, hurry; pattle, a plough-staff; daimen-icker in a thrave, an ear of corn now and then; lave, rest ; snell, biting; cranreuch, hoar-frost; a-gley, aslant; no thy lane, not alone.

WEE, sleekit, cow'rin', tim'rous beastie,
    O what a panic's in thy breastie !
Thou need na start awa sae hasty,
        Wi' bickering brattle!
I wad be laith to rin an' chase thee
        Wi' murd'ring pattle!

I'm truly sorry man's dominion
Has broken Nature's social union,
An' justifies that ill opinion
        Which makes thee startle
At me, thy poor earth-born companion
        An' fellow-mortal!

I doubt na, whiles, but thou may thieve;
What then? poor beastie, thou maun live!
A daimen-icker in a thrave
        'S a sma' request:
I'll get a blessin' wi' the lave,
        And never miss 't!

Thy wee bit housie, too, in ruin!
Its silly wa's the win's are strewin'!
An' naething now to big a new ane,
        O' foggage green!
An' bleak December's winds ensuin',
        Baith snell an' keen!

Thou saw the fields laid bare and waste,
An' weary winter comin' fast,
An' cozie here, beneath the blast,
        Thou thought to dwell,
Till crash! the cruel coulter past
        Out-thro' thy cell.

That wee bit heap o' leaves an' stibble
Has cost thee mony a weary nibble!
Now thou's turned out, for a' thy trouble,
        But house or hald,
To thole the winter's sleety dribble,
        An' cranreuch cauld!

But, Mousie, thou art no thy lane
In proving foresight may be vain;
The best-laid schemes o' mice an' men
        Gang aft a-gley,
An' lea'e us nought but grief an' pain
        For promised joy.

Still thou art blest compared wi' me!
The present only toucheth thee:
But oh! I backward cast my e'e
        On prospects drear!
An' forward though I canna see,
        I guess an' fear!

I AM

There are no more pathetic lines than these in the English tongue. They were written by John Clare, a poor peasant who spent much of his life in a workhouse asylum. We hear in them the cry of a forsaken genius who was sufficiently sane to shape his plaint into a poignant song.

I AM ! yet what I am who cares, or knows ?
    My friends forsake me like a memory lost.
I am the self-consumer of my woes;
They rise and vanish, an oblivious host,
Shadows of life, whose very soul is lost.
And yet I am—I live—though I am tossed

Into the nothingness of scorn and noise,
Into the living sea of waking dream,
Where there is neither sense of life, nor joys,
But the huge shipwreck of my own esteem
And all that's dear. Even those I loved the best
Are strange—nay, they are stranger than the rest.

I long for scenes where man has never trod,
For scenes where woman never smiled or wept,
There to abide with my Creator, God,
And sleep as I in childhood sweetly slept,
Full of high thoughts, unborn. So let me lie,
The grass below; above, the vaulted sky.

TO THE SMALL CELANDINE

Wordsworth was a lover of flowers, yet it took him thirty years to discover the modest celandine. When he did notice it as a herald of Spring, he gave it long withheld fame in these bright, easy, and enthusiastic verses. They were written in 1802. The book name of the lesser celandine is the ranunculus ficaria, and its popular name the pilewort.

Pansies, lilies, kingcups, daisies,
  Let them live upon their praises;
Long as there's a Sun that sets,
Primroses will have their glory;
Long as there are violets,
They will have a place in story:
There's a flower that shall be mine,
Tis the little Celandine.

Eyes of some men travel far
For the finding of a star;
Up and down the heavens they go,
Men that keep a mighty rout!
I'm as great as they, I trow,
Since the day I found thee out,
Little flower, I'll make a stir,
Like a sage astronomer.

Modest, yet withal an elf
Bold, and lavish of thyself;
Since we needs must first have met
I have seen thee, high and low.
Thirty years or more, and yet
Twas a face I did not know;
Thou hast now, go where I may,
Fifty greetings in a day.

Ere a leaf is on a bush,
In the time before the thrush
Has a thought about her nest,
Thou wilt come with half a call,
Spreading out thy glossy breast
Like a careless prodigal;
Telling tales about the Sun
When we've little warmth, or none.

Poets, vain men in their mood,
Travel with the multitude:
Never heed them; I aver
That they all are wanton wooers;
But the thrifty cottager,
Who stirs little out of doors,
Joys to spy thee near her home;
Spring is coming, thou art come!

Comfort have thou of thy merit,
Kindly, unassuming spirit!
Careless of thy neighbourhood,
Thou dost show thy pleasant face
On the moor, and in the wood,
In the lane; there's not a place,
Howsoever mean it be,
But tis good enough for thee.

Ill befall the yellow flowers,
Children of the flaring hours!
Buttercups, that will be seen,
Whether we will see or no;
Others, too, of lofty mien;
They have done as worldlings do,
Taken praise that should be thine,
Little, humble Celandine.

Prophet of delight and mirth,
Ill-requited upon Earth;
Herald of a mighty band,
Of a joyous train ensuing,
Serving at my heart's command,
Tasks that are no tasks renewing,
I will sing, as doth behove,
Hymns in praise of what I love!

THE UNSEEN PLAYMATE

Robert Louis Stevenson in this poem (reprinted from A Child's Garden of Verses by permission of Messrs Longmans) has written a beautiful piece of fancy. He almost makes us see this unseen playmate. He means, of course, the gentle spirit of happiness and of true childhood joy which makes each little boy or girl never feel lonely.

When children are playing alone on the green
In comes the playmate that never was seen.
When children are happy and lonely and good
The Friend of the Children comes out of the wood.

Nobody heard him and nobody saw,
His is a picture you never could draw;
But he's sure to be present, abroad or at home,
When children are happy and playing alone.

He lies in the laurels, he runs on the grass,
He sings when you tinkle the musical glass;
Whene'er you are happy and cannot tell why,
The Friend of the Children is sure to be by!

He loves to be little, he hates to be big,
Tis he that inhabits the caves that you dig;
Tis he, when you play with your soldiers of tin,
That sides with the Frenchmen and never can win.

Tis he, when at night you go off to your bed,
Bids you go to your sleep and not trouble your head;
For wherever they're lying, in cupboard or shelf,
Tis he will take care of your playthings himself!

TO A BULLDOG

It is not strange that the terrible burden of the world's loss of millions of glorious dead through war should find expression in literature that melts the heart. Among the few war poems that sound the depths of unavailing sorrow this address to a bulldog by Sir John Squire stands conspicuous. Captain W. H. Squire (Acting Major), Royal Field Artillery, was killed in 1917. What it meant to one household is reflected, through the dog that missed him, with a pathos that makes reading aloud almost impossible. Sir John Squire, distinguished as a poet and a literary critic, published the volume containing the poem through Messrs. Hodder & Stoughton, and we warmly commend his poems to the rising generation.

WE shan't see Willy any more, Mamie,
  He won't be coming any more:
He came back once and again and again,
  But he won't get leave any more.

We looked from the window and there was
    his cab,
  And we ran downstairs like a streak,
And he said, " Hullo, you bad dog," and
    you crouched to the floor,
  Paralysed to hear him speak.

And then let fly at his face and his chest
  Till I had to hold you down,
While he took off his cap and his gloves
    and his coat,
  And his bag and his thonged Sam
    Browne.

We went upstairs to the studio,
  The three of us, just as of old,
And you lay down and I sat and talked
    to him
  As round the room he strolled.

Here in the room where, years ago
  Before the old life stopped,
He worked all day with his slippers and
    his pipe,
  He would pick up the threads he'd
    dropped.

Fondling all the drawings he had left
    behind,
  Glad to find them all still the same,
And opening the cupboards to look at his
    belongings
  . . . Every time he came.

But now I know what a dog doesn't know,
  Though you'll thrust your head on my
    knee,
And try to draw me from the absent-
    mindedness
  That you find so dull in me.

And all your life you will never know
  What I wouldn't tell you even if I could,
That the last time we waved him away
  Willy went for good.

But sometimes as you lie on the hearthrug
  Sleeping in the warmth of the stove,
Even through your muddled old canine
    brain
  Shapes from the past may rove.

You'll scarcely remember, even in a dream,
  How we brought home a silly little pup,
With a big square head and little crooked
    legs
  That could scarcely bear him up;

But your tail will tap at the memory
  Of a man whose friend you were,
Who was always kind, though he called
    you a nasty dog
  When he found you on his chair.

Who'd make you face a reproving finger
  And solemnly lecture you
Till your head hung downwards and you
    looked very sheepish!
  And you'll dream of your triumphs too.

Of summer evening chases in the garden
  When you dodged us all about with a
    bone:
We were three boys, and you were the
    cleverest,
  But now we're two alone.

When summer comes again,
  And the long sunsets fade,
We shall have to go on playing the feeble
    game for two
  That since the war we've played.

And though you run expectant as you
    always do
  To the uniforms we meet,
You'll never find Willy among all the
    soldiers
  In even the longest street.

Nor in any crowd; yet, strange and bitter
    thought,
  Even now were the old words said,
If I tried the old trick and said " Where's
    Willy? "
  You would quiver and lift your head,

And your brown eyes would look to ask if
    I were serious,
  And wait for the word to spring.
Sleep undisturbed: I shan't say that again,
  You innocent old thing.

I must sit, not speaking, on the sofa,
  While you lie asleep on the floor;
For he's suffered a thing that dogs couldn't
    dream of,
  And he won't be coming here any more.

WOODMAN, SPARE THAT TREE

This long, popular sentimental song had an American origin. It springs from an incident witnessed by George P. Morris, the writer of the song. A friend with whom he was riding turned aside to see a tree planted by his grandfather, and by it they found a man sharpening his axe to cut it down. The friend interposed by buying the tree and arranging for its preservation. Morris, on reaching home, at once expressed his friend's appeal in the words of the song, which attained a world-wide circulation. George P. Morris, who was born in 1802, was an American brigadier-general and a writer of many songs. He died in New York in 1864.

WOODMAN, spare that tree! Touch not
    a single bough!
In youth it sheltered me, and I'll protect
    it now.
'Twas my forefather's hand that placed
    it near his cot;
There, woodman, let it stand; thy axe
    shall harm it not!

That old familiar tree, whose glory and
    renown
Are spread o'er land and sea. And
    wouldst thou hew it down?
Woodman, forbear thy stroke! Cut not
    its earth-bound ties;
O, spare that aged oak, now towering to
    the skies.

When but an idle boy I sought its grateful
    shade;
In all their gushing joy here, too, my
    sisters played.
My mother kissed me here, my father
    pressed my hand;
Forgive the foolish tear; but let that old
    oak stand.

My heart-strings round thee cling, close
    as thy bark, old friend;
Here shall the wild bird sing, and still thy
    branches bend.
Old tree, the storm still brave! And,
    woodman, leave the spot;
While I've a hand to save, thy axe shall
    harm it not.

PIPPA'S SONG

This lovely and famous early morning song is from a poem by Robert Browning called Pippa Passes. Pippa is an Italian girl who works hard and rarely has a holiday, but when the looked-for day comes, she goes out and sings songs wherever she goes, and her passing by has an influence for good on all the people who hear her voice.

THE year's at the spring,
    And day's at the morn;
Morning's at seven;
The hillside's dew-pearled;
The lark's on the wing;
The snail's on the thorn;
God's in His heaven;
All's right with the world.

INFANT JOY

William Blake, who always had a good deal of the child in him, here babbles and coos as child to child.

I HAVE no name;
    I am but two days old.
What shall I call thee?
" I happy am,
Joy is my name."
Sweet joy befall thee!

Pretty Joy!
Sweet Joy, but two days old.
Sweet Joy I call thee;
Thou dost smile,
I sing the while,
Sweet joy befall thee!

THE DAYS GONE BY

This poem by James Whitcomb Riley is a natural echo from a very happy boyhood. There are some points in it which are not true to English conditions. We cannot imagine a quail being as sweet as the nightingale, for instance. But remembrance of our earliest youth is the last to leave us, and most pitiable are they by whom it is not joyous.

O THE days gone by! O the days gone
    by!
The apples in the orchard, and the path-
    way through the rye;
The chirrup of the robin, and the whistle
    of the quail
As he piped across the meadows sweet as
    any nightingale;
When the bloom was on the clover, and
    the blue was in the sky,
And my happy heart brimmed over, in the
    days gone by.

In the days gone by, when my naked feet
    were tripped
By the honeysuckle tangles where the
    water-lilies dipped,
And the ripples of the river lipped the moss
    along the brink
Where the placid-eyed and lazy-footed
    cattle came to drink,
And the tilting snipe stood fearless of the
    truant's wayward cry,
And the splashing of the swimmer, in the
    days gone by.

O the days gone by! O the days gone by!
The music of the laughing lip, the lustre
    of the eye;
The childish faith in fairies, and Aladdin's
    magic ring,
The simple, soul-reposing, glad belief in
    everything;
When life was like a story holding neither
    sob nor sigh,
In the golden olden glory of the days
    gone by.

THE MAN WITH THE HOE

This grim poem is from the pen of Charles Edwin Markham (1852–1940), an outstanding American poet. It was written after the poet had seen the celebrated painting by the great French artist Jean François Millet entitled The Man with the Hoe, of which a reproduction is given on this page. The poet was so struck with the attitude of the man in the painting, the hopelessness of his life, the misery of his ill-rewarded toil, his utter lack of all the bright intellectual gifts that lift man so immeasurably above the brute creation, that in a passion of pity he wrote this poem. It has been said that the poet exaggerates the debasing influence of field labour, but there is much truth in his outburst.

BOWED by the weight of centuries, he leans
Upon his hoe, and gazes on the ground,
The emptiness of ages in his face,
And on his back the burden of the world.

To trace the stars and search the heavens for power;
To feel the passion of Eternity?
Is this the dream He dreamed who shaped the suns
And pillared the blue firmament with light?
Down all the stretch of hell to its last gulf
There is no shape more terrible than this,
More tongued with censure of the world's blind greed,
More filled with signs and portents for the soul,
More fraught with menace to the universe.
What gulfs between him and the seraphim!
Slave of the wheel of labour, what to him
Are Plato and the swing of Pleiades?

THE MAN WITH THE HOE—BY JEAN FRANÇOIS MILLET

Who made him dead to rapture and despair,
A thing that grieves not, and that never hopes,
Stolid and stunned, a brother to the ox?
Who loosened and let down this brutal jaw?
Whose was the hand that slanted back this brow?
Whose breath blew out the light within this brain?
Is this the thing the Lord God made and gave
To have dominion over sea and land;

What the long reaches of the peaks of song,
The rift of dawn, the reddening of the rose?
Through this dread shape the suffering ages look;
Time's tragedy is in that aching stoop;
Through this dread shape humanity betrayed,
Plundered, profaned, and disinherited,
Cries protest to the Judges of the World,
A protest that is also prophecy.
O masters, lords, and rulers in all lands,
Is this the handiwork you give to God—
This monstrous thing distorted and soul-quenched?

How will you ever straighten up this shape;
Touch it again with immortality;
Give back the upward looking and the
light;
Rebuild in it the music and the dream;
Make right the immemorial infamies,
Perfidious wrongs, immedicable woes?
O masters, lords, and rulers in all lands,
How will the Future reckon with this Man?
How answer his brute question in that hour
When whirlwinds of rebellion shake the
world?
How will it be with kingdoms and with
kings—
With those who shaped him to the thing
he is—
When this dumb Terror shall reply to God,
After the silence of the centuries?

A MATCH

This is one of the most popular of the poems of Algernon
Charles Swinburne, most of which are exercises in verbal
melody. It sounds melodious, and as if it ought to have a
meaning as sweet as the sound, but it is a poem that does
not easily condense into clear thought.

IF love were what the rose is,
    And I were like the leaf,
Our lives would grow together
In sad or singing weather,
Blown fields or flowerful closes,
    Green pleasure or grey grief;
If love were what the rose is,
    And I were like the leaf.

If I were what the words are,
    And love were like the tune,
With double sound and single
Delight our lips would mingle
With kisses glad as birds are
    That get sweet rain at noon;
If I were what the words are,
    And love were like the tune.

If you were life, my darling,
    And I your love were death,
We'd shine and snow together
Ere March made sweet the weather
With daffodil and starling
    And hours of fruitful breath;
If you were life, my darling,
    And I your love were death.

If you were thrall to sorrow,
    And I were page to joy,
We'd play for lives and seasons
With loving looks and treasons
And tears of night and morrow
    And laughs of maid and boy;
If you were thrall to sorrow,
    And I were page to joy.

If you were April's lady,
    And I were lord in May,
We'd throw with leaves for hours
And draw for days with flowers,
Till day like night were shady
    And night were bright like day;
If you were April's lady,
    And I were lord in May.

If you were queen of pleasure,
    And I were king of pain,
We'd hunt down love together,
Pluck out his flying-feather,
And teach his feet a measure,
    And find his mouth a rein;
If you were queen of pleasure,
    And I were king of pain.

HUNTING SONG

This hunting song by Sir Walter Scott appeared in the
preface to his first novel, Waverley. It is in tune with the
breezy life he loved in the country. At that time men had
only half emerged from the period when they hunted for a
living, and animal slaughter was regarded as the finest form
of sport. Many think differently now, but Scott, though an
animal lover, appears to have no such qualms.

WAKEN, lords and ladies gay,
    On the mountain dawns the day;
All the jolly chase is here,
With hawk, and horse, and hunting-spear!
Hounds are in their couples yelling,
Hawks are whistling, horns are knelling,
Merrily, merrily, mingle they,
Waken, lords and ladies gay.

Waken, lords and ladies gay,
The mist has left the mountain grey,
Springlets in the dawn are steaming,
Diamonds on the brake are gleaming:
And foresters have busy been
To track the buck in thicket green;
Now we come to chant our lay,
Waken, lords and ladies gay.

Waken, lords and ladies gay,
To the greenwood haste away;
We can show you where he lies,
Fleet of foot, and tall of size;
We can show the marks he made
When 'gainst the oak his antlers frayed;
You shall see him brought to bay,
Waken, lords and ladies gay.

Louder, louder chant the lay,
Waken, lords and ladies gay!
Tell them youth, and mirth, and glee,
Run a course as well as we;
Time, stern huntsman! who can baulk,
Staunch as hound, and fleet as hawk:
Think of this, and rise with day,
Gentle lords and ladies gay.

LITTLE VERSES FOR VERY LITTLE PEOPLE

THE DIFFERENCE

Eight fingers,
  Ten toes,
Two eyes,
  And one nose.
Baby said,
  When she smelt the rose,
" Oh ! what a pity
  I've only got one nose."

Ten teeth
  In even rows,
Three dimples,
  And one nose.
Baby said,
  When she smelt the snuff,
" Deary me!
  One nose is enough."

Laura E. Richards

EYES AND NO EYES

What, Charles returned! Papa ex-
    claimed.
  " How short your walk has been!
But Thomas—Julia—where are they?
  Come, tell me what you've seen."

" So tedious, stupid, dull a walk ! "
  Said Charles; " I'll go no more;
First stopping here, then lagging there,
  O'er this and that to pore.

" I crossed the fields near Woodland House
  And just went up the hill;
Then by the river-side came down,
  Near Mr. Fairplay's mill."

Now Tom and Julia both ran in;
  " Oh, dear Papa ! " said they,
" The sweetest walk we both have had!
  Oh, what a pleasant day!

" Near Woodland House we crossed the
    fields,
  And by the mill we came."
" Indeed! " exclaimed Papa, " how's this ?
  Your brother did the same;

" But very dull he found the walk.
  What have you there ? Let's see!
Come, Charles, enjoy this charming treat,
  As new to you as me."

" First look, Papa, at this small branch,
  Which on a tall oak grew,
And by its slimy berries white
  The mistletoe we knew.

" A bird all green ran up a tree,
  A woodpecker we call,
Who, with his strong bill, wounds the
    bark,
  To feed on insects small.

" And many lapwings cried pee-wit;
  And one among the rest
Pretended lameness to decoy
  Us from her lonely nest.

" Young starlings, martins, swallows, all
  Such lovely flocks so gay;
A heron, too, which caught a fish,
  And with it flew away.

" This bird we found, a kingfisher;
  Though dead, his plumes how bright!
Do have him stuffed, my dear Papa,
  'Twill be a charming sight.

" When reached the heath, how wide the
    space!
  The air, how fresh and sweet!
We plucked these flowers and different
    heaths,
  The fairest we could meet.

" The distant prospect we admired,
  The mountains far and blue;
A mansion here, a cottage there ;
  See, here's the sketch we drew.

" A splendid sight we next beheld,
  The glorious setting sun,
In clouds of crimson, purple, gold;
  His daily race was done."

" True taste with knowledge," said Papa,
  " By observation's gained;
You've both well used the gift of sight,
  And this reward obtained.

" My Julia in this desk will find
  A drawing-box quite new;
This spy-glass, Tom, you oft desired,
  I think it now your due.

" And pretty toys and pretty gifts
  For Charles, too, shall be bought
When he can see the works of God,
  And prize them as he ought."

Adelaide O'Keeffe

INTO THE WORLD AND OUT

Into the world he looked with sweet
    surprise;
The children laughed so when they saw
  his eyes.

Into the world a rosy hand in doubt
He reached—a pale hand took one rosebud out.

" And that was all—quite all ! " No,
    surely! But
The children cried so when his eyes were
  shut.

Sarah M. B. Piatt

THE MONTHS

JANUARY brings the snow,
  Makes our feet and fingers glow.

February brings the rain,
Thaws the frozen lake again.

March brings breezes sharp and chill,
Shakes the dancing daffodil.

April brings the primrose sweet,
Scatters daisies at our feet.

May brings flocks of pretty lambs,
Sporting round their fleecy dams.

June brings tulips, lilies, roses,
Fills the children's hands with posies.

Hot July brings thunder-showers,
Apricots, and gilly-flowers.

August brings the sheaves of corn:
Then the harvest home is borne.

Warm September brings the fruit;
Sportsmen then begin to shoot.

Brown October brings the pheasant,
Then to gather nuts is pleasant.

Dull November brings the blast—
Hark! the leaves are whirling fast.

Cold December brings the sleet,
Blazing fire, and Christmas treat.

Sarah Coleridge

FIDDLE-DEE-DEE

THERE once was a bird that lived up in
  a tree,
And all he could whistle was Fiddle-dee-
dee!—
A very provoking, unmusical song
For one to be whistling the summer day
long!
Yet always contented and busy was he
With that vocal recurrence of Fiddle-
dee-dee!

Hard by lived a brave little soldier of four,
That weird iteration annoyed him to sore:
" I prithee, Dear-Mother-Mine, fetch me
my gun,
For, by our St. Didy, the deed must be
done
That shall presently rid all creation and me
Of that ominous bird and his Fiddle-dee-
dee! "

Then out came Dear-Mother-Mine, bring-
ing her son
His awfully truculent little red gun;
The stock was of pine and the barrel of tin,
The " bang " it came out where the bullet
went in:
The right kind of weapon, I think you'll
agree,
For slaying all fowl that go Fiddle-dee-dee!

The brave little soldier quoth never a word
But he up and he drew a straight bead on
that bird;
And while that vain creature provokingly
sang
The gun it went off with a terrible bang !
Then loud laughed the youth, " By my
Bottle," cried he,
" I've put a quietus on Fiddle-dee-dee! "

Out came then Dear-Mother-Mine, say-
ing : " My son,
Right well have you wrought with your
little red gun!
Hereafter no evil at all need I fear
With such a brave soldier as You-My-Love
here! "
She kissed the dear boy. *The bird in the
tree
Continued to whistle his Fiddle-dee-dee!*

Eugene Field

I THINK WHEN I READ

I THINK when I read that sweet story of
  old,
  When Jesus was here among men,
How He called little children as lambs to
  His fold,
  I should like to have been with Him then.
I wish that His hands had been placed on
  my head,
  That His arm had been thrown around
  me,
And that I might have seen His kind look
  when he said:
  " Let the little ones come unto Me."

Yet still to His footstool in prayer I may go,
  And ask for a share in His love;
And if I thus earnestly seek Him below
  I shall see Him and hear Him above,
In that beautiful place He has gone to
  prepare
  For all that are washed and forgiven;
And many dear children are gathering
  there,
  " For of such is the kingdom of heaven."

Jemima Thompson Luke

BYE, BABY BUNTING

Bye, Baby Bunting,
    Daddy's gone a-hunting
To get a little rabbit-skin
To wrap my Baby Bunting in.

JOHNNY'S FROLIC

Ho! for a frolic!
    Said Johnny the stout :
"There's coasting and sledding;
    I'm going out! "
Scarcely had Johnny
    Plunged in the snow
When there came a complaint
    Up from his toe.
" We're cold," said the toe,
    " I and the rest;
There are ten of us freezing,
    Standing abreast."

Then up spoke an ear:
    " My! but it's labour
Playing in winter. Eh,
    Opposite neighbour? "

" Pooh! " said his nose,
    Angry and red;
" Who wants to tingle?
    Go home to bed! "

Eight little fingers,
    Four to a thumb,
All cried together,
    ' Johnny, we're numb! "

But Johnny the stout
Wouldn't listen a minute;
Never a snow-bank
    But Johnny was in it.

Tumbling and jumping,
    Shouting with glee,
Wading the snow-drifts
    Up to his knee.

Soon he forgot them,
    Fingers and toes,
Never once heeded
    The ear and the nose.

Ah, what a frolic!
    All in a glow,
Johnny grew warmer
    Out in the snow.

Often his breathing
    Came with a joke:
" Blaze away, Johnny!
    I'll do the smoke."

" And I'll do the fire,"
    Said Johnny the bold,
" Fun is the fuel
    For driving off cold."

CUCKOO IN THE PEAR-TREE

The Cuckoo sat in the old pear-tree.
                    Cuckoo!
Raining or snowing, naught cared he.
                    Cuckoo!
Cuckoo, cuckoo, naught cared he.

The Cuckoo flew over a housetop nigh.
                    Cuckoo!
" Dear, are you at home, for here am I ?
                    Cuckoo!
Cuckoo, cuckoo, here am I."

" I dare not open the door to you.
                    Cuckoo!
Perhaps you are not the right cuckoo?
                    Cuckoo!
Cuckoo, cuckoo, the right cuckoo! "
" I am the right Cuckoo, the proper one,
                    Cuckoo!
For I am my father's only son,
                    Cuckoo!
Cuckoo, cuckoo, his only son."
" If you are your father's only son—
                    Cuckoo!
    The bobbin pull tightly,
    Come through the door lightly —
                    Cuckoo!
If you are your father's only son—
                    Cuckoo!
It must be you, the only one—
Cuckoo, cuckoo, my own Cuckoo!
                    Cuckoo! "

                William Brighty Rands

THERE WAS A LITTLE MAN

There was a little man
    Who wooed a little maid;
And he said: " Little maid, will you wed,
    wed, wed?
I have little more to say,
    So will you ay or nay?
For the least said is soonest men-ded, ded,
    ded."

Then the little maid replied:
    " Should I be your little bride,
Pray what must we have for to eat, eat,
    eat?
Will the flame that you're so rich in
    Light a fire in the kitchen?
Or the little God of Love turn the spit,
    spit, spit? "

THE DOVE AND THE WREN

The dove says, 'Coo, coo; what shall I do?
    I can scarce maintain two.'
' Pooh, pooh! ' says the wren; ' I have
    got ten,
And keep them all like gentlemen.'

What's the news of the day,
    Good neighbour, I pray?
They say the balloon
Is gone up to the Moon!

⊡   ⊡

March winds and April showers
    Bring forth May flowers.

⊡   ⊡

There is a rainbow in the sky,
    On the arch where the tempests trod;
God wrote it ere the world was dry:
'Tis the autograph of God.

⊡   ⊡

The Hart he loves the high wood,
    The Hare he loves the hill,
The Knight he loves his bright sword,
    The Lady loves her will.

⊡   ⊡

Every lady in this land
    Has five nails upon her hand,
Twenty on her hands and feet;
All this is true, without deceit.

⊡   ⊡

If all the world were apple pie,
    And all the sea were ink,
And all the trees were bread-and-cheese,
    What should we have to drink?

⊡   ⊡

Good-morrow to you, Valentine!
    Curl your locks as I do mine;
Two before and three behind,
Good-morrow to you, Valentine!

⊡   ⊡

For want of the nail the shoe was lost;
    For want of the shoe the horse was lost;
For want of the horse the rider was lost;
For want of the rider the battle was lost;
For want of the battle the kingdom was
    lost;
And all for the want of a horse-shoe nail.

⊡   ⊡

Here's a poor widow from Babylon,
    With six poor children all alone;
One can bake and one can brew,
One can shape and one can sew,
One can sit by the fire and spin,
One can bake a cake for a king.
Come choose you East, come choose you
    West,
Come choose you the one that you love
    the best.

⊡   ⊡

Little Boy Blue, come blow your horn,
    The sheep's in the meadow, the cow's
    in the corn;
But where is the boy that looks after the
    sheep?
He's under a haycock, fast asleep.

Georgie Porgie, Pudding and Pie,
    Kissed the girls and made them cry.
When the boys came out to play
Georgie Porgie ran away.

⊡   ⊡

Sing, sing, what shall I sing?
    The cat has eaten the pudding-string!
Do, do, what shall I do?
The cat has bitten it quite in two.

⊡   ⊡

Queen Anne, Queen Anne, she sits in
    the sun,
As fair as the lily, as white as the swan.

⊡   ⊡

There was a little boy went into a field,
    And lay down on some hay;
An owl came out and flew about,
    And the little boy ran away.

⊡   ⊡

The girl in the lane that couldn't speak
    plain
    Cried gobble, gobble, gobble;
The man on the hill that couldn't stand
    still
    Went hobble, hobble, hobble.

⊡   ⊡

Sea-gull, sea-gull, sit on the sand;
    It's never good weather when you're
on the land.

⊡   ⊡

Baa, baa, black sheep, have you any
    wool?
Yes, sir, yes, sir, three bags full;
One for the master, and one for the dame,
And one for the little boy that cries down
    the lane.

⊡   ⊡

To market, to market, to buy a fat pig,
    Home again, home again, Jiggety
    Jig.
To market, to market, to buy a fat hog,
Home again, home again, Jiggety Jog.

⊡   ⊡

There were two blackbirds sitting on a
    hill,
The one named Jack, the other named
    Jill.
Fly away, Jack! Fly away, Jill!
Come again, Jack! Come again, Jill!

⊡   ⊡

Four-and-twenty tailors went to kill a
    snail;
The best man amongst them durst not
    touch her tail;
She put out her horns like a little Kyloe
    cow;
Run, tailors, run, or she'll kill you all e'en
    now!

Imperishable Thoughts of Men Enshrined in the Books of the World

Tennyson's Masterpiece

AS printed among Tennyson's works, In Memoriam is a long poem of one hundred and thirty-one sections, with a prologue and an epilogue. It is really a collection of short poems written on different occasions over a period of about sixteen years, dedicated to the memory of a dear friend of the poet, Arthur Henry Hallam, who was expected by all who knew him to become one of the most notable men of England, but who died suddenly at Vienna on September 15, 1833, and was brought back by sea and buried at Clevedon, on the Bristol Channel. Tennyson's grief at the loss of his friend was so intense that for many years it had a constant influence on the poet's life, turning his thoughts to the contemplation of man's destiny, and the effect of grief in purifying the mind of man.

IN MEMORIAM

STRONG Son of God, immortal Love,
  Whom we, that have not seen thy
    face,
  By faith, and faith alone, embrace,
Believing where we cannot prove:

Thine are these orbs of light and shade;
  Thou madest Life in man and brute;
  Thou madest Death; and lo, thy foot
Is on the skull which thou hast made.

Thou wilt not leave us in the dust:
  Thou madest man, he knows not why.
  He thinks he was not made to die;
And thou hast made him: thou art just.

Thou seemest human and divine,
  The highest, holiest manhood, thou:
  Our wills are ours, we know not how;
Our wills are ours, to make them thine.

Our little systems have their day;
  They have their day and cease to be:
  They are but broken lights of thee,
And thou, O Lord, art more than they.

We have but faith: we cannot know;
  For knowledge is of things we see;
  And yet we trust it comes from thee,
A beam in darkness: let it grow.

Let knowledge grow from more to more,
  But more of reverence in us dwell;
  That mind and soul, according well,
May make one music as before

But vaster. We are fools and slight;
  We mock thee when we do not fear:
  But help thy foolish ones to bear:
Help thy vain worlds to bear thy light.

Forgive what seemed my sin in me;
  What seemed my worth since I began;
  For merit lives from man to man,
And not from man, O Lord, to thee.

Forgive my grief for one removed,
  Thy creature, whom I found so fair.
  I trust he lives in thee, and there
I find him worthier to be loved.

Forgive these wild and wandering cries,
  Confusions of a wasted youth;
  Forgive them where they fail in truth,
And in thy wisdom make me wise.

IN GRIEF'S FIRST HOUR

The poem begins with the above verses, dated 1849, and they strike at once a note of confident hope in the goodness and mercy of God. Overshadowed by the loss of his friend, he asks himself whether they will live again, and continue in another life the friendship of this. He has been studying works of philosophy, but from them he only comes to know that we cannot understand the inner mysteries of life, and must be content with faith. Yet he finds himself wandering sorrowfully in the street where his friend had lived.

DARK house, by which once more I stand
  Here in the long, unlovely street,
  Doors where my heart was used to beat
So quickly, waiting for a hand,

A hand that can be clasped no more—
  Behold me, for I cannot sleep,
  And like a guilty thing I creep
At earliest morning to the door.

He is not here; but far away
  The noise of life begins again,
  And ghastly through the drizzling rain
On the bald street breaks the blank day.

ROMANCE · HISTORIES · DRAMAS · ESSAYS · WORLD CLASSICS

THE LAST JOURNEY

"Every pleasant spot" where the friends had been now seems dark, and despair has driven hope and faith away. The poet's soul has now begun to feel with a new keenness in his grief, but his thoughts are gentle when he contemplates the last journey of his friend over seas to the quiet waters of the River Severn in his native land.

FAIR ship, that from the Italian shore
  Sailest the placid ocean-plains
  With my lost Arthur's loved remains,
Spread thy full wings, and waft him o'er.

So draw him home to those that mourn
  In vain; a favourable speed
  Ruffle thy mirrored mast, and lead
Through prosperous floods his holy urn.

All night no ruder air perplex
  Thy sliding keel, till Phosphor, bright
  As our pure love, thro' early light
Shall glimmer on the dewy decks.

.   .   .   .   .   .

I hear the noise about thy keel;
  I hear the bell struck in the night:
  I see the cabin window bright;
I see the sailor at the wheel.

Thou bring'st the sailor to his wife,
  And travelled men from foreign lands;
  And letters unto trembling hands;
And, thy dark freight, a vanished life.

So bring him: we have idle dreams:
  This look of quiet flatters thus
  Our home-bred fancies: O to us,
The fools of habit, sweeter seems.

To rest beneath the clover sod,
  That takes the sunshine and the rains.
  Or where the kneeling hamlet drains
The chalice of the grapes of God;

Than if with thee the roaring wells
  Should gulf him fathom-deep in brine;
  And hands so often clasped in mine
Should toss with tangle and with shells.

IF THE LOST CAME BACK

"Is this the end of all my care?" the poet asks himself when the body of his friend has been hidden in the dark grave. In the depth of his grief his reason is not calm enough to answer him, and he can only resign himself to his sorrow and to what time may teach him. In these verses he expresses the commonest feelings of humankind, the difficulty at first of believing that a friend who has died will never meet us and speak to us again in this world.

IF one should bring me this report,
  That thou hadst touched the land to-day,
  And I went down unto the quay,
And found thee lying in the port;

And standing, muffled round with woe,
  Should see thy passengers in rank
  Come stepping lightly down the plank
And beckoning unto those they know;

And if along with these should come
  The man I held as half divine;
  Should strike a sudden hand in mine,
And ask a thousand things of home;

And I should tell him all my pain,
  And how my life had drooped of late,
  And he should sorrow o'er my state
And marvel what possessed my brain;

And I perceived no touch of change,
  No hint of death in all his frame,
  But found him all in all the same,
I should not feel it to be strange.

NATURE'S SOOTHING INFLUENCE

"Calm despair and wild unrest" are now the two opposing feelings struggling within him, but when he comes again to the grave of his friend, the very gentleness of the natural scenes has a soothing influence on his spirit, and he writes:

THE Danube to the Severn gave
  The darkened heart that beat no more;
  They laid him by the pleasant shore,
And in the hearing of the wave.

There twice a day the Severn fills;
  The salt sea-water passes by,
  And hushes half the babbling Wye,
And makes a silence in the hills.

The Wye is hushed nor moved along,
  And hushed my deepest grief of all,
  When filled with tears that cannot fall,
I brim with sorrow drowning song.

The tide flows down, the wave again
  Is vocal in its wooded walls;
  My deeper anguish also falls,
And I can speak a little then.

MEMORIES OF THE LOST FRIEND

His grief is still a purely personal emotion, and has not yet led him into the wider and deeper feelings which we call "universal," because they embrace mankind as a whole. It is still of their old remembered companionship he sings.

THE path by which we twain did go,
  Which led by tracts that pleased us well,
  Through four sweet years arose and fell,
From flower to flower, from snow to snow:

And we with singing cheered the way,
  And, crowned with all the season lent,
  From April on to April went,
And glad at heart from May to May:

But where the path we walked began
  To slant the fifth autumnal slope,

As we descended following Hope,
There sat the Shadow feared of man,

Who broke our fair companionship,
And spread his mantle dark and cold,
And wrapt thee formless in the fold,
And dulled the murmur on thy lip.

And bore thee where I could not see
Nor follow, though I walk in haste,
And think that, somewhere in the waste,
The Shadow sits and waits for me.

THE SACRIFICE OF LOVE

But in the presence of this " Shadow cloaked from head to foot," which is, of course, Death, " who keeps the keys of all the creeds," the poet begins to ponder over the great mysteries of man's life and destiny. His thoughts of life, however, are always involved with memories of his friend.

I know that this was Life—the track
Whereon with equal feet we fared;
And then, as now, the day prepared
The daily burden for the back.

But this it was that made me move
As light as carrier-birds in air;
I loved the weight I had to bear,
Because it needed help of Love:

Nor could I weary, heart or limb,
When mighty Love would cleave in twain
The lading of a single pain,
And part it, giving half to him.

THE LESSONS OF LIFE

From his personal feelings he now begins to draw the real lessons of life, and as the wildness of despair gives place at length to more reasonable and calmer thoughts, he is able to contemplate his loss with calmness and resignation.

I envy not in any moods
The captive void of noble rage,
The linnet born within the cage,
That never knew the summer's woods:

I envy not the beast that takes
His license in the field of time,
Unfettered by the sense of crime,
To whom a conscience never wakes;

Nor, what may count itself as blest,
The heart that never plighted troth
But stagnates in the weeds of sloth;
Nor any want-begotten rest.

I hold it true, whate'er befall,
I feel it when I sorrow most;
'Tis better to have loved and lost
Than never to have loved at all.

THE MESSAGE OF THE BELLS

Then, with the approach of Christmastide, and all its holy memories, he finds his very sorrow touched with joy. New feelings of hope, and a serene happiness, born of his rising faith in God's Mercy, now dwell in that breast where so recently the wildness of sorrow and despair had reigned.

The time draws near the birth of Christ:
The moon is hid; the night is still;
The Christmas bells from hill to hill
Answer each other in the mist.

Four voices of four hamlets round,
From far and near, on mead and moor,
Swell out and fail, as if a door
Were shut between me and the sound:

Each voice four changes on the wind,
That now dilate, and now decrease,
Peace and goodwill, goodwill and peace.
Peace and goodwill, to all mankind.

This year I slept and woke with pain,
I almost wished no more to wake,
And that my hold on life would break
Before I heard those bells again;

But they my troubled spirit rule,
For they controlled me when a boy;
They bring me sorrow touched with joy,
The merry merry bells of Yule.

THE POET'S FAITH AND DOUBT

His faith in the promises of God, as revealed to us in the teachings of Jesus, is not yet absolute, and his mind is not without its doubts, but he has emerged from his darkest sorrow with the conviction that the grave is not the end.

My own dim life should teach me this,
That life shall live for evermore,
Else Earth is darkness at the core,
And dust and ashes all that is;

. . . .

What then were God to such as I ?
'Twere hardly worth my while to choose
Of things all mortal, or to use
A little patience ere I die;

'Twere best at once to sink to peace,
Like birds the charming serpent draws.
To drop head-foremost in the jaws
Of vacant darkness and to cease.

DO THE DEPARTED THINK OF US ?

It is springtime again, and the poet still is singing his mournful songs in memory of his friend. For the first time we find him wondering whether the spirit of the departed takes any interest in the life on Earth, and, if so, he cannot but think these songs of his will be grateful to the spirit's ear.

No joy the blowing season gives,
The herald melodies of spring,
But in the songs I love to sing
A doubtful gleam of solace lives.

If any care for what is here
  Survive in spirits rendered free,
  Then are these songs I sing of thee
Not all ungrateful to thine ear.

THE PURPOSE OF ALL LIFE

From this thought he goes on to speculate upon the life of
the departed. " How fares it with the happy dead ? " he
asks, and suggests that theirs is indeed the larger life, to
which all the joys and sorrows and good and evil of this
world we live in are but the dim and bungling preparations.

OH, yet we trust that somehow good
  Will be the final goal of ill,
  To pangs of nature, sins of will,
Defects of doubt, and taints of blood;

That nothing walks with aimless feet;
  That not one life shall be destroyed,
  Or cast as rubbish to the void,
When God hath made the pile complete;

That not a worm is cloven in vain;
  That not a moth with vain desire
  Is shrivelled in a fruitless fire,
Or but subserves another's gain.

Behold, we know not anything;
  I can but trust that good shall fall
  At last—far off—at last, to all,
And every winter change to spring.

. . . .

Dost thou look back on what hath been,
  As some divinely gifted man,
  Whose life in low estate began
And on a simple village green;

Who breaks his birth's invidious bar,
  And grasps the skirts of happy chance,
  And breasts the blows of circumstance,
  And grapples with his evil star;

. . . .

And moving up from high to higher,
  Becomes on Fortune's crowning slope
  The pillar of a people's hope,
The centre of a world's desire;

Yet feels, as in a pensive dream,
  When all his active powers are still:
  A distant dearness in the hill,
A secret sweetness in the stream,

The limit of his narrower fate,
  While yet beside its vocal springs
  He played at counsellors and kings,
With one that was his earliest mate;

Who ploughs with pain his native lea
  And reaps the labour of his hands,
  Or in the furrow musing stands;
" Does my old friend remember me ? "

WHEN GRIEF IS PAST

This, then, is the wide and universal hope that has grown
within the soul of the poet, as he has turned from his own
personal sorrows to contemplate the sorrows of all mankind,
and to look with clearer faith upon the work of God. He
has no longer any doubt that God has created man not as
the mere creature of a passing day, but as an inheritor of
immortal life. He begins also to feel half ashamed of his
grief, saying that " The song of woe is, after all, an earthly
song," and in the larger love of mankind, which Jesus came
to teach, he finds the joy that far outweighs the loss of a
friend. Another year has passed; it is Christmas once more.

AGAIN at Christmas did we weave
  The holly round the Christmas
    hearth;
  The silent snow possessed the earth,
And calmly fell our Christmas-eve:

The Yule-clog sparkled keen with frost,
  No wing of wind the region swept,
  But over all things brooding slept
The quiet sense of something lost.

As in the winters left behind,
  Again our ancient games had place,
  The mimic picture's breathing grace,
And dance and song and hoodman-blind.

Who showed a token of distress?
  No single tear, no mark of pain:
  O sorrow, then can sorrow wane?
O grief, can grief be changed to less?

O last regret, regret can die!
  No—mixt with all this mystic frame,
  Her deep relations are the same,
But with long use her tears are dry.

THE COMING OF SPRING

The poet is thus uneasy at the thought that his sorrow for
his friend has lessened. It is personal feeling again pushing
against the wider love of humanity, and in the following
beautiful song of spring he calls upon the warmer season of
the year to thaw his frozen sorrow and let it flower again.

DIP down upon the northern shore,
  O sweet new year delaying long;
  Thou doest expectant Nature wrong;
Delaying long, delay no more.

What stays thee from the clouded noons,
  Thy sweetness from its proper place?
  Can trouble live with April days,
Or sadness in the summer moons?

Bring orchis, bring the foxglove spire,
  The little speedwell's darling blue,
  Deep tulips dashed with fiery dew,
Laburnums, dropping-wells of fire.

O thou, new year, delaying long,
　Delayest the sorrow in my blood,
　That longs to burst a frozen bud
And flood a fresher throat with song.

WHAT MIGHT HAVE BEEN

His mind is back again entirely with his friend, when he
sings thus of what might have been had the lost one lived
to marry the poet's sister, to whom he had been engaged.

WHEN I contemplate all alone
　The life that had been thine below,
　And fix my thoughts on all the glow
To which thy crescent would have grown.

I see thee sitting crowned with good,
　A central warmth, diffusing bliss
　In glance and smile, and clasp and kiss,
On all the branches of thy blood;

Thy blood, my friend, and partly mine;
　For now the day was drawing on
　When thou shouldst link thy life with one
Of mine own house, and boys of thine

Had babbled " Uncle " on my knee;
　But that remorseless iron hour
　Made cypress of her orange flower,
Despair of Hope, and earth of thee.

I seem to meet their least desire,
　To clap their cheeks, to call them mine,
　I see their unborn faces shine
Beside the never-lighted fire.

I see myself an honoured guest,
　Thy partner in the flowery walk
　Of letters, genial table-talk,
Or deep dispute, and graceful jest;

While now thy prosperous labour fills
　The lips of men with honest praise,
　And sun by sun the happy days
Descend below the golden hills

With promise of a morn as fair;
　And all the train of bounteous hours
　Conduct by paths of growing powers,
To reverence and the silver hair;

Till slowly worn her earthly robe,
　Her lavish mission richly wrought,
　Leaving great legacies of thought,
Thy spirit should fail from off the globe;

What time mine own might also flee,
　As linked with thine in love and fate,
　And, hovering o'er the dolorous strait
To the other shore, involved in thee,

Arrive at last the blessed goal,
　And He that died in Holy Land
　Would reach us out the shining hand,
And take us as a single soul.

What reed was that on which I leant ?
　Ah, backward fancy, wherefore wake
　The old bitterness again, and break
The low beginnings of content.

FAMILIAR SCENES REVISITED

For a time the thoughts of the poet are again entirely with
the departed; then comes a visit to Cambridge, where they
had been at college together, but the sense of personal loss
is no longer felt, the gloom has lifted from the poet's mind.

I PASSED beside the reverend walls
　In which of old I wore the gown;
　I roved at random through the town,
And saw the tumult of the halls;

And heard once more in college fanes
　The storm their high-built organs make,
　And thunder-music, rolling, shake
The prophets blazoned on the panes;

And caught once more the distant shout,
　The measured pulse of racing oars
　Among the willows; paced the shores
And many a bridge, and all about

The same grey flats again, and felt
　The same, but not the same; and last
　Up that long walk of limes I passed
To see the rooms in which he dwelt.

Another name was on the door:
　I lingered; all within was noise
　Of songs, and clapping hands, and boys
That crashed the glass and beat the floor;

Where once we held debate, a band
　Of youthful friends, on mind and art,
　And labour, and the changing mart,
And all the framework of the land;

When one would aim an arrow fair,
　But send it slackly from the string;
　And one would pierce an outer ring,
And one an inner, here and there;

And last the master-bowman, he,
　Would cleave the mark.　A willing ear
　We lent him.　Who but hung to hear
The rapt oration flowing free

From point to point, with power and grace
　And music in the bounds of law,
　To those conclusions when we saw
The God within him light his face,

6929

And seem to lift the form, and glow
  In azure orbits heavenly-wise;
  And over those ethereal eyes
The bar of Michael Angelo.

RING OUT WILD BELLS

Through many sections of the poem the writer recalls events
in his friendship with his lost companion, but there is
always a feeling of joy now in his expressions of grief, no
wavering note of doubt when he sings of the greater things
of life and immortality; until at last a Christmas comes
that finds him calm in mind and strong in faith, and in a
great song of triumph the poem reaches its climax.

Ring out, wild bells, to the wild sky,
  The flying cloud, the frosty light;
  The year is dying in the night;
Ring out, wild bells, and let him die.

Ring out the old, ring in the new,
  Ring, happy bells, across the snow:
  The year is going, let him go;
Ring out the false, ring in the true.

Ring out the grief that saps the mind,
  For those that here we see no more;
  Ring out the feud of rich and poor,
Ring in redress to all mankind.

Ring out a slowly dying cause,
  And ancient forms of party strife;
  Ring in the nobler modes of life,
With sweeter manners, purer laws.

Ring out the want, the care, the sin,
  The faithless coldness of the times;
  Ring out, ring out my mournful rhymes,
But ring the fuller minstrel in.

  . . . .

Ring out old shapes of foul disease;
  Ring out the narrowing lust of gold,
  Ring out the thousand wars of old,
Ring in the thousand years of peace.

Ring in the valiant man and free,
  The larger heart, the kindlier hand;
  Ring out the darkness of the land,
Ring in the Christ that is to be.

JOY COMES WITH SPRING

The poet's new mood is reflected, as spring follows the
winter cold, in the lovely sights and sounds with which
Nature renews the beauty of the Earth.

Now fades the last long streak of snow,
  Now burgeons every maze of quick
  About the flowering squares, and thick
By ashen roots the violets blow.

Now rings the woodland loud and long,
  The distance takes a lovelier hue,
  And drowned in yonder living blue
The lark becomes a sightless song.

Now dance the lights on lawn and lea,
  The flocks are whiter down the vale,
  And milkier every milky sail
On winding stream or distant sea ;

Where now the seamew pipes, or dives
  In yonder greening gleam, and fly
  The happy birds, that change their sky
To build and brood; that live their lives

From land to land; and in my breast
  Spring wakens too; and my regret
  Becomes an April violet,
And buds and blossoms like the rest.

WHAT TIME HAS TAUGHT THE POET

So at last the poet's personal grief has passed; " been lived
down," as we say. Time has indeed taught him wisdom, and
he is wise in the confident hope that far better than unavailing sorrow for the dead is the steady faith in the reunion
of friends in after life, " some strong bond which is to be."

Is it, then, regret for buried time
  That keenlier in sweet April wakes,
  And meets the year, and gives and takes
The colours of the crescent prime?

Not all: the songs, the stirring air,
  The life re-orient out of dust,
  Cry through the sense to hearten trust
In that which made the world so fair.

Not all regret; the face will shine
  Upon me while I muse alone;
  And that dear voice I once have known
Still speak to me of me and mine:

Yet less of sorrow lives in me
  For days of happy commune dead;
  Less yearning for the friendship fled
Than some strong bond which is to be.

THAT ONE DIVINE EVENT

The last thoughts of the poet, freed from all contemplation
of his own feelings, are with mankind as a whole, and in his
vision he sees the ultimate triumph of life over death, of
good over evil. Man is no mere animal, but capable of
love and suffering and hope, and these are but the seeds of
what will flower and bear fruit in the after life of the soul.
Nature, the poet says, is like an open book.

No longer half-akin to brute,
  For all we thought and loved and did,
  And hoped, and suffered, is but seed
Of what in them is flower and fruit.

Whereof the man, that with me trod
  This planet, was a noble type
  Appearing ere the times were ripe,
That friend of mine who lives in God,

That God, which ever lives and loves,
  One God, one law, one element,
  And one far-off divine event,
To which the whole creation moves.

The Story of the Most Beautiful Book in the World

The Growth of Christianity

WE have finished our survey of the Bible stories. Their continuation is to be found in the story of Christianity to which the Bible led. The Bible was finished over eighteen centuries ago. The Christianity that grew out of it, and still finds its inspiration in it, goes on, and will go on, with a development like that which can be traced throughout the Bible. Here we shall follow, in outline, the changeful growth of the Christianity that at last will complete the reconciliation of humanity with God which the Bible began. Religion entered upon an entirely new stage when Jesus left to His disciples the spreading throughout the world of his Divine revelation.

THE WINNING OF THE WORLD

THE rapid spread of Christianity, after the earthly presence of the Master was withdrawn, dwarfs all recorded miracles. Failure could not seem more complete than when Jesus, rejected by the priests of his own race, was denounced by them to the Roman Government of Judea as a dangerous revolutionist, crucified as a criminal, and his few inconspicuous disciples all forsook Him and fled. To human wisdom that seemed the end—the disgraceful end—of the Galilean carpenter who had been felt to be a marvellous teacher by crowds of simple countrymen.

Against any revival of the excitement caused by His powers of healing, His compelling personality, His tender teaching, and His shining purity, were the resentment of the closely-organised Jewish priesthood, the paganism of the non-Jewish elements in the population, and the mighty Government of the Roman Empire which, with a kind of lofty contempt, always supported organised local opinion in its distant provinces. And yet, before the generation to which Jesus had belonged had passed away, the gentle religion of the meek and pure in heart, that saw God as a Heavenly Father and all men as brethren, had spread over western Asia, penetrated to Athens, the home of philosophy in Greece, and was permeating silently the imperial city of Rome itself.

The western world, made bankrupt of spirituality by the trivialities and superstitions of outworn paganism, was waiting in expectancy for a Messiah, a deliverer, with a new faith that would satisfy the loftiest hopes of humanity ; and, as the story of Him who brought life and immortality to light passed from land to land, the finest souls in every race that heard the good news felt that in very truth a Messiah had come.

The complete destruction of Jerusalem, and the shattering of the priestly system of the Jews by the army of Titus, had some effect, no doubt, on the most religious race in the world. No longer could it be hoped by Jews that the Chosen People would ever attain to an earthly kingship. The long cherished belief in a conquering Messiah perished. Rome ruled the world. A spiritual sway was the only possibility left. The Master's teaching that the Kingdom of God is within the hearts of men appealed alike to disillusioned Jews and to the many races who bowed the knee, in temporal affairs, to the all-embracing might of Rome. The thoughts of men widened to something like the breadth of the Master's own outlook and reached to the Eternal Beyond. It was the immortal Christ who conquered the imagination of a generation that had well-nigh lost hope.

For a time the disciples held firmly the belief that Jesus would quickly return and visibly inaugurate a new era. Even Paul, the greatest of all the preachers of the Christian faith, held this view; but, as we can see in his letters, if we understand when each of them was written, he began to realise that Christ's kingdom was

GREAT FIGURES OF THE OLD TESTAMENT · THE LIFE OF JESUS

to be in the hearts of men till the whole world had been reached by His Gospel. And this spiritual aspect of Christianity, as bringing men into a right relationship to God through succeeding ages, was at last accepted by nearly all Christians.

THE GREAT WAVE OF ENTHUSIASM WHICH WOULD NOT BE STAMPED OUT

No doubt the early mistake of a swift triumphant reappearance of Christ had a great effect in making the first Christians earnest and faithful; but the most real cause of the marvellous spread of the new faith, for centuries after Jesus finished His earthly life, was a passionate devotion aroused by the truth and loveliness of the revelation He had made to mankind, and a feeling of the difference He had made to the world by the glorious outlook He had disclosed. His spirit thrilled men to a sublime enthusiasm that knew no fear.

And, indeed, there was need for such an enthusiasm, for persecution soon did its worst to stamp out the swiftly spreading faith. The Roman Empire, which dominated the world almost as far as India by force of arms, demanded that its august Emperors should be acknowledged as divine, according to the old pagan ideas, and, of course, Christians could not make any such acknowledgment. They were willing to render to Caesar the things which were Caesar's, but not to render to him the adoration that was God's. So from time to time the Emperor tried to abolish Christianity altogether by making life intolerable for followers of Christ.

HOW CHRISTIANITY GREW UP ROUND TWO GREAT CENTRES IN EUROPE

If a Roman nobleman was a Christian he was degraded from his rank, and not allowed to hold any honourable office. If he was one of the people he was deprived of citizenship, and insults and cruelties were heaped upon him without any hope of redress. If he was a slave he must remain a slave for life. Christians were not allowed to assemble together for worship. Their churches were destroyed; their books were burned, and they were themselves tortured and martyred. These sufferings were borne with patience; death was met with exaltation, for to them it meant " being with Christ, which is far better." Men who had known little of Christianity before, or had been deceived by false accounts of it, wondered at such heroism, admired it, tried to find out the secret of it, and Christianity flourished more and more.

In less than 300 years after the Crucifixion the position had altered so greatly that the Emperor Constantine formally granted toleration to Christians. He moved his capital to Byzantium, later called Constantinople, now Istanbul, and here Christianity organised itself in eastern Europe as the Greek Orthodox Church; while the Christianity of western Europe, centring on Rome, became the Roman Catholic Church and claimed the headship of the faith for the bishop of Rome as the successor of St. Peter, under the name of the Pope, or Holy Father, of Christendom. Gradually the Roman Empire ceased to exist as a Power dominating the world, and the closely organised Christian Church of the West became the most far-reaching and uniting influence. While the Roman Empire was shrinking, the Church which had made Rome its capital was expanding beyond what had been regarded as the borders of civilisation, and in course of time it became the religion favoured by the temporal Government.

THE FOUNDING OF THE FIRST CHURCHES OF THE EARLY CHRISTIANS

Warlike races who knew nothing of either Christianity or the fanciful poetical religions of Greece and Rome were pressing from the north and east on the nations that lived around the northern Mediterranean shore. As they gradually crushed the Roman Empire they were met by something stronger than the imperial legions. They were themselves conquered by the gentle religion of Christ.

By the time the Christian religion had established itself firmly everywhere around the great sea of southern Europe, and in the Near East its method of worship and expansion had greatly changed. The early disciples went forth from place to place in the simplest manner, preferably in pairs, and sometimes, like Paul, earned their own living on their journeys. As the Christians grew in numbers they organised churches and took the Jewish synagogues as their first models. During periods of persecution they met in secrecy. But later, as security was attained, they felt that the arts of architecture and painting might fitly be used to give dignity to their adoration of the Almighty; and many devout men separated themselves from the ordinary work of the world and

THE LITTLE POOR MAN OF ASSISI

FRANCIS OF ASSISI, LOVING THE LITTLE BIRDS AS HIS BROTHERS AND SISTERS, BROUGHT THE SELFLESSNESS OF JESUS INTO HIS AGE

pledged themselves to a holy life, while as missionaries they spread the faith throughout the heathen lands by which the Roman Empire was surrounded.

The separation of Christian people into those who, on the one hand, tilled the soil, or traded by land and sea, or engaged in useful industries, or served as soldiers under kings or nobles, and, on the other hand, those who made religion their principal concern by being church dignitaries, or parish priests, or monks in monasteries, or wandering friars, constituted the most vital division of human society in those days.

A GREAT BODY WITH A POWER MIGHTIER THAN KINGS

The Church became rich and powerful, owner of large estates, and with vast influence apart from its religious duties. The clergy were almost the only people who had the leisure and means for acquiring the knowledge contained in books, and that added to their power. So, instead of Christians being a scattered body of loyal followers of Christ, they were compactly formed into a mighty Institution more powerful than the greatest of kings. It was, however, very earnest in spreading the Gospel everywhere, as we may see by studying how it Christianised the British Islands at an early date.

When did Christianity first reach our country? No one knows exactly, but it seems probable that in less than fifty years after Christ was crucified outside Jerusalem Roman soldiers brought the Christian faith to this distant island in the northern seas.

HOW CHRISTIANITY CAME TO BRITAIN FIFTY YEARS AFTER CALVARY

About thirty years after the Crucifixion, Paul, who had been preaching throughout Palestine, Asia Minor, and Greece for a quarter of a century, was brought a prisoner to Rome, where he continued his work in captivity, till his martyrdom, probably in A.D. 62. We know that his teaching had appealed to the Roman soldiery. Between A.D. 70 and A.D. 80 Julius Agricola came twice to Britain to complete the conquest of the country. First he came as a general and then as governor, and, after putting down rebellions, he made Roman influence permanent by establishing towns here and there. Among the towns apparently founded at this time was Silchester, on

the main road from London to the west, and excavations of the foundations of this early Roman settlement suggest that it had a Christian church.

If this reading of the ruins of Silchester be true, it is evident that less than fifty years after Paul had finished his course, having kept the faith, the seeds of Christianity were sown in Britain. No doubt they were supplemented by the work of missionaries from Gaul, where Christianity quickly became rooted.

That the British who lived for three hundred and fifty years under Roman rule were in a large degree Christian is proved abundantly. Before Constantine, who was first proclaimed Roman Emperor at York, adopted Christianity as the Imperial religion, and before he founded Constantinople as a Christian capital, the Christians of Britain were so well organised that they sent three bishops to represent them at a great council at Arles, in the south of France, in 314.

HOW BRITAIN CAME TO BE BLOTTED OUT OF THE RECORDS OF THE CHURCH

St. Patrick, the patron saint of Ireland, was a Briton who went there as a missionary. A Briton began missionary work among the Picts. Pelagius, a religious thinker whose views raised arguments among Christians throughout the world, was a Briton. All the traditions of the legendary British King Arthur picture him as a Christian prince in a Christian land, fighting bravely against the incursions of heathen from over the sea. It is clear that when the Romans left Britain they left Christianity in all its more civilised parts, in close touch with the great Church organised from Rome.

Yet, a hundred and fifty years later, when Pope Gregory saw slaves from England in the Roman streets, he gazed on them with strange eyes, and only saw in them handsome heathens of an unknown race. The land was blotted out of the records of the Church. It had to be re-missioned.

No wonder we have little knowledge of the story of our land under the Romans, except from Roman books written at a distance, and the slender records dug out of the ruins of a world overthrown. Our fierce English forefathers, in ruthless hordes, obliterated the religion, social life, language, the very existence of the Britons of the fertile lowlands, and established heathenism in new forms.

A hundred years of oblivion followed, tempered only by the dim faith which survived in the mountainous borderlands of Wales and in Devon and Cornwall. The very alphabet in which records were made was changed. The Britons had accepted Latin as the language of learning. The English brought with them their rude Runic alphabet, which even yet we can only interpret doubtfully. The overthrow was complete. Christianity was uprooted.

THE CHURCH'S GOOD WORKS GIVE IT A FRESH HOLD ON THE PEOPLE

It is usual to say that the second Christianising of England came through Gregory sending Augustine and a body of monks from Rome into Kent in 597, when Ethelbert, the chief English king of his day, was converted, but this is only partly true. The re-missioning of Britain had begun thirty years before the arrival of Augustine. Ireland, Christianised from Britain, repaid the debt by sending Columba and his successors to the islands of Scotland, the lowlands, and the north of England. As soon as the heathen conquerors settled down and ceased to be plundering rovers, the monks of Iona approached them from islands in the west, where they had founded lonely retreats for prayer and a religious life. Thus England was Christianised afresh by simultaneous advances from north and south. The methods used were different. The southern missionaries were organisers and politicians and worked through the Courts of kings; the northern missionaries relied on the quiet influence of good lives, and their work though less rapid was more sure.

A time came when the two movements merged into one; but a sign of the existence of two movements remains to this day in the fact that there is an Archbishop of York as well as an Archbishop of Canterbury.

HOW THE SOUTH HELD THE FORT FOR CHRISTIANITY IN BRITAIN

As the men of English race became more settled, and passed more fully under the influence of Christianity the Church gained a fresh hold on the people by being the repository of learning, the centre of all education, the reliever of the poor, and the protector of the oppressed. In this work the Church movement in the north distinguished itself, producing the fine scholars Bede and Alcuin. It became known through Europe for its learning and missionary zeal.

Then came the second heathen invasion. New hordes of Northmen ravaged every coast. Their fury, directed most fiercely against churches and monasteries, fell disastrously on the north. Northumbria and central England were swamped by the Danish hosts. The overthrow was not so complete as the overthrow of Celtic Christianity had been, for the whole kingdom was never engulfed at one time, and these later invaders were more nearly akin to the English than the English had been to the Britons, and so were more susceptible to absorption. But religion and learning went down for the time being in the north, and this time it was the south that held the fort for Christianity, and achieved a second revival of learning, and a gradual re-expansion of the Christian faith.

Not, however, till the story of these fluctuations in British Christianity had filled nine hundred years was it finally established beyond peril. Surely a country that has been Christianised at such a cost ought never to flag in its efforts to pass on its faith to less fortunate lands.

THE BEAUTIFUL AND USEFUL LIFE OF POPE GREGORY THE GREAT

We have mentioned the names of Pope Gregory, Bede, and Alcuin as notable in the early religious history of Great Britain. Pope Gregory the First bears in history the name of the Great, and right well he deserves it. He was a Roman noble who might easily have become one of the greatest officers of the Roman Empire; but he chose rather the life of prayer and of service to God, with no thought of his own honour, yet, out of his self-denial the highest honour came to him unsought. Gregory's wisdom and goodness won him such love in Rome that when Pope Pelagius died all men said no other man should be pope but Gregory, and though he strove hard to be excused, no other man would they have. He wished to come himself to Britain as a missionary, but the rulers of the Church would not allow him to leave Rome, where he was much needed. It was Gregory who gave the Church the fine, stately chants that are called Gregorian.

The life of Bede was a beautiful one, spent far from the din of the battlefield, the bargaining of the market, and the pleasures of the Court.

All his days were passed, though he was the greatest scholar and teacher of Anglo-Saxon times, in the peaceful monasteries at Wearmouth and at Jarrow. There he studied, wrote, and taught the six hundred youths who gathered round him. For them he wrote text-books covering the then known field of knowledge ; for them, and for the people, he wrote a history of the English Church, telling how Christianity was brought into the country.

So earnest and noble-minded a scholar could not bear to think that the greatest book ever written should remain a sealed book to every person unable to read Latin ; and he was determined, if God gave him strength to do it, to translate at least the Gospel of St. John into Anglo-Saxon, that all might hear and understand it in their own tongue. Forty-four works, mostly in Latin, he had written during his busy life of teaching ; one more, the Gospel of Love, he would leave behind him. He was getting ill and feeble, but he would not leave even to the ablest pupil a work so important as the translation of the Gospel. " I will not have my boys read a lie," he declared, " nor labour fruitlessly after my death."

THE LAST DAYS OF THE BEAUTIFUL LIFE OF THE VENERABLE BEDE

Day by day Bede grew weaker ; but, refusing to rest, he continued cheerfully, dictating to his scribe. One of his scholars, Cuthbert, wrote a description of the last hours of his revered master, and an artist has painted a beautiful picture of the old man on his couch in his little cell, with a youth before him eagerly taking down his words.

In his History of the English People, John Richard Green thus describes the scene:

The dawn broke on another sleepless night, and again the old man called his scholars round him and bade them write.

" There is still a chapter wanting," said the scribe as the morning drew on, " and it is hard for thee to question thyself any longer."

" It is easy done," said Bede. " Take thy pen, and write quickly."

Amid tears and farewells the day wore on to eventide.

" There is yet one sentence unwritten, dear master," said the boy.

" Write it quickly," said the dying man.

" It's finished now," said the little scribe at last.

" You speak truth," said the master. " All is finished now."

Placed upon the pavement, his head supported in his scholars' arms, his face turned to the spot where he was wont to pray, Bede chanted the solemn " Glory to God." As his voice reached the close he passed quietly away.

THE GREAT SCHOLAR WHO CARRIED ON THE WORK OF BEDE

Alcuin, who was born in 735, the year when Bede died so gloriously, was the great scholar who carried on in the north of England the educational work of Bede, and then accepted the invitation of the Emperor Charlemagne to go to the Frankish Court at Aix-la-Chapelle; and there, and later at Tours, established a school of Continental education, which survived when the storm of Danish barbarism had swept away the culture of Yorkshire and Durham.

There were other remarkable men who were connected with the Church in England in early times, and by their actions and disputes showed what was going on in other countries also, as questions of power and privilege arose between the rulers of the Church and the rulers of the different States. One, Bishop Dunstan, who was born in 925, was the real ruler of England for many years. He made numerous changes, increasing the power of the clergy, and setting them apart from the rest of the people. One of his rules was that they should not marry.

A very good thing he did was to give protection to slaves, and to teach their owners that it was good to set them free. For in those days there were many slaves in England, and the law suffered their masters to kill them, and laid but light penalties on anyone who slew a slave.

DUNSTAN, THE GOOD FRIEND OF THE SLAVES OF ENGLAND

Dunstan taught men that slaves are quite as good as other men in God's sight, and that the priests could not pronounce the words of pardon for wrong done to a slave unless the wrongdoer repented of his sin and did penance for it as much as if he had wronged a free man.

When William the Conqueror made himself King of England, nearly a hundred years later, he was ill-pleased with the state of the Church, for the clergy had gone back from the strict ruling of Dunstan; and he brought over, to be Archbishop of Canterbury, an Italian who had been the head of the Abbey of Bec, in Normandy. His name was Lanfranc. William wished to have the Church to help him in keeping the Norman barons from becoming too powerful and troublesome, and he knew that Lanfranc would assist him.

To this end Lanfranc persuaded William to increase the power and wealth of the Church, and to separate the clergy from the laity even more than Dunstan had tried to do. Therefore, in the bishoprics and at the head of the great monasteries, called abbeys or priories, he set, whenever it was possible, not Englishmen, but foreigners who lived by the stricter rule.

Lanfranc put an end to the practice of the clergy marrying, and he arranged with the king that from this time the clergy should not be subject to the ordinary laws of the land in their private doings, but only to the law of the Church, and should be judged only by courts made up of clergy; and that, moreover, if there were disputes between clergy and laity, these Church courts should judge.

LANFRANC PERSUADES WILLIAM TO BUILD UP THE POWER OF THE CHURCH

Soon after William Rufus succeeded William the Conqueror, Lanfranc died, and the new king not only neglected to appoint a new archbishop, but seized for himself the money which the archbishop should have had for the Church. Yet when William fell sick and thought he was about to die, he feared for his soul because he had robbed the Church, and so he appointed a new archbishop. Yet he fancied he could save his soul if he died, and continue in his evil courses if he lived, if he chose for archbishop someone whom he could frighten into working his own will; and so he would have a certain very gentle and pious scholar named Anselm, another Italian, who was now Abbot of Bec as Lanfranc had been. Anselm soon showed William how he had misjudged his gentleness. The great Anselm was a very lion for boldness in the cause of justice and righteousness, and would in no wise obey the king's behests when they were evil, as they commonly were. Nor would he suffer William to rob the Church or to set up bishops and abbots who would do his bidding and pay him great sums of money.

The strife between them became so hot that Anselm had to leave England. When the Red King was dead, and the wise King Henry the First reigned in his stead,

Anselm came back to England, and made agreement with the king readily that the bishops and abbots should do the king homage for their lands as the barons did, but should be appointed according to the rules of the Church, and not according to the will and pleasure of a king whose intent might be evil.

THE QUARREL BETWEEN CHURCH AND STATE THAT WENT ON FOR YEARS

This quarrel between the king and the archbishop was a part of a great quarrel between Church and State which had been going on for many years. There had been at Rome a monk named Hildebrand, who had been the chief adviser of more than one of the popes, and then himself became Pope Gregory the Seventh. Gregory held that it was the will of God to rule the world through two powers—the temporal power, which means the emperors and kings of the different countries, and the spiritual power, which means the Church ruled over by the Pope. Of these two powers he accounted the spiritual power the greater, and so it seemed to him that the reign of God upon Earth would be made manifest only when emperors and kings humbled themselves before the Pope. This he believed all the more because he knew that he himself loved righteousness and hated iniquity, whereas the emperors and kings sought their own advantage more than the glory of God.

THE PENITENT EMPEROR WHO STOOD IN THE SNOW FOR THREE DAYS

Accordingly Pope Gregory would have the Church set wholly free from the rule of emperors and kings. But these were in no wise ready to believe that the bidding of popes and bishops was in very truth the sound of the voice of God; they would have all men in their realms obey them, priests as well as laymen. So there was deadly strife between Pope Gregory and the Emperor Henry the Fourth of Germany.

Seeing that those who wished ill to the emperor were ready enough to aid Gregory against him, the emperor was forced to humble himself for a time, and to stand in the snow in the garb of a penitent for three days, praying for the Pope's pardon at a place called Canossa, though in after time he defied Gregory again and got the better of him. Yet Gregory had taught so many men to believe that in this quarrel the cause of the Church was the cause of God that for nearly two hundred years it often seemed that the Pope was mightier than emperor or king.

It will be seen that the Church had travelled far away from the state of things when it was persecuted by kings. It now claimed to call them to obedience and rule them in the name of God. This attitude culminated during the life of a Pope whom some people reckon was the greatest who ever claimed to be a successor of Peter; while others think that, though he was undoubtedly a sincere man, he was far from seeing at times what was righteousness and what was iniquity. This was Innocent the Third, who was the youngest man ever to be made Pope. Like Gregory, he believed that the Pope was set over the Church and over all men, having all sceptres and thrones subject to him.

STEPHEN LANGTON WHO NEVER FLINCHED AS THE CHAMPION OF FREEDOM

So great was Innocent's power that he was able to decide which of two princes who claimed to be emperor should be acknowledged. When Philip Augustus, King of France, committed sin, he made him cease from his wrong-doing, and the King of Leon, in Spain, in like manner. Also he placed England under an interdict, and would have taken away King John's crown and given it to the King of France if John had not made submission. Therein Innocent thought he was doing right, though in England there were few who were ready to admit that any foreign priest, were he the Pope himself, had power and authority to choose their king.

One thing, however, Innocent did for which all Englishmen should respect his memory. He chose as Archbishop of Canterbury Stephen Langton, a man who feared neither Pope Innocent nor King John, but stood up manfully for justice and right, claiming from the king for the Church no more than the Church's due, and yielding to the Pope's bidding no more than was his due. For what he had at heart was the good of the whole people of England.

When Innocent was reconciled to John by the king's submission, Langton was none the readier to suffer John to play the tyrant, but himself took the chief part in uniting the barons to demand from the king the great Charter of English liberties. This he did, though Innocent himself bade him desist. When John was dead, and some of the barons disliked the Charter because it hindered them from playing the tyrant over their vassals, it was by Langton's influence that the Charter was again confirmed in spite of them.

Pope Innocent the Third not only claimed the right to rule kings but also forcibly to rule the inmost and most sacred beliefs of every individual man.

A TERRIBLE DAY IN THE BITTER HISTORY OF PERSECUTION

The freedom of men to obey, on their own account, the loftiest thoughts and aspirations that come to them was at stake. Terrible persecution, as bad as the early Christians ever suffered, was started against good men by the Church, and was enforced by war and by law. The crime punished was heresy: that is, not believing what one cannot believe.

Most strangely, at the very time when wholesale slaughter was being practised on the Albigenses—Christians in the south of France—a movement began within the Church, and gained the approval of Innocent the Third, for returning to the simple purity and loving kindness of Jesus Himself, as they shone forth from His life and teaching.

A young man named Francis, son of a rich merchant of the Italian town of Assisi, after an early life of gaiety and thoughtlessness, became deeply impressed by the need for a simple, wholly unselfish, joyous goodness. He took as his ideal, in fact, the life of our Lord as we have it preached in the Gospels. Never has there been a more Christ-like life than that lived by Saint Francis of Assisi.

FRANCIS OF ASSISI, THE CHRIST-LIKE FOLLOWER OF THE MASTER

He insisted on assuming poverty, living with the poor, and making loving kindness towards all living creatures the motive force of his whole being. In seven years a brotherhood of 5000 men had been formed accepting the same vows that he had taken. Thus the Franciscan Order was established within the Roman Catholic Church. It illustrated the original and simple Christianity of Christ, side by side with the form of Christianity which had been built up through the ages—the Kingdom of Heaven within the heart, and the Kingdom of Earthly Pomp.

The war between these two ideals has been going on ever since in Christianity, and its progress will be traced in the last chapter which begins on page 7075.

The Interests and Pleasures of Life for All Indoors and Out

SIMPLE LEATHERWORK

Some really beautiful things can be made with leather, and it takes years of study and training to become a skilled craftsman. However, there is no need for us to learn all the details of the craft before we are able to make useful little things with leather, so this page and the next are devoted to showing us how easily we can make them from odd pieces of material.

First of all let us consider what is required before we start. We shall want some materials—odd pieces of thin leather, such as baghide, basil, or suede can be bought fairly cheaply, or we can cut some quite good pieces from an old handbag, leather coat, jerkin, or other discarded leather goods. Some thonging is also required. These narrow lengths of leather or plastic can also be bought, but if we have a piece of leather long enough, we can cut them ourselves. As we are not stitching, but working in a simpler manner by thonging, needles and thread are not needed.

Tools are the next things to think about, and we shall want a flat steel ruler, or a strip of metal with a straight edge, a very sharp penknife, and a small punch to make the holes to take the thonging. As we are making only small articles, a small punch is required, such as one used for punching holes

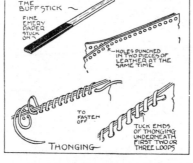

in paper. A knitting needle can be used for this purpose in very small work. A very sharp knife always makes the cutting of leather much easier and neater, so we keep our penknife sharp by rubbing it occasionally on a "buff-stick." This can be made by sticking a strip of fine emery paper on a flat piece of wood as shown in the sketch.

Every care should be taken when cutting the leather. For straight cuts, lay the material on a flat piece of wood. Place the steel ruler along the line where the leather is to be cut, and keep it firmly pressed down. Then we take the knife, hold it like a pen, but with the handle almost vertical, and keeping the blade close to the ruler, press downwards and draw it towards us. It is important to lay the leather across the grain of the wood, as the knife blade is liable to run with the grain and slip away from the ruler. When making a long cut, we keep the ruler pressed down right to the very end, otherwise the leather will stretch and the bottom corner will not be cut square. Curves, after being marked out in pencil, can be cut with a pair of scissors.

Now for punching the holes. To ensure that this is done evenly, the two pieces of leather should be held firmly together. This can be

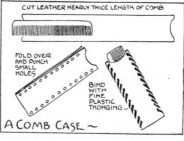

A COMB CASE ~

CRAFTS · GAMES · NEEDLEWORK · PUZZLES · SCIENCE EXPERIMENTS

done by sticking the two edges together first, or by roughly stitching with large stitches, the thread being pulled out after the holes are punched through. Paper clips can also be used to keep the two pieces of leather together.

One of the simplest things to make is a comb case, which is made from one piece of leather. First take the comb and lay this on the piece of leather and mark round with pencil, as shown in the sketch on the preceding page, allowing for the holes to be punched round. Cut off the strip, which should be twice the length of the comb. Now fold over the leather, neatly keeping both edges together, and punch the holes round the sides, making them in both thicknesses of leather at once. All that is necessary now is the thonging; the method of working is shown in the first picture on the previous page. When this is completed, fasten the ends off strongly.

The purse is made in a manner similar to that of the comb case, and can be used as a school purse, with a loop attached for hanging round the neck.

An armchair ash tray is a very useful present, and the illustration shows clearly how it is made. The actual ash tray can be a very small one, which can be bought, or the lid off a tin or the aluminium top of a small carton can be used. The tray can be fixed to the leather by making two or three small holes in the bottom of the tin or aluminium ash tray with a thin nail, then sewing the tray to the leather as if sewing on a button. A "turn-over" paper fastener can be used if a small slit is made in the bottom of the tray and in the leather. The fastener is then passed through the two slits and turned over in the usual manner.

In making the simple woven belt, care should be taken when cutting the slits to see that they are all an equal distance apart and

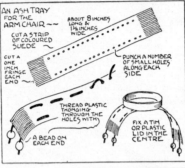

AN EASILY-MADE PURSE —

AN ASH TRAY FOR THE ARM CHAIR ~~

A SIMPLE WOVEN BELT ~

are all the same length. If we are using three or four thongs, the length of the slits should be the width of all the thongs plus a little over to allow for the bending when the thongs are woven in and out. The buckle should be sewn or riveted on. Riveting is easily done by first sticking the end of the leather down after the buckle has been placed in position, then punching two small holes. Insert a small rivet in each hole, turning over the ends of the rivet with a hammer, and flatten them out. Two or three small holes should be made at the other end of the belt to tighten or loosen when it is worn.

After we have made all these things in leather with a ruler, a knife, and a small punch as the only tools, we may like, as pocket-money will allow, to add to our equipment and go in for leathercraft in a big way. Then we should first get a good book on the subject—the local library is quite likely to have one—and study this carefully.

Thonging, as already shown, is the simplest way to join leather. Next comes stitching, and for this we shall need some needles and thread. Hand sewing is usually done with the aid of two needles, one on each end of the thread. One needle is pushed through one side of the leather, then the other is pushed through the same hole in the opposite direction and the ends of the thread pulled tightly together. Thus a double stitch is obtained. Sewing-thread should be treated first by rubbing it over with shoe-maker's wax or beeswax. This makes it much stronger and prevents its fraying.

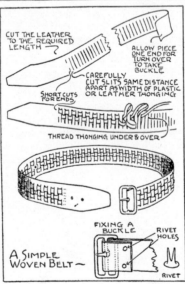

ANSWER TO THE PUZZLE OF THE BROKEN PLATE ON PAGE 6806—All the pieces were found, but the owner could not put them together to make a perfect plate. The picture shows how the puzzle was solved.

A PAPER-KNIFE MADE IN PLASTIC

PATIENCE is the quality most needed when handling plastics for the first time. There is a knack in dealing with this modern material in all its different forms, but many attractive things can be made from it.

Plastic thread and thonging, sold in hanks, and " ribbon," " tape," belting, and material for making pretty aprons and other fancy articles, can be bought by the yard at almost every store, and may be used in much the same way as similar sewing materials.

Plastics which can be cut with a saw, and then, if necessary, softened by heat and moulded to shape—the kind from which the paper-knife was made—are available at handicraft shops, either transparent or in lovely opaque shades.

Plastics of this type can be obtained in sheets of varying thicknesses and sizes and are sold by the pound, a piece about nine inches square and one eighth of an inch thick weighing about ten ounces. They make up delightfully into boxes, trays, ornaments, and many other useful and decorative things. Where two pieces of plastic have to be joined, as in making a box, a special cement is used, and this should be bought at the same time as the material.

These plastic " off-cuts," as the pieces are termed, are protected with a paper covering, for the highly-polished surface is easily marked, and though the marks can generally be removed with a polish sold for the purpose, it is simpler to avoid making any.

The paper-knife shown was cut from a nine-inch square off-cut, three-sixteenths of an inch thick, and turquoise blue in colour, leaving enough over to make two more like it. Thus the knives make cheap presents, though we should warn the receivers that the objects must not be washed or left to soak in very hot water, or they may lose their shape.

No pattern is needed for the paper-knife, as the picture is one-third its original size, so that it is quite a simple matter to draw a pattern the right size using squared paper. From this pattern, the outline is drawn on the protective covering of the plastic, leaving a little margin all round for finishing, as in woodwork. The cutting-out is done with a fretsaw, though had the outline been straight, a small saw could have been used.

Do not be tempted, for quickness, to try a treadle saw if one is available, as the greater friction will cause the plastic to soften. This in itself might not matter, but as plastic cools it sets very quickly, and the edges of the cut may partially rejoin ; also, when the sawing stops, the plastic is likely to set around the fretsaw and break it.

After the article has been cut, the rough edges must be smoothed off with a file. Then the long curved side of the knife and its point

THE FINISHED PAPER-KNIFE

have to be fined down equally on both sides to make a thin edge which can be used to open and slit envelopes neatly. This also is done with a file, and when the knife is properly shaped, a final smoothing-down is given with very fine glasspaper.

There is now nothing left to do but polish the knife until it has an equal gloss all over. Special polishes can be bought, or plate powder, whitening, or metal polish can be used in the ordinary way, but it takes patience, perseverance, and " elbow grease."

Making an article which has to be bent to shape is quite a craftsman's work. After cutting the article out to a flat pattern, the plastic must be soaked in boiling water until it is pliable enough to bend to the required shape. The minute or two taken for this varies according to thickness.

The moulding should be done round a pattern cut out in wood first. Work deftly, and if possible do all the shaping at one time to avoid heating again to remould.

HINTS FOR THE YOUNG RIDER

RIDING a horse is a knack which can only be acquired by practice, but there are a few things the beginner should know before he starts.

The most important thing is that the reins are for guiding the horse, not for helping the rider to keep himself in the saddle. They must be lightly held and never jerked or tugged.

Riding a horse is a combination of grip and balance, gripping with one's knees and developing an instinct of balance—" daylight " should never be seen between the rider's knees and his saddle. The first knack to be acquired is that of rising in the saddle when trotting. It is best not to make a deliberate attempt to rise, but to let the horse throw one up and down. When cantering the rider sits down in the saddle all the time, and this is another accomplishment that can only be developed by practice.

It is a good thing to begin by making friends with the horse, patting him and fussing over him. But there is only one way to horsemanship, as with so many other things, and that is to have confidence in oneself.

PIGEONS AND HOW TO KEEP THEM

PIGEON-KEEPING is one of the oldest of hobbies, having been followed by the ancient Egyptians and by the Greeks and Romans. Many of the present-day breeders and exhibitors of fancy and racing pigeons began in their boyhood by keeping a single pair of pet birds, and any boy can start in the same way.

The first essential is a weatherproof cote, which is also protected from, or out of reach of, the pigeon's natural enemies, cats and rats. A shed, an outhouse, or an old chicken house would convert very well.

If the ground is at all damp a raised floor should be built so that air may circulate underneath, and a wire run like that of a fowl-house may be constructed, but considerably higher, and fitted here and there with branches or perches for the pigeons to rest on. This will make a useful flight, and it should certainly not be less than eight feet high. The size will be regulated by the space available, but the bigger the better.

There must be an adequate opening between the house and the flight, with a landing-place on each side. Of course, a flight is not absolutely necessary, but it is safer, as in some of the best birds the homing instinct is not strong. Though when they have come to know their home and have nested, they may be allowed to fly freely, as they will return to their nesting-boxes.

Inside the pigeon-house a series of nesting-boxes must be arranged in tiers, and these should be placed on one side, and short perches fixed round the other sides. In the middle of the floor should be kept a vessel of fresh drinking water, such that the birds cannot bathe in it, and in different parts of the house boxes filled with grit. The floor must be strewn with sand or sawdust.

The short perches should be so arranged that the pigeons on one cannot reach those on another. The birds will quickly select their own perches. If the perches are placed one above another, two pieces of wood fastened together, gable fashion, must be attached to the wall just below, to prevent anything falling on the pigeons below.

Each nesting-box for a pair of pigeons should be divided into two compartments.

This enables the hen-pigeon to lay a second clutch in one division while young birds are occupying the other. There should be entrance holes to each compartment, side by side with a short platform in front, to do duty as an alighting board for both.

Long platforms serving several nesting-boxes must be avoided, as they lead to quarrelling among the birds. The size of each compartment should range from 12 inches by 12 inches by 10 inches high to 14 inches by 14 inches by 12 inches high, according to the breed of pigeon kept. These vary considerably in size.

The interior of the pigeon-house should be fairly well lighted, and thoroughly ventilated without being draughty. It must be frequently cleaned out to keep everything sweet and wholesome. In the open-air flight, cover the floor with fine gravel or shingle, and have a drinking vessel and also a large, shallow bath full of water for bathing.

The pigeons may be fed by hand at regular intervals—two meals a day is sufficient, and only as much as the birds will eat up should be given at one time. Or another suitable arrangement is to have in the house a self-supplying hopper, so that the birds can feed themselves. Small

RACING PIGEONS HOMEWARD BOUND

maize, wheat, grey peas, barley, tares, and buckwheat should be given; beans, peas, and maize being increased in quantity in winter, and wheat, barley, and tares in the summer. Household scraps are appreciated, and hemp seed should be given sometimes as medicine.

Grit can be bought, or can be made up of half a peck of gritty sand, half a peck of old lime mortar, and three and a half pounds of coarse salt, well mixed together. Such a supply will be sufficient for a year, and will help to keep the birds healthy.

The hen-pigeon lays a clutch of two eggs, and the period of incubation is about seventeen days, during which the hen covers the eggs at night and the cock-bird by day.

It is largely a matter of taste which breeds to keep, but it is wise to start with the long-faced and hardier breeds, as these will bring up their young without any assistance and are easier to manage. Suggestions for the beginner are the carrier, magpie, and nun.

BOATS ANY BOY CAN MAKE

There are many ways of making sailing boats and steamers, and metal, wood, cardboard, and even paper can be used in their construction.

Water-line models are quite easy to make. These all have flat bottoms and are cut from flat pieces of wood, with decks and other fittings fixed on the top. The more solid kind of model is made by carving the hull from a solid block of wood. This is more difficult. Another way of making a model is by building it up from strips of wood all screwed together. By this method a hollow hull can be made.

Cardboard and paper are used for models meant for show only, although these will float quite successfully if they are well varnished. Metal, of course, is more difficult to use because the parts have to be soldered together.

Here are some very simple models which any boy can make. First there is the little flat-bottomed sailing boat which can be taken to the seaside or to a pond, and which, with the addition of a small metal rudder fixed at the back, will sail quite straight. The metal rudder can be cut from an empty aluminium tin.

The sail of the boat should be made from stiff material such as thick drawing paper. The mast can be made from an old knitting needle pushed firmly into a small hole in the hull. The bottom ends of the sail should be held down with pins. Do not make the sail too large or the mast too high. A small

cut in the stern is all that is needed to fix in the rudder as shown in the sketch.

The model steamer which will float illustrates how to build up a model by using thin wood stripped off plywood. The material bends easily and can be tacked round the hull. Cut out the hull first, then carefully fasten on the sides with panel pins, as shown. This forms the bulwarks. The panel pins can be bought at any ironmongers very cheaply. Do not use tinned tacks as these will split the wood.

The deck fittings, such as the upper decks and bridge, are just pieces of wood pinned on with panel pins. Sandpaper all these parts to make them neat and smooth. The masts can be made of knitting needles and the derricks of pieces of wire pushed into holes made in the deck. To add rails on the upper deck, use small pins and cotton or very thin wire twisted round them, putting in the bottom rail first. A piece of dowel rod can be used for a funnel. When the model is finished it should be painted, the deck being white and the hull another colour.

The last sketch shows how to make a model lighter, like those used on rivers. Quite a lot of fun can be had with a large model of this craft by loading it up with sand, stones, or other material and pulling it across the water on a long string.

In all cases, models which are to be used for floating should be given a good coat of paint, especially if any glue is used for fixing deck fittings, such as funnels and ventilator shafts.

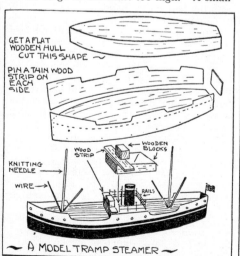

A MODEL TRAMP STEAMER

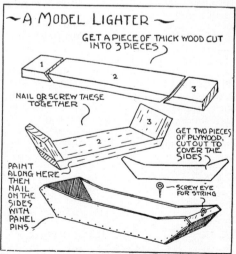

A MODEL LIGHTER

HOW TO PLAY ROUNDERS

ROUNDERS, modest ancestor of the national American game of baseball, has been a popular pastime in Britain since the early 18th century. It was played in a haphazard fashion for many years, but the National Rounders Association has now standardised the rules and given the game a new dignity.

The equipment required is of the simplest character—a stick, 18 inches in length and $5\frac{1}{2}$ inches in circumference at its thickest part; a soft ball; and four posts, each four feet in height. The pitch should be marked out with white lines, as shown in the plan.

Teams consist of nine players each, and the captains toss to decide which shall bat first. The team which scores the greater number of rounders in two innings wins the game. If one team is leading by ten or more rounders in the first innings, the captain has the option of requiring the opponents to follow on.

The batting team having decided its sequence of players, the first batsman takes her place with both feet in the 6-foot batting square. Facing her is the bowler, with both feet in the 8-foot bowling square. Behind the batsman is the backstop, the equivalent of a wicket keeper in cricket. Four fielders guard the four posts and the remaining three take their places in the deep.

It is advisable to have two umpires. One should stand behind the bowler at a point just beyond the second post; the other should stand to the batsman's right. Players waiting to bat should form a line and as each batsman completes the course she should take her place at the end of this line, thus preserving the proper sequence.

The bowler must bowl underarm, keeping her feet within her square until the ball has left her hand. It is a no-ball if it is not delivered underarm; if it is jerked; if it is out of reach of the batsman; if it is higher than the top of the head or lower than the knee as it passes the batsman; or if it is directed straight at the batsman. The penalty for three consecutive no-balls is half a rounder to the batsman.

A batsman is allowed only one good ball and, having received it, she must run, whether she hits it or not. Having hit it, she scores a rounder if she succeeds in running round the track, passing outside posts 1, 2, 3, and 4 in their proper order and touching the fourth post with her hand. If she fails to hit the

good ball and completes the track she is awarded half a rounder. A rounder cannot be scored if the batsman overtakes another member of her own team standing at a post ahead of her.

We will assume that the first batsman has scored a rounder. The second player in the line takes her place in the batting square, but succeeds in reaching only the first post as the result of her strike. The third batsman then strikes and as she, too, must make for the first post, it follows that the player already standing there must move on. So the game proceeds, with each player preserving her correct place in the batting sequence and yet making as much ground as possible.

When standing at a post, a batsman must maintain contact with it with her hand.

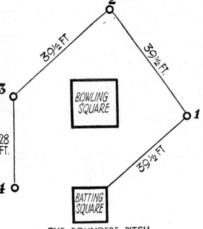

THE ROUNDERS PITCH

There are seven ways in which a batsman may be given out : 1, If the ball be caught, unless "no-ball" has been called by the umpire. 2, If she leaves the batting square before she has either hit the good ball or allowed it to pass her. 3, If she runs to the inside of a post. 4, If a fielder with the ball in her hand touches the post to which she is running, before she makes contact. 5, If, after having tried to hit the ball (unless a no-ball has been called), a fielder touches her with the ball in her hand while she is still in the batting square. 6, If a fielder with the ball in her hand touches her as she is running between the posts. 7, If she obstructs a fielder or intentionally deflects the course of the ball. In all cases the hand holding the ball shall count as the ball.

Two or more batsmen can be put out before the ball is returned to the bowler, and the last few batsmen can be dismissed in a body if none has reached the fourth post when a fielder throws the ball, full pitch, into the batting square.

When only one batsman is left, she is entitled to one minute's rest between each rounder she scores. She also has the choice of three good deliveries from the bowler, but, naturally, forfeits the right to any remaining balls if she is caught out or starts to run.

The above are the most important rules, and from them you should have gained a fair idea of how rounders is played under modern conditions.

ENID AND GERAINT—FROM THE PAINTING BY ROWLAND WHEELWRIGHT

THE KNIGHTS OF KING ARTHUR—FROM A TAPESTRY DESIGNED BY SIR EDWARD BURNE-JONES
AND MADE BY MORRIS & COMPANY

LANCELOT AND ELAINE OF ASTOLAT—FROM THE PAINTING BY SIDNEY PAGET

SIR TRISTRAM IS ADMITTED AS A KNIGHT OF THE ROUND TABLE—FROM A FRESCO IN THE
KING'S ROBING-ROOM IN THE PALACE OF WESTMINSTER

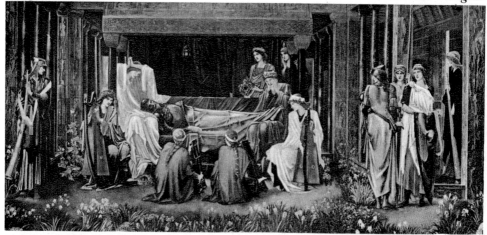

KING ARTHUR IN AVALON—FROM THE PAINTING BY SIR EDWARD BURNE-JONES

QUEEN GUINEVERE IN THE NUNNERY GARDEN—FROM THE PAINTING BY MARY F. RAPHAEL

THE VISION OF THE HOLY GRAIL—FROM THE PAINTING BY EDWIN A. ABBEY

Reproduced from a Copley print by courtesy of Messrs. Curtis & Cameron

SIR GALAHAD
BY ALLAN STEWART

THE BEGUILING OF MERLIN
BY SIR EDWARD BURNE-JONES

SIR GALAHAD
BY G. F. WATTS

THE PASSING OF ARTHUR—FROM THE PAINTING BY JAMES ARCHER

The pictures in these pages are reproduced by courtesy of Mr. Frederick Hollyer, the Bristol Art Gallery, and others

The Great Stories of the World That Will Be Told for Ever

ORPHEUS AND EURYDICE

ORPHEUS was a mortal, but people said that his mother must have been Calliope, the muse of heroic poetry, and his father Apollo, the god of music.

He was one of the heroes who sailed in the Argo, and he made a chant telling of their wonderful adventures in quest of the Golden Fleece.

But he was even greater as a musician than as a poet. When his neighbours tried to give strangers an idea of his lovely art they would say that it was magical. Trees bent their boughs to hear him. Hawks and doves, sheep and wolves, forgot cruelty and fear as they listened.

Perhaps the ancient Greeks hid a parable in that story; Orpheus stands for Art, which reconciles men of all politics and creeds, though war-mongers try to separate them into camps of hatred.

Orpheus married Eurydice, a lovely woman who was dearer to him than his fame as an Argonaut or music itself. They had not been married long when Eurydice, walking alone in the woods, saw a man hiding in a thicket. Fearing a robber or a madman, she turned to flee. He pursued. The terrified woman ran blindly, not looking where she went, and trod on a snake.

Hours later Orpheus, after seeking everywhere, found her dead body. One foot was swollen, and bore the unmistakable fang-marks of a serpent's bite.

So great was the woe of Orpheus that he vowed to follow her to the under-world, and dwell there with her if he could not win her back to life.

With his lyre on his back Orpheus wandered far and wide till he came to the gateway of Hades. It was guarded by the three-headed dog monster Cerberus, but at the sound of Orpheus's lyre the creature fawned, and let him pass.

Down a long tunnel Orpheus went till he came to a swift, black river. The banks were crowded with ghosts begging Charon, the grim old ferryman, to take them across to King Pluto. He carried over those who had received burial in the ancient manner, with a coin placed under the dead man's tongue as Charon's fee; but those who had not were obliged to shiver on the banks for a hundred years before he would bring them over free. All ancient religions paid great heed to funerals, and believed that the soul's welfare depended on these ceremonies which propitiated the gods of death.

IMAGINATION · CHIVALRY · LEGENDS · GOLDEN DEEDS · FAIRY TALES

Charon would have refused to carry a mortal if Orpheus had not sung and played as he stood on the banks. The lovely strains melted even that hard heart, and Orpheus passed over into the dark kingdom of King Pluto.

It was divided by four great rivers, Acheron, Styx, Phlegethon, whose floods were of fire, and Lethe, whose waters brought forgetfulness. Three judges, Minos, Aeacus, and Rhadamanthus, examined all the new-comers, and weighed their good and bad actions in the scales of Themis, the blindfold goddess of justice.

If good outweighed bad the soul was led to the Elysian Fields, a beautiful country where friends and lovers wandered in meadows and groves like those on Earth.

If bad outweighed good, the soul was driven to Tartarus, a place of punishment. Here cruel King Tantalus, tormented by hunger and thirst, stood up to his chin in a stream of water, with a branch of fruit hanging just above his head. But every time he stooped to drink the water flowed back from his mouth, and every time he snatched at the fruit it swung out of reach. Here wicked Sisyphus was compelled to roll a great stone to the top of a hill, but every time he reached the summit the stone slipped from his grasp and ran to the bottom. Here Tityus was chained flat to the ground, while a vulture continually fed on his living flesh. Here Ixion was bound to a wheel, which whirled him round and round in endless misery.

Between Tartarus and the Elysian Fields sat King Pluto, Lord of the Dead, black-bearded, black-robed, and stern. Beside him sat beautiful Queen Proserpine, whom he had stolen from the Earth.

Orpheus made his way to their throne. He did not speak but sang his story, and all the under-world listened to that heart's song. Pluto's black eyes grew dim. The wheel of Ixion and the stone of Sisyphus stood still. The flood ceased to torment Tantalus, and the vulture forgot to prey on the tortured Tityus.

When Orpheus was silent Pluto spoke. For the sake of that song he would reverse all the iron laws of his kingdom and let Eurydice return to Earth, on condition that Orpheus did not look at her till they had left the kingdom of the under-world.

Orpheus waited joyfully with lowered eyes till the ghost of Eurydice was fetched. Then he set out on the return journey. It seemed very long, and his impatience to look back at the dear one who followed grew greater at every step. At length he crossed into the upper world, and turned at once with a triumphant cry. Alas! He should have waited till Eurydice, too, had set foot on Earth. No sooner had he seen her than she vanished.

This time he sought to enter Hades in vain. For seven days he wandered on the banks of Acheron, beseeching Charon to give him a passage. Then he returned to Earth, and, sitting by the banks of a river, poured out his grief in a last song.

It was at the time of the feast of Bacchus. Some women called to him to play them a dance measure, and when he paid no heed they began to stone him. At first the stones turned aside harmlessly. But the women drowned the lyre by their shrieks, and then the stones fell true.

Orpheus was killed, and flung into the river with his lyre. As the lyre sank its strings cried " Eurydice! Eurydice! " The gods would not let the great musician's instrument lie in the mud of a river; they set it in the heavens, and it became the constellation called Lyra.

Some say that his body was afterwards drawn ashore and buried, and that nightingales sang about the grave. As for his spirit, it joined Eurydice in the Elysian Fields.

THE SHAM IMMORTAL

Salmoneus was the most important person in the universe, to Salmoneus.

He was a king, but that did not content him. He wished his subjects to fall down and worship him. He proclaimed that he was divine. He had a great bridge of bronze built before his palace, and made slaves flash torches about his chariot wheels as they rumbled over it, so that his people should think it thundered and lightened when Salmoneus went forth.

Some rustics were so simple as to believe that their king was really a god, and some courtiers thought it good policy to pretend that they believed it. Then Jove said: " I will show them the difference between god and man, lightning and torches, chariot wheels and thunder."

As Salmoneus rode out in triumph, and men fell on their knees by the roadside, Jove hurled a thunderbolt from Heaven, and the sham immortal fell dead.

KING ARTHUR AND HIS KNIGHTS

The tale of King Arthur should be as dear to us as the hills of home. Hector, Siegfried, and Roland are foreigners, but Arthur is our own British hero, whose story has been told in the inglenook to generation after generation of British children. It has coloured their dreams and games, shaped their ideas of courage and faithfulness, become part of their characters ; and so it has influenced history. When Caxton printed the story in one of the first English books, the good craftsman owned that " divers men hold opinion that there was no such Arthur." Historians incline to believe that the legend sprang from the true story of a Celtic chieftain of the fifth or sixth century, who beat off Saxon invaders and made many other British kings his vassals. Round his memory a wonderful group of fables grew up, and when the British were conquered by the Saxons this story became their great comfort. They handed it down like an heirloom. In time it was arrayed in all the trappings of fourteenth-century chivalry, and bedizened with magic jewels. In that form it was written down about 1469 by Sir Thomas Malory, for the pleasure of Edward the Fourth.

THE COMING OF ARTHUR

WHEN King Uther Pendragon was at war there appeared in his capital a ragged man called Merlin, who soon convinced the King of his magic powers. Through the wizard's counsel the King overthrew his enemies and obtained the hand of Igraine, Duchess of Tintagil. Merlin served the King on condition that the heir to the throne should be given him, unchristened, to bring up.

When a son was born King Uther told his servants to carry it to the beggar man at the gate. Merlin took the babe to a knight called Sir Ector, who was richer in honesty than in this world's goods, and bade him bring up the prince as his son, calling him Arthur.

So the boy grew up far from the flatteries and pomps of a Court, submissive to the good knight and his son Kaye, whom Arthur took for his elder brother.

Some fifteen years passed, and King Uther died. Many of his barons desired to seize the throne, and the land seemed on the eve of civil war, when lo, there appeared a miracle ! In the churchyard of the greatest church in London a mighty stone was found with an anvil on it, and a sword embedded in the anvil. On the sword were inscribed the following words : " Whoso pulleth out this sword is rightful King of England."

All the lords of the land gathered to the place, and strove in vain to pull out the sword. They encamped near by, and held tournaments to pass the time till one of their number should succeed in plucking it from its resting-place.

Sir Ector came to London and brought his sons. One day, as they rode out to the jousts, Kaye discovered that he had left his sword at home. Arthur offered to return and fetch it. But the house where they lodged was locked, for everyone had gone to the tournament. Arthur determined that his brother should not be disappointed in the tournament for lack of a weapon. He remembered hearing of the sword in the churchyard. Arthur hurried thither, drew it out easily, and carried it to Kaye.

When Kaye saw what was written on it he went to his father and said, " I must be rightful King of England." His father led him to a church, and made him swear on the altar to tell the truth. Then Kaye owned that it was Arthur who had given him the sword.

Sir Ector knew the time had come to tell the prince who he was. Arthur's first thought was one of grief because those he had loved as father and mother were not his true parents.

At first the barons refused to accept the boy as their king. The sword was put back in the anvil, and once more no one could pull it out save Arthur. For a year pretexts of delay were made, but at last the boy was crowned amid the acclamations of the common folk.

EXCALIBUR

MERLIN became Arthur's counsellor. One day the wizard took the young king to a lake. A boat was moored to the bank. Suddenly in the midst of the lake an arm appeared holding a scabbarded sword. Then a maiden rose from the waters near by. Arthur called to her, " O Lady of the Lake ! If that sword be yours I pray you give it to me, and I will give you treasure in return."

" Take the sword, King," said the Lady. " I will ask my gift in my own time."

She sank beneath the waves. Arthur rowed out to the midst of the lake, and the hand yielded up the sword to him. Merlin told him that the sword was called Excalibur, and in battle it would shine like fire, dazzling the enemy. The scabbard was as wonderful as the sword, for it would save its wearer from losing blood, however terrible his wounds might be.

With the aid of these weapons, Arthur conquered Scotland, Ireland, Gaul, Norway, and Muscovy. He ruled wisely and justly, righting the wrongs of the poor, and giving the realm peace. No crown was more glorious than his in all Christendom. His fame spread far and wide, so that his enemies began to plot his ruin.

THE ROUND TABLE

THE most beautiful lady in the world was said in those days to be Guinevere, daughter of the King of Cameliard. Arthur sent Lancelot, most renowned and most courtly of his knights, to offer her the crown of an English Queen. Her father was proud that his daughter should be consort to the heroic King Arthur, so Guinevere was forced to leave her home and follow Lancelot into a strange land. On the journey he was so kind, and cheered the exile so gently, that she grew to love him. Lancelot loved her also, but he held his peace, thinking he loved her in vain. So she was wedded to King Arthur amid great rejoicings. Because he had done his embassy so well Lancelot was appointed the Queen's champion, bound to take her part in any quarrel and guard her life.

Guinevere's father had sent Arthur a great round table, at which a hundred and fifty knights could feast together. The King vowed that only the worthiest knights should have a seat at it. There was no higher honour in the land than to be one of the Knights of the Round Table. Wealth or lineage could not obtain a place there without worth.

When anyone was oppressed by tyrant or witch he would send to King Arthur for help, and one of the Knights of the Round Table would ride to the rescue. Their adventures fill many books. Here we can only name some of the most famous.

Gareth came disguised to the Court, and lived there in the kitchen, taunted by Kaye, but kindly treated by the King's nephew Gawain and by Lancelot, who pitied him. At last came the boy's chance to prove his mettle. A lady arrived seeking help against her enemies, and the scullion claimed the boon of helping her. She was angry and loaded him with insults, but he followed her in spite of all she could say, overpowered her enemies, and then, when he had won glory, revealed himself as Arthur's nephew, son of the King of the Orkneys.

Geraint, the Knight Errant, wedded Enid, whose father was a poor knight. Suspecting her of a wrong she had not done, Geraint made her suffer cruelly, but in the end he discovered her innocence.

Tristram, nephew of King Mark of Cornwall, fell in love with Iseult of Ireland. When he told his uncle of her beauty King Mark determined to marry her himself. The King of Ireland consented. Tristram went, broken-hearted, to live in exile. He married Iseult of Brittany. After many years he fell ill, and a soothsayer declared that he could only be cured by Iseult Queen of Cornwall, who was a skilful physician. Tristram sent a messenger to Cornwall, bidding him hoist white sails on his return if he were successful. Iseult of Cornwall hastened to save his life, but Tristram's wife was jealous, and told the sick man that she saw the vessel returning with black sails. At this news Tristram gave up hope, and died.

Lancelot was invincible in war and tourney, but he loved the world too well to be a peerless knight like young Galahad, whose name has stood for manly purity ever since those days. All men were eager to be Lancelot's friends. Many maids loved him in vain, and Elaine of Astolat, at whose father's castle he had lodged awhile, died of grief when he returned to Court. Elaine's dead body was laid on a barge, which drifted down to Camelot.

THE QUEST OF THE HOLY GRAIL

ON the eve of Pentecost, as the knights of the Round Table were at supper, a crashing like thunder shook the roof. Then a sunbeam, brighter than anything in the world, entered the hall, and in it floated a cup. By its glory they knew it for the cup our Lord used at the Last Supper, called the Holy Grail. The air was filled with sweet scents, and a great peace stole into men's hearts.

Suddenly the Grail vanished. King Arthur thanked Heaven that he and his knights had been vouchsafed this vision. " Amen! " cried Sir Gawain, Arthur's nephew, called the Courteous. Then he vowed to set out to seek the Grail on the morrow. If after a year and a day he could not see it he would know that the Quest was not for him. All the other knights vowed the same thing.

The brave men rode far and wide, meeting with strange adventures, but faring for the most part like Lancelot. He one day came on a tournament between two companies of knights, one mounted all on black horses and the other on white. The black seemed the weaker side, so Lancelot joined with them, confident of bringing victory by his prowess. But he was overborne, and stunned. Some men carried him aside into a wood, where they left him. When he recovered, Lancelot was filled with shame at his defeat. He mounted his horse painfully, and rode away. Soon he met a nun. " Ah, Lancelot," she said, " you are without peer among earthly knights, but in heavenly adventures you have been worsted. The tournament was a parable. The white knights battled for holiness, the black for sin and pride. You chose the worldly side. Beware of everlasting pain."

Then Lancelot's shame was greater than ever, and, deeming himself unworthy of the Quest, he returned to Camelot.

News came of the death of many knights, but none knew what had become of Sir Percivale, Sir Bors, and Sir Galahad. More than three years passed, and then Sir Bors returned with a marvellous tale.

The three lost knights, though they had set out separately, were led together by many strange signs. They wandered on, encountering many perils, till they came to the sea, and there they found an empty ship, with an altar on it, and the Holy Grail shining through a veil.

The vessel sailed away of its own accord to Sarras. They went ashore, carrying their holy treasure. The king of the place seized the Grail, and flung the knights into a dungeon, where they lay for six months, comforted by visions. Then the king fell sick and died. He had no heir. While his counsellors debated who should be king, a mysterious voice bade them choose the youngest of the captive knights. So Galahad became king, and righted all the wrongs in that land.

A year after his crowning he wakened his friends, telling them to haste with him to the room where the Grail was kept. They saw a great company of angels about it. Galahad held up his hands to heaven crying, " Now, blessed Lord, there is such joy in my heart I would live no more on Earth if it be Thy will."

His companions saw the whole flock of angels take flight, with the likeness of Galahad in their midst. When they looked down, the Grail had vanished, and Galahad's body lay dead.

THE TREACHERY OF VIVIEN AND MORGAN LE FAY

MERLIN, the wise counsellor, fell in love like any foolish boy. His lady was called Vivien, and she is said to have been not mortal, but the child of a lake. She pretended to love Merlin, till she had learned all his magic arts. Then she told him of great treasure lying in an underground cave, and begged him to get it for her. No sooner had he descended than she, by strong enchantments, sealed up the mouth with a great boulder, so that Merlin was imprisoned for evermore.

Arthur had a sister called Morgan le Fay, who practised magic. She was angry with Arthur, who had slain her lover, and she determined to steal Excalibur. She never found an opportunity for that, but she managed to unbuckle the magical scabbard, and flung it into a deep lake.

Now Arthur was no longer proof against wounds; he had lost his wise counsellor, and many of his knights had perished in the Quest of the Grail. Shadows gathered over the sunlight of his reign.

THE PASSING OF ARTHUR

MORDRED, one of the king's nephews, was an evil man, jealous of Lancelot's prowess and the King's splendour. He spread abroad a lie that the Queen was a wicked woman, and so cunningly did he contrive that she was condemned to be burned to death. King Arthur could not alter the course of justice; lover or stranger, queen or scullion, must suffer the same punishment.

Lancelot was away, but the tidings reached him. He galloped up with a company of knights as the Queen was led to death, struck down her guards, and carried her off to a strong castle. In the encounter he had, though quite unknowingly, killed Sir Gareth.

The Pope sent a letter to King Arthur telling him to take back his Queen, who was innocent. Guinevere returned to Court, but Lancelot was banished because he had slain Sir Gareth. Gawain, Gareth's brother, would not permit Arthur to make peace with him. Lancelot went beyond the seas, and his friends with him.

Then Mordred gathered all his followers together and rebelled against Arthur. He was twice defeated in battle, but rallied again. Gawain got his death stroke in the first fight. He lived long enough to write to Lancelot making peace with him, telling of Mordred's treachery, and asking Lancelot to come to the King's aid. Many who should have aided Arthur stood aside because they were indignant at Lancelot's banishment. Before Lancelot could get Gawain's message, however, a third battle took place.

So terrible was this fight that at dusk Arthur and two brothers, Lucan and Bedivere, were all that was left of the two hosts. Arthur had killed Mordred, but the stricken traitor had gathered his strength for a blow which had cleft the King's helmet, and given him a frightful wound. Lucan and Bedivere carried the King to a little deserted chapel near by, and there Lucan fell dead of his wounds.

Arthur lamented the death of his good knights, saying, " Were I to live after them my life would only be sorrow. Weep not, Bedivere, but take my sword Excalibur and throw it into the lake near by."

Bedivere took the sword, but its hilt was gorgeous with jewels, and its blade was famous through the world. He had not the heart to throw it into the dark lake. Justifying his action to himself, he hid it and returned to the King. Arthur asked what he had seen.

" Sir," answered Bedivere, " I saw nothing but the wind and the waves."

" You have not dealt truly with me," said the King, reproachfully. " Go, do a dying man's behest."

Bedivere went, but again he disobeyed; and then Arthur was moved to wrath and cried, " Ah, traitor, you care more for the sword than your king! "

At that Bedivere ran out, seized the sword quickly, and hurled it far into the lake. Before it fell an arm, " clothed in white samite, mystic, wonderful," came out of the water. It caught the sword and brandished it before both disappeared beneath the waves.

When Arthur heard that, he told Bedivere to help him to the lake, and when he had done so the knight marvelled to see before him a barge, containing many fair ladies robed in black.

" Lay me in the barge," said the King. The ladies received him with loud lamentations. Then they rowed him away.

So ends the tragic story of the King's last desperate fight against overwhelming odds. Some say that Arthur sleeps in a flowery land, whose entrance is a cave in the Welsh hills, and that he will return to his people in their sorest need.

THE END OF THE KNIGHTS

GUINEVERE became a nun at Almesbury, and spent six sad years praying for the King's soul.

When Lancelot returned to England and found all that had befallen he remembered what Galahad had said of this unstable world. He became a hermit, and seven others who had been his comrades in arms joined him in a life of humility and prayer. One night he had a vision bidding him and his companions go to Almesbury. He obeyed the vision, and on arrival two days later learned that Guinevere had been dead half an hour. The hermit knights bore her body back to Glastonbury, where they buried her.

A little while after Lancelot fell sick. One morning Sir Bors found him dead on his bed, and the smile on his countenance was like the smile of Galahad.

Old Sir Ector, who had seen the beginning and end of Arthur's glory, came to the burying. He looked at the dead man, whose face, according to custom, was uncovered, and said: "Ah, Lancelot, thou wert the courtliest knight that ever drew sword, and the faithfullest friend that ever bestrode a horse. Thou wert the head of all Christian Knights."

With the old man's words the story of King Arthur and the Knights of the Round Table was fitly finished.

THE BRAVE FRENCH MAID OF NOYON

AT a house in the little town of Noyon, in France, something had gone wrong with the drains, and workmen had to be sent down to open the drains and clean out the sewer. That is a dangerous thing to do because of the poisonous gases.

In this case four men were busily at work when they were overcome by the sewergas, and were unable to give the signal to be drawn up.

The people in the house wondered what was the matter and grew alarmed, but no one dared venture down.

Then a brave servant maid, a girl of seventeen, begged to be tied to the rope and let down into the sewer.

This was done, and she reached the group of men lying helpless down below. As quickly as her trembling hands would allow her she tied one man to the rope, and jerked it as a signal for him to be drawn up. Willing hands hauled up the burden, and on reaching the surface the unconscious man was still alive.

A second time the girl tied a man to the rope, and he was drawn into safety.

But the next time the dangling rope came down for the girl to catch she was gasping for breath. She struggled against the feeling of suffocation, and tried to fasten the third man to the rope.

This she managed to do, but she herself was on the verge of unconsciousness, so, with a desperate effort, she wound her long hair round the rope and tied it tightly. Then she lost consciousness; but the watchers above carefully, very carefully, pulled the double burden up into safety just in time.

The fresh air soon revived the girl, and then she bethought her of the fourth man down in the dangerous sewer. It was hardly likely that he would still be alive, but there was a slight chance, and so again this noble girl risked her life. But this time her effort was in vain, for the poor man was drawn up lifeless.

The French nation loves to reward a brave action, and some handsome gifts found their way to the unselfish maid who so cheerfully and readily risked her own life for the sake of others.

THREE CUPS OF COLD WATER

THERE is a saying of Jesus which has woven itself into all the history of humanity, into the periods of famine, the days of battle, and the hours of death. It is the saying that we do Christ service even when we give only a cup of cold water to those who thirst.

Our brave English soldier Sir Philip Sidney, who lived at Penshurst in Kent, and wrote tender poems under the noble oaks which we may still see spreading their wide arms over Penshurst Park, was one of those who have lived to fulfil Christ's exhortation.

Sir Philip Sidney was called by Queen Elizabeth " the jewel of her times." He was a great scholar and traveller, a poet and musician, an athlete and horseman, above everything else a great gentleman. The nobility of his nature, the bravery of his spirit, and the graciousness of his manner rendered him the most notable and romantic figure of the age in which he lived.

This noble man was mortally wounded at the battle of Zutphen, Holland, in 1586. He had fought like a hero. Two horses had been killed under him, and still he led his soldiers with a dauntless courage into the thick of the fight. But at last a bullet struck him, and as he reeled in the saddle his horse turned and bolted with him from the field.

When he was in the camp he called for a cup of water. The day was excessively hot; he was in a raging fever; the agony of his wound was indescribable.

With great trouble a little water was brought to him. He lifted himself up, took the bottle, and was about to place it to his lips when his gaze caught the eyes of a poor wounded soldier fixed longingly upon the water.

The look in the man's eyes made Sidney forget his pain. With a noble smile he stretched out his arm and handed the bottle to the dying man, with the immortal words: " Soldier, thy need is greater than mine! "

Such was the glory of Sidney that the epitaph of one of his friends was in these words:

Fulke Greville,
Servant to Queen Elizabeth,
Counsellor to King James,
Friend to Sir Philip Sidney.

Another hero is famous for a deed somewhat similar. This is the generous

Rudolf of Hapsburg, whose descendants ruled over Austria, a kingdom made by his power. On one occasion Rudolf was with his army in a place where everyone was afflicted by terrible thirst. Somebody was able to find a cupful of water, which was brought to Rudolf as a great and priceless treasure. He took the prized cup in his hands, but exclaimed: "I cannot drink alone. All cannot share this little draught. I thirst not for myself but for my whole army." And, so saying, he tipped up the cup and emptied the water on the ground.

One more story we may give because it shows in some measure, but not fully, the Christlike spirit.

During the seventeenth-century wars between Denmark and Sweden a wounded Dane was about to raise a wooden bottle of water to his lips when a cry reached him from a wounded Swede.

The good Dane, using the words of our own Sidney, stumbled to the side of his enemy, and saying "Thy need is greater than mine," kneeled down and held the water to his lips. But the Swede, suddenly raising a pistol, fired and wounded the Dane in the shoulder.

"Rascal!" cried the twice-wounded soldier of Denmark. "I would have befriended you, and you would murder me! Now will I punish you. I would have given you the whole bottle, but now you shall have only half."

He raised the bottle to his lips, drank of it, and then gave it into the hand that had tried to kill him.

THE DOG THAT DID ITS DUTY

A COLLIE was once fastened to its kennel by so short a chain that it could move out only a few feet, and the kennel was in an open garden.

One bitter, wet night a female dog found her way from the street to the kennel, and evidently begged for shelter, for in the morning the collie was found outside his kennel, dying from cold, while the female dog, an entire stranger, was comfortably installed inside the kennel, with five newly-born puppies.

To match that pathetic incident we must turn to a snowy night in the life of James Hogg, the Ettrick shepherd poet. The snow was coming down heavily and the flocks were out, so the shepherd called up his faithful collie, talked to her, and sent her off to search one side of the moors while he scoured the other.

She went her way and he went his; and late at night he returned, exhausted, bringing his share of the sheep. But there was no sign of the collie or her sheep, so he sat down in his cabin to wait.

Hour after hour passed, and then came a low whine and a feeble scratching at the door. The poet rushed out. There was the collie's share of the sheep, every one of them safe and sound, and there was the collie, in her mouth a tiny puppy. She laid her baby at her master's feet, then disappeared into the night. Presently she returned, bringing another puppy.

Her babies had been born in the snow, yet she had done her duty, and not a sheep was missing. She brought the second of her babies to her master, placed it in his lap, looked pitifully into his face, and then lay down and died!

THE MAN WHO SAVED HIS SON

A FRENCH merchant named Labat was taken ill in the early years of the last century, and retired to a beautiful house on the banks of the River Adour.

Here, one morning, his gaze was attracted by a rider struggling with a restive horse on the opposite bank. The old merchant, who was wearing a dressing-gown, peered across the distance and watched the battle between man and horse with anxious eyes. Suddenly he was horrified to see the rider hurled violently from the back of the plunging horse and thrown into the river.

The merchant never hesitated. He forgot his age and his own safety, and, hurrying down, dived in after the drowning stranger. Such is the call of Humanity.

He was a good swimmer, but the heavily-booted horseman was hard to save, and it was only after a terrible struggle that the merchant succeeded in bringing him safely to shore.

Then, with a cry which must have startled the morning echoes, the grand old man exclaimed fervently:

"Sacred Humanity, what do I not owe you? I have saved my son!"

THE FABLES OF PILPAY

About five hundred years after Christ the Persian King Nushirwan sent one of his courtiers to India to obtain a book called The Fables of Pilpay. The fame of these stories was well known, but the Indians were jealous of their possession, and would not allow the fables to be turned into other languages. However, by stealth and bribery the courtier managed to obtain a copy. After this the fables were soon translated into every dialect of the East and many European languages. It is said that the Bible alone surpasses it in this particular. The general teaching of the fables is that *Love is strength.* The fables, in the original, are all linked together like the stories of the Arabian Nights. A king is warned in a dream to search for treasure in a certain place; he finds in a jewelled casket a piece of satin on which is written several wise proverbs. The proverbs are explained in a series of fables by a wise old Brahmin called Pilpay. Another name for them is Kalilah and Dimnah.

THE FOX AND THE HEN

A HUNGRY fox, spying a fine fat hen, made up his mind to eat her. But as he was about to spring on her he heard a great noise, and, looking up, saw a drum hanging on a tree. As the wind blew, the branches beat upon the drum.

" Ah! " said he. " A thing that can make so much noise must certainly have more flesh upon it than a miserable hen."

So, allowing the hen to escape, he sprang upon the drum; but when he tore the parchment open he found that there was nothing whatever inside.

" Wretched being that I am! " said he. " I have missed a meal for nothing."

By being too greedy we may miss everything that is worth having.

THE IRON-EATING RATS

A MERCHANT once had to make a long journey, and first of all sold all his property and bought bars of iron, because he thought this the safest form of wealth. Moths could not devour them nor thieves run off with them. He asked a friend to lock them in his treasure chamber, and set off with an easy mind.

When the traveller returned he went to his friend, who met him with an air of mingled insolence and hypocrisy.

" Oh, yes," he said, " I locked your iron up safely enough, but who can keep rats out with bolts and bars? Unfortunately they have eaten it all up! "

The traveller had trusted his friend, and had no proof to show that the iron had been left in his charge; it was useless to seek justice. He therefore went his way.

On passing out of the house alone he saw one of his friend's children, whom he picked up and carried off without being seen.

That evening he met his friend rushing through the streets nearly mad with grief.

" My son is lost! " he cried.

" Well," said the traveller, " that must be the child I saw carried off by an owl. What a country this is, where a little bird can carry off a great child of five and rats eat bars of iron! "

At this his friend suddenly looked less terrified, and greatly ashamed.

He went his way in silence, to give orders that the merchant's iron should be carried to his house and the child brought back.

Deceivers are usually as unsuccessful as they deserve to be.

THE THREE FISHES

THREE fishes lived in a pond. The first was wise, the second had a little sense, and the third was foolish. A fisherman saw the fish, and went for his net.

" I must get out of this pond at once," said the wise fish. And he threw himself into a little channel that led to a river.

Presently the fisherman returned with his net, and stopped up the channel leading to the river. The second fish wished he had followed the example of the wise fish; but he soon thought of a plan to escape. He floated upside down on the surface of the water, and the fisherman, thinking he was dead, did not trouble about him any more.

But the foolish fish was caught, and taken home to be eaten.

We should all endeavour to be wise.

FOUR FRIENDS

THERE were once four good friends—a little goat, a tortoise, a rat, and a raven. One morning the others were anxious because the goat did not meet them at the brook as usual. The raven flew up into the air, and presently came down with the news that their friend was entangled in a hunter's net.

" I'll gnaw through it," said the rat.

" I'll carry you there," said the raven.

Away they flew, and the last cord had been bitten when the tortoise toiled up.

" Oh, friend," cried the goat, " why did you come? The hunter may be here any moment, and how can you escape? "

The tortoise was about to say that she could not endure safety while her friend's life was in danger when, sure enough, the hunter arrived. The goat galloped off, the raven flew, the rat slipped into a hole, but the poor tortoise had not crawled two inches before the man picked her up and put her in a bag. He was very angry, but he had at least got *something* for the pot.

The three friends now met in a great state of misery, but the goat said: " Our tears will do the tortoise no good. We must act quickly. I have a plan by which we may rescue our comrade."

The others heard and approved it. Soon after the hunter saw a little goat limp out from behind a clump of bushes. She went slowly and seemed an easy prey. Throwing down the bag, that he might run faster, the man set off in pursuit.

Several times the goat let him come quite close, and then, seeming to make a painful effort, escaped him. " It is only a matter of tiring her out," said the man; " I must have patience." So he was led far from his bag.

Meanwhile the rat was gnawing the string that tied up its mouth. The tortoise was soon free, and then, with many exclamations of thankfulness and relief, she crept into hiding under the bush.

When the goat thought that time enough had been given to accomplish the rat's task she suddenly set off for the hills at a canter. The hunter was amazed to see her lameness suddenly cured. When he returned to find the tortoise gone he gaped more than ever; then, thinking that he had been tricked by goblins, he hurried from the place and never harried the four friends again.

Love is strength.

THE MAN WHO WAITED TO BE FED

A RELIGIOUSLY minded man was once walking in a forest when he saw a falcon carrying food to a young raven, which he had taken under his protection.

" Ah," cried the man, " what a lesson is here! The goodness of Heaven is unbounded. The parents of this poor fledgling have met with some accident, but it is not allowed to starve. How greedy I am to run about searching for food instead of trusting to Providence! "

He decided to give up his time to prayer alone, and so betook himself to a cave, where he stayed, without food, for three days. However, no bird or beast came to bring him anything to eat.

On the third night he had a dream, in which a voice said to him, " Son, the goodness of Heaven is unbounded, for it has given you the means with which to feed yourself. There was indeed a lesson in what you saw in the forest nest; imitate not the fledgling, but the merciful falcon who worked harder in order that he might have something to give to the needy."

God helps those who try to help themselves.

THE FALCON AND THE HEN

SAID a falcon to a hen, " How ungrateful you must be! You are fed with the best of food, you have a snug bed provided for you at night, you are protected from foxes, and yet, when the men who do all this for you want to take hold of you, you run away and do not return their caresses. Now, I do not receive anything like so many benefits, and yet I allow the men to hold me, and I serve them when they go hunting in the field."

" Ah! " said the hen. " What you say is true. But, remember, you never see a hawk roasting in front of the fire, whereas you see hundreds of good fat hens treated in that way."

Circumstances alter cases.

THE KING WHO GREW KIND

A CRUEL king was riding one day when he saw a fox attack a hen. But just then a dog ran after the fox and bit his leg. The fox, however, lame as he was, managed to escape into his hole, and the dog ran off. A man who saw him threw a stone at the dog, and cracked his head; but at this moment a horse passing by ran against the man and trod on his foot. A minute later the horse's foot slipped on a stone, and his ankle was broken.

" Ah! " said the king. " This will be a lesson to me. I see that misfortunes always overtake those who ill-use others."

And from that time the king became a kind and wise ruler of his people.

Punishment sooner or later overtakes those who wrong others.

THE ADDER IN A BURNING BUSH

A MAN was once travelling with his camel through the desert when he saw a bush on fire, and heard a small voice crying from the midst of it imploring help.

He dismounted, and saw an adder ringed in with flames. The man emptied his money from a small bag, which he fastened to his spear, and stretched it out through the flames. The adder jumped in, and was borne out of danger.

"I want no thanks," said the man, as the snake crawled out, "but I think gratitude should make you promise never to hurt mankind again."

"On the contrary," returned the snake, "I intend to bite you and your camel. That is the way men return a good action."

"No, no!" cried the man, seeing the adder ready to strike with venomous fangs; "men return kindness for kindness. Only consult some witness, and I will abide by his judgment."

"Agreed," said the snake, and they set off together.

The first creature they met was a cow, who replied to their question: "It is the custom to reward a kind action by a cruel one. All my life I have supplied my mistress with milk, butter, and cheese. She has sold my calves to the butcher, and is having me fatted for the same customer."

The snake gave the man a look, but he said, "One witness is not enough! The cow is prejudiced; let us ask another."

"Very well," said the snake, and asked the tree above for its opinion.

"Men always return evil for good," said the tree. "My race gives them fruit and shade from the sun, yet they cut us down and burn us."

"Are you satisfied now?" asked the snake, with a triumphant smile.

"Give me one more chance!" pleaded the man, and the snake agreed, for he felt sure the answer would always be the same.

The next creature they met was a fox, to whom the adder briefly told the story, asking if his ingratitude was not customary and right.

The fox looked at him severely.

"It is not likely that I should give judgment in your favour," he said, "when you begin by telling a lie. Of course you could never have got into that little bag."

"Don't trust me, trust your own eyes!" cried the adder. "Open the bag!"

In jumped the snake, the fox winked, and the man drew up the strings that fastened the neck of the bag.

"My judgment," said the fox, "is that the man shall pound the ungrateful snake to death with a large stone."

Avoid the company of sly and vicious people, for they are never to be trusted.

THE BRAVE DIVER OF TOR BAY

ONE summer's day a torpedo-boat came to grief in Tor Bay, Devonshire, for her propeller shaft snapped and pierced her plating, so that the water rushed in.

Some other boats came to her aid, but she sank in about half an hour. The crew had taken to the boats, and there, 150 feet down, the boat remained until it was decided to send divers to examine it.

Two men, Sidney Leverett and Walter Trapnell, came forward, and one light evening they were taken out to where the wrecked boat lay.

Trapnell was let down first, and he soon sent up a telephone message that he had found the wreck. He was told to note the damage and to signal when he could be drawn up.

But no signal came, and the full twenty minutes, beyond which time it is dangerous for a diver to stay down at such a depth, had passed. The men in the boat pulled the life-lines but all they felt was a heavy weight.

Sidney Leverett, recognising that something serious was the matter, sent down a message to ask what was wrong. Then, to his horror, he heard that Trapnell's lines were fouled, and he was unable to get clear. That meant that his friend was caught like a fly in a spider's web.

Without a moment's delay he slipped over the edge of the boat, and dropped down to the wreck. There he found his friend standing on the bottom, his lifeline and precious air-tube entangled in the wreck. He worked hard to free him.

Every instant's delay added danger, for Trapnell had used up all the air available to him, and if he could not be freed soon Leverett knew he would become unconscious and die. Every moment he himself was getting weaker and weaker, yet his friend's life depended on his quickness and skill. So he struggled on patiently.

At last he set Trapnell free. Leverett signalled, and sank into unconsciousness, while the men in the boat drew up the two divers very slowly, lest the rush of fresh, pure air should kill them both. When they were at last freed from their diver's dress Leverett slowly recovered, but his poor friend, for whom he had risked so much, died the next day.

THE GIRL WHO HELD THE FORT

THE history of the early French settlers in Canada provides us with many a story of courage and devotion. Foremost among those whose names have become famous for heroic deeds in those perilous times was Madeleine de Verchères, a girl of fourteen, who saved a fort.

The fort consisted of several houses surrounded by palisades, and a strong blockhouse. One day, Madeleine was standing by the riverside, some distance from the fort, when she heard the cry: "Run, Mademoiselle, run! The Iroquois!"

She turned, and saw a band of Iroquois Indians. Swiftly she ran back to the fort. Nearly all the people of the place were away in the fields when the attack was made, and were killed. There were left in the fort two soldiers, an old man, some women and children and Madeleine's two brothers, boys of ten and twelve.

At the first sign of the danger the soldiers fled to hiding. As the Indians delayed their attack Madeleine went round to inspect the defences. In the blockhouse she found the two soldiers preparing to set light to the gunpowder and blow up the fort. Madeleine's courage shamed them, and they set themselves to defend the place. They and Madeleine's two brothers opened fire from the loopholes, while Madeleine fired a cannon as a signal of distress. This signal was repeated from post to post till the warning of danger reached the city of Montreal.

Night came on, and had the Indians attacked them in the darkness all would have been lost. Madeleine ordered her elder brother and the soldiers to guard the women and children in the blockhouse while she posted her young brother, the old man, and herself as sentinels.

Throughout the dread night they passed the cry "All's well," and the Indians, finding the place so well guarded, refrained from attacking it.

For a week the Indians besieged the fort, but, not knowing how weak the defenders were, dared not attack it. At the end of the week, during which time Madeleine had scarcely rested, she was dozing with her gun under her arm when she heard the sentry cry that either Frenchmen or Indians were moving up the river. Help had come from Montreal!

The brave little leader marched to the river, and saluted the officer in command. "Monsieur," she said, "I surrender my arms to you."

The relief was accomplished. The Indians had fled. Madeleine could now rest secure. The news of her bravery spread far and wide, and her heroism was rewarded by a pension.

THE LEAK IN THE DYKE

IN Holland the people have continually to keep watch on the sea, as parts of the country are below its level at high tide. To keep the sea from flooding the land, great banks called dykes were built.

This is the story of a little Dutch boy who saved the low-lying district where he lived from being flooded. His name was Peter, and one evening his mother sent him to take some cakes to an old blind man who lived near the dyke.

On his way back, Peter walked below the tall bank, on the other side of which the sea was muttering. "You're a wicked old sea," said Peter. "You would like to break through and spoil our lands and homes, but our strong dyke keeps you in your place!"

Just then he was startled at hearing a trickle of water on his side of the bank and, running to the spot, he was horrified to see a stream no wider than his hand running out from the bank. Young as he was Peter knew what that meant, a leak in the dyke-wall, which, though small now, could grow to a flood in a single night.

He knew, too, that to leave it and run for help might mean that it would widen beyond control before men could reach the place. Scooping up handfuls of sand he stopped up the crack and at the same time shouted for help. But there were no houses near by and no one heard his cries.

The sun sank and still he shouted—more feebly now—and worked to keep the crack closed. As the night wore on he wondered whether he would die out there in the cold. But he stuck to his post and continued working to prevent that tiny breach from being disastrously widened.

They found him next morning, senseless but still alive, one arm in the breach—the boy who had saved their lands.

This story was written by Mary Dodge, the American author, in 1865, and came to be regarded as fact, not fiction.

THE NOBLE ALCESTIS

IN the old simple days of shepherd kings a prince of Thessaly called Admetus met a handsome stranger on the plain. It was Apollo, who had been banished from Heaven, but he saluted the mortal with humility, and asked for work.

Admetus needed a shepherd, so for many years afterwards the god of light and music and poetry kept the king's flocks. Admetus was a good master, indeed he was the friend rather than the tyrant of his servants, so that Apollo grew to love him. When Jove's anger had passed, and Apollo was recalled from exile, the Sun god sought to do Admetus a service. He journeyed to the great cavern where the Parcae, or the three Fates, were spinning human lives.

These three aged sisters, clad in white and crowned with narcissus, presided over human birth and death. Clotho, who held a distaff, was the Fate who directed whether a man should be born in palace or hovel, Lachesis spun out the actions of his life on her spindle, while Atropos cut the thread with her great shears when she decided that his hour for death had come. They were inexorable, and even Jove, king of heaven, could not intervene when they cut the life-thread of a hero he loved.

But the beautiful Apollo, with his music and sweet voice, softened their hearts, and persuaded them to promise not to cut the thread of Admetus's life, on one condition: when Death came for him some friend must be willing to die in his stead.

The news was brought to the shepherd king by a soothsayer. Perhaps he smiled and said, " Then I shall not live longer than other men. Who, except in the heat of battle, would go down to the dark realm of King Pluto that his friend might live on in the light of the Sun ? "

A little later Prince Jason set out in the good ship Argo to recapture the Golden Fleece. Among the heroes who went with him was Admetus. He bore himself bravely, but this is not the place to tell again their adventures. It suffices to say that he returned in safety.

Jason brought home with him the beautiful witch Medea as his wife. Now, Jason had been unjustly deprived of his kingdom by old King Pelias, but on his return he stayed at the usurper's Court, and all seemed friendship. Pelias was an old, sickly man. One day his four daughters were telling Medea how it saddened them to see his weakness. The witch said she could renew his youth by magic. First, however, she would prove her powers to the eager girls.

She got an old ram, had it killed, and put the body in a huge cauldron. She threw strange herbs into the pot, and chanted weird ditties. By and by she lifted out a young, playful lamb.

" I can turn your father into a radiant youth," she said, " but it requires courage and secrecy."

The daughters were so anxious to renew the old man's life that they made a slave stab him that night. But when he was dead Medea only laughed at them, and refused to use her magic to restore him. In vain were all their cries and tears. They were driven into exile as murderers.

But Admetus believed their innocence, and offered them shelter in his Court. One of them, called Alcestis, became his wife. After time had dimmed the tragedy in her memory they were happier than most kings and queens have ever been.

At length Admetus was stricken down by a deadly fever that no physician could cure. Alcestis watched by his side day and night, for she had heard the prophecy.

One night, as she watched by torchlight, Alcestis saw Death approach. He was a tall, grave man, clad in black. Alcestis felt no fear as he glided from the doorway to the bedside. She rose and said, " Take my life for his ! "

Death held out his hand; she took it without lament, and he led her down to the sunless world where King Pluto ruled with his fair wife Proserpine, and heroes wandered on the banks of the Styx. For, to the loving Alcestis, the upper world without her husband would have been as dismal as this grey country.

Admetus began to grow well from the moment that his wife spoke her noble words. All Greece joined with him in celebrating the lovely memory of Alcestis. She was the pattern of womanhood, the most fragrant name in history.

But they say that the king found life as heavy as death without her, and that Hercules, pitying his grief, went to the underworld. The hero offered to wrestle with Death if Alcestis should be the prize. After a desperate tussle Hercules triumphed, and brought Alcestis back to Thessaly.

ARACHNE AND HER TAPESTRIES

In all Colophon there was no needle-woman so skilful as Arachne, daughter of Idmon the dyer. Her tapestries were masterpieces of beauty. Great and small flocked to see her at work. The townsfolk boasted of their clever citizen, saying, "There is not such another in the world."

Arachne grew dizzy with such praise. In her conceit she said: "Truly, I am ready to challenge all needle-workers to a contest, from Minerva downward."

As she spoke an old woman, a stranger, who stood in the crowd of admiring neighbours, said gently: "Child, such talk is rash and irreverent. Mortals cannot hope to rival the gods."

Arachne tossed her head and exclaimed: "I would say it to Minerva herself!"

"She is here," said the old woman, suddenly growing upright, young, and beautiful. "She accepts your challenge."

Arachne was not frightened, but only made more proud than ever because a goddess had descended from heaven to meet her. Arachne's vanity made her feel sure of victory, for she was certainly the finest worker that ever depicted heroes and queens, woods and seas, with a needle. But she was not a goddess.

"Let us begin now," she cried. "Here are two looms, and thread enough for a mile of tapestries."

Long they worked in silence. Arachne chose as her subject a group of incidents showing the gods at fault—for in Greek Legend the gods were subject to the weaknesses of man, though they were immortal. It was indeed a beautiful picture, and in every way perfect as mortal could make it. But when the neighbours who praised it turned to Minerva's work, which showed her battle with Neptune, everyone cried out in astonishment. The sea looked so real that women drew back for fear of being wetted by the spray, and the needle-work people were so lifelike that a child ran screaming from their warlike attitude.

Arachne could not be blind to the difference. She fled from the humiliating sight of her work hung by Minerva's. Then, because pride was the very breath of life to her, and she could not bear to live without it, she hanged herself. But Minerva, pitying her foolish rival, turned her into a spider hanging on the end of its thread.

The descendants of that first spider still go by the family name of Arachnidae, and are famous for their spinning.

THE PRINCE WHO BECAME A GRASSHOPPER

Never be cruel to a grasshopper. It might be a prince, as you shall hear. Laomedon, first king of Troy, had a handsome son called Tithonus. The boy's mother was a daughter of the River Scamander, but history does not tell us whether the water-baby was found among the reeds or discovered in a giant lily. How ever it was that she came to live among men, she was beautiful as the famous river, and her son took after her.

Tithonus was fond of hunting, and was often abroad before the stars had faded from the sky. So Aurora, the dawn goddess, grew to know and love him. One dewy morning she appeared to him suddenly in her rose-coloured gown and her wreath of sunbeams. Tithonus fell in love with her, as the shepherd prince Endymion had fallen in love with the Moon goddess. After that there was only one part of the day he cared for: it was the brief, lovely moment when Dawn came to Earth.

But at length a cloud spread over his happiness. It was the thought that death must one day part him from his immortal lady. He begged her to ask this boon of the king of the gods, that he should live for ever. After much supplication by Aurora, Zeus granted her request, and the unchangeable decree went forth that Tithonus should never die.

Years sped quickly, and Tithonus began to get wrinkled, grey, and stiff. He had asked eternal life and not eternal youth from the gods. He was no longer the handsome lover of the Dawn; but they remained faithful friends. Tithonus enjoyed the wise pleasures of middle age.

Alas! middle age could not last for ever. Hundreds of years passed, and Tithonus was a helpless old weakling whose life was a burden to him. One day, with tears running from his sightless eyes, he begged Aurora to reverse the decree and let him die. But the word of the king of the gods could not be altered.

Yet Aurora gained permission to change the old man's form. He became a lively grasshopper, leaping and singing among the thyme flowers.

Somewhere he must be chirping still.

DAEDALUS AND HIS SON ICARUS

DAEDALUS was an Athenian inventor who gave the world the wedge, the axe, and sails. He made, besides these useful things, many cunning toys, such as statues which moved by themselves.

He had not, alas, that greatness of heart which should have gone with such cleverness of mind. When he saw that his nephew Talus showed signs of the same genius, Daedalus gave himself up to the vilest jealousy. One day, as the boy watched his uncle at work, a sudden rage seized Daedalus, and he hurled the boy down to the courtyard below. Talus was killed instantly.

Daedalus fled from justice with his son Icarus. They came to Crete, where King Minos sent for Daedalus, and employed him at the Court in various ways. He made the famous labyrinth in which Theseus afterwards fought the bull-headed man who then dwelled there and devoured human beings. But when his work was finished, Daedalus and his son were imprisoned by the treacherous king.

Young Icarus despaired, but Daedalus, the ingenious, contrived a way of escape. With wax and feathers he made two huge pairs of wings. One day the two captives strapped them on, and sailed over the prison walls and the sentinels, away to freedom.

The delight of Icarus in his new power was boundless. He soared and swooped instead of flying steadily as his father bade him. Now he wanted to see how high he could ascend. Up and up he climbed, till the hot Sun melted the wax, and his strong pinions were destroyed.

He dropped like a stone in the ocean, and was drowned. That part was called the Icarian Sea after him.

Now Daedalus felt the same anguish as the father of Talus. Helplessly he flew round and round over his beloved son's blue grave, and then he winged his mournful way to Sicily.

Here for a while his talents brought him favour and money, but his story soon became known. King Minos was angry with the King of Sicily for harbouring the runaway. Fearing a war, the Sicilian had Daedalus executed. This time the inventor did not try to escape. Life was not sweet to him without Icarus.

SITS-BY-THE-DOOR

English children all know the story of Una and the Lion. Red Indian children have a legend very like it. Here it is.

ONCE upon a time there was a beautiful girl, who belonged to the Blackfoot tribe, called Sits-by-the-door. She was her parents' darling, and had many friends.

But one day the tribe changed camp. First went a party of warriors in single file, then came the women and children, and more warriors brought up the rear. Suddenly a party of Crow Indians sprang out upon the middle of the line. They seized many women and children, while their comrades shot down the first Blackfoot warriors who sprang to the rescue. Then they made off swiftly with the captives. Sits-by-the-door was among them.

It was a long, painful journey to the Crow camp by Yellowstone River, and at every step the poor prisoners thought of the terrors before them. When they arrived some were burned, others made slaves.

Sits-by-the-door was given to a cruel man who ill-used her brutally. Every night he tied her wrists and ankles together lest she should escape. But his old wife was kind to the slave in secret.

One day when the Indian was hunting she told Sits-by-the-door that her husband had decided to kill her.

" If he spares you till tonight," she said, " I will help you to escape."

The Indian came in weary, gulped his supper, and fell asleep. The old woman cautiously untied the ropes. Then she gave Sits-by-the-door a flint, a bag of pemmican, and a pair of moccasins.

The poor girl sped out. All night she ran through the woods, and merciful Heaven sent snow to cover her tracks. Through the day she had to lie hidden, but at dusk she set off again.

Days passed ; her moccasins were in ribbons and her store of pemmican was exhausted. Soon she began to weaken from hunger, and could only totter a little way at a time. All at once she heard a noise behind her; a great grey wolf was swiftly following her !

Sits-by-the-door began to run, but she was too exhausted to go far, and at last she dropped down in despair. She expected to feel the wolf spring on her shoulders, but nothing happened. She looked up. He lay at her feet like a dog.

Then Sits-by-the-door knew he was no ordinary beast of prey, but an animal that had been sent by the Great Spirit to watch over and guard her.

" Brother," she said, " I hunger! "

Instantly the wolf bounded off into the woods to seek food.

Sits-by-the-door thought she was far enough from the Crows to light a fire in safety, so she gathered brushwood and kindled a flame with the flint; then she lay down to wait.

Before long the wolf returned with a little dead fawn. Sits-by-the-door cooked it, and shared it with the wolf. From the skin she made moccasins for her torn feet. She slept fearlessly, guarded faithfully by her strange friend.

In this manner the two travelled together for several days, till at last they reached the Blackfoot camp.

It is impossible to imagine the joy of the girl's parents at seeing her again, for they thought she must have perished by fire and torture.

Sits-by-the-door was worn out by the long journey and the excitement of her homecoming. She bade her kinsmen be kind to her friend the wolf; but that night she fell ill, and while her parents were busy tending her the Indian dogs attacked it, and drove it out of the village.

Every evening for some time it would come to a hill overlooking the camp and howl. The girl's friends brought it meat, but it ran away from them. It wanted Sits-by-the-door, who was too ill to come. At last it came no more.

Sits-by-the-door recovered, and lived a long, happy life. Perhaps it was in honour of her friend that Indians started to call the Milky Way the Wolf Trail.

THE POACHER'S SILENCE

Some thirty years ago a gamekeeper was killed in the east of England, and two poachers were arrested for the crime and brought to trial.

There was no difficulty as to which of the poachers was the guilty party. One of the men confessed that he and he alone had done the horrible deed. But for some reason or another there was a general feeling that he was innocent.

When the verdict was given, and the judge had pronounced sentence of death, the friends of the prisoner bestirred themselves, and, raising the plea that he suffered from a deformity of the neck which would make it a torture to hang him, they succeeded in getting a respite.

But after the respite had been granted the law ordered a medical examination of the prisoner, and none of the doctors could find any reason why he should not meet the punishment for the crime he had committed. He was, therefore, for the second time, condemned to die.

But the people in his part of the world were utterly unconvinced that he was guilty, and immediately set about getting up fresh petitions for his reprieve. So numerous and so earnest were these petitions that the law again granted a respite, and the poacher was sentenced to penal servitude for life.

Think what those words " penal servitude for life " mean. They mean that a man ceases to be a man, and becomes a number; that every tomorrow has the same soul-killing monotony as yesterday; that the life of the world is shut out from him by frowning walls.

Perhaps this poacher many times wished that the law had put him to death, for he lay in prison day after day, week after week, month after month, for nearly thirty years. Then he was released. He went into prison a strong and vigorous man; he came out white and bowed, and marked for ever with the grey pallor of the prison cell.

And when he came out and found that his fellow-poacher was dead the true story of the crime was told. It was not he, but his fellow-poacher, who had killed the keeper—struck him down with the butt of a gun, and thrown the body into a pond. He himself had had no hand in the crime. But why did he take upon himself the guilt ?

The answer shows us that even in bad men there is a spark of goodness. This rough English poacher held his peace because the real murderer was a married man with a wife and children dependent on him for support. He himself was unmarried and had no dependents.

And so, for the sake of the other man's wife and children, this simple, rough-hearted poacher did what he could, and willingly offered his life.

A FELLOW BY THE NAME OF ROWAN

WHEN war broke out between America and Spain in 1898 the first thing for America to do was to send a message from the President of the United States to the leader of the insurgents in Cuba. This leader, Garcia by name, had to be reached at all costs and told what America meant to do. It was also necessary to know definitely that he would fight on the side of America against Spain.

But could he be reached? Where was Garcia? He was somewhere in the wild mountains of war-stricken Cuba—somewhere, miles from cities, miles from postmen and telegraph boys, miles from everything. How could the President of the United States reach him?

With all the vast wealth and power at his disposal, the great President was helpless. He could not say to Garcia: " Help me, and I will help you." He could not say so simple a thing as that, although he was surrounded by telegraph and telephone wires, and had thousands of men to obey his commands.

But someone came to him and said: " There's a fellow by the name of Rowan who will find Garcia for you."

This fellow Rowan was summoned into the President's presence. He was asked if he could find Garcia. He said he would try. The President liked the look of the man, liked his way of speaking, and gave him a letter for Garcia.

Rowan took the letter and placed it in an oilskin pouch, which he strapped round his waist, next to the skin. Then he walked out and disappeared. In four days an open boat crept toward the coast of Cuba under the blackness of a midnight sky. The boat was shot forward on a wave, it grounded on the beach, and before a second wave reached it a fellow by the name of Rowan was walking up the shingle to the cliffs.

Three weeks passed away rapidly. At the end of that time a man appeared on the opposite side of the island, entered a boat, and was rowed away. He had walked from shore to shore, evading a thousand dangers in a land hostile to his race and country, and he had found Garcia.

Thus appeared for a brief moment on the stage of history a fellow by the name of Rowan; and as silently as he appeared he disappeared again into the darkness and the silence, the hero of a flashing moment. All he told of his adventure was in these few simple words:

April 23. I received the cipher cable despatch " Join Garcia as soon as possible." At 10 a.m., dressed as an English hunter, I crossed Jamaica, and reached St. Ann's Bay at 1 a.m.

Boarded small sailboat, and by daylight entered the Caribbean Sea, kept well off the Cuban coast until dark, then landed about 11 p.m. Next morning proceeded through forest.

About noon, May 1, reached insurgents' headquarters. Conferred with Garcia, and arranged to be accompanied back by envoys with information.

Crossed the island of Cuba astride meridian 77 degrees, and reached coast about sunset May 5. Passed under guns of Spanish fort at 11 p.m., and by daylight was out of sight of Cuba on our way to Key West.

That is how Lieutenant Rowan described his journey through Spanish patrol vessels and the Spanish lines, through Cuban swamps, mud, fever, and mosquitoes—a deed which an American general described as " a most perilous undertaking, and an act of cool daring that has rarely been equalled in the annals of warfare."

But such deeds are not allowed to be buried in this world, and a great American journalist, Elbert Hubbard, who went down in the Lusitania, chose another way of telling the story of A Message to Garcia. His story of it has been printed millions of times, and we print it below because it should never be forgotten.

A Message to Garcia, By Elbert Hubbard

IN all this Cuban business there is one man stands out on the horizon of my memory like Mars at perihelion.

When war broke out between Spain and the United States it was very necessary to communicate quickly with the leader of the insurgents. Garcia was somewhere in the mountain fastnesses of Cuba—no one knew where. No mail or telegraph message could reach him. The President must secure his co-operation, and quickly. What to do?

Someone said to the President: " There is a young fellow by the name of Rowan will find Garcia for you if anybody can."

Rowan was sent for, and given a letter to be delivered to Garcia.

How "the fellow by the name of Rowan"

took the letter, sealed it up in an oilskin pouch, strapped it over his heart, in four days landed by night off the coast of Cuba from an open boat, disappeared into the jungle, and in three weeks came out on the other side of the island, having traversed a hostile country on foot, and delivered his letter to Garcia, are things I have no special desire now to tell in detail. The point I wish to make is this: McKinley gave Rowan a letter to be delivered to Garcia; Rowan took the letter, and did not ask " Where is he at? "

By the Eternal! there is a man whose form should be cast in deathless bronze and the statue placed in every college of the land. It is not book-learning young men need, but a stiffening of the vertebrae, which will cause them to be loyal to a trust, to act promptly, concentrate their energies; do the thing.

Put this matter to a test: You are sitting now in your office—six clerks are within call. Summon any one of them and make this request: " Please look in the encyclopedia and make a brief memorandum for me concerning the life of Correggio."

Will the clerk quietly say, " Yes, sir," and go and do the task?

On your life he will not. He will ask one or more of the following questions:

Who was he?

Which encyclopedia?

Where is the encyclopedia?

Was I hired for that?

Don't you mean Bismarck?

Is he dead?

Is there any hurry?

Shan't I bring you the book and let you look it up yourself?

And after you have answered the questions and explained how to find the information and why you want it, the clerk will go off and get one of the other clerks to help him to find Correggio—and come back and tell you there is no such man.

Now, if you are wise you will not bother to explain to your assistant that Correggio is indexed under the Cs, not in the Ks, but will smile and say, " Never mind," and look it up yourself.

" You see that book-keeper? " said the foreman to me in a large factory.

" Yes; what about him? "

" Well, he's a fine accountant, but if I sent him up to town on an errand he might accomplish the errand all right, and, on the other hand, might stop at four saloons on the way and forget what he had been sent for."

We have recently been hearing much sympathy expressed for the " downtrodden denizen of the sweat-shop " and the " homeless wanderer searching for honest employment," and with it all often go many hard words for the men in power.

Nothing is said about the employer who grows old before his time in the vain attempt to get ne'er-do-wells to do intelligent work.

I know one man of really brilliant parts who has not the ability to manage a business of his own, and yet who is absolutely worthless to anyone else because he carries with him constantly the insane suspicion that his employer is oppressing or intending to oppress him.

Tonight this man walks the street looking for work, the wind whistling through his threadbare coat.

Have I put the matter too strongly? Possibly I have; but when all the world has gone a-slumming I wish to speak a word of sympathy for the man who, against great odds, has directed the efforts of others, and, having succeeded, finds there is nothing in it; nothing but bare board and clothes. I have carried a dinner pail and worked for a day's wages, and I have also been an employer of labour, and I know there is something to be said on both sides.

There is no excellence in poverty; rags are no recommendation, and all employers are not rapacious and high-handed any more than all poor men are virtuous. My heart goes out to the man who does his work when the " boss " is away as well as when he is at home.

And the man who, when given a letter for Garcia, quietly takes the message without asking any idiotic questions, and with no lurking intention of doing aught else but deliver it, never has to go on strike for higher wages.

Civilisation is one long, anxious search for just such individuals. Anything such a man asks shall be granted. He is wanted in every city, town, and village—in every office, shop, store, and factory.

The world cries out for such; he is needed, and needed badly—the man who can carry a message to Garcia.

THE PHANTOM CATS

THERE was once a Japanese hunter who had strayed far from home in the pursuit of a deer.

At dusk he was passing through the woods which clothed a steep mountain. Very far below he saw lights; but he did not try to reach the village lest in the darkness he should fall over some precipice. However, he saw a ruined temple a little higher up the mountain, and there in a corner he lay down to sleep.

He was suddenly awakened by a terrible din. The moonlight shone through the broken roof and showed him twelve cats, all dancing and yelling, gambolling and shrieking. The most dreadful thing about it was that they were using human words. The hunter understood that they were rejoicing over some feast which would soon take place, and they kept crying, " Tell it not to Shippeitaro ! "

At dawn next day the hunter set off for the village below. The first person he met was a little boy who was crying. When the hunter asked what was the matter the child said: " My sister will be given to the demon tonight ; my dear Plum Blossom will be torn to pieces by the demon."

" What demon is it who would do this ? " asked the huntsman.

" He lives on the mountain. He sends terrible plagues upon us unless we sacrifice a maiden to him each year. It is now our family's turn to give a victim. Plum Blossom will be put in a great box

and carried to the temple on the hill. At midnight he will come to kill her."

The hunter did not say one sympathetic word. He simply asked, " Who is Shippeitaro ? "

" He is a big dog belonging to the Prince," said the boy.

The huntsman then made the boy tell him where the Prince lived. Without waiting for breakfast he hurried off to the palace, unfolded his hastily-made plans, and borrowed Shippeitaro. Then he went back again to the village.

It was easy to find the house of the stricken family; a few words from the hunter changed this grief to hope.

At nightfall a party of young men climbed the mountain, carrying a great box. They put it down in the ruined temple, and nothing could persuade them to wait, so great was their terror. But the hunter hid behind a pillar.

Midnight came, and with a horrible miaowing the cats rushed in, led by a huge tom with eyes like live coals. He ran up to the box and seized the lid with his teeth. Out sprang Shippeitaro and caught the monster by his throat. The huntsman ran up to cut off his wicked head. Then man and dog made short work of the other cats, which had been too stupefied with fright to escape.

After that no more demons troubled the district, and Shippeitaro was the best-loved four-footed thing in the place.

THE BOY WHO KEPT BACK AN ARMY

IN the warfare which the French made upon the Tirolese, a people living in the north-east of Italy, the French soldiers attacked a village on the bank of the River Ard. The village could only be reached by crossing a swiftly-flowing river rushing along the bottom of a deep ravine. Across the ravine lay the huge trunk of a tree, which had been cut down on the bank and allowed to fall so that its trunk rested on the farther side, and the tree, therefore, formed a bridge.

Three hundred Tirolese men and a boy guarded the bridge. The boy was Albert Speckbacher. As the French advanced the Tirolese began to hew down the bridge with axes, but the bullets from the rifles of the French soldiers fell thick and fast, and one after another the brave men fell. Among the dead was Albert's father.

The brave boy took his father's place. The bridge was nearly down; a few more strokes of the axe and there would be no way for the French to cross. Seizing an axe, Albert Speckbacher faced the fire from the French guns, and hewed the tree at the peril of his life. He cut it all but through—there was only a thin piece of wood holding the bridge together.

At that moment Albert Speckbacher gave up his life for his people. He threw down his axe and jumped on the tree with such force that his weight snapped the thin piece still holding it in its place, and the bridge and the boy fell together into the swift river below.

The French were stirred by this act of bravery, and they buried the boy's body with honour, and set up a monument to tell how nobly he died.

KATE BARLASS OF THE BROKEN ARM

JAMES THE FIRST of Scotland was a good king; but when he came to the throne, about 500 years ago, the country was in such disorder that he had to be stern and severe; so many of the nobles hated him and conspired to kill him.

It happened that the king went one winter to Perth, with his queen and her ladies, and abode in the Abbey of Perth, while his followers were scattered over the city; and here was the traitors' chance.

To make matters easier, some servants were bribed to remove the bolts and bars from the doors. And so it befell one night, when the king was sitting quite unarmed with the queen and her ladies, that a great clatter of weapons was heard, and he knew his foes had come to murder him.

But as he knew that there was a vault under the chamber where he was, he wrenched up the boards from the floor and leaped down, and the ladies quickly put them back just before the traitors entered the room. And they, not finding him, searched for him high and low. Then the king and the ladies in the chamber, thinking the danger was over, began to move the boards; but just at that moment they heard the traitors returning. There was no time to cover all up, and on the door was no lock or bolt to stay them— only the iron rings of the bolt.

Quick as thought one of the queen's maidens, Katherine Douglas, sprang to the door and thrust her arm through the rings of the bolt, crying out that there was no one in the room but ladies.

But the fierce men outside paid no heed, and poor Katherine's arm was snapped, and the men burst in and slew the king.

For her brave deed the name of Katherine Douglas found its way throughout the land, and men called her Kate Barlass, the lass who barred the door with her arm.

THE TWO DAUGHTERS OF JAPAN

THERE was once a Japanese sportsman who loved shooting with the bow and arrow. He took no pleasure in shooting at targets, but desired always a living mark.

Now, he had two daughters who were devoted followers of the gentle lord Buddha, whose teaching forbids men to take life except in cases of strict necessity. Their father was, in outward forms, a Buddhist too, but he brushed aside that part of Buddha's teaching which it did not suit him to follow.

The two girls often tried to dissuade him from this disobedience, fearing that Heaven would punish their father's soul in the next world.

One day a friend said to their father : "There are two storks which come every night to the lake beyond my garden. You ought to try to get them."

"I will shoot them tonight," cried the archer. His daughters overheard.

When it was quite dark he set off for the lake, and waited. Before long he saw two white things moving by the shore. Two skilful shots brought them to the ground. He ran up, and saw that he had killed his own daughters. They had taken this way of showing him the sacredness of life.

In his grief and horror he flung away bow and arrows for ever.

THE RACE WITH THE FLOOD

THE most famous engine-driver in America, Hiram Free, has gone on his last ride, but long will his name be remembered. Every American boy knew of his race with the flood which swept away Johnstown, in Pennsylvania.

A huge dam, 700 feet long, held up the waters of the River Conemaugh in a reservoir, twelve miles from Johnstown. The railway ran down the valley and crossed the river by a bridge below the town.

From his engine Hiram Free saw the dam bursting, and a great wall of water, seven yards deep, come rushing down the valley. Putting on full speed, he dashed down the valley, with the waters tearing up the railway track behind, and his warning whistle gave hundreds of people time to escape. Outrunning the waters, he passed Johnstown and crossed the railway bridge, shrieking the alarm.

The town was almost entirely destroyed by the flood, and so were seven villages lower down the valley, but the railway bridge stood firm.

This terrible accident showed American engineers the need of strong embankments to hold up great reservoirs of water ; but most people remember it best by Hiram Free's heroic race for life.

BLUE JAY

On the north-west coast of America there used to dwell a powerful race of Indians called the Chinooks. As they hollowed out their cedar-tree canoes, or feathered their arrows, they were fond of telling tales, particularly tales of Blue Jay.

Whether Blue Jay was a man, or a bird, or a will o' the wisp no one could say. He seemed to take it in turn to be all three. But, in any shape, it was mischief that delighted him.

One evening when Blue Jay returned from hunting he found that his sister Ioi had disappeared. Blue Jay was incapable of affection; he had never done anything but tease Ioi all her life. But as they had lived alone together, and there was now no one to cook for him, Blue Jay soon missed Ioi very much.

The days passed, and there was still no sign of her. Blue Jay began to wish he had behaved better. He made inquiries; no one knew anything about the missing girl. At length Blue Jay set out himself in search of her.

He wandered far and wide without ever getting news. Then, one day, when he was fishing, his canoe suddenly began to move of its own accord. He was swept swiftly over the sea until he came to a foreign land.

He drew up his canoe, and walked inland till he came to a village. In the biggest lodge he found Ioi surrounded by several heaps of bones.

She greeted him kindly, and then, pointing to the heaps, she said:

" This is my husband, this is my mother-in-law, this is my little brother-in-law, who is kinder than ever you were, Blue Jay. At sunset they will turn into men and women, but at the sound of a loud voice they will become like this again till the next sunset."

She explained that the Shadow People had come when Blue Jay was out, and asked her to marry their chief. She was only too glad to leave her brother, even for a foreign land.

Very soon it became twilight, and Blue Jay found himself surrounded by a crowd of handsome, courteous people, who made him very welcome. But as soon as the merriment was at its height Blue Jay suddenly gave a loud shout. The fine folk disappeared, and there were only heaps of bones to be seen.

Some time after he had returned to his own place a man died, leaving his wife and two children terribly poor. The Shadow People were sorry for them, and used to leave whale meat at the door of their little hut by the creek.

Blue Jay smelt delicious odours coming from the place; he called the other men, and the worthless crew burst in upon the widow, and carried off the meat.

Next day the elder of the two children, a girl, had disappeared.

" The Shadow People have taken her, like Ioi," said Blue Jay. " Let us go and fetch her back!"

So they all set off in their canoes.

They reached a different part of Shadow Land. Not a person was to be seen except the stolen girl, who said she was happily married to one of the Shadow People, and invited them home.

Blue Jay had no sooner got into the house than he complained that he was hungry. Suddenly a queer creature appeared with a long beak. He used this to split wood, and soon a fire was kindled. It began to smoke. Now another queer creature with a huge stomach appeared, and swallowed it all.

A little piece of meat was cooked, but when it was set on the table another creature appeared and began to slice it. It became a canoe-load of meat.

After the guests had eaten the Shadow People challenged them to a diving match; the loser was to be slain.

" I will be the Chinook champion," said Blue Jay.

So he fastened bushes to the side of his canoe, and when he felt he could breathe no more he would come up, hidden by the bushes, and get some fresh air. By this means he seemed to stay under for a remarkable time, and won the match.

Next they had a climbing contest Blue Jay and a chipmunk were set to climb a piece of ice that reached from the Earth to the clouds. Blue Jay crawled round to the side on which no one was looking, changed himself into a bird, and flew to the top, where he took on his man's form again and was acclaimed victor.

By many other trials of strength and agility did the Shadow People try to get rid of their unwelcome guests, but they were always defeated by Blue Jay's dishonesty. At last the Chinooks returned, for no one wanted them, and the girl was devoted to her Shadow kin.

Now Blue Jay took a wife, and in time had some children whom he treated as callously as Ioi. Once there was a fearful famine, and the people only had roots and mussels to eat. All the men went out in their canoes to seek food. The chief was dead, but his little son was a spirited boy who desired to serve his people. He begged to go hunting with the men.

" It is too dangerous," said Blue Jay.

The boy clung to his canoe, up to the armpits in water, but Blue Jay struck his hands till he was obliged to leave go.

The men were lucky enough to kill a sea-lion. They were near a rocky island.

" Let us drag it ashore and cut it up here," said Blue Jay. Then, when that was done, he said: " There is not enough here for all the tribe! We had better eat it ourselves, and say nothing about it."

That evening they returned, and there was a great pattering of feet as the women and children rushed down to hear if they had brought anything back.

" No," said Blue Jay. " You must gather mussels."

This happened again the next day, and the day after. Always the chief's son begged to be taken, and always Blue Jay refused, knowing that the youth would insist on bringing back the kill.

On the fourth day, as they sat at their feast, the men suddenly heard a whirring in the air, and a flock of birds flew round and round overhead uttering cries that almost sounded like human shouts of scorn.

That evening there was no rush of pattering feet when the canoe party returned. The men rushed to their homes. All were deserted. Not one of them ever saw his wife and children again—nor did they deserve that they should do so.

THE INVENTION OF MEDICINE

IT is all very well to grumble at being dosed: just listen to me a minute, and learn what would have happened if there had been no medicine.

At the beginning of things men and beasts lived together like brothers. But gradually they drifted apart. What was the first little squabble, I wonder, which led to the great separation? Certain it is that men made huts for themselves in clearings, while the animals kept to the woods. Then, one day, when his aged wife was shivering with cold, a man went out with a stone and sling. He came back with the warm skin of an animal. After that there was open war.

The animals met together for counsel. How could they punish these clever wretches who were able to strike down the strongest beast and use its fur to warm their miserable hairless bodies? The animals could not make bows and arrows, hatchets and spears, slings and snares. But they were something of magicians, and so they invented disease.

Before that time there was no such thing as illness. But those angry animals now invented and sent into the world all the sicknesses there are, from measles to lumbago. I do not know who thought of mumps, but it is said that the deer are responsible for rheumatism.

As these fearful curses streamed out into the world it seemed as though the human race must soon be wiped out. But a piece of ivy hung over the mouth of the council cave, and he heard the plot. He crawled away and told it to the oak, who whispered it to the wind, who told the grass and the reeds. The news spread like wild-fire. Now the plants held a council in their turn.

It was in a forest glade. A beech said: " I do not think men should be killed like this. I have a feeling that one day they may do marvellous things. Although they are poor and naked now, I believe that one day they will be as glorious as tigers or pine trees!"

The cowslip said: " Their young ones are almost as pretty as buds. Let us help them against the animals."

Nearly every leaf rustled its approval. One or two plants, such as the deadly nightshade and hemlock, were unfriendly, and the nettle said: " I shall blister them whenever I get the chance!"

But the dock replied: " And I will heal the place!"

Thereupon the plants set out to make remedies for all the diseases invented by the animals. If you look in your botany book you will find that nearly every herb has a medicinal use besides its beauty. If you screw up your face the next time your mother begins to shake the bottle, you are very ungrateful, and you hurt the feelings of the whole vegetable kingdom.

Nature's Wonderful Living Family in Earth and Air and Sea

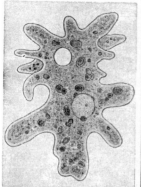  

An Amoeba, Protozoa with spines, and Foraminifera from the Adriatic Sea, seen through the microscope

THE WORLD OF THE PROTOZOA

EVERYWHERE Man can go the Protozoa were there before him and may survive him. Living, they may shape his life ; dead, they lift the mountains from the ocean bed, building them on their dead bodies. They are as many as the sands of the sea; as many as the visible stars of the universe; and yet they were unknown to us till on a day three centuries ago a Dutch lensmaker in Delft, Leeuwenhoek, saw through one of the first microscopes a new world of them in a drop of dirty water.

For these microscopic creatures the name was found, in 1820, of Protozoa, meaning thereby that they were the first created, the most primitive of living animals. This definition of them has not stood the test of time, because, though the vast majority of them have animal characteristics, it is impossible to exclude from among them many which live, temporarily or permanently, after the manner of the vegetable kingdom, and which are plants to all intents and purposes, albeit not descending from the simplest plants in an unbroken series. The term Protista was suggested, so as to unite in one vast assemblage the simple and primitive living things from which the animal and vegetable kingdoms have taken their origin.

By something else we may know these Protozoa. They have only one living cell. All their life, all their structure, all their development is implicit in it; though even this restriction has to be modified to make room for living creatures which are colonies of single cells, each cell alike to every other. These are the Metazoa, which have been evolved from simpler one-celled ancestors.

The Metazoa are tissue-like animals; the primitive sponges are examples. The resemblances in form and life and living of the Protozoa, and their differences, are so multitudinous that a small Encyclopedia would hardly be enough to enumerate them; but their extremely small size is a quality that all have, and yet is so graduated that while a few can be seen with the naked eye, the majority can be viewed only as Leeuwenhoek saw them under a microscope, and some are all but invisible.

Another quality they have which sets them apart from other living creatures : it is their staggering power of multiplication and its swiftness in action. An elephant requires 25 years to attain maturity and become a parent. A single Protozoan, if no fatal accident attended the lengthening out of the chain, would become the ancestor of a million of its kind in four days. It is this fecundity or

PREHISTORIC LIFE · MAMMALS · BIRDS · REPTILES · FISHES · INSECTS

teeming productivity which enables the Protozoa to set their mark on the structure of the Earth.

In the depths of the ocean lie billions upon billions of dead Protozoa—Foraminifera and Radiolaria—which have left their skeletons over vast tracts of the ocean floor as almost the sole constituents of the ooze on which the deep-sea cables rest, and through which the words of men flicker and flutter and beat. The Radiolaria are a group of a great many species, and the same was true in past ages, since in many geological deposits the rocks are constituted of the same materials.

THE MINUTE BODIES WHICH HAVE BUILT UP THE MIGHTY MOUNTAINS

From the Radiolaria and Foraminifera and other forms contributing to their numbers has been built a great part of the solid surface of the Earth's crust. They are the mountain builders. Their bodies rising from the deep have become the limestone rocks of mountain ranges. Their monuments are the Alps and the Carpathians, the Mountains of the Moon in Morocco. Their mausoleums were rising in Egypt millions of years before there was a Pharaoh or any human being; they crowned the heights of Persia before Persia was; and supplied the Miliolite limestones for noble buildings in Paris before there was a France.

This building activity is conferred on them by their ability to add to their number in such a way as to impart to them a restricted immortality. No waiting for them. The single cell splits into two single cells, and these two split again almost as fast as two ticks of a clock. The protozoan Paramecium, one of those infusoria that Leeuwenhoek spied through his lens, has been experimentally set going and kept going for some thirty years, always the same Paramecium replacing the ancestor, till at last something happens to the life-force and the clock runs down. Otherwise the Paramecium progeny might overwhelm the world.

PAYING GUESTS WHO PAY NEXT TO NOTHING FOR THEIR KEEP

After the consideration of the Protozoa as mountain builders comes that of inquiring how their life, while they live, affects the life of the world; that is to say, the existence of the higher animals, those who, like ourselves, have to suffer them.

Let us be fair; they may do us a good turn here and there, but as parasites, a quality in them which first focused attention to their habits, they are paying guests paying next to nothing, and harder to evict than any squatter. They must have food, and in face of their numbers no Food Controller can prevent them. After all the majority nourish themselves as all animals must; that is to say they are entirely dependent for food and sustenance on other living organisms which they capture, devour, and digest.

Such animals, protozoa or other, are said to be " holozoic," a word signifying " completely animal-like "; they are unable to build up the calories they need, and require proteins ready made. A number, assigned to the Mastigophora (from the Greek, mastix, a whip) have slender whip-like filaments, or flagella, that enable them to move along and capture food. To this section belong the Trypanosomes, parasites of which there will be more to be said, but nothing to praise.

THE PROTOZOA WHICH CONTAIN CHLOROPHYLL LIKE THAT OF GREAT PLANTS

A certain number of Protozoa, all, with rare exceptions, belonging to the class Mastigophora, possess in their bodies peculiar coloured corpuscles, containing chlorophyll like the green chlorophyll of plants, by which in sunlight they can split up carbon dioxide, freeing the oxygen and using the carbon to build up protein. Such are in this way similar to the ordinary green plants, and are called holophytic, meaning " completely plant-like." It was in order to combine the holozoics and the holophytes that the new term Protista was suggested, uniting the vast assemblage of simple and primitive living beings from which the animal and vegetable kingdoms have taken origin.

Some Protozoa that have no such apparatus are spared the need of devouring other creatures, because they live on decaying organic substances they encounter. They are termed saprophytic because their mode of life is like that of the fungus—a saprophyte. They do not need ready-made protein, because they can build it up from other chemical substances as they go. The Flagella free-lances are cf their company.

Among the Mastigophora is a sub-section comprising a small number of marine forms, of which the best known is the common Noctiluca miliaris of our coasts. It is about the size of a pin's-head, but its body, much smaller than that, is inflated with a watery gelatinous substance, from which noctiluca derives its remarkable power of light production, probably the result of oxidation within it. This power reveals itself in warmer seas than ours in magnificent displays of phosphorescence covering at night square miles of ocean, so that a ship sailing in it appears to float on a living floor of light,

become so engrained that in structure it has become a vegetable. Otherwise a parasitic Protozoan is entirely dependent on its particular host or hosts. It may live on or in the host. If outside it may do no harm and may use the host only as offering shelter and transport while looking for a living. On the other hand it may bite the hand that feeds it, as one of the parasites of fishes does by leaving a permanent wound on the skin; and fish are not the only victims, for some human diseases have been attributed to the same insidious penetration.

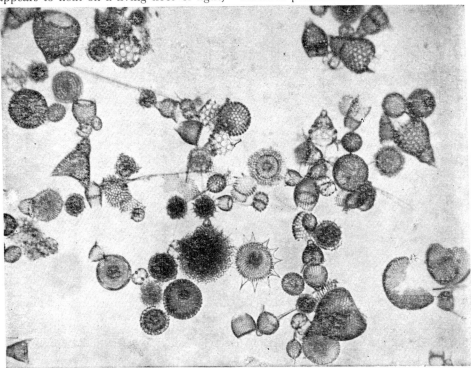

SILICEOUS SHELLS OF RADIOLARIANS, MINUTE MARINE ANIMALS INVISIBLE TO THE NAKED EYE
This greatly enlarged photograph clearly shows the beautiful structure of the shells of protozoa

that is in fact a living floor of billions of noctiluca. The display comes unexpectedly and disappears as suddenly as it comes. Stirring increases it as experiments show.

Finally, Protozoa of all classes live as parasites, at the expense of some other living creature, their willing or unwilling host. The varying modes of life are of less value in classifying them because of their differences: all four ways of life and living are to be found in the one order of the Flagellata, and in one subdivision of it the holophytic habit has

The vast majority of parasites that live inside the host are there for no good or useful purpose. If a few offer compensation as house cleaners, the others are like the housebreaker whose presence is alone sufficient to make him suspect. Two modes of parasitism may be distinguished. The parasite may intercept the food of its host and so rob it of its sustenance, but the food robbers are in general harmless otherwise. But the parasites which nourish themselves on the substance of the host may produce the most dangerous effects; and like the Kea, the big New Zealand parrot which was originally a herbivorous or insect-eating bird and became almost accidentally carnivorous, and began, and continues, to kill sheep for its food, so in protozoan parasites of the hungrier kind is an ascending capacity for harmfulness, culminating in species which bring about the death of their host.

It is far from clear in what way the poisonous effects of parasitic Protozoa are produced. The effect may depend on the host as well as the parasite effecting it. Nor need it depend on the number of the parasites. They may be present in force on an insect and the insect no worse for it, yet on the other hand a large mammal may succumb to the effect of microscopic parasites so scanty in number as hardly to be detected, as when the Trypanosome gambiense kills thousands of native Africans by Sleeping Sickness. It might seem that a specific poison is produced by the parasite, but up to the present scarcely more than one such poison has been isolated.

THE IDEAL HOST FROM THE PARASITE'S POINT OF VIEW

The poison bears the sinister name of Sarcocystis, in one of the Sarcosporidia, and the Sarcosporidia are a section of the Sporozoa. They are very common in domestic animals, and found frequently in Man. They usually damage only by force of numbers, and do not do much harm otherwise. They are visible to the naked eye and often very large. The sheep supports big ones, and the roebuck one nearly one-twentieth of an inch long.

The parasite, one might say, does not seek to kill its host, because by doing so it would deprive itself of visible means of support ; the death of the host might be the greatest disaster that could befall itself. The ideal host from the parasite's point of view is one that is tolerant of it, going on imperturbably content with its company. But either before or after it fails them there must be some escape to another host. Active migration can only be effected when the host leads an aquatic life, not when it is a land animal. The way of escape must be one to enable the parasite to find a host elsewhere. There are several such ways and the most complicated is like that of the malarial parasite *Plasmodium malariace* which spends one part of its life cycle in an insect and the other part in Man where, as surely as a tiger, it may become a man-killer.

The Protozoan parasite, like any single-celled thing, is more or less a minute mass of the living substance protoplasm, containing within it other substances, fluid, solid, even gaseous, which are the product of its own activity or have been taken up from outside. A drop of a fluid substance when suspended in another fluid tends immediately to become a perfect sphere, and this may be regarded as the primary form of a living cell.

THE ENDLESS FANTASTIC SHAPES WHICH THE PROTOZOA ASSUME

A great many Protozoa have this spherical form, especially those which, like the Radiolaria, float freely in water; but the majority depart, for various reasons, more or less from it. A first reason would be that the Protozoan could not maintain it. Thus an amoeba in which the protoplasm is quite naked can keep the spherical form while at rest, but when it becomes active it may assume new appearances, such as that of thrusting out the protoplasm in spines or protuberances varying in size, length, width, and activity. If not wanted they can disappear.

These protuberances—spines, flagella, or whatever form they assume or whatever purpose they serve, whether to aid movement or whip up food—are conspicuous in the endless fantastic shapes the Protozoa assume. Fantastic as some of them are, they have all been evolved in the long eras since life appeared on the planet to serve best the interests of these living parasites if not those of any other creature. This assertion may do the Protozoa something less than justice, for without some of them as scavengers, the life of the world would soon be choked with its own refuse.

PROBLEMS OF CLASSIFICATION WHICH FACE THE SCIENTISTS

The unravelling of the aim and value of these diversities of form is a task that the Protozoologists undertake and must pursue unceasingly ; and it has to begin with the tedium of classification. The first classification is that between species which move freely and those that are fixed or attached. Of the freely-moving some float or swim, and some creep along on a firm foundation. The swimmers become egg-shaped, the creepers are more or less flattened and spread over the surface. Sitters, or attachés, are more or less vase-shaped, with an attachment drawn out into a stalk. A frequent peculiarity is that the Protozoan, whether fixed or free, acquires a spiral twist—though it need not be a vicious spiral.

The second consideration is to discern how the form developed and is maintained, and on what principles. The answer has to be sought in the structure of the individual. The structure may be external like an envelope, or internal like a framework or interior scaffolding. Some of the naked bodies form shells about themselves, others build about themselves walls formed of spicules of sponge ; and an experimental zoologist induced one of the Difflugia to set up housekeeping with particles of coloured glass.

The Difflugia are in fact only a very small item in a system of classification which is not founded on any of these diversities that have been mentioned, nor on others arising out of the physiology, the life cycles, the sex, the tendency or ability to change the shape ; but regards only the larger differences in shape or size or the processes of life. The Difflugia, for example, are set among the Sarcodina, a term derived originally from "sarcode" and employed for the living substance, the "life-stuff," before protoplasm was substituted. The Sarcodina are those in which the protoplasmic body is naked, as in the amoeba.

The second ruling class are the Mastigophora, or those in which, as already stated, the organs of locomotion and food-capture are the lashing, whip-like flagella. The protoplasmic body may be naked or may have a cortex, or a sort of

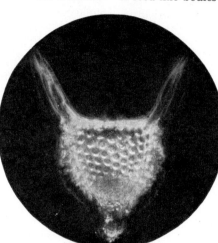
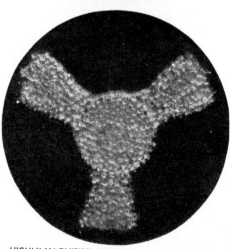

HIGHLY-MAGNIFIED PICTURES OF RADIOLARIA, SHOWING THE DELICACY OF THEIR STRUCTURE

bark, as the brain has. The Trypanosomes are in this company.

Let us take the Sporozoa. These are protozoa occurring always as parasites of other living organisms, and without means of locomotion or of taking food into their stomachs or other digestive apparatus. Reproduction takes place by the formation of seed-like bodies or spores, within which are one or two minute germs. Spore, from the Greek sporos, means a seed, and was at first applied by botanists to its appearance in ferns, but they are not true seeds ; but each is merely a single cell in a protective covering. But this single cell encloses a sporozoite, which escapes and, finding a new host, begins to act there with all the vigour of a commando. It absorbs its nutriment through its skin, and may increase its numbers very rapidly.

The Sporozoa are a very extensive group, and a vast miscellaneous assemblage of forms that have little in common except the parasitic habit and the ability to perpetuate the race by spores. The most deadly of the spores or sporozoites are those which become parasites of the blood corpuscles, red or white, and destroy them. They penetrate and destroy the corpuscles of fish, amphibia, and reptiles ; occurring among any vertebrate or backboned animals, preferably cold-blooded ones, but not sparing mammals. The intermediate hosts among the mammals are insects which are porters or carriers of the sporozoites; mosquitoes, flies, ticks, and leeches. Respect for these parasites falls to its lowest in considering the

Haemosporidia, the blood-corpuscle devourers.

Of the other main classes, the Sarcodina and Mastigophora are the primitives, comprising the main stock from which the others have been evolved. They are descended from an ancestral type common to both but lost in the abyss of time, and since modified in two divergent directions. The Sarcodina types are those which grow to a large size, many visible to the naked eye. As adults, the permanent organs are wanting and the naked body moves and captures food by thick limbs pushed out from it. The young may be amoeba-like and have thread-like extensions like flagella.

FLAGELLA WHICH STICK OUT LIKE PINS IN A PINCUSHION

The Mastigophora are usually of very small size, and their flagella remain with them while they live. Their bodies are of the amoeba type. They are the pygmies of the Protozoa, but though so minute they are lavishly equipped with flagella. Some, it is true, may have only one flagellum, but in others they abound.

Last but one of the classifications are the Infusoria. They are fallen from the high estate which they occupied after Leeuwenhoek first espied them, when they had a realm as wide as that of all the Protozoa together, and were simply " animalculae." Now, just as the word " insect " is applied only to the six-legged kind, so the term infusoria has become narrowed to denote only the Infusoria Ciliata, and Suctoria.

The Ciliata are the most abundant and familiar of microscopic forms of life, and in one sense the highest of the Protozoa, since in no other has the body so elaborate a structure, and one so adapted to all the functions of life. The cilia, the slender thread-like protrusions from the body, form a sort of furry covering, though some may be developed to serve, like flagella, for food capture or locomotion. In the sub-class of Suctoria the sedentary adults have no cilia, though in their youth they may be swimmers. The Paramecium is included in the Ciliata.

TINY FORMS WHICH WERE BEYOND THE POWERS OF MICROSCOPES

Changes in the interpretation of these classes are continually made and must be, seeing that the material is on the way to infinity. The Chlamydozoa, which was the last to be admitted as a class by itself

in the earlier years of this century, are now in danger of being displaced altogether. The Chlamydozoa, from the Greek " chlamys," a scarf, were so exceedingly small as either to be microscopic or beyond the powers of the microscope; and though the electron microscope may now reveal them, their structure remains a matter for speculation. It was first proposed to include them among the Protozoa because, as parasites, they were believed to be the causes of certain diseases not produced by visible germs. Among such diseases were vaccinia, trachoma, and others in human beings, and diphtheria in birds ; and other diseases afterwards added to the list were hydrophobia, scarlet fever, measles, foot and mouth disease in domestic animals, and a disease of silk-worms.

These diseases will be recognised as those now attributed to viruses. The Chlamydozoa were in those days the first to be named as " filter passers," because they passed through the porcelain filters used in laboratories to filter visible disease germs; and attention was more closely focused on them because they were producers of disease, and no means of preventing them was to be found. That is roughly true of the virus as it is now known and as it remains to be better known. But the parasitic habit which is common to the Chlamydozoa of yesterday and the virus of today establishes a link, and possibly a clue to what the disease poison is and how it acts.

IN ITS DEATH AS IN ITS LIFE THE PARASITE ADDS TO HUMAN KNOWLEDGE

Partly because of the minute size of the virus, measured in millionths of an inch, it became doubted whether it were a living thing at all or whether it was, especially where it produced disease in plants, only a chemical molecule. The conflict is still maintained, but a suggestion made by the foremost defender of the virus as a living entity, is that the parasite, however it may be classed, is one that so degenerated by living on some other living thing that it became so nearly the complete parasite that it could exist in no other way. The body of the parasite shrank in millions of years almost to extinction, but its evil purpose remained. So in its death as in its life, the parasite adds to human knowledge, and that is something attempted, something done by the simplest living thing.

The Story of the Things We See About Us Every Day

NATIONAL FLAGS AND EMBLEMS

STRANGE are the ways of man. In the day of extreme national peril, the thing he prizes most is not his gold, his goods, his land, or his life, but a piece of cloth fluttering from a pole. It is worth a few shillings at most, but millions of men would rather perish than lose it. It is their flag, their national symbol.

In these pages we give in full colour the flags of the nations of the World.

Standards and ensigns, often with flag-like streamers, were used by the ancient peoples of the East, and are referred to in the Bible. But the Red Dragon of Wales is perhaps the oldest surviving standard in the western world. The Romans adopted it from the Parthians, and used it as the ensign of their foreign auxiliaries. The Roman warriors brought it to Britain, and after they left it was often carried into battle to oppose the White Horse of the Saxons.

Of all national flags, the Union Flag is to us the most interesting, and its history is written on its face. Its very name is interesting, for the word Union commemorates the Union of the Crowns of England and Scotland. The Union Flag is popularly called the Union Jack, but strictly the term Jack can only be applied to the small Union Flag flown at the bow of a ship. It is made up of the English flag of St. George, the Scottish flag of St. Andrew, and the Irish flag of St. Patrick.

St. George, who lived about 300 years after Christ, was a heroic soldier who gave up his life rather than deny his faith at the bidding of a Roman emperor. When the red cross of St. George became the English flag is not known, but it was certainly used in Edward the First's time.

St. Andrew was one of the twelve Apostles and was crucified on a cross. Some relics of the Apostle are supposed to have been carried to Scotland, and the white cross of St. Andrew on a blue ground long ago became the national flag of Scotland.

St. Patrick was carried to Ireland as a slave at the beginning of the fifth century. He founded schools and monasteries, and died there a very old man. Many centuries afterward the cross of St. Patrick became the Irish national flag.

The three flags became one by the union of the three countries. In the year 1603 the crowns of England and Scotland were united, and so in 1606 the cross of St. Andrew was added to the cross of St. George as the first Union flag of Great Britain. At the beginning of last century the cross of St. Patrick was added to the Union flag, after the Parliament of Ireland had been united with that of Great Britain.

When we see this flag flying, at home on our public buildings, or at sea on our ships, or in foreign countries at the British embassies, or in far-off parts of the Earth, we

INDUSTRIES · HOW THINGS ARE MADE · WHERE THEY COME FROM

should remember what it means. It is not a flag of war, or of boasting; it stands particularly for the memory of three good and brave men, and it stands generally for us all as a sign that we love freedom, justice, and peace.

HOW THE RED AND WHITE CROSSES CAME TO BE UNITED

The flag has had a curious history as a national banner. The original English flag was white and bore the plain red cross of St. George. Such flags originated on land, but it was at sea that they became significant. To fly the national flag at the mast head was an act of defiance, to lower it was evidence of submission, and to hoist a false flag was dishonourable.

Scotland had then as its own ensign the banner of St. Andrew. Tradition says that when the Picts and Scots were hard pressed by the Saxons they prayed to St. Andrew for help, and, seeing in the blue sky a white cross formed by the clouds, they took this as an answer of victory, they rushed into battle and defeated their foes. After the victory they adopted the St. Andrew's cross as their emblem.

When James Stuart came from Scotland to the English throne, a curious difficulty arose. What flag was to be used on the king's ships, common to both countries? English sailors objected to St. Andrew's flag and Scots to St. George's.

THE FIRST STEP IN THE MAKING OF THE UNION FLAG

It was decided, therefore, to join the red cross and the white, and this was known as the " Union Flagge," and was to be flown on the main-top. But it was not to supersede the older national emblems, for the proclamation went on to say that " in their fore-toppe all subjects of South Britaine shall weare the Red Crosse onely, as they were wont, and our subjects of North Britaine in their fore-toppe the White Crosse onely."

The Admirals of the Navy, however, soon began to object to merchant ships using the Union flag, their argument being that foreign vessels were never sure which was a king's ship and so might fail to salute. Another proclamation was therefore issued in the time of Charles the First ordering that only naval vessels should fly the Union flag, and that English merchant ships should fly St. George's cross, and Scottish merchant vessels St. Andrew's cross as of old.

After Charles had lost his throne, however, the Union flag was discarded in favour of St. George's. Cromwell did not recognise Scotland, because the Scottish peoples had sided with the Stuarts. But when Charles the Second came back, the people began to use the Union flag, and a proclamation was necessary to remind them that this was the king's jack, not to be used by unauthorised persons. The proclamation seems to have had little effect, however, for the Union flag was still much used, and at last, when the Parliaments of England and Scotland were united in 1707, a new Union Flag was designed to supersede the old flags.

This flag was one of the greatest in the world, for it was under it that the British built up their mighty Empire.

It was the flag raised at Plassey when Clive won India; it flew in Nova Scotia and Newfoundland when the French fleur-de-lys was lowered. Under it Wolfe won Quebec, and Nelson the Battle of the Nile.

THE ENSIGN THAT GOES ROUND THE WORLD ON OUR MERCHANT SHIPS

In addition to the Union Jack there are various British ensigns. The Red Ensign is a red flag with a Union Jack in the upper corner, and this is used as a national emblem by all British merchant ships. The White Ensign is a white flag with the St. George's cross, and the Union Jack in the upper corner. This is used at sea only by the Royal Navy or by the Royal Yacht Squadron. The Blue Ensign is a blue flag with the Union Jack in the upper corner, and is used only by ships of the Royal Naval Reserve, merchantmen commanded by officers of the Reserve, and certain yacht clubs.

The British Royal Standard, the flag of the monarch, has undergone many changes. Its heraldry is described on page 4983.

The flag of the United States, though so much more recent than the Union Jack, has an interesting history. When the Colonies resisted the Mother Country, it became necessary to have a flag under which to fight, should fighting be necessary. But the Americans did not want to break away from England if they could get fair treatment, and they designed a flag called the Grand Union, with thirteen stripes of white and red; and in the upper corner they placed the Union Jack.

The arms of Washington's ancestors in England had been made up of stars and stripes, and later the Union Jack was removed from the top corner and in its place was put, on a blue background, a circle with thirteen stars representing the thirteen original colonies or States.

Later still the flag was changed again, and on the blue background the stars were arranged in rows, a new star being added for every new State admitted to the Union.

The thirteen stripes still remain to represent the original States, but in the Stars and Stripes there are now forty-eight stars to correspond with the forty-eight States comprising the Union.

Curiously enough, in the upper corner of the Hawaiian flag the Americans still retain the Union Jack, which thus has the rare distinction of flying over a foreign land.

FLAGS & EMBLEMS OF THE BRITISH COMMONWEALTH

We give below notes on the significance of the design on the flags of the British Commonwealth, except where the meaning is obvious.

EUROPE

GREAT BRITAIN AND NORTHERN IRELAND. The Union Jack is made up of the three crosses of St. George of England, St. Andrew of Scotland, and of the Irish Geraldines, commonly called the cross of St. Patrick.

CHANNEL ISLANDS. Three lions form the emblem of Jersey and Guernsey, as they formed the Royal Arms of England 700 years ago. Alderney has one lion.

ISLE OF MAN. Three armour-clad legs. An ancient emblem of the Manx people, who borrowed it from the arms of Sicily.

GIBRALTAR. A fortress with arched gateway, under which is a key, standing for the key of the Mediterranean Sea.

MALTA. A half-red, half-white shield of the old knights of Malta, and a George Cross.

AMERICA

DOMINION OF CANADA. A shield with the arms of England, Scotland, and Ireland, with the lilies of France, and below a sprig of maple.

QUEBEC. The three fleurs-de-lis are part of the old flag of France, and are a relic of the days when Quebec was under French sovereignty.

NEW BRUNSWICK. The vessel is a "lymphad," or ancient galley, and represents the important fisheries of the province.

NOVA SCOTIA. The name means New Scotland, and its origin is represented by the St. Andrew's Cross in reverse—blue on white—and the Royal Arms of Scotland on the shield.

PRINCE EDWARD ISLAND. Although the maple is the national emblem of Canada it is the oak which is shown on the small island. The motto "Parva sub ingent" means "Small but great," and is a reference to the

island being the smallest of the Canadian provinces.

NEWFOUNDLAND. Symbolical figures with the words "Terra Nova," meaning New Land, and "Haec tibi dona fero," meaning "I bring these gifts to thee."

BERMUDAS. A red lion holding a shield, with an old ship in a rough sea off a rock-bound coast.

BAHAMAS. The inscription on the garter reads "Commercia expulsis piratus restituta," meaning "Commerce restored by the defeat of pirates."

BRITISH HONDURAS. The set of woodcutter's tools refer to the colony's mahogany industry.

ST. LUCIA. Roses and heraldic lilies, with crossed sugar-canes.

FALKLAND ISLANDS. The ship represents the Desire, in which Captain John Davis discovered the islands in 1592.

AFRICA

UNION OF SOUTH AFRICA. With representations of the Union Jack, the old Orange Free State flag, and the old Transvaal Vierkleur.

GHANA. Red for those who worked for independence; gold for the country's wealth; green for forests and farms. The black star represents the lodestar of African freedom.

RHODESIA-NYASALAND FEDERATION. Sun represents Nyasaland; wavy lines, suggesting the Victoria Falls, are from Northern Rhodesia's arms. Those of Southern Rhodesia have a lion (included in Federation arms) and thistles from the arms of the Rhodes family; the pick represents gold-mining.

GAMBIA. Representing the valuable ivory and palm-oil.

UGANDA. The bird is the African Balearic Crane.

SOMALILAND. The head is of a kudu, a beautiful antelope.

MAURITIUS. The supporters of the shield are the extinct dodo and a sambur deer. Each supports a sugar cane.

ASIA

INDIA. Blue wheel represents the Chakra of Asoka, a Buddhist ruler of the third century B.C.

PAKISTAN. The crescent and star is the traditional emblem of Mohammedanism. The broad white stripe at the hoist refers to those of other religions.

CEYLON. This republic uses a royal flag, that of the last King of Kandy.

FEDERATION OF MALAYA. The 11 stripes and the 11-pointed star represent the nine States (Johore, Kedah, Kelantan, Negri Sembilan, Pahang, Perlis, Perak, Selangor, and Trengganu) and the two Settlements (Malacca and Penang) which form the Federation.

AUSTRALASIA

COMMONWEALTH ENSIGN. The large seven-pointed star of the union (six points representing the six States and the seventh the Commonwealth of Australia) with the star group known as the Southern Cross.

QUEENSLAND. A blue Maltese cross, with the British crown.

NEW SOUTH WALES. St. George's Cross, with a star on each arm, and a lion.

VICTORIA. The white stars of the Southern Cross on a blue sky, with the British crown.

SOUTH AUSTRALIA. A handsome heraldic bird, representing the white-backed piping shrike.

WESTERN AUSTRALIA. The black swan found in this country.

DOMINION OF NEW ZEALAND. The stars making up the Southern Cross.

GILBERT AND ELLICE ISLANDS. The frigate bird is represented.

FLAGS OF THE UNITED STATES OF AMERICA

We give below notes on the State flags and arms of America, except where the meaning of the flag is obvious from the picture. The number of stars usually indicates the order in which the State joined the Union.

ALASKA. The stars form the constellation of the Great Bear.

ALABAMA. A St. Patrick's Cross, the national flag of the Confederacy between 1863 and 1865.

CALIFORNIA. The famous bear flag of the American settlers who revolted against Mexico.

COLORADO. The red C is the initial of the name of the State, and the golden disc is the Sun.

CONNECTICUT. The three grape vines represent the three original colonies of the State.

DELAWARE. A sheaf of wheat and an ear of corn with an ox below, a ship in full sail for crest, and a husbandman and rifleman.

DISTRICT OF COLUMBIA. The three stars are taken from the arms of George Washington.

FLORIDA. An Indian woman scattering flowers, with the Sun's rays and a highland, a coconut tree, and a steamboat.

GEORGIA. An arch labelled Constitution is upheld by three pillars of Government. Under the arch is an armed defender.

IDAHO. The circle enclosing a shield shows the Snake River with mountains. The supporters are a miner with pick and shovel, and a woman with scales and torch of Liberty.

ILLINOIS. The scroll in the beak bears the motto, "State Sovereignty—National Union."

INDIANA. The 13 outer stars represent the original 13 states of the Union; the other 5 stars represent the 5 States admitted to the Union before Indiana.

IOWA. A flying eagle with the motto, "Our liberties we prize and our rights we will maintain."

KANSAS. A prairie with buffalo pursued by Indians, a cabin, a river with a steamboat.

KENTUCKY. Two men shaking hands, in a circle with the motto, "United we stand, divided we fall."

LOUISIANA. A pelican protecting her nest and feeding her young; with the motto, "Union, Justice, and Confidence."

MAINE. A shield with a pine tree and a moose lying at its foot, and the motto "I direct."

MARYLAND. The escutcheon of Lord Baltimore, to whom a patent was issued in 1632 to found a colony there.

MASSACHUSETTS. An Indian holding a bow and arrow, and in the upper corner a silver star. The crest is a wreath with a hand and sword.

MICHIGAN. A shield bearing a hunter, with the rising sun, supported by an elk and a moose.

MINNESOTA. The Falls of St. Anthony in the background, a pioneer ploughing, an Indian fleeing toward the setting sun, the whole surrounded by a scroll.

MISSISSIPPI. The Confederate battle flag with blue, white, and red stripes.

MISSOURI. A grizzly bear, a crescent, and the arms of U.S.A., with a helmet supporting a cloud for a crest, and two bears.

MONTANA. The sun setting behind the mountains, and a plough, pick, and spade.

NEBRASKA. A steamboat ascending the Missouri River, a smith, a settler's cabin and wheat sheaves, and a train.

NEVADA. A star with two sprigs of sagebrush below, and above a scroll with the motto "Battle born."

NEW HAMPSHIRE. A rising sun with a ship on the stocks, and the American flag flying.

NEW JERSEY. Three ploughs on a shield with figures of Liberty and Prosperity. The horse is suggestive of stock-raising.

NEW MEXICO. The ancient Zia Sun symbol in red on the yellow of old Spain.

NEW YORK. Vessels in the Hudson River, with a rising sun at the back and the eagle on a globe, with Liberty and Justice.

NORTH CAROLINA. Scrolls giving the date of independence, and of victory over the English.

NORTH DAKOTA. The original of this flag is believed to have been that of the territorial militia and was first flown in South Dakota.

OHIO. The O is the initial of the name of the State. The red disc inside represents the Sun.

OKLAHOMA. A Red Indian rawhide shield with pendant feathers, a pipe of peace, and an olive branch.

OREGON. A landscape with an emigrant wagon and a deer,

and at the back the sea with a steamship and a brig. Below is a scroll with the words "The Union," and a plough, rake, and pick.

PENNSYLVANIA. A ship in full sail, two ploughs, and sheaves of wheat, a bald eagle, and two harnessed horses.

RHODE ISLAND. A gold anchor and a blue ribbon with the motto "Hope," and 13 golden stars in a circle, representing the original 13 States of the Union.

SOUTH CAROLINA. A white palmetto typical of the State.

TENNESSEE. This was the 16th State to be admitted to the Union, but the three stars denote that it was the third to join after the original 13 States.

TEXAS. A single white star commemorates the name of The Lone Star State, the pet name of the old republic of Texas.

UTAH. A beehive suggesting industry, and sego lilies, which are common in the State.

VERMONT. A green landscape with a red cow, yellow sheaves, and a tall pine. At the back are the mountains of the State.

VIRGINIA. Virtus, the genius of the Commonwealth, dressed as an Amazon, treading on Tyranny. This design is as old as the Independence, for it was adopted only one day after the Declaration.

WASHINGTON. On the green field is Washington's portrait.

WEST VIRGINIA. An ivy-clad rock, the date of the State's foundation, a farmer with plough and axe, a miner with his pick. Below are two rifles crossed and a cap of Liberty.

WISCONSIN. A shield supported by a sailor and miner, containing the U.S.A. arms in a scroll, an anchor, a workman's hand with a hammer, a spade and pickaxe crossed, and a plough.

HAWAII. The Union Jack in the corner is a relic of the first flag of the United States, and is the only flag now flying over United States soil which retains the British emblem.

PANAMA CANAL. The shield shows 13 red and white stripes and a Spanish galleon in full sail. The motto on the scroll is "The land divided, the world united."

1000 FLAGS OF THE WORLD
BRITISH COMMONWEALTH & EMPIRE

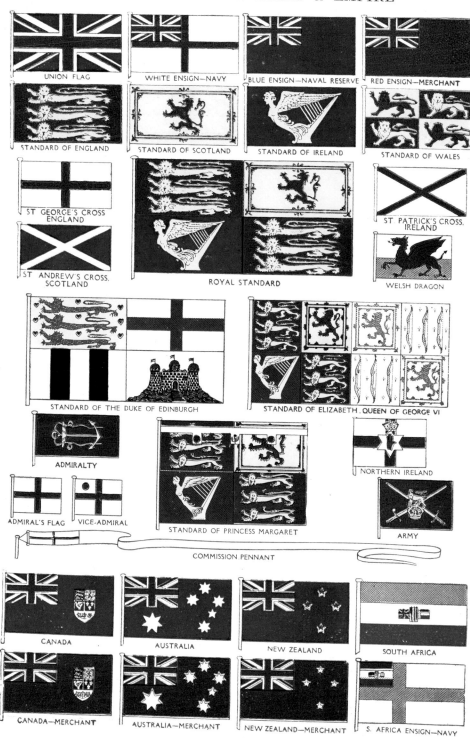

UNION FLAG

WHITE ENSIGN—NAVY

BLUE ENSIGN—NAVAL RESERVE

RED ENSIGN—MERCHANT

STANDARD OF ENGLAND

STANDARD OF SCOTLAND

STANDARD OF IRELAND

STANDARD OF WALES

ST GEORGE'S CROSS ENGLAND

ST PATRICK'S CROSS, IRELAND

ST ANDREW'S CROSS, SCOTLAND

ROYAL STANDARD

WELSH DRAGON

STANDARD OF THE DUKE OF EDINBURGH

STANDARD OF ELIZABETH, QUEEN OF GEORGE VI

ADMIRALTY

NORTHERN IRELAND

ADMIRAL'S FLAG

VICE-ADMIRAL

STANDARD OF PRINCESS MARGARET

ARMY

COMMISSION PENNANT

CANADA

AUSTRALIA

NEW ZEALAND

SOUTH AFRICA

CANADA—MERCHANT

AUSTRALIA—MERCHANT

NEW ZEALAND—MERCHANT

S. AFRICA ENSIGN—NAVY

28 L 10

GOVERNOR OF NORTHERN IRELAND   LORDS LIEUTENANT OF COUNTIES   DIPLOMATIC OFFICIALS   ARMY COUNCIL

CONSULS ASHORE   CONSULS AFLOAT   GENERAL OFFICERS AFLOAT   OTHER RANKS AFLOAT

NAVAL ORDNANCE   WAR OFFICE ORDNANCE   ADMIRALTY VESSELS   WAR OFFICE ENGINEERS

CUSTOMS   BOARD OF TRADE   POST OFFICE   FISHERY RESEARCH

FISHERIES BOARD, SCOTLAND   COMMISSIONERS OF NORTHERN LIGHTHOUSES   NORTHERN LIGHTHOUSE FLAG   COMMISSIONERS OF IRISH LIGHTS

CINQUE PORTS   QUEEN'S HARBOURMASTER   PACIFIC CABLE BOARD   LLOYD'S SIGNAL STATIONS

ROYAL MAIL   CUSTOMS COMMISSIONERS   PORT OF LONDON AUTHORITY   NORTH SEA FISHERIES GUARD   LLOYD'S BURGEE

CITY OF LONDON   LONDON COUNTY COUNCIL   THAMES CONSERVANCY   HUMBER CONSERVANCY   MERSEY DOCKS BOARD

ISLE OF MAN   JERSEY   GUERNSEY   POSITION OF BADGE   ALDERNEY   GIBRALTAR   MALTA, G.C.

PILOT FLAG

TRINITY HOUSE— ENSIGN   BRITISH BROADCASTING CORPORATION   TRINITY HOUSE— MASTER'S FLAG

ONTARIO QUEBEC NOVA SCOTIA NEW BRUNSWICK

GOVERNOR-GENERAL OF CANADA

MANITOBA BRITISH COLUMBIA PRINCE EDWARD ISLAND ALBERTA

SASKAT-CHEWAN JAMAICA ST. LUCIA

GOVERNOR-GENERAL OF CANADA

ST. VINCENT GRENADA BERMUDAS

BARBADOS BRITISH GUIANA BAHAMAS NEWFOUNDLAND WINDWARD ISLANDS BRITISH HONDURAS LEEWARD ISLANDS

TRINIDAD & TOBAGO FIJI FALKLAND ISLANDS COMMISSIONER, NEW HEBRIDES SOLOMON ISLANDS TURKS & CAICOS ISLANDS PAPUA

GOVERNOR-GENERAL OF AUSTRALIA WESTERN PACIFIC, HIGH COMMISSIONER SOMBRERO & BAHAMA LIGHTS GILBERT AND ELLICE ISLANDS GOVERNOR-GENERAL OF NEW ZEALAND

VICTORIA NEW SOUTH WALES SOUTH AUSTRALIA QUEENSLAND WESTERN AUSTRALIA TASMANIA BRITISH NORTH BORNEO

TONGA—STANDARD TONGA—ENSIGN TONGA—CUSTOMS RARATONGA SARAWAK BRITISH N. BORNEO NATIVE CHIEFS

SINGAPORE LABUAN CEYLON SEYCHELLES MAURITIUS CYPRUS

BRUNEI FEDERATION OF MALAYA KEDAH PERAK PAHANG SELANGOR

JOHORE SULTAN OF JOHORE NEGRI SEMBILAN AUSTRALIAN NAVAL BOARD KELANTAN PERLIS TRENGGANU

RHODESIA-NYASALAND FEDERATION

GHANA

KENYA COLONY

ZANZIBAR BRITISH RESIDENT

GAMBIA

NORTHERN RHODESIA

SOMALILAND

SOUTHERN RHODESIA

HIGH COMMISSIONER SOUTH AFRICA

S.A.H.C.

KENYA

TANGANYIKA

SIERRA LEONE

NIGERIA

NYASALAND

ADEN

UGANDA

ST. HELENA

BRITISH CIVIL AIR ENSIGN

EDINBURGH

DUBLIN

BELFAST

R.A.F. ENSIGN

INDIA

WESTMINSTER ABBEY

PAKISTAN

BRITISH HISTORICAL FLAGS

ROYAL STANDARDS

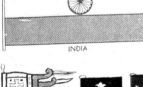

GONFANON AND RELIGIOUS FLAG OF WILLIAM I 1066

EDWARD CONFESSOR (POSTHUMOUS)

RICHARD I, 1189

RICHARD I, 1194

ST. GEORGE, RICHARD I, 1194

ST. ANDREW ANCIENT SCOTTISH

EDWARD III TO HENRY IV, 1340-1405

HENRY IV TO ELIZABETH 1405-1603

DOUGLAS STANDARD, CHEVY CHASE, 1388

A STANDARD OF HENRY VII

1st SQUADRON   2nd SQUADRON   3rd SQUADRON   4th SQUADRON
FLAGS OF VICE-ADMIRALS AT THE BATTLE OF CADIZ, 1596

ENSIGN, JAMES I 1615

STANDARD OF THE STUART KINGS

LONDON TRAINED BANDS, 1643—BLUE, GREEN, & YELLOW REGIMENTS

COMMONWEALTH 1653

ADMIRAL 1653

COMMONWEALTH ENSIGN

CROMWELL'S GREAT UNION

IRISH ENSIGN, 1686

UNION JACK OF ANNE, 1707

FOR THE PROTESTANT RELIGION AND THE LIBERTY OF ENGLAND

JE MAINTIENDRAY

WILLIAM III (ON LANDING) 1688

FLAGS OF THE UNITED STATES OF AMERICA

NATIONAL FLAG & ENSIGN

FLAG OF THE PRESIDENT

SECRETARY OF THE ARMY

SECRETARY OF THE TREASURY

ASSISTANT SEC-RETARY, TREASURY

SECRETARY OF STATE

SECRETARY OF COMMERCE

ADMIRAL SENIOR

ADMIRAL JUNIOR

VICE-ADMIRAL

JACK

REAR-ADMIRAL

COMMODORE

SENIOR OFFICER

NAVAL ARTIL-LERY ASHORE

NAVAL INFANTRY ASHORE

NAVAL MILITIA

LIEUT. GENERAL

MAJOR-GENERAL

BRIGADIER GENERAL

CONSULS

CAVALRY STANDARD

FIELD ARTILLERY STANDARD

MOUNTED ENGINEERS' STANDARD

SIGNAL CORPS STANDARD

CHIEF OF STAFF COLOURS

INFANTRY COLOURS

COAST ARTILLERY COLOURS

ENGINEERS COLOURS

TRANSPORT SERVICE

SUBMARINE DEFENCE

NAVAL RESERVE

ORDNANCE VESSELS

ENGINEER VESSELS

ASSISTANT SEC-RETARY, NAVY

ASSISTANT SEC-RETARY, COMMERCE

MARINE CORPS

MAJOR-GENERAL MARINES

BRIGADIER-GENERAL MARINES

ARTILLERY DISTRICT COMMANDER

COMMISSIONER OF NAVIGATION

BUREAU OF NAVIGATION

COMMISSIONER OF FISHERIES

BUREAU OF FISHERIES

COMMISSIONER OF LIGHTHOUSES

BUREAU OF LIGHTHOUSES

PUBLIC HEALTH SERVICE

SURGEON-GENERAL PUBLIC HEALTH

COAST-GUARD

COAST-GUARD JACK

COAST-GUARD ANCHORAGE

POWER SQUADRONS

CUSTOMS

SUPERINTENDENT COAST SURVEY

COMMODORE NAVAL MILITIA

COAST SURVEY

YACHT ENSIGN

DELAWARE   PENNSYLVANIA   NEW JERSEY   GEORGIA

CONNECTICUT   MASSACHUSETTS   MARYLAND   SOUTH CAROLINA

NEW HAMPSHIRE   VIRGINIA   NEW YORK   NORTH CAROLINA

RHODE ISLAND   VERMONT   KENTUCKY   TENNESSEE

OHIO   LOUISIANA   INDIANA   MISSISSIPPI

ILLINOIS   ALABAMA   MAINE   MISSOURI

ARKANSAS   MICHIGAN   FLORIDA   TEXAS

IOWA   WISCONSIN   CALIFORNIA   MINNESOTA

OREGON

KANSAS

WEST VIRGINIA

NEVADA

NEBRASKA

COLORADO

NORTH DAKOTA

SOUTH DAKOTA

MONTANA

WASHINGTON

IDAHO

WYOMING

UTAH

OKLAHOMA

NEW MEXICO

ARIZONA

DISTRICT OF COLUMBIA

HAWAII

ALASKA

GOVERNOR OF PANAMA CANAL ZONE

SECRETARY OF THE INTERIOR

HISTORICAL FLAGS OF THE UNITED STATES

HUDSON'S FLAG, 1609

DUTCH WEST INDIA COMPANY, 1650

BUNKER HILL 1775

ENSIGN WASHINGTON'S CRUISERS, 1775

LIBERTY TREE 1776

FIRST NAVY ENSIGN, 1775

MERCHANT ENSIGN, 1776

FIRST "STARS & STRIPES," 1777

"STAR-SPANGLED BANNER," 1795

NATIONAL FLAG, 1818

U.S. NATIONAL FLAG CIVIL WAR

U.S. INFANTRY REGIMENTAL CIVIL WAR

U.S. ARTILLERY NATIONAL—CIVIL WAR

CONFEDERATE "STARS & BARS," 1861

CONFEDERATE JACK, 1861

CONFEDERATE NAVAL ENSIGN 1862

CONFEDERATE BATTLE FLAG 1861, & NAVY JACK, 1863

CONFEDERATE BATTLE FLAG 1863

CONFEDERATE NATIONAL FLAG, 1863

CONFEDERATE NATIONAL FLAG, 1865

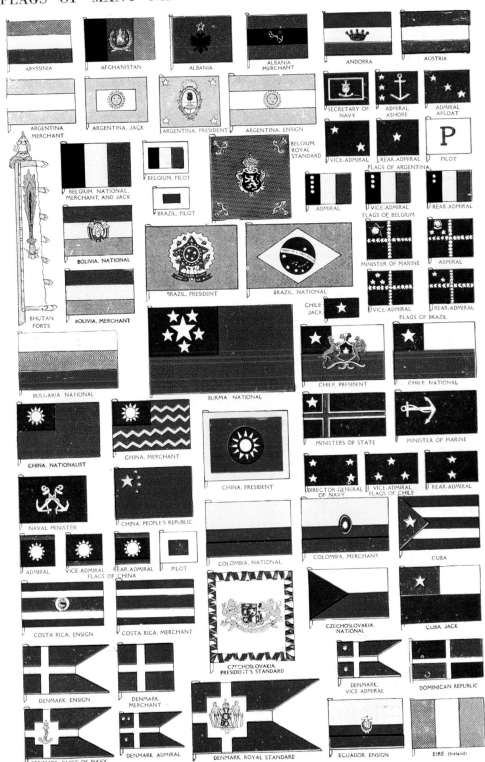

ABYSSINIA

AFGHANISTAN

ALBANIA

ALBANIA MERCHANT

ANDORRA

AUSTRIA

ARGENTINA, MERCHANT

ARGENTINA, JACK

ARGENTINA, PRESIDENT

ARGENTINA, ENSIGN

SECRETARY OF NAVY

ADMIRAL ASHORE

ADMIRAL AFLOAT

VICE-ADMIRAL

REAR-ADMIRAL

PILOT

FLAGS OF ARGENTINA

BELGIUM ROYAL STANDARD

BELGIUM, PILOT

BELGIUM NATIONAL, MERCHANT, AND JACK

BRAZIL, PILOT

ADMIRAL

VICE-ADMIRAL

REAR-ADMIRAL

FLAGS OF BELGIUM

BOLIVIA, NATIONAL

BOLIVIA, MERCHANT

BHUTAN FORTS

BRAZIL, PRESIDENT

BRAZIL, NATIONAL

MINISTER OF MARINE

ADMIRAL

CHILE JACK

VICE-ADMIRAL

REAR-ADMIRAL

FLAGS OF BRAZIL

BULGARIA NATIONAL

BURMA NATIONAL

CHILE, PRESIDENT

CHILE, NATIONAL

CHINA, NATIONALIST

CHINA, MERCHANT

CHINA, PRESIDENT

MINISTERS OF STATE

MINISTER OF MARINE

NAVAL MINISTER

CHINA, PEOPLE'S REPUBLIC

DIRECTOR-GENERAL OF NAVY

VICE-ADMIRAL

REAR-ADMIRAL

FLAGS OF CHILE

ADMIRAL

VICE-ADMIRAL

REAR-ADMIRAL

PILOT

FLAGS OF CHINA

COLOMBIA, NATIONAL

COLOMBIA, MERCHANT

CUBA

COSTA RICA, ENSIGN

COSTA RICA, MERCHANT

CZECHOSLOVAKIA, NATIONAL

CUBA, JACK

DENMARK ENSIGN

DENMARK, MERCHANT

CZECHOSLOVAKIA, PRESIDENT'S STANDARD

DENMARK, VICE-ADMIRAL

DOMINICAN REPUBLIC

DENMARK, CHIEF OF NAVY

DENMARK ADMIRAL

DENMARK, ROYAL STANDARD

ECUADOR, ENSIGN

EIRE (Ireland)

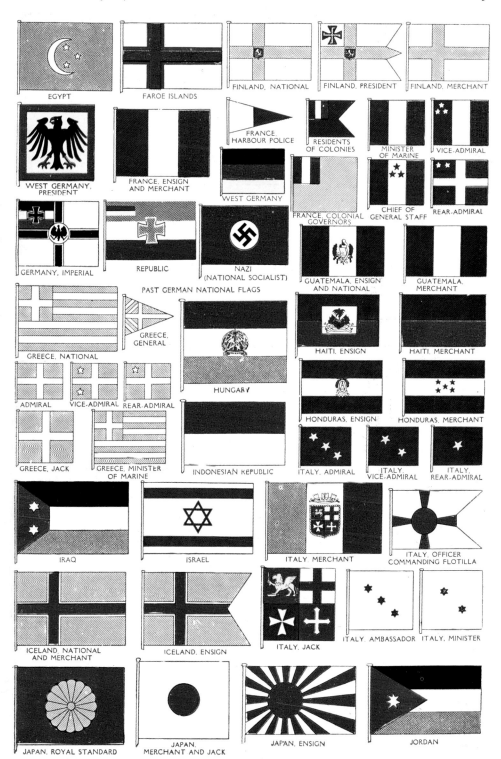

EGYPT

FAROE ISLANDS

FINLAND, NATIONAL

FINLAND, PRESIDENT

FINLAND, MERCHANT

WEST GERMANY, PRESIDENT

FRANCE, ENSIGN AND MERCHANT

FRANCE, HARBOUR POLICE

RESIDENTS OF COLONIES

MINISTER OF MARINE

VICE-ADMIRAL

WEST GERMANY

FRANCE, COLONIAL GOVERNORS

CHIEF OF GENERAL STAFF

REAR-ADMIRAL

GERMANY, IMPERIAL

REPUBLIC

NAZI (NATIONAL SOCIALIST)

PAST GERMAN NATIONAL FLAGS

GUATEMALA, ENSIGN AND NATIONAL

GUATEMALA, MERCHANT

GREECE, GENERAL

GREECE, NATIONAL

HUNGARY

HAITI, ENSIGN

HAITI, MERCHANT

ADMIRAL

VICE-ADMIRAL

REAR-ADMIRAL

HONDURAS, ENSIGN

HONDURAS, MERCHANT

GREECE, JACK

GREECE, MINISTER OF MARINE

INDONESIAN REPUBLIC

ITALY, ADMIRAL

ITALY, VICE-ADMIRAL

ITALY, REAR-ADMIRAL

IRAQ

ISRAEL

ITALY, MERCHANT

ITALY, OFFICER COMMANDING FLOTILLA

ICELAND, NATIONAL AND MERCHANT

ICELAND, ENSIGN

ITALY, JACK

ITALY, AMBASSADOR

ITALY, MINISTER

JAPAN, ROYAL STANDARD

JAPAN, MERCHANT AND JACK

JAPAN, ENSIGN

JORDAN

LEBANON

LIBERIA NATIONAL

LIBERIA, PRESIDENT

LIBYA

LIECHTENSTEIN

LUXEMBURG

MEXICO ENSIGN

NETHERLANDS PRINCE

NETHERLANDS, ROYAL STANDARD

NETHERLANDS PRINCESS

MALDIVE ISLANDS

PILOT

MEXICO ADMIRAL

MEXICO REAR-ADMIRAL

NETHERLANDS, ENSIGN AND MERCHANT

ADMIRAL

VICE-ADMIRAL

REAR-ADMIRAL

NETHERLANDS JACK

GOVERNORS OF DUTCH COLONIES

MONACO, PRINCE

NICARAGUA, ENSIGN

NORWAY, ROYAL STANDARD

NORWAY ENSIGN

DISTRICT GOVERNOR, DUTCH EAST INDIES

MONACO, NATIONAL

MOROCCO

SENIOR ADMIRAL

ADMIRAL

NORWAY, MERCHANT

NORWAY COMMANDER-IN-CHIEF COASTAL DEFENCE

NEPAL

PANAMA

PHILIPPINE REPUBLIC

VICE-ADMIRAL NORWAY

MINISTER OF DEFENCE

REAR-ADMIRAL

NORWAY, JACK

NORWAY PILOT

PARAGUAY, ENSIGN

PARAGUAY, VICE-ADMIRAL

PAPAL STATE

NORWAY, G.O.C. DIVISION

PERU, PILOT

POLAND, PRESIDENT

POLAND, NATIONAL

PERSIA

PERSIA, IMPERIAL STANDARD

PERU, MINISTER OF MARINE

VICE-ADMIRAL

PERU ENSIGN AND NATIONAL

PERU MERCHANT

REAR-ADMIRAL OR GENERAL

PORTUGAL, JACK

POLAND, DIPLOMATIC AND MERCHANT

PORTUGAL, PRESIDENT

PORTUGAL, NATIONAL

MINISTER OF MARINE

GOVERNOR OF PROVINCE

GOVERNOR OF OVERSEAS DISTRICT

ADMIRAL

VICE ADMIRAL

REAR-ADMIRAL

POLAND JACK

RUMANIA, ENSIGN

RUMANIA, MERCHANT

SALVADOR

SAN MARINO

SAUDI ARABIA

SIAM, ROYAL STANDARD

SIAM, NATIONAL

SIAM, ENSIGN

MINISTER OF MARINE AND ADMIRALTY

ADMIRAL SIAM

VICE-ADMIRAL

REAR-ADMIRAL

SUDAN

SPAIN PRESIDENT

SWEDEN ROYAL STANDARD

SWEDEN MINISTER OF DEFENCE

SWEDEN, MERCHANT

SWITZERLAND

SPAIN NATIONAL

TIBET

PILOT

ADMIRAL

SYRIA

TUNIS, BEY'S STANDARD

ADMIRAL

SWEDEN, ENSIGN

VICE-ADMIRAL

UNION OF SOVIET SOCIALIST REPUBLICS

TUNIS, ENSIGN AND MERCHANT

TURKEY, ENSIGN AND MERCHANT

TURKEY, PILOT

TURKEY VICE-ADMIRAL

TURKEY MINISTER OF MARINE

URUGUAY ENSIGN AND MERCHANT

VENEZUELA, MERCHANT

NORTH ATLANTIC TREATY ORGANISATION

YEMEN

YUGOSLAVIA

COUNCIL OF EUROPE

UNITED NATIONS ORGANISATION

OLYMPIC GAMES

FLAGS OF THE YACHT CLUBS OF THE WORLD

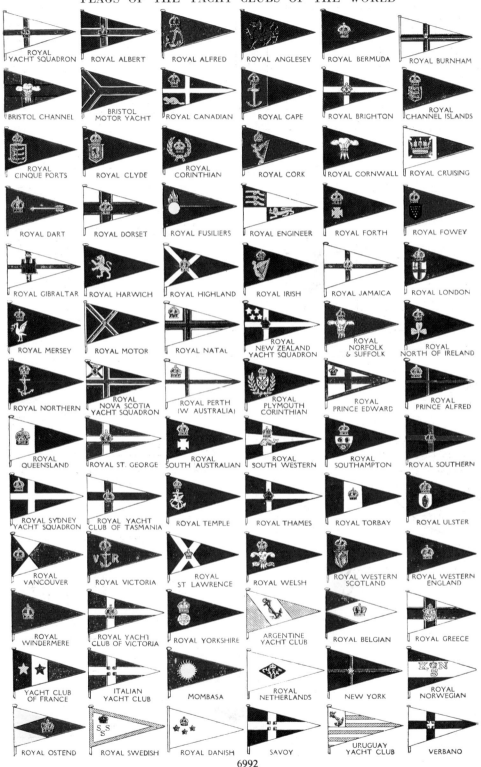

ROYAL YACHT SQUADRON · ROYAL ALBERT · ROYAL ALFRED · ROYAL ANGLESEY · ROYAL BERMUDA · ROYAL BURNHAM

BRISTOL CHANNEL · BRISTOL MOTOR YACHT · ROYAL CANADIAN · ROYAL CAPE · ROYAL BRIGHTON · ROYAL CHANNEL ISLANDS

ROYAL CINQUE PORTS · ROYAL CLYDE · ROYAL CORINTHIAN · ROYAL CORK · ROYAL CORNWALL · ROYAL CRUISING

ROYAL DART · ROYAL DORSET · ROYAL FUSILIERS · ROYAL ENGINEER · ROYAL FORTH · ROYAL FOWEY

ROYAL GIBRALTAR · ROYAL HARWICH · ROYAL HIGHLAND · ROYAL IRISH · ROYAL JAMAICA · ROYAL LONDON

ROYAL MERSEY · ROYAL MOTOR · ROYAL NATAL · ROYAL NEW ZEALAND YACHT SQUADRON · ROYAL NORFOLK & SUFFOLK · ROYAL NORTH OF IRELAND

ROYAL NORTHERN · ROYAL NOVA SCOTIA YACHT SQUADRON · ROYAL PERTH (W AUSTRALIA) · ROYAL PLYMOUTH CORINTHIAN · ROYAL PRINCE EDWARD · ROYAL PRINCE ALFRED

ROYAL QUEENSLAND · ROYAL ST. GEORGE · ROYAL SOUTH AUSTRALIAN · ROYAL SOUTH WESTERN · ROYAL SOUTHAMPTON · ROYAL SOUTHERN

ROYAL SYDNEY YACHT SQUADRON · ROYAL YACHT CLUB OF TASMANIA · ROYAL TEMPLE · ROYAL THAMES · ROYAL TORBAY · ROYAL ULSTER

ROYAL VANCOUVER · ROYAL VICTORIA · ROYAL ST LAWRENCE · ROYAL WELSH · ROYAL WESTERN SCOTLAND · ROYAL WESTERN ENGLAND

ROYAL WINDERMERE · ROYAL YACHT CLUB OF VICTORIA · ROYAL YORKSHIRE · ARGENTINE YACHT CLUB · ROYAL BELGIAN · ROYAL GREECE

YACHT CLUB OF FRANCE · ITALIAN YACHT CLUB · MOMBASA · ROYAL NETHERLANDS · NEW YORK · ROYAL NORWEGIAN

ROYAL OSTEND · ROYAL SWEDISH · ROYAL DANISH · SAVOY · URUGUAY YACHT CLUB · VERBANO

OCEAN FLAGS OF FAMOUS STEAMSHIP LINES

HISTORICAL FLAGS—FOURTEENTH CENTURY

These flags of the world in the middle of the fourteenth century are adapted from a contemporary
manuscript written and illustrated by a Franciscan friar of Spain who had travelled widely.

SEVENTEENTH AND EIGHTEENTH CENTURIES

ENGLISH UNION | SCOTTISH UNION | ENGLAND, ENSIGN ADMIRAL | VICE-ADMIRAL WHITE SQUADRON | REAR-ADMIRAL BLUE SQUADRON | VICE-ADMIRAL OF ENGLAND

REAR-ADMIRAL OF ENGLAND | FLAG OF DEFIANCE | SCOTLAND, ENSIGN | IRELAND, ENSIGN | EAST INDIA COMPANY | GUINEA COMPANY

NEW ENGLAND | HOLLAND, JACK | DOUBLE PRINCE HOLLAND | HOLLAND, ENSIGN | AMSTERDAM | FLUSHING

PETER THE GREAT OF RUSSIA | OSTEND, ENSIGN | OSTEND, WAR FLAG | SPAIN | BISCAY | FRANCE, STANDARD

FRANCE, ENSIGN | FRANCE, GALLEYS | PICARDY | MARSEILLES | DUNKIRK & CALAIS | PROVENCE

HELIGOLAND | HAMBURG | HAMBURG MERCHANT | BREMEN | MIDDLEBURG | ROSTOCK

DANZIG | ZEALAND | SWEDEN, NAVAL | SWEDEN, MERCHANT | LUNEBURG | MALTA

JERUSALEM | DENMARK NAVAL | DENMARK MERCHANT | SEVILLE | GENOA & CORSICA | LEGHORN

VENICE | NAPLES | PAPAL FLAG | PAPAL ADMIRAL | PORTUGAL NAVAL | PORTUGAL MERCHANT

SAVOY | CONSTANTINOPLE | ALGIERS | TRIPOLI | TUNIS | TETUAN

MOCHA | SALLEE | SURAT, GRAND MOGUL | BENGAL, GRAND MOGUL | AMOY, CHINA | TONQUIN

The collection of flags on this page first appeared in an old book printed more than 200 years ago. Colour-printing not having then begun, the colours were indicated by initial letters.

FLAGS OF OTHER DAYS THAT ARE NO LONGER FLOWN

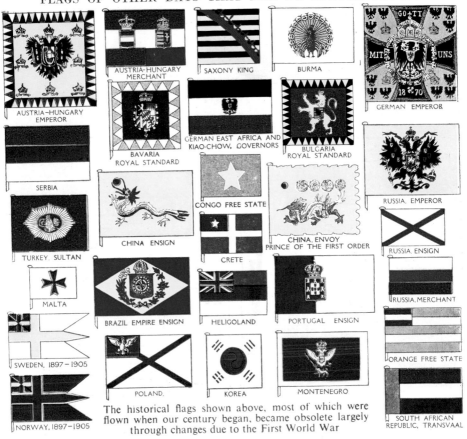

AUSTRIA-HUNGARY MERCHANT

SAXONY KING

BURMA

GERMAN EMPEROR

AUSTRIA-HUNGARY EMPEROR

BAVARIA ROYAL STANDARD

GERMAN EAST AFRICA AND KIAO-CHOW, GOVERNORS

BULGARIA ROYAL STANDARD

SERBIA

CONGO FREE STATE

RUSSIA, EMPEROR

CHINA ENSIGN

CHINA, ENVOY PRINCE OF THE FIRST ORDER

RUSSIA, ENSIGN

TURKEY, SULTAN

CRETE

MALTA

BRAZIL EMPIRE ENSIGN

HELIGOLAND

PORTUGAL ENSIGN

RUSSIA, MERCHANT

SWEDEN, 1897–1905

POLAND.

KOREA

MONTENEGRO

ORANGE FREE STATE

NORWAY, 1897–1905

The historical flags shown above, most of which were flown when our century began, became obsolete largely through changes due to the First World War

SOUTH AFRICAN REPUBLIC, TRANSVAAL

INTERNATIONAL CODE OF SIGNALS

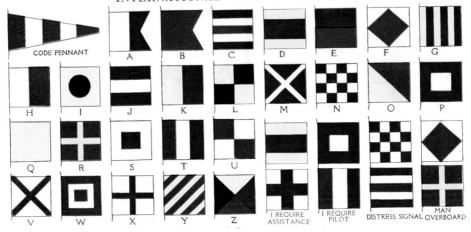

CODE PENNANT

A B C D E F G

H I J K L M N O P

Q R S T U

V W X Y Z

I REQUIRE ASSISTANCE

I REQUIRE PILOT

DISTRESS SIGNAL

MAN OVERBOARD

MARKS ON MILITARY PLANES

UNITED STATES   FRANCE   NETHERLANDS   U.S.S.R   ROYAL AIR FORCE   BELGIUM

Plain Answers to the Questions of the Children of the World

Let the thick curtain fall; I better know than all
How little I have gained, how vast the unattained.

Others shall sing the song, others shall right the wrong,
Finish what I begin, and all I fail of win.

What matter I or they? Mine or another's day,
So the right word be said, and life the sweeter made?

Whittier

MUST ALL THINGS END ?

ALL things do not end. The Preacher wrote long ago that there was no new thing under the Sun, and yet it is very difficult to say what really does end and what does not.

We can think in a moment of a hundred things that do end—such as, say, a piece of string, a stick, a fire that dies out, a river, or a race. These have the sort of ending that we can see with our eyes. We can think in a moment of a hundred things that end *for us*—such as, for example, a storm, which comes to an end as far as we are concerned, though we cannot say that the rain really ends, because the storm may have gone somewhere else. Or we may be watching a ship pass at sea, and the beautiful sight may come to an end because the ship passes from our view; but the vision is ended only for us, because, of course, others may watch the ship from beyond where we happen to be.

There are other things which we may allow to end or not, as the case may be, because we can control them. There are many cruel things in the world which men might bring to an end if they would, such as bull-fighting in Spain, or forced labour camps, or even war. Men could stop these things if they would, as they can stop the running of an engine or the ticking of a watch.

A clock has been made which is expected to run for ten thousand years, so that we might think that that clock, at any rate, has no end. We may be sure, however, that the stuff of which the clock is made will crumble away in less than ten thousand years, and that brings us to what this question really means. For are we to say that when the clock no longer tells the time it is ended? We know that nothing can be utterly destroyed, and so we know, therefore, that nothing can be utterly ended. *But the form and shape of everything that we can see or handle may end.*

The stuff of which the clock is made may crumble; but, though it is no more a clock, it is still stuff of another kind which we may call dust; and no doubt it might change, in millions and millions of years, through the action of natural forces that are always at work, into stuff of which another clock might be made. And so, of course, if a clock can end as a clock, the wall on which it hangs may end as a wall; the house which the wall supports may cease to be a house; the street in which the house stands may cease to be a street; the town through which the street runs may cease to be a town; and the very Earth itself may cease to be *as we know it now.*

After all, the Earth has not always been as it is today. As Tennyson says:

There rolls the deep where grew the tree,
  O Earth, what changes hast thou seen!
There where the long street roars hath been
  The stillness of the central sea.

But, although man has not yet learned all that he has to learn, everything that

FIRE · WIND · WATER · LIFE · MIND · SLEEP · HOW · WHY · WHERE

man does know tells us in the plainest possible words that the Earth can never be destroyed, however much its form may change. We speak of a thing wearing away, but nothing really wears away; its form changes, that is all. So that what comes to an end is not a thing itself, but the form of a thing.

This book may end, in the form in which we hold it in our hands; but the thoughts this book has put into our minds, the feelings that have grown in our hearts as we have read it, will remain and influence our lives. And we, in turn, will influence the lives of our successors. Of one thing let us be sure for ever—that goodness never ends, that all this beautiful world, this wonderful life of ours, was not created by God to exist for a few years and then to die. The changes of Nature are sometimes more than we can understand, and the last change that we know, the sleep that we call death, is the strangest of all. But it is a sleep, and not an end.

What is the Biggest Single Thing in the Universe ?

Astronomers down the ages have given many estimates of the size of the universe. How vast it is may be gathered from the fact that, not satisfied with the 100-inch telescope on Mount Wilson, astonomers have constructed and set up on Mount Palomar in California a 200-inch telescope. This huge instrument will penetrate 1000 million light years into space and therefore be able to reveal objects within a circle which has a diameter of more than 11,500,000,000,000,000,000,000 miles.

Now in this universe the biggest single thing must be the greatest of the nebulae, though which this is we are at present unable to say owing to the possibility of new discoveries. These nebulae, which appear in the sky as hazy patches of light, are vast masses of cosmic dust and light gases. Even if the great nebula in Orion were no farther away from us than the nearest fixed star, it would cover an expanse many times as great as the diameter of our whole Solar system, which is about 7000 million miles wide. But as the gaseous nebulae are more distant than the nearest stars, while the spiral nebulae are beyond the Galactic universe, their size must be inconceivable.

Apart from them the biggest object in the universe is the giant star Antares, which has been found to have a diameter of between 360 and 420 million miles, as against our own Sun's diameter of only 866,000 miles. The Earth's orbit round the Sun is 186 million miles in diameter, so that the Sun could be placed in the very centre of Antares, and the Earth could revolve round in its present orbit, and there would still be 120 million miles all round this orbit inside the giant star. Or, to put it in another way, two orbits such as the Earth's path round the Sun could be placed side by side inside Antares.

What is a Hall Mark ?

Many of us have in our homes treasured articles of gold or silver which, we have often heard the grown-ups say, are " genuine ; you can see the hall mark on it," and we may have wondered just what those tiny marks stamped on the article have to do with its value.

The term hall mark comes from Goldsmith's Hall in London, where, since ancient times, gold and silver articles have been tested and stamped. There are six other Assay Offices in the British Isles—at Birmingham, Chester, Sheffield, Edinburgh, Glasgow, and Dublin.

A silver article that has been tested in London bears a leopard's head, which was first used when King Edward I in 1300 introduced the testing for their quality of gold and silver articles. It is now called the Town Mark for London, articles tested at the Assay Offices in the other places having different Town Marks.

Since 1363 every maker of gold and silver articles has put his own mark beside the King's Mark. In 1478 another, now called the Date Mark, was introduced. It is a letter indicating the year in which the assay was made.

About 1544 the Lion Passant was added to satisfy the public that articles were not being made of coins melted down—the coinage having been debased by Henry VIII ! This is now the standard mark for silver.

Gold articles do not bear the lion, but have figures showing the carat standard of the metal. These are : 22 carat, shown with a crown ; 18 carat, also with a crown ; 14 carat, with the decimal 585; and 9 carat, with the decimal 375. The last two standards have no crown.

Down the centuries articles so stamped have been recognised as beyond suspicion.

What are Logarithms ?

Logarithms are a series of numbers representing, or used in the place of, other numbers. They make it possible for long and tedious calculations to be done with great rapidity by substituting the addition and subtraction of logarithms for the multiplying and dividing of the numbers they represent.

They are an invention of the time of Shakespeare, and we owe them to John Napier, Baron of Merchiston, near Edinburgh. Used in all the higher calculations of advanced mathematics, they are of inestimable value, for without them few of the great and marvellous discoveries of modern astronomy or physics could have been made.

Logarithms are partly a discovery and partly an invention. Napier arranged a series of numbers in *geometrical progression*, which he called anti-logarithms, and then, corresponding to them, a series of numbers in *arithmetical progression*, these being called logarithms; and he found that by adding together two logarithms the result was *the logarithm of the product of two anti-logarithms* represented by the logarithms.

A series of numbers is said to be in geometrical progression when each is derived from the preceding number by multiplying by a constant factor. Thus 2 6 18 54 162 and so on, are in geometrical progression because 6 is 2 multiplied by 3, 18 is 6 multiplied by 3, 54 is 18 multiplied by 3, and so on. A series of numbers is said to be in arithmetical progression when the numbers increase or decrease by a common difference, as in 1 3 5 7 9 11 13.

Now, if we take a series of figures in geometrical progression, and place under it a series in arithmetical progression, we have a simple set of anti-logarithms and logarithms, thus :

1	2	4	8	16	32	64	128	256
0	1	2	3	4	5	6	7	8

Suppose we now wish to multiply 32 by 8. Instead of doing this in the ordinary way, we add together the logarithms of those numbers, found in the bottom line, 5 and 3, which give 8, and then we look for 8 in the table and find that its anti-logarithm in the upper line is 256, which is the product of 32 multiplied by 8. Of course for such small and simple calculations we do not need logarithms, but when dealing with large numbers the amount of time saved by Napier's invention is incalculable.

The logarithms, as originally invented by Napier in 1614, were soon improved, he himself having much to do with the improvements. Any base may be taken from which to work out a table of logarithms, but for convenience 10 is used, and the logarithm of 10 is 1. Then the logarithm of 100 is 2, of 1000 is 3, and so on. The logarithm of 1 is 0, and obviously any number between 1 and 10 must have for its logarithm a number between 0 and 1.

It must be understood that the logarithms of most numbers have decimal fractions which cannot be represented completely, and so an approximate value is found by working out the logarithms to several decimal places. There are tables of logarithms worked out to four figures, five figures, and so on, the extra figures giving greater accuracy, but being more difficult and complicated to use. Thus the logarithm of 200 to five places of decimals is 2·30103.

This brief description of logarithms simply shows the principle of this astonishing invention, but, as used in higher mathematics, logarithms are very complicated and too difficult to explain here. All kinds of calculations, besides multiplication and division, can be worked out by logarithms. The word itself is made up from two Greek words and means the *number of the ratios*.

What is a Synod ?

Sometimes we read of people attending a Synod and we wonder what it is. The word comes from Greek and means an assembly, and it is a meeting of churchmen to discuss all sorts of affairs to do with their Church.

In the early days of the Christian Church there would be a universal Synod, or Oecumenical Council, to which all the world bishops were summoned. We come across the word Synod again today in the expression the full Synod of the Convocation of Canterbury. Convocation means to call together, and is the word used for the assemblies of the clergy of the Church of England. There is a Convocation of Canterbury and a Convocation of York.

WHAT ARE THE CROWN JEWELS?

THEY are the historic crowns, regalia, and royal ornaments of our British Kings and Queens, and some of them are used at the Coronation Ceremony in Westminster Abbey. Most of them have some symbolic meaning, and their worth to the British peoples far exceeds their value as gold and gems, great as that is.

They are kept in the Jewel House at the Tower of London, where everyone may see them, and a glittering scene they present in their huge plate glass case.

The two most important items are St. Edward's Crown and the Imperial Crown of State. St. Edward's Crown, which takes its name from Edward the Confessor, is used only for the actual crowning ceremony, resting on the Sovereign's head for just a few minutes. The Imperial State Crown is worn by the new king or queen when leaving Westminster Abbey, and on special Royal occasions afterwards.

St. Edward's Crown is the older. Made for Charles II, it is a replica of the ancient crown of England which, together with much of the regalia, was broken up in Oliver Cromwell's time. It is studded with jewels, and its base is a gold circlet with four crosses and four fleurs-de-lys. From this circlet rise two golden arches, the actual badge of sovereignty, and resting on these is a golden globe surmounted by a cross.

At a coronation, St. Edward's Crown is placed on the Monarch's head by the Archbishop of Canterbury, but the Imperial State Crown later replaces it and is the one seen by the cheering multitudes amid the pageantry of the Royal procession from Westminster Abbey to Buckingham Palace.

The reason for the exchange of crowns in the Abbey dates back to the Coronation of Queen Victoria. She was only 18 at the time, and it was considered that St. Edward's Crown, weighing nearly seven pounds, was too heavy for her young head to support for long. So it was decided to make a lighter one for her to wear.

Truly magnificent is the Imperial Crown of State, with a platinum frame containing no fewer than 3095 precious stones—diamonds, pearls, rubies, sapphires, and emeralds, all set in silver and gold. Prominent in one of the four Maltese crosses above the rim of the Crown is the Black Prince's ruby, given to him by Pedro the Cruel of Castile in 1367, and later worn by Henry the Fifth at Agincourt.

The arches of the crown are composed of 783 diamonds designed as oak leaves, with pearl acorns. Beneath a fifth Maltese cross, on the top of the crown, is a globe formed of 581 diamonds.

Nearly a thousand years of history are spanned by the treasures in the Imperial State Crown; it holds the sapphire said to have been worn by Edward the Confessor at his Coronation, and also the 309-carat diamond cut from the famous Cullinan stone presented to Edward VII by South Africa. Another of its historic gems is the Stuart sapphire which James II took with him into exile.

Next in importance among the many lustrous Crown Jewels is one shaped like an eagle. This is the Ampulla (Latin for flask), and it contains the Holy Oil used for anointing the Sovereign—an ancient ritual and the central act of the whole Coronation Ceremony. The Ampulla and the Golden Spoon used with it are the oldest pieces in the regalia, for they were probably used at the Coronation of Henry IV in 1399.

After the sacred act of Anointing, the rest of the regalia is presented as symbols to the Monarch: the Golden Spurs for Chivalry; the Sword, thickly encrusted with precious stones, which symbolises Justice; the golden Orb, ornamented with pearls and surmounted by a cross, which stands for the hope of a world united in Christianity; the Ring of Kingly Dignity; and the two Sceptres representing Authority.

One of these sceptres contains what is perhaps the brightest gem in all this dazzling collection, the enormous 516-carat diamond cut from the same Cullinan stone which contributed to the Imperial State Crown.

A daring attempt to steal the Crown Jewels was made in 1671 by a desperate character known as Colonel Blood. Disguised as a clergyman, he entered the Tower with three of his confederates and asked if his friends might be shown the Crown Jewels. All four attacked the keeper of the regalia, and ran off with the Crown and the Orb. They were soon captured, however, and imprisoned in the Tower.

REGALIA USED AT THE CORONATION

St. Edward's Crown, with which the Sovereign is crowned

The Imperial State Crown, worn on all State occasions

The Orb, with the Globe dominated by the Cross

The Ampulla, which holds the Holy Oil for the Anointing

The Anointing Spoon, into which the Holy Oil is poured

Royal Sceptre with the Dove

The Golden Spurs of Knighthood

The Armills, or gold bracelets

Royal Sceptre with the Cross

The Ring of Kingly Dignity

The Jewelled Sword of State, thickly encrusted with precious stones

Can We Drink Sea Water ?

We can, of course, drink sea water if it has been distilled, that is, if it has been boiled and the steam from it cooled into liquid. But there is another way by which salt water can be turned into fresh, and that is by mixing with it a mineral called silver zeolite.

This method was developed during the Second World War for the benefit of thirsty shipwrecked sailors, and airmen whose planes had been brought down. These unlucky men often drifted at sea for long periods in rafts or small boats.

Each man carried a small collapsible bag, made of waterproof material, which had a filter and a sucking tube. On the raft were supplies of zeolite. The castaway would fill the bag with sea water and then drop into it a tablet of zeolite. This would dissolve in about 20 minutes and by its chemical action render the salt water fresh.

Zeolite consists mainly of silicates of lime, soda, and alumina, and is usually found where there are igneous rocks.

How is Easter Fixed ?

In early times all countries did not keep Easter on the same date. The churches of Asia Minor celebrated it on the same day as the Jews kept their Passover, while the Churches of the West, remembering that Jesus rose on a Sunday, kept Easter on the Sunday following the Passover day. Various attempts to reconcile these two practices failed, and then the Council of Nicaea passed a decree that everywhere the great feast should be observed upon the same day, that day to be the Sunday following the Jewish Passover. To prevent further disputes, four rules were laid down for the fixing of the date.

It was decided that March 21 should be regarded as the Spring Equinox—the time in spring when day and night are equal; that the full Moon on that date, or the next after that date, should be taken for the full Moon of the Passover month: that the Sunday following full Moon should be Easter Day; and that if the full Moon happened on a Sunday, Easter should be the Sunday after. This plan has been observed ever since, and by it the date of Easter is fixed.

In carrying out the arrangement for the fixing of Easter various difficulties have arisen during the centuries owing to the fact that the moons do not correspond exactly with the calendar. A series, or cycle, of 19 years has therefore been taken and numbered from 1 to 19, the numbers being known as Golden Numbers. Then to each of these years has also been given a number which is the age, reckoned in days, of the Moon at the beginning of the year. The numbers in this second series are known as Epacts, and from the Golden Number and Epact the full Moon for deciding the date of Easter in any year may be worked out.

It is curious that in arranging the date of Easter according to rule, the Spring Equinox is a calculated date and not the actual Spring Equinox; the moon referred to is not the actual Moon shining in the sky, but a mathematically calculated moon; and full Moon does not mean a complete circular Moon, but a supposed full Moon according to certain averaging over a course of years. All this is due to the imperfections of the calendar, which never corresponds exactly with the real movements of the Sun and Moon.

By means of the Golden Number and the Epact, which can always be found set forth in any good almanac, a clever boy or girl can work out the date of Easter for any year. The earliest date on which Easter Sunday can fall is March 22, but that will not occur till the year 2285, and the latest possible date is April 25, which occurred in 1943.

The reason 19 years are taken to form a cycle for reckoning the Golden Numbers is that after nineteen years on a given day of the month the Moon is approximately in the same position in the sky as it was nineteen years before, so that nineteen forms a complete series.

What is Hydroponics ?

Hydroponics is a method of growing plants without soil by supplying to them the chemicals which, in their natural manner of growth, they derive from the earth. The roots of the plants grown in this artificial manner must, of course, be supported, and for this purpose a porous litter-bed composed of wood-wool, peat, straw, moss, or some other material is used. This litter bed is arranged on a frame with a wire mesh or perforated bottom through which the plant's roots can reach down to the solution of nutrient chemicals below the frame.

The Story of the Beautiful Things in the Treasure-House of the World

| Pottery vase from Phaestus, Crete | Lead figure from Troy | Bronze lamp-stand from Aegion, Greece | Bronze mirror from Sunium, Attica, in Greece |

DIGGING UP THE ANCIENT WORLD—2
CRETE, TROY, AND ANCIENT GREECE

In this chapter we continue our story of the exploration of ancient civilisations. We go first to Crete, Mycenae, and Greece; then to Syria and Palestine. In Italy we complete our survey of the Mediterranean countries. Then we visit Eastern lands and America. Finally we come to what the spade has revealed in our own island.

IT was in the island of Crete, whose story has been dealt with already in the History and Art sections of this work, that the civilisation next in time and importance to that of Egypt appeared. It began as far back as the first Pyramid builders and rose and waned in unison with Egyptian art and culture. It had a great period of renaissance about 3000 B.C., and between 2250 B.C. and 1200 B.C. was the centre of a great island Empire which stretched over the Aegean Sea to the mainland, where it had considerable power.

Though its history is so old, the story of its excavation belongs to the last 100 years. It begins with the search for the relics of a people and an art which were young when Crete was old. Part of the story belongs to the work of Schliemann, who unearthed Troy, and found, though he hardly realised it, the remains of a mighty empire which had been lost. All

that was known of it was vaguer than the stories of Homer, nothing more than legends of the Minotaur with the eye in its forehead and the Labyrinth, Minos the King, and Daedalus who sought the sky with uplifted wings.

Today these fairy tales are real. When Schliemann had turned his attention from Troy to Mycenae the archaeologists began to ask whence this unexampled civilisation had come, for it had no complete affinity with that of the Hittites, its nearer neighbours, or with that of the more distant Egyptians. It was not a Mycenean civilisation, but something wider, perhaps that of the Achaeans, who were more widely scattered; and more certainly that of a sea-going people, for the sea continually appears in their art. In 1883 a German writer, Milchöfer, suggested that perhaps Crete was the centre, and in 1886 Schliemann tried to secure the site of Knossos for excavation. He had heard of the discovery of a grotto to Zeus by a Cretan on the south coast. But the Cretans put obstacles in his way, and for some years nothing was attempted.

Then in the nineties of last century Sir Arthur Evans saw some curious seals with

PICTURES · STATUES · CARVINGS · BUILDINGS · IVORIES · CRAFTS

figures on them which he announced to be an unknown form of picture-writing. Thereupon he revived the idea that Crete had been the centre of the civilisation of an island people who had represented Europe in the long struggle against Asia. He was more successful than Schliemann had been with the Cretans, and he secured the Knossos area for excavation. In this century he uncovered the great dwelling of King Minos—not one palace but many.

LIFE AS IT WAS IN THE PALACE OF MINOS OF CRETE

We can sit on the king's throne. We can, as Professor Macalister says, turn over the tablets on which his stewards recorded the household accounts and inventories, though as yet we may not pry into their secrets. Broad stairs lead from court to court, from anteroom to bedroom, or bathroom to light-wells and concert-halls, on one of which is a picture of ladies in flounced skirts and low-cut bodices. There are treasure chambers and great cellars stored with jars for provisions.

There are underground chambers revealing that an earthquake once wrecked them, the throne where the king sat in judgment, and abundant evidence of a cruel pastime where boys played the part of unarmed matadors with bulls. There are other houses and altars outside the Palace of King Minos, and a remarkable dancing floor in its precincts. Sir Arthur Evans found the best of all the sites in the island of Crete.

There are other sites and other Mediterranean islands, among which Malta, with its chambers for some unknown ritual sunk far underground and its huge stone altars for worship or sacrifice, offers another problem of prehistoric civilisation.

THE GREAT OPPORTUNITY WHICH CAME TO A POOR GROCER'S BOY

Troy and Mycenae proved important sites and they attracted the German-born Heinrich Schliemann.

Schliemann was a poor lad who began to hear about Hector and Achilles from his father sooner than he could read, and in return wrote for him a Latin essay on them when he was ten! Not for this eager boy was the scientific career he wanted, but a hard apprenticeship in a grocer's shop, where he swept the floor and ground the potato flour, and sold butter, salt, and herrings from five in the morning till eleven at night.

He was released from his servitude by an accident that threatened his health, and he settled in Hamburg as a clerk, still dreadfully poor but with opportunity, hardly purchased, to study, especially languages. At last his fortunes turned, he became rich, and he turned joyfully to his first love.

He was nearing forty but he learned Greek in six weeks, and the man who had been a grocer's boy and was now a prosperous merchant in the Russian capital set about turning himself into an archaeologist. He read everything about Greece he could lay his hands on; he travelled in Egypt, Palestine, and Syria, acquiring Arabic on the way, and visited Athens as a prelude to retiring from business; and at last, a man in the mid-forties, he set out to find the Troy of his dreams and to prove that he was right about its site.

NINE CITIES THAT WERE BURIED ONE ABOVE THE OTHER

He proved it. Others had asserted that the Troy of Homer stood on the heights of Bunarbashi where the River Scamander enters the plain. But Schliemann chose Hissarlik as the place, and turned the first sod there in 1870. He found more than he sought, for here were nine cities buried one on top of the other; and though we know now that he was mistaken in his identification of the actual city he sought for, his discoveries startled the world. In 1872 he dug down to a wondrous collection of gold and silver ornaments and jewellery which in his book figures as the Treasure of Priam and is displayed in the engraving as "golden diadems, fillets, earrings, silver talents, and vessels of silver and gold," with actually a key of the treasure chest. Priam probably never saw them, but their significance to knowledge was unmistakable, and even the Turks saw they were worth something as bullion and made some strong objections to their removal. In 1932 new excavations began to discover the tombs of the Trojan kings, which the Turks prohibited Schliemann from seeking.

The prohibition was a blessing. It drove Schliemann to Mycenae, where again his good fortune stood by him, for misled by a word in the Greek historian Pausanias he selected the burial ground behind the Lion Gate in which to dig and there drove down to discover five shaft graves, in two of which the dead were completely covered with gold and the gold vessels were far more numerous and beautiful than those at Troy. Gold dishes with the most exquisite designs, a little gold sanctuary of Aphrodite and her doves, gold cups and golden masks to cover the faces of the dead. Many of the gold ornaments disclosed designs of seaweed and shellfish, cuttle-fish and fantasies of the sea. It was an art different from any other known, and it was the examination of it, then and thereafter, when it was found repeated elsewhere and on other materials, that led scholars to seek some country or civilisation from which it had spread across the Mediterranean. That origin was found, as we have said, in Crete.

Schliemann was assisted by Dörpfeld, who first made the architecture of Troy clear, and in excavating the Homeric stronghold of Tiryns had much to do in keeping it from clumsy destruction at the hands of the workmen.

Tiryns is a little gem, a citadel built on a rock, and is Schliemann's greatest contribution to an understanding of the heroes who throng the pages of the Iliad. But his most enduring gift to knowledge lay in awakening from its sleep of some four thousand years that Mediterranean civilisation the centre of which proved to be Crete, and which continued to reveal itself in every coast of the tideless sea, in Cyprus, and as far west as the shores of Spain. Tiryns, Mycenae, and Crete with the Aegean Islands under its sway were the cradle of Greek Art, an art which to this day inspired mankind. Its supreme age was that of Phidias the Athenian, some of whose sculptures on the Parthenon were sent to England in 1803. Known as the Elgin marbles, these magnificent treasures are in the British Museum as we read on another page.

So numerous and widespread have been the excavations in Greece and her colonies during the past century and more that we can only mention a few outstanding names and dates.

The Greek remains of Sicily, the island richest in temple ruins, were first examined in 1812. In 1820 a Greek peasant, Georgios of Melos, found there in several pieces the wondrous Aphrodite of Melos which now stands in the Louvre at Paris and was first bought for 750 francs. In 1840 Charles Fellows discovered in a rocky peninsula on the south coast of Asia Minor the ancient Greek Lycia; in 1855 Charles Newton, aided by Lord Stratford de Redcliffe, began the work which added the statue of Demeter at Cnidus to the treasures of the British Museum.

Newton's additions to the collection of Greek sculpture are second only to those of Elgin. He was one of the founders of the School for Hellenic Studies, which has served the work of excavation well. The Winged Victory of Samothrace was found in fragments at Kaballa in the island of Samothrace; the statue by Champoiseau in 1863, the ship's prow twelve years later.

And here is a comparatively recent example. On the north coast of Africa archaeologists have uncovered the ancient city of Cyrene with a great Greek temple in which was found a statue of Aphrodite carved in the Hellenistic Age. These are only a few of the fragments of Greek art which the years have found and the seekers have put together. Delos, Olympia, Eleusis, the Temple at Aegina, Delphi, are among the great names which have received a second birth.

DISCOVERIES IN SYRIA AND PALESTINE

In our survey we now turn back to those ancient civilisations of Syria and Palestine which link geographically the civilisations of Asia with Egypt. It was through Palestine that the wandering tribes from the north reached Egypt and that Egyptian invaders came into contact with that Hittite civilisation of which we read in a previous chapter.

Syria has not been adequately surveyed, but after the close of the First World War the French, who held the Mandate over this country, began excavations on the north Syrian coast. Near the head of the Gulf of Alexandretta they revealed a settlement which proved to be a cosmopolitan port as mixed in population as that of Marseilles today. Tablets in eight languages show that Cretans, Babylonians, Phoenicians, and, probably, Cypriotes used this ancient place as a port of exchange for the goods that came from Asia to the Mediterranean along one of the most ancient highways in the world.

Palestine has been better served. The first explorer was Seetzen in 1801; he was followed by Burckhardt, who in 1809 found in the Sinai Peninsula the rock city of Petra, " the rose-red city half as old as Time," as Dean Burgon called it, the capital of Edom. The Dead Sea was explored in 1835 by Costigan, who died of Palestine fever.

Tyrwhitt Drake was one of the victims, and it was his death which gave an opening to the young engineer officer who was afterwards known as Lord Kitchener, and who for a number of years surveyed for the Palestine Exploration Fund, having at least one narrow escape from death during his work.

The Rev. Edward Robinson, an American Congregationalist minister whose studies extended over fourteen years (1838–52) first put the geography of the Holy Land on a sound basis. But most of all are we indebted to the Palestine Exploration Fund, whose maps were superseded only by the photographic survey made during the First World War.

Palestine and Syria were the meeting ground on which the two civilisations of the Semites and the Egyptians warred or met to exchange their products; they were the cockpit and the highway of the peoples of Africa and the fertile crescent of Semitic Asia, the region bounded on the north by the Taurus Mountains and the Aramaeans

of north Syria; on the south by the Arabs of Arabia, to the east by the Assyrians and Babylonians as far as the Persian Gulf; to the west as far as the Mediterranean, by the Phoenicians, the Moabites, and the Hebrews.

In Palestine for long years the most interesting discovery was the Moabite Stone of Mesha, King of Moab, found as long ago as 1868. It begins " I Mesha King of Moab," and recounts Mesha's successful revolt against the Israelites. In the neighbourhood of Jerusalem were found a few cuneiform inscriptions, some of which refer to the time when the Assyrians conquered Israel; and at Lachish, where was established the value of Palestinian pottery in fixing dates, Leslie J. Starkey discovered a series of objects of great value to archaeology. Sir Flinders Petrie's excavations at Gaza were of the utmost value in showing the civilisation of peoples overlapping one another since the Stone Age, and at Jericho Professor John Garstang laid bare the story of the city, even to the fire-stricken walls that fell before Joshua.

The most beautiful Palestinian relic, the Alexander sarcophagus, which is now in Istanbul, was bought by a merchant of Sidon in the fourth century. A picture of this fine sculpture is on page 4402.

THE DISCOVERIES IN ITALY

Etruria and the Etruscans, who were a powerful people in Italy before the Romans, with a rarer civilisation and art, have a history still mysterious. They invaded Rome. Lars Porsena was one of their generals and a real person, but references to them by Roman or Greek historians are rare or flimsy or contradictory.

A people of great gifts artistically, of organising power and military ability, the Etruscans differed from the Italians and the Romans in almost everything. Their language was unlike any other in Europe, and though written in Greek characters and though hundreds of inscriptions exist it has never been fully understood or translated. Their religion was strange, their art their own with a touch of Greek influence. It was anciently maintained that the Etruscans came to Italy from Asia Minor something less than a thousand years B.C. No

certain proof of this has been found; and many other suppositions exist, but on the whole it seems most likely that the Etruscans were part of an unknown Asiatic race who reached Umbria about the ninth century before the Christian era. What is all but certain is that the Etruscans burst on the Italian world complete in the elements of civilisation, not as conquerors, but quite simply as complete strangers among a not unfriendly people—as inhabitants of Ireland made themselves at home in Britain. In the island of Lemnos are traces that some halted there on their way to the West; and some French excavations near Ras Shamra in Syria have disclosed tablets which in one of the new languages they reveal may afford a link with the lost Etruscan tongue.

The first Etruscan settlements were on the west coast, north of Rome, with their capital on the site of the modern town of

LINKS WITH DAYS LONG PAST

THE STREET OF MERCURY IN POMPEII TODAY

A HOUSE IN POMPEII

RUINS OF THE SECOND CITY OF TROY

STAIRS IN THE PALACE OF PHAESTUS IN CRETE

THE ROMAN THEATRE AT TAORMINA IN SICILY

THE ROCK TEMPLE OF ED-DEIR
AT PETRA

A BEAUTIFUL VASE FROM
POMPEII

THE MOABITE
STONE

A SCULPTURED BOULDER FROM
GUATEMALA

AN ANCIENT VASE
FROM CRETE

THE THRONE OF MINOS AT
KNOSSOS

THE PERISTYLE OF THE SO-CALLED HOUSE OF CLEOPATRA AT DELOS

A STAIRCASE IN THE PALACE AT KNOSSOS

ROMAN MOSAIC PAVEMENT AT ST. ALBANS

IN THE HOUSE OF THE GLADIATORS, POMPEII

RUINS OF THE WALLS OF ANCIENT ILION

A ROMAN THEATRE UNCOVERED AT ST. ALBANS, WITH ONE OF THE PILLARS RECONSTRUCTED

GOLD CLASP WITH GARNETS AND GLASS, FROM SUTTON HOO

JEWELLED AND GOLD-INLAID PURSE-LID, FROM SUTTON HOO

ROMAN POT SHOWING A COMBAT WITH A LION, FROM COLCHESTER

GOLD BUCKLE WITH NIELLO INLAY, FROM SUTTON HOO

ROMAN VASE SHOWING A HUNT-ING SCENE, FROM COLCHESTER

A ROMAN SPHINX FOUND AT COLCHESTER

A ROMAN CENTURION AT COLCHESTER

MONUMENT TO A ROMAN CAVALRY OFFICER AT COLCHESTER

A WINGED FIGURE FROM
ETRURIA

AN OLD MAYA GOD AND
HIGH PRIEST

AN ETRUSCAN DRINKING
VESSEL

THE ANCIENT TEMPLE OF BORO BUDUR IN JAVA

RELIEFS ON THE WALLS OF ANGKOR THOM
AT ANGKOR

THE TOMB OF AGAMEMNON
AT MYCENAE

*Some of the pictures on these pages are from Dörpfeld's Troja and Ilion ; others are reproduced by courtesy of the British
Museum, Colchester Museum, E.N.A., Messrs. Burton Holmes, Ewing Galloway, Herbert G. Ponting, and others*

Corneto Tarquinia. This was in southern Etruria. Later they spread to towns which are now Perugia, Chiusi, Cortona, Arezzo, Volterra, and Fiesole outside Florence, and at all these places their relics have been found. As we have said, they fought with Rome, but they were at last thrust back. They were perhaps not exterminated by war, but by the spreading scourge of malaria, which undermined their vitality. But all that is known certainly about the Etruscans has been found from the excavation of their old cities, such as Marzabotto, which had a wall, paved streets, elaborate houses, fine temples, and a system of drainage; as well as their tombs and the treasures found therein.

The perception of the origins of Etruscan art first arose when Niebuhr, the regenerator of Roman history, became Prussian minister at the Papal Court about 1820. Niebuhr contemplated a work which was to describe the antiquities of Rome, and secured the services of Gerhard, who became one of a band of brilliant young German antiquaries in Italy. Gerhard catalogued the museums, established an international association of all archaeologists, and at its beginning examined the tombs of southern Etruria afresh.

THE HISTORY OF GREEK PAINTING FOUND IN THE ETRUSCAN TOMBS

Insignificant grottoes were found by him to be filled with the most beautiful Greek vases, many of them painted. In a few months there was found one of the finest collection of vases known; there were vases for storing, mixing, pouring, and drinking wine, and what most stamped them, apart from the astonishing designs painted on them, was their combination of the greatest utility with the simplest form. The painted designs had another value, for by their number and variety they interpreted Grecian mythology, and it became possible by noting the pictorial development to date the origin of vases.

In short, the Etruscan tombs wrote for the archaeological world the history of Greek painting. By comparison with that the identification of old Etruria with a Greek settlement was unimportant. The most beautiful vase of all, the François vase, was found at Chiusi, the old Etruscan capital of Clusium, but paintings came from places as far apart as Pisa and Pompeii.

Nor were vases and paintings the only things sought and found; mosaics, jewels, statuary, tombs, and funerary inscriptions and sarcophagi were gathered together.

WHAT THE CATACOMBS IN ROME HAVE TOLD US OF THE EARLY CHRISTIANS

The collecting craze by foreign visitors awakened Italy and Rome to a sense of their hidden treasures. The Archaeological Institute in Rome was founded, and it recruited many indefatigable scholars and workers, among whom was Giambattista de Rossi, whose investigation of the Roman catacombs put the history of the Early Christians on a new foundation.

This was one of the many examples of scientific exploration and research which enriched the archaeological study of Rome during the last century. Among the chief discoveries was that by De Rossi of the catacomb of Calixtus, in 1862. The excavations on the Palatine then begun revealed the temple on the Capitoline and the House of Livia. In 1872 the Forum, long used for Roman cattle and sunk in débris, was so far cleared that the reliefs of the tribune could be seen. The ancient house in the Farnesina, the Ludovisi marble throne, the statue of Apollo found in the Tiber, are also landmarks of discovery.

At Ostia, in the years of Mussolini's dictatorship, the complete plan of the great port was revealed, and in Rome Mussolini had the distinction of having ordered the excavation which led to the discovery of the Forum of Augustus and part of the Library of the Forum of Trayjan ; so that he left Ancient Rome more venerable than he found it.

WONDERFUL DISCOVERIES IN THE CITIES OF POMPEII AND HERCULANEUM

Napoleon gave the greatest impulse to the exploration of Egypt and its history, and by establishing in Paris the Musée Napoléon stimulated the search in other lands for the treasures of antiquity. His favourite sister Caroline was the most energetic excavator of Pompeii. The discovery of Pompeii was much older; its ruins had been known since 1748, when the mysterious production by Neapolitan peasants of antiquities for sale led to their disclosure. Herculaneum had yielded prizes since the first excavations in 1711, including the wonderful Villa dei Papiri in 1753, where a hundred statues in bronze and marble, as well as the library of its first owner, had been got out. But work at Herculaneum was very difficult because lava flung over by the eruption of Vesuvius had hardened to stone, and it was abandoned in 1766.

Pompeii was easier to deal with because its ashes were looser. About 1764 two theatres, the three-cornered Forum with its remains of early temples and the sanctuaries of Isis, were uncovered. The Neapolitans went on with the work in leisurely manner for some thirty years, burying houses again after the spoil had been taken from them and leaving decorations to decay. At last concerted digging stopped altogether. It was revived in Napoleonic times by Miot, the minister of Joseph Bonaparte, the new king of Naples, who employed 150 men and spent £900 a year; but Caroline, the wife of Marshal Murat, who succeeded Joseph, put her heart and soul into it, and found employment for 600 workmen. Then were uncovered the solemn Street of Tombs and the Market Place with the colonnade. Some other temples and the stately

Basilica saw again the light of day. The Bourbons continued the work after Ferdinand re-entered Naples as its king. The two different points of the excavations at the Forum and the Street of Tombs were connected, and the climax of these efforts was reached at the Temple of Fortuna Augusta and the baths near the Forum. In 1860 the Italians infused a new spirit into the examination of the city, putting Fiorelli in charge; and he, beginning on the Pompeian houses, was able first to show how and when they were built, and to establish the existence of four distinct periods in Pompeian art, one or other of which shows derivation from Greece or from Egypt. The most important single discovery was that of the House of the Vettii in 1894, with 188 paintings.

Work has been carried on steadily at Herculaneum and Pompeii in this century. A few fine artistic treasures have been added from Pompeii, but research proves that the two towns, of which Herculaneum was the better built, were neither rich, nor, with few exceptions, cultured.

DISCOVERIES IN THE FARTHER EAST

Having brought the older civilisations of Europe and the Near East almost to our own doors, we may now glance at others in the Farther East and in the Newer West before looking at our own land. In India there is little yet to be discerned of the more ancient civilisations of Mesopotamia, Egypt, Crete, or Syria. But at least one astonishing piece of statuary hints at an origin far older than Greek sculpture.

About 1700 B.C. the Aryan Kassites invaded Babylonia, probably impelled thereto by changes in the climate of Asia, which formed new deserts, and others of the same invaders flowed into India, where they found no old civilisation to adopt, and so set up a less advanced one of their own. Nothing more emerges till Buddhism and the sainted Asoka emerge in the sixth century B.C.; and Asoka's wisdom, his edicts, and his sayings are the most priceless antiquities of the wide Empire he governed. The later relics of art and architecture compare with those of the Roman Empire; and the offshoots, the buried temples of Ceylon, the tremendous temples and palaces of Angkor in Cochin China, and the pyramidical shrine at Boro Budur

in Java, are more imposing but later than the ruined Roman cities of North Africa.

Farther East is the civilisation of China, which is next in age to that of Crete, and may have begun before 2000 B.C. It also may have been created by incursion from Persia or Babylonia; but the seed thus planted there found fertile soil and developed in a way all its own. Nor was the seed long in development, and the bronzes, both those which have been discovered and those which were pictured by the early Chinese antiquaries, some of whom published engravings of them about the time of our William the Conqueror, show that in 1600 B.C. the metal work was fine and beautiful.

But the surface of China has been no more than scratched by the antiquaries. The most important work of all was done by Sir Aurel Stein in excavating the buried cities of Khotan in Chinese Turkestan, or Sinkiang. The ruins were buried by the sand and preserved by it, and it was here that evidence was found of the spread of Indian and Scythian art to China. Khotan was a little kingdom, an oasis, on the route from the valley of the Oxus to China, and so was a link in the chain from India and the West to the Farthest East. Khotan as a region struggled against the most formidable of deserts, the Taklamakan, and at last the Khotan settlements went down in the fight against its encroachments. But Stein's spade brought to sight a uniform and well-defined civilisation stretching in a straight line for 300 miles. Fine statuary; decorated woodcarving of the Greek and

Buddhist style which showed later the influence of Roman taste also, and which flourished in the north-west of India; early Persian influences, as well as frescoes on Buddhist shrines resembling ancient Indian art—all these were found.

Since then excavations in the provinces of Honan and Shansi have given further evidence, with hopes of more, of a period when China was in touch with the prehistoric cultures of the Near East.

THE LOST CIVILISATION OF THE MAYAS

When the Spanish conquistadores ravaged Mexico they had only a thirst for plunder The blight has not wholly lifted from those lands, but the wonder has grown, and in Yucatan in Mexico, and in Central America to Honduras, antiquaries find a people by the side of whom the Aztecs are modern.

In many parts their traces are found in fragments of brick and stone; in others, where the forest, as pervading and intrusive as the desert sands of Central Asia, has hidden temples and sculptured pyramids and palace walls, there is evidence of a people, the Mayas, older than the Toltecs, who were before the Aztecs.

The Maya people were first made known in Europe by A. P. Maudslay, who spent thirteen years in visits to Central America to bring back moulds and casts of their buildings and monuments. These were eventually accepted by the British Museum, where still they are. At last they attracted the attention which they merited as the records of a civilisation older than that of the Aztecs or the Toltecs or any other in the region from Yucatan to Honduras and from Palenque to Guatemala City.

But they also attracted the attention of

more than one unbridled theorist, and their origin was ascribed variously to the lost Tribes of Israel, to Egypt, and by one imaginative authority to the year 5000 B.C. But unromantic and patient investigation not yet at an end shows them to have been a race apart who built great cities, who reached high levels in art in stone carvings, paintings, pottery manufacture, and architecture. They had small acquaintance with metals, their tools being stone or wood, and yet had a mathematical turn of mind which enabled them to form a calendar more exact than any before our own.

The Mayas also possessed a system of syllables (but no alphabet), and this enabled them to express by signs their dating. These alone have been read, largely by aid of documents salved from destruction and obtained from their degenerate descendants in Yucatan. For the Spaniards had put an end to the Mayas as a people and to everything associated with them except their monuments. It is now clear that they and their flowering life lasted rather less than five centuries, beginning roughly with the first years of the Christian era. Rather strangely they were the only ancient people who invented a sign for zero.

OUR OWN LAND BEFORE THE NORMANS CAME

It has been reserved for the 20th century to discover more of the history of these islands during the 20 centuries before the Christian era began than had been learned in any century since the Romans came and went.

The curtain that closed down after the last Roman legion had left and did not rise again till Saxon history had begun, when all interest in the ancient inhabitants of Britain was extinguished or dispersed

in legend, has again been lifted at its far corners by excavations at the Roman cities of St. Albans and Colchester. In each a separate Celtic city has been disclosed, that at Colchester being the city of Cymbeline, or Cunobelinus.

At St. Albans, which the Romans named Verulamium and made the south midland capital, some of the finest Roman works of art have been found; but at Colchester the discovery of pottery kilns and their products shows that the people living there were quite capable of assimilating Roman art and industry and of adding it to an art of their own far from negligible. In short, we now learn that the pre-Roman Britons were not woad-painted barbarians, but were a people with a high culture of their own. On that side of the island they were, like the Romans themselves, newcomers who had subdued a native population and were in their turn to fall before Rome's superior military organisation. They were one of several waves of invasion from the Continent—from the Rhine, from France and Belgium which provided the Belgae whom Julius Caesar saw, or from Brittany and Spain.

RELICS OF BRITAIN'S EARLIEST MEN FOUND IN KENT AND SUFFOLK

The earliest men in Britain were those of the Old Stone Age, and how far back that is no one can with certainty tell, for Benjamin Harrison's Eolithic flint implements in Kent and Reid Moir's discoveries in Suffolk put the date back hundreds of thousands of years. But the more strictly archaeological discoveries in England are associated with the New Age of the men of the stone axe merging into the Bronze and Iron Ages. These Neolithic men were here before the first waves of invasion which reached south-east Britain from across the North Sea and the south-west in Cornwall, and the Welsh coast and Ireland from the Atlantic lands of Spain, Portugal, and Brittany. These were the people who made the Long Barrows which were family vaults and raised the dolmens in the west.

CIRCLES OF WOOD AND STONE FROM BRITAIN'S FAR DISTANT PAST

To about the year 2000 B.C. belongs the most ancient of the British big monuments, Avebury Circle, which was raised about the same time as the invasion of the round-headed Beaker Folk, the primitive John Bulls who amalgamated with the tribes they found and began the Bronze Age. To the middle of the Bronze Age, 500 years later, belongs the great circle built of wood and known as Woodhenge. It has six concentric circles of posts and was the forerunner of Stonehenge, the greatest of all our prehistoric monuments, having been built at different times through several centuries.

But there were, both before and after, other tides of invasion attracted from the Continent by the great wealth of gold in the Wicklow Mountains. Excavations in Ireland by Harvard University have taught us a great deal about these adventurers and settlers. Cornwall imported a great deal of the gold, and a remarkable find of gold ornaments was found at Towednack near St. Ives in 1931. More or less belonging to this period were the people who began the tin-mining industry in Cornwall, built the miners' settlements and circular hill fortresses, and ultimately reached the lake villages of Glastonbury and Meare in Somerset. Here we may see the art of the Celtic Bronze Age which survived the Roman occupation and came to light again in Saxon times. Even the Roman occupation did not submerge these villages; rather did they, or the people who occupied them, absorb what the Romans brought. In the excavated dwellings at Meare, flint implements have been found by the side of Roman-British pottery.

A RACE AS DEVOTED TO THE CULT OF THE DEAD AS THE ANCIENT EGYPTIANS

The excavations in northern England suggest that the people there were chiefly influenced by the culture of Scandinavia and the Baltic. But throughout the several waves of invasion the New Stone Age men of the south seem to have remained a distinct people, affected by the same impulses in their monuments and imbued with the same religious belief. As in a much later age Christianity was sown and flowered in the south, so in the Bronze Age all Britain south of the Trent was persuaded to a way of religion like that of prehistoric Portuguese and Spaniards and other dwellers on the Atlantic shores.

They were as devoted to the cult of the dead as the Egyptians, raising huge monuments of earth and stone in which to bury their great leaders.

In Anglesey, a round chambered tomb at Bryn Celli Dhu, carefully examined in 1925, revealed the ceremonial accompanying a burial. In the tomb was a pillar carefully cut and clearly sacred, and a stone rudely sculptured and engraved with spirals was buried beside a pit outside the chamber. There are indications that human sacrifice was made when the chief was entombed.

About this time a change is seen in some of the habits of these Bronze Age Britons of whose burial customs we know so much more than of their lives, and this is generally attributed to the thin edge of the Iron Age spreading like a wedge from central Europe, where the weapon of iron was beating down the defensive bronze as Alexander's iron-fronted phalanx burst through Persia.

ONE OF THE GREATEST DISCOVERIES OF THIS CENTURY

The discovery of the link between the British Iron Age and that of Europe is one of the most important of this century. The iron invasion went on for hundreds of years, and its earliest traces are found in that land of prehistoric ghosts, the Wiltshire Downs. The reason for the Wiltshire occupation both then and before is clear, for these Downs were uplifted above the vast forest covering most of Britain to the north. It was one or other of these waves which built the great hill camps like a chain of fortresses from Wiltshire to the far west.

Most of these hill fortresses are quite different from the earlier earthworks of the men of the Stone Age, and we may find it strange to think that they were the work of men who were of the highest skill in metalwork and enamelling and had actually caught some of the inspiration of the far-off Greeks. All that the conquering Roman left to them was the defence of some of the coastal camps in the far west and in Wales. The camp of Trer Ceiri in North Wales is one of them.

Of the mingling of the Romans with the Britons they found in possession much has been learned, and much more is known of Roman Britain than of any period without written record. The military camp of Richborough, where for nearly three centuries a Roman army made its Aldershot, has added much to knowledge which continued excavation in London and a number of small sites has enlarged.

A SECOND FLOWERING OF THE LOST CELTIC ART

But when we come to Saxon times, the most astonishing discovery is the emergence of a second flowering of the lost Celtic art.

In the year 1939, on the sandy heath between the Estuary of the River Deben, Suffolk, and the sea six miles away, a tall barrow was excavated which revealed what the Keeper of British Antiquities at the British Museum described as the most marvellous find in the archaeological annals of England. It was a large ship, of which clear traces remained though the timbers had disappeared, and it belonged to the Anglo-Saxon, not the later Viking, age, and was of a kind unparalleled in British archaeology. Not only were gold jewellery, silver plate, dishes of bronze and iron found in the ship, but its discovery shed important light on the history of the migrations of the Teutonic peoples, of which the settlement in England by the Saxons was only an episode.

The ship was a great open rowing boat 80 feet long by 14 feet wide and 4 feet 6 inches deep, drawing two feet of water when light, and manned by 38 oarsmen. It has been suggested that it may have been the burial ship of the East Anglian King Aethelhere between the 6th and 7th centuries; but while that is uncertain, what seems likely is that this was the richest of such burials (of which others are known), many of the objects being family or tribal heirlooms.

A WEALTH OF GOLD NEVER BEFORE SEEN IN AN ANGLO-SAXON GRAVE

The gold is the most striking; such a wealth of gold had never been seen before in an Anglo-Saxon grave—the great gold belt buckle, the sword with a gold pommel, and 22 other gold pieces, buckles, hinges, clasps, studs, gold coins, and billets, and nearly all jewelled with garnets, over 9000 of these stones. After the gold, a long way after, comes the silver, a miscellaneous collection, probably coming by way of trade from Eastern Europe or the Near East. The most outstanding is the great Anastasius Dish, covered with small incised ornament. Lastly, the " purse lid," the most gorgeous of the finds, with a gold outer frame, and jewelled with bars and panels of garnet and mosaic glass.

Furthermore, the discovery goes to show that the Anglo-Saxons not only absorbed all that the ancient Britons and Roman Britons had left, but that they had preserved and added to it the culture with which they had been in contact on the mainland before they became invaders. Before they were submitted, like the Briton they had conquered, to the law of the sword, they had an artistic achievement superior to that of most European nations, and in nothing but architecture had they anything to learn from their Norman conquerors.

British archaeology is a palimpsest with characters written by Celt, Iberian, Scandinavian, and even Byzantine genius.

The Story of the Peoples of All Nations and Their Homelands

The Sugar Loaf Mountain dominating the harbour of Rio de Janeiro, capital of Brazil

CENTRAL AND SOUTH AMERICA

THE New World was not discovered by men from the Old World until the end of the fifteenth century ; and it is still in the making.

Since Columbus first set foot in the Bahama Islands, in 1492, the power and wealth of America have grown mighty beyond words ; far mightier than those of the Old World countries from which came those intrepid men who followed in the footsteps of Columbus. But the European adventurers and conquerors took with them their racial and religious differences, and the course of history has made not one but two Americas—the north, Teutonic and Protestant ; the central and south, Latin and Catholic.

While the north marched forward as the United States and Canada, the greater part of Central and Southern America lay for two centuries under the hand of Spanish colonial dominion. That dominion, however, did not destroy the native tribes. The Spaniards went in search of gold and treasure, not to till the ground, and therefore the native Indians remained, though in a state of subjection ; so that today the countries of Central and South America are inhabited by a mixture of races, neither European nor Indian, but Mexican, Peruvian, Chilean, Brazilian, and so on.

The conquerors of South America never really opened up the interior, so that all these Latin-American republics are young countries. Their real development began only about a century ago.

These countries occupy some nine million square miles of the Earth's surface, stretching from the Rio Grande, whose waters divide the plains of Texas from the Mexican highlands, down through the narrow mountainous lands which divide the Caribbean Sea from the wide waters of the Pacific, and through the vast pear-shaped continent which we call South America to the " land of fire," that island of mountain, forest, and cloud which ends at Cape Horn. Thus Latin America begins at latitude 30°, away to the north of the Tropic of Cancer, embraces the whole tropical region, and stretches away beyond the 55th parallel of latitude south.

The modern history of this continent begins round one of the narrowest necks of land and water in the world, at the Isthmus of Panama, now pierced by that great American artificial waterway which

THE FIVE CONTINENTS & 100 NATIONS & RACES THAT INHABIT THEM

links the Atlantic with the Pacific and is itself a rival to the Suez Canal as one of the engineering wonders of the modern world. For the later conquerors from Spain thought, as Columbus had done, that in reaching America they had reached the fringe of Asia and were on their way to the Spice Islands. Keats has put into immortal lines their amazement when they saw on the other side of that fateful isthmus the wide stretches of the Pacific, though he mistook Cortes for Balboa :

> Or like stout Cortes when, with eagle eyes,
> He stared at the Pacific—and all his men
> Looked at each other with a wild surmise :
> Silent, upon a peak in Darien.

THE MIGHTY SPECTACLE WHICH MET THE GAZE OF BALBOA

It was in fact Vasco Nunez de Balboa who was the first European to stand, in 1513, on that peak and see that mighty spectacle. We do not know what height this was—certainly not the Balboa Hill marked on our maps today ; but Balboa marched across the isthmus, strode into the sea, and with drawn sword claimed the Pacific for the monarchs of Castile and Aragon. Four years later, on March 4, 1517, a Spanish sailor touched at Yucatán ; and a year later Cortes sailed to Mexico from Cuba, roused the subject peoples of Mexico against their Aztec rulers, and on Tuesday, November 8, 1519, entered the city now known as Mexico City. The vast treasure which the Spaniards found there, though the royal treasure was thrown into the lake and lost, during the two years that followed, inspired the Spaniards to further conquests. Mexico became " New Spain."

Pizarro made his first hazardous and dangerous voyage on the unknown western coasts of America in 1527, when he reached Túmbez, lying to the north of Cape Blanco.

PIZARRO'S CONQUEST OF THE ANDES AND THE CITY OF THE SUN

He returned to Spain to tell of El Dorado, the golden country he had found, and received the commission for the conquest of Peru, which he carried out with such brilliancy of conception, such daring in execution, such disdain of hardship and danger, and, alas, with so much cruelty.

His second landing was in 1531, with a tiny force of 183 men and 27 horses, and in two years he had scaled the mighty natural fortress of the Andes and taken the Inca capital of Cuzco, the City of the Sun. Thus the great colonial empire of Spain in South America was founded, and to the end the Peruvian city of Lima, founded by Pizarro, was the centre of the Spanish government of South America.

The stories of the conquest of Mexico by Cortes and of Peru by Pizarro are two of the most heroic and marvellous episodes anywhere to be found in modern history. They are told elsewhere in this book, and at length by William Prescott, the nineteenth-century historian, in his two books The Conquest of Mexico and The Conquest of Peru, which must be read if we want to study the beginnings of modern history in Latin America.

Cortes and Pizarro were not the only Spanish heroes among the Conquistadores, as the Spanish conquerors were called. There were Sebastian de Benalcazar and Ximenes de Quesada, who conquered the country between Panama and Peru ; Diego de Almagro and Pedro de Valdivia, who occupied Chile ; and Pedro de Mendoza who founded the first Spanish settlement at Buenos Aires in 1536. Meanwhile Portugal brought Brazil, or at least the coastal districts of it, into subjection ; the Portuguese sailor Cabral had sighted the land as early as 1500, and taken " possession " in the name of his monarch.

EXHAUSTED TRAVELLERS DRIFTING HELPLESS DOWN THE AMAZON

By 1550, in the short space of about 20 years, the vast continent of South America was appropriated by a handful of soldiers for the Spanish and Portuguese monarchs.

Some rough idea of the geographical situation was now available, for in 1520 Magellan had sailed through the Strait of Magellan into the Pacific, and the world knew that America was a continent far distant from the Indies. In 1541 Francis Orellana made that marvellous voyage through the dense tropical forest from Peru down the head waters of the Amazon. Fifty sick and weak men failed to keep in touch with the stronger members of the party, who were marching on the banks on the way from Quito to the Rio Napo. So Orellana and his men could do nothing but let the rafts drift on, day after day, through the forest and its enchanting wonders, getting what food they could, till, in seven months time, they reached the ocean, and a little farther north found a European settlement.

Hardly less adventurous was the expedition of Quesada on the Orinoco in 1537. Though avarice and cruelty marked the conquest, it remains a marvellous achievement.

What sort of people and what sort of government did the conquerors find? In Mexico and Yucatán, in Honduras, and other parts of Central America they found the remains of great cities belonging to an older Maya civilisation of great antiquity. The strangely impressive remains of those buildings of great stones hewn not with iron (for iron tools were still unknown in America when Europeans set foot there), but with stone tools, and ornamented with fantastic carvings and hieroglyphics, have no parallel for massiveness, not even in Egypt, in the Old World.

There was also, in Mexico, the Aztec civilisation, highly organised in military matters, in religion, and in education of a kind, but having for its foundation a cruel religion. Human beings as well as animals were sacrificed on its altars, and there were cannibal feasts to complete the ceremonies of high feast days. The men and women were specially trained and their sacrifice was held as a great honour by their families.

THE INCAS, CHILDREN OF THE SUN, WHOSE EMPIRE HAD STOOD FOR 300 YEARS

The conquistadores of Peru found the highlands of the Andes and the country as far down as Chile under the rule of the Incas, the Children of the Sun, whose empire had then lasted for about 300 years.

The Inca rule was a despotic one, but gentler and more advanced in the ordinary arts of life than the Mexican. The great temples and palaces of their cities were also built of mighty hewn stones, put together without mortar, but so exquisitely balanced and shaped that the great Inca walls still form the foundation of the streets of Cuzco.

These Inca temples and palaces were adorned with quantities of gold and silver exquisitely wrought. Indeed, from Mexico and along the whole coast the Spaniards found wonderful gold and silver work, and never succeeded in discovering how the work had been accomplished with the primitive appliances at the disposal of the people.

The Incas had, like the Aztecs of Mexico, succeeded a still older civilisation of great builders, the remains of whose work are still to be seen at Tihuanaco and other places in Peru and Bolivia. They made great roads over the mountains with marvellous flying bridges over the deep gorges; they terraced the sides of those gorges so as to grow roots and grain wherever irrigation was possible in that arid land; and if they kept the people in subjection, they also maintained them in prosperity.

THE LAND BRIDGE BY WHICH MAN MAY HAVE REACHED AMERICA

The Incas were held in more reverence by their subjects than any rulers have ever been, and faint recollections of their greatness linger among the Indians today.

The invaders in both North and South America found a thinly-peopled continent; otherwise the conquest would have been much more difficult.

Some people think that the Indian tribes which inhabit America came from Eastern Asia in the first instance. Certainly, whether they are tall or short, long or broad-headed, these tribes are more like the inhabitants of eastern Asia than any other type. They may have journeyed there when America and Asia were still linked by land in the far north, or they may possibly have crossed by way of the Aleutian Islands.

The Aztec and the Inca civilisations extended over only a part of the whole area. The great majority of the Indians lived, as they live today, in the simplest fashion. In the Gulf of Maracaibo and on the Amazon and Orinoco rivers there are still lake dwellings, perched on lofty piles standing in the water. They are reached by canoe, and the ladder is a notched tree trunk.

THE INDIAN WHO LIGHTS A FIRE UNDER HIS HAMMOCK FOR WARMTH

The ordinary forest house of the Indian of the north has open sides and a sloping roof thatched with palm leaves and reaching almost to the ground; it is more a shelter than a house. The Indian hut of the plains is round or oval, with thatched roof and wall built of wattle and plastered with clay.

The Brazilian tribes differ very much in their degrees of skill and culture. Many of them have no better habitation than a miserable bamboo structure, but the oblong shelter is the rule, with a couple of separate huts for sleeping and cooking. Some Brazilian huts have bunks, but the hammock, which seems to have been invented by the Guiana Indians, has been introduced practically throughout the continent. The Indian of British Guiana will sometimes light a fire under his hammock by way of protection against the chills of night!

In some districts the Indians live under good conditions, and are educated and well-to-do members of the community; but conditions vary from State to State and from province to province. In Paraguay the Indians form the bulk of a well-organised community with land and houses of their own; in Brazil, where slave raids persisted until comparatively recent times, many tribes are still uncivilised. Generally the Indian is polite and hospitable, but the remote districts of the Amazon are believed still to harbour cannibal tribes.

DRAKE'S ADVENTURES WITH THE SPANIARDS OF SOUTH AMERICA

It must not be thought that the Spaniards and the Portuguese had it all their own way in the sixteenth century, and were unmolested by their European rivals. French corsairs from St. Malo harassed the Spanish fleets, and French Protestants tried to make a settlement in Brazil. The Dutch long contested Portuguese supremacy in Brazil, and English gentlemen adventurers, openly or secretly assisted by Queen Elizabeth, hung on the sea-routes waiting for the Spanish treasure-ships.

Drake landed on the Isthmus, took Nombre de Dios, and ambushed the mule trains carrying Peruvian silver to Panama; and in 1578 he sailed through the Strait of Magellan and laid waste the coasts of Peru. During the short formal war which began in 1585 he ravaged the Spanish Indies, and captured Cartagena, the great treasure port and market centre. Raleigh and others sought to make settlements in the fever-haunted districts of the Orinoco, and eventually the English, Dutch, and French established themselves in Guiana. For thirty years in the seventeenth century the Dutch fought for the possession of Brazil, and France attacked Rio in 1710.

But generally, from Mexico southwards, the Spaniards and the Portuguese held dominion except in the recesses of the inaccessible forests, where even today the wild tribes still stand outside the law.

Neither Spaniards nor Portuguese had the racial antipathy to the dark man which prevents most British colonists from intermarrying with inhabitants of the places where they settle. The colonial governors assigned tracts of land to their soldiers and to settlers from Spain, and these in many cases intermarried with the Indian population.

THE STRANGE MIXTURE OF PEOPLES IN CENTRAL AND SOUTH AMERICA

The Mexican nation of today is a Spanish-Indian nation; the Brazilians are Portuguese-Indian stock with much Negro admixture, those Negroes brought in many cases from Africa in English slave-ships; in Argentina and Uruguay the population is of Spanish-Indian, Italian, German, and British stock. The Spanish colonial families which have no Indian blood are very few anywhere. Paraguay, alone of all the States, is almost purely Indian, with a small admixture of Spanish blood.

But if you take the whole of South America there are still vast areas in which you may go for miles without finding a human habitation. There are no really reliable figures of population, but there may now be in South America 113 million people, or in the whole of Latin America, including Mexico and the central republics, some 180 million. These consist of pure Indians, Negroes (in Brazil), mestizos (mixed European and Indian blood), mulattos and quadroons (mixed European and Negro blood), Spanish and Portuguese colonists, descendants of families long settled in America, and newcomers from Italy, Germany, Great Britain, and Spain.

A Spanish chronicler says that the Chibchas of Bogota (now Colombia) numbered nearly a million at the time of conquest, and were almost exterminated in twenty years. The number of Indians in Peru and Bolivia was reduced from eight to four million in two hundred years of Spanish rule. The natives of north-eastern Brazil who were not enslaved were practically exterminated at the end of the sixteenth century.

THE HORRORS CHARLES DARWIN WITNESSED IN ARGENTINA

Charles Darwin, who was in Argentina in 1832 at the time of an expedition by General Rosas against an Indian rising, tells of the slaughter which accompanied its repression. Many Indians perished in the hard toil in the mines and on the land to which their masters put them, and in modern times the tribes on the Putumayo suffered from the severities of the rubber gatherers; but the agents which tend to thin them out today are strong drink and the diseases they may take from the white man. Everywhere they brew intoxicating drink from maize, sugar-cane, and other plants. The important fact to remember is that though Spanish rule was corrupt, intolerant from the religious point of view, and a barrier to development because of the strict trade monopoly with Spain, it did not completely destroy the native peoples. Some of them were absorbed; those who remained Indians received, not education, but a simple form of Christianity.

Order. In Paraguay they taught colonies of Indians to make rich and prosperous settlements where they grew all kinds of grain, tobacco, sugar, and yerba maté, the Paraguayan substitute for tea, and kept herds of cattle and sheep. When they were driven out the settlements fell into decay, and progress was put back for over half a century. Here and there European Protestant missions carry on the same work. One Peruvian English mission is a small colony of Indians who are able to produce all that is necessary for the little community.

In the last years of the eighteenth century the Spaniards began to improve their methods, and above all they withdrew

THE MODERN AIRPORT OF GUATEMALA CITY, FIVE THOUSAND FEET ABOVE SEA LEVEL

Above all, Spanish rule gave the continent a common language, Spanish, so that the Colombian or the Mexican can understand the speech of the Chilean or the Argentino. In Brazil, however, Portuguese is spoken. The mestizos speak Spanish or Portuguese, and every Indian who becomes educated learns one or the other.

Latin America has not the " colour " question in the same acute form in which it is known in the United States, and in many parts of South Africa. But centuries of oppression have left the Indians reserved and impassive, and they have never had equal opportunity with the whites. Their best friends in Spanish colonial days were the Jesuit missionaries, who sought to raise the level of their culture; but jealousies led to the expulsion of the

their veto on trade through the River Plate, the great estuary of the Paraná and Uruguay rivers, and the only route to the central plains. They still appointed newcomers from Spain to the higher offices, thus arousing great discontent among the colonial Spanish aristocracy. But the Spanish concessions came too late. The power of the Spaniards in Europe was shaken by Napoleon's conquest of Spain, and revolt against their rule blazed up all over Central and South America.

It is not possible to tell here the history of that great struggle, nor of the national heroes who freed Latin America from foreign dominion in the years between 1800 and 1826. There was San Martin, who led the revolution in Argentina and conducted the Army of Liberation in 1817 across the lofty pass over the Andes into

Chile, now pierced by the railway; Bolivar, who delivered the northern republics, together with Peru and Bolivia, and is honoured in all four countries for the purity and disinterestedness of his action even more than for his military achievements; Hidalgo, Morelos, Yturbide, and the unscrupulous Santa Anna in Mexico; and a host of others, among whom we find some of English and Irish birth, notably Bernardo O'Higgins, who became a President of Chile.

THE LONG YEARS OF TROUBLE IN THE HISTORY OF MEXICO

The course of history in Mexico was much more complicated than that of the South American States, partly because its territory ran side by side with the United States, to which Mexico had to yield Nevada, Arizona, New Mexico, and Upper California. Then there were long civil wars, and in later years intervention by Spain, Britain, and France.

France took separate action after the first two Powers had retired, and established on the throne of Mexico the Archduke Maximilian, a son-in-law of King Leopold of Belgium. He was Emperor of Mexico for the troubled years between 1864 and 1867. In 1867 the United States Government told France plainly that her army must be removed, and that they would recognise no Government in Mexico but a republican one. Maximilian was foolish enough to remain, and was shot by the Republicans on June 19, 1867.

Brazil, too, only gained real independence after a long and chequered struggle between conflicting factions within and with neighbouring States throughout the years from the Declaration of Independence in 1822 to the final abdication of the Portuguese dynasty and the Declaration of the Republic in 1889. Even after this long period of war and revolution when the republic was established, disorders and local risings made progress in Brazil very slow indeed.

THE HISTORIC DECLARATION WHICH GAVE LATIN AMERICA ITS CHANCE

Generally speaking, the Latin-American States had the sympathy of the United States and of Britain in their fight for freedom. Britain was sympathetic because of her anger with Spain. In 1823 the absolute power of the Spanish king was restored by French arms, and Britain thought that France once more was making a bid for world power, and she threw her great influence and her naval strength on the side of the revolted colonies.

"If France has Spain," cried George Canning in a famous speech, "at least it shall be Spain without the Indies. *We have called a new world into existence to redress the balance of the old.*" On December 22, 1823, President Monroe of the United States made the historic declaration that no part of America was henceforth open for colonisation. The Monroe Doctrine has come to mean that, while existing European colonies will be respected, the United States, vastly more powerful than the younger American States, will not allow European domination of any existing independent American country. This, with the declaration of British Foreign Minister Canning, gave Latin America its chance.

The new republics did not quite satisfy their more enthusiastic supporters in the United States and Britain. They had adopted democratic institutions in countries where a great proportion of the population were and are absolutely illiterate, and in States where the great body of the citizens were Indians, with no inkling of the meaning of the vote, but who were prepared to fight wherever they were required to do so.

THE SUCCESSION OF REVOLUTIONS WHICH HELD BACK PROGRESS

The result was a succession of revolutions made by ambitious dictators, elections faked by the military party in power, wars between the States, and a general state of chaos from which orderly government only evolved later.

Now there are signs of a better understanding between the individual States, though there is still some jealousy between them, and the old dispute about the North Chaco, an area of some 100,000 square miles between the River Pilcomayo and the Paraguay, led to an outbreak of war between Bolivia and Paraguay which lasted many years.

Argentina and Chile, after quarrelling for half a century over their boundary, followed a wiser course. They agreed to the arbitration of King Edward VII of Britain, and, after accepting the decision, they set up a solemn monument on the summit of the pass over the Andes, under which the transcontinental railway now bores its way, as the evidence of their determination never again to go to war one with another. It is a gigantic figure of Christ, with the inscription, *Sooner shall these mountains crumble than the people of Argentina and Chile break the peace which, at the feet of Christ the Redeemer, they have sworn to maintain.*

At intervals the States hold a pan-American congress, at which they can discuss the many interests they have in common. The Pan-American Union, too, which had been established in 1890, convened a conference at Petropolis, near Rio de Janeiro, in 1947, at which the American republics signed a treaty of collective security with the United States.

THE VOLCANIC RANGES WHICH RUN DOWN THE WESTERN COAST

Now let us look at the physical conditions out of which the wealth, the prosperity, the advantages, and the difficulties of this great continent spring.

The dominating physical feature is the volcanic range, or parallel ranges, of mountains running down the whole of the western coast. In Mexico the main chain, the Sierra Madre, runs southward from the Rocky Mountains, but practically the whole of the country is a great table-land, varying in height from 4000 to 8000 feet, from which rise numerous ranges of mountains. The principal volcanoes lie in a line between Colima and Vera Cruz. Of these Citlaltepec (Orizaba) and Popocatepetl are about the 18,000 feet level. The former is no longer active, but there are some peaks in Mexico which were thrown up in the eighteenth century, and one, Paricutia, as late as 1943.

At each side the slope to the narrow coastal plain is steep. In the south the mountains are compressed into a narrow space, filling, indeed, the whole area of the Mexican province of Oaxaca, and they stretch right away through Central America. Many of the volcanoes are active, and have had devastating eruptions within recent times.

THE COLOSSAL CUT BETWEEN THE MOUNTAINS JOINING TWO OCEANS

At Panama the great series of mountain ranges sink at one point to the level of about 3000 feet, and there is a saddle between the peaks of only a few hundred feet. It is in this fold that American engineers cut the canal linking the Atlantic and Pacific Oceans. The moun-

tains continue down the whole of the west coast of the continent, sometimes in three distinct ranges and sometimes in two, enclosing in Peru and Bolivia wide and lofty tablelands on which lies the high inland sea of Titicaca, once much greater in extent than it is today.

The eastern chain is called Los Andes, and the western La Cordillera. The Andes contain the highest volcanic peaks in the world, Cotopaxi reaching 19,344 feet. Aconcagua, in the extreme west of Argentina, is one of the giant mountains of the world, reaching 23,080 feet. The South American chain has seven peaks over 20,000 feet high, and eight of 16,000 feet and over. If we remember the height of Mont Blanc, 15,782 feet, we have some idea of the gigantic height of the Andes.

In southern Argentina the parallel ranges give place to one, which ends in the rocks of Tierra del Fuego. Along a great part of the coast there is a low coastal range. Short and rapid torrents descend here and there, but the greatest rivers flow eastward across the plains, traversed in Brazil by a series of lower ranges, which form the water partings between the rivers running north to the Amazon, and between the Amazon and River Plate systems.

THE GREAT RIVER SYSTEM LOOKING LIKE AN INLAND SEA

The Amazon is the largest river system of the world, the main stream having a navigable length of 3000 miles and a total length of 3900 miles to one of its principal sources, the Lake of Lauricocha, which lies to the north-east of Lima in Peru. Many of its great tributaries are also navigable. If we look at the map we see how numerous these are, their great length, and the way in which they widen out here and there into lakes.

In the wet season the Amazon spreads over great areas, and in many places has the aspect of an inland sea dotted with forest islands. At all seasons of the year it has many parallel arms, which make it rather a system of waterways than a single waterway. Ocean-going steamers go up as far as Manaos, which is 850 miles upstream from the coast, and is the centre of the rubber trade; ordinary steamers go as far as Iquitos in Peru.

Everywhere the Amazon and its tributaries form practically the only means of communication over a vast area, and the

Indians who live there have always been expert watermen and clever in the construction of the canoes and little flat boats with which they navigate the river. Except for the upper course of the Amazon which is called the Marañon, the whole of its basin is forest, with only small patches of cultivated land; and the same conditions apply to many of its tributaries.

A part of Colombia and the whole of Venezuela lie in the basin of the Orinoco and its feeders, which form the principal highways of the country. The Orinoco is also bordered by forests, but the high lands north and south are covered with a rough pasturage and are known as the Llanos.

HOW THE INSECTS HOLD A WATERWAY AGAINST THE APPROACH OF MAN

Western Colombia is watered by another great river, the Magdalena. South of the Orinoco system, and in the northern part of Brazil, there are more grassy plains before the great forests begin. There is a curious natural canal connecting one of the feeders of the Rio Negro, a northern tributary of the Amazon, with the Orinoco, but it is infested with insects to an even greater degree than the Amazon itself, and is little used even by native canoes. There is, a little higher up the valley, a short water parting where canoes can be hauled across and communication established.

There are two other important factors to be taken into account in the climate and rainfall of South America beside the actual latitude. They are the lie of the mountains, the trade winds, and the cold Antarctic current called after the scientist Humboldt, which comes up the Pacific along the Chilean and Peruvian coasts.

A DISTRICT WHERE IT RAINS EVERY DAY OF THE YEAR

From the Isthmus of Panama down to a little below the Equator, at the Gulf of Guayaquil, the tropical summer rains give everywhere the rank, abundant, and varied vegetation of tropical countries. In the Choco district on the Pacific coast of Colombia it rains every afternoon and evening every day of the year. But from the Gulf of Guayaquil down to a point a little north of Valparaiso the west coast is practically rainless, because the trade winds blow south-east from the Atlantic, and after traversing the continent yield up the remnant of their moisture on the high eastern range of the Andes, leaving none for the plateau, the western range, and the west coast. That is why there are very few rivers and practically no rain in this district.

Curiously enough, that same coast is often buried in cloud and mist, due to the contact between the cold air arising from the Humboldt current and the heated land. The sea itself is not the blue sea you expect to see in the tropics, but often cold and grey. Only where a torrent comes down to the sea is there any mitigation of the barrenness of these shores, rich as we shall see, nevertheless, because of the guano deposited by sea-birds on the rocky islands of the coast, which would in a wet climate be washed away and wasted, and the valuable nitrate deposits of the desert of Atacama, which are shipped from Antofagasta. As soon as you are out of the zone of the trade winds, that is, in the neighbourhood of Valparaiso, the position is reversed. The winds are westerly from the Pacific, and give southern Chile abundant rains, while Patagonia, on the eastern side, is a thirsty land.

THE SPACIOUS AND IMPOSING GRANDEUR OF THE MOUNTAIN SCENERY

The Andes themselves have a grandeur to be found nowhere else except in the Himalayas. Throughout their whole length right through the tropics, the summits are clad with snow. But the foothills from the west are bare and dry, without the forests which add to the magnificence of the Himalayas. There is little grass and, except in the deeper valleys, no wood on the western side, and on the east in many places one plunges direct from the mountain into thick forest, so that no view of the mountains or anything else can be obtained.

What redeems the scenery of the High Andes (wrote Lord Bryce in his book on South America) is the richness and delicacy of the colours which the brilliant desert light gives to distant objects. A black peak becomes deep purple ; a slope of dry grey earth takes a tender lilac; and evening as it falls transfigures the stones which strew the sides of a valley with a soft glow. The snow sparkles and glitters at noonday and flushes in sunset with a radiance unknown to our climate. . . . Yet this cannot make them inspire the sort of affection we feel for the mountains of temperate countries, with their constant changes from rain to sunlight, their fresh streams and bubbling springs, and flowers starring the high pastures.

There is grandeur and stark beauty of line ; there are immense heights and yawning depths. The rainless mountain tableland of Peru and Bolivia is awe-inspiring and imposing in the grandeur of its scenery ; but the loveliest mountain prospects in Latin America are to be found on the Mex'can plateau. Here there is sufficient rainfall to give abundant vegetation, there is the bright sunshine of the tropics, with the coolness and clearness of high elevations, and ranges of lower hills, and beyond them the towering snow-clad volcanic cones ; while far away to the southward in Chile there is the added beauty of deep-cut sea fiords running up into the land.

Bearing in mind the physical conditions of each region, we can see, if we look at the map, the reasons for the economic circumstances of life. Maize, wheat, coffee, cotton, every kind of fruit, oranges, lemons, grape-fruit, mangoes, bananas, alligator pears—all these flourish in different parts of Mexico, and navel oranges grow wild in perfection. In the north ranching is very important, both for cattle, sheep, and horses.

THE MINERALS WHICH HAVE BROUGHT WEALTH TO MEXICO

The great forests on the coasts of Mexico and in the nearby States supply all kinds of tropical hard woods, mahogany, ebony, sandalwood, and rosewood. But the great wealth of Mexico, a wealth which has brought her much trouble and jealousy for 400 years, lies in her minerals ; gold, silver, copper, lead, iron, and many others.

Another source of wealth has been her petroleum deposits, which at one time provided as much as a quarter of the world's supplies, although her output now is nothing like this proportion.

The Mexican oilfields were once to a great extent owned by American, British, and Dutch companies. But not long before the Second World War, Mexico decided to take over her oilfields, and she paid large sums of money to the American, British, and Dutch owners for them.

Mexico has many excellent harbours on her western coasts, especially at Acapulco and San Blas. But on the Gulf of Mexico the harbours are not good. The Atlantic current swirls through the Caribbean Sea, forming sand banks and lagoons, the channels of which could be kept clear, though at a great cost. Vera Cruz is the principal port on this coast ; it has a good harbour. The greatest of Mexican rivers is the Rio Grande, which forms the boundary between the United States of America and Mexico.

With other rivers, the Rio Grande is being increasingly used for hydro-electric power and irrigation works.

A COUNTRY FULL OF INTEREST FOR TRAVELLER AND ARCHAEOLOGIST

Mexico City, the capital of the Republic, is also its commercial centre. The city stands on the plateau at an elevation of 7000 feet on the site of the Aztec city. The museum there is full of interest for the archaeologist. There is the Stone of the Sun with its calendar, and the monstrous image in basalt known as the Idol Huitzilopochtli, the Aztec war god. In Yucatán there are extensive remains of Maya buildings with wonderful sculptures.

As might be expected, Mexico's principal trade is with her greater neighbour the United States, but Britain sends her a considerable quantity of goods and British engineers have carried out many great works in Mexico.

In the Central American republics and in Venezuela, Colombia, and Ecuador you have the heavy rains of the tropics and their rich, rank vegetation. Until the advance of science taught man how to defend himself against his most deadly enemy, the mosquito, the swampy ground around the rivers and on the coast was a death-trap for Europeans, and even for the natives who had been habituated to it for centuries. General Gorgas made the building of the Panama Canal possible by destroying the mosquitos in their breeding places and screening the huts of the labourers ; and since then Mexico, Venezuela, and Brazil have learned how to fight yellow fever, adopting the methods of Gorgas, with the result that the plague has almost disappeared. (There are fine doctors and specialists in all these countries.)

THE HEALTHY HIGHLANDS AND THE DANGEROUS VALLEYS

This was the first step to a real development of these districts. In all of them the highlands are healthy and relatively cool, the deep valleys and lowlands, too rich in vegetation, are dangerous to humanity. Throughout them the same great range of produce which we have mentioned in Mexico, with the exception, of course, of wheat, grows profusely, and the coconut palm provides the native Indian with food, intoxicating drink, and fibre. Costa Rica provides one of the best coffees, and exports some millions of bunches of bananas every year. Honduras has the finest mahogany trees in the world, and is one of the places from which we get our bananas.

THE SIX LITTLE REPUBLICS AND ONE COLONY OF CENTRAL AMERICA

Costa Rica and Honduras are two of the seven small states of Central America, the long isthmus between Mexico and South America. Of these seven, one is the Colony of British Honduras and the others are little republics. Costa Rica, which means the Rich Coast, has an area of only 19,695 square miles and a population of less than a million. Honduras is more than twice as big ; its area is some 44,411 square miles, but its population is one-and-a-half million.

Guatemala is much the same size and has a population approaching three million. Nicaragua is larger, with an area of 57,145 square miles, but it is thinly populated, having little more than a million people.

Salvador is the baby of Central America, with an area of only 13,176 square miles but it has a population of nearly two million. Panama has an area of 28,575 square miles and a population of less than a million. A small strip on each side of its great canal is controlled by the United States.

In South America the dense forests are the chief obstacles which man has to overcome, and there are vast regions in the tropical area which have so far defied Europeans. You cannot " wander " in a tropical forest, not even in a sub-tropical one, for in an instant you are closed in, and the growth is so dense that a way can only be hacked by using tools.

THE AMAZING VEGETATION OF THE GREAT TROPICAL FORESTS

That is why the upper reaches of the Amazon are still inhabited by savage and even cannibal tribes. Perhaps the great forest region which covers eastern Colombia and Ecuador, a part of eastern Peru, and a vast area in Brazil, would be more untouched than it is if it were not for the rubber seekers, who in pursuit of this product have made their way into the forest where the rivers have cut a path through the dense growth.

The forest has an amazing variety of great trees, many of them with vivid blossoms of all sorts of colours; there is an undergrowth of palms, bamboos, and other plants, and even the tree fern will grow to the height of 20 feet; then there are the climbing and parasitic plants, from the thick monkey-ladder to the brilliant orchid which add to the profusion of life. Even keeping to the trees and the monkey-ladder as the monkeys usually do, they are still not safe from their enemies, for the boa constrictor winds itself around the trees and catches its prey in this way. Similarly the rivers swarm with alligators which prey on the smaller animals.

The spotted jaguar is the tiger of the new world, and the fiercest of the forest animals. There are many kinds of wild cats. Henry Walter Bates, the traveller and naturalist, records 38 species of monkeys on the Amazon. The Brazilians keep the coaita, or red-faced spider monkey as a pet. Other wild animals of tropical America are the ocelot, a prettily marked beast which lives in the trees and preys on birds; the puma, the Mexican lion, which sometimes attacks horses and cattle; the tapir; the sloth; and the ant-eater.

THE SMALL HUMMING-BIRD AND THE GREAT CONDOR OF THE ANDES

The birds are brilliant in colour but not generally musical in song. Parrots and macaws abound, and the humming-birds, some no bigger than bees and others as large as wrens, flash their lovely wings in the sunshine. Oddest of all South American birds is the toucan of Guiana and Brazil. Its huge beak, like the claw of a lobster, is orange in colour and is 8 inches long; the head is blue and orange, the throat white, and the plumage black with red and white on the tail, altogether an amazing creature. Of the birds of prey the most extraordinary is the condor of the Andes, a kind of South American eagle which figures largely in Peruvian sculptures and pottery. The tortoise is a valuable item of commerce, and on the upper Amazon a staple food.

In northern Brazil the same kind of produce is found as in the northern republics. In the eastern highlands cotton is widely cultivated. Rio de Janeiro the capital, São Paulo, and Santos, the coffee port, all lie near the line of Capricorn. But the trade winds from the Atlantic and the height of the land—for the whole district is traversed by a series of mountain ranges—make the climate comparatively

PICTURES OF LATIN AMERICA

THE TOWN OF ROSARIO IN ARGENTINA, SEEN FROM THE RIVER PARANÁ

A STREET IN HAVANA, CAPITAL
OF CUBA

COLUMBUS CATHEDRAL
AT HAVANA

THE EXCHANGE AT HAVANA
IN CUBA

THE LAW COURTS AT
BUENOS AIRES

NATIONAL CONGRESS PALACE AT
BUENOS AIRES

A PLANTER'S HOME NEAR MATANZAS IN CUBA

A PARK IN THE CENTRE OF BUENOS AIRES

THE TOWN OF MANAOS ON THE RIO NEGRO IN BRAZIL

AN OLD INDIAN POSES FOR
HIS PORTRAIT

INDIANS OF BRAZIL
AT HOME

AN INDIAN OF BRAZIL
ENJOYS A SMOKE

THE NATIONAL LIBRARY AT RIO DE JANEIRO

THE OPERA HOUSE AT MANAOS

SANTOS, A PORT OF SÃO PAULO IN BRAZIL

RIO DE JANEIRO, THE CAPITAL OF BRAZIL

BARRANQUILLA, THE CHIEF PORT OF COLOMBIA, ON THE MAGDALENA RIVER

THE AVENUE OF PALMS IN VERA CRUZ, MEXICO

AN INDIAN MOTHER AND HER CHILD OF YUCATAN IN MEXICO

THE BASILICA OF JESUS DEL RIO AT PASTO IN COLOMBIA

THE SEBANA CENTRAL RAILWAY STATION AT BOGOTÁ IN COLOMBIA

THE GOVERNMENT PALACE AT QUITO, CAPITAL OF ECUADOR

A FOUNTAIN NEAR BOGOTÁ, FEDERAL CAPITAL OF COLOMBIA

A TYPICAL GOLD MINE IN NICARAGUA

A CLOTH MARKET IN
MEXICO CITY

THE LEGISLATIVE PALACE AT LA PAZ,
CAPITAL OF BOLIVIA

INDIANS IN LA PAZ,
BOLIVIA

AN AYMARA INDIAN
OF BOLIVIA

AN INDIAN MOTHER AND
CHILD IN LA PAZ

THE CITY OF PUEBLA IN MEXICO

TAMPICO, A MEXICAN SEAPORT

POPOCATEPETL, THE GREAT MEXICAN VOLCANO

A STREET SCENE IN TIERRA DEL FUEGO

THE GOVERNMENT PALACE AT ASUNCION,
CAPITAL OF PARAGUAY

SAN JOSÉ CATHEDRAL IN
COSTA RICA

A HOUSE AT CARACAS
IN VENEZUELA

TWO LITTLE NATIVES OF
PANAMA

A MAYA GOD IN A
TEMPLE IN MEXICO

A NATIVE VILLAGE IN PANAMA

OX-CARTS ON THE ROAD IN COSTA RICA

A WATER-CART IN A STREET IN SAN SALVADOR,
CAPITAL OF SALVADOR

LOOKING DOWN ON THE PANAMA CANAL
FROM THE HILL OF BALBOA

INCA MASONRY IN
CUZCO, PERU

" CHRIST THE REDEEMER " AT
RIO DE JANEIRO, BRAZIL

A NATIVE STREET
IN CHILE

THE PLAZA VICTORIA AT VALPARAISO IN CHILE

THE CATHEDRAL AT JULIACA IN PERU

THE PORT OF ANTOFAGASTA
IN CHILE

A BRIDGE ON ONE OF THE WORLD'S HIGHEST
RAILWAYS, IN THE PERUVIAN ANDES

LOOKING DOWN ON
GUATEMALA CITY

THE GREAT STATUE OF CHRIST
IN THE ANDES

GRANADA, THE LANDING-PLACE
ON LAKE NICARAGUA

A CART DRAWN BY OXEN IN
GUATEMALA CITY

A MAN OF
MEXICO

WATER-CARRIERS NEAR
CULIACAN IN MEXICO

POCITOS BEACH AT MONTEVIDEO,
CAPITAL OF URUGUAY

THE NATIONAL PALACE OF THE PRESIDENT AND
CABINET OF GUATEMALA, AT GUATEMALA CITY

THE CENTRAL RAILWAY STATION,
MONTEVIDEO

MONTEVIDEO CATHEDRAL
IN URUGUAY

THE TOWN OF PAYSANDU
IN URUGUAY

THE PALACE OF THE PRESIDENT & GOVERNMENT
BUILDING AT LIMA, CAPITAL OF PERU

The pictures on these pages are reproduced by courtesy of Messrs. Burton-Holmes, Ewing Galloway, the E.N.A., and others

cool and pleasant. This is one of the greatest coffee-producing countries in the world, providing three-quarters of the world's supply.

THE FOODS WHICH GROW IN THE SOUTHERN STATES OF BRAZIL

In the southern States the tropical produce, the sugar, the rice, the cocoa, and the nut-bearing palms—from which the famous Brazil nuts are gathered—give way to the crops of more temperate climates. Maize grows in all the provinces, and manioc, the root from which the farina used by Brazilians in breadmaking is derived, is universal. In Paraná there is still coffee, but also a great acreage under wheat, potatoes, and yerba maté, the leaf from which a liquid resembling tea is brewed all over the southern States of South America. In Rio Grande do Sul we are in a warm temperate climate, and find enormous stretches of alfalfa or lucerne, the great fodder crop of the continent. Here is the beginning of the ranching industry which makes the wealth of the countries to the south.

The towns of Brazil are modern, with wide streets, electric light, buses, and the rest of the apparatus of civilisation, but within a mile or two of any of them you may find yourself in a wild and impenetrable forest. Rio de Janeiro, known generally simply as Rio, the capital, is one of the most beautifully situated cities of the world, with its wide bay flanked by the Sugar Loaf mountain and the curious pointed peaks of the Organ Mountains.

HOW THE COFFEE IS TAKEN ACROSS THE MOUNTAINS FOR EXPORT

São Paulo, which is a centre of the coffee plantations, stands high on the plateau and is connected with Santos, the port from which the coffee is exported, by a mountain railway. Pará, at the mouth of the Amazon, has a large trade up the river down which the rubber from the forests is brought. Pernambuco, built partly on an island at the extreme easterly point of Brazil, is sometimes called by the Brazilians the American Venice. Bahia, once the capital, is now famous for its cocoa and tobacco.

Brazil, far and away the biggest of the Latin American republics, has an area of 3,288,000 square miles, and a population of about 55 million.

South of Brazil and westward in the heart of the continent lie the great southern plains of Paraguay, Uruguay, and Argentina.

Paraguay, watered by the Paraná and the Paraguay rivers, is the most Indian of all the States, and outside Asunción and the two or three other towns the spoken language is Guarani. Ranching is the principal source of wealth.

Paraguay has an area of 150,500 square miles, and a population of about 1,450,000.

Uruguay is a progressive little State with advanced legislation and a determination to bring the standard of government and of education up to European levels. It has a magnificent river, the Uruguay, and a fine natural seaport in Montevideo. Though smaller than Paraguay—the area of Uruguay is 72,153 square miles—its population is well over two million. Both Uruguay and its larger and more powerful neighbour Argentina, are primarily stock-raising countries. The Indian element is less in these two States than anywhere else in South America, and there has been during the past century a steady stream of immigrants from the United States, Germany, England, Scotland, Italy, and Spain, who have brought energy and modern industrial methods with them.

BUENOS AIRES, THE BUSIEST CITY IN LATIN AMERICA

Argentina's capital, Buenos Aires, is busy and bustling, and more like a North American city than any other place in Latin America. The people of Buenos Aires are very wealthy, and they make frequent trips to Europe, especially to Paris, bringing back French fashions, French books, and French amusements. The city is rich, smart, and expensive, with nothing of the quiet Spanish city about it. Its citizens will tell you, with pride, that it is the largest city south of the Equator, the largest Spanish-speaking city anywhere, and rapidly becoming one of the largest ports of the world, though it has not the natural advantages of Montevideo, and has been constructed with much labour. Argentina has taken its constitution and its business methods from the United States, but its literary and artistic culture is Spanish and French.

It is the second largest of the Latin American countries, having an area of 1,078,769 square miles. Its population is over 18 million, nearly all of the people being of European descent. The native Indians are decreasing in numbers, and there are fewer than 30,000 of them in the whole country.

The pampas or plains of southern Argentina are really flat, without the undulation which relieves the plain of Uruguay. But away in the west and north you will see that the High Andes are partly in Argentine territory, and that the country stretches away inland to the north.

In these northern districts sugar and tobacco are grown. Argentina is more subject to drought than Uruguay, and also suffers from locusts, which do enormous damage in spite of the strong measures that have been—and still are—taken against them.

THE SKILLED GAUCHOS WHO ROUND UP THE CATTLE ON THE PLAINS

In the south there is a tract which gets very little rain at any time, as the prevailing winds there are westerly and precipitate their moisture on the Andes. In many districts water is not too plentiful, and it is necessary to sink deep wells, the water being run along the fields in troughs for the use of the cattle.

Argentina is mainly a country of ranching and farming on a large scale, exporting through Buenos Aires to Europe immense quantities of meat, wheat, linseed, and maize.

Originally the Spanish landowners had big holdings which covered a square league, or about six thousand acres. There were practically no enclosures, and great herds of cattle and horses wandered over the plains, marked with their owners' marks and brought in from time to time by the gauchos, who are as skilled with the lasso and the bolas as any American cowboy. Holdings or estancias of this size are still common ; but as settlement becomes closer, it is found necessary to find smaller holdings for new men.

THE GREAT STOCK FARMS WHICH SUPPLY THE WORLD WITH MEAT

The romantic day of the unenclosed pampas is past. The estancias are being broken up into fields for the better management of the stock, and wire fencing is everywhere. The herds are carefully bred, and the Argentine landowner spends enormous sums on pedigree animals from Britain, which are kept in good quarters and generally pampered as pets of the family.

Many estancias are owned by the great meat companies of Buenos Aires and Montevideo. There are some estancias for the breeding of big herds of cattle, and others where the young stock brought from the breeding ranches are fattened for the freezing works, large areas being kept under maize and alfalfa for feeding them. On the stock-raising farms the labour is provided by the peon, or native Argentino, but on the farms devoted to arable culture many of the workers are Italians.

There is not much variety of life on the estancia, less than there used to be when there were no enclosures and there was the excitement of catching the stock with the lasso, but on high days and holidays the peon will go off on his horse to the nearest town and get a little amusement. But the town is far away, and though there is a network of railways all over the more thickly settled districts, travelling is expensive and the distances long. The manager and his family themselves get to town but seldom, for hotel accommodation is usually dear.

Education under these conditions is difficult. Progress, however, has been made, and the number of people unable to read and write has been considerably reduced in recent years. A tax is imposed on employers to support the universities.

THE MANY FLOURISHING CITIES OF ARGENTINA

Argentina is a great producer of wool and mutton as well as beef, and sheep-raising is the chief industry in southern regions of the country.

The republic has had plenty of troubles. The trade unions are a powerful element in the nation's political life, but periods of dictatorship as well as violent labour disputes have been a frequent experience of the Argentine people.

There are many flourishing cities in Argentina besides Buenos Aires. Tucumán in the north is the centre of the sugar industry, and is about 25 hours by rail from Buenos Aires ; the old town of Santa Fé on the Paraná ; La Plata, founded in 1882, when the first big boom in Argentina began, was a proverb for its rapid growth, and now it has become important again as a centre of the oil-refining industry ; Bahia Blanca is the great shipping port for grain from the south ; Cordobá, with its university, set in lovely scenery on the edge of the western highlands, is the city of learning ; Comodoro Rivadavia in the south is an important oil centre and even supplies natural gas to the capital, 1000 miles away.

There is also the town of Mendoza, on the transcontinental railway from Buenos Aires to Santiago in Chile, just at the point where the railway begins to ascend toward the mountains. This part of Argentina is bare and arid, but Mendoza, watered by a torrent which descends here from the Andes, is a little oasis where the vine flourishes. Here too is one of the centres of the petroleum industry, which became more and more important as wells were found in different parts of the country, from Jujuy in the north to the extreme south. The town of Mendoza has a magnificent view of the high Andes towards the south-west, from Tupungato southwards, especially at sunrise when the light touches the snow with red.

From Mendoza the line passes through a plain, and then up the imposing Valley of Desolation to the point, fifteen hundred feet below the summit of the pass, where the mountain is pierced by the railway tunnel. The line is a wonderful piece of engineering, and for the last part of the ascent to the tunnel the journey is by rack rail.

THE COLOSSAL FIGURE OF JESUS STANDING AS A SYMBOL OF PEACE

Far above on the old mule track stands the gigantic figure of the Christ, to symbolise the determination of the two nations to live at peace. Descending towards Chile you pass through some of the finest rock scenery in the world, and presently descend to a lovely watered country very different from the arid plains of the coast farther north ; for here the winds are westerly, and the dry tract is on the Argentine side. Bright sun, mountain air, vineyards, rushing torrents, forest trees, brilliant flowering cactus, and flowers of every hue greet the eye.

At Los Andes the traveller will see men in crimson ponchos—the universal Indian garb in the west, a brightly coloured woollen, oblong cloth, with a hole through which to put the head—galloping along with curiously made and ornamented saddles ; he will see teams of oxen drawing the haycarts ; droves of pack mules ; women carrying baskets of pomegranates ; dark, low houses with no windows visible from the street, for the windows open to the court, or patio, round which the house is built ; and behind all—the Andes.

Chile, spread like a ragged ribbon up the south-west coast of South America, has an area of 286,397 square miles and a population approaching six million. Santiago, the capital of Chile, is a beautiful old Spanish town, and Valparaiso, its port, is one of the busiest places on the Pacific coast.

CENTRAL CHILE AND ITS DANGER FROM EARTHQUAKES

Central Chile is one of the loveliest countries in the world, with its indented coast, its islands, its mountains, its sunshine, and its rich variety of flowers and fruit. The people are energetic and enterprising. The Chilenos had a fierce and long struggle with the Araucanian Indians of this district, who are still among the finest of the native races, and are themselves bold and active. The Chilean cities are not so modern in pattern as some in the Atlantic States, and there is always the danger of earthquakes, like the one which devastated Santiago and Valparaiso in 1906 ; but great advances are made every year. The whole of the coast is more Spanish, less touched with modern European manners and ways than are to be found on the other side of the Andes.

Chile has one great natural source of wealth beside her agriculture, and that is in her nitrate fields, which lie a little to the north of Valparaiso, where the desert begins. In the higher regions of this desert, about 20 miles from the coast, at a height of from 3000 to 5000 feet, occur the nitrate deposits, producing the nitrate of soda or saltpetre which is so valuable a fertiliser, though scientific development of substances has greatly affected its supremacy. The district is a barren country, where everything has to be imported for the use of the population which has grown up around the industry.

ANTOFAGASTA, THE SEA-GATE FOR TWO COUNTRIES

All the food for man and beast, even the water, has to be brought from without, and such little gardens as have been made are made of imported soil. But the district, possession of the whole of which was only obtained by Chile after a war with Peru and Bolivia in 1881, has brought capital and great wealth to Chile.

The nitrates are exported from the port of Antofagasta, which fetches its water from a spot 193 miles away. From

Antofagasta, too, is exported the copper which is mined in the mountains of Bolivia and Chile. This port serves Bolivia as well as Chile, and from there runs a railway right up to La Paz, the real, though not the official, capital of Bolivia, which is Sucre.

Two other important seaports in Chile are Iquique, a town which has suffered terribly from earthquakes, and from which nitrates and iodine are exported; and far away in the south Punta Arenas, on the Strait of Magellan, the centre of a flourishing sheep and wool trade.

But to return to Antofagasta. You may either ascend to La Paz from this Chilean port, taking 48 hours, or you may take a shorter route from Arica. Or again there is a railway from Mollendo in Peru to Puno on the Peruvian side of Lake Titicaca, and thence the traveller can go by boat to Guaqui, and on to La Paz by rail. It is possible to approach Bolivia from the Atlantic Ocean from Pará, at the mouth of the Amazon. The Amazon and the Madeira rivers are navigable as far as the falls on the Madeira River near San Antonio, from which place there is a little railway leading to Villa Bella in Bolivia, and from this point it is possible to travel by river and on muleback to La Paz.

LONG STRINGS OF LLAMAS CARRYING GOODS IN THE MOUNTAINS

Bolivia, one of the only two landlocked republics of Latin America (the other is Paraguay), has an area of about 416,000 square miles and a population of about three million.

The mule is the standard way of travel in the whole of this high region. For the transport of goods the people of Bolivia and Peru use strings of llamas. The llama is useful for his wool as well, and is shorn every three or four years; but his chief service to humanity is to do their carrying for them. He is a curious beast, and has more than his hump in common with the camel. He knows exactly how much a llama is expected to carry—about 100 pounds—and nothing in the world will induce him to do more than his share. He simply lies down, and will not get up if more is put on his back.

But by whatever route La Paz is reached the traveller finds it a wonderful place. To begin with, it is the highest capital in the world, standing at an elevation of 12,700 feet. That is more than twice as high as Ben Nevis. Nevertheless, La Paz does not lie on the top of a hill, but in a deep depression of the plateau, and to reach it you descend into a basin about 1500 feet deep.

For the traveller approaching the city by train from Guaqui there is no sign whatever of the existence of the place until he notices llamas, donkeys, and pedestrians moving along to a spot where they suddenly disappear from view.

HOW THE INDIANS OF BOLIVIA AND PERU KEEP ALOOF FROM THE WHITE MAN

La Paz is so high that the visitor is apt to suffer from the mountain sickness which is one of the difficulties of life on the Peruvian and Bolivian plateau.

La Paz is really an Indian city and Bolivia is primarily an Indian country. But there is little intercourse between the Indians and the white people. The Indian does the actual manual work. Next above him comes the mestizo, or half-breed, who commonly wears European clothes, and is reckoned, by himself at any rate, as a white man. He directs the Indian labour. The Indian is nominally a Christian, but he has adopted the saints of the Church without abandoning the old beliefs and superstitions which he held under the Incas. This is the case, too, with the Quichua Indians who form the country population of Peru. They neither love nor hate the white man, but they fear him and keep aloof.

So they live their own lives, keep their own native dances, the real secrets of which are hidden from the white man, though in some places you may now and then see a public dance, when the Indian dresses himself in the most terrible looking masks, adorns himself with all his fine clothes and feathers, and, accompanied by wild and barbarous music, dances as his forefathers have done for centuries.

THE ANCIENT RUINS WHICH HELPED TO MAKE A RAILWAY

La Paz is very cold after sundown, but the Indian seems well acclimatised. He wears a cotton shirt and loose trousers, surmounted by a gay poncho and a felt hat; the women wear a multitude of woollen petticoats, red, orange, and other bright colours. There are no fireplaces in their houses, because the little available solid fuel must be reserved for cooking purposes.

The little railway which leads from La Paz to Guaqui on the shores of Lake Titicaca is interesting, because in the building of it the engineers used quantities of the stones of one of the oldest and strangest ruins in the world. These stand on the plain of Tihuanaco, and date from a period long before the coming of the Incas. There are still standing immense walls and doorways, with carvings of human figures, and of the condor and the puma.

RICH PRODUCTS OF THE MOUNTAINS, PLAINS, AND FORESTS OF BOLIVIA

Bolivia is not all mountainous country. On the inland side of the Andes there is some good grazing country where the land descends to the Chaco, the plain which continues under that name into northern Argentina, while the north-east forms part of the selvas or forests of the upper waters of the Amazon, and is a rich rubber country. The mountainous region is rich in tin, copper, silver, and other minerals, which are only partially developed. The silver mountain of Potosi is in Bolivian territory. The chief mineral exported is tin. Other valuable products are coca, from which cocaine is derived, and the beautiful furs of the little chinchilla and the fox. Some of the fine wool of the alpaca and the vicuña goat is exported; but much of it, both here and in Peru, is spun and woven by the people themselves for their own use. Ponchos of vicuña wool are valued all over South America, as they are proof against heavy rain, and practically never wear out.

THE MASSIVE WALLS OF CUZCO WHICH HAVE STOOD FOR THOUSANDS OF YEARS

Crossing Lake Titicaca in the excellent boats which ply between Guaqui and Puno the traveller is in Peru. The natives use a boat made of reeds, called a balsa. Titicaca, South America's biggest lake (3200 square miles), contains the islands of the Sun and the Moon held sacred by the Incas. It is a beautiful lake, with a view of the range in which Illimani and Sorata are the giants. One of the most charming things about it is the presence of the great flocks of pink flamingoes, which look as if they had come straight out of a fairy tale. There are quantities, too, of many other sorts of wild fowl.

Away to the north-west the railway carries you to Cuzco, the City of the Sun and the capital of the old Inca empire. It is a Spanish city, but the inhabitants are mainly Indians. The Spaniards destroyed the ancient city as far as they could, but they could not destroy the vast walls. Some of these walls, built of huge stones fitted together with amazing skill, remain, and in some cases modern houses are built on them. The church and convent of St. Dominic is built out of the remains of the Temple of the Sun, and the west end of the church is evidently an old Inca wall. Outside the city rise the ruins of the ancient fortress of Sacsahuaman, on a hill about 650 feet high. The walls on the side away from Cuzco, where the ascent is less steep, are built in three parallel lines, and the whole forms one of the most imposing remnants in the world of prehistoric times. On the hillside stand seats cut out of the solid rock of the hillside.

The presence of these indications of past greatness arouses endless questions when one sees the abject condition of the people whose forefathers built them. The contrast between the past and the present is more startling here than anywhere else.

TERRACES MADE IN THE HILLSIDES BY THE QUICHUA INDIANS

The people here are Quichuas, and speak the Quichua language. They are most diligent cultivators. Where they are unable to get good land they cultivate terraces made in the hillsides. At some time Peru must have been thickly populated. But the Spaniards allowed the irrigation works to get out of repair, and with that the possibility of supporting a large population on the soil in the more arid districts was destroyed. The population today is over 8,700,000, and the area of the republic is 514,059 square miles.

Excellent cotton of the long-staple Sea Island variety is grown in some districts of Peru. The conditions are similar to those which make the growing of long-staple cotton possible in Egypt. The torrents which come down from the mountains overflow their banks at certain seasons of the year, and when they return to their beds they leave behind them a fine silt which is admirable for cotton-growing. The main crop is similar to American cotton. Sugar is grown in the irrigated districts. Other crops are tobacco, coffee, cocoa, and rice.

On the Peruvian coast are the guano islands. This deposit is a rich manure; but supplies are not so abundant as they were. Peru has anthracite coal, copper, silver, and gold mines, and oilfields on the Ecuador frontier. Rubber comes from the forests to the east of the sierra and from the forests on the banks of the rivers which flow down to the waters of the Amazon. It is exported by river through Pará in Brazil. Cinchona bark, from which quinine is made, was once an important trade, but now Europe takes its supplies chiefly from Java.

The chief port of Peru is Callao, and eight miles away stands Lima the capital, the city founded by Pizarro on the banks of the Rimac river. Everywhere throughout the continent the towns show considerable art in the laying out of the squares and the streets. Every Spanish town has its great plaza, where the principal churches and buildings are. The plaza is generally planted with trees and has a fountain in the middle. The churches in the older towns date from the early days of the conquest; some of them are admirable examples of Spanish sixteenth and seventeenth-century art. The interiors are richly and rather gaudily decorated, and nearly all the principal ones have silver altars. The old colonial houses are built round a patio, with a fountain in the middle and orange trees or vines or gay flowers.

THE FAMILY LIFE OF THE PEOPLE OF PERU

Here the family live and eat. To the street the house presents a blank wall, sometimes with a carved wooden balcony jutting out into the street, often gay with flowers. The closed-in Spanish house is significant of the social life, which is very much more strict and formal than ours. The visitors to the house are chiefly the whole circle of relations, and it is with difficulty that a stranger is admitted.

The lovely little city of Arequipa is a good example of the Spanish colonial town. It stands on the Rio Chile, and lies about 50 miles from the coast in an amphitheatre of mountains, which includes the three great peaks of El Misti, Chachani, and Pichu Pichu. It stands over 7000 feet above the sea out of reach of the sea mists, in beautiful desert air in a bright light which gives full value to the shadows in the streets bordered by the blank walls of the low houses, broken here and there with fast-shuttered windows. There is something reminiscent of a

Moorish city in the place, because it is in effect a desert city, and the same ways of living are prescribed by the climate as prevail in the East. That is the real reason for the darkened houses, for their flat roofs, for the courts where the family can sit out in the cool of the evening undisturbed by curious eyes, and for the arcades in which the shopping can be done in protection from the glare of the sun. Arequipa has a cathedral and a magnificent Jesuit church built of red-grey sandstone, with a finely carved façade and an interior rich in wood-carving of every kind. The city is perhaps the most ecclesiastical place in the whole of South America.

THE CAPITAL OF ECUADOR NINE THOUSAND FEET ABOVE THE SEA

The little republic of Ecuador is mountainous and still somewhat undeveloped. Its area is about 176,000 square miles and its population is about 3,200,000. From the port of Guayaquil a railway runs to Quito, the capital, which stands at a height of 9350 feet, and a motor-road, 375 miles long, runs to the Colombian border. There are over 3000 miles of good roads in the State, but much communication is still effected by mules travelling over rough tracks. The country is well watered by rivers which flow down to the River Marañon; some of these are navigable.

Colombia, with an area estimated at 440,000 square miles and a population of over 11 million, is enormously rich in her natural resources, but here again there is inadequate communication. The main artery is still the Magdalena river. River travelling is slow, and it may take as many as 14 days to get from the port of Cartagena to the capital, Bogotá. Modern governments, however, are pressing on with better air, road, and rail communications, as well as various schemes for building factories.

THE SPANISH TOWN CAPTURED BY SIR FRANCIS DRAKE

Cartagena is an interesting place to English people, because it is there that in 1585 Francis Drake crept into the harbour in the night, and at daybreak broke through the fortifications and captured the town.

It is a white city rising straight from the sea, with its streets and houses in the Spanish colonial fashion. The coast is bordered by mangrove swamps. Every kind of tropical produce is grown in

Colombia, which is said to have the best mild coffee in the world, and exports large quantities. She has also big oilfields in the Magdalena Valley.

One of the minor industries of Colombia (as well as of Ecuador) is the making of genuine panama hats, manufactured from the fronds of a certain variety of palm.

Venezuela, which has an area of 352,143 square miles and a population of over five million, lies entirely within the tropics, yet it is one of the most prosperous countries in the world. Americans, British, and Dutch have been busy developing its oilfields, and immense iron ore deposits are being opened up in the south. Venezuela also has the advantage of the Orinoco being navigable throughout the whole of its length in the State, and even beyond its borders into Colombia. Caracas, the capital, is a beautiful modern city, and as it stands on high ground the climate is not oppressive in spite of its tropical position.

East of Venezuela lie the three Colonies of British, Dutch, and French Guiana with a combined area of over 175,000 square miles. These have been described elsewhere in this book (see Index).

TWO WEST INDIAN ISLANDS AND THEIR THREE REPUBLICS

There are three Latin-American Republics on Cuba and Hispaniola, the biggest islands of the West Indies. Cuba, 44,206 square miles in area with some 5,800,000 people, was discovered by Columbus and remained Spanish until 1898, when the United States won independence for it by war. After many political and economic troubles Cuba adopted a very democratic Constitution in 1940. Havana, a seaport with a fine harbour, is the capital.

Hispaniola is divided between the Dominican Republic and the Republic of Haiti, Haiti being the western third. Discovered by Columbus, with its capital, now called Ciudad Trujillo, founded by his brother, the present Dominican Republic has a Spanish-speaking population of some 2,300,000 in its 19,332 square miles. It won independence from Spain in 1821. Haiti was a French Colony, whose Negro population, led by Toussaint l'Ouverture, revolted, winning freedom in 1804. Its area is 10,714 square miles and population 3,100,000. Both these republics have received financial and other help from the United States and have revised their Constitutions in recent years. Sugar is the mainstay of both islands, but they also have mineral wealth, including coal, which is scarce in Latin America.

THE PROBLEM OF THE VAST UNPEOPLED SPACES OF LATIN AMERICA

The future of Latin America no man can safely tell. Where European capital has been abundantly available and backed by a constant immigration of colonists from progressive European countries, as in the case of Uruguay and Argentina, the country is prosperous, and adds substantially to the wealth of the world by the export of food and other commodities. But the case is not quite so simple in hotter countries like Colombia and Ecuador. In Brazil, too, are huge tracts that have not been thoroughly explored.

Many people think, nevertheless, that Brazil, so rich in nearly every kind of natural resource, and with a climate that in many districts is nearly perfect, is one of the great countries of the future, and will be able to absorb large numbers of people from Europe.

The United States, however, realising that their future was decisively linked with her own, undertook at the Pan-American Conference of 1940 to support all the Latin-American States in trade as well as in defence questions. These conferences continue, to mutual benefit.

On the whole, then, development since the Wars of Liberation has been rapid. Education is still backward, and must be where the population is scattered. There are State universities, however, and many young men and women attend the universities of the United States and Europe. Many Latin Americans have become world famous.

THE PLACE OF SOUTH AMERICA IN THE FUTURE OF THE WORLD

Nature has given South America such a magnificent country that she may yet redress the balance of the Old World; but she lacks the tradition of good government and of freedom which we are so fortunate to inherit from our forefathers. It may be that, with her statesmen taking part in the Pan-American Conference and in the political and social work of the United Nations, both the ideas and the practice may improve, and in due course bring health and happiness to the peoples of this vast and varied continent.

MAPS OF SOUTH & CENTRAL AMERICA

THIS BIRD'S-EYE VIEW OF SOUTH AMERICA SHOWS THE COUNTRIES, CHIEF TOWNS, MOUNTAINS, AND RIVERS

PICTURE-MAP OF SOUTH AMERICA SHOWING ITS PHYSICAL FEATURES

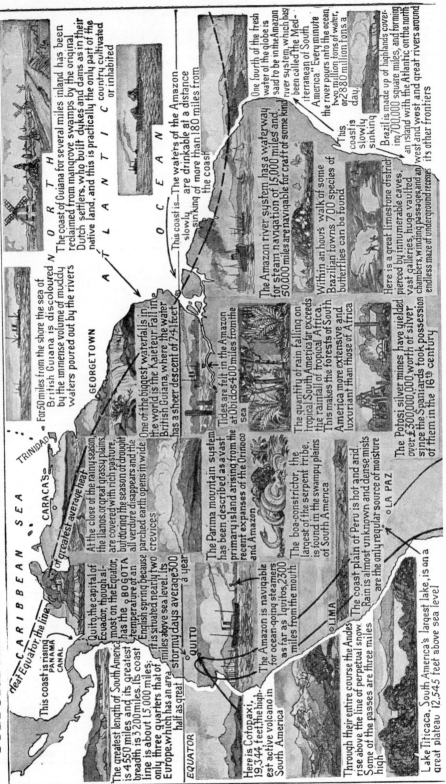

CARIBBEAN SEA

West Equator the line

TRINIDAD

CARACAS

GEORGETOWN

N O R T H

A T L A N T I C

O C E A N

EQUATOR

QUITO

LIMA

LA PAZ

PANAMA CANAL

This coast is rising

For 50 miles from the shore the sea of British Guiana is discoloured by the immense volume of muddy waters poured out by the rivers

The coast of Guiana for several miles inland has been reclaimed from mangrove swamps by the original Dutch settlers, who built dukes and dams as in their native land, and this is practically the only part of the country cultivated or inhabited

This coast is.—The waters of the Amazon are drinkable at a distance sinking of more than 180 miles from the coast

One fourth of the fresh water of the globe is said to be in the Amazon river system, which has been called the Mediterranean of South America." Every minute the river pours into the ocean two million tons of water, or 2,880 million tons a day.

This coast is slowly sinking

Brazil is made up of highlands covering 700,000 square miles, and forming an island with the Atlantic on the north and west and great rivers around its other frontiers

The greatest length of South America is 4,550 miles and its greatest breadth is 3,200 miles. Its coast line is about 15,000 miles; only three quarters that of Europe, which has an area half as great

Quito, the capital of Ecuador, though almost on the Equator, has the temperature of an English spring because it is situated nearly two miles above sea level. Its average 300 stormy days a year

At the close of the rainy season, the llanos, or great grassy plains, are covered with rich pasture, but during the season of drought all verdure disappears and the parched earth opens in wide crevices

One of the biggest waterfalls in the world is the Kaieteur Fall in British Guiana, where the water has a sheer descent of 741 feet

The Parima mountain system has been described as a vast primary island arising from the recent expanses of the Orinoco and Amazon

The Amazon river system has a waterway for steam navigation of 15,000 miles and 50,000 miles are navigable for craft of some kind

Tides are felt in the Amazon at Obidos 400 miles from the sea

The boa-constrictor, the largest of the serpent tribe, is found in the swampy plains of South America

The quantity of rain falling on tropical South America far exceeds the rainfall of tropical Africa. This makes the forests of South America more extensive and luxuriant than those of Africa

Within an hour's walk of some Brazilian towns 700 species of butterflies can be found

Here is a great limestone district pierced by innumerable caves, vast galleries, huge vaulted chambers, winding passages and an endless maze of underground recesses

Here is Cotopaxi, 19,344 feet, the highest active volcano in South America

The Amazon is navigable for ocean-going steamers as far as Iquitos, 2,300 miles from the mouth

The coast plain of Peru is hot and arid. Rain is almost unknown and dense mists are the only regular source of moisture

The Potosi silver mines have yielded over £300,000,000 worth of silver since the Spaniards took possession of them in the 16th century

Through their entire course the Andes rise above the line of perpetual snow. Some of the passes are three miles high

Lake Titicaca, South America's largest lake, is on a great plateau 12,545 feet above sea level

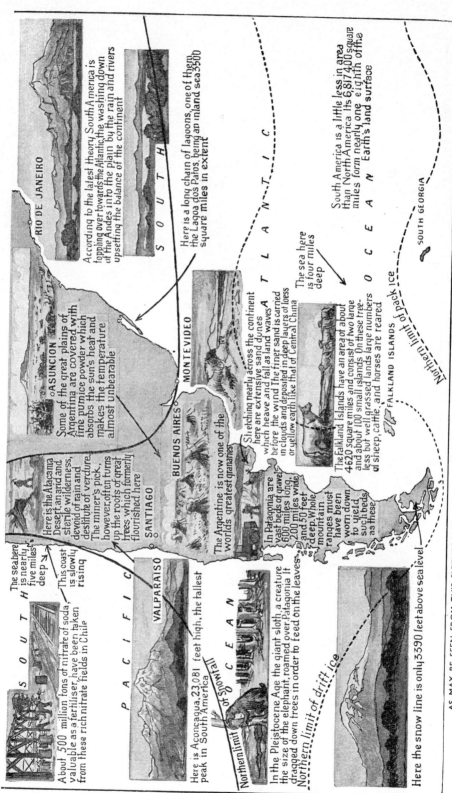

RIO DE JANEIRO

According to the latest theory, South America is toppling over towards the Atlantic, the washing down of the Andes into the plain by the rain and rivers upsetting the balance of the continent

S O U T H

Here is a long chain of lagoons, one of them, the Lagoa dos Patos, being an inland sea 3500 square miles in extent

South America is a little less in area than North America. Its 6,817,400 square miles form nearly one-eighth of the Earth's land surface

SOUTH GEORGIA

A T L A N T I C

O C E A N

The sea here is four miles deep

ASUNCION

Some of the great plains of Argentina are covered with fine pumice powder which absorbs the sun's heat and makes the temperature almost unbearable

MONTEVIDEO

Stretching nearly across the continent here are extensive sand dunes which heave and fall as land waves before the wind. The finer sand is carried in clouds and deposited in deep layers of loess or yellow earth like that of Central China

The Falkland Islands have an area of about 4620 square miles and consist of two large and about 100 small islands. On these treeless but well-grassed lands large numbers of sheep, cattle, and horses are reared

FALKLAND ISLANDS

Northern limit of pack ice

Here is the Atacama Desert, an arid and sterile wilderness, devoid of rain and destitute of verdure. The miner's pick, however, often turns up the roots of great trees which formerly flourished here

SANTIAGO

BUENOS AIRES

The Argentine is now one of the world's greatest granaries

In Patagonia are vast beds of gravel, 600 miles long, 200 miles wide, and 50 feet deep. Whole mountain ranges must have been worn down to yield such beds as these

The sea here is nearly five miles deep

This coast is slowly rising

About 500 million tons of nitrate of soda, valuable as a fertiliser, have been taken from these rich nitrate fields in Chile

S O U T H

VALPARAISO

P A C I F I C   O C E A N

Here is Aconcagua, 23,081 feet high, the tallest peak in South America

Northern limit of snowfall

In the Pleistocene Age the giant sloth, a creature the size of the elephant, roamed over Patagonia. It dragged down trees in order to feed on the leaves

Northern limit of drift ice

Here the snow line is only 3390 feet above sea level

AS MAY BE SEEN FROM THIS PICTURE-MAP, THE FACE OF SOUTH AMERICA ABOUNDS IN THE MOST INTERESTING PHYSICAL FEATURES

THE INTERESTING PLANT LIFE OF SOUTH AMERICA

NORTH ATLANTIC OCEAN

CARIBBEAN SEA

PANAMA CANAL

EQUATOR

TRINIDAD

GEORGETOWN

CARACAS

BOGOTA

QUITO

LIMA

LA PAZ

Coconuts

Vanilla

Rice

Tobacco

Cotton

Coffee

Lemons

Caesalpinia

Cedar

Cacao

Sugar cane

Tonka bean

Mimusops

Galipea

Bananas

Ivory Nut Palm

Cinchona

Bananas

Himennea

Mangrove

Mango

Cotton

Rice

Smilax

Ipecacuanha

Tamarind

Coca

Sugar cane

Grapes

Ground nuts

Maize

Cedar

Quebracho

Maté

Oranges

Cinchona

Coffee

Cacao

Mahogany

Rubber forests

Rubber trees

Sassafras

Brazil nuts

Logwood

Altalea

Pine

Maize

Lancewood

Bananas

Copaiva

Coca

Tobacco

Cinchona

Rice

Rubber

Manioc

Cacao

Rice

Coffee

Sugar

Maize

Coffee

Grapes

Guava

Cotton

Sugar

Bixa

Quassia

Altalea

Castor oil plant

Tobacco

Rosewood

Rubber trees

Cedar

Leopoldinia Palm

Sugar

Altalea Palm

Manioc

Rice

Coconuts

Peaches

Sugar

Rice

Cotton

Coconuts

No coconuts grow farther inland or south of this line

Rubber does not grow south of this line

7044

AMONG THE PLANTS WHICH THRIVE IN SOUTH AMERICA ARE COFFEE, COTTON, RICE, ORANGES, LEMONS, BESIDES BANANAS AND RUBBER TREES

THE GREAT VARIETY OF THE ANIMAL LIFE OF SOUTH AMERICA

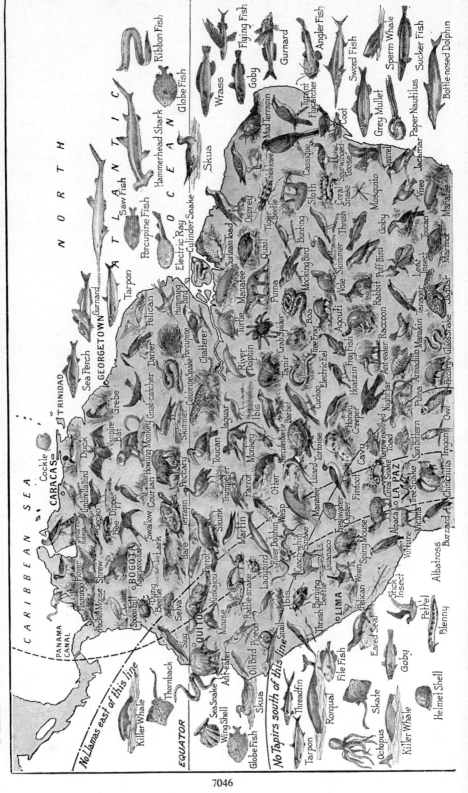

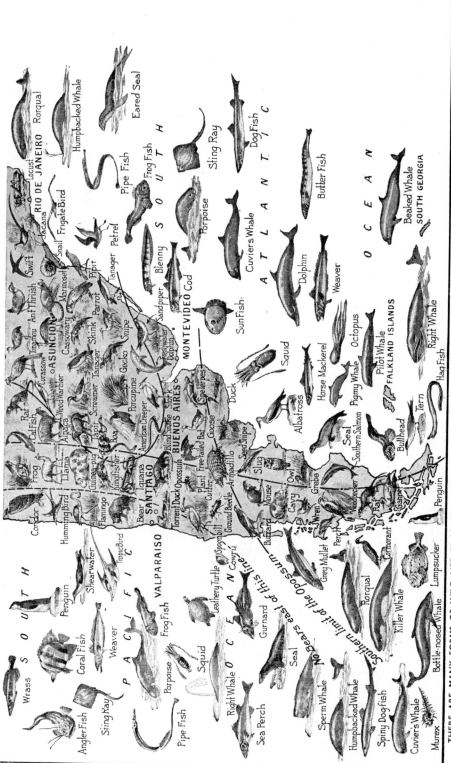

THERE ARE MANY FORMS OF WILD LIFE IN SOUTH AMERICA, RANGING FROM THE CHINCHILLA TO THE ARMADILLO AND FROM THE IGUANA TO THE BOA

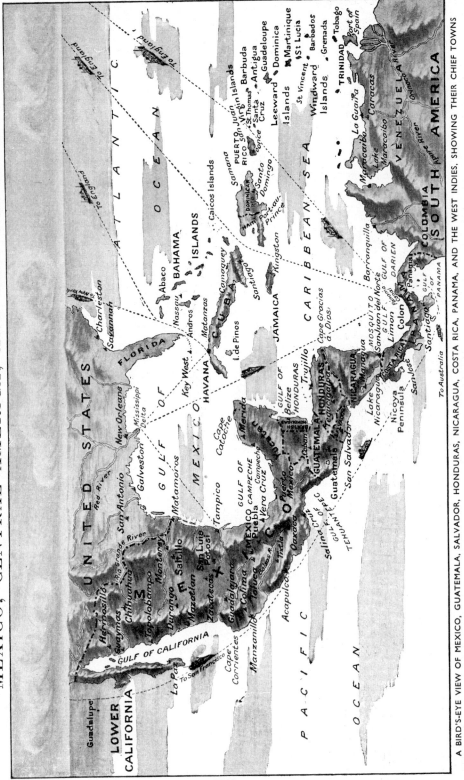

MEXICO, CENTRAL AMERICA, AND THE WEST INDIES

A BIRD'S-EYE VIEW OF MEXICO, GUATEMALA, SALVADOR, HONDURAS, NICARAGUA, COSTA RICA, PANAMA, AND THE WEST INDIES, SHOWING THEIR CHIEF TOWNS

One Thousand Poems of All Times and All Countries

Wordsworth's Ode On Immortality

WILLIAM WORDSWORTH is known by this poem more universally than by
any other of his writings, for it appeals, with great beauty of thought and
language, to a common human experience. Looking back, the man remembers
how the fresh sights of the natural world thrilled him when he was a boy. It was as
if a glow rested on it from other worlds. The poet suggests that a child brings into
the world lingering recollections—mere hints—of lives lived before, and though
they fade away they leave us spiritual longings to the end of our days. The title of
the poem is Intimations of Immortality from Recollections of Early Childhood.

WORDSWORTH RECALLS HIS CHILDHOOD

*The poet begins by stating that the dreams and visions of
his youth had made the Earth, and all his eyes had looked
upon in early years, so beautiful to him that in later life,
when the commoner sights had become so familiar, they
seemed to lose some of the qualities they once possessed.*

THERE was a time when meadow, grove,
    and stream,
The earth, and every common sight,
      To me did seem
      Apparelled in celestial light,
The glory and the freshness of a dream.
It is not now as it hath been of yore:—
      Turn whereso'er I may,
      By night or day,
The things which I have seen I now can
    see no more.

*His knowledge tells him that Earth and all its wonders are
not less fair than when he was young; but they have lost the
" glory " which they had when his eyes first beheld them.*

THE Rainbow comes and goes,
    And lovely is the Rose;
The Moon doth with delight
Look round her when the heavens are
    bare;
Waters on a starry night
Are beautiful and fair;
The sunshine is a glorious birth;
But yet I know, where'er I go,
That there hath passed away a glory from
    the earth.

*But there are times in our later years when the singing of
the birds and the frisking of the lambs suddenly bring up
before us, as in a flash, our childhood's happy visions.*

NOW, while the birds thus sing a joyous
    song,
And while the young lambs bound
    As to the tabor's sound,
To me alone there came a thought of grief:
A timely utterance gave that thought relief,
    And I again am strong;
The cataracts blow their trumpets from
    the steep;

No more shall grief of mine the season
    wrong;
I hear the echoes through the mountains
    throng,
The Winds come to me from the fields of
    sleep,
    And all the earth is gay;
    Land and sea
Give themselves up to jollity,
    And with the heart of May
Doth every beast keep holiday;
    Thou Child of Joy,
Shout round me, let me hear thy shouts,
    thou happy Shepherd-boy !

*Yet, in the midst of his delight in thus living over again his
childhood's joys, the poet finds himself making note of
some things—a tree and a field—that seemed to be different
now as compared with his early visions of them; thus the
spell is broken; he is a man again, and trained thought
takes the place of simple natural feeling and delight.*

YE blessèd creatures, I have heard the call
    Ye to each other make; I see
The heavens laugh with you in your jubilee;
    My heart is at your festival,
    My head hath its coronal,
The fulness of your bliss, I feel—I feel it all.
    O evil day! if I were sullen
    While Earth herself is adorning,
    This sweet May-morning,
    And the children are culling
      On every side,
    In a thousand valleys far and wide,
    Fresh flowers; while the sun shines
    warm,
And the babe leaps up on his mother's arm.
    I hear, I hear, with joy I hear!
    But there's a tree, of many one,
A single field which I have looked upon;
Both of them speak of something that is
    gone:
    The Pansy at my feet
    Doth the same tale repeat:
Whither is fled the visionary gleam?
Where is it now, the glory and the dream?

POEMS · SONGS · BALLADS · VERSES AND RHYMES WITH MUSIC

Then he begins to think what these remembered visions of his vanished childhood may mean. In this great stanza he sets forth his thoughts. We may have lived before, and as in manhood we catch fleeting visions of our childhood, so may we have faint visions of a previous existence.

OUR birth is but a sleep and a forgetting:
  The Soul that rises with us, our life's
        Star,
    Hath had elsewhere its setting,
      And cometh from afar:
    Not in entire forgetfulness,
    And not in utter nakedness,
But trailing clouds of glory do we come
    From God, who is our home;
Heaven lies about us in our infancy!
Shades of the prison-house begin to close
      Upon the growing Boy,   [flows,
But He beholds the light, and whence it
      He sees it in his joy;
The Youth, who daily farther from the east
    Must travel, still is Nature's priest,
      And by the vision splendid
      Is on his way attended;
At length the Man perceives it die away,
And fade into the light of common day.

It may be, the poet suggests, that our present existence here on Earth, with all its distractions and pleasures, has dulled in us the memory of the "imperial palace," or heaven, whence our souls have come, just as the experience of manhood and age dulls in us the memories of our childhood.

EARTH fills her lap with pleasures of her
      own;
Yearnings she hath in her own natural
      kind,
And, even with something of a mother's
      mind,
      And no unworthy aim,
    The homely Nurse doth all she can
To make her foster-child, her innate Man,
    Forget the glories he hath known,
And that imperial palace whence he came.

The thought expressed in the previous stanza is followed farther in the next. But we are to remember that the poet never asserts as a fact that he believes in a past existence. The idea is a very old one and is a feature of some religions, such as Buddhism, and the poet suggests it for a poetic purpose which will presently be made clear to us.

BEHOLD the Child among his new-born
      blisses,
A six years' darling of a pigmy size!
See, where 'mid work of his own hand he
      lies,
Fretted by sallies of his mother's kisses,
With light upon him from his father's eyes!
See, at his feet, some little plan or chart,
Some fragment from his dream of human
    · life,
Shaped by himself with newly-learnèd art;
      A wedding or a festival,
      A mourning or a funeral;
      And this hath now his heart,

And unto this he frames his song:
      Then will he fit his tongue
To dialogues of business, love, or strife;
      But it will not be long
      Ere this be thrown aside,
      And with new joy and pride
The little actor cons another part;
Filling from time to time his " humorous
      stage "
With all the Persons, down to palsied Age,
That Life brings with her in her equipage;
      As if his whole vocation
      Were endless imitation.

The poet now addresses the child. The little boy, the little girl, is the greatest wonder of the world ! For in its little body is the seed of everlasting life; it is " glorious in the sight of heaven-born freedom "; but, as the years grow upon it and make the wonders of the world commonplaces to it, it will become ever less conscious of these wonders.

THOU, whose exterior semblance doth
      belie
      Thy soul's immensity;
Thou best Philosopher, who yet dost keep
Thy heritage; thou Eye among the blind,
That, deaf and silent, read'st the eternal
      deep,
Haunted for ever by the eternal mind :
      Mighty Prophet!   Seer blest!
      On whom those truths do rest
Which we are toiling all our lives to find,
In darkness lost, the darkness of the grave;
Thou, over whom thy Immortality
Broods like the Day, a master o'er a slave,
A presence which is not to be put by;
Thou little Child, yet glorious in the might
Of heaven-born freedom on thy being's
      height,
Why with such earnest pains dost thou
      provoke
The years to bring the inevitable yoke,
Thus blindly with thy blessedness at strife?
Full soon thy soul shall have her earthly
      freight,
And custom lie upon thee with a weight,
Heavy as frost, and deep almost as life!

Yet, just as at times these visions of our childhood rise again in our mind, so must we in our later years, when our knowledge is ripened, realise that these visions have a mighty power in opening for us the very gateways of immortality. They are not so much to be regarded as glimpses of a life that is past as of an immortal life of the soul which endures for ever. The very fact that such thoughts ever arise in us is a proof that there exists for us some other life beyond the life we are living in this world today. They are like the echoes of a great sea; that sea is the immortal life of the soul, and death is but the beginning of our heavenly voyage.

O JOY! that in our embers
      Is something that doth live,
    That nature yet remembers
      What was so fugitive !
The thought of our past years in me doth
      breed

Perpetual benediction; not indeed
For that which is most worthy to be blest:
Delight and liberty, the simple creed
Of childhood, whether busy or at rest,
With new-fledged hope still fluttering in
    his breast:
      Not for these I raise
      The song of thanks and praise;
      But for those obstinate questionings
      Of sense and outward things,
      Fallings from us, vanishings;
      Blank misgivings of a Creature
Moving about in worlds not realised,
High instincts before which our mortal
    Nature
Did tremble like a guilty thing surprised:
      But for those first affections,
      Those shadowy recollections,
    Which, be they what they may,
Are yet the fountain-light of all our day,
Are yet a master-light of all our seeing;
    Uphold us, cherish, and have power to
      make
Our noisy years seem moments in the being
Of the eternal Silence; truths that wake,
    To perish never;
Which neither listlessness, nor mad en-
    deavour,
    Nor Man nor Boy,
Nor all that is at enmity with joy,
Can utterly abolish or destroy!
    Hence in a season of calm weather,
      Though inland far we be,
Our souls have sight of that immortal sea
    Which brought us hither,
    Can in a moment travel thither,
And see the children sport upon the shore,
And hear the mighty waters rolling ever-
    more.

Thus at last, in our old age, even when worldly knowledge may have dulled our childhood's memories, the joyous feelings of our early years may yet awaken within us, and our ripened senses should tell us that these feelings are the very truth of God speaking to us, not in words, but in a way no words can speak, of the immortal life to which we are born, if we only have " the faith that looks through death.'

THEN sing, ye Birds, sing, sing a joyous
      song!
    And let the young Lambs bound
    As to the tabor's sound!
We in thought will join your throng,
    Ye that pipe and ye that play,
    Ye that through your hearts today
    Feel the gladness of the May!
What though the radiance which was once
    so bright
Be now for ever taken from my sight,
    Though nothing can bring back the
      hour

Of splendour in the grass, of glory in the
    flower;
    We will grieve not, rather find
    Strength in what remains behind;
    In the primal sympathy
    Which having been must ever be;
    In the soothing thoughts that spring
    Out of human suffering;
    In the faith that looks through
      death,
In years that bring the philosophic mind.

So that in the end, when we are old, if we have preserved our faith, though we may have lost the keen sense of wonder and delight we enjoyed in childhood, we shall still, in a different way, rejoice in all God's creation; and find it touching our hearts with feelings of deeper beauty.

AND O, ye Fountains, Meadows, Hills,
    and Groves,
Forbode not any severing of our loves!
Yet in my heart of hearts I feel your might;
I only have relinquished one delight
To live beneath your more habitual sway.
I love the Brooks which down their
    channels fret,
Even more than when I tripped lightly as
    they;
The innocent brightness of a new-born
    Day is lovely yet;
The Clouds that gather round the setting
    sun
Do take a sober colouring from an eye
That hath kept watch o'er man's mortality;
Another race hath been, and other palms
    are won.
Thanks to the human heart by which we
    live,
Thanks to its tenderness, its joys, and fears,
To me the meanest flower that blows can
    give
Thoughts that do often lie too deep for
    tears.

FREEDOM

The idea that freedom is something which, once for all, can be gained, held, and kept as a fixed possession, is combated by James Russell Lowell, the famous American poet, in these lines from one of his poems. Freedom, he says, must be constantly renewed to suit new circumstances.

WE are not free: doth Freedom, then,
    consist
In musing with our faces toward the Past,
While petty cares and crawling interests
    twist
Their spider-threads about us, which at last
Grow strong as iron chains, to cramp and
    bind
In formal narrowness heart, soul, and mind.
Freedom is recreated year by year,
In hearts wide open on the Godward side.

HOW LANG AND DREARY IS THE NIGHT

The poet's habit of attributing his own feelings to his
surroundings is often seen in the songs of Robert Burns, and
in these longing memories we are given an example of it.

How lang and dreary is the night
    When I am frae my dearie!
I restless lie frae e'en to morn,
    Tho' I were ne'er sae weary.

For oh, her lanely nights are lang;
    And oh, her dreams are eerie;
And oh, her widowed heart is sair,
    That's absent frae her dearie.

When I think on the lightsome days
    I spent wi' thee, my dearie,
And now that seas between us roar,
    How can I be but eerie!

How slow ye move, ye heavy hours;
    The joyless day how drearie!
It wasna sae ye glinted by
    When I was wi' my dearie.

LINES WRITTEN IN KENSINGTON GARDENS

Matthew Arnold was a singularly all-round man, a scholar,
a critic, a poet, but far more than only a man of books. In
this poem we see him lying in Kensington Gardens, in the
season when sheep are turned into that great London park
to crop the grass among the stately trees. And there, en-
circled by London, he finds himself one with Nature, that
never betrays the heart that loves her, and feels a larger
peace than is known in the busy racket of the world of men.
It is a lesson sweet and true, and is put by the poet into
words that constantly have a surprising grace.

In this lone open glade I lie,
    Screened by deep boughs on either
        hand;
And at its end, to stay the eye,
    Those black-crowned, red-boled pine
        trees stand.

Birds here make song, each bird has his,
    Across the girdling city's hum.
How green under the boughs it is!
    How thick the tremulous sheep-cries
        come!

Sometimes a child will cross the glade
    To take his nurse his broken toy;
Sometimes a thrush flit overhead
    Deep in her unknown day's employ.

Here at my feet what wonders pass,
    What endless, active life is here!
What blowing daisies, fragrant grass!
    An air-stirred forest, fresh and clear.

Scarce fresher is the mountain sod
    Where the tired angler lies, stretched
        out,
And, eased of basket and of rod,
    Counts his day's spoil, the spotted trout.

In the huge world which roars hard by
    Be others happy, if they can!
But in my helpless cradle I
    Was breathed on by the rural Pan.

I, on men's impious uproar hurled,
    Think often, as I hear them rave,
That peace has left the upper world,
    And now keeps only in the grave.

Yet here is peace for ever new!
    When I who watch them am away!
Still all things in this glade go through
    The changes of their quiet day.

Then to their happy rest they pass;
    The flowers upclose, the birds are fed,
The night comes down upon the grass,
    The child sleeps warmly in his bed.

Calm soul of all things! make it mine
    To feel, amid the city's jar,
That there abides a peace of thine
    Man did not make, and cannot mar!

The will to neither strive nor cry,
    The power to feel with others give!
Calm, calm me more! nor let me die
    Before I have begun to live.

BREATHES THERE THE MAN

These are the opening lines of the final Canto of Sir Walter
Scott's Lay of the Last Minstrel. The aged harper is asked
why he, being so skilful, does not journey to England,
where he would be better rewarded. His reply is this outburst of patriotic fervour. Such national pride is felt by
men of almost every country, but it has seldom been expressed so ardently as it is by Scott in these lines.

Breathes there the man with soul so
        dead,
Who never to himself hath said,
    This is my own, my native land?
Whose heart hath ne'er within him burned
As home his footsteps he hath turned
    From wandering on a foreign strand?
If such there breathe, go, mark him well;
For him no Minstrel raptures swell;
High though his titles, proud his name,
Boundless his wealth as wish can claim;
Despite those titles, power, and pelf,
The wretch, concentred all in self,
Living, shall forfeit fair renown,
And, doubly dying, shall go down
To the vile dust from whence he sprung,
Unwept, unhonoured, and unsung.

O Caledonia! stern and wild,
Meet nurse for a poetic child!
Land of brown heath and shaggy wood,
Land of the mountain and the flood,
Land of my sires! what mortal hand
Can e'er untie the filial band
That knits me to thy rugged strand!

THE BELLS OF HEAVEN

Ralph Hodgson has made himself one of the most sympathetic interpreters of animal life among our poets. Here is a bold outburst against the cruel and shameful oppression of animals, wild and tame.

'TWOULD ring the bells of Heaven,
  The wildest peal for years,
If Parson lost his senses
And people came to theirs,
And he and they together
Knelt down with angry prayers
For tamed and shabby tigers,
And dancing dogs and bears,
And wretched, blind pit-ponies,
And little hunted hares.

IT WILL END IN THE RIGHT

Gerald Massey, who in youth was a working man, and became a vigorous patriotic poet with a noble love of freedom and a firm faith in the triumph of goodness, wrote verses which have found splendid fulfilment in the present day. Here is an example. Massey lived from 1828 to 1907.

NEVER despair, O my comrades in
  sorrow!
I know that our mourning is ended not.
  Yet
Shall the vanquished today be the victors
  tomorrow,
Our star shall shine on in the tyrant's
  sunset.
Hold on, though they spurn thee, for
  whom thou art living
A life only cheered by the lamp of its love;
Hold on! Freedom's hope to the bounden
  ones giving;
Green spots in the waste wait the worn
  spirit-dove.
Hold on—still hold on—in the world's
  despite,
Nurse the faith in thy heart, keep the lamp
  of Truth bright,
And, my life for thine, it shall end in the
  Right.

What though the martyrs and prophets
  have perished!
The Angel of Life rolls the stone from their
  graves;
Immortal's the faith and the freedom they
  cherished,
Their lone triumph cry stirs the spirits of
  slaves!
They are gone, but the glory is left in
  our life,
Like the day-god's last kiss on the darkness of even,
Gone down on the desolate seas of their
  strife,
To climb as star-beacons up Liberty's
  heaven.

Think of the wrongs that have ground us
  for ages!
Think of the wrongs we have still to
  endure!
Think of our blood, red on history's
  pages!
Then work, that our reckoning be speedy
  and sure.
Slaves cry to their gods, but be our God
  revealed
In our lives, in our works, in our warfare
  for man;
And bearing—or born upon—Victory's
  shield,
Let us fight battle-harnessed, and fall in
  the van.
Hold on, still hold on, in the world's
  despite,
Nurse the faith in thy heart, keep the
  lamp of Truth bright,
And, my life for thine, it shall end in the
  Right.

A FAREWELL

These verses were written by Tennyson to the brook at Boxley, in Kent, where he lived for a time—the brook which he described in his Ode To Memory. The permanence of Nature contrasted with the short life of man has been a theme for all poets.

FLOW down, cold rivulet, to the sea,
  Thy tribute wave deliver;
No more by thee my steps shall be,
  For ever and for ever.

Flow, swiftly flow, by lawn and lea,
  A rivulet, then a river:
Nowhere by thee my steps shall be,
  For ever and for ever.

But here will sigh thine alder tree,
  And here thine aspen shiver;
And here by thee will hum the bee,
  For ever and for ever.

A thousand suns will stream on thee,
  A thousand moons will quiver;
But not by thee my steps shall be,
  For ever and for ever.

MUSIC, WHEN SOFT VOICES DIE

This charming little song, illustrating the delights of happy memories, is a scrap by Shelley published after his death.

MUSIC, when soft voices die,
  Vibrates in the memory;
Odours, when sweet violets sicken,
Live within the sense they quicken.

Rose leaves, when the rose is dead,
Are heaped for the belovèd's bed;
And so thy thoughts, when thou art gone,
Love itself shall slumber on.

THE THREE GIVERS

The fact that he had the blessing of an Irish wife helped Sir William Watson to one of the most graceful compliments ever paid by a poet-husband. These verses are from Sir William's own selection of a hundred of his poems, which are published by Messrs. Hodder and Stoughton.

ENGLAND gave me sun and storm,
  The food whereon my spirit throve;
America gave me hand-clasps warm,
  And Ireland gave me her I love.

Heirs of unequal wealth they are,
  These noble lands, these givers three;
And it was the poorest one by far
  That gave the richest gift to me.

TO THE CUCKOO

These verses to the cuckoo, written by Wordsworth in 1802, and containing some admirable touches of description, transport the poet, as was his custom, to his boyhood, when all Nature's sights and sounds thrilled him with a sense of romance. But it is strange that, often as he heard the bird, he never happened to see it in his boyhood. Like the corn-crake, the cuckoo seems to be something of a ventriloquist, but, unlike that ground bird, it can be easily seen.

O BLITHE new-comer! I have heard,
  I hear thee and rejoice.
O Cuckoo! shall I call thee bird,
  Or but a wandering voice?

While I am lying on the grass
  Thy twofold shout I hear;
From hill to hill it seems to pass,
  At once far off and near.

Though babbling only to the vale
  Of sunshine and of flowers,
Thou bringest unto me a tale
  Of visionary hours.

Thrice welcome, darling of the Spring!
  Even yet thou art to me
No bird, but an invisible thing,
  A voice, a mystery;

The same whom in my schoolboy days
  I listened to; that cry
Which made me look a thousand ways
  In bush, and tree, and sky.

To seek thee did I often rove
  Through woods and on the green;
And thou wert still a hope, a love;
  Still longer for, never seen.

And I can listen to thee yet;
  Can lie upon the plain
And listen, till I do beget
  That golden time again.

O blessèd bird! the earth we pace
  Again appears to be
An unsubstantial, fairy place;
  That is fit home for thee!

LET US WITH A GLADSOME MIND

When he was a schoolboy of fifteen, as he himself tells us, John Milton wrote this paraphrase of Psalm 136. We omit twelve verses of Israelitish history. The paraphrase, though it does not follow the original closely and has not the full melody of the poet's later style, shows signs of the imagination that was to be fully displayed in later life, and is an interesting example of boyish workmanship.

LET us with a gladsome mind
  Praise the Lord, for he is kind,
    For his mercies ay endure,
    Ever faithful, ever sure.

Let us blaze his name abroad,
For of Gods he is the Lord:

O let us his praises tell
Who doth the wrathful tyrants quell.

Who with his miracles doth make
Amazèd heaven and earth to shake:

Who by his wisdom did create
The painted heavens so full of state:

Who did the solid Earth ordain
To rise above the watery plain:

Who by his all-commanding might
Did fill the new-made world with light:

And caused the golden-tressèd Sun
All the day long his course to run:

The hornèd Moon to shine by night
Amongst her spangled sisters bright:

All living creatures he doth feed,
And with full hand supplies their need:

Let us therefore warble forth
His mighty majesty and worth:

That his mansion hath on high
Above the reach of mortal eye:
  For his mercies ay endure,
  Ever faithful, ever sure.

ORPHEUS AND HIS LUTE

This song, describing the power of music according to ancient fables, is from the play of Henry the Eighth, printed in Shakespeare's works but only partly written by Shakespeare. The song is from the scene which was probably not written by him. Killing is here an adjective.

ORPHEUS with his lute made trees,
  And the mountain-tops that freeze,
  Bow themselves when he did sing:
To his music plants and flowers
Ever sprung; as sun and showers
  There had made a lasting spring.

Everything that heard him play,
Even the billows of the sea,
  Hung their heads, and then lay by.
In sweet music is such art,
Killing care and grief of heart
  Fall asleep, or, hearing, die.

RHYMES OF THE CHILDREN OF FRANCE

An English version of these rhymes appears side by side with the French

FAIS DODO, COLAS

Fais dodo, Colas, mon petit frère,
 Fais dodo, t'auras du lolo.
Maman est en haut
Qui fait du gâteau ;
Papa est en bas,
Qui fait du chocolat;
Fais dodo, Colas, mon petit frère,
Fais dodo, t'auras du lolo.

HUSH-A-BYE, COLIN

Hush-a-bye, Colin, brother of mine,
 Mustn't cry, hush-a-bye.
Mamma's up above,
Making cakes for you, love;
And Daddy, downstairs,
Nice choc'late prepares.
Hush-a-bye, Colin, brother of mine,
Mustn't cry, hush-a-bye.

SUR LE PONT D'AVIGNON

Sur le pont d'Avignon,
 L'on y danse, l'on y danse ;
Sur le pont d'Avignon,
L'on y danse tous en rond.
Les beaux messieurs font comm' ça,
Et puis encore comm' ça,
Sur le pont d'Avignon,
L'on y danse, l'on y danse;
Sur le pont d'Avignon
L'on y danse tous en rond.
Les belles dames font comm' ça,
Et puis encore comm' ça;
Sur le pont d'Avignon
Tout le monde y danse en rond !

ON THE BRIDGE OF AVIGNON

On the bridge of Avignon,
 See them dance, see them dance!
On the bridge of Avignon,
They trip around, retire, advance;
Gallant swains bend low, like this,
And once again do so, like this.
On the bridge of Avignon,
See them dance, see them dance !
On the bridge of Avignon,
They trip around, retire, advance;
Fair ladies curtsey low, like this,
And once again do so, like this.
See them dance, see them dance,
On the bridge of Avignon.

RAMÈNE TES MOUTONS

La plus aimable à mon gré
 Je vais vous la présenter.
Nous lui ferons passer barrière.
" Ramène tes moutons, bergère;
Ramène, ramène, ramène, donc,
Tes moutons à la maison."

BRING BACK YOUR SHEEP

I'll introduce—just wait awhile—
 A charming maiden by yon stile.
" Ho ! pass this way," aloud we'll mock,
" Shepherdess, lead back your flock;
Lead back, lead back, as you are told,
Your pretty sheep within the fold."

LA MÈRE MICHEL

C'est la mère Michel qui a perdu son
 chat,
Qui crie par la fenêtre à qui le lui rendra,
Et le compère Lustucru qui lui a ré-
 pondu;
" Allez, la mère Michel, votre chat n'est
 pas perdu."
C'est la mère Michel qui lui a demandé:
" Mon chat n'est pas perdu ! vous l'avez
 donc trouvé? "
Et le compère Lustucru qui lui a ré-
 pondu :
" Donnez une récompense, il vous sera
 rendu."
Et la mère Michel lui dit : " C'est décidé,
Si vous rendez mon chat, vous aurez un
 baiser."
Le compère Lustucru, qui n'en a pas
 voulu,
Lui dit: " Pour un lapin votre chat est
 vendu ! "

MOTHER MITCHELL

Mother Mitchell one day lost her
 pussy, alack !
And cried out of window: " Oh, who'll
 bring her back ? "
Then old Gaffer Lustucru smilingly said:
" Your cat isn't lost—she is merely mis-
 laid."
Mother Mitchell cried, hopefully gazing
 around her ;
" My pussy not lost ! Oh, pray, have
 you found her ? "
Then old Gaffer Lustucru answered her pat:
" If you give a reward you will soon get
 your cat."
Said old Mother Mitchell : " 'Twould
 not be amiss,
If you find me my pussy, to give you a
 kiss."
But sly Gaffer Lustucru much preferred
 gold,
And said : " For a rabbit your pussy is
 sold ! "

KEEL ROW

This is one of the North Country sea-songs that have grown up nobody knows how, so that both words and music are inherited from past generations without the authorship being known. The words in these verses move to the sound of the oars in the rowlocks of a moving boat.

As I came thro' Sandgate,
  Thro' Sandgate, thro' Sandgate,
As I came thro' Sandgate
  I heard a lassie sing.
O weel may the keel row,
The keel row, the keel row,
O weel may the keel row,
  That my laddie's in.

O wha's like my Johnnie,
Sae leith, sae blythe, sae bonny?
He's foremost among the mony
  Keel lads o' coaly Tyne;
He'll set and row so tightly,
Or in the dance, so sprightly,
He'll cut and shuffle sightly;
  Tis true, were he not mine.

He wears a blue bonnet,
Blue bonnet, blue bonnet;
He wears a blue bonnet,
  And a dimple in his chin.
And weel may the keel row,
The keel row, the keel row,
And weel may the keel row,
  That my laddie's in.

ON A LITTLE LADY'S THIRD BIRTHDAY

This was written by the modern poet Sir William Watson to his little daughter, when she had been three times round the Sun, as her father daintily says.

My tiny lady, can it
  Be true that you and I,
On something called a planet,
Are somewhere in the sky?

Yes—and at such a tearing
And madcap speed we've spun,
That you, with dreadful daring,
Have thrice been round the Sun.

Nay, it yet more amazes,
That my far-venturing girl
Can be as fresh as daisies
After so wild a whirl!

And now 'neath western billow
The Sun is put to bed,
And you, too, on your pillow
Must lay a golden head.

Ah, tears—they come so quickly,
For grief so quickly gone!
Yet joys have rained as thickly,
For you to dream upon.

FOR THE FALLEN

The First World War, with its terrible slaughter of young men, many of them the finest spirits of their time, deeply moved all sympathetic and thoughtful men and women, and many poets tried to express the national feeling. It was felt widely that this poem in a wonderful degree put into a musical measure the pride and sorrow and remembrance of the country. The writer, Laurence Binyon, who died in 1943, was, besides being a poet, the author of excellent books on art, and one of the Keepers of Oriental prints in the British Museum. The poem was written for The Times.

With proud thanksgiving, a mother for
    her children,
  England mourns for her dead across the
    sea.
Flesh of her flesh they were, spirit of her
    spirit,
  Fallen in the cause of the free.

Solemn the drums thrill; Death august and
    royal
  Sings sorrow up into immortal spheres.
There is music in the midst of desolation
  And a glory that shines upon our tears.

They went with songs to the battle, they
    were young,
  Straight of limb, true of eye, steady and
    aglow.
They were staunch to the end against odds
    uncounted,
  They fell with their faces to the foe.

They shall grow not old, as we that are
    left grow old;
  Age shall not weary them, nor the years
    condemn.
At the going down of the sun and in the
    morning
  We will remember them.

They mingle not with their laughing com-
    rades again;
  They sit no more at familiar tables at
    home;
They have no lot in our labour of the day-
    time:
  They sleep beyond England's foam.

But where our desires are and our hopes
    profound,
  Felt as a well-spring that is hidden from
    sight,
To the innermost heart of their own land
    they are known
  As the stars are known to the Night.

As the stars that shall be bright when we
    are dust,
  Moving in marches upon the heavenly
    plain,
As the stars that are starry in the time of
    our darkness,
  To the end, to the end, they remain.

TODAY

Thomas Carlyle was deeply impressed by the idea of Time. Here he puts some of his impressions into rhyme, making them useful as warnings but insignificant as verse.

So here hath been dawning
　Another blue day:
Think wilt thou let it
　Slip useless away?

Out of Eternity
　This new day was born;
Into Eternity
　At night will return.

Behold it aforetime
　No eye ever did;
So soon it for ever
　From all eyes is hid.

Here hath been dawning
　Another blue day:
Think wilt thou let it
　Slip useless away?

TO ALTHEA, FROM PRISON

This graceful lyric by Richard Lovelace, a Royalist poet of the reign of Charles the First, was written in prison to his lady-love. Its gay strains finally merge into serious truth.

WHEN Love with unconfinèd wings
　Hovers within my gates,
And my divine Althea brings
　To whisper at the grates,
When I lie tangled in her hair
　And fettered to her eye,
The birds that wanton in the air
　Know no such liberty.

When flowing cups run swiftly round
　With no allaying Thames,
Our careless heads with roses bound,
　Our hearts with loyal flames;
When thirsty grief in wine we steep,
　When healths and draughts go free,
Fishes that tipple in the deep
　Know no such liberty.

When, like committed linnets, I
　With shriller throat shall sing
The sweetness, mercy, majesty,
　And glories of my king;
When I shall voice aloud how good
　He is, how great should be,
Enlargèd winds, that curl the flood,
　Know no such liberty.

Stone walls do not a prison make,
　Nor iron bars a cage;
Minds innocent and quiet take
　That for an hermitage;
If I have freedom in my love
　And in my soul am free,
Angels alone, that soar above,
　Enjoy such liberty.

WEST LONDON

This striking sonnet by Matthew Arnold is in its first eight lines a fine example of condensed and vivid description. The street picture of the begging family is complete in spectacle and in feeling. But the moral drawn in the last six lines is not as natural as the picture painted. It was not pride that made the woman beg of the poor rather than of the rich. Experience had taught her it is the poor who give quickest sympathy to the pain of poverty.

CROUCHED on the pavement close by
　　Belgrave Square
A tramp I saw, ill, moody, and tongue-
　　tied;
A babe was in her arms, and at her side
A girl; their clothes were rags, their feet
　　were bare.

Some labouring men, whose work lay
　　somewhere there,
Passed opposite; she touched her girl,
　　who hied
Across, and begged, and came back satis-
　　fied.
The rich she had let pass with frozen stare.

Thought I: "Above her state this spirit
　　towers;
She will not ask of aliens, but of friends,
Of sharers in a common human fate.

" She turns from that cold succour, which
　　attends
The unknown little from the unknowing
　　great,
And points us to a better time than ours."

HE IS NOT A POET

Wilfrid Scawen Blunt (1840-1922) was a Sussex squire, traveller, poet, and politician. He had led an adventurous life. The sixteen lines that follow tell of his boyish aims, his longing for a life of adventure. They are not quite sincere, for Blunt succeeded best as a poet.

I WOULD not, if I could, be called a poet.
　I have no natural love of the chaste
　　muse.
If aught be worth the doing I would do it;
And others, if they will, may tell the news.
I care not for their laurels, but would
　　choose
On the world's field to fight or fall or run.
My soul's ambition would not take excuse
To play the dial rather than the sun.
The faith I held I hold, as when a boy
I left my books for cricket-bat and gun.
The tales of poets are but scholars'
　　themes.
In my hot youth I held it that a man
With heart to dare and stomach to enjoy
Had better work to his hand in any plan
Of any folly, so the thing were done,
Than in the noblest dreaming of mere
　　dreams.

THE EVE OF SAINT MARK

John Keats published volumes of poems in 1817 and 1820,
and wrote a number of poems that were not published till
after his death, in 1821. The poem which follows is a fragment found among the poet's papers. No doubt it was the
beginning of a tale. The legend of St. Mark's Day is that
the wraiths of people who are in peril of death accompany
them to church on that day. If their ghost comes out with
them they will live; if it remains behind in the church they
are doomed. Probably the poet was about to introduce this
legend, for there was a version of it among his notes. All
we have in the poem is a description of people going to
church decorously in a romantic old city, while a young girl
reads from a quaint ancient volume. Every line gives a
clear picture with a suggestion of romance in it. The
poem is one of the most fascinating of literary fragments.

UPON a Sabbath day it fell;
   Twice holy was the Sabbath bell
That called the folk to evening prayer;
The city streets were clean and fair
From wholesome drench of April rains;
And, on the western window panes,
The chilly sunset faintly told
Of unmatured green valleys cold,
Of the green, thorny, bloomless hedge,
Of rivers new with spring-tide sedge,
Of primroses by sheltered rills,
And daisies on the aguish hills.
Twice holy was the Sabbath bell:
The silent streets were crowded well
With staid and pious companies,
Warm from their fireside orat'ries;
And moving, with demurest air,
To evensong and vesper prayer.
Each arched porch and entry low
Was filled with patient folk and slow,
With whispers hush and shuffling feet,
While played the organ loud and sweet.

The bells had ceased, the prayers begun,
And Bertha had not yet half done
A curious volume, patched and torn,
That all day long, from earliest morn,
Had taken captive her two eyes
Among its golden broideries;
Perplexed her with a thousand things:
The stars of Heaven, and angels' wings,
Martyrs in a fiery blaze,
Azure saints in silver rays,
Moses' breastplate, and the seven
Candlesticks John saw in Heaven,
The winged Lion of Saint Mark,
And the Covenantal Ark,
With its many mysteries,
Cherubim and golden mice.

Bertha was a maiden fair,
Dwelling in the old Minster square;
From her fireside she could see,
Sidelong, its rich antiquity,
Far as the Bishop's garden wall;
Where sycamores and elm trees tall,

Full-leaved, the forest had outstript,
By no sharp north wind ever nipt,
So sheltered by the mighty pile.
Bertha arose, and read awhile,
With forehead 'gainst the window-pane.
Again she tried, and then again,
Until the dusk eve left her dark
Upon the legend of Saint Mark.
From plaited lawn-frill, fine and thin,
She lifted up her soft warm chin,
With aching neck and swimming eyes,
And dazed with saintly imageries.

All was gloom, and silent all,
Save now and then the still footfall
Of one returning homewards late,
Past the echoing minster gate.

The clamorous daws that all the day
Above tree-tops and towers play,
Pair by pair had gone to rest,
Each in its ancient belfry nest,
Where asleep they fall betimes
To music of the drowsy chimes.

All was silent, all was gloom,
Abroad and in the homely room:
Down she sat, poor cheated soul!
And struck a lamp from the dismal coal;
Leaned forward, with bright drooping hair
And slant book, full against the glare.
Her shadow, in uneasy guise,
Hovered about, a giant size,
On ceiling-beam and old oak chair,
The parrot's cage, and panel square;
And the warm angled winter screen
On which were many monsters seen,
Called doves of Siam, Lima mice,
And legless birds of Paradise,
Macaw, and tender Avadavat,
And silken-furred Angora cat.
Untired she read, her shadow still
Glowered about, as it would fill
The room with wildest forms and shades,
As though some ghostly queen of spades
Had come to mock behind her back,
And dance, and ruffle her garments black.

Untired she read the legend page
Of holy Mark, from youth to age,
On land, on sea, in pagan chains,
Rejoicing for his many pains.
Sometimes the learned eremite,
With golden star, or dagger bright,
Referred to pious poesies
Written in smallest crow-quill size
Beneath the text; and thus the rhyme
Was parcelled out from time to time:
" Als writith he of swevenis,
Men han beforne they wake in bliss,

Whanne that hir friendes thinke hem
    bound
In crimped shroude farre under grounde;
And how a litling child mote be
A saint er its nativitie,
Gif that the modre (God her blesse!)
Kepen in solitarinesse,
And kissen devoute the holy croce.
Of Goddes love, and Sathan's force,
He writith; and thinges many mo:
Of swiche thinges I may not show.
Bot I must tellen verilie
Somdel of Saintè Cicilie,
And chieflie what he auctorethe
Of Saintè Markis life and dethe."

At length her constant eyelids come
Upon the fervent martyrdom;
Then lastly to his holy shrine,
Exalt amid the tapers' shine
At Venice,—

THE SOLE BIDDER

The fleetingness of time and pleasure is here contrasted by Harold Begbie, in a homely way, with the lasting power of noble sacrifice through love. All are willing to buy pleasure, but who will bid for the crown of thorns?

THE company was gathered,
    And Life, the auctioneer,
Stands up before the bidders,
    His hammer lying near.
" Lot One," he cries, " I offer
    Is Time that's passing on,
And Time, my friends, remember,
    Is going, going : *gone !* "

Two bidders fight to buy it,
    But not with gold accurst:
They offer all their efforts,
    Their hunger and their thirst.
One means to use it nobly,
    The other for his boast;
The hammer falls—he had it
    Who longed to get it most.

Once more the crowd sways forward,
    And Life, with hammer high,
Puts up the lots of Satan,
    All things that rot and die,
Rich dainties for the palate,
    Proud, garish things to don;
With sin and shame men buy them,
    Hark! Going, going: *gone !*

And now cries Life, " I offer
    A thing that Mammon scorns,
Yet centuries have praised it—
    Last lot, a crown of thorns."
Ah, most have spent their fortunes,
    One laughs, another fears;
Love bows his head, sole bidder,
    And buys it with his tears.

THE WORLD'S MAY QUEEN

We must expect poets to attribute choice qualities to their own lands. It is the universal habit of poets of all nations. In these lines, which form the second stanza of a longer poem, Alfred Noyes makes Spring choose England from all countries as her permanent May Queen. It is a daring choice, considering the weather, but we hope it is true. Alfred Noyes (1880–1958) was one of the most travelled of poets and a most sensitive writer.

WHEN Spring comes back to England
    And crowns her brows with May,
Round the merry moonlit world
    She goes the greenwood way:
She throws a rose to Italy,
    A fleur-de-lys to France;
But round her regal morris-ring
    The seas of England dance.

When Spring comes back to England
    And dons her robe of green,
There's many a nation garlanded,
    But England is the Queen;
She's Queen, she's Queen of all the world
    Beneath the laughing sky,
For the nations go a-Maying
    When they hear the New Year cry:

" Come over the water to England,
    My old love, my new love,
Come over the water to England,
    In showers of flowery rain;
Come over the water to England,
    April, my true love;
And tell the heart of England
    The Spring is here again! "

CONTENT

Pleas for quietness and contentment, with the modest ambitions of the simple life, abound in early English poetry. This is an example from Robert Greene, a 16th-century poet.

SWEET are the thoughts that savour
    of content;
    The quiet mind is richer than a crown;
Sweet are the nights in careless slumber
    spent;
    The poor estate scorns Fortune's angry
    frown.
Such sweet content, such minds, such
    sleep, such bliss,
Beggars enjoy when princes oft do miss.

The homely house that harbours quiet
    rest;
    The cottage that affords no pride, nor
    care;
The mean that 'grees with country music
    best;
    The sweet consort of mirth and music's
    fare;
Obscurèd life sets down a type of bliss,
A mind content both crown and kingdom
    is.

NOW THANK WE ALL OUR GOD

Martin Rinkart, who wrote this fine hymn of thanksgiving, was a German pastor who lived from 1586 to 1649,
through a period of great suffering, and yet kept a joyful
heart. He was a brave man in face of war and pestilence.
The translator, Miss Catherine Winkworth (1829–1878),
issued her English version of German hymns in 1858.
The tune (Wittenberg) to which the hymn is usually sung
is German, by Johann Cruger, and was contemporary with
the hymn and probably written specially for it.

Now thank we all our God
  With heart, and hands, and voices,
Who wondrous things hath done,
In Whom His world rejoices;
  Who from our mother's arms
    Hath blessed us on our way
  With countless gifts of love,
    And still is ours today.

O may this bounteous God
Through all our life be near us,
  With ever joyful hearts
And blessed peace to cheer us;
  And keep us in His grace,
    And guide us when perplexed,
  And free us from all ills
    In this world and the next.

All praise and thanks to God
The Father now be given,
  The Son, and Him who reigns
With them in highest heaven,
  The One Eternal God,
    Whom earth and heaven adore,
  For thus it was, is now,
    And shall be evermore.

I STOOD AND WATCHED

This poetic fancy, which appeared in an American newspaper, tells very prettily the triumph of faith; for without
faith in the goodness and mercy of God many other virtues
will not help us greatly. That, at least, is the message of
this very beautiful poem.

I stood and watched my ships go out,
  Each, one by one, unmooring, free,
What time the quiet harbour filled
  With flood tide from the sea.

The first that sailed, her name was Joy;
  She spread a smooth, white, shining
    sail,
And eastward drove, with bending spars,
  Before the sighing gale.

Another sailed, her name was Hope;
  No cargo in her hold she bore;
Thinking to find in western lands
  Of merchandise a store.

The next that sailed, her name was Love;
  She showed a red flag at her mast,
A flag as red as blood she showed,
  And she sped south right fast.

The last that sailed, her name was Faith;
  Slowly she took her passage forth,
Tacked, and lay to; at last she steered
  A straight course for the north.

My gallant ships, they sailed away
  Over the shimmering summer sea;
I stood at watch for many a day,
  But one came back to me.

For Joy was caught by pirate Pain;
  Hope ran upon a hidden reef;
And Love took fire, and foundered fast
  In whelming seas of grief.

Faith came at last, storm-beat and torn;
  She recompensed me all my loss,
For, as a cargo safe, she brought
  A crown linked to a cross.

SHE WAS A PHANTOM OF DELIGHT

No poet has ever described womanhood more apprecia-
tively than Wordsworth. He himself has told us how this
progressive picture of womankind from youth to middle age
was composed. The first stanza is a description of a Highland girl, whose sprite-like beauty suddenly enchanted
him and his sister Dorothy when they were visiting Scotland.
To this were added two verses describing the revelation of
full womanhood in his wife, expanding into homely
helpfulness, and yet retaining its early charm.

She was a phantom of delight
  When first she gleamed upon my sight,
A lovely apparition, sent
To be a moment's ornament;
Her eyes as stars of twilight fair;
Like twilight's, too, her dusky hair;
But all things else about her drawn
From May-time and the cheerful dawn;
A dancing shape, an image gay,
To haunt, to startle, and waylay.

I saw her upon nearer view,
A spirit, yet a woman too!
Her houshold motions light and free,
And steps of virgin liberty;
A countenance in which did meet
Sweet records, promises as sweet;
A creature not too bright or good
For human nature's daily food;
For transient sorrows, simple wiles,
Praise, blame, love, kisses, tears, and
  smiles.

And now I see with eye serene
The very pulse of the machine;
A being breathing thoughtful breath,
A traveller between life and death;
The reason firm, the temperate will,
Endurance, foresight, strength, and skill;
A perfect woman, nobly planned,
To warn, to comfort, and command;
And yet a spirit still, and bright
With something of angelic light.

THE CROWNING OF DREAMING JOHN

Dreaming John, one of the finest poems of our matchless countryside, is taken from the Collected Poems of John Drinkwater, and is given here by courtesy of his publishers, Sidgwick and Jackson.

SEVEN days he travelled
    Down the roads of England,
Out of leafy Warwick lanes
Into London Town.
Grey and very wrinkled
Was Dreaming John of Grafton,
But seven days he walked to see
A king put on his crown.

DOWN the streets of London
    He asked the crowded people
Where would be the crowning
And when would it begin.
He said he'd got a shilling,
A shining silver shilling,
But when he came to Westminster
They wouldn't let him in.

DREAMING John of Grafton
    Looked upon the people,
Laughed a little laugh, and then
Whistled and was gone.
Out along the long roads,
The twisting roads of England,
Back into the Warwick lanes
Wandered Dreaming John.

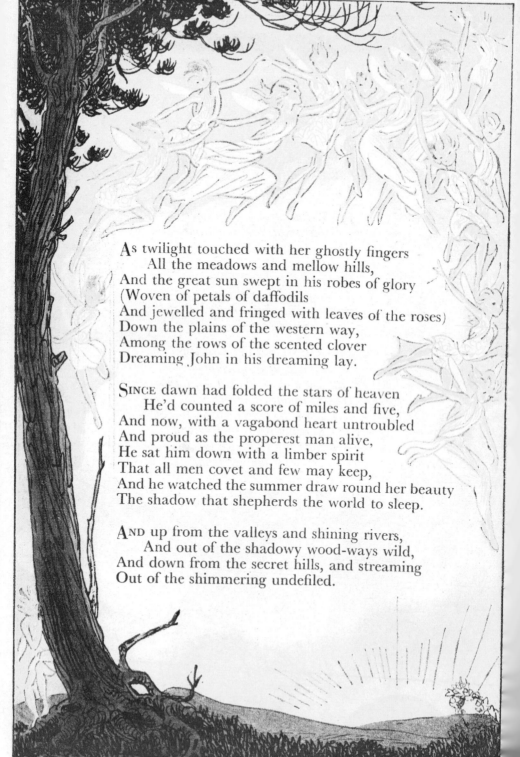

As twilight touched with her ghostly fingers
    All the meadows and mellow hills,
And the great sun swept in his robes of glory
(Woven of petals of daffodils
And jewelled and fringed with leaves of the roses)
Down the plains of the western way,
Among the rows of the scented clover
Dreaming John in his dreaming lay.

Since dawn had folded the stars of heaven
    He'd counted a score of miles and five,
And now, with a vagabond heart untroubled
And proud as the properest man alive,
He sat him down with a limber spirit
That all men covet and few may keep,
And he watched the summer draw round her beauty
The shadow that shepherds the world to sleep.

And up from the valleys and shining rivers,
    And out of the shadowy wood-ways wild,
And down from the secret hills, and streaming
Out of the shimmering undefiled.

Wonder of sky that arched him over,
Came a company shod in gold
And girt in gowns of a thousand blossoms,
Laughing and rainbow-aureoled.

Wrinkled and grey and with eyes a-wonder
    And soul beatified, Dreaming John
Watched the marvellous company gather
While over the clover a glory shone;
They bore on their brows the hues of heaven,
Their limbs were sweet with flowers of the fields,
And their feet were bright with the gleaming treasure
That prodigal earth to her children yields.

They stood before him, and John was laughing
    As they were laughing; he knew them all.
Spirits of trees and pools and meadows,
Mountain and windy waterfall,
Spirits of clouds and skies and rivers,
Leaves and shadows and rain and sun,
A crowded, jostling, laughing army,
And Dreaming John knew every one.

Among them then was a sound of singing
　　And chiming music, as one came down
The level rows of the scented clover,
Bearing aloft a flashing crown;
No word of a man's desert was spoken,
Nor any word of a man's unworth,
But there on the wrinkled brow it rested,
And Dreaming John was king of the Earth.

Dreaming John of Grafton
　　Went away to London,
Saw the coloured banners fly,
Heard the great bells ring,
But though his tongue was civil
And he had a silver shilling,
They wouldn't let him in to see
The crowning of the King.

So back along the long roads,
　　The leafy roads of England,
Dreaming John went carolling,
Travelling alone;
And in a summer evening,
Among the scented clover,
He held before a shouting throng
A crowning of his own.

John Drinkwater

HIS PILLAR

Robert Herrick's poetry was often light as thistledown, but he knew that, by its grace, it was likely to preserve his name in human memory, as indeed it has done. So he lets us know that in these verses, simple though they may be, he expects to leave for himself a lasting memorial.

ONLY a little more
    I have to write,
      Then I'll give o'er,
And bid the world good-night.

'Tis but a flying minute
    That I must stay,
      Or linger in it ;
And then I must away.

O Time, that cut'st down all,
    And scarce leav'st here
      Memorial
Of any men that were;

How many lie forgot
    In vaults beneath,
      And piecemeal rot
Without a fame in death!

Behold this living stone
    I rear for me,
      Ne'er to be thrown
Down, envious Time, by thee.

Pillars let some set up,
    If so they please;
      Here is my hope,
And my Pyramides.

NAPOLEON'S FAREWELL

Lord Byron put these words into the mouth of Napoleon when he surrendered and was sent into exile. They do not represent the true relations between Napoleon and France, for Napoleon was the betrayer of liberty in that great country; but they are the kind of thoughts which Napoleon, dazzled by the idea of personal glory, probably cherished.

FAREWELL to the land where the gloom of
    my glory
  Arose and o'ershadowed the earth with
    her name;
She abandons me now, but the page of her
    story,
  The brightest or blackest, is filled with
    my fame.
I have warred with a world which van-
    quished me only
  When the meteor of conquest allured
    me too far;
I have coped with the nations which dread
    me thus lonely,
  The last single captive to millions in war.

Farewell to thee, France! when thy
    diadem crowned me
  I made thee the gem and the wonder of
    earth;

But thy weakness decrees I should leave
    as I found thee,
  Decayed in thy glory, and sunk in thy
    worth.
Oh, for the veteran hearts that were wasted
    In strife with the storm, when their
    battles were won;
Then the eagle, whose gaze in that moment
    was blasted,
  Had still soared with eyes fixed on
    victory's sun!

Farewell to thee, France! but when
    Liberty rallies
  Once more in thy regions, remember me
    then:
The violet still grows in the depth of thy
    valleys;
  Though withered, thy tear will unfold
    it again.
Yet, yet, I may baffle the hosts that
    surround us,
  And yet may thy heart leap awake to
    my voice;
There are links which must break in the
    chain that has bound us,
  Then turn thee and call on the Chief of
    thy choice!

THE WORLD IS TOO MUCH WITH US

This glorious sonnet, calling on us to appreciate the romantic loveliness of Nature, was written by Wordsworth in 1806. But is it true that the Greek, with his mythological poetry of Nature, loved the outdoor world and everything belonging to it more than we love it? Certainly no Greek drew more deeply than Wordsworth on the riches of Nature. Perhaps the verse was truer in Wordsworth's day than in ours, except that the first two lines may be always true.

THE world is too much with us; late
    and soon,
Getting and spending, we lay waste
    our powers:
Little we see in Nature that is ours;
We have given our hearts away, a sordid
    boon!
This sea that bares her bosom to the moon;
The winds that will be howling at all
    hours,
And are up-gathered now like sleeping
    flowers;
For this, for everything, we are out of
    tune;
It moves us not. Great God! I'd rather be
A Pagan suckled in a creed outworn;
So might I, standing on this pleasant lea,
Have glimpses that would make me less
    forlorn;
Have sight of Proteus rising from the sea;
Or hear old Triton blow his wreathèd
    horn.

MY OLD FRIEND

It is curious that poetry has not provided many close and intimate studies of friendship. The romances of friendship have been told, but not much has been said about the ordinary effects of a friendly presence. This charming study is by Dr. Arthur Christopher Benson (1862–1925), who was graceful in prose, verse, and friendship.

IT seems the world was always bright
  With some divine unclouded weather
When we, with hearts and footsteps light,
  By lawn and river walked together:

There was no talk of me and you,
  Of theories with facts to bound them,
We were content to be and do,
  And take our fortunes as we found them.

We spoke no wistful words of love,
  No hint of sympathy and dearness,
Only around, beneath, above,
  There ran a swift and subtle nearness.

Each inmost thought was known to each
  By some impetuous divination:
We found no need of flattering speech,
  Content with silent admiration.

I think I never touched your hand,
  I took no heed of face or feature,
Only, I thought on sea or land
  Was never such a gracious creature.

It seems I was not hard to please,
  Where'er you led I needs must follow;
For strength you were my Hercules,
  For wit and lustre my Apollo.

The years flew onward: stroke by stroke
  They clashed from the impartial steeple,
And we appear to other folk
  A pair of ordinary people.

One word, old friend: though fortune flies,
  If hope should fail, till death shall sever,
In one dim pair of faithful eyes
  You seem as bright, as brave as ever.

ODE TO THE WEST WIND

In this ode Shelley reaches the summit of his achievement as a poet. It was written in 1819, near Florence, when the west wind was collecting vapours for the autumnal rains. The poet, now 27, and with less than three years more to live, had run through a wildly impractical youth, and was beginning to feel his responsibility to the world as a poet, and this consciousness is here expressed with a magnificent poetic fervour. Two stanzas of the poem are here omitted.

O WILD West Wind, thou breath of Autumn's being,
Thou, from whose unseen presence the leaves dead
Are driven, like ghosts from an enchanter fleeing,

Yellow, and black, and pale, and hectic red,
Pestilence-stricken multitudes: O thou,
Who chariotest to their dark wintry bed

The wingèd seeds, where they lie cold and low,
Each like a corpse within its grave, until
Thine azure sister of the Spring shall blow

Her clarion o'er the dreaming earth, and fill
(Driving sweet buds like flocks to feed in air)
With living hues and odours plain and hill:

Wild Spirit, which art moving everywhere;
Destroyer and preserver; hear, oh, hear;

If I were a dead leaf thou mightest bear;
If I were a swift cloud to fly with thee;
A wave to pant beneath thy power, and share

The impulse of thy strength, only less free
Than thou, O uncontrollable! If even
I were as in my boyhood, and could be

The comrade of thy wanderings over Heaven,
As then, when to outstrip thy skiey speed
Scarce seemed a vision; I would ne'er have striven

As thus with thee in prayer in my sore need.
Oh, lift me as a wave, a leaf, a cloud!
I fall upon the thorns of life! I bleed!

A heavy weight of hours has chained and bowed
One too like thee : tameless, and swift, and proud.

Make me thy lyre, even as the forest is:
What if my leaves are falling like its own!
The tumult of thy mighty harmonies

Will take from both a deep, autumnal tone,
Sweet though in sadness. Be thou, Spirit fierce,
My spirit ! Be thou me, impetuous one!

Drive my dead thoughts over the universe
Like withered leaves to quicken a new birth!
And, by the incantation of this verse,

Scatter, as from an unextinguished hearth
Ashes and sparks, my words among mankind!
Be through my lips to unawakened earth

The trumpet of a prophecy! O, Wind,
If Winter comes, can Spring be far behind?

LITTLE VERSES FOR VERY LITTLE PEOPLE

THE LOVABLE CHILD

Frisky as a lambkin,
  Busy as a bee:
That's the kind of little girl
  People like to see.

Modest as a violet,
  As a rosebud sweet:
That's the kind of little girl
  People like to meet.

Bright as a diamond,
  Pure as any pearl:
Everyone rejoices in
  Such a little girl.

Happy as a robin,
  Gentle as a dove:
That's the kind of little girl
  Everyone will love.

Fly away and seek her,
  Little song of mine,
For I choose that very girl
  As my valentine.   Emilie Poulsson

FAITHLESS SALLY BROWN

Young Ben he was a nice young man,
  A carpenter by trade;
And he fell in love with Sally Brown,
  That was a lady's maid.

But as they fetched a walk one day
  They met a press-gang crew;
And Sally she did faint away,
  While Ben he was brought to.

The Boatswain swore with wicked words,
  Enough to shock a saint,
That, though she did seem in a fit,
  'Twas nothing but a feint.

"Come, girl," said he, "hold up your head,
  He'll be as good as me;
For when your swain is in our boat
  A boatswain he will be."

So when they'd made their game of her,
  And taken off her elf,
She roused, and found she only was
  A coming to herself.

"And is he gone, and is he gone?"
  She cried, and wept outright;
"Then I will to the waterside,
  And see him out of sight."

A waterman came up to her;
  "Now, young woman," said he,
"If you weep on so you will make
  Eye-water in the sea."

"Alas! They've taken my beau Ben
  To sail with old Benbow."
And her woe began to run afresh
  As if she'd said Gee woe!

Says he, "They've only taken him
  To the Tender ship, you see."
"The Tender-ship!" cried Sally Brown.
  "What a hard-ship that must be!"

Now Ben had sailed to many a place
  That's underneath the world;
But in two years the ship came home,
  And all her sails were furled.

But when he called on Sally Brown,
  To see how she went on,
He found she'd got another Ben,
  Whose Christian name was John.

"Oh, Sally Brown! Oh, Sally Brown!
  How could you serve me so?
I've met with many a breeze before,
  But never such a blow."

Then reading on his bacco box,
  He heaved a bitter sigh;
And then began to eye his pipe,
  And then to pipe his eye.

And then he tried to sing "All's well,"
  But could not, though he tried;
His head was turned, and so he chewed
  His pigtail till he died.

His death, which happened in his berth,
  At forty-odd befell;
They went and told the sexton, and
  The sexton tolled the bell.   Thomas Hood

THE OWL AND THE EEL

The owl and the eel and the warming-pan,
They went to call on the soap-fat man.
The soap-fat man he was not within:
He'd gone for a ride on his rolling-pin.
So they all came back by the way of the town,
And turned the meeting-house upside down.
                              Laura E. Richards

CITY MOUSE AND GARDEN MOUSE

The city mouse lives in a house,
  The garden mouse lives in a bower;
He's friendly with the frogs and toads,
  And sees the pretty plants in flower.

The city mouse eats bread and cheese,
  The garden mouse eats what he can;
We will not grudge him seeds and stocks,
  Poor little timid, furry man.
              Christina Georgina Rossetti

MOON, SO ROUND AND YELLOW

Moon, so round and yellow,
    Looking from on high,
How I love to see you
    Shining in the sky.
Oft and oft I wonder,
    When I see you there,
How they get to light you,
    Hanging in the air:

Where you go at morning,
    When the night is past,
And the sun comes peeping
    O'er the hills at last.
Sometime I will watch you
    Slyly overhead,
When you think I'm sleeping
    Snugly in my bed.
                        Matthias Barr

BABY SLEEPS

The baby wept;
    The mother took it from the
        nurse's arms,
And hushed its fears, and soothed its vain
    alarms,
And baby slept.

Again it weeps,
And God doth take it from the mother's
    arms,
From present griefs, and future unknown
    harms,
And baby sleeps.
                        Samuel Hinds

LETTY'S GLOBE

When Letty had scarce passed her third
    glad year,
    And her young artless words began to
        flow,
One day we gave the child a coloured
    sphere
    Of the wide earth, that she might mark
        and know,
By tint and outline, all its sea and land.
    She patted all the world; old empires
        peeped
Between her baby fingers; her soft hand
    Was welcome at all frontiers.   How she
        leaped
And laughed and prattled in her world-
    wide bliss:
But when we turned her sweet unlearned
    eye
On our own isle she raised a joyous cry:
    Oh! yes, I see it, Letty's home is there!
And, while she hid all England with a kiss,
Bright over Europe fell her golden hair.
                Charles Tennyson Turner

THE SHEPHERD

How sweet is the shepherd's sweet lot.
    From the morn to the evening he
        strays;
He shall follow his sheep all the day,
    And his tongue shall be filled with praise.

For he hears the lamb's innocent call,
    And he hears the ewe's tender reply;
He is watchful while they are at peace,
    For they know when their shepherd is
        nigh.   William Blake

THE FROST LOOKED FORTH

The Frost looked forth one still, clear
    night,
And whispered: " Now I shall be out of
    sight,
So through the valley and over the height
    In silence I'll take my way;
I'll not go on like that blustering train,
The wind and the snow, the hail and the
    rain;
They make so much bustle and noise in
    vain,
    But I'll be as busy as they."

Then he flew to the mountain and
    powdered its crest;
He lit on the trees, and their boughs he
    dressed
In diamond beads, and over the breast
    Of the quivering lake he spread
A coat of mail, that it need not fear
The downward point of many a spear
That hung on its margin far and near,
    Where a rock could rear its head.

He went to the windows of those who slept,
And over each pane like a fairy crept;
Wherever he breathed, wherever he stept,
    By the light of the moon were seen
Most beautiful things: there were flowers
    and trees,
There were bevies of birds and swarms of
    bees,
There were cities with temples and towers,
    and these
All pictured in silver sheen.

But he did one thing that was hardly fair,
He peeped in the cupboard, and finding
    there
That all had forgotten for him to prepare,
    " Now, just to set them a-thinking,
I'll bite this basket of fruit," said he;
" This costly pitcher I'll burst in three,
And the glass of water they've left for me
    Shall tchich to tell them I'm drinking."
                        Hannah Flagg Gould

THE REAL HISTORY OF THE APPLE-PIE

A APPLE-PIE, B bit it,
  C cut it, D dealt it,
E ate it, F fought for it,
G got it, H had it,
I iced it, J joked about it,
K kept it, L longed for it,
M mourned for it,
N nodded at it,
O opened it, P peeped in it,
Q quartered it, R ran for it,
S stole it, T took it,
U upset it, V viewed it,
W wanted it, X expected it,
Y yearned for it, Z had a zest for it;
And when they came to ampersand
They all desired a piece in hand.

At last they every one agreed
Upon the apple-pie to feed;
But as there seemed to be so many
Those who were last might not have any
Unless some method could be thought out
To stop their squabbles being fought out.
They all agreed to stand in order
Around the apple-pie's fine border,
Take turn as they in school-book stand,
From great A down to ampersand,
In equal parts the pie dividing,
A fair plan they were all deciding,

Says A, give me a good large slice,
Says B, a little bit, but nice,
Says C, cut me a piece of crust,
Take it, says D, it's dry as dust,
Says E, I'll eat it fast, I will,
Says F, I vow I'll have my fill,
Says G, give it me good and great,
Says H, a little bit I hate,
Says I, it's ice I must request,
Says J, the juice I love the best,
Says K, let's keep it up above,
Says L, the border's what I love,
Says M, it makes your teeth to chatter,
N said, it's nice, there's nought the matter,
O others' plates with grief surveyed,
P for a large piece begged and prayed,
Q quarrelled for the topmost slice,
R rubbed his hands and said " it's nice,"
S silent sat, and simply looked,
T thought, and said, it's nicely cooked,
U understood the fruit was cherry,
V vanished when they all got merry,
W wished there'd been a quince in,
X here explained he'd need convincing,
Y said, I'll eat, and yield to none,
Z, like a zany, said he'd done,
While ampersand purloined the dish,
And for another pie did wish.

PEMMY WAS A PRETTY GIRL

PEMMY was a pretty girl,
  But Fanny was a better;
Pemmy looked like any churl
  When little Fanny let her.

Pemmy had a pretty nose,
  But Fanny had a better;
Pemmy oft would come to blows,
  But Fanny would not let her.

Pemmy had a pretty doll,
  But Fanny had a better;
Pemmy chattered like a poll
  When little Fanny let her.

Pemmy had a pretty song,
  But Fanny had a better;
Pemmy would sing all day long,
  But Fanny would not let her.

Pemmy loved a pretty lad,
  But Fanny loved a better;
And Pemmy wanted for to wed,
  But Fanny would not let her.

THERE'S NOTHING LIKE A DADDY

I DO not want a puppy-dog, although I
    know they're nice,
For my papa can romp with me in ways
    that quite suffice.
He'll bark just like a St. Bernard, and
    like a mastiff growl,
And you would feel like laughing when he
    imitates its howl.

I do not want a pussy-cat. I like cats
    pretty well.
But Daddy beats them all, and plays
    better than I can tell.
He'll purr and siss like anything; his
    mewing you should hear;
It makes more noise than any cat, and, oh,
    I shake with fear!

I do not want a pony small. Of course
    they're lots of fun,
But what's the use of ponies when you're
    my dear daddy's son?
He takes me on his shoulders broad, or
    puts me on his knees,
And sets me off a-galloping as madly as
    you please.

In short, I don't want anything as long as
    Daddy's here;
He's pretty much of everything, and don't
    get out of gear.
And best of all the things boys have, I'm
    sure you'll find it true,
There's nothing like a daddy who will
    always play with you !

MR. NOBODY

I KNOW a funny little man,
    As quiet as a mouse,
Who does the mischief that is done
    In everybody's house.
There's no one ever sees his face,
    And yet we all agree
That every plate we break was cracked
    By Mr. Nobody.

'Tis he who always tears our books,
    Who leaves the door ajar;
He pulls the buttons from our shirts,
    And scatters pins afar.
That squeaking door will always squeak,
    For, prithee, don't you see,
We leave the oiling to be done
    By Mr. Nobody.

He puts damp wood upon the fire,
    That kettles cannot boil;
His are the feet that bring in mud
    And all the carpets soil.
The papers always are mislaid:
    Who had them last but he?
There's no one tosses them about
    But Mr. Nobody.

The finger-marks upon the door
    By none of us are made;
We never leave the blinds unclosed
    To let the curtains fade.
The ink we never spill, the boots
    That lying round you see
Are not our boots; they all belong
    To Mr. Nobody.

THE WASP AND THE BEE

A WASP met a bee that was buzzing by,
    And he said: "Little cousin, can
you tell me why
You are loved so much better by people
than I?

"My back shines as bright and yellow as
gold,
And my shape is most elegant, too, to
behold;
Yet nobody likes me for that, I am told."

"Ah, cousin," the bee said, "'tis all very
true;
But if I had half as much mischief to do,
Indeed they would love me no better than
you.

"You have a fine shape and a delicate
wing;
They own you are handsome; but then
there's one thing
They cannot put up with, and that is your
sting.

"My coat is quite homely and plain, as
you see,
Yet nobody ever is angry with me,
Because I'm a humble and innocent bee."

From this little story let people beware,
Because, like the wasp, if ill-natured they
are
They will never be loved if they're ever
so fair.

THE KILKENNY CATS

THERE were once two cats of Kilkenny,
    Each thought there was one cat too
many;
So they fought and they fit,
And they scratched and they bit,
Till, excepting their nails
And the tips of their tails,
Instead of two cats there weren't any.

THE LITTLE MOUSE

I HAVE seen you, little mouse,
    Running all about the house,
Through the hole your little eye
In the wainscot peeping sly,
Hoping soon some crumbs to steal,
To make quite a hearty meal.
Look before you venture out,
See if pussy is about;
If she's gone you'll quickly run
To the larder for some fun;
Round about the dishes creep.
Taking into each a peep,
To choose the daintiest that's there,
Spoiling things you do not care.

WHAT CAN THE MATTER BE?

O DEAR, what can the matter be?
    O dear, what can the matter be?
O dear, what can the matter be?
    Johnnie's so long at the fair.

He promised to buy me a bunch of blue
ribbon,
He promised to buy me a bunch of blue
ribbon,
He promised to buy me a bunch of blue
ribbon,
To tie up my bonnie brown hair.

He promised to bring me a basket of
posies,
A garland of lilies, a garland of roses,
A little straw hat to set off the blue
ribbons
    That tie up my bonnie brown hair.

THE OLD WOMAN AND HER PIG

An old woman was sweeping her house, and she found a crooked sixpence.

"What," she said, "shall I do with this little sixpence? I shall go to market and buy a little pig."

As she was coming home she came to a stile. The piggy would not go over the stile. She went a little farther, and she met a dog, so she said to the dog:

Dog, dog, bite pig;
Piggy won't get over the stile,
And I shan't get home tonight!
But the dog would not.

She went a little farther, and she met a stick. So she said:

Stick, stick, beat dog;
Dog won't bite pig;
Piggy won't get over the stile,
And I shan't get home to-night!
But the stick would not.

She went a little farther, and she met a fire. So she said:
Fire, fire, burn stick;
Stick won't beat dog;
Dog won't bite pig;
Piggy won't get over the stile,
And I shan't get home tonight!
But the fire would not.

She went a little farther, and she met some water. So she said:
Water, water, quench fire;
Fire won't burn stick;
Stick won't beat dog;
Dog won't bite pig;
Piggy won't get over the stile,
And I shan't get home tonight!
But the water would not.

She went a little farther, and she met an ox. So she said:
Ox, ox, drink water;
Water won't quench fire;
Fire won't burn stick;
Stick won't beat dog;
Dog won't bite pig;
Piggy won't get over the stile,
And I shan't get home tonight!
But the ox would not.

Then she met a butcher, and she said:
Butcher, butcher, kill ox;
Ox won't drink water;
Water won't quench fire;
Fire won't burn stick;
Stick won't beat dog;
Dog won't bite pig;
Piggy won't get over the stile,
And I shan't get home tonight!
But the butcher would not.

She went a little farther, and met a rope. So she said:
Rope, rope, hang butcher;
Butcher won't kill ox;
Ox won't drink water;
Water won't quench fire;
Fire won't burn stick;
Stick won't beat dog;
Dog won't bite pig;
Piggy won't get over the stile,
And I shan't get home tonight!
But the rope would not.

She went a little farther, and she met a rat. So she said:
Rat, rat, gnaw rope;
Rope won't hang butcher;
Butcher won't kill ox;
Ox won't drink water;
Water won't quench fire;
Fire won't burn stick;
Stick won't beat dog;
Dog won't bite pig;
Piggy won't get over the stile,
And I shan't get home tonight!
But the rat would not.

She went a little farther, and she met a cat, so she said:
Cat, cat, kill rat;
Rat won't gnaw rope;
Rope won't hang butcher;
Butcher won't kill ox;
Ox won't drink water;
Water won't quench fire;
Fire won't burn stick;
Stick won't beat dog;
Dog won't bite pig;
Piggy won't get over the stile,
And I shan't get home tonight!
But the cat said to her, "If you will go to yonder cow, and fetch me a saucer of milk, I will

kill the rat." So the old woman said to the cow:

Cow, cow, give me a saucer of milk;
Cat won't kill rat;
Rat won't gnaw rope;
Rope won't hang butcher;
Butcher won't kill ox ;
Ox won't drink water;
Water won't quench fire;
Fire won't burn stick;
Stick won't beat dog;
Dog won't bite pig;
Piggy won't get over the stile,
And I shan't get home tonight!

But the cow said to her, " If you will go to yonder haymakers, and fetch me a wisp of hay, I'll give you the milk." So away went the old woman to the haymakers, and said;

Haymakers, give me a wisp of hay;
Cow won't give milk;
Cat won't kill rat;
Rat won't gnaw rope;
Rope won't hang butcher;
Butcher won't kill ox;
Ox won't drink water;
Water won't quench fire;
Fire won't burn stick;
Stick won't beat dog;
Dog won't bite pig;
Piggy won't get over the stile,
And I shan't get home tonight!

But the haymakers said to her, " If you will go to yonder stream, and fetch us a bucket of water, we'll give you the hay." So away the old woman went.

But when she got to the stream she found the bucket was full of holes. So she covered the bottom with pebbles and then filled the bucket with water, and she went back with it to the hay. As soon as the cow had eaten the hay she gave the old woman the milk; and away she went with it in a saucer to the cat. As soon as the cat had lapped up the milk;

The cat began to kill the rat;
The rat began to gnaw the rope;
The rope began to hang the butcher;
The butcher began to kill the ox;
The ox began to drink the water;
The water began to quench the fire;
The fire began to burn the stick;
The stick began to beat the dog;
The dog began to bite the pig;
The little pig in a fright jumped over the stile;

So the old woman got home that night!

THE OLD MAN WHO LIVED IN A WOOD

There was an old man who lived in a wood,
    As you may plainly see;
He said he could do as much work in a day
    As his wife could do in three.
" With all my heart, the old woman said,
    If that you will allow,
Tomorrow you'll stay at home in my stead
    And I'll go and drive the plough.

" But you must milk the Tidy cow,
    For fear that she go dry;
And you must feed the little pigs
    That are within the sty;
And you must mind the speckled hen,
    For fear she lay away;
And you must reel the spool of yarn
    That I spun yesterday."

The old woman took a staff in her hand
    And went to drive the plough;
The old man took a pail in his hand,
    And went to milk the cow;

But Tidy hinched and Tidy flinched,
    And Tidy broke his nose,
And Tidy gave him such a blow
    That the tears ran down to his toes.

" High, Tidy, ho!   High, Tidy, high!
    Tidy, do stand still!
If ever I milk you, Tidy, again,
    'Twill be sore against my will."

He went to feed the little pigs
    That were within the sty;
He hit his head against the beam,
    And he made the tears to fly.
He went to mind the speckled hen,
    For fear she'd lay astray,
And he forgot the spool of yarn
    His wife spun yesterday.

So he swore by the sun and the moon and the stars,
    And the green leaves on the tree,
If his wife didn't do a day's work in her life
    She should ne'er be ruled by he.

Doodle, doodle, doo,
The princess lost her shoe;
Her highness hopped,
The fiddler stopped,
Not knowing what to do.

⊡ ⊡

A FARMER's dog leaped over the stile,
His name was little Bingo;
There was B with an I, I with an N,
N with a G, G with an O,
There was B, I, N, G, O,
And his name was little Bingo.

⊡ ⊡

THERE was an old man in a tree
Who was horribly bored by a bee;
When they said, " Does it buzz? "
He replied, " Yes, it does!
It's a regular brute of a bee! "

⊡ ⊡

LITTLE Polly Flinders
Sat among the cinders,
Warming her pretty little toes;
Her mother came and caught her,
And whipped her little daughter
For spoiling her nice new clothes.

⊡ ⊡

SEE-SAW, Margery Daw,
Baby shall have a new master;
She shall have but a penny a day
Because she can't work any faster.

⊡ ⊡

SHALL I sing? says the Lark,
Shall I bloom? says the Flower;
Shall I come? says the Sun,
Or shall I? says the Shower.

Sing your song, pretty Bird,
Roses bloom for an hour;
Shine on, dearest Sun;
Go away, naughty Shower.

⊡ ⊡

COCK ROBIN got up early,
At the break of day,
And went to Jenny's window
To sing a roundelay.

He sang Cock Robin's love
To little Jenny Wren,
And when he got unto the end
Then he began again.

⊡ ⊡

THE rose is red, the violet's blue,
The pink is sweet, and so are you!

⊡ ⊡

YOUNG lambs to sell!
Young lambs to sell!
If I'd as much money as I could tell
I never would cry Young lambs to sell!

CURLY LOCKS! Curly Locks! wilt thou
be mine?
Thou shalt not wash dishes, nor yet feed
the swine;
But sit on a cushion, and sew a fine seam,
And feed upon strawberries, sugar, and
cream.

⊡ ⊡

THERE was an old woman who lived in a
shoe;
She had so many children she didn't know
what to do;
She gave them some broth without any
bread,
She whipped them all round, and sent
them to bed.

⊡ ⊡

FIRST the farmer sows his seeds,
Then he stands and takes his ease;
Stamps his foot and claps his hands,
And turns him round to view his lands.

⊡ ⊡

PETER PIPER picked a peck of pickled
pepper;
A peck of pickled pepper Peter Piper
picked;
If Peter Piper picked a peck of pickled
pepper,
Where's the peck of pickled pepper Peter
Piper picked?

⊡ ⊡

A LITTLE old man and I fell out;
How shall we bring this matter
about?
Bring it about as well as you can;
Get you gone, you little old man.

⊡ ⊡

WHAT are little boys made of, made of?
What are little boys made of?
Snaps and snails and puppy-dogs' tails;
And that's what little boys are made of,
made of.

What are little girls made of, made of?
What are little girls made of?
Sugar and spice, and all that's nice;
And that's what little girls are made of,
made of.

⊡ ⊡

LAVENDER blue and rosemary green,
When I am king you shall be queen.
Call up my maids at four of the clock,
Some to the wheel and some to the rock,
Some to make hay and some to thresh corn,
And you and I will keep the bed warm.

THERE was a king met a king
    In a narrow lane.
Says this king to that king:
    ' Where have you been? '
' Oh, I've been a-hunting
    With my dog and my doe.'
' Pray lend him to me,
    That I may do so.'
    ' There's the dog, *take* the dog.'
      ' What's the dog's name? '
    ' I've told you already.'
      ' Pray tell me again.'

PUSSY sits beside the fire:
    How can she be fair?
In comes the little dog:
    " Pussy, are you there?
So, so, Mistress Pussy,
    Pray, how do you do? "
" Thank you, thank you, little dog,
    I'm very well just now."

THERE was a man, and he went mad,
    And he jumped into a biscuit bag;
The biscuit bag it was so full,
So he jumped into a roaring bull;
The roaring bull it was so fat,
So he jumped into a gentleman's hat;
The gentleman's hat it was so fine,
So he jumped into a bottle of wine;
The bottle of wine it was so dear,
So he jumped into a barrel of beer;
The barrel of beer it was so thick,
So he jumped into a walking-stick;
The walking-stick it was so narrow,
So he jumped into a wheelbarrow;
The wheelbarrow began to crack,
So he jumped into a haystack;
The haystack began to blaze,
So he did nothing but cough and sneeze!

JOHN COOK he had a little grey mare; he,
    haw, hum!
Her back stood up, and her bones they
    were bare; he, haw, hum!
John Cook was riding up Shunter's Bank;
    he, haw, hum!
And there his nag did kick and prank;
    he, haw, hum!
John Cook was riding up Shunter's Hill;
    he, haw, hum!
His mare fell down and she made her will;
    he, haw, hum!
The bridle and saddle were laid on the
    shelf; he, haw, hum!
If you want any more you may sing it
    yourself; he, haw, hum!

A BUTTERFLY perched on a mossy brown
    stile,
And a little maid saw him and cried, with
    a smile:
" O beautiful butterfly, yellow and blue,
Stop, stop; let me sit on the stile with
    you! "
But the beautiful butterfly, yellow and
    blue,
Opened his wings, and away he flew;
And when he'll return I really can't say,
But the little maid sits on the stile to
    this day!

I KNOW a child, and who she is
    I'll tell you by and by.
When Mamma says Do this, or that,
    She says What for? and Why?
She'd be a better child by far
    If she would say I'll try.

OLD Abram Brown is dead and gone,
    You'll never see him more;
He used to wear a long brown coat
    That buttoned down before.

As I was going to sell my eggs
    I met a man with crooked legs;
Crooked legs and turned-up toes.
I tripped up his heels, and he fell on his
    nose.

A LITTLE cock sparrow sat on a green
    tree,
And he chirruped, he chirruped, so merry
    was he.
A naughty boy came with his wee bow
    and arrow,
Determined to shoot this little cock
    sparrow.

" This little cock sparrow shall make me
    a stew,
And his giblets shall make me a little pie
    too."
" Oh, no," said the sparrow, " I won't
    make a stew! "
So he flapped his wings, and away he flew.

HECTOR PROTECTOR was dressed all in
    green;
Hector Protector was sent to the Queen;
The Queen did not like him,
    No more did the King;
So Hector Protector was sent back again.

The Story of the Most Beautiful Book in the World

Carrying on the Great Ideal

WE have read together the wonderful narrative of the Bible, the life of Jesus, the great story of Paul. We have seen how the ideas of Jesus, carried to Antioch and Rome by His servant Paul, opposed by all that hate, cruelty, and evil could do to destroy them, endured through the decay of the Roman Empire, and became the chief influence in the progress of the world when Rome had become but the shadow of a name. For us it remains to carry on the work that began in Galilee, that Paul brought to Europe, and that men have built up through ages of suffering and toil. It is for us to carry forward the influence of Jesus by the gentleness of our lives, to spread goodness and hopefulness everywhere, to keep for ever shining in our lives, undimmed and unbroken, the beautiful Light of the World.

CHRISTIANITY IN THE WORLD

WE have traced what happened to Christianity after the disciples went forth into many parts of the world to proclaim the good news; how two chief churches were formed in Rome and in Constantinople; how the Church of Rome grew to be a most powerful institution under the Pope, and a rival to the government of nations by their kings. Gradually the Church undertook to fix what all Christians should believe, and what ought not to be believed in religion; and this was followed by punishments, including death, for Christians who doubted whether some of the Church's teachings were the pure teachings of Christ.

The differences of opinion and belief as to what Christianity is, and the use of force to secure uniformity, make up one of the saddest chapters to be recorded in human history.

We cannot conceive of Jesus doing what was done by the Churches adopting his name. He was no persecutor; he was content to be persecuted. In all the Christian Churches of all ages there have been men truly reflecting Christ's spirit, and they, by whatever name they may be called, are his true Church; but also in all the churches, in churches of almost every creed, there have been men with a persecuting spirit, and unfortunately they have often been the leading spirits, harsh and implacable.

The truth is they simply did not understand the mind of Christ. So, within His Church (within the Protestant churches as in others) came wars and bloodshed, massacres and burnings alive—a terrible retrospect! All this came about because men were not allowed the liberty to be honest in their inmost beliefs.

We shall be unjust in looking back on these things if we think it was only one part of the Church that was cruel. Cruelty was common. Gentleness was at a discount among men who had power. Religion was infected by it, even the religion called by the name of the Lord of Love. Only gradually has the mind that was in Jesus dominated His Church, as only gradually is it dominating the world.

The difficulty began when the Church attempted by force to crush out such forms of Christianity as did not quite agree with the forms it had said were the only right forms. It is impossible to conquer thought and belief by force. Persecution only made men who were seeking the truth the more resolute. They died gladly for the faith that was dear to them, as the earlier Christians had died rather than submit to the official religion of pagan Rome.

As time went on men of a thoughtful and independent tone of mind claimed to go back to the teachings of Scripture to find out what Christianity was as it was taught by Christ and the Apostles.

GREAT FIGURES OF THE OLD TESTAMENT · THE LIFE OF JESUS

The man who began to preach a greater freedom of inquiry was a learned English priest named John Wycliffe, who lived most of his life while Edward the Third was King of England. He has been called the Morning Star of the Reformation. It grieved him to see that so many of the clergy seemed to care little for the souls of the people, so he sent out his disciples to preach the Gospel for the truth's sake, without earthly reward.

HOW WYCLIFFE'S FOLLOWERS WERE PERSECUTED IN ENGLAND

He also translated the Scriptures so that the people could read them—the Bible in England having been available only in Latin for the learned to read. His teaching made the rulers of the Church angry, though it was pleasing enough to some of the great lords, such as John of Gaunt; and therefore they protected Wycliffe from the bishops, who would have had him punished as a heretic. And so John Wycliffe himself died in peace.

But after his death his disciples in England, who were called Lollards—from a word which means to chant or sing— were persecuted as heretics, and Wycliffe's doctrines were declared to be heresies; and a fearful thing was done, his body being taken from the grave and burned, and the ashes cast into the river. Yet his doctrines came to be held in other lands, and there arose in Bohemia a teacher named John Huss, who taught the things that Wycliffe taught; and many of the people of Bohemia believed these things and held them for truth.

FIERCE WARS THAT WERE CAUSED BY AN EMPEROR'S BROKEN PROMISE

In those days there was held a great Council at Constance, in Switzerland, to put an end to the quarrels that were going on as to which of two men who claimed to be pope was really pope, and Huss was bidden to come before this Council to answer for his doctrines. He would not have gone except that the Emperor Sigismund gave him a written promise that he should be suffered to come and to depart unhurt. But the emperor, to his great shame, broke his word, and Huss was condemned to be burned. The folk of Bohemia were very angry at these things, and would in no wise deny the truth of what Huss had taught them; and there followed long and fierce wars, in which the Hussites were often victorious.

Among the men who sought to spread knowledge and gain greater freedom for honest thought, but yet drew back when they feared that great and violent change might come, the most famous and the cleverest, was Erasmus, the Dutchman who greatly loved Sir Thomas More, and was beloved by him.

The learned Erasmus was born in 1466 at Rotterdam, in Holland. It was meant that he should be a monk, and he was brought up among monks. Yet though he became a priest, a monk he would not be, but spent his time in studying and lecturing and talking and writing. His witty words threw scorn and contempt upon corruption and superstition and all manner of folly, and his wise words taught men to understand the writings of Paul and the evangelists, and to insist on the right interpretation of them.

At last a time was reached when many men felt that a firm stand must be made at any cost against religion being imposed on them by authority. The greatest of these was Martin Luther, whose name is most closely associated with the widespread, epoch-making movement known in history as the Reformation.

THE MINER'S SON WHO LED THE REFORMATION IN GERMANY

Luther was very humbly born, for his father was no more than a poor miner; yet, being a frugal man with a wise wife, and both of them God-fearing folk, they prospered enough to be able to send their son to school, which poor folk could not always do in those days. The boy, being clever, did so well in his studies that he hoped to become a lawyer; but his thoughts were turned more zealously to religion, as the story goes, by the sudden death of his dearest friend.

Therefore he resolved to become a monk, thinking that it was only in the quiet of the cloister that a man could lead a truly spiritual and holy life. Then he was chosen to be one of the teachers at the new university of Wittenberg, in Saxony; and there it was not long before men began to flock to his lectures and his sermons, as he said strange things that went home to people's hearts, for he loved truth and spoke it fearlessly.

But as yet he had not thought at all that any man would ever call him heretic; for there was nothing that he taught or believed which he had not found either in the words of Paul or of the great Bishop St. Augustine, after whom the order of monks to which Martin Luther belonged was named.

It was a sore grief to him when he found that the interpretation which he gave to the Bible was not that of the Church, and a greater grief still when he felt compelled to denounce the practice of offering forgiveness for sins for money, as was sometimes done.

In the end the authorities of the Church found it necessary to oppose Luther with all their power; and the Pope sent a bull, which means a paper with a seal fixed to it, declaring that Luther was a heretic (an unbeliever), and Luther burned the Pope's bull before the citizens of Wittenberg, who, for the most part, were on his side. This act was as much as to say that he denied the Pope's authority altogether.

Just at this time what was called a Diet, an assembly of the princes and nobles of the German Empire, was held at Worms, and Luther was bidden to appear before it and answer for himself. Thither he went, though none knew whether his fate might not be that of John Huss; many men urged him not to risk his life, seeing that Duke George of Saxony was bitter against him.

But Luther said: " I will go, though it rain Duke Georges," and he stood before the gathered princes and nobles and bishops, and showed a great courage, saying that the words charged against him were true, and while he held them to be true he would not withdraw them, but would himself be true to his conscience. " Here stand I," he said boldly, " God help me! I can do no other."

However, before the Diet passed its judgment against him, declaring him an

READING FROM A CHAINED BIBLE IN ELIZABETHAN DAYS

outlaw, certain of his friends made a prisoner of him and carried him off secretly to a secure place where none could find him, and so his life was saved. From that time the princes of the German Empire were divided, some being for Luther and others for the Pope; and those who were for Luther would not yield him up.

It was while he was in hiding that Luther began his translation of the Bible into the German tongue, as Wycliffe had translated it into English; but now that the printing press had been invented thousands of people had the chance of reading Luther's Bible where only one had had the chance of reading Wycliffe's, and Luther's followers in Germany multiplied.

It was because they wanted to *protest* against oppression that Luther's followers were first called Protestants. All the rest of his days, throughout the Protestant parts of Germany, no man was held in such honour as Martin Luther. Though we should not find it possible to accept all his views today, he stood for much of what we now believe. By the great influence he had he used to keep the peace between his own followers and the zealous Romanists, though after he died they went to war with each other.

Now, although it is certain that there was none other who wrought so mighty a work as Luther, there were others who set out on the same path. One of these was the Swiss Ulrich Zwingli, of Zurich, who, before Martin had begun, was already teaching much that Luther was to preach.

But in some matters he departed from the Roman doctrine even more than Luther, so that Luther himself would not admit him to his friendship. However, the men who spread the reformed doctrine in England and Scotland were disciples of Zwingli rather than of Luther. Zwingli died as a soldier in defence of Zurich.

Soon afterwards there arose another champion of the Reformation, John Calvin, Frenchman, who lived for the most part at Geneva. The teaching of Calvin was very stern, and he ruled with a harsh discipline over the manner of life of his followers, and set up a new form of rule for the Church, not by bishops, but by presbyters, so that the name given to it is Presbyterianism. He, too, differed very much from Luther, and outside of England the Protestants came to be generally divided into Calvinists and Lutherans.

In England the Reformation took a different way, for its leaders held that in rejecting the Pope's authority they were in no wise ceasing to be a branch of the Catholic Church, but were a branch of the Church which had freed itself from errors. They suffered men to hold different opinions about many doctrines, so that some might incline towards Luther and others towards Calvin if, in their manner of worship, they gave heed to the ordinances of the Church as declared by the law.

THE COURSE OF THE REFORMATION IN ENGLAND AND SCOTLAND

The man who did most in making changes, and in checking them from extremes, was Thomas Cranmer, the Archbishop of Canterbury, who died at the stake in the terrible reign of Queen Mary.

In Scotland the Reformation was given its shape for the most part by a great disciple of Calvin, John Knox. He was a priest in the Roman Church when he was taught Luther's ideas by George Wishart, who became a Protestant martyr. By reason of his zeal and his powerful preaching the Protestant Scots, who had rebelled and were besieged at St. Andrews, took John Knox for their pastor. And so it was that when the French came to help Mary they took St. Andrews, and John Knox was carried off as a prisoner.

By the French Knox was sent to the galleys for a time and afterwards removed to prison. But when he was set free he returned to Scotland, and from that time to the day of his death all the reformers looked to him as their guide. He was a stern man, hating all things that had to do with vanity, and when the young Queen Mary came back to Scotland from France he had no fear of reproving her and all her courtiers, as Elijah reproved King Ahab, speaking words bold and bitter because she was much given to gaiety.

Knox taught a stern religion, and made the Scots, who were ever a rough and hardy people, a sterner folk than before; but he wrought a great work among them by the care he took for the teaching of children all over the land. He died full of years and honours, and, though for his hardness men scarcely love his memory, they still hold it in reverence.

THE LONG STRUGGLE IN ENGLAND FOR RELIGIOUS FREEDOM

Since that time Britain has been on the whole a Protestant country. Only gradually, however, did it allow full religious freedom to those who held the Roman Catholic faith, for early Protestantism was tainted by the idea of repressing beliefs contrary to its own. It was not until nearly our own time, indeed, that full liberty of religion was established throughout the land, and the victory completely won.

Growing freedom in religion has been followed by a growth of various forms of worship and differences in belief, though now there is a tendency towards greater unity. It is felt increasingly that in what is most essential, as judged by the teachings and life of Jesus, Christians are of one Church inwardly, though they may call themselves by different names.

In one respect all branches of the Church of Christ have followed the example of the earliest Christians, and have sought to spread the faith throughout all lands. That was a form of service the Roman Catholic Church has never lost sight of, and its missionary record has many noble pages.

HOW THE SPIRIT OF CHRISTIANITY HAS QUIETLY MADE ITS WAY

Christianity, in its many forms, is by far the most widely diffused of all religions. Other faiths are found widely held in large territories, as with Mohammedanism, Brahminism, Buddhism, and the religions of China; but Christianity is spreading everywhere. There is no land where its voice is not heard. And, best of all, its spirit is quietly permeating lands and influencing lives even where its teachings are not accepted as a religion; and many who do not openly enlist under the banner of Christ are in deed faithful unawares.

GOODBYE TO THE

My Little Travellers

TRAVELLERS through the world are we all, and you and I have been companions once again in this journey through the realms of knowledge.

INTO the homes of millions of people this Book of my Heart has gone since it began with a little child so long ago, and from a great multitude all over the Earth has come back to me the love that is more precious than gold. For it has been read by millions throughout our Empire and the United States of America. It has been translated into many languages and so has delighted children who speak French and Italian, Portuguese and Spanish, and even Chinese. Now we come to the last page of all. It is the time to say Goodbye to this old friend, and turn to something new.

YET with a book as with a friend, it is surely not the sadness of farewell, for the spirit of a book grows into our lives and will not die. So it is that this book goes on. It has been made out of the hearts of men and women, and it grows

To face page 7079

BOOK OF MY HEART

into the hearts and lives of a great multitude. It carries through the world those things that do not die, those things without which life would not be worth while.

IT will go on in your own life, as long as you see with these eyes and feel with these hands; and when these eyes no longer see, and these hands no longer feel, all that this book has meant to you will go on working in the lives of those who remember you. And after them, for ages after them, whatever is good in this book will live.

SHALL we let its last word breathe the spirit that I like to feel is in it everywhere, the spirit of goodwill to all mankind, and the faith that, whatever may betide us, nothing ill can happen to those who put their trust in God? He is our Refuge and our Strength, and underneath us are His Everlasting Arms.

AND so, little travellers, Goodbye, and God be with us till our journey's end.

Arthur Mee

Children's Encyclopedia

GUIDE TO KNOWLEDGE

including

Reference Tables

Atlas of the World

Index to this Book

so forming a quick guide to

LIVES OF FAMOUS PEOPLE
SCIENTIFIC AND GEOGRAPHICAL FACTS
A THOUSAND POEMS AND RHYMES
STORIES OF ALL AGES AND RACES
ABOUT TWENTY THOUSAND PICTURES

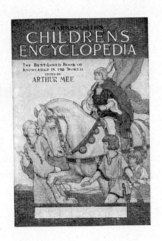

WORLD FACTS AND FIGURES IN TABLE FORM
COUNTRIES OF THE WORLD

Here we give the countries of the world, with their capitals or chief towns, approximate areas (in square miles), and populations. Where a country is made up of a number of States, these are also given.

Country	Capital	Area	Population
Aden Colony	Crater	75	130,000
Aden Protectorate		112,000	800,000
Afghanistan	Kabul	250.000	12.000,000
Alaska	Juneau	586,400	129,000
Albania	Tirana	10,700	1,200,000
Algeria	Algiers	848,000	9,500,000
Andorra	Andorra	191	5200
Arabian States			
Bahrain	Manamah	250	120,000
Kuwait	Kuwait	5800	200,000
Muscat & Oman	Muscat	82,000	550,000
Qatar	Dona	8000	18,000
See also Saudi-Arabia and Yemen			
Argentina	Buenos Aires	1,079,000	18,000,000
Australia	Canberra	2,974,581	9,000,000
Austria	Vienna	32,370	6,930,000
Basutoland	Maseru	11,720	600,000
Bechuanaland	Serowe	275,000	295,000
Belgian Congo	Leopoldville	904,750	11,260,000
Ruanda Urundi	Usumbura	19,540	3,800,000
Belgium	Brussels	11,770	11,000,000
Bermuda	Hamilton	21	39,000
Bolivia	La Paz	416,000	3,100,000
Brazil	Rio de Janeiro	3,288,000	54,660,000
British Guiana	Georgetown	83,000	453,000
British Honduras	Belize	8870	73,000
British Solomons	Honiara	11,500	100,000
Brunei	Brunei Town	2226	41,000
Bulgaria	Sofia	42,800	7,160,000
Burma	Rangoon	262,000	19,000,000
Cambodia	Phnôm-Penh	88,780	3,250,000
Canada	Ottawa	3,845,774	16.000.000
Ceylon	Colombo	25,332	8,000,000
Chile	Santiago	286,400	6,000,000
China	Peking	6,000,000	600,000,000
Colombia	Bogota	440,000	11,260,000
Costa Rica	San José	19,700	825,000
Cuba	Havana	44,200	5,815,000
Cyprus	Nicosia	3572	506,000
Czechoslovakia	Prague	49,380	12,600,000
Denmark	Copenhagen	16,580	4,500,000
Faroe Islands		540	29,180
Greenland	Godthaab	827,000	21,400
Dominican Rep.	Cuidad Trujillo	19,330	3,000,000
Ecuador	Quito	175,580	3,200,000
Egypt	Cairo	386,000	23,000,000
Eire	Dublin	27,047	2,960,000
England	London	50,337	41,148,000
For separate Counties see page 7082			
Ethiopia	Addis Ababa	350,000	20,000,000
Eritrea	Asmara	48,350	1,100,000
Falkland Islands	Stanley	4620	2230
Fiji	Suva	7080	312,000
Finland	Helsinki	130,165	4,165,000
France	Paris	212,660	42,750,000
French Equatorial Africa	Brazzaville	959,260	4,386,000
Chad (Fort Lamy); Gabun (Libreville); Middle Congo (Point-Noire); and Ubangi-Shari (Bangui).			
French Guiana	Cayenne	37,340	29,000
French West Africa		1,925,700	18,000,000
Dahomey	Porto Novo	43,230	1,570,000
French Sudan	Bamoko	591,000	3,445,000
Guinea	Conakry	98,890	2,257,000
Ivory Coast	Abidjan	184,180	2,170,000
Mauritania		323,300	546,000
Niger	Niamey	499,400	2,165,000
Senegal	St. Louis	77,700	2,100,000
Upper Volta		110,000	3,117,000
Gambia	Bathurst	4000	280,000
Germany	Berlin	143,200	70,000,000
Ghana	Accra	92,000	4,500,000
Gibraltar		2¼	23,000
Gilbert and Ellice Islands		370	36,000
Greece	Athens	51,250	7,603,000
Dodecanese Is.	Rhodes	1586	122,000
Guatemala	Guatemala City	45,450	2,900,000
Haiti	Port-au-Prince	10,710	3,112,000
Holland	The Hague	12,600	10,500,000
Honduras	Tegucigalpa	44,410	1,510,000
Hong Kong	Victoria	390	2,250,000
Hungary	Budapest	33,900	10,000,000
Iceland	Reykjavik	39,760	148,000
India	New Delhi	1,260,640	360,000,000
Indonesia	Djakarta	700,000	78,000,000
Iraq	Baghdad	116,600	5,000,000
Israel	Jerusalem	7800	1,430,000
Italy	Rome	116,230	47,000,000
Sardinia	Cagliari	9283	1,274,000
Sicily	Palermo	9927	4,462,000
Japan	Tokyo	147.690	89,000,000
Jordan	Amman	37,500	1,500,000
Kenya	Nairobi	225,000	6,250,000
Korea		85,260	27,650,000
North	Pyong-Yang	49,110	8,230,000
South	Seoul	36,150	19,420,000
Laos	Vientiane	69,480	1,190,000
Lebanon	Beirut	4000	1,500,000
Liberia	Monrovia	43,000	2,750,000
Libya	Tripoli	700,000	1,100,000
Liechtenstein	Vaduz	65	13,500
Luxemburg	Luxemburg	999	300,000
Madagascar	Tananarive	228,650	4,350,000
Malaya	Kuala Lumpur	50,690	5,705,000
Johore (Johore Bahru); Kedah (Alor Star); Kelantan (Kota Bahru); Malacca (Malacca); Negri Sembilan (Sereban); Pahang (Kuala Lipis); Penang (George Town); Perak (Ipoh); Perlis (Kangar); Selangor (Kuala Lumpur); Trengganu (Kuala Trengganu).			
Malta	Valletta	95	315,000
Mauritius	Port Louis	720	520,000
Mexico	Mexico City	760,370	26,930,000
Monaco		368 acres	20,200
Morocco	Rabat	154,000	8,500,000
Nepal	Katmandu	54,000	7,000,000
Netherlands : see Holland			
„ Guinea	Hollandia	151,000	700,000
„ Antilles	Willemstad	381	164,200
„ Guiana : See Surinam			
New Guinea	Rabaul	93,000	1,109,000
New Hebrides	Vila	5700	52,000
New Zealand	Wellington	103,736	2,037,500
Nicaragua	Managua	57,140	1,100,000
Nigeria	Lagos	373,250	31,000,000
North Borneo	Jesselton	29,400	350,000
Northern Ireland	Belfast	5328	1,370,000
For separate Counties see page 7082			
Norway	Oslo	124,700	3,340,000
Spitsbergen and Bear Island		25,000	3200
Pakistan	Karachi	364,740	82,000,000
Panama	Panama	25,580	817,000
Papua	Port Moresby	90,540	303,000
Paraguay	Asuncion	157,000	1,500,000
Persia	Tehran	628,060	20,000,000
Peru	Lima	514,060	8,715,000
Philippine Islands	Quezon City	115,600	20,620,000
Poland	Warsaw	120,360	27,000,000
Portugal	Lisbon	35,470	9,000,000
Azores	Angra	888	287,000
Portuguese Africa			
Angola	Loanda	481,300	4,150,000
Guinea	Bissau	13,950	523,000
Madeira	Funchal	308	208,000
Mozambique	Lourenço Marques	297,730	5,846,000
Puerto Rico	San Juan	3435	2,211,000
Rhodesia & Nyasaland	Salisbury	475,100	7,000,000
Southern Rhodesia (Salisbury); Northern Rhodesia (Lusaka); Nyasaland (Zomba).			
Rumania	Bucharest	91,670	17,500,000
Salvador	San Salvador	13,180	1,986,000
Samoa		1209	106,000
American	Pago Pago	76	19,000
Western	Apia	1133	87,230
San Marino	San Marino	38	12,100
Sarawak	Kuching	47,070	590,000
Saudi Arabia	Mecca	870,000	6,500,000
Scotland	Edinburgh	30,410	5,100,000
For separate Counties see page 7082			
Seychelles Islands	Victoria	156	37,000
Sierra Leone	Freetown	28,000	2,000,000
Singapore	Singapore City	224	1,000,000
Somaliland, British	Hargeisa	68,000	640,000
„ French Jibuti		9070	65,000
Somalia	Mogadishu	194,000	1,250,000
South Africa, Union	Pretoria	472,500	14,000,000
Cape of Good Hope (Cape Town); Natal (Pietermaritzburg); Transvaal (Pretoria); Orange Free State (Bloemfontein).			
South-West Africa	Windhoek	317,800	420,000
Spain	Madrid	195,500	28,300,000
Balearic Islands	Palma	1935	386,000
Canary Islands		2800	800,000
Spanish Guinea	Santa Isabel	10,036	140,000
Sudan	Khartoum	970,000	8,000,000
Surinam	Paramaribo	55,400	223,000
Swaziland	Mbabane	6700	200,000
Sweden	Stockholm	173,400	7,200,000

Switzerland	.. Berne	15,950	4,820,000
Syria	.. Damascus ..	66,050	3,780,000
Tanganyika	.. Dar-es-Salaam	362,690	8,100,000
Thailand ..	.. Bangkok ..	200,150	18,000,000
Tibet	.. Lhasa	475,000	1,000,000
Tonga ..	.. Nukualofa ..	269	51,000
Tunisia ..	.. Tunis	48,300	3,500,000
Turkey ..	.. Ankara	296,500	21,000,000
Uganda ..	.. Entebbe ..	94,000	5,400,000

Union of Soviet Soc-
ialist Republics Moscow.. .. 8,534,750 195,000,000
Armenia (Erivan); Azerbaijan (Baku); Byelo-Russia
(Minsk); Estonia (Tallinn); Georgia (Tbilisi); Karelo-
Finnish (Petrozavodsk); Kazakhstan (Alma-Ata); Kirgh-
izia (Frunze); Latvia (Riga); Lithuania (Vilnius);
Moldavia (Kishinev); Russian Soviet Federal Socialist
Republic (Moscow); Tadzhikistan (Stalinabad); Turk-
menistan (Ashkhabad); Ukraine (Kiev); Uzbekistan
(Tashkent).
United Kingdom London .. 93,990 50,215,000
For Counties of the United Kingdom, see below
United States of
America .. .. Washington .. 3,022,390 170,000,000
Alabama (Montgomery); Arizona (Phoenix); Arkansas
(Little Rock); California (Sacramento); Colorado
(Denver); Connecticut (Hartford); Delaware (Dover);
Florida (Tallahassee); Georgia (Atalanta); Idaho
(Boise); Illinois (Springfield); Indiana (Indianapolis);
Iowa (Des Moines); Kansas (Topeka); Kentucky
(Frankfort); Louisiana (Baton Rouge); Maine (Augusta);
Maryland (Annapolis); Massachusetts (Boston); Michi-
gan (Lansing); Minnesota (St. Paul); Mississippi

(Jackson); Missouri (Jefferson City); Montana (Helena);
Nebraska (Lincoln); Nevada (Carson City); New
Hampshire (Concord); New Jersey (Trenton); New
Mexico (Santa Fe); New York (Albany); North Carolina
(Raleigh); North Dakota (Bismarck); Ohio (Columbus);
Oklahoma (Oklahoma City); Oregon (Salem); Penn-
sylvania (Harrisburg); Rhode Island (Providence);
South Carolina (Columbia); South Dakota (Pierre);
Tennessee (Nashville); Texas (Austin); Utah (Salt Lake
City); Vermont (Montpelier); Virginia (Richmond);
Washington (Olympia); West Virginia (Charleston);
Wisconsin (Madison); Wyoming (Cheyenne).

Uruguay ..	.. Montevideo ..	72,150	2,350,000
Venezuela ..	.. Caracas ..	352.150	5,280,000
Vietnam (South)	Saigon	68,000	10,000,000
,, (North)	Hanoi	65,000	13,000,000
Wales ..	.. Cardiff	8006	2,026,150

For separate Counties, see below

West Indies ..		12,480	2,850,000
Bahamas ..	.. Nassau	4404	84,000
Barbados ..	.. Bridgetown ..	166	220,000
Cayman Islands	Georgetown ..	100	7600
Jamaica ..	.. Kingston ..	4410	1,450,000
Leeward Islands	St. John (Antigua)	423	120,000
Trinidad &			
Tobago ..	.. Port of Spain	1860	640,000
Turks & Caicos			
Islands ..	.. Grand Turk ..	166	6600
Windward Is.	.. St. George's ..	826	292,000
Yemen ..	.. Sanaa	75,000	5,000,000
Yugoslavia..	.. Belgrade ..	96,260	17,000,000
Zanzibar ..	.. Zanzibar Town	640	150,000

COUNTIES OF THE UNITED KINGDOM

Here is a list giving every County in the four Countries which form the United Kingdom, with its chief town, approximate area in square miles, and population.

COUNTIES OF ENGLAND

Bedfordshire	.. Bedford ..	473	311,850
Berkshire ..	.. Reading ..	725	402,940
Buckinghamshire	Aylesbury ..	750	386,160
Cambridgeshire..	Cambridge ..	867	255,900
Cheshire ..	.. Chester	1015	1,258,050
Cornwall ..	.. Bodmin ..	1356	345,610
Cumberland	.. Carlisle	1520	285,350
Derbyshire..	.. Derby	1006	826,340
Devonshire..	.. Exeter	2610	798,280
Dorsetshire..	.. Dorchester ..	973	291,160
Durham ..	.. Durham	1014	1,463,420
Essex	.. Chelmsford ..	1528	2,043,570
Gloucestershire	.. Gloucester ..	1259	938,620
Hampshire..	.. Winchester ..	1650	1,196,620
Herefordshire	.. Hereford ..	842	127,090
Hertfordshire	.. Hertford ..	632	609,740
Huntingdonshire	Huntingdon ..	366	69,270
Kent	.. Maidstone ..	1525	1,563,290
Lancashire..	.. Lancaster ..	1878	5,116,010
Leicestershire	.. Leicester ..	832	630,890
Lincolnshire	.. Lincoln	2662	706,570

County is divided into three administrative areas: Holland
(418 sq. miles; 101,550; chief town, Boston); Kesteven
(724 sq. miles; 131,560; chief town, Seaford); and Lindsey
(1520 sq. miles; 473,460; chief town, Lincoln).

London		117	3,348,340
Middlesex ..	.. Brentford ..	232	2,268,780
Norfolk ..	.. Norwich ..	2053	546,550
Northamptonshire	Northampton ..	997	423,330
Northumberland	Alnwick.. ..	2018	798,180
Nottinghamshire	Nottingham ..	847	841,080
Oxfordshire	.. Oxford	749	275,770
Rutlandshire	.. Oakham ..	152	20,510
Shropshire	.. Shrewsbury ..	1347	289,840
Somersetshire	.. Taunton ..	1613	551,190
Staffordshire	.. Stafford ..	1154	1,621,010
Suffolk ..	.. Ipswich ..	1482	442,440

County is divided into two administrative areas: East
Suffolk (871 sq. miles; 321,850; chief town, Ipswich);
and West Suffolk (610 sq. miles; 120,590; chief town,
Bury St. Edmunds).

Surrey ..	.. Kingston ..	722	810,560
Sussex	.. Lewes	1457	936,740

County is divided into two areas: East Sussex (829 sq. miles;
618,080; chief town, Lewes); and West Sussex (638 sq.
miles; 318,660; chief town, Chichester).

Warwickshire	.. Warwick ..	983	1,960,870
Westmorland	.. Appleby ..	789	67,380
Wiltshire ..	.. Salisbury ..	1345	387,380
Worcestershire	.. Worcester ..	699	522,970
Yorkshire ..	.. York	6079	4,516,370

County is divided into three areas: East Riding (1172 sq.
miles; 510,000; chief town, Beverley); North Riding
(2127 sq. miles; 525,500; chief town, Northallerton); and
West Riding (2780 sq. miles; 3,480,070; chief town,
Wakefield).

COUNTIES OF SCOTLAND

Aberdeenshire ..	Aberdeen ..	1971	308,050
Angus ..	.. Forfar ..	973	274,870
Argyllshire..	.. Inveraray ..	3124	63,270
Ayrshire ..	.. Ayr ..	1132	321,180
Banffshire ..	.. Banff	630	50,140
Berwickshire	.. Duns	457	25,060
Buteshire ..	.. Rothesay ..	218	19,290
Caithness ..	.. Wick	685	22,710
Clackmannanshire	Clackmannan ..	55	37,530
Dumfriesshire	.. Dumfries ..	1072	85,660
Dunbartonshire..	Dumbarton ..	246	164,260
East Lothian ..	Haddington ..	267	52,240
Fife	.. Cupar	504	306,860
Invernessshire ..	Inverness ..	4211	84,920
Kincardineshire	Stonehaven ..	382	47,340
Kinrossshire	.. Kinross	82	7420
Kirkcudbrightshire	Kirkcudbright	900	30,740
Lanarkshire	.. Lanark	848	1,614,130
Midlothian ..	.. Edinburgh ..	366	565,750
Morayshire	.. Elgin	476	48,210
Nairnshire ..	.. Nairn	163	8720
Orkney ..	.. Kirkwall ..	376	21,260
Peeblesshire	.. Peebles	347	15,230
Perthshire ..	.. Perth	2493	128,070
Renfrewshire	.. Renfrew ..	240	324,650
Ross and Cromarty	Dingwall ..	3089	60,500
Roxburghshire	.. Jedburgh ..	660	45,560
Selkirkshire	.. Selkirk	267	21,720
Shetland ..	.. Lerwick.. ..	550	19,340
Stirlingshire	.. Stirling	451	187,430
Sutherlandshire..	Dornoch ..	2028	13,660
West Lothian ..	Linlithgow ..	120	88,580
Wigtownshire	.. Wigtown ..	487	311,630

COUNTIES OF WALES

Anglesey ..	.. Beaumaris ..	276	50,640
Brecknockshire ..	Brecon	735	56,480
Caernarvonshire	Caernarvon ..	568	124,070
Cardiganshire ..	Cardigan ..	691	56,270
Carmarthenshire	Carmarthen ..	920	171,740
Denbighshire ..	Denbigh ..	669	170,700
Flintshire ..	.. Mold	255	145,110
Glamorganshire	.. Cardiff	817	1,201,990
Merionethshire ..	Dolgelley ..	660	41,460
Monmouthshire	.. Monmouth ..	542	424,650
Montgomeryshire	Montgomery..	798	45,990
Pembrokeshire ..	Haverfordwest	614	90,900
Radnorshire	.. Presteign ..	470	20,000

COUNTIES OF NORTHERN IRELAND

Antrim ..	.. Belfast	1176	683,500
Armagh ..	.. Armagh.. ..	489	114,000
Down ..	.. Downpatrick..	952	243,000
Fermanagh ..	Enniskillen ..	653	53,000
Londonderry ..	Londonderry	804	160,000
Tyrone	Omagh	1218	133,000

POPULATIONS OF THE WORLD
Rough Estimates

Asia	1,323,000,000
Europe	406,500,000
North America	233,000,000
Africa	216,000,000
U.S.S.R.	214,500,000
South America	121,100,000
Australasia and Oceania	14,200,000
Total	2,528,300,000

WORLD'S BIGGEST ISLANDS
Square Miles

Australia	2,974,581
Greenland	827,300
New Guinea	316,861
Borneo	290,012
Madagascar	228,642
Baffin (Canada)	197,754
Sumatra	167,620
Honshu (Japan)	88,919
Great Britain	88,752
Victoria (Canada)	80,340
Ellesmere (Canada)	77,392
Celebes	73,000
South Island (New Zealand)	58,093
Java	48,534
North Island (New Zealand)	44,281
Cuba	44,206
Newfoundland	42,734
Luzon (Philippines)	40,420
Iceland	39,758
Mindanao (Philippines)	36,537

WORLD'S BIGGEST SEAS
Square Miles

Caribbean	1,667,762
Mediterranean	1,145,000
Bering	876,000
Okhotsk	590,000
East China	482,000
Yellow	480,000
Hudson Bay	476,000
Japan	389,000
Andaman	308,000
North	222,000
Red	169,000
Caspian	168,890
Black	164,000
Baltic	163,000

WORLD'S LONGEST RIVERS

River	Flowing into	Miles
Nile	Mediterranean	4160
Amazon	Atlantic	3900
Mississippi-Missouri	Gulf of Mexico	3870
Yangtse	East China Sea	3100
Congo	Atlantic	2720
Amur	Tartary Strait	2700
Hwangho	Yellow Sea	2700
Lena	Laptev Sea	2650
Niger	Gulf of Guinea	2600
Mekong	South China Sea	2600
Ob	Gulf of Ob	2500
Paraná	Rio de la Plata	2450
Yenisei	Kara Sea	2350
Murray	Lake Alexandria	2310
Volga	Caspian Sea	2290
Madeira	Amazon River	2000
Yukon	Bering Sea	1980
St. Lawrence	Gulf of St. Lawrence	1950
Rio Grande	Gulf of Mexico	1880
Irtyish	Ob River	1850
Purus	Amazon River	1850
Sao Francisco	Atlantic	1800
Syr Darya	Aral Sea	1770
Salween	Gulf of Martaban	1750
Danube	Black Sea	1725

The longest river in the British Isles is the Shannon, which rises in Co. Cavan and flows for 240 miles to Limerick and the Atlantic coast. The Severn, rising on Plynlimmon (2468 feet) in Cardiganshire to flow for 220 miles to the Bristol Channel, is the longest in Great Britain. The Thames, England's longest, rises near Coates, Gloucestershire, and runs eastward for 210 miles to the North Sea. The Clyde is Scotland's longest river, flowing westward from Lanark for 106 miles.

AREA OF EARTH'S SURFACE
Square Miles

Asia	17,000,000
Africa	11,500,000
Europe	3,750,000
North America	8,300,000
South America	6,800,000
Oceania	4,000,000
Antarctica	6,000,000
Total Land	57,350,000
Total Ocean Area	139,405,000
Total Area of Earth's surface	196,755,000

AVERAGE DEPTHS OF THE OCEANS

	Feet		Feet
Pacific	14,050	Indian	13,000
Atlantic	12,880	Arctic	4000

WORLD'S BIGGEST LAKES

		Square Miles
Superior	N. America	31,820
Victoria	Africa	26,640
Huron	N. America	23,010
Michigan	N. America	22,400
Tanganyika	Africa	12,700
Baikal	Asia	12,150
Great Bear	N. America	12,000
Great Slave	N. America	11,170
Nyasa	Africa	11,000
Erie	N. America	9940
Winnipeg	N. America	9398
Ontario	N. America	7540
Ladoga	Europe	7100
Balkhash	Asia	6670
Chad	Africa	6300
Onega	Europe	3820
Eyre	Australia	3700
Rudolf	Africa	3475
Titicaca	S. America	3200
Nicaragua	N. America	3089
Athabaska	N. America	3058

There are besides these the two great inland seas, the Caspian (168,890 square miles) between Europe and Asia, and the Aral (24,600 square miles) in Asia. In South America there is also Lake Maracaibo (6300 square miles), classed among the lakes although it is not enclosed by land.

HEIGHTS OF FAMOUS WATERFALLS

	Feet
Angel, Venezuela	3212
Tegula, Natal	3110
Kukenaan, Venezuela	2000
Sutherland, New Zealand	1904
Takakkaw, British Columbia	1650
Ribbon, California	1612
King George VI, British Guiana	1600
Upper Yosemite, California	1430
Gavarnie, France	1385
Krimml, Austria	1300
Wollomombie, New South Wales	1100
Staubbach, Switzerland	980
Mardola, Norway	974
Trummelbach, Switzerland	950
Tully, Queensland	920
Chirombo, Northern Rhodesia	880
Vettis, Norway	850
King Edward VIII, Br. Guiana	840
Gersoppa, India	830
Kaieteur British Guiana	741
Kalambo, Tanganyika	726
Maradals, Norway	650
Skykje, Norway	650
Feather, California	640
Maletsunyane, Basutoland	630
Bridalveil, California	620
Multnomah, Oregon	620
Nevada, California	594
Wentworth, New South Wales	578
Bowen, New Zealand	540
Voring, Norway	529
Skjaeggedals, Norway	525
Marina, British Guiana	500
Victoria, Rhodesia	354
Horseshoe, Niagara, Canada	167

The highest waterfall in Great Britain is the Glomach (370 feet) in Ross and Cromarty.

AVERAGE HEIGHTS OF THE CONTINENTS

	Feet		Feet
Asia	3000	N. America	2000
Africa	1900	S. America	1880
Europe	980	Australia	1000

Average height of all the Earth's land surface is 2800 feet

WORLD'S HIGHEST MOUNTAINS

	Feet
Everest, Himalayas	29,028
Godwin-Austen, K 2, Himalayas	28,250
Kanchanganga, Himalayas	28,166
Lhotse I, Himalayas	27,890
Makalu, Himalayas	27,790
Lhotse II, Himalayas	27,560
Cho Oyu, Himalayas	26,867
Dhaulagiri, Himalayas	26,810
Nanga-Parbat, Himalayas	26,660
Anapurna, Himalayas	26,503
Gasherbrum, Himalayas	26,470
Gosainthan, Himalayas	26,289
Distegil, Himalayas	25,869
Nuptse, Himalayas	25,680
Masherbrum, Himalayas	25,660
Nanda Devi, Himalayas	25,645
Rakaposhi, Himalayas	25,550
Kamet, Himalayas	25,447
Namcha Barwa, Himalayas	25,446
Gurla Mandhata, Himalayas	25,355
Ulug Mustagh, Kwenlun	25,340
Tirich Mir, Hindu Kush	25,230
Kungur, Pamirs	25,200
Minya Konka, Szechwan	24,900
Kula Kangri, Himalayas	24,780
Changtse, Himalayas	24,760
Stalin Peak, Tien Shan	24,590
Jonsong, Himalayas	24,416
Pobedy Peak, Sinkiang	24,406
Mustagh Ata, Sinkiang	24,388
Huascaran, Andes	22,211
Sorata (Illampu), Andes	21,500
Sahama, Andes	21,480
Illimani, Andes	21,221
Huandoy, Andes	20,855
McKinley Alaska	20,269
Llullaillaco, Andes	20,244
Mount Logan, Rockies	19,850
Demavend, Persia	18,600
Tolima, Cordilleras	18,320
Mount St. Elias, Rockies	18,008
Charles Louis, New Guinea	18,000
Ararat, Armenia	17,160
Mount Lucania, Rockies	17,150
King's Peak, Rockies	17,130
Sangay, Ecuador	17,124
Kosh'an Tau, Caucasus	17,096
Kenya, Kenya	17,040
Ruwenzori, Uganda	16,794
Kluchevskaya, Kamchatka	16,124
Mont Blanc, Alps	15,781

Highest peak in the British Isles is Ben Nevis (4406 feet) in the Grampian Range in Scotland. England's highest point is the 3210-feet Scafell Pike in the Cumbrians, while Snowdon (3560 feet) in Caernarvonshire is the highest peak in Wales. Carrantuohill (3414 feet) in County Kerry is the highest mountain in Ireland.

VOLCANOES

	Feet
Cotopaxi, Ecuador	19,344
Popocatepel, Mexico	17,887
Mount Wrangell, Alaska	14,005
Mauna Loa, Hawaii	13,680
Mount Erebus, Antarctica	13,200
Smeru, Java	11,500
Nyiragongo, Belgian Congo	11,384
Etna, Sicily	10,741
Mount Lassen, United States	10,435
Ruapehu, New Zealand	9175
Asama, Japan	8340
Hecla, Iceland	4747
Vesuvius, Italy	3891

Now Believed Extinct

Aconcagua, Argentina	23,081
Chimborazo, Ecuador	20,577
Kilimanjaro, Tanganyika	19,340
Antisana, Ecuador	19,260
Citlaltepec (Orizaba), Mexico	18,700
Elbruz, U.S.S.R.	18,526
Fujiyama, Japan	12,425

FOREIGN MONEY

The Second World War played havoc with the finances and money systems of most nations, and the rates of exchange even now continue to fluctuate. Furthermore, there have been currency reforms in many countries, and in others new units of currency have been introduced. This table gives the units of currency of many foreign countries and their approximate value in British money.

	Approximate Value
Argentina : 1 Peso (100 Centavos)	2d.
Austria : 1 Schilling (100 Groschen)	3½d.
Belgium : 1 Franc (100 Centimes)	1¾d.
Brazil : 1 Cruzeiro (100 Centavos)	1d.
Bulgaria : Leva (100 Stotinki)	1s. 0d.
Burma : 1 Kyat (100 Pyas)	1s. 6d.
Canary Islands: Spanish money is the currency in use. (See Spain)	
Ceylon: 1 Rupee (100 Cents)	1s. 6d.
Chile: 1000 Pesos (100,000 Centavos)	11s. 0d.
China: 1 Yuan (New currency)	2s. 11d.
Colombia: 1 Peso (100 Centavos)	1s. 4d.
Costa Rica: 1 Colon (100 Cents)	1s. 3d.
Crete: The currency is the same as for Greece, but local notes are issued; also silver and copper coins of equal value to the Greek currency.	
Cuba: 1 Peso (100 Centavos)	7s. 0d.
Czechoslovakia: 1 Crown (100 Heller)	1s. 0d.
Denmark: 1 Krone (100 Ore)	1s. 0d.
Ecuador: 1 Sucre (100 Centavos)	4½d.
Egypt: Egyptian £ (100 Piastres) (1 Piastre=10 Milliemes)	20s. 6d.
Eire: The monetary unit and system are the same as for Great Britain, but there is a separate issue of notes and coins.	
Finland: 100 Markkas (10,000 Penni)	3s. 1d.
France: 100 Francs	1s. 8½d.
Germany (W.): Mark (100 Pfennig)	1s. 8d.
Greece: 1 Drachma (100 Lepta)	3d.
Guatemala : 1 Quetzal (100 Centavos)	7s. 0d.
Haiti: 1 Gourde (100 Centimes)	1s. 5d.
Holland : 1 Gulden (100 Cents)	1s. 11d.
Hong Kong : 1 Dollar (100 Cents)	1s. 3d.
Hungary: 1 Forint (100 Filler)	8d.
India: 1 Rupee (16 Annas)	1s. 6d.
Indonesia: 1 Roepiah or Gulden (100 Sen or Cents)	7½d.
Iran: 1 Rial (100 Dinars)	1d.
Iraq: 1 Dinar (1000 Fils)	20s. 0d.

	Approximate Value
Israel: 1 Israel Pound (1000 Prutot)	5s. 0d.
Italy : 100 Lire	1s. 2d.
Java: See Indonesia	
Japan: 100 Yen (10,000 Sen)	2s. 0d.
Luxemburg: The currency is the same as for Belgium	
Madeira: Portuguese currency is used (see Portugal)	
Mauritius: 1 Rupee (100 Cents)	1s. 6d.
Mexico: 1 Peso (100 Centavos)	7d.
Monaco : French currency is used (see France)	
Norway: 1 Kroner (100 Ore)	1s. 0d.
Pakistan: 1 Rupee (16 Annas)	1s. 6d.
Panama : 1 Balboa (100 Centimos)	7s. 2d.
Paraguay : 1 Guarani (100 Centimos)	1d.
Peru: 1 Sol (100 Centavos)	5d.
Philippine Islands : 1 Peso (100 Centavos)	3s. 6d.
Poland: 1 Zloty (100 Groszy)	1s. 0d.
Portugal : 1 Escudo (100 Centavos)	3d.
Rumania: 1 Leu (100 Bani)	1s. 2d.
Russia (U.S.S R.): 1 Rouble	1s. 9d.
Import and Export of Russian money is prohibited, so that the currency has no value outside Russia.	
Salvador : 1 Colon (100 Centavos)	2s. 10d.
Seychelles: 1 Rupee (100 Cents)	1s. 6d.
Spain : 1 Peseta (100 Centimos)	2d.
Surinam: 1 Gulden (100 Cents)	3s. 10d.
Sweden: 1 Krona (100 Ore)	1s. 5d.
Switzerland : 1 Franc (100 Centimes)	1s. 8d.
Syria and Lebanon: Syrian or Lebanon Pound (100 Piastres)	2s. 0d.
Thailand: 1 Baht (100 Satang)	4d.
Turkey: Piastre of 40 Paras; 100 Piastres=1 £ T	2s. 6d.
United States of America : 1 Dollar (100 Cents)	7s. 2d.
Uruguay: 1 Peso (100 Centesimos)	4s. 8d.
Venezuela: 1 Bolivar (100 Centimos)	2s. 0d.
Yugoslavia: 100 Dinars	2s. 4d.

WORLD'S TALLEST BUILDINGS

	Feet
Empire State Building, New York	1248
Chrysler Building, New York	1046
Palace of the Soviets, Moscow	1037
Eiffel Tower, Paris	985
60 Wall Tower, New York	950
Bank of Manhattan, New York	927
R.C.A. Building, New York	850
Woolworth Building, New York	792

On top of the Empire State Building there is a 222-foot television mast. Above the Palace of the Soviets is a 328-foot statue of Lenin.

New York has 36 buildings more than 500 feet high. Chicago has nine, the highest being the Board of Trade building, which is 605 feet high.

In addition to the Palace of the Soviets and the Eiffel Tower there are only two buildings over 500 feet in Europe. These are Ulm Cathedral, 529 feet, and Cologne Cathedral, 512 feet. In England there are Blackpool Tower, 500 feet, and Salisbury Cathedral, 404 feet high.

APPROXIMATE AREAS AND GREATEST KNOWN DEPTHS OF THE OCEANS

Ocean	Square miles	Depth in feet
Pacific	63,802,000	35,640
Atlantic	31,831,000	30,246
Indian	28,350,000	22,968
Antarctic	7,500,000	14,274
Arctic	5,440,000	17,850

CHIEF LANGUAGES OF THE PEOPLES

Chinese	600,000,000
English	300,000,000
Russian	200,000,000
Spanish	102,700,000
Japanese	97,700,000
German	78,947,000
Western Hindi	72,000,000
French	68,895,000
Bengali	51,000,000
Portuguese	48,800,000
Italian	43,700,000
Javanese	42,000,000

AREAS OF RIVER BASINS

River	Location	Square Miles
Amazon	S. America	2,053,318
Congo	Africa	1,339,923
Mississippi	N. America	1,243,700
La Plata	S. America	1,198,000
Nile	Africa	1,119,652
Yenisei	Asia	1,042,000
Ob	Asia	934,000
Lena	Asia	932,000
Amur	Asia	709,000
Mackenzie	N. America	699,400
Yangtse	Asia	689,000
Niger	Africa	580,000
St. Lawrence	N. America	565,200
Volga	Asia	531,000
Zambesi	Africa	513,000
Orinoco	S. America	430,000
Orange	Africa	400,000
Hwangho	Asia	400,000
Yukon	N. America	330,000
Danube	Europe	320,300
Colorado	N. America	246,000
Rio Grande	N. America	171,890

NOTABLE SHIP CANALS

The first column of figures gives the length in miles, the second column gives the width of the canal at the bottom in feet, and the third the depth in feet.

Göta	115	47	10	Sweden
Suez	100	197	34	Egypt
Kiel	61	150	45	Germany
Panama	50½	300	45	Panama
Elbe and Trave	41	72	10	Germany
Manchester	35½	120	29	England
Welland	26¾	200	25	Canada
Princess Juliana	20	52	16	Holland
Amsterdam	16½	88	23	Holland
Corinth	4	72	26	Greece
Sault Ste. Marie, U.S.A.	1½	100	22	U.S.A.
Sault Ste. Marie	1	142	20	Canada

WORLD'S LONGEST BRIDGES

(With length, in feet, of waterway)

Lower Zambesi	Africa	11,322
Storsstromsbroen	Denmark	10,499
Tay Bridge	Scotland	10,289
Upper Sone	India	9839
Godavari	India	8881
Forth Bridge	Scotland	8291
Rio Salado	Argentina	6703
Golden Gate	San Francisco U.S.A.	6260
Rio Dulce	Argentina	5866
Hardinge	India	5384
Victoria Jubilee	Montreal	5325
Moerdijk	Holland	4698
Harbour	Sydney, N.S.W.	4124
Jacques Cartier	Montreal	3888
Queensborough	U.S.A.	3720
Brooklyn	U.S.A.	3451
Torun	Poland	3291
Quebec Bridge	Quebec	3205

THE WORLD'S BIGGEST LINERS

		Length	Breadth	Tonnage
Queen Elizabeth	British	987 feet	118 feet	83,673
Queen Mary	British	975 „	118 „	81,237
United States	American	917 „	101 „	53,329
Liberté	French	893 „	102 „	51,839
Ile de France	French	763 „	92 „	44,356
Nieuw Amsterdam	Dutch	714 „	88 „	36,667
Mauretania	British	739 „	89 „	35,674
Caronia	British	687 „	91 „	34,183
Pasteur	French	671 „	88 „	30,447
Arcadia	British	687 „	91 „	29,734
Iberia	British	686 „	91 „	29,614
Cristoforo Colombo	Italian	656 „	90 „	29,191
Orsova	British	690 „	90 „	28,790
Edinburgh Castle	British	718 „	84 „	28,705
Pretoria Castle	British	718 „	84 „	28,705
Orcades	British	681 „	91 „	28,164

The biggest ship in the world is the Universe Leader, an oil-tanker of 84,730 tons. She is 850 feet long and 124 feet wide, and is owned by an American company. There are also a number of oil-tankers of more than 25,000 tons.

ASTRONOMY TABLES—PLANETS AND STARS

Heat and Light Received by the Planets

Reckoning the heat and light received by the Earth from the Sun as 1000, the amounts received by the planets are as follows:

Mercury	6800	Jupiter ..	40
Venus ..	1900	Saturn ..	10
Earth ..	1000	Uranus ..	3
Mars ..	440	Neptune ..	1

Distances of Planets From Earth

	Greatest Distance in miles
Mercury	137,910,000
Venus	162,229,000
Mars	249,384,000
Jupiter	601,540,000
Saturn	1,030,912,000
Uranus	1,960,583,000
Neptune.. ..	2,913,644,000

	Least Distance in miles
Mercury	48,020,000
Venus	23,701,000
Mars	34,900,000
Jupiter	365,816,000
Saturn	742,646,000
Uranus	1,606,183,000
Neptune.. ..	2,674,357,000

Relative Gravitation on the Surfaces of Sun and Planets

The pull of gravitation on the surface of other planets varies very much from the pull of the Earth, and reckoning the Earth's gravitation as 100 the relative pull on the Sun and other planets is:

Sun ..	2770	Mars ..	38
Mercury	38	Jupiter ..	261
Venus ..	86	Saturn ..	119
Earth ..	100	Uranus ..	88
		Neptune ..	110

Sun Statistics

Mean distance of Sun from the Earth, 92,965,000 miles

Greatest distance of Sun from the Earth, 94,524,000 miles

Least distance of Sun from the Earth, 91,406,000 miles

Diameter, 867,000 miles

Mass, reckoning the Earth as 1, 333,000

Density, reckoning the Earth as 1, ·25

Volume, reckoning the Earth as 1, 1,305,000

Force of gravity at the surface, reckoning the Earth as 1, 27·7

Period of rotation on its axis 25 days, 7 hours, 48 minutes

Speed of rotation at its equator, 4407 miles an hour

Surface in square miles 2,283,621,466,000

Surface area equals 12,000 times that of the Earth

Volume, 339,300,000,000,000,000 cubic miles

Total attraction between Earth and Sun equals the pull of 3,600,000,000,000 tons

Energy radiated from each square foot of surface equals 15,000 horse-power

Temperature about 10,000 degrees Fahrenheit

Mass of the Sun in tons 1,998,000,000,000,000,000,000,000,000

Candle power 1,575,000,000,000,000,000,000,000

Height some flames rise from the surface, 286,000 miles

Speed of Planets Round the Sun

	Per second Miles		Per day Miles
Mercury ..	29	..	2,505,000
Venus ..	21·7	..	1,873,000
Earth ..	18	..	1,555,000
Mars ..	14·9	..	1,287,000
Jupiter ..	8	..	771,000
Saturn ..	6·2	..	536,000
Uranus ..	4·3	..	372,000
Neptune ..	3·1	..	268,000
Pluto ..	2	..	173,000

Statistics of the Earth

Polar diameter, 7899·6 miles

Equatorial diameter, 7926·6 miles

Circumference at the Equator, 24,899 miles

Area of the surface, 196,950,000 square miles

Volume, 260,000,000,000 cubic miles

Mass (weight) 6,000,000,000,000,000,000,000 tons

Earth's orbit, 580,000,000 miles

Speed travelling round the Sun, 66,000 miles an hour

Amount of the Sun's energy received, one two-thousand-millionth

Weight of the atmosphere, estimated, 11,600,000,000,000,000,000 pounds

Area of the sea, 139,440,000 square miles

Area of the land, 57,510,000 square miles

Distance in Miles of the Planets from the Sun

	Mean Distance
Mercury	35,987,000
Venus	67,245,000
Earth	92,965,000
Mars	141,650,000
Jupiter	483,678,000
Saturn	886,779,900
Uranus	1,783,000,000
Neptune	2,790,000,000
Pluto	3,675,000,000

	Greatest Distance	Least Distance
Mercury	43,386,000	28,588,000
Venus	67,705,000	66,787,000
Earth	94,524,000	91,406,000
Mars	154,860,000	128,440,000
Jupiter	507,016,000	460,340,000
Saturn	936,388,000	837,170,000
Uranus	1,866,059,000	1,700,707,000
Neptune	2,819,120,000	2,768,881,000

Years of the Planets

The period of revolution round the Sun of the planets varies enormously, and is given here, this period being the length of the planet's year in each case.

	Days	Hours	Minutes
Mercury	87	23	15
Venus ..	224	16	48
Earth ..	365	6	9
Mars ..	686	23	31
Jupiter ..	4332	14	2
Saturn ..	10,759	5	16
Uranus ..	30,688	7	12
Neptune..	60,180	20	38
Pluto ..	248 years		

Twenty Brightest Stars

The twenty brightest stars in the heavens are known as First Magnitude Stars, and are as follow:

Star	Constellation
Sirius ..	.. Canis Major or the Great Dog
Canopus ..	.. Argo or the Ship Argo
Alpha Centauri	Centaurus or the Centaur
Arcturus	.. Boötes
Rigel ..	.. Orion
Capella ..	.. A u r i g a or the Wagoner
Vega ..	.. Lyra, or the Lyre
Procyon ..	.. Canis Minor or the Little Dog
Betelgeuse	.. Orion
Achernar	.. Eridanus or the River Eridanus
Aldebaran	.. Taurus or the Bull
Beta Centauri	Centaurus or the Centaur
Alpha Crucis ..	Crux or the Southern Cross
Antares	.. Scorpio or the Scorpion
Altair ..	.. Aquilla or the Eagle
Spica ..	.. Virgo or the Virgin
Fomalhaut	.. Piscis Australis or the Southern Fish
Pollux ..	.. Gemini or the Twins
Regulus ..	.. Leo or the Lion
Deneb ..	.. Cygnus or the Swan

Brightness of the Stars

It is estimated that the other stars are brighter than one of the sixth magnitude by the number of times shown here:

A star of the:

Fifth magnitude ..		2 times
Fourth magnitude ..		6 times
Third magnitude ..		12 times
Second magnitude ..		25 times
First magnitude ..		100 times
Sirius, the brightest star		400 times
The Sun, our nearest star,		2,400,000,000,000 times

Volume, Mass, Density, and Areas of the Planets

This table shows the relative volumes, or bulk, the mass, or weight, the density, or compactness, and the surface, or area, of the various planets, reckoning the Earth as 100 in each case.

	Volume	Mass	Density	Surface
Mercury	5·6	4·7	85	14
Venus	92	82	89	93
Earth	100	100	100	100
Mars	15	10·8	71	28
Jupiter	130,900	31,770	24	11,690
Saturn	76,000	9480	13	8330
Uranus	6500	1460	22	1590
Neptune	8500	1700	20	1890

Relative Sizes of the Orbits of the Planets

If the orbit of Mercury round the Sun is represented by a circle one inch in diameter, the relative sizes of the diameters of the orbits of the planets are as follow:

Orbit of	Inches	Orbit of	Inches
Mercury ..	1	Jupiter ..	13·4
Venus ..	1·9	Saturn ..	24·6
The Earth	2·6	Uranus ..	49·5
Mars ..	3·9	Neptune ..	77·5

Diameters of the Sun and Moon and Planets

	miles			miles
Sun ..	864,000	Mars ..		4200
Moon ..	2163	Jupiter ..		88,700
Mercury	3200	Saturn ..		71,100
Venus ..	7600	Uranus ..		30,900
Earth ..	7927	Neptune		33,000
		Pluto ..		3600

Facts and Figures About the Moon

Diameter, 2163 miles

Circumference, 6795 miles

Surface area, 14,660,000 square miles

Volume, 5,300,000,000 cubic miles

Mass, 78,000,000,000,000,000,000 tons

Mean Distance from Earth, 238,000 miles

Greatest Distance from Earth, 252,970 miles

Least Distance from Earth, 221,600 miles.

Circumference of Moon's Orbit, 1,500,680 miles

Speed in its orbit, 2288 miles per hour, or 3357 feet per second

Full Moon's light is one-618,000th of sunlight

Amount of sunlight reflected, 17 per cent

Estimated day temperature, 200° Fahrenheit

Estimated night temperature, minus 200° Fahrenheit

Diameter of Bailly, the biggest crater, 180 miles

Depth of deepest crater, Newton, 29,000 feet

Height of tallest mountain, Leibnitz, 30,000 feet

Time of one revolution round Earth 27 days 7 hours 43 minutes 11 seconds

Force of gravity at Moon's surface is four-twenty-fifths that of the Earth

Weight of a terrestrial pound on the Moon, 2¼ ounces.

FOUR HUNDRED INVENTIONS & DISCOVERIES

Here we give a list of over 400 important inventions and discoveries in the history of the world, with names, nationality, and dates

Aberration of Light, James Bradley (British) 1727

Accordion, Damian (Austrian) 1829

Acetylene, Edmund Davy (British) 1836

Acrostic, Porphyrius Optatianus (Roman) 4th century

Actinometer, Sir John Herschel (British) 1825

Aerated Waters, first made in Europe about 1767

Aerograph, or Air-brush, C. L. Burdick (British) 1893

Aeroplane. A development from a successful glider by Sir George Cayley (British) in 1809 to the first successful man-carrying, power-driven aeroplane by the brothers Wilbur and Orville Wright (American) 1903

Aga Light (or Dalen Light) for gaslight buoys, Gustaf Dalén (Swedish) about 1907

Air-gun, Rinault or Marin (French) 1656

Air-pump, Otto von Guericke (German) 1654

Algebra, Drophantus of Alexandria, 4th century

Alum, at Roccha in Syria, about 1300

Aluminium, Frederick Wöhler (German) 1827

Ambrine, Barthe de Sandfort (French) 1904

American Organ, invented by a French workman in Paris, 1835

Anchors, by the Tuscans before 600 B.C.

Aniline, Unverdorben (German) 1826

Aniline Dye, Sir William Perkin (British) 1856

Antipyrine, Knorr (German) 1883

Aquatint, Abbé St. Non (French) in early 18th century, perfected by Jean Baptiste Le Prince (French) 1750

Archeopteryx, Herman von Meyer and Dr. Häberlein (German) 1861

Archimedean Screw, Archimedes of Syracuse, about 236 B.C.

Argand Lamp, Aimé Argand (Swiss) about 1782

Argon, Lord Rayleigh and Professor Ramsay (British) 1893

Artesian Well, first sunk in Europe at Artois, in France, in 1126, but previously known in China and Egypt

Artificial Satellite, first launched from Earth by Russia, October 1957

Artificial Silk, Sir Joseph Swan (British) 1883

Atmosphere, composition of, Joseph Priestley (British) 1774

Atmospheric Pressure, 15 pounds to square inch, Galileo (Italian) 1564

Atomic Bomb, first used in warfare, August 1945

Atomic Theory, J. Dalton (British) 1808

Audiometer, D. E. Hughes (British) 1879

Audiphone, R. G. Rhodes (American) 1880

Autogyro, Senor de la Cierva (Spanish) 1920

Avogadro's Law, Count Amedeo Avogadro (Italian) about 1837

Bacteria, Antonius von Leeuwenhoek (Dutch) 1680

Baily's Beads, Francis Baily (British) 1836

Balloon, Joseph Montgolfier (French) 1782. Previously Joseph Black (British) had made a small balloon in a room, 1767

Barium, Sir Humphry Davy (British) 1808

Barker's Mill, Dr. Robert Barker (British) 18th century

Barometer, Torricelli (Italian) about 1643

Barrage in War, first used by British in Battle of the Somme, 1916

Bassoon, Afranio (Italian) 16th century

Battering-ram, Artemon (Lacedemonian) about 441 B.C.

Bayonet, at Bayonne, France, about 1647

Beet Sugar : see Sugar

Bellows reputed to have been invented by Anacharsis (Scythian) about 569 B.C.

Benzene, or Benzol, Michael Faraday (British) 1825

Bessemer Steel, Sir Henry Bessemer (British) 1855

Bicycle, Safety, J. Kemp Starley (British) 1880

Billiards, Henrique Devigne (French) about 1571

Bismuth, Basil Valentine (German) 1450

Blasting Gelatine, Alfred Nobel (Swedish) 1875

Bleaching with Chlorine, Claude Berthollet (French) about 1785

Blood Corpuscles, Red, Antonius von Leeuwenhoek (Dutch) about 1700

Bobbinet Machine, John Heathcoat (British) 1809

Bode's Law, named after Johann E. Bode (German), but first announced by Johann Titius (German) 1772

Bombs, at Venlo in the Netherlands, 1495

Bone Oil, Johann K. Dippel (German) 17th century

Boracic, or Boric, Acid, Wilhelm Homberg (German) 1702

Boulle Work, Charles Boulle (French) about 1672

Boyle's Law, Robert Boyle (British) 1662

Braille System for the Blind, Louis Braille (French) 1834

Bramah Hydraulic Press, Joseph Bramah (British) 1795

Bromine, Antoine Balard (French) 1826

Brontometer, George J. Symons (British) 1890

Buhl Work : see Boulle

Bunsen Burner, Robert Bunsen (German) about 1852

Cadmium, F. Stromeyer (German) 1817

Calcium, Sir Humphry Davy (British) 1808

Calculating Machine, Blaise Pascal (French) about 1650

Camera Obscura, attributed to Roger Bacon (British) 1297

Cannon, Berthold Schwarz (German) early 14th century

Cannon, Modern Breech-loading, Sir W. Armstrong (British) 1859

Capstan, reputed inventor Sir Samuel Morland (British) about 1690

Carbide of Calcium, first made by F. Wöhler (German) 1862 ; first cheap commercial process of manufacture T. L. Willson (American) and H. Moissan (French) 1892

Carbolic Acid, Runga (German) 1834

Carbon Bisulphide, Wilhelm Lampadius (German) 1796

Carbon Dioxide (Carbonic Acid Gas), Joseph Black (British) 1755

Catapult, for sieges, Dionysius, the tyrant of Syracuse, 399 B.C.

Cathode Rays, Julius Plucker (German) about 1847

Cell Theory of Life, Theodor Schwann (German) 1839

Cellular Structure of Plants, Robert Hooke (British) 1665

Celluloid, Alexander Parkes and Daniel Spill (British) before 1870; perfected by John Hyatt (American) 1872

Cement (Roman), Parker (British) 1796

Cephalic Index, Anders Retzius (Swedish) about 1842

Ceres, the first asteroid, or minor planet, Giuseppe Piazzi (Italian) 1801

Chain Shot, invented in Europe about 1665

Chanting, St. Ambrose (Gallic) about 386

Chassepot Rifle, Antoine Chassepot (French) 1870

Chlorine, Karl Scheele (Swedish) 1774

Chloroform, simultaneously by Eugène Soubeiran (French) and Baron Liebig (German) 1831. First used as an anaesthetic by Sir James Simpson (British) 1848

Chromium, Vauquelin (French) 1798

Chronometer, John Harrison (British) 1761

Cigarette, invented in France about 1799

Cinema, a gradual development. Zoetrope, or wheel of life, described by W. G. Horner (British) about 1833 ; first instantaneous photographs of motion, Edward Muybridge (British) 1872; first satisfactory film, George Eastman (American) 1885; first moving picture camera, William Friese-Greene (British) 1889; first satisfactory moving picture projector, Robert W. Paul (British) 1895

Circulation of the Blood, William Harvey (British) about 1628

Clocks, invented by the French in the 13th century

Coal Tar Dyes, Sir William Perkin (British) 1856

Coal Tar Perfumes, Sir William Perkin (British) 1868

Cobalt, George Brandt (Swedish) 1733

Coins, said to have been invented by the Lydians before 860 B.C.

Cold Storage for Meats, Francis Bacon (British) 1626

Collodion, Christian Schönbein (German) 1845

Comet, first photographic discovery of, Edward E. Barnard (American) 1892

Concertina, Sir Charles Wheatstone (British) about 1825

Copying Machine for Letters, James Watt (British) 1778

Cordite, Sir F. A. Abel and Sir James Dewar (British) 1889

Cotton Saw Gin, Eli Whitney (American) 1793

Creosote, Baron Karl von Reichenbach (German) about 1833

Crookes's Tube, Sir William Crookes (British) 1879

Dalen Light (or Aga Light), Gustaf Dalén (Swedish) about 1907

Daylight Saving, William Willett (British) 1908

WITH NAMES, NATIONALITY, AND DATES

Diesel Engine, Rudolf Diesel (German) 1893 to 1897

Dissolving Views, Henry L. Childe (British) 1874

Diving Dress, Augustus Siebe (German) 1829

Drilling Machine in Agriculture, Jethro Tull (British) early 18th century

Drum Capstan for Anchors, Sir Samuel Morland (British) about 1690

Dualin, Explosive, Carl Ditmar (German) 1870

Duplex Telegraphy, two messages along one wire at same time, Dr. Gintl (Austrian) 1853

Dynamite, Alfred Nobel (Swedish) 1867

Dynamo, Michael Faraday (British) 1831

Electric Clock, Sir Charles Wheatstone (British) and Alexander Bain (British) 1840

Electric Condenser, Alessandro Volta (Italian) 1782

Electric Furnace, Robert Hare (American) 1781, but first made a commercial success by Sir William Siemens (German) 1880

Electric Light (carbon), Sir Humphry Davy (British) 1800

Electric Light (incandescent), J. W. Swan (British) 1880

Electric Lighthouse, Michael Faraday (British) 1859

Electric Machine, first, Otto von Guericke (German) 1647

Electric Motor, Moritz Jacobi (German) 1834

Electric Welding, Professor Elihu Thomson (American) 1887

Electro - magnetism, Hans Oersted (Danish) 1802

Electron, Von Helmholtz (German) 1881

Electrophorus, Volta (Italian) 1775

Electro-plating, Thomas Spencer (British) 1837

Encke's Comet, Jean Louis Pons (French) 1818

Epsom Salts, Nehemiah Grew (British) 1695

Eros, minor planet, Herr Witt (German) 1898

Esperanto, Dr. Zamenhof (Polish) 1887

Etching, Francis Mazzuoli, also called Parmigiano (Italian) about 1532

Ethane, Sir Edward Frankland (British) and Adolf Kolbe (German) 1848

Ether, of space, Johann Encke (German) 1829

Ether, a chemical, Valerius Cordus (German) 1540

Finsen Light, Niels Finsen (Danish) about 1900

Fire-arms, Berthold Schwarz (German) 1378

Fire Brigade, in London, 1798

Fire-engine, attributed to Ctesibius of Alexandria about 250 B.C.

Fire-engine, steam, John Braithwaite (British) 1830

Fleming Valve : see Thermionic Valve

Flintlock, invented 1588

Flora, minor planet, John R. Hind (British) 1847

Fluorine, Sir Humphry Davy (British) 1813

Flying-shuttle in weaving, John Kay (British) 1733

Fog Siren : see Siren

Formic Acid, John Ray (British) 1670

Fraunhofer's Lines, Joseph von Fraunhofer (German) 1814

Fulminate of Mercury, Luke Howard (British) 1799

Galvanising, Paul Jacques Malouin (French) 1742

Galvanometer, André-Marie Ampère (French) 1820

Gas Engine, John Barber (British), about 1780, but first made practical by Etienne Lenoir (French) 1860

Gas-lighting, William Murdock (British) 1779

Gaslight Printing Paper in photography, first made in America about 1897

Gas Mantle, Baron Welsbach (Austrian) 1885

Gas-meter, John Malam (British) 1820

Gatling Gun, R. J. Gatling (American) 1862

Gegenshein or Counterglow of Zodiacal Light, Brorsen (German) about 1846

Geissler Tube, Heinrich Geissler (German) about 1860

Glass, first made in Egypt about 1550 B.C.

Glauber Salts, Johann Glauber (German) about 1650

Glycerine, Karl Scheele (Swedish) 1779

Gnome Engine, first successful aero-engine, a French invention about 1909

Golliwog, Bertha Upton (English) 1896

Gramophone (originally called Phonograph), Thomas Alva Edison (American) 1877

Gravitation Laws, Sir Isaac Newton (British) 1685

Greek Fire, Callinicus of Heliopolis, A.D. 668

Grenade, in France about 1536

Guillotine, Antoine Louis (French) 1792

Gun-cotton, Christian Schönbein (German)1845

Gun, Modern Big, built up of wrought iron and steel, Lord Armstrong (British) 1856

Gunpowder, Roger Bacon (British) about 1292, or Bertholdus Schwartz (German) about 1320. Some say it was used by the Hindus 333 B.C.

Gunpowder, Smokeless, Falkenstein (German) 1889

Gyroscope, Jean Foucault (French) 1852

Hammurabi's Code of Laws, found at Susa by J. de Morgan, 1901

Hansom Cab, Joseph Hansom (British) 1833

Harvey Process, for hardening steel plates, H. A. Harvey (American) 1891

Hebe, minor planet, Hencke (German) 1847

Helicopter, first designed by Leonardo da Vinci (Italian) about 1500

Heliograph, H. Mance (British) 1875

Heliometer, Auguste Savary (French) 18th century

Helium, in the Sun, Sir Norman Lockyer (British) 1868; in the Earth, Sir William Ramsay (British) 1895

Homeopathy, Samuel Hahnemann (German) 1810

Hot-blast, in iron smelting, James Neilson (British) 1828

Hotchkiss Gun, Benjamin Hotchkiss (American) 1881

Hydraulic Crane, Sir William Armstrong (British) 1846

Hydraulic Press, Joseph Bramah (British) 1846

Hydrochloric Acid, Le Comte (French) about 1510

Hydrogen, Paracelsus (German Swiss) about 1500; recognised as an element by Henry Cavendish (British) 1766

Hypnotism, Franz Mesmer (German) about 1766

Ice, Artificial, made chemically, Walker (English) 1782

Inoculation for Smallpox, first practised in India 1500 B.C.

Insulin, Dr. Frederick Banting (Canada) 1923

Iodine, Courtois (French) 1811

Iridium, Smithson Tennant (British) 1804

Iris, minor planet, John R. Hind (British) 1847

Iron smelting with coal instead of charcoal, Dr. John Roebuck (British) 1762

Jacquard loom, Joseph Marie Jacquard (French) 1801

Jet Propulsion for aircraft. Frank Whittle (British) 1930–41

Juno, minor planet, Carl Harding (German) 1804

Jupiter, four of his moons first seen by Galileo (Italian) 1610

Jupiter's great red spot, Professor Pritchett (American) 1878

Kaleidoscope, Sir David Brewster (British) 1816

Key bugle (also called Kent bugle), James Halliday (British) 1810

Kinetoscope, Thomas A. Edison (American) 1893

Koenig's flame, Rodolphe Koenig (German) 1876

Lace-making machine, Hammond (British) about 1768

Laryngoscope, Manuel Garcia (Spanish) 1855

Lathe, attributed to Talus, grandson of Daedalus, about 1240 B.C.

Laughing gas (nitrous oxide), Joseph Priestley (British) 1772

Leonids, meteors, first seen in A.D. 902

Lewis gun, Colonel Isaac Newton Lewis (American) 1915

Leyden jar, E. G. Von Kleist (German) 1746

Lifeboat, Henry Greathead (British) 1789

Life-saving net for fire brigades, The Haulon Brothers (American) about 1884

Lightning conductor, Benjamin Franklin (American) about 1752

Lightning's identity with electricity, Benjamin Franklin (American)1752

Light valve: see Sun valve

Limelight, Thomas Drummond (British) 1826

Linoleum, Elijah Galloway 1843

Linotype machine in printing, Ottmar Mergenthaler (German - American), 1889

Liquefaction of gases, Sir Humphry Davy (British) 1823

Lithography, Alois Senefelder (German) about 1796

Logarithms, John Napier (British) 1614

Lucifer matches, Walker (British) 1827

Continued on next page

7087

400 INVENTIONS AND DISCOVERIES WITH

Continued from previous page

Macadamised roads, John MacAdam (British) 1819

Machine gun, earliest type first used in American Civil War, 1861

Magic lantern, Athanasius Kircher (German) 1646

Magnesium, Sir Humphry Davy (British) 1808

Magnesium light, Robert Bunsen (German) 1860

Magnetic needle, dip of, Robert Norman (British) about 1576

Majolica, Luca della Robbia (Italian) about 1440

Malaria germ, true life-story of, Sir Ronald Ross (British) 1898

Manganese, Joseph Gahn (Swedish) 1774

Manometric flames: see Koenig's flames

Margarine, Mege-Mouries(French) 1869

Mars, canals of, Giovanni Schiaparelli (Italian) 1877

Mars, moons of, Asaph Hall (American) 1884

Matchlock, invented about 1460; first used in battle at Rhejan, 1525

Maxim gun, Sir Hiram Maxim (American)1884

Maximite, high explosive, Hudson Maxim (American) about 1890

Meat Extract, Baron Liebig (German) 1848

Megaphone, Thomas Alva Edison (American) 1878

Melinite, Eugène Turpin (French) 1886

Mendelism, law of heredity, Gregor Mendel (Austrian) 1854

Mercerised cotton, John Mercer (British) 1844

Mercurial pump, Emanuel Swedenborg (Swedish) 1722

Mercury vapour lamp, Peter C. Hewitt (British) 1902

Mesmerism, Franz Mesmer (German) about 1766

Metric system, a committee of seven Frenchmen 1790 to 1799

Mezzotint engraving, Colonel Von Siegen (German) 1643

Micrometer, William Gascoigne (British) 1638

Microphone, Professor D. E. Hughes (British) 1878

Microscope, Zacharias Jansen (Dutch) about 1590

Mimeograph, Thomas Alva Edison (American) 1878

Mineral waters: see Aerated waters

Mines at sea, first used by Americans in 1775

Minor planet, first photographic discovery of, Max Wolf (German) 1891

Minor planets, first one, Ceres, discovered by Giuseppe Piazzi (Italian) 1801

Minor planets, smallest 550 yards across, discovered by James E. Keeler (American) 1900

Monitor, John Ericsson (Swedish) 1862

Monotype machine, Talbot Lanston (American) about 1887

Morphia, Serturner (German) 1816

Morse code, Samuel Morse and Alfred Vail (American) 1837

Morse telegraph instrument, Samuel Morse (American) 1832

Motor-car, a gradual development. First self-propelling road vehicle by Nicolas Cugnot (French) 1768; first petrol-driven motor car by Gottlieb Daimler (German) 1885

Mulready penny postage envelope, William Mulready (British) 1840

Mustard gas, Guthrie (British) 1860

Naphthalene, A. Garden (British) 1819

Nebula in Andromeda, Abdurrahman Al-Sufi (Persian), middle of tenth century

Nebula in Orion, Jean Baptiste Cysatus (Swiss) about 1618

Nebular hypothesis, Pierre Laplace (French) 1796

Neon, Sir William Ramsay (British) 1898

Neptune, discovered by mathematical calculation, independently by John Adams (British) and U. J. J. Leverrier (French) 1846; actually seen by Dr. Johann Galle (German) and James Challis (English) 1846

Neptune's moon, William Lassell (British) 1846

Nernst lamp, Walther Nernst (German) 1897

Nickel, Axel Cronstedt (Swedish) 1751

Nitrogen, Daniel Rutherford (British) 1772

Nitro-glycerine, Sobrero (Italian) 1847

Nuclear fission, American and British scientists 1940 to 1945

Okapi, Sir Harry Johnston (British) 1901

Omnibus, first used in Paris 1818

Ophthalmoscope, Hermann Helmholtz (German) 1851

Optophone, Dr. E. E. Fournier d'Albe (British) 1914

Orrery, fourth Earl of Orrery (British) 18th century

Oxygen, Joseph Priestley (British) 1774

Oxy-hydrogen blowpipe, Robert Hare (American) 1801

Ozone, Christian Schönbein (German) 1839

Paddle-wheels, William P. Miller (British) 1787

Pallas, minor planet, Heinrich Olbers (German) 1802

Panorama, Robert Barker (British) 18th century

Pantograph, Christopher Scheiner (German) about 1603

Paper-making machine, Louis Robert (French) about 1690

Paraffin, Baron Karl von Reichenbach (German) 1830

Paravane, Commander C. D. Burney (British) 1916

Parchment, Eumenes of Pergamus, about 190 B.C.

Penicillin, Sir Alexander Fleming (British) 1929

Pens, steel, Wise (British) 1803

Phonograph, Thomas Alva Edison (American) 1877

Phonography (Pitman's shorthand) Sir Isaac Pitman (British) 1837

Phosphorus, George Brandt (Swedish) 1670

Photography, a gradual development. Thomas Wedgwood and Sir Humphry Davy (British) made sensitised paper and took prints of objects 1802; Joseph Niepce (French) improved this process 1814; Louis Daguerre (French), who had worked with Niepce, produced daguerrotype photographs in 1839;

first negative photograph made by Henry Fox Talbot (British) 1839; first flash-light photograph by Mr. Brothers (British) 1864; first dry plate by Dr. R. L. Maddox (British) 1871; first colour photography, Franz Veress (Austrian) 1890

Pianoforte, attributed variously to Cristofalli (Italian), J. C. Schroeter (German), and Marius (French) early in 18th century. Really evolved from earlier instruments

Picric acid, Peter Woulfe (British) 1771

Picture postcards, first used at Royal Naval Exhibition, London, 1891

Piltdown Skull, Charles Dawson (British) 1912

Pistol, invented at Pistoja, Italy, about 1500

Pithecanthropus, Eugène Dubois (French) 1894

Pitman's shorthand, Sir Isaac Pitman (British) 1837

Planimeter, Hermann (German) 1814

Pluto, the planet, Lowell Observatory (American) 1930

Pneumatic tyre, J. B. Dunlop (British) 1888

Pompeii, by an Italian peasant, 1748

Portland cement, Joseph Aspden (British) 1824

Postage stamps, adhesive, James Chalmers (British) 1834

Potassium, Sir H. Davy (British) 1807

Potter's wheel, said to be invented by Anacharsis the Scythian, about 569 B.C.

Printing (in Europe), Johann Gutenberg (German) about 1420. Printing from movable types was practised in China centuries earlier

Printing from cast type, Peter Schoeffer (German) about 1440

Printing machine, steam, with a revolving cylinder of paper, Friedrich Koenig (German) 1810

Precession of the equinoxes, Hipparchus (Greek) 130 B.C.

Prussian blue, Johann K. Diffel (German) early 18th century

Quinine, Pierre Pelletier and Joseph Caventou (French) 1820

Radar, or radio-location, British scientists, 1934

Radiometer, Sir William Crookes (British) 1875

Radiotonogram, Dr. E. E. Fournier d'Albe (British) 1924

Radium, Madame Curie (Polish) and M. Curie (French) 1898

Railways, began as wooden rails for horse-drawn trucks in 17th century. First steam locomotive by Trevithick (British) 1801; George Stephenson's first locomotive 1814 ; first steam railway, Stockton and Darlington, opened 1825

Reaping machine, Rev. Patrick Bell (British) 1826

Refrigerator, Jacob Perkins (British) 1834

Regelation, of ice, Michael Faraday (British) 1850

Regenerative furnace, Sir William Siemens (British) 1856

Repeating watches and clocks, Edward Barlow, sometimes called Booth (British) 1676

Revolver, Samuel Colt (American) 1835

Rifled barrels for firearms, August Kotter (German) about 1520

Rocket apparatus for saving life. Idea invented by Sergeant Bell (British)

1791, first practical apparatus, Captain W. Manby (British) 1807

Röntgen rays: see X-rays

Rope-making machine, Richard Marsh (British) 1784

Rosetta stone, by a French officer near Rosetta, Egypt, 1799

Rotor Boat: see Sailless Sailing Ship

Ruling machine, by a Dutchman in London 1782

Saccharine, Fahlberg and Remsen (American) 1886

Safety fuse, William Bickford (British) 1831

Safety lamp, Sir Humphry Davy (British) 1815

Sailless sailing ship, Anton Flettner (German) 1924

Sam Browne Belt, General Sir Samuel Browne (British) before 1900

Saraband, a stately dance, Sarabanda (Spanish) 16th century

Saturn's dusky ring, William Bond (American) 1850

Saturn's moons, four of them first seen by Giovanni Cassini (Italian) 1671, 1672, 1684

Saturn's rings first seen as handles by Galileo (Italian) 1610

Saturn's rings, with the dark division, first recognised by Giovanni Cassini (Italian) 1675

Saw, band, William Newberry (British) 1808

Saw, circular, Samuel Muller (British) 1777

Screw-auger, William Henry (American) about 1755

Screw propeller, Robert Hooke (British) 1681

Sedan chair, first used at Sedan in France, early 17th century

Seismometer or seismograph, Robert Mallet (British) 1858

Selenium, John Berzelius (Swedish) 1817

Serpent, musical instrument, Canon Guillaume (French) 16th century

Sewing machine, Thomas Saint (English) 1792; first practical machine, Barthélemy Thimmonier (French) 1830; but first to be widely used, Elias Howe (American) about 1841

Shell in warfare, first used about 1600

Shrapnel shell, H. Shrapnel (British) 1784

Siren, C. C. Daboll (American) 1870

Slide rule, Edmund Gunter (British) 1620 and Edmund Wingate (British) 1626

Soda Water, first manufacture at Geneva at end of 18th century

Sodium, Sir Humphry Davy (British) 1807

Sonnet, form of verse, Guido d'Arezzo (Italian) about 1024

Sound photography, Dr. E. E. Fournier d'Albe (British) 1924

Spectacles attributed to Alexander de Spina (Italian) about 1285

Spectroscope, Sir Isaac Newton (British) about 1672

Spinning jenny, James Hargreaves (British) about 1764

Spinning mule, Samuel Crompton (British) 1779

Spinning roller, Sir Richard Arkwright (British) 1769

Spiral nebula, first, Sir John Herschel (British) 1845

Spirit-level, attributed to Robert Hooke (British) about 1660 and J. M. Thevenot (French) about 1690

Sprengel pump, H. J. P. Sprengel (German) 1865

Springs for watches and clocks, Dr. Hooke (British) 1735

Steam engine, a gradual development from the aeolipile of Hero of Alexandria about 130 B.C.; Marquis of Worcester (British) describes a steam engine 1663; first steam engine with a piston by Denis Papin (French) 1690; first steam engine used regularly by Thomas Savery (British) 1698; first self-acting steam engine by Thomas Newcomen (British) 1712; James Watt's first engine, the real parent of modern engines, 1769. See Turbine

Steam hammer, James Nasmyth (British) 1842

Steam plough, John Heathcot, M.P. (British) 1832

Steamship, a gradual development. In 1736 Jonathan Hulls (British) took out a patent for a steamboat, but this was only designed, never made; Count de Jouffroy (French) built a steamboat which ran on the Saone at Lyons 1783; John Fitch (American) built a paddle steamer in 1790; William Symington (British) successfully tried a steamboat in 1788, and in 1802 made the first steamboat for practical use

Stereoscope, Sir Charles Wheatstone (British) 1838

Stethoscope, René Laennec (French) 1816

Stocking frame, in weaving, William Lee (British) 1589

Stokes gun, or mortar, Sir George Stokes (British) 1915

Submarine, a development. One said to have been invented in 1578, various improvements led to first really successful submarine by Torsten Nordenfelt (Swedish) 1885

Sugar from beetroot. Andres Marggraff (German) 1747

Sunshine recorder, J. F. Campbell (British) 1857

Sun-valve for unattended lighthouses, Gustaf Dalén (Swedish) about 1900

Tartaric acid, Karl Scheele (Swedish) 1770

Taximeter, A. Gruner (German) 1895

Telegraph, electric, Sir W. Cooke and Sir C. Wheatstone (British) 1837 and about the same time S. Morse (American)

Telegraph, semaphore system, Claude Chappe (French) 1792

Telephone, A. Graham Bell (British) 1877

Telescope, reflecting, Sir Isaac Newton (British) 1668

Telescope, refracting, a development. First suggested by Roger Bacon about 1250; arrangement of lenses to bring things near by Leonard Digges, before 1570; telescopes first constructed by John Lipperhay, Zacharias Jansen, and James Metius (Dutch) about 1608

Tel-el-Amarna tablets, found by Professor Flinders Petrie (British) 1888

Television, first image televised by John L. Baird (British) 1923

Tellurium, John Muller (German) 1782

Thallium, Sir William Crookes (British) 1861

Thermionic valve, J. A. Fleming (British) 1904. Grid added by Lee de Forest (American) 1907

Thermometer, attributed to Galileo before 1597

Thorium, John Berzelius (Swedish) 1828

Threshing machine, Michael Menzies (British) about 1732

Timber-bending machine, T. Blanchard (American) about 1854

T.N.T. (trinitrotoluene), Wilbrand (German) 1863

Tonic-sol-fa system of music, Miss Glover (British) about 1841

Tonometer, H. Scheibler (German) 1834

Torpedo, Robert Whitehead (British) 1866

Torpedo boat destroyer, John Ericsson (Swedish) about 1870

Torsion balance, Charles Coulomb (French) 1786

Tourniquet, Morel (French) 1674

Tramways, a development from colliery tramways. First modern tramway by G. F. Train (American) at New York, 1832

Transit of Venus, first observed by Jeremiah Horrocks (British) 1639

Transporter bridge, Charles Smith (British) middle of 19th century

Tread-mill for prisons, Sir William Cubitt (British) 1817

Tuberculin, Professor Robert Koch (German) 1890

Tungsten, Don Fausto D'Elhuyar (Spanish) 1783

Tunnelling, shield for, Sir Marc Isambard Brunel (British) about 1825

Turbine, steam, Hero of Alexandria 130 B.C. In modern times the cupped turbine was invented by De Laval (Swedish) in 1888, and the bladed turbine by Sir Charles Parsons in 1884

Tutankhamen's tomb, Howard Carter (British) 1922

Typewriter, Mills (British) 1714, but first practical machine Charles Thurber (British) 1843

Typographic etching, Dawson Brothers (British) 1873

Uranium, Martin Klaproth (German) 1789

Uranus, Sir William Herschel (British) 1781; previously seen twenty times, but supposed to be a small star

Uranus, two moons of, Sir William Herschel (British) 1781. Two others found by William Lassell (British) 1851

Vaccination for smallpox, Dr. Edward Jenner (British) 1796

Venetian glass, at Venice about 1100

Vesta, minor planet, Heinrich Olbers (German) 1807

Vitamins, Dr. Eugene Wildiers (Belgian) 1901

Vocalion, James B. Hamilton and John Farmer (British) 1875

Volapuk, universal language, J. M. Schleyer (German) 1879

Voltaic pile, Alessandro Volta (Italian) 1800

Wall-paper, first used in Europe, in Spain and Portugal about 1555, used earlier in China and Japan

Weaving power-loom, Edmund Cartwright (British) 1785

Wireless, a development, made practical by Marconi (Italian) 1895

Wool carding machine in spinning, Lewis Paul (British) 1748

Wool-combing machine, Edmund Cartwright (British) 1789

X-rays, Wilhelm Konrad Röntgen (German) 1895

A.A. Automobile Association

A.A.A. Amateur Athletic Association

A.A.I. Associate of the Auctioneers' Institute

A1. At Lloyd's a ship that is classed as A1 is a ship that is almost new or as good as new

A.B. Able-bodied seaman

A.C. Ante Christum — before Christ ; Alternating Current

A.C.A. Associate of the Institute of Chartered Accountants

A.D. Anno Domini—In the year of Our Lord

A.D.C. Aide-de-camp, an army officer who acts as personal assistant to a general

A.F.C. Air Force Cross

A.F.M. Air Force Medal

A.F.R.Ae.S. Associate Fellow of the Royal Aeronautical Society

A.G. Adjutant-General

A.H. Anno Hegirae. The Mohammedans reckon their years from the Hegira, or the flight of Mohammed in 622 A.D. Anno means In the year

A.I.C.E. Associate of the Institution of Civil Engineers

A.L.A. Associate of the Library Association

A.M. Ante meridiem—before noon; Anno mundi—in the year of the world

A.M.I.C.E. Associate Member of the Institution of Civil Engineers

A.M.I.E.E. Associate Member of the Institution of Electrical Engineers

A.O.C. Air Officer Commanding

A.Q.M.G. Adjutant - Quartermaster - General

A.R.A. Associate of the Royal Academy

A.R.A.M. Associate of the Royal Academy of Music

A.R.B.S. Associate of the Royal Society of British Sculptors

A.R.C.A. Associate of the Royal Cambrian Academy; Associate of the Royal College of Art

A.R.C.O. Associate of the Royal College of Organists

A.R.C.S. Associate of the Royal College of Science

A.R.I.B.A. Associate of the Royal Institution of British Architects

A.R.P.S. Associate of the Royal Photographic Society

A.R.S.A. Associate of the Royal Scottish Academy; Associate of the Royal Society of Arts

A.R.S.L. Associate of the Royal Society of Literature

A.R.S.M. Associate of the Royal School of Mines (now Royal College of Science)

A.R.W.S. Associate of the Royal Society of Painters in Water-Colours

A.S.A.A. Associate of the Society of Incorporated Accountants and Auditors

A.T.C. Air Training Corps

B.A. Bachelor of Arts

B.B. Boys Brigade

B.B.C. British Broadcasting Corporation

B.C. Before Christ

B.Ch. Bachelor of Surgery (Latin, Baccalaureus Chirurgiae)

B.C.L. Bachelor of Civil Law

B.D. Bachelor of Divinity

B.E. Bachelor of Engineering

B.E.A. British European Airways

B.E.M. British Empire Medal

B.L. or **LL.B.** Bachelor of Laws

B.M. Bachelor of Medicine

B.M.A. British Medical Association

B.Mus. Bachelor of Music

B.O.A.C. British Overseas Airways Corporation

B.R.C.S. British Red Cross Society

B.Sc. Bachelor of Science

B.S.T. British Summer Time

C. Centigrade, the markings on the French or decimal thermometer

C.A. Chartered Accountant

C.B. Companion of Order of the Bath

C.B.E. Commander of the Order of the British Empire

C.C. County Council; Cricket Club; Cycling Club

c.c. Cubic centimetres

C.E. Civil Engineer

C.E.T.S. Church of England Temperance Society

Cf. A contraction of Confer, it is used in the sense of compare

C.f.i.c. Cost, freight, insurance, and commission

C.G.M. Conspicuous Gallantry Medal

C.H. Companion of Honour

C.I.D. Criminal Investigation Department

C.I.E. Companion of the Order of the Indian Empire

C.I.Mech.E. Companion of the Institution of Mechanical Engineers

C.M. Master in Surgery (Latin, Chirurgiae Magister); Common metre

Cm. Centimetre, French measurement

C.M.G. Companion of the Order of St. Michael and St. George

C.O. Commanding Officer

Co. Company; County

C.O.D. Cash on delivery

C.P.R. Canadian Pacific Railway

C.P.R.E. Council for the Preservation of Rural England

Cr. Credit or creditor

C.S. Chemical Society; Civil Service; Clerk of the Signet; Court of Session; Keeper of the Seal (Latin, Custos Sigilli)

C.S.C. Conspicuous Service Cross

C.S.I. Companion of the Order of the Star of India

C.T.C. Cyclists Touring Club

C.V.O. Commander of the Royal Victorian Order

Cwt. Hundredweight (Latin, C, centum), wt., weight

D. Penny or pence (Latin, denarius)

D.B.E. Dame Commander of the Order of the British Empire

D.C. Repeat from the beginning. A contraction used in music, standing for the Italian words, Da capo; Direct Current

D.C.L. Doctor of Civil Law

D.C.M. Distinguished Conduct Medal

D.D. Doctor of Divinity

D.D.S. Doctor of Dental Surgery

Del. He or she drew it (Latin, Delineavit)

D.F. Defender of the Faith; Dean of the Faculty

D.F.C. Distinguished Flying Cross

D.F.M. Distinguished Flying Medal

D.G. By the Grace of God (Latin, Dei Gratia)

D.Litt. Doctor of Literature

D.L.O. Dead Letter Office

D.M. Doctor of Medicine, Oxford University; Doctor of Music

D.Sc. Doctor of Science

D.S.O. Companion of the Distinguished Service Order

D.V. God Willing (Latin, Deo Volente)

dwt. Pennyweight

E.R. Elizabeth Regina (Queen Elizabeth)

F. or **Fahr.** Fahrenheit

F.A. Football Association

F.A.I. Fellow of the Chartered Auctioneers' and Estate Agents' Institute

F.A.N.Y. First Aid Nursing Yeomanry

F.A.O. Food and Agriculture Organisation

F.B.I. Federation of British Industries; Federal Bureau of Investigation

F.C.A. Fellow of the Institute of Chartered Accountants

F.C.P. Fellow of the College of Preceptors

F.C.S. Fellow of the Chemical Society

F.D. or **Fid.Def.** Defender of the Faith (Latin, Fidei Defensor)

F.G.S. Fellow of the Geological Society

F.I.A. Fellow of the Institute of Actuaries

F.L.S. Fellow of the Linnaean Society

F.M. Field-Marshal

F.P. Fire plug

F.P.S. Fellow of the Pharmaceutical Society

F.R.Ae.S. Fellow of the Royal Aeronautical Society

F.R.A.M. Fellow of the Royal Academy of Music

F.R.A.S. Fellow of the Royal Astronomical Society; Fellow of the Royal Asiatic Society

F.R.B.S. Fellow of the Royal Society of British Sculptors

F.R.C.O. Fellow of the Royal College of Organists

F.R.C.P. Fellow of the Royal College of Physicians

F.R.C.S. Fellow of the Royal College of Surgeons

F.R.C.V.S. Fellow of the Royal College of Veterinary Surgeons

F.R.G.S. Fellow of the Royal Geographical Society

F.R.Hist.Soc. Fellow of the Royal Historical Society

F.R.H.S. Fellow of the Royal Horticultural Society

F.R.I.B.A. Fellow of the Royal Institute of British Architects

F.R.I.C.S. Fellow of the Royal Institution of Chartered Surveyors

F.R.Met.S. Fellow of the Royal Meteorological Society

F.R.P.S. Fellow of the Royal Photographic Society

F.R.S. Fellow of the Royal Society

F.R.S.A. Fellow of the Royal Society of Arts

F.R.S.E. Fellow of the Royal Society of Edinburgh

F.R.S.L. Fellow of the Royal Society of Literature

F.R.S.S. Fellow of the Royal Statistical Society

F.S.A. Fellow of the Society of Antiquaries

F.Z.S. Fellow of the Zoological Society

G.A.T.T. General Agreement on Tariff and Trade

G.B.E. Knight (or Dame) Grand Cross of the Order of the British Empire

G.C. George Cross

G.C.B. Knight Grand Cross of the Order of the Bath

G.C.I.E. Knight Grand Commander of the Order of the Indian Empire

G.C.M.G. Knight Grand Cross of the Order of St. Michael and St. George

G.C.S.I. Knight Grand Commander of the Order of the Star of India

G.C.V.O. Knight Grand Cross of the Royal Victorian Order

G.M. George Medal

G.M.T. Greenwich Mean Time

G.O.C. General Officer Commanding

G.P.O. General Post Office

H.E. His Excellency; His Eminence

H.G. His (or Her) Grace; Horse Guards

H.H. His (or Her) Highness

H.I.H. His (or Her) Imperial Highness

H.M. Her (or His) Majesty

H.M.C. Her Majesty's Customs

H.M.I.S. Her Majesty's Inspector of Schools

H.M.S. Her Majesty's Ship

H.M.S.O. Her Majesty's Stationery Office

H.Q. Headquarters

H.R.H. His (or Her) Royal Highness

H.S.H. His (or Her) Serene Highness

H.W.M. High Water Mark

ib or **ibid.** Ibidem, Latin for in the same place

id. Idem, the same

i.e. Id est, Latin for that is

I H S. Jesus, from the first three letters of the name when written in Greek capitals. With full points between, as **I.H.S.**, the letters stand also for the Latin words Jesus Hominum Salvator (Jesus Saviour of Men)

USE, AND WHAT THEY STAND FOR

I.L.O. International Labour Organisation

I.N.R.I. Jesus of Nazareth, King of the Jews. The letters stand for the Latin words Jesus Nazarenus Rex Judaeorum, which were written above the Cross. J and I are the same in Latin

inst. Instant (of the current month)

I.O.U. I owe you

I.Q. Intelligence Quotient

I.S.O. Imperial Service Order

I.T.A. Independent Television Authority

J.P. Justice of the Peace

K.B.E. Knight of the Order of the British Empire

K.C.B. Knight Commander of the Order of the Bath

K.C.M.G. Knight Commander of the Order of St. Michael and St. George

K.C.S.I. Knight Commander of the Order of the Star of India

K.C.V.O. Knight Commander of the Royal Victorian Order

K.G. Knight of the Garter

K.P. Knight of Order of St. Patrick

K.T. Knight of Order of the Thistle

lb. Pound or pounds (Latin, libra)

L.C.C. London County Council

L.C.J. Lord Chief Justice

L.C.P. Licentiate of the College of Preceptors

L.D.S. Licentiate in Dental Surgery

Litt.D. Doctor of Letters (Literature)

LL.B. Bachelor of Laws (Latin, Legum Baccalaureus)

LL.D. Doctor of Laws (Latin, Legum Doctor)

L.P.T.B. London Passenger Transport Board

L.R.C.P. Licentiate of the Royal College of Physicians

L.R.C.P.E. Licentiate of the Royal College of Physicians, Edinburgh

L.R.C.S. Licentiate of the Royal College of Surgeons

L.S. Linnaean Society

L.S.A. Licentiate of the Society of Apothecaries

L.s.d. Pounds, shillings, and pence (Latin, librae, solidi, denarii)

L.T.A. Lawn Tennis Association

Ltd. Limited Liability

M.A. Master of Arts

M.B. Bachelor of Medicine (Latin, Medicinae Baccalaureus)

M.B.E. Member of the Order of the British Empire

M.C. Military Cross

M.C.C. Marylebone Cricket Club

M.Ch. Master in Surgery (Latin, Magister Chirurgiae)

M.C.M.E.S. Member of the Civil and Mechanical Engineers Society

M.D. Doctor of Medicine (Latin, Medicinae Doctor)

Mgr. Monsignor or Monsignore, an Italian title of prelates

M.I.E.E. Member of the Institute of Electrical Engineers

M.I.Mar.E. Member of the Institute of Marine Engineers

M.I.M.E. Member of the Institution of Mining Engineers

M.I.Mech.E. Member of the Institution of Mechanical Engineers

M.I.M.M. Member of the Institute of Mining and Metallurgy

M.Inst.C.E. Member of the Institution of Civil Engineers

M.Inst.M.E. Member of the Institution of Mining Engineers

M.Inst.Met. Member of the Institute of Metals

M.J.I. Member of the Institute of Journalists

M.L. Licentiate in Medicine

MM. Messieurs, French for gentlemen, plural of Monsieur ; Military Medal

mm. Millimetre

M.O.H. Medical Officer of Health

M.P. Member of Parliament

m.p.h. Miles per hour

M.P.S. Member of the Pharmaceutical Society

M.R.A.S. Member of the Royal Academy of Science ; Member of the Royal Asiatic Society

M.R.C.C. Member of the Royal College of Chemistry

M.R.C.P. Member of the Royal College of Physicians

M.R.C.S. Member of the Royal College of Surgeons

M.R.C.V.S. Member of the Royal College of Veterinary Surgeons

M.R.I. Member of the Royal Institution

MS. Manuscript, the plural being MSS.

M.S. Master of Surgery

Mus.B. Bachelor of Music

Mus.D. Doctor of Music

Mus.M. Master of Music

M.V.O. Member of the Royal Victorian Order

N.A.A.F.I. Navy, Army, and Air Force Institute

NALGO National and Local Government Officers Association

N.A.T.O. North Atlantic Treaty Organisation

N.B. Note well (Latin, Nota bene) ; North Britain or Scotland

N.C.O. Non-commissioned Officer

N.C.U. National Cyclists Union

Nem. Con. No one contradicting (Latin, Nemine contradicente)

No. Number. (Latin, Numero)

N.P.L. National Physical Laboratory

N.S.P.C.C. National Society for the Prevention of Cruelty to Children

N.U.T. National Union of Teachers

Ob. Died (Latin, Obit)

O.B.E. Officer of the Order of the British Empire

O.E.E.C. Organisation for European Economic Co-operation

O.H.M.S. On Her Majesty's Service

O.M. Order of Merit

O.S. Old Style, referring to the calendar before its change in George II's reign ; Ordnance Survey

Oz. Ounce. The z represents a curious character in old manuscripts to denote an abbreviation

P. & O. Peninsular and Oriental Steam Navigation Company

P.C. Police Constable ; post card ; Privy Councillor

Ph.B. Bachelor of Philosophy (Latin, Philosophiae Baccalaureus)

Ph.D. Doctor of Philosophy (Latin, Philosophiae Doctor)

P.M. Afternoon (Latin, Post Meridiem)

P.M.G. Postmaster-General

P.O. Patent Office ; Post Office ; Postal Order

P.S. Pharmaceutical Society ; Philological Society

P.T.O. Please turn over

P.W.D. Public Works Department

Q.C. Queen's Counsel

Q.E.D. Which was to be demonstrated (Latin, Quod erat demonstrandum)

Q.E.F. Which was to be done (Latin, Quod erat faciendum)

Q.M.G. Quartermaster-General

q.v. Which see (Latin, Quod vide)

R. King or Queen (Latin, Rex or Regina)

R.A. Royal Academy ; Royal Artillery

R.A.C. Royal Automobile Club

R.Ae.S. Royal Aeronautical Society

R.A.F. Royal Air Force

R.A.M. Royal Academy of Music

R.A.M.C. Royal Army Medical Corps

R.A.O.C. Royal Army Ordnance Corps

R.B.A. Royal Society of British Artists

R.B.S. Royal Society of British Sculptors

R.C.M. Royal College of Music

R.C.S. Royal College of Surgeons

R.E. Royal Engineers

R.E.M.E. Royal Electrical and Mechanical Engineers

R.F. République Français ; Royal Fusiliers

R.G.S. Royal Geographical Society

R.H.A. Royal Hibernian Academy

R.H.G. Royal Horse Guards

R.H.S. Royal Historical Society ; Royal Horticultural Society ; Royal Humane Society

R.I. Royal Institute of Painters in Water Colours ; Royal Institution

R.I.B.A. Royal Institute of British Architects

R.I.P. Rest in peace (Latin, Requiescat in pace)

R.M. Royal Mail ; Royal Marines

R.Met.S. Royal Meteorological Society

R.M.S. Royal Mail Steamer ; Royal Microscopical Society ; Royal Society of Miniature Painters

R.N. Royal Navy

R.N.R. Royal Naval Reserve

R.N.V.R. Royal Naval Volunteer Reserve

R.O.I. Royal Institute of Oil Painters

R.S. Royal Signals ; Royal Society

R.S.A. Royal Scottish Academy

R.S.E. Royal Society of Edinburgh

R.S.L. Royal Society of Literature

R.S.M. Royal School of Mines

R.S.P.C.A. Royal Society for the Prevention of Cruelty to Animals

R.S.V.P. Reply, if you please, from the French Répondez, s'il vous plaît

R.S.W. Royal Scottish Water-Colour Society

Rt. Hon. Right Honourable

R.U. Rugby Union

R.W.S. Royal Society of Painters in Water Colours

R.Y.S. Royal Yacht Squadron

S. Saint ; Señor ; Signor ; South

s. Shillings (Latin, solidi) ; seconds

s.g. Specific gravity

S.J. Society of Jesus (Jesuits)

S.P.C.K. Society for the Promotion of Christian Knowledge

S.P.G. Society for the Propagation of the Gospel

S.S.A.F.A. Soldiers', Sailors', and Airmen's Families Association

T.D. Territorial Officers Decoration

Toc. H. Talbot House

T.U. Trade Union

T.U.C. Trades Union Congress

U.D.C. Urban District Council

U.K. United Kingdom

U.N. United Nations

U.N.E.S.C.O. United Nations Educational, Scientific, and Cultural Organisation

U.P. United Presbyterian (Church)

U.S.A. United States of America

U.S.S.R. Union of Soviet Socialist Republics

V. Roman numeral, five ; versus, against ; vide, see

V.C. Vice-Chancellor ; Vice-Consul ; Victoria Cross

Viz. Namely (Latin, videlicet)

W.D. War Department

W.H.O. World Health Organisation

W.O. War Office ; Warrant Officer

W.R.A.C. Women's Royal Army Corps

W.R.A.F. Women's Royal Air Force

W.R.N.S. Women's Royal Naval Service

W.V.S. Women's Voluntary Services

X. An unknown quantity

Y.M.C.A. Young Men's Christian Association

Y.W.C.A. Young Women's Christian Association

KINGS AND QUEENS OF BRITAIN (since A.D. 829)

(The figures give the date of the reign)

SAXONS AND DANES

EGBERT 829–839
(Became king of the West Saxons in 802. He defeated the king of Mercia in 825, and annexed Kent. In 829 he became overlord of all the English kings, and may thus be regarded as the first King of England.)

ETHELWULF 839–858

ETHELBALD 858–860
ETHELBERT 858–866

ETHELRED I 866–871

ALFRED THE GREAT 871–901

EDWARD THE ELDER 901–924

ATHELSTAN 924–940

EDMUND I (The Elder) 940–946

EDRED 946–955

EDWY 955–959

EDGAR 959–975

EDWARD THE MARTYR 975–978
(He was about 15 when he succeeded, but was stabbed to death three years later. Edward was styled martyr in 1001.)

ETHELRED II (The Unready) 978–1016

EDMUND II (Ironside) 1016–1016

CANUTE 1017–1035

HAROLD I (Harefoot) 1035–1040

HARDICANUTE 1040–1042

EDWARD THE CONFESSOR 1042–1066

HAROLD II 1066–1066
(Killed at Battle of Hastings on October 14, 1066.)

HOUSE OF NORMANDY

WILLIAM THE CONQUEROR 1066–1087

WILLIAM II (Rufus) 1087–1100

HENRY I (Beauclerk) 1100–1135

STEPHEN 1135–1154

HOUSE OF PLANTAGENET

HENRY II (of Anjou) 1154–1189
(Son of Matilda, daughter of Henry I, and Geoffrey Plantagenet, Count of Anjou.)

RICHARD I (Coeur-de-Lion) 1189–1199
(Son of Henry II and Eleanor of Aquitaine.)

JOHN (Lackland) 1199–1216
(Brother of Richard I.)

HENRY III (of Winchester) 1216–1272
(Son of John and Isabella of Angoulême.)

EDWARD I 1272–1307
(Son of Henry III and Eleanor of Provence.)

EDWARD II (of Caernarvon) 1307–1327
(Son of Edward I and Eleanor of Castile. Created first Prince of Wales on February 7, 1301, when he was seven.)

EDWARD III 1327–1377
(Son of Edward II and Isabella of France.)

RICHARD II 1377–1399
(Grandson of Edward III. Son of Edward the Black Prince, and Joan, the Fair Maid of Kent. He was forced to resign the Crown.)

HOUSE OF LANCASTER

HENRY IV (Bolingbroke) 1399–1413
(Grandson of Edward III. Son of John of Gaunt and Blanche, daughter of Henry, first Duke of Lancaster.)

HENRY V 1413–1422
(Son of Henry IV and Mary de Bohun.)

HENRY VI (of Windsor) 1422–1461
(Son of Henry V and Katherine of Valois.)

HOUSE OF YORK

EDWARD IV 1461–1483
(Great-great-grandson of Edward III. Son of Richard, Duke of York, and Cicely Neville.)

EDWARD V 1483–1483
(Son of Edward IV and Elizabeth Woodville. When 13, he and his 11-year-old brother Richard, were murdered in the Tower, probably by order of their uncle, Richard of Gloucester, who became king.)

RICHARD III (Crouchback) 1483–1485
(Brother of Edward IV. Killed on Bosworth Field on August 23, 1485.)

HOUSE OF TUDOR

HENRY VII 1485–1509
(Son of Edmund Tudor and Margaret Beaufort. By his marriage to Elizabeth of York, daughter of Edward IV, in 1486, the Houses of York and Lancaster were united and the Wars of the Roses ended.)

HENRY VIII 1509–1547
(Son of Henry VII and Elizabeth of York.)

EDWARD VI 1547–1553
(Son of Henry VIII and his third wife, Jane Seymour.)

MARY I 1553–1558
(Daughter of Henry VIII and his first wife, Catherine of Aragon.)

ELIZABETH I 1558–1603
(Daughter of Henry VIII and his second wife, Anne Boleyn.)

HOUSE OF STUART

JAMES I 1603–1625
(Son of Mary, Queen of Scots, and Henry Stuart, Lord Darnley. Born Edinburgh Castle, June 19, 1566. Proclaimed King of Scotland when his mother abdicated in 1567. He ascended the English throne as a descendant of Henry VII's eldest daughter, thus uniting the two kingdoms.)

CHARLES I 1625–1649
(Son of James I and Anne of Denmark. His differences with Parliament led to the Civil War (1642–1648. Beheaded on January 30, 1649.)
Following the execution of Charles, a Commonwealth was proclaimed, with Oliver Cromwell as Lord Protector.

CHARLES II 1660–1685
(Son of Charles I and Henrietta Maria.)

JAMES II 1685–1688
(Brother of Charles II.)

WILLIAM III 1689–1702
MARY II 1689–1694
(William : son of William II, Prince of Orange, and Mary Stuart, daughter of Charles I. Mary : daughter of James II and Anne Hyde.)

ANNE 1702–1714
(Sister of Mary II.)

HOUSE OF HANOVER

GEORGE I 1714–1727
(Son of Ernest Augustus of Hanover and Sophia of Bohemia, granddaughter of James I.)

GEORGE II 1727–1760
(Son of George I and Sophia Dorothea of Celle.)

GEORGE III 1760–1820
(Grandson of George II. Son of Frederick Louis, Prince of Wales, and Augusta of Saxe-Gotha.)

GEORGE IV 1820–1830
(Son of George III and Charlotte Sophia of Mecklenburg-Strelitz.)

WILLIAM IV 1830–1837
(Brother of George IV.)

VICTORIA 1837–1901
(Niece of William IV. Daughter of Edward, Duke of Kent, and Mary Louise Victoria of Saxe-Coburg-Gotha.)

HOUSE OF SAXE-COBURG

EDWARD VII 1901–1910
(Son of Victoria and Albert the Prince Consort.)

HOUSE OF WINDSOR

GEORGE V 1910–1936
(Son of Edward VII and Alexandra of Denmark.)

EDWARD VIII 1936–1936
(Son of George V and Mary of Teck. Born June 23, 1894. Abdicated December 11, 1936, and is H.R.H. the Duke of Windsor.)

GEORGE VI 1936–1952
(Brother of Edward VIII.)

ELIZABETH II 1952
(Daughter of George VI and H.M. Elizabeth the Queen Mother. Born April 21, 1926.)

LONG MAY SHE REIGN

KINGS AND QUEENS OF SCOTLAND (1057–1603)

MALCOLM III (Canmore) 1057–1093

DUNCAN II 1093–1094

DONALD BANE 1094–1097

EDGAR 1097–1107

ALEXANDER I 1107–1124

DAVID I 1124–1153

MALCOLM IV (The Maiden) 1153–1165

WILLIAM I (The Lion) 1165–1214

ALEXANDER II 1214–1249

ALEXANDER III 1249–1285

MARGARET, MAID OF NORWAY 1285–1290

JOHN BALIOL 1292–1296
(Scotland and England were constantly at war for the next ten years, and no king of Scotland was proclaimed until 1306, when Robert Bruce crushed the English under Edward I.)

ROBERT BRUCE 1306–1329

DAVID II 1329–1371

ROBERT II (The Steward) 1371–1390

ROBERT III 1390–1406

JAMES I 1406–1437

JAMES II 1437–1460

JAMES III 1460–1488

JAMES IV 1488–1513

JAMES V 1513–1542

MARY 1542–1567

JAMES VI 1567–1625
(James I of England.)

WEIGHTS AND MEASURES
COMPREHENSIVE SERIES OF TABLES
FOR QUICK AND READY REFERENCE
The abbreviations commonly used are given with each weight or measure

AVOIRDUPOIS WEIGHT
16 drams, dr.	= 1 ounce, oz.
16 ounces	= 1 pound, lb.
14 pounds	= 1 stone, st.
28 pounds	= 1 quarter, qr.
4 quarters	= 1 hundredweight, cwt.
20 hundredweights	= 1 ton, t.
100 pounds	= 1 cental, or short cwt.
2000 pounds	= 1 short ton
7000 grains	= 1 pound

TROY WEIGHT
3·1683 grains	= 1 carat
24 grains, gr.	= 1 pennyweight, dwt.
20 pennyweights	= 1 ounce, oz.
12 ounces or 5760 grains	= 1 pound, lb.

APOTHECARY'S WEIGHT, DRY
20 grains, gr.	= 1 scruple, ℈
3 scruples	= 1 drachm, ℨ
8 drachms	= 1 ounce, ℥
12 ounces	= 1 pound, ℔.

APOTHECARY'S MEASURE, LIQUID
60 minims or drops, ℳ	= 1 fluid drachm, f℈
8 fluid drachms	= 1 fluid ounce, f℥
20 fluid ounces	= 1 pint, O
8 pints	= 1 gallon, Cong.

LINEAR MEASURE
12 inches, ins.	= 1 foot, ft.
3 feet	= 1 yard, yd.
5½ yards	= 1 rod, rd., pole, po., or perch, per.
40 poles	= 1 furlong, fur.
8 furlongs	= 1 mile, mi.
3 miles	= 1 league

LAND MEASURE
7·92 inches	= 1 link, li.
25 links	= 1 rod, rd.
4 rods or 100 links	= 1 chain, ch.
80 chains	= 1 mile, mi.

SQUARE MEASURE
144 square inches, sq. in.	= 1 square foot, sq. ft.
9 square feet	= 1 square yard, sq. yd.
30¼ square yards	= 1 square rod, sq. rd.; square pole, sq. po.; or square perch, sq. per.
40 square poles	= 1 rood, r.
4 roods	= 1 acre, ac.
640 acres	= 1 square mile, sq. mi.

LAND SQUARE MEASURE
625 square links, sq. li.	= 1 square rod, sq. rd.
16 square rods	= 1 square chain, sq. ch.
10 square chains	= 1 acre, ac.
640 acres	= 1 square mile, sq. mi.

CUBIC OR SOLID MEASURE
1728 cubic inches, cu. in.	= 1 cubic foot, cu. ft.
27 cubic feet	= 1 cubic yard, cu. yd.

LIQUID MEASURE
4 gills, gill	= 1 pint, pt.
2 pints	= 1 quart, qt.
4 quarts	= 1 gallon, gal.

DRY MEASURE
2 pints, pt.	= 1 quart, qt.
4 quarts	= 1 gallon, gal.
2 gallons	= 1 peck, pk.
4 pecks	= 1 bushel, bush.
8 bushels	= 1 quarter, qr.
36 bushels	= 1 chaldron, chal.
5 quarters	= 1 wey
2 weys	= 1 last

CIRCULAR MEASURE
60 seconds, "	= 1 minute, '
60 minutes	= 1 degree, °
30 degrees	= 1 sign, s.
90 degrees	= 1 right angle, rt. L, or quadrant, ⌐
180 degrees	= 1 semi-circle, ◖
360 degrees	= 1 circle, ⊙

HAY AND STRAW WEIGHT
36 pounds of straw	= 1 truss
56 pounds of old hay	= 1 truss
60 pounds of new hay	= 1 truss
36 trusses	= 1 load
1 load of straw	= 11 cwts. 64 lb.
1 load of old hay	= 18 cwts.
1 load of new hay	= 19 cwts. 32 lb.

WOOL WEIGHT
7 pounds avoirdupois	= 1 clove
14 pounds	= 1 stone
28 pounds	= 1 tod
182 pounds	= 1 wey
364 pounds	= 1 sack
4368 pounds	= 1 last
20 pounds	= 1 score
12 score	= 1 pack

MEASURES OF TIME
60 seconds, sec.	= 1 minute, min.
60 minutes	= 1 hour, hr.
24 hours	= 1 day, dy.
7 days	= 1 week, wk.
2 weeks	= 1 fortnight
4 weeks	= 1 lunar month, mo.
365 days or 52 weeks. or 12 calendar months or 13 lunar months	= 1 year
366 days	= 1 leap year
100 years	= 1 century
1000 years	= 1 millennium

NAUTICAL MEASURES
6 feet	= 1 fathom, fa.
100 fathoms	= 1 cable's length
10 cable's lengths or 1000 fathoms	= 1 nautical mile
60 nautical miles	= 1 degree
360 degrees	= the Earth's circumference
1 knot (a measure of speed)	= 1 nautical mile per hour

QUARTER DAYS
In England and Ireland
Lady Day	..	March 25
Midsummer	..	June 24
Michaelmas	..	September 29
Christmas	..	December 25

In Scotland
Candlemas	..	February 2
Whitsun	..	May 15
Lammas	..	August 1
Martinmas	..	November 11

LEAP YEAR
Thirty days hath September,
April, June, and November.
All the rest have thirty-one
Except February, alone,
Which has twenty-eight days clear,
And twenty-nine days each Leap Year.

Leap Years are those for which the last two digits of the year are divisible by four exactly, and have 366 days instead of the normal 365. Thus 1956 was a Leap Year because 56 is divisible by four. If, however, the year is an exact number of centuries it is not normally a Leap Year unless the two first digits are divisible by four. For instance, 1900 was not a Leap Year, but 2000 will be.

MISCELLANEOUS MEASURES
8 pounds	= 1 stone of meat
56 pounds	= 1 firkin of butter
12 articles	= 1 dozen
12 dozen	= 1 gross
12 gross	= 1 great gross
20 articles	= 1 score
24 sheets	= 1 quire
20 quires	= 1 ream
2 reams	= 1 bundle
10 bundles	= 1 bale
10 gallons	= 1 anker of wine
18 gallons	= 1 runlet
42 gallons	= 1 tierce
63 gallons	= 1 hogshead
2 hogsheads	= 1 pipe

ARITHMETICAL TERMS
SUM—The amount or aggregate of two or more numbers.

DIFFERENCE—The result of the subtraction of one number from another.

PRODUCT—The result of multiplying two numbers together. For example, $40 = 8 \times 5$, 40 being called the product, 8 the multiplicand, and 5 the multiplier.

QUOTIENT—The result of dividing one number by another. For example, $40 \div 5 = 8$, 40 being called the dividend, 5 the divisor, and 8 the quotient.

H.C.F. (Highest Common Factor) or G.C.M. (Greatest Common Measure)—This means the greatest number which can exactly divide each of two or more numbers. For example, the H.C.F. of 35 and 15 is 5.

L.C.M. (Lowest Common Multiple). This means the smallest number which is exactly divisible by each of two or more numbers. For example, the L.C.M. of 5 and 2 is 10.

FACTORS—Numbers which, when multiplied together, make up another number, such as $3 \times 5 = 15$. Thus 3 and 5 are factors of 15.

PRIME NUMBER—A number which can have no factors other than itself and unity, such as 5 and 17.

COMPOSITE NUMBER—Any number which can be divided into other factors besides itself and unity. For example, 6 can be divided by 3 and 2 as well as by 6 and 1.

PRIME FACTOR—A factor which is also a prime number. For example, 3 is a factor of 6, and is also a prime number.

WEIGHTS AND MEASURES TABLES

OLD ENGLISH COINS

1 groat	=		4 pence
1 tester	=		6 pence
1 noble	=	6s.	8d.
1 angel	=	10s.	
1 half guinea	=	10s.	6d.
1 mark	=	13s.	4d.
1 guinea	=	£1	1s.
1 Carolus	=	£1	3s. 9d.
1 Jacobus	=	£1	5s.
1 Moidore	=	£1	7s.
1 Joannes	=	£1	16s.

RELATIVE CONDUCTIVITY OF METALS

Metals are conductors of heat, but they conduct it in very various degrees. Silver is the best, and, reckoning its conductivity as 100, here are the other metals in order.

Silver	100·0
Copper	91·8
Gold	74·3
Aluminium	56·1
Magnesium	36·0
Zinc	26·6
Nickel	20·8
Pure Iron	17·4
Platinum	16·9
Chromium	16·5
Tin	14·8
Cast Iron	12·7
Mild Steel	11·3
Lead	8·1
Mercury	2·3
Bismuth	1·9

MELTING POINTS OF METALS

The fusion point of a metal is the temperature at which it melts and becomes a liquid. This varies greatly for different metals as we see here.

Metal	Degrees Fahrenheit	Degrees Centigrade
Tungsten	6120	3380
Tantalum	5432	3000
Osmium	4892	2700
Iridium	4429	2443
Platinum	3216	1769
Iron	2786	1530
Nickel	2647	1453
Steel	2552	1400
Copper	1983	1083
Gold	1945	1063
Silver	1761	960·8
Aluminium	1220	660·1
Zinc	787·1	419·5
Lead	621·1	327·3
Tin	449·4	231·9
Mercury	− 38·0	− 38·9

STRENGTHS OF MATERIALS

Here is the tensile strength or resistance, reckoned in pounds per square inch, which various materials offer to separation.

Cast Aluminium	14,300
Cast Brass	21,400–27,200
Brass wire	50,000–78,600
Phosphor Bronze	25,700–40,000
Cast Copper	17,100–24,300
Copper wire	57,200–65,800
Cast Iron	14,300–32,900
Wrought Iron	41,500–64,400
Cast Lead	1700–2400
Mild Steel	61,500–70,000
Steel wire	about 157,000
Cast Tin	2900–5000
Rolled Zinc	15,700–21,400
Hard wood	8600–15,700
Soft wood	4300–11,400
Cat gut	6000
Spider thread	25,700
Piano wire	266,000–333,000

MONEY TABLE

4 farthings	=	1 penny
12 pence	=	1 shilling
20 shillings	=	1 pound, or sovereign
2 shillings	=	1 florin
2s. 6d.	=	1 half-crown
5 shillings	=	1 crown

STRENGTH OF ICE

1½ inches thick will support a man
4 inches thick will support horsemen
10 inches thick will support a crowd
18 inches thick will support a railway train.

THE METRIC SYSTEM

MEASURES OF WEIGHT

10 milligrammes, mg.	=	1 centigramme, cg.
10 centigrammes	=	1 decigramme, dg.
10 decigrammes	=	1 gramme, g.
10 grammes	=	1 decagramme, Dg.
10 decagrammes	=	1 hectogramme, Hg.
10 hectogrammes	=	1 kilogramme, Kg.
10 kilogrammes	=	1 myriagramme, Mg.
10 myriagrammes	=	1 quintal, Ql.
10 quintals	=	1 tonne, T.

LINEAR MEASURE

10 millimetres, mm.	=	1 centimetre, cm.
10 centimetres	=	1 decimetre, dm.
10 decimetres	=	1 metre, m.
10 metres	=	1 decametre, Dm.
10 decametres	=	1 hectometre, Hm.
10 hectometres	=	1 kilometre, Km.
10 kilometres	=	1 myriametre, Mm.

SQUARE MEASURE

100 square millimetres, sq. mm. or mm.²	=	1 square centimetre, sq. cm. or cm.²
100 square centimetres	=	1 square decimetre, sq. dm. or dm.²
100 square decimetres	=	1 square metre or 1 centiare, sq. m. or m.², ca.
100 square metres (centiares)	=	1 square decametre or 1 are, sq. Dm. or Dm.², a.
100 square decametres (ares)	=	1 square hectometre or 1 hectare, sq. Hm. or Hm.², Ha.
100 square hectometres (hectares)	=	1 square kilometre, sq. Km. or Km.²

CUBIC MEASURE

1000 cubic millimetres, cu.mm. or mm.³	=	1 cubic centimetre, cu.cm. or cm.³
1000 cubic centimetres	=	1 cubic decimetre, cu.dm. or dm.³
1000 cubic decimetres, cu.m.. or m.³	=	1 cubic metre,

MEASURE OF CAPACITY

10 millimetres, ml.	=	1 centilitre, cl.
10 centilitres	=	1 decilitre, dl.
10 decilitres	=	1 litre, l.
10 litres	=	1 decolitre, Dl.
10 decolitres	=	1 hectolitre, Hl.
10 hectolitres	=	1 kilolitre, Kl.
10 kilolitres	=	1 myriolitre, Ml.

OLD ENGLISH MEASURES

72 points	=	1 inch
12 lines	=	1 inch
3 barley corns	=	1 inch
¾ inch	=	1 digit
2¼ inches	=	1 nail, n.
3 inches	=	1 palm
4 inches	=	1 hand, hd.
9 inches	=	1 span
1¼ yards	=	1 English ell
1⅓ yards	=	1 French ell
37·2 inches	=	1 Scottish ell
18 inches	=	1 cubit
3 feet or 5 feet	=	1 pace
4 bushels	=	1 coomb

1 yoke of land is a day's work for two oxen

YARDS IN A MILE IN MANY COUNTRIES

Most European countries now use the Metric units of measurement. Some other measures in use are

	yards
International Mile	2030
England and U.S.A. (Mile)	1760
England (Geographical)	2027
England (Nautical Mile)	2027
Austria (Postal Mile)	8297
China (Li)	705
Denmark (Mil)	8237
Greece (Stadion)	1094
Italy (Miglio)	1628
Japan (Ri)	4294
Portugal (Milha)	2283
Russia (Verst)	1167
Sweden (Mil)	11,689
Switzerland (Stunde)	5249
Turkey (Berri)	1826

WATER FACTS AND FIGURES

One gallon occupies 277·4 cubic inches or 0·16 cubic feet

One gallon weighs ten pounds

One cubic foot weighs 62·29 pounds

One cubic foot of sea water weighs 64·2 pounds

One cubic foot of fresh water contains 6·229 gallons

One cubic foot is equal to 28·32 litres

One cubic inch of water weighs 0·036 pounds

One cubic yard contains 168·2 gallons

One cubic yard weighs approximately 15 hundredweight

One ton of sea water occupies 34·9 cubic feet

One ton of fresh water occupies 36·0 cubic feet

One cubic foot of ice weighs 57·3 pounds

One ton of fresh water contains 224 gallons

Water boils at 100° Centigrade; 212° Fahrenheit; 80° Réaumur

Water freezes at 0° Centigrade; 32° Fahrenheit; 0° Réaumur

Sea water freezes at 28·6° Fahrenheit

Sea water is equal to 1·03 the weight of pure water

Pure water is equal to 0·97 the weight of sea water

VELOCITY OF WATER NEEDED FOR REMOVING MATERIALS

3 ft. a second will move				fine clay
6 "	"	"	"	fine sand
8 "	"	"	"	coarse sand
12 "	"	"		gravel
				(one inch in diameter)
36 "	"			move stones
				(as large as hen's eggs

CONVERSION TABLES

LINEAL MEASURES FOR TURNING

millimetres into inches multiply by 0·03937
inches into millimetres multiply by 25·40
centimetres into inches multiply by 0·3937
inches into centimetres multiply by 2·540
decimetres into inches multiply by 03·937
inches into decimetres multiply by 0·2540
metres into inches multiply by 39·37
inches into metres multiply by 0·02540
metres into feet multiply by 3·281
feet into metres multiply by 0·3048
metres into yards multiply by 1·094
yards into metres multiply by 0·9144
metres into poles multiply by 0·1988
poles into metres multiply by 5·029
hectometres into yards multiply by 109·4
yards into hectometres multiply by 0·009144
kilometres into yards multiply by 1094
yards into kilometres multiply by 0·0009144
kilometres into miles multiply by 0·6214
miles into kilometres multiply by 1·609

SUPERFICIAL MEASURES FOR TURNING

square millimetres into square inches multiply by 0·001550
square inches into square millimetres multiply by 645·2
square centimetres into square inches multiply by 0·1550
square inches into square centimetres multiply by 6·452
square decimetres into square inches multiply by 15·50
square inches into square decimetres multiply by 0·06452
square decimetres into square feet multiply by 0·1076
square feet into square decimetres multiply by 9·290
square metres into square feet multiply by 10·76
square feet into square metres multiply by 0·09290
square metres into square yards multiply by 1·196
square yards into square metres multiply by 0·8361
square decametres into square yards multiply by 119·6
square yards into square decametres multiply by 0·008361
square decametres into square poles multiply by 3·954
square poles into square decametres multiply by 0·2529
square decametres into roods multiply by 0·09884
roods into square decametres multiply by 10·12
square hectometres into acres multiply by 2·471
acres into square hectometres multiply by 0·4047
square hectometres into square miles multiply by 0·003861
square miles into square hectometres multiply by 259·0
square kilometres into square miles multiply by 0·3861
square miles into square kilometres multiply by 2·590

CUBIC MEASURE FOR TURNING

cubic millimetres into cubic inches multiply by 0·00006102
cubic inches into cubic millimetres multiply by 16390
cubic centimetres into cubic inches multiply by 0·06102
cubic inches into cubic centimetres multiply by 16·39
cubic decimetres into cubic inches multiply by 61·020
cubic inches into cubic decimetres multiply by 0·01639

These factors are based on the following fundamental conversion factors
1 metre = 39·3701 inches
1 yard = 0·914398 metres
1 kilogramme = 2·20462 pounds
1 pound = 0·453592 kilogrammes
1 gallon = 277·420 cubic inches = 4·54596 litres = 4546·09 cubic centimetres
1 litre = 1000·028 cubic centimetres = 0·219976 gallons = 61·026 cubic inches
1 calorie = 4·1855 Joules
1 B.t.u. = 1054·54 Joules

---

cubic metres into cubic feet multiply by 35·31
cubic feet into cubic metres multiply by 0·02832
cubic metres into cubic yards multiply by 1·308
cubic yards into cubic metres multiply by 0·7646

WEIGHTS

To Turn

milligrammes into grains multiply by 0·01543
grains into milligrammes multiply by 64·80
centigrammes into grains multiply by 0·1543
grains into centigrammes multiply by 6·480
decigrammes into grains multiply by 1·543
grains into decigrammes multiply by 0·6480
grammes into grains multiply by 15·43
grains into grammes multiply by 0·06480
grammes into drams (avoirdupois) multiply by 0·5644
drams (avoirdupois) into grammes multiply by 1·772
grammes into pennyweights (troy) multiply by 0·6430
pennyweights (troy) into grammes multiply by 1·555
grammes into scruples (apothecary's) multiply by 0·7716
scruples (apothecary's) into grammes multiply by 1·296
grammes into drachms (apothecary's) multiply by 0·2572
drachms (apothecary's) into grammes multiply by 3·888
grammes into ounces (avoirdupois) multiply by 0·03527
ounces (avoirdupois) into grammes multiply by 28·35
grammes into ounces (troy) multiply by 0·03215
ounces (troy) into grammes multiply by 31·10
grammes into ounces (apothecary's) multiply by 0·03215
ounces (apothecary's) into grammes multiply by 31·10
hectogrammes into ounces (avoirdupois) multiply by 3·527
ounces (avoirdupois) into hectogrammes multiply by 0·2835
kilogrammes into grains multiply by 15430
grains into kilogrammes multiply by 0·00006480
kilogrammes into ounces (avoirdupois) multiply by 35·27
ounces (avoirdupois) into kilogrammes multiply by 0·02835
kilogrammes into pounds (avoirdupois) multiply by 2·205
pounds (avoirdupois) into kilogrammes multiply by 0·4536
kilogrammes into hundredweights multiply by 0·01968
hundredweights into kilogrammes multiply by 50·80
kilogrammes into tons multiply by 0·0009843
tons into kilogrammes multiply by 1016

CAPACITY

To Turn

decilitres into gills multiply by 0·7040
gills into decilitres multiply by 1·421
decilitres into pints multiply by 0·1760
pints into decilitres multiply by 5·683
litres into pints multiply by 1·760
pints into litres multiply by 0·5682
litres into quarts multiply by 0·8799
quarts into litres multiply by 1·136
litres into gallons multiply by 0·2200
gallons into litres multiply by 4·546
decalitres into gallons multiply by 2·200
gallons into decalitres multiply by 0·4546
kilolitres into gallons multiply by 220·0
gallons into kilolitres multiply by 0·004546
centilitres into fluid ounces multiply by 0·3520
fluid ounces into centilitres multiply by 2·841
decilitres into fluid ounces multiply by 3·520
fluid ounces into decilitres multiply by 0·2841
decalitres into bushels multiply by 0·2750
bushels into decalitres multiply by 3·637
hectolitres into bushels multiply by 2·750
bushels into hectolitres multiply by 0·3637
hectolitres into quarters multiply by 0·3437
quarters into hectolitres multiply by 2·909
kilolitres into bushels multiply by 27·50
bushels into kilolitres multiply by 0·03637
kilolitres into quarters multiply by 3·437
quarters into kilolitres multiply by 0·2909

COMPOUND FACTORS

To Turn

pounds per lineal foot into kilogrammes per lineal metre multiply by 1·488
kilogrammes per lineal metre into pounds per lineal foot multiply by 0·6720
pounds per lineal yard into kilogrammes per lineal metre multiply by 0·4961
kilogrammes per lineal metre into pounds per lineal yard multiply by 2·016
tons per lineal foot into kilogrammes per lineal metre multiply by 3333
kilogrammes per lineal metre into tons per lineal foot multiply by 0·0003000
tons per lineal yard into kilogrammes per lineal metre multiply by 1111
kilogrammes per lineal metre into tons per lineal yard multiply by 0·0009000
pounds per mile into kilogrammes per kilometre multiply by 0·2818
kilogrammes per kilometre into pounds per mile multiply by 3·548
pounds per square inch into kilogrammes per square centimetre multiply by 0·07031
kilogrammes per square centimetre into pounds per square inch multiply by 14·22
tons per square inch into kilogrammes per square millimetre multiply by 1·575
kilogrammes per square millimetre into tons per square inch multiply by 0·6350
pounds per square foot into kilogrammes per square metre multiply by 4·882
kilogrammes per square metre into pounds per square foot multiply by 0·2048
tons per square foot into tonnes per square metre multiply by 10·94
tonnes per square metre into tons per square foot multiply by 0·09143
tons per square yard into tonnes per square metre multiply by 1·215
tonnes per square metre into tons per square yard multiply by 0·8229

pounds per cubic yard into kilogrammes per cubic metre multiply by 0·5933

kilogrammes per cubic metre into pounds per cubic yard multiply by 1·685

pounds per cubic foot into kilogrammes per cubic metre multiply by 16·02

kilogrammes per cubic metre into pounds per cubic foot multiply by 0·06243

tons per cubic yard into tonnes per cubic metre multiply by 1·329

tonnes per cubic metre into tons per cubic yard multiply by 0·7526

pounds per gallon into kilogrammes per litre multiply by 0·09978

kilogrammes per litre into pounds per gallon multiply by 10·02

inch-tons into kilogrammetres multiply by 25·80

kilogrammetres into inch-tons multiply by 0·03876

foot-pounds into kilogrammetres multiply by 0·1383

kilogrammetres into foot-pounds multiply by 7·231

foot-tons into tonne-metres multiply by 0·3096

tonne-metres into foot-tons multiply by 3·230

B.t.u. into K-calories multiply by 0·2519

K-calories into B.t.u. multiply by 3·970

B.t.u. per square foot into K-calories per square metre multiply by 2·712

K-calories per square metre into B.t.u. per square foot multiply by 3·3687

CONVERTING ENGLISH WEIGHTS AND MEASURES

To Turn

feet into links multiply by 1·515

links into feet multiply by 0·66

chains into miles multiply by 0·0125

miles into chains multiply by 80

Russian versts into English miles multiply by 0·6629

English miles into Russian versts multiply by 1·508

square feet into acres multiply by 0·00002296

acres into square feet multiply by 43,560

square yards into square miles multiply by 0·0000003228

square miles into square yards multiply by 3,097,600

square miles into acres multiply by 640

acres into square miles multiply by 0·001652

cubic feet into bushels multiply by 0·7786

bushels into cubic feet multiply by 1·284

cubic inches into gallons multiply by 0·003605

gallons into cubic inches multiply by 277·4

cubic feet of water into pounds multiply by 62·29

pounds of water into cubic feet multiply by 0·01605

cubic feet of water into tons multiply by 0·02781

tons of water into cubic feet multiply by 35·96

QUICK WAYS OF RECKONING

The formulae given above enable us to get exact figures, but there are rough and ready ways of changing one measure or weight into another so as to give us approximate results, and some of the more useful are given here.

To Turn

metres into feet multiply by 3¼

feet into metres multiply by 0·3

metres into yards add one-tenth

yards into metres deduct one-tenth

kilometres into miles multiply by five-eighths

miles into kilometres multiply by 1⅝

square metres into square yards add one-fifth

square yards into square metres deduct one-fifth

square kilometres into square miles multiply by 0·4

square miles into square kilometres multiply by 2⅜

cubic metres into cubic yards add one-third

cubic yards into cubic metres deduct one-quarter

kilogrammes into pounds (avoirdupois) multiply by 2¼

pounds into kilogrammes deduct a tenth and divide by 2

litres into pints multiply by 1¾

pints into litres multiply by three-fifths

UNITS OF MEASUREMENT

BASIC UNITS

These are the units of Length, Mass, and Time and most other units may be derived from these, with the addition of heat units. The English units are the Foot, the Pound and the Second. The Metric units are the Centimetre, the Gram and the Second.

FORCE UNITS

One Poundal is the force which, acting on a mass of one pound, gives it an acceleration of one foot per second per second

One Dyne is the force which, acting on a mass of one gram, gives it an acceleration of one centimetre per second per second

WORK OR ENERGY UNITS

One Foot-Pound is the energy required to raise one pound one foot vertically

One Foot-Poundal is the work done by a force of one Poundal in moving its point of application by one foot

One Erg is the work done by a force of one Dyne in moving its point of application by one centimetre

One Joule is equal to ten million Ergs

POWER

One Horse-Power is a rate of working of 550 foot-pounds per second, or 33,000 foot-pounds per minute

One Watt is a rate of working of one Joule per second

PRESSURE UNITS

Pressure is the force acting on unit area of surface and is measured in pound's weight per square inch or dynes per square centimetre. It is also measured in centimetres of mercury and Atmospheres

One Atmosphere is a pressure of 76 centimetres of mercury under specified conditions, equal to 14·7 pounds' weight per square inch

HEAT UNITS

One Degree of Fahrenheit temperature (° F.) is a one-hundred-and-eightieth part of the rise in temperature between the temperature of melting ice (32° F.) and the temperature of water boiling at a pressure of one atmosphere (212° F.)

One Degree of Centigrade (Celsius) temperature (° C.) is one-hundredth part of the rise in temperature between the temperature of melting ice (0° C.) and the temperature of water boiling at a pressure of one atmosphere (100° C.)

One British Thermal Unit (B.t.u.) is the quantity of heat required to raise the temperature of one pound of water at 60·5° F. by one degree Fahrenheit

One Therm is equal to 100,000 British Thermal Units

One Calorie is the quantity of heat required to raise the temperature of one gram of water at 15° C. by one degree Centigrade

One K-Calorie or Large Calorie equals 1000 calories

LIGHT UNITS

The Illuminating Power, Candle-power or Intensity of a source of light is measured in Candle-power (Candela)

One Standard English Candle is one-tenth of the intensity of a Harcourt lamp burning pentane

One Foot-Candle is the illumination at a point on a surface produced by a source of one candle power one foot away from the point in a direction perpendicular to the surface

ELECTRICAL UNITS

One International Ampere is the current of electricity that will deposit 0·0011180 grams of silver per second when flowing through a silver nitrate solution

One International Ohm is the resistance of a column of mercury at 0° C., the length of which is 106·3 cms. and the mass of which is 14·45 grams,

contained in a tube having an area of cross-section of one square millimetre

One International Volt is the electrical pressure or potential difference which, applied across a conductor of resistance one ohm, will maintain a current of one ampere

One Coulomb is the quantity of electricity which passes a given point in a conductor when one ampere flows for one second

One Watt is also a unit of electrical power and is the power developed when a current of one ampere is maintained by a pressure of one volt

One Watt-hour is the unit of electrical energy and is the energy supplied when a power of one watt is maintained for one hour

One Kilowatt-hour or Board of Trade Unit is 1000 watt-hours, being the electrical energy supplied in one hour by a source working at the rate of 1000 watts

One Farad is the capacity of a condenser in which a charge of one coulomb produces a potential difference of one volt between the plates.

One Microfarad is the more usual unit of capacity and is equal to one millionth of a Farad.

OTHER UNITS

One Micron is a millionth of a metre

One Angstrom is a hundred-millionth of a centimetre

One Oersted is the unit of magnetising force and is the strength of a magnetising field in which a unit magnetic pole is acted upon by a force of one dyne

One Gauss is the unit of magnetic induction and is equal to one line of magnetic induction per square centimetre

One Light-year is 9,500,000,000,000 kilometres or 5,900,000,000,000 miles

One Parsec is 30,800,000,000,000 kilometres or 19,100,000,000,000 miles

The mean radius of the earth's orbit is 149,000,000 kilometres or 92,900,000 miles.

WEIGHTS AND MEASURES TABLES

The Elements with their Chemical Symbols and Atomic Weights

Element	Symbol	Atomic Weight
Actinium	Ac	227·05
Aluminium	Al	26·98
Americium	Am	243
Antimony	Sb	121·76
Argon	A	39·944
Arsenic	As	74·91
Astatine	At	210
Barium	Ba	137·35
Berkelium	Bk	245
Beryllium	Be	9·013
Bismuth	Bi	209·00
Boron	B	10·82
Bromine	Br	79·916
Cadmium	Cd	112·41
Caesium	Cs	132·91
Calcium	Ca	40·08
Californium	Cf	246
Carbon	C	12·011
Cerium	Ce	140·13
Chlorine	Cl	35·457
Chromium	Cr	52·01
Cobalt	Co	58·94
Copper	Cu	63·54
Curium	Cm	245
Dysprosium	Dy	162·46
Erbium	Er	167·2
Europium	Eu	152·0
Fluorine	F	19·00
Francium	Fr	223
Gadolinium	Gd	156·9
Gallium	Ga	69·72
Germanium	Ge	72·60
Gold	Au	197·0
Hafnium	Hf	178·6
Helium	He	4·003
Holmium	Ho	164·94
Hydrogen	H	1·008
Indium	In	114·76
Iodine	I	126·91
Iridium	Ir	192·2
Iron	Fe	55·85
Krypton	Kr	83·80
Lanthenum	La	138·92
Lead	Pb	207·21
Lithium	Li	6·940
Lutetium	Lu	174·99
Magnesium	Mg	24·32
Manganese	Mn	54·94
Mercury	Hg	200·61
Molybdenum	Mo	95·95
Neodymium	Nd	144·27
Neon	Ne	20·183
Neptunium	Np	237
Nickel	Ni	58·69
Niobium	Nb	92·91
Nitrogen	N	14·008
Osmium	Os	190·2
Oxygen	O	16
Palladium	Pd	106·7
Phosphorus	P	30·975
Platinum	Pt	195·23
Plutonium	Pu	239
Polonium	Po	209
Potassium	K	39·100
Praseodymium	Pr	140·92
Promethium	Pm	145
Protactinium	Pa	231
Radium	Ra	226·05
Radon	Rn	222
Rhenium	Re	186·31
Rhodium	Rh	102·91
Rubidium	Rb	85·48
Ruthenium	Ru	101·1
Samarium	Sm	150·43
Scandium	Sc	44·96
Selenium	Se	78·96
Silicon	Si	28·09
Silver	Ag	107·880
Sodium	Na	22·991
Strontium	Sr	87·63
Sulphur	S	32·066
Tantalum	Ta	180·95
Technetium	Tc	99
Tellurium	Te	127·61
Terbium	Tb	158·93
Thallium	Tl	204·39
Thorium	Th	232·05
Thulium	Tm	168·94
Tin	Sn	118·70
Titanium	Ti	47·90
Uranium	U	238·07
Vanadium	V	50·95
Wolfram (formerly Tungsten)	W	183·92
Xenon	Xe	131·3
Ytterbium	Yb	173·04
Yttrium	Y	88·92
Zinc	Zn	65·38
Zirconium	Zr	91·22

Einsteinium, Fermium, Mendelevium, and Nobellium are new-found elements

Mathematical, Geometrical, and Astronomical Signs

- **+** plus, the sign of addition
- **−** minus, the sign of subtraction
- **×** the sign of multiplication
- **÷** the sign of division
- **:** is to
- **::** as
- **∴** because
- **∴** therefore
- **=** equals
- **∞** infinity
- **√** square root
- **∛** cube root
- **∜** fourth root, and so on
- **%** per cent
- **≠** is unequal to
- **>** is greater than
- **≯** is not greater than
- **<** is less than
- **≮** is not less than
- **∥** is parallel to
- **∦** is not parallel to
- **⊥** is perpendicular to
- **△** equilateral
- **∠** angle
- **∠s** angles
- **∟** right angle
- **≜** equiangular
- **≛** equality
- **△** triangle
- **□** square
- **▭** rectangle
- **Sol□** parallelopiped
- **⊙** circle
- **○** circumference
- **◖** semicircle
- **⌒** arc
- **@** at
- **☉** sun
- **●** new moon
- **☽** first quarter of moon
- **○** full moon
- **☾** last quarter of moon
- **○** Planet
- **⊕** Earth
- **☿** Mercury
- **♀** Venus
- **♂** Mars
- **♃** Jupiter
- **♄** Saturn
- **♅** Uranus
- **♆** Neptune
- **☄** Comet
- **✳** Fixed Star
- **☌** conjunction
- **☍** opposition

Pounds in a Cubic Foot of Material
Average figures are given where necessary

Material	lb	Material	lb
Aluminium	170	Granite	170
Brass	530	Limestone	170
Copper	550	Portland Stone	150
Cast Iron	440	Quartz	160
Wrought Iron	490	Sandstone	150
Steel	490	Wet Sand	130
Lead	704	Marble	170
Tin	455	Dry Clay	120
Cement	90	Wet Clay	135
Concrete	140	Dry Earth	100
Coal	93·5	Wet Earth	120
Glass	160	Dry Garden Mould	70
Coke	45	Dry Peat	30
Tar	62	Wet Peat	70
Air	0·080	Dry Sand	100
Water	62	Ice	57
Sea Water	64	Slate	170
Steam	0·038	Loose Snow	4–15
Asphalt	87	Moist Snow	15–20
Chalk	170	Rock Salt	140
Flint	160		

Pounds in a Cubic Foot of Timber

Timber	lb	Timber	lb
Alder	33	Hickory	50
Ash	46	Hornbeam	45
Balsa	8	Jarrah	57
Bamboo	25	Larch	38
Beech	46	Lime	32
Birch	45	Maple	42
Boxwood	76	Oak (English)	50
Cherry	38	Pine	32
Chestnut (horse)	35	Plane	35
Chestnut (Spanish)	41	Poplar	26
Cork	16	Spruce (Norway)	30
Cypress	30	Sycamore	41
Ebony	73	Teak	50
Elm (English)	43	Walnut	41
Fir (Silver)	30	Willow	33
Hazel	39	Yew	52

Roman Numerals

I—1	C—100
II—2	CC—200
III—3	CCC—300
IV—4	CD—400
V—5	D—500
VI—6	IƆ—500
VII—7	DC—600
VIII—8	IƆC—600
IX—9	DCC—700
X—10	M—1000
XI—11	CIƆ—1000
XII—12	MC—1100
XIII—13	MD—1500
XIV—14	MM—2000
XV—15	CIƆCIƆ—2000
XVI—16	IICIƆ—2000
XVII—17	IIM—2000
XVIII—18	
XIX—19	V̄—5000
XX—20	IƆƆ—5000
XXX—30	
XL—40	V̄I—6000
L—50	
LX—60	X̄—10,000
LXX—70	CCIƆƆ—10,000
LXXX—80	IƆƆƆ—50,000
XC—90	C̄—100,000
	CCCIƆƆƆ—100,000
	CCCCIƆƆƆ—1,000,000

THE QUICKEST WAY OF FINDING THINGS

The Area of a Triangle

The area of a triangle is equal to the base multiplied by half the perpendicular height; or if we know the length of the three sides AB, BC, CA, and half their sum is represented by S, we can find the area by using the formula S (S—AB) (S—BC) (S—CA), and by taking the square root of the result.

The Area of an Equilateral Triangle

The area of an equilateral triangle can be found by multiplying the square of the length of one side by ·433.

If we have the Length of Two Sides of a Right-Angled Triangle, how can we find the Third Side?

If we have the base and perpendicular we should square each of these, add the results together, and take the square root of the sum; that will give us the length of the hypotenuse, or side opposite the right angle. If we have the length of the hypotenuse and one other side, we should square them both, subtract the smaller number from the larger, and take the square root of the result. That will be the third side.

The Area of a Parallelogram

To find the area of a parallelogram, we have to multiply the base by the perpendicular height.

The Area of a Rhombus or Square

In addition to the last-mentioned method we may multiply the two diagonals together and divide the result by two.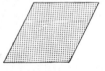

The Area of a Trapezium

A trapezium is a four-sided figure having two of its sides parallel, and we find the area by taking half the sum of the two parallel sides and multiplying by the perpendicular distance between them.

The Area of a Trapezoid

A trapezoid is a four-sided figure of which no two sides are parallel. We find its area by multiplying the longest diagonal by half the sum of the two perpendiculars falling on it from the opposite angles. Another method of finding the area of any figure of four or more unequal straight sides is to divide it into triangles and find the area of each, adding these together for the result.

The Area of a Hexagon, Octagon, or any Regular-sided Figure

Take half the radius of the inscribed circle (that is, the circle drawn *inside* the figure and touching all its sides), multiply this by the length of one side, and then multiply the result by the number of the sides.

The Circumference of a Circle

Multiply the diameter of the circle by 3·1416, or, more roughly, by 3⅐.

The Diameter of a Circle

If we have the length of the radius we multiply that by two to find the diameter of a circle; if we have the length of the circumference we multiply that by ·31831.

The Area of a Circle

There are many ways of finding the area of a circle. We may multiply half the radius by the circumference; or we may square the radius and multiply by 3·1416; or we may square the diameter and multiply by ·7854; or we may square the circumference and divide by 3·1416 multiplied by four; or we may square the circumference and multiply by ·07958; or we may find the area of a triangle having a base equal to the circumference and a height equal to the radius.

The Circumference of an Ellipse

Take half the sum of the long and short diameters and multiply by 3·1416. The answer gives the circumference.

The Area of an Ellipse

Take the long diameter, multiply it by the short diameter, and multiply the result by ·7854.

The Length of the Arc of a Circle

The simplest way to find this is to subtract the chord of the whole arc from eight times the chord of half the arc, and divide the remainder by three.

The Area of the Sector of a Circle

Multiply the length of the arc by one half the radius and the result is the area of the sector.

The Area of the Segment of a Circle

We find the area of a sector having the same arc by the method given in the last paragraph, and then subtract from the result the area of the triangle formed by the radii and the chord.

The Area of the Surface of a Sphere

This is found by squaring the diameter and multiplying by 3·1416; or by multiplying the diameter by the circumference.

The Cubic Contents of a Sphere

To find this we must cube the diameter and multiply by ·5236; or we take the area of the surface and then multiply it by one-third of the radius.

The Area of the Surface of a Cylinder

Add the areas of the two ends to the result of the circumference of one end multiplied by the length. This will give the area of the surface.

The Cubic Contents of a Cylinder

Multiply the area of one end by the length of the cylinder; the result is the cubic contents.

The Area of the Surface of a Prism

To find this add the areas of the two ends to the perimeter, or distance round one end multiplied by the length.

The Cubic Contents of a Prism

Multiply the area of one end by the length of the prism and the result is the cubic contents.

The Cubic Contents of a Prismoid

A prismoid is a body that approaches to the form of a prism without being actually a prism; that is, its sides are not parallelograms. To find its contents we proceed thus: to the sum of the area of the two ends we add four times the middle area and multiply the sum by one-sixth the height.

The Area of the Surface of a Cone

To find this multiply the slant height by the circumference of the base, and divide the result by two. Then to the result add the area of the base.

The Cubic Contents of a Cone

To find this multiply one-third of the perpendicular by the area of the base.

The Area of the Surface of a Pyramid

Multiply the slant height by the perimeter of the base, divide by two, and add the area of the base. The result will give the area of the surface.

The Cubic Contents of a Pyramid

Multiply one-third of the perpendicular height by the area of the base to find the cubic contents.

The Length of a Ring

There are various ways of finding the length of a ring. We may multiply the sum of the radii of the outer and inner boundaries by 3·1416; or we may take half the sum of the outer and inner boundaries; or we may subtract the circumference of the cross section from the outer boundary; or we may add the inner boundary to the circumference of the cross section.

The Area of the Surface of a Plane Ring

The surface of a plane ring is the space between two concentric circles, and its area is found by adding the two radii together, multiplying by their difference, and then multiplying the result by 3·1416.

The Area of the Surface of a Solid Ring

Multiply the circumference of the circular section of the ring by the length of the ring, and the result is the area of the surface.

The Cubic Contents of a Ring

To find this multiply the area of the cross section by the length of the ring.

The Cubic Contents of a Spherical Shell

This means the space occupied by the actual material of a hollow ball, and we find it by subtracting the cube of the inner diameter from the cube of the outer diameter and multiplying the result by ·5236.

The Cubic Contents of the Frustum of a Sphere

The frustum of a sphere is the part between two parallel planes. Its contents are found by squaring the radius of the base, adding the square of the radius of the top, multiplying by three, adding result to square of height, and multiplying by ·5236 of the height.

The Cubic Contents of the Segment of a Sphere

The segment of a sphere is the part cut off by a single plane, and its contents are found by squaring the radius of the base, multiplying the result by three, then adding that result to the square of the height, and multiplying the whole by ·5236 of the height.

The Area of the Surface of a Frustum

A frustum is also the part of a solid figure next to the base left after cutting off the top part by a plane parallel to the base. The area of its surface is found by multiplying the slant height by the perimeter of the two ends added together, dividing by two, and then adding to the result the areas of both ends.

The Cubic Contents of a Frustum

To the area of the two ends add the square root of their product and multiply by one-third of the height to find the cubic contents.

The Area of a Parabola

A parabola is formed when we intersect or cut a cone with a plane parallel with its side. The area of the surface thus exposed is found by multiplying the base by two-thirds the height.

The Length of the Side of a Square Inscribed in a Circle

Multiply the diameter of the circle by ·707 and the result gives the side of the inscribed square.

The Diameter of a Circle Circumscribing a Square

Multiply the side of the square by 1·414.

The Length of the Side of a Square Circumscribing a Circle

This square of course has a side exactly equal to the diameter of the circle that it circumscribes, or fits round.

The Length of the Side of a Square Equal in Area to a Circle

Multiply the diameter of the circle by ·8862.

The Diameter of a Circle Equal in Area to a Square

Multiply the side of the square by 1·1284.

The Cubic Contents of a Cube

Multiply the length by the breadth and the result by the height; in other words, cube the side, and the result is the volume or cubic contents.

PHYSIOLOGY TABLES—MAN & THE ANIMALS

Rate of the Heart-beat in Various Animals each Minute

Elephant	25 to 28
Horse	26 to 40
Ass	46 to 50
Ox	40 to 50
Man	70 to 80
Sheep	70 to 80
Goat	70 to 80
Pig	70 to 80
Dog	90 to 100
Cat	120 to 140
Rabbit	120 to 150
Birds	120 to 180

Time Occupied in Circulation of the Blood in Seconds

Dog	15 to 17
Goat	14
Rabbit	8
Squirrel	4½
Man	23

Average Amount of Blood in Various Animals

	Part of total Body Weight
Adult Man	one-thirteenth
Horse	one-eighteenth
Ox	one-thirtieth
Sheep	one-twenty-fifth
Goat	one-twenty-fifth
Pig	one-twenty-eighth
Dog	one-eighteenth
Cat	one-twentieth
Rabbit	one-thirty-second
Birds	one-twenty-ninth

Number of Respirations a Minute

Horse	6 to 10
Ox	10 to 15
Sheep	12 to 20
Goat	12 to 20
Dog	15 to 28
Cat	20 to 30
Rabbit	50 to 60
Whale	4 to 5
Man	12 to 19

Average Age when the Teeth Come

First Teeth

Central incisors (lower)	6th month
Central incisors (upper)	7th ,,
Lateral incisors (upper)	9th ,,
Lateral incisors (lower)	10th ,,
First molars	12th ,,
Canines	18th ,,
Second molars	2nd year, or later

Permanent Teeth

First molars	6½ years
Lower central incisors	7 ,,
Upper central incisors	8 ,,
Lateral incisors	9 ,,
First bicuspid	10 ,,
Second bicuspid	11 ,,
Canines	12 ,,
Second molars	13 ,,
Third molars (wisdom)	17 to 25, or later.

The full set of permanent teeth is 32; 16 in each jaw.

Temperature of Various Animals in Fahrenheit

Ape	104	Monkey	104
Bat	100	Ox	102
Cat	102	Oyster	82
Chicken	111	Panther	102
Crow	109	Parrot	106
Dog	102	Pig	105
Donkey	98	Pigeon	109
Duck	111	Porpoise	100
Elephant	100	Rabbit	100
Fox	102	Rat	102
Glowworm	74	Shark	77
Goat	104	Sheep	104
Goose	107	Snail	76
Guinea-pig	100	Snake	88
Hare	100	Sparrow	108
Hen	108	Squirrel	102
Horse	99	Tiger	99
Jackal	101	Turkey	109
Jackdaw	107	Woodcock	108
Man	99	Wolf	105

Average Height and Weight of Human Beings

Age	Height of Male ft.	in.	Height of Female ft.	in.	Weight of Male st.	lb.	Weight of Female st.	lb.
1	2	5½	2	3½	1	4½	1	4
2	2	8½	2	7	2	4½	1	11¼
3	2	11	2	10	2	6	2	3½
4	3	1	3	0	2	9	2	8
5	3	4	3	3	2	12	2	11
6	3	7	3	6	3	2	2	13¾
7	3	10	3	8	3	7¾	3	5½
8	3	11	3	10½	3	13	3	10
9	4	1¾	4	0¾	4	4½	3	13½
10	4	3¾	4	3	4	11½	4	6
11	4	5½	4	5	5	2	4	12
12	4	7	4	7½	5	6¾	5	6½
13	4	9	4	9¾	5	12½	6	3
14	4	11¼	4	11¾	6	8	6	12¾
15	5	2¼	5	1	7	4¾	7	8¼
16	5	4¼	5	1¾	8	7	8	1
17	5	6¼	5	2½	9	5	8	3½
18	5	7	5	2½	9	11½	8	9
19	5	7¼	5	2¾	9	13½	8	12
20	5	7½	5	3	10	3¼	8	11½
21	5	7½	5	3	10	5	8	10
22	5	7½	5	3	10	7	8	11½
23	5	7½	5	3	10	7½	8	12
24	5	7¾	5	2¾	10	8	8	9
25	5	7¾	5	2	10	12¼	8	8
26	5	7¾	5	2	10	12¼	8	8
27	5	7¾	5	2	10	12¼	8	8
28	5	7¾	5	2	10	12¼	8	8
29	5	7¾	5	2	10	12¼	8	8
30	5	7¾	5	2	11	6	8	8
31	5	8	5	1	11	6	8	9
32	5	8	5	1	11	6	8	9
33	5	8	5	1	11	6	8	9
34	5	8	5	1	11	6	8	9
35	5	8	5	1	11	6	8	9

Average Weight and Chest Measurement for Height of a Man of Thirty

Height ft.	in.	Weight st.	lb.	Chest Circumference in.
5	0	8	0	33½
5	1	8	4	34
5	2	9	0	35
5	3	9	7	35
5	4	9	13	36
5	5	10	2	37
5	6	10	5	37½
5	7	10	8	38
5	8	11	1	38½
5	9	11	8	39
5	10	12	1	39½
5	11	12	6	40
6	0	12	10	40½
6	1	13	0	41

Average Height and Weight of a Woman (Dressed)

Height ft.	in.	Weight st.	lb.
4	10	7	0
4	11	7	4
5	0	7	7
5	1	7	12
5	2	8	2
5	3	8	9
5	4	9	2
5	5	9	9
5	6	9	13
5	7	10	8
5	8	11	4

Average Weight of Human Organs

	oz.
Heart	
Male	10 to 12
Female	8 to 10
Lungs	
Right	23
Left	19
Stomach	4½ to 5
Liver	45 to 60
Pancreas	3
Spleen	5 to 7
Kidney	4½ to 5½
Brain	
Male	50
Female	44

Weight of the Brain of Various Nationalities

	ounces		ounces
Scottish	50	Pawnee	47·1
German	49·6	Italian	46·9
English	49·5	Hindu	45·1
French	47·9	Gipsy	44·8
Zulu	47·5	Bushman	44·6
Chinese	47·2	Eskimo	43·9

Weight of the Brain in Various Races of Man

	grammes
European Man	1367
Woman	1204
Oceanian Man	1319
Woman	1219
American Man	1308
Woman	1187
Asiatic Man	1304
Woman	1194
African Man	1293
Woman	1211
Australian Man	1214
Woman	1111

Weight of the Brain Compared with the Rest of the Body

Small Singing Bird	one part out of	12
Marmoset	,, ,,	22
Capuchin Monkey	,, ,,	25
Magpie	,, ,,	28
Rat	,, ,,	28
Gibbon	,, ,,	28
Woman	,, ,,	35
Mole	,, ,,	36
Man	,, ,,	36
Lemur	,, ,,	42
Half-grown Chimpanzee	,, ,,	51
Cat	,, ,,	82
Adult Gorilla	,, ,,	104
Tapir	,, ,,	104
Pigeon	,, ,,	160
Eagle	,, ,,	160
Lizard	,, ,,	160
Frog	,, ,,	172
Dog	,, ,,	214
Carp	,, ,,	248
Fowl	,, ,,	347
Sheep	,, ,,	351
Goose	,, ,,	360
Horse	,, ,,	400
Young Elephant	,, ,,	500
Tiger	,, ,,	500
Lion	,, ,,	500
Ox	,, ,,	500
Ostrich	,, ,,	1200
Land Turtle	,, ,,	2240
Shark	,, ,,	2496
Sea Turtle	,, ,,	5680
Tunny	,, ,,	37,440

Time Required for Digestion of Various Foods

	Hrs.	Min.
Rice	1	0
Raw Eggs	1	30
Apples	1	30
Boiled Sago	1	45
Boiled Milk	2	0
Stale Bread	2	0
Boiled Turkey	2	25
Broiled Lamb	2	30
Baked Potatoes	2	30
Boiled Beans	2	30
Boiled Parsnips	2	30
Raw Oysters	2	55
Boiled Eggs	3	0
Boiled Mutton	3	0
Roast Beef	3	0
New Bread	3	15
Boiled Carrots	3	15
Boiled Turnips	3	30
Boiled Potatoes	3	30
Butter	3	30
Cheese	3	30
Stewed Oysters	3	30
Hard-boiled Eggs	3	30
Boiled Pork	3	30
Roast Fowl	4	0
Roast Goose	4	30
Cabbage	4	30
Roast Pork	5	15
Roast Veal	5	30

ATLAS OF THE WORLD

37 Colour Maps of All Countries

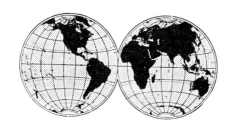

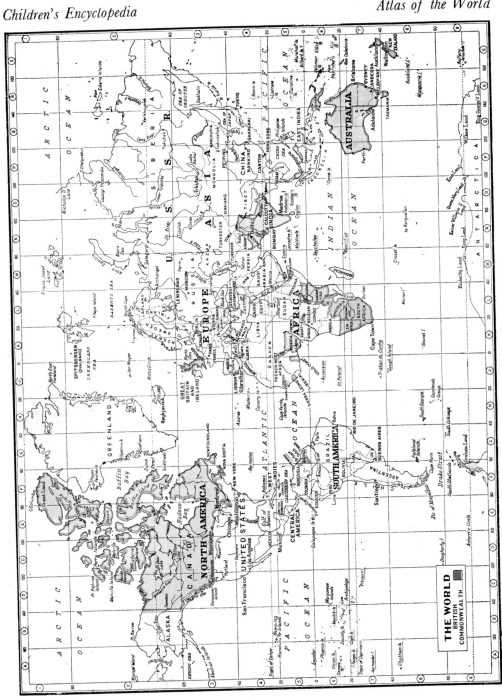

THE WORLD
BRITISH
COMMONWEALTH......

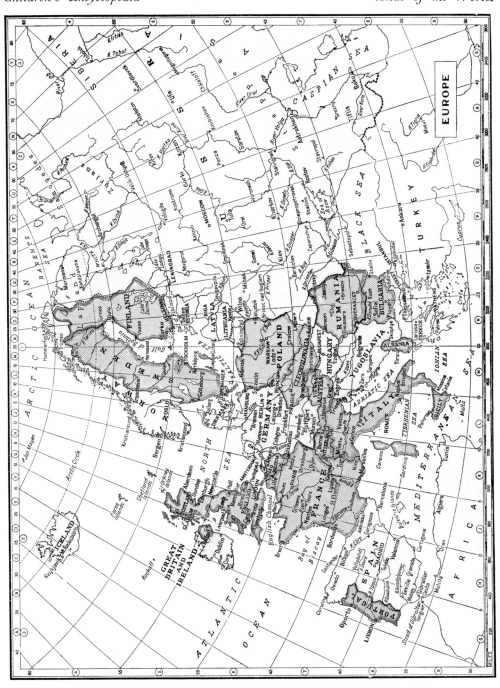

EUROPE

ENGLAND AND WALES

SCOTLAND

IRELAND

FRANCE

MILES

7108

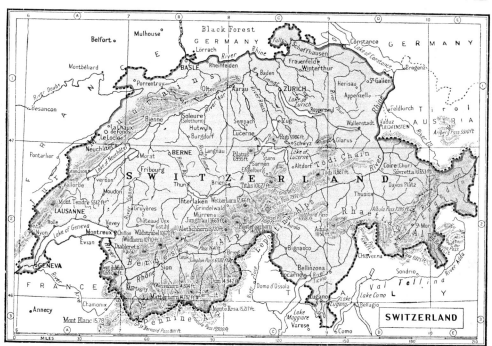

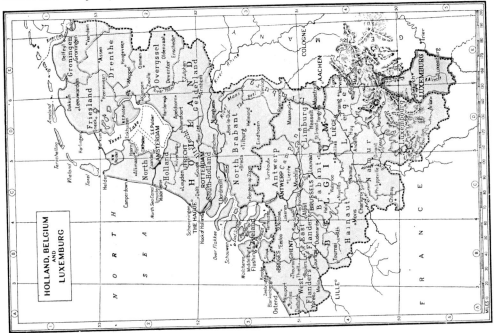

HOLLAND, BELGIUM
AND
LUXEMBURG

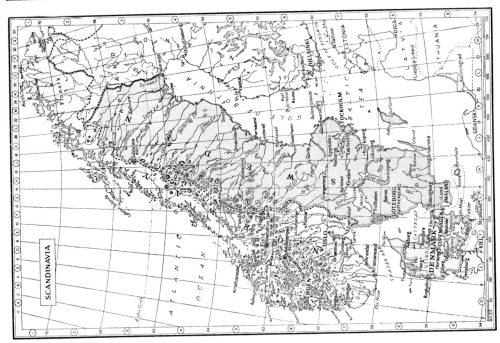

SCANDINAVIA

GERMANY

BALKANS

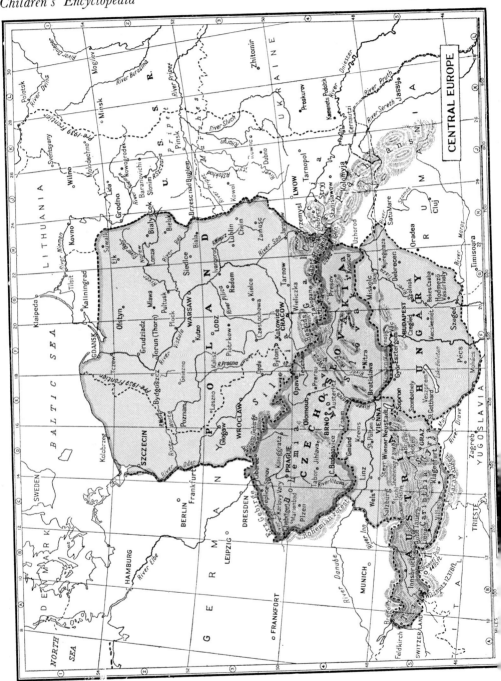

CENTRAL EUROPE

WESTERN U.S.S.R.
AND FINLAND

ANCIENT GREECE
Ionians [   ]   Dorians [   ]   Aeolians [   ]

MILES   50   100   150   200   250   300   350   400   450   500   550   600

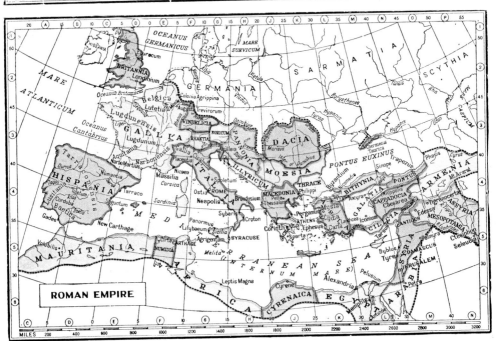

ROMAN EMPIRE

MILES   200   400   600   800   1000   1200   1400   1600   1800   2000   2200   2400   2600   2800   3000   3200

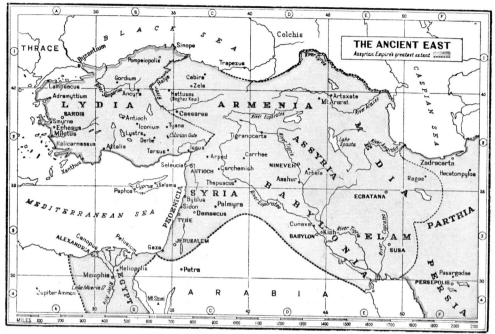

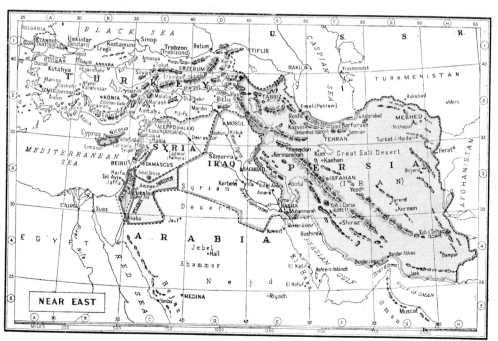

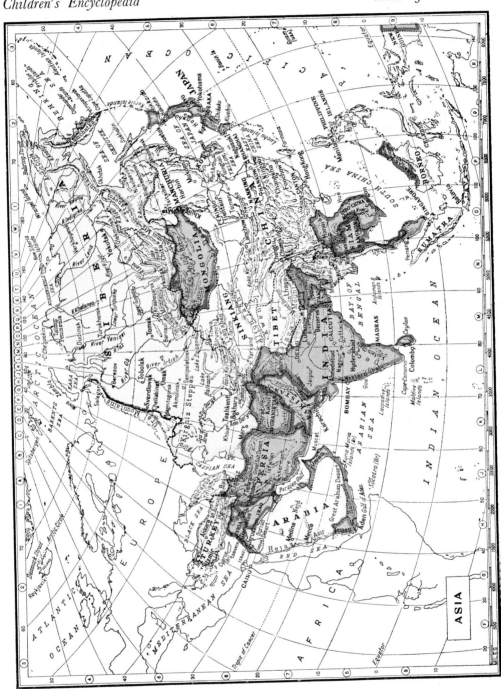

ASIA

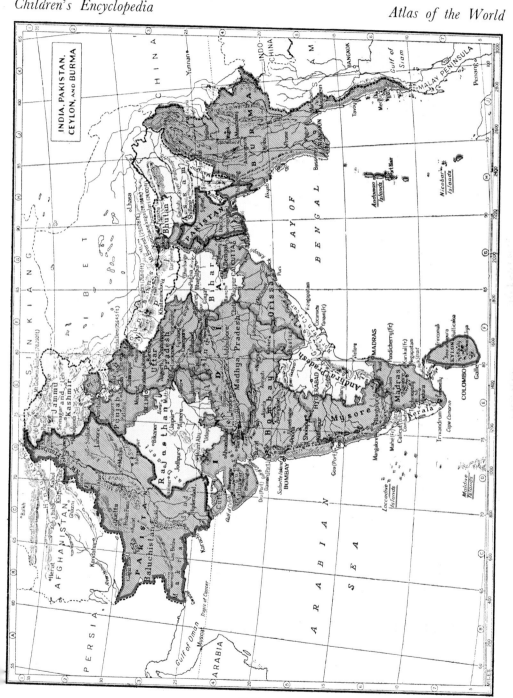

INDIA, PAKISTAN,
CEYLON, AND BURMA

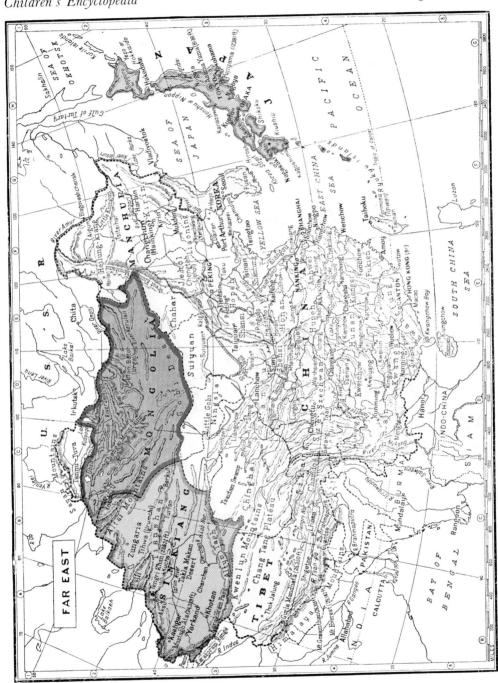

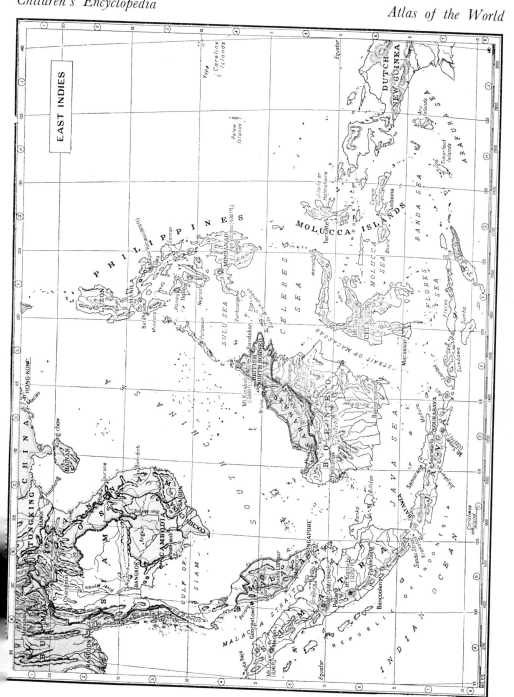

EAST INDIES

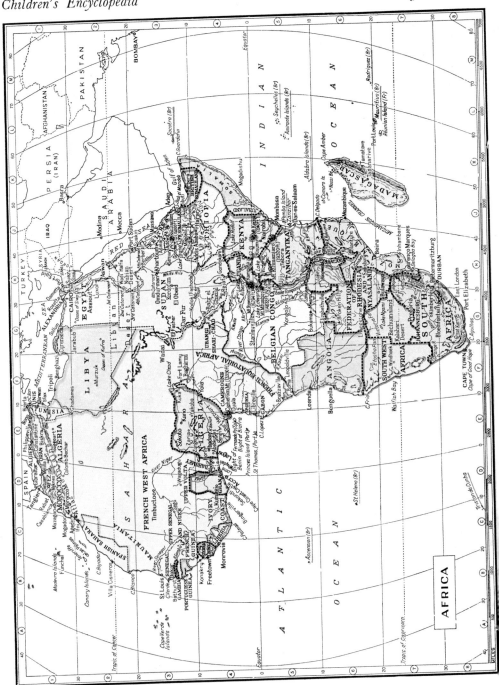

AFRICA

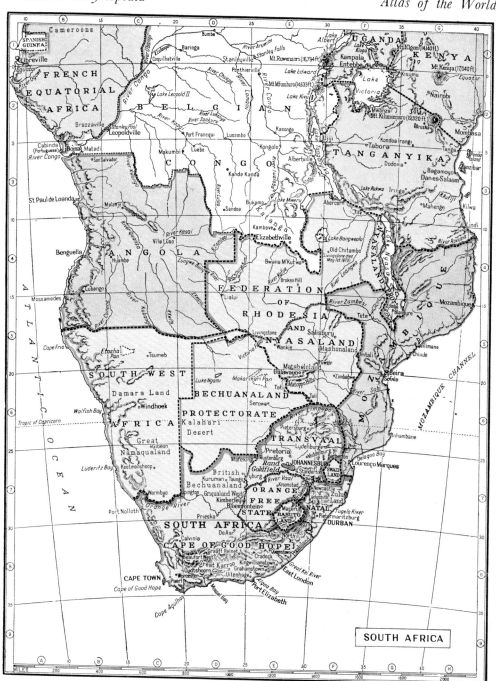

SOUTH AFRICA

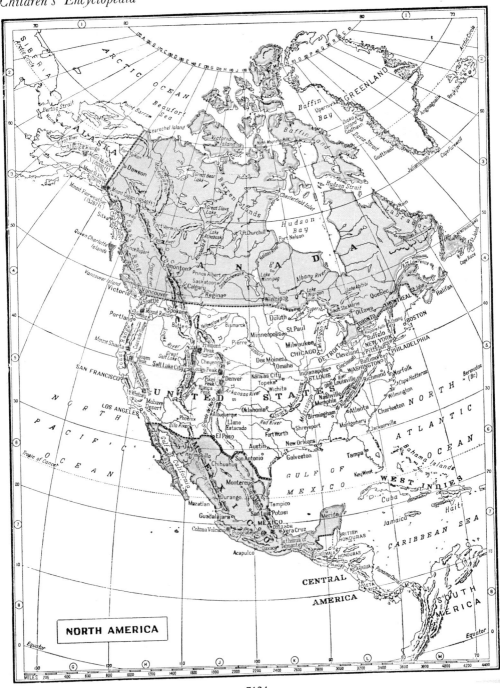

NORTH AMERICA

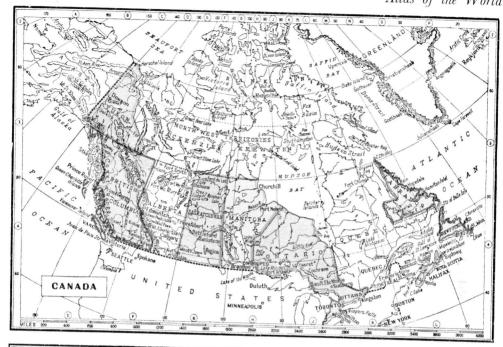

CANADA

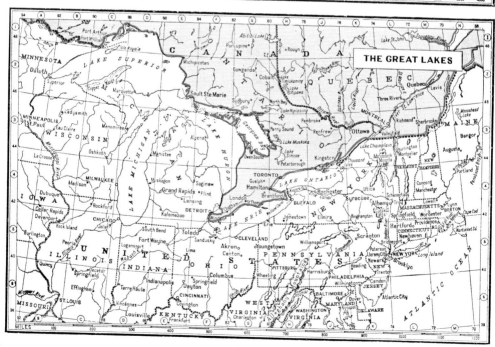

THE GREAT LAKES

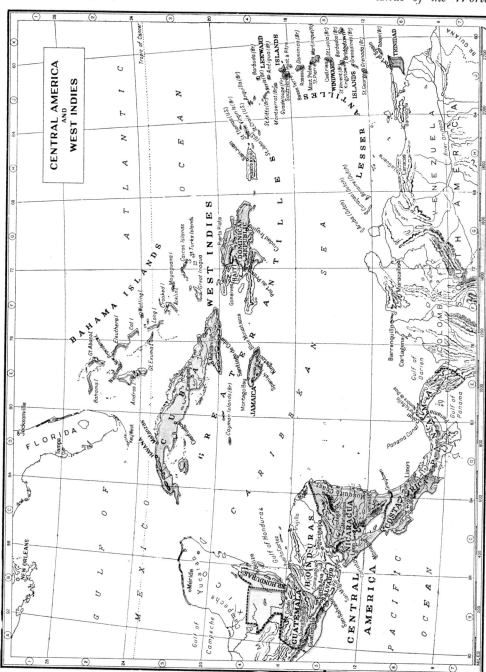

CENTRAL AMERICA
AND
WEST INDIES

SOUTH AMERICA

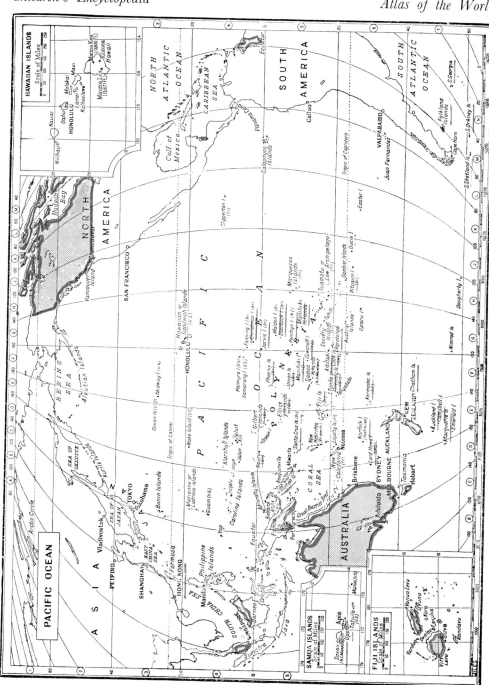

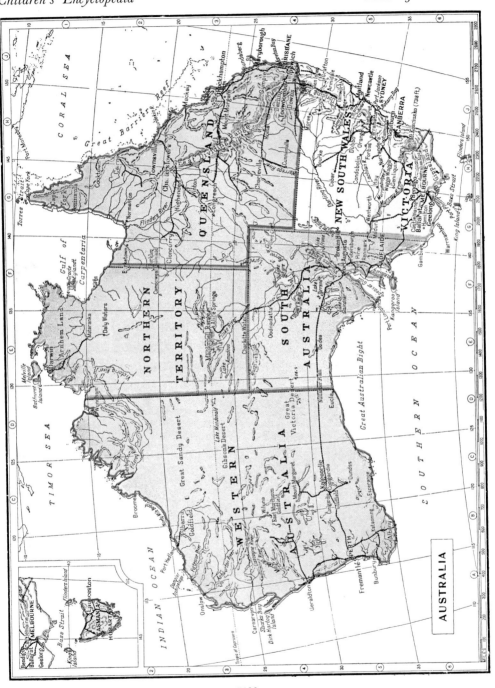

AUSTRALIA

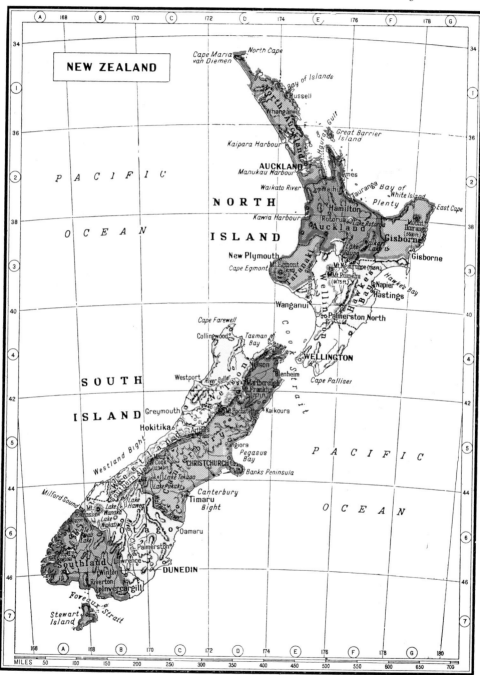

NEW ZEALAND

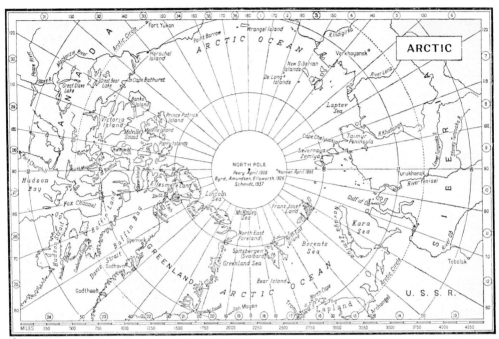

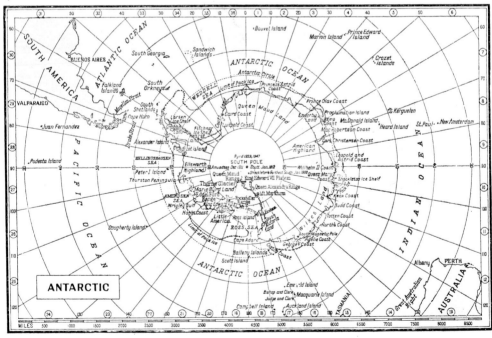

INDEX OF
THIS WORK

GROUPS OF PICTURES IN THIS BOOK
in Colour, Photogravure, and Black and White

SHAKESPEARE AND SOME OF HIS IMMORTAL CHARACTERS

INDEX OF POEMS AND RHYMES

THIS is probably the most complete index of verses for boys and girls appearing in any book. A poem is entered three times, so that it can be found if we know either the title, the first line, or the author's name.

The collection of poetry in the Children's Encyclopedia is made up of separate pieces, and they represent every kind of verse. There are sonnets, songs, odes, dramatic pieces, humorous verses, hymns, and psalms ; nursery rhymes in English and French ; folk-lore songs of Germany ; songs set to music ; nonsense verses ; and selections from Shakespeare and many other poets whose works are too long to quote as a whole.

All the poems of an author are together under his name. They are *indented* under the name ; that is to say, the titles begin a little way on in the line, not straight with the other lines. All poems with these indented lines are by the author whose name is above them.

To find a poem, look under the first line, the title, or the author's name. No notice is taken of *A* or *The*, so that if you are looking for *The Spider and the Fly* you should look up *Spider*.

THE BOOK, BY HENRI MORISSET

INDEX TO THE CHILDREN'S ENCYCLOPEDIA

THIS Index will guide you to whatever you want in this book. If you want something about the Sun, turn to S and find the word Sun. Many subjects are indexed many times. It is best to look under any heading you can think of until you find it.

The order of the Index is strictly alphabetical, every phrase, or title of a book or story, counting as one word. The key-word or phrase comes first in black type, the main article on the subject follows immediately, and then come references scattered throughout the work. All pages referring to reading matter are in **Black type**. Pictures and maps come next with the page figures in light type, and at the end of the group is an indication where to look for extra information.

A phrase is indexed under its first word : Act of God is under Act.

Saints are under their names, but a town like St. John's is under St. John's.

In indexing titles such words as **The** and **A** are omitted ; The Comedy of Errors is under C. The words **Common** and **Wild** are also ignored.

Think of what you want and look under the most important word. If you want a man look under his name. If you want a country look under its name. If you want a story and do not remember the title look under Stories. For Poetry see Poetry Index on page 7141

evolution of animals, **79**
fossils, map, 222
in Heraldry, in colour, 927
migration map, 220
prehistoric animals, clock diagram, 10
procession of prehistoric life, 39
scientific classification, 2298–99
　　See also Bird, Fish, Insect, Invertebrate, Vertebrate, and the individual names of animals.
Animalcule, 4856
seen through microscope, 1910, 1915
Animal Friends, story, **3252**
Animal shadows, how to make them, with pictures, 126
Aniseed, obtained from anise plant, **2808**
Anisota, caterpillars of American species of moth, in colour, 6209
Anjou, old French province in the valley of the Loire, 835
Ankara, capital of Turkey, **6135**
people and scenes, 6131, 6143–45
Ankle, arch of, how supported, **1695**
bones of described, 1695
Anna Karenina, Tolstoy's novel, **4818**
Annals, of Ennius, **5426**
Annam, former State, now part of Vietnam, **6512**
Annas, priest who tried Jesus, **4588**
Anne, queen of England, **6470**
Nassau arms dropped by, 4984
Union of England and Scotland, **1214**
Anne, of Cleves, fourth wife of Henry VIII, **1076**
Anne, empress of Russia, **5895**
Anne, Princess, daughter of Queen Elizabeth II, **1941**, 1941
Annecy, city of French Savoy, chateau on hilltop near, 4055
Annie Laurie, the two versions of the song, **1265**
Annigoni, Pietro, his portrait of Queen Elizabeth II, frontis. Volume I
Anning, Mary, discovered ichthyosaurus fossil, **1508, 1509**
Anno Domini, what it means, **2295**
Anno Hegirae, what it means, **2295**
Anno Mundi, what it means, **2295**
Anno Urbus Conditae, what it means, **2295**
Annual plant, what it is, **3179, 4541**
Annual sea blite, what it is like, **5762**
Annunciation, Rossetti's painting, 2550
sculpture by Donatello, **4725**
Anoa, dwarf buffalo of Celebes, **1156**
Anointing Spoon, in Crown Jewels, used in Coronation ceremony, **7000, 7001**
Anolis, Cuban, reptile, **4493**
Anomala, Frisch's beetle, in colour, **6336**
Anomia shell, 6580
Anopheles mosquito, 1913, 1916
　　See also Malaria and Yellow Fever
Anselm, St., Archbishop of Canterbury, **6937**
Ant, its story, **5959**
formic acid in body, **61, 5967**
number of facets on eyes, **5001**
seeds collected by, **945**
South American acacia protected by, **5964**
termite, known as white ant, **5715**
watching ants at work, **3231**
wisdom of, **5968**

Pictures of Ants

carrying cocoons, 5965
corn-root aphides tended by, **5711**
milking aphis, 5959
nests, 5965
solitary, in colour, **5714**
swarm removing dead queen, 5961
swarm working, 5961
various species, 5959, 5961, 5965, 5967
white ant, or termite, **5721**
wood-ant, in colour, **5714**
Ant and the Grasshopper, fable, **3990**
Antarctica, 2127, 6551, **6859, 6860**
Australian base at Mawson Harbour, 6562
explorers of, 2380, 6549, 6860
first crossing by land, **6860**
International Geophysical Year expedition, **6562, 6860**
Ross Dependency, **2697**
are there flowers in the Antarctic? **5978**
map, in colour, **7132**
penguins of all kinds, 4001
　　See also names of explorers

Antarctic wolf: see Wolf
Antares, star, **3849, 3852**
size compared with Sun, **6998**
Ant-bear: see Aard-vark
Ant-eater, family of, **2273**
great, 2275
lesser, or tamandua, 2275
Antelope, its life-story, **1398**
how fast can it run? **6864**
varieties, 1400, 1401
　　See also Addax
Antelopine kangaroo, 2393
Anthemius, of Tralles, Lydia, Greek architect, **5742**
Anther, what it is, 332
of meadow fox-tail grass, 581
Ant-hill, section, 5965
ant-bears feeding, 2271
Anthony: see Mark Antony
Anthracite coal, 2834
mines in Peru, 7039
vast anthracite field in China, 6502
what it is, **3772**
Anthrax, Pasteur's treatment for, 2624
Antibiotics, what are they? **3890**
Anticline, rock formation which forms oil-trap, 2963
Anti-cyclone, meaning of, in weather chart, **6721**
Anticyra combusta, Indian moth, caterpillar, in colour, 6210
Antigone, Sophocles's drama, 5184
story, **6691**
Antigua, West Indian island, 3554
St. John harbour, 3562
Antimony, Australia's production, 2448
China's great output, **6502**
picture, in colour, 1302
Antinous, friend of Emperor Hadrian to whom statues were erected, 4404
Roman bust, 5130
sculptured head, 4398
Antioch, statue in Vatican which is fine example of late Greek art, **4403**
Antioch, ancient Syrian city, **6297, 6417**
general view, 6297
Antiochus Epiphanes, king of Syria and persecutor of the Jews, **890**
Antipholus, in Shakespeare's play, The Comedy of Errors, **6033**
Antiquary, the novel by Scott, **2722**
painting by Richard Bonington, 2421
Antirrhinum, genus of order Scrophularineae, **6493**
flower, 6383
Antisthenes, cynic sect formed by, **5002**
Anti-toxin, diphtheria and tetanus treated with, 2628
Ant lion, insect, **6458, 6461**
Antofagasta, Chilean port, **7036, 7032**
Antonello of Messina, Sicilian painter, 277, 932
portrait by, 938
portrait of himself, 933
Antonine Column, Rome, its height, 3284
Antoninus Pius, Roman Emperor, portraits of himself and his wife, 2878
Antonio, in Merchant of Venice, **6040**
Shylock refuses his plea, 6041
Antonio, in The Tempest, **6296**
Antonio's Wonderful Lion, story and picture, 5466
Antony, Mark: see Mark Antony
Antrim, county of Northern Ireland, Carron Tower, 2004
Lough-a-veema peaty bed, 2006
old bridge near Antrim Castle, 3070
Ant-thrush, or pitta, 3148
bird, in colour, 3143
Antwerp, Belgium's great port, **5648**
cathedral, finest in Belgium, **5991**
Musée Plantin, **6371**
Quentin Matsys's famous picture, The Descent from the Cross, **1057**
Rubens's life at, **6674**
Rubens's paintings at, **1421, 5652**

Pictures of Antwerp

cathedral, exterior, 5985, 5997
cathedral, nave and choir, 5987
Hotel de Ville, 6367
Hotel de Ville, Salle de Leys, 6365
Plantin Museum, 6361
Rubens's statue, 5649
view across Schelde, 5655

Antwerp pigeon, 4118
Anubis baboon, 161
Anuradhapura, Ceylon, ancient jungle city, **2813**
ancient bo tree, **3052**
ruined temple, 2818
Anvil, why is the end tapered? **6230**
Apathus bee, insect, in colour, **5714**
Apatite, phosphate of lime, 1302
Ape, resemblance to Man, **159**
Barbary, with young one, 162
black, 161; head, 3047
Ape and the Wedge, story, **3495**
Apennine Chain, on Moon, **3486**
Apennines, mountain range running through Italy, **4909**
Aphaia, Temple of, at Aegina, **4028, 5497, 5510**
sculptured figures from, 4029–31
Aphis, or green-fly, insect pest, **5721**
kept by ants for honey dew, **5963**
grape-vine aphis, life-story, **4519**
insect on leaf, 5721
milked by ant, 5959
rose-tree aphis, 5719
woolly aphis, life-story, **5365**
Aphrodite, goddess of ancient Greece and Rome, **3517**
　　See also Venus
Aphrodite of Cnidus, statue by Praxiteles, **4272,** 4271
Aphrodite of Melos: see Venus of Milo
Apo, Mount, volcano in Philippines, 6514
Apocrypha, Hebrew writings, **5677, 6869**
Apoderus, hazel, beetle, in colour, **6336**
Apollo, god of ancient Greece and Rome, **3516**
god of self-restraint followed by Pythagoras, **1040**
how Apollo and Mercury became friends, story, **4964**
Phaethon and Apollo, **6598**
temple stood on Wiltshire plain long after fall of Rome, **2398**

Pictures of Apollo

ancient statues, 4029, 5010, 5130
Apollo and Daphne, painting by Henrietta Rae, 3525
Apollo and Daphne, sculpture by Bernini, 5013
painting by Briton Rivière, 3524
Apollo, Temple of, at Miletus, **5500**
sculptures from frieze, 4146–47
Apollo Belvedere, famous Greek statue, now in the Vatican, **4403,** 4400
Apollo Citharoedus, wonderful statue by Scopas, copy of which is in Vatican, **4277,** 4274
Apollo of Amphipolis, coin, 5391
Apophyllite, silicate of aluminium, 1303
Apostles, life stories, **6732**
belief in Christ's return to Earth, **6932**
did any of the Apostles come to Britain? **6103,** 2400
　　See also under separate names; Disciples; Bible, and so on
Apothecary's Measure, liquid, **7093**
Apothecary's Weight, dry, **7093**
Apotheosis of Homer, Ingres's classical painting in the Louvre, 1806
Apoxyomenus, The, famous statue by Lysippus, **4278,** 4273
Appalachian Mountains, North America, 3674, 2192
Apparent noon, what it is, **5122**
Apparent time, what it is, **5122**
Apparition, The, Moreau's fine painting, 2930
Appaumée, heraldic charge, 926
Appetite, why it varies, **2184**
Appian Way, catacombs in, 444
what was the Appian Way? **2157, 5488**
reconstruction, 5499
view, 1780
Appius Claudius, made the Appian Way, **5488**
Apple, member of genus Pyrus, **6492**
Australia grows many apples, **2443**
floating ball and lively apple, trick, **3232**
how to cut an apple inside without peeling it, 1622
how to make an apple-picker, with picture, **3597**

ART
The following are the actual headings of the chapters in this group ; the subjects dealt with will be found in their proper places in the index

ART (School Lessons)
The following are actual headings of the chapters in this group ; the subjects dealt with will be found in their proper places in the index.

Canova, Antonio, Italian sculptor of the classical school, classic statue of Napoleon, 4647
how he modelled a lion from butter, 5466, 5467
athlete, in the Vatican, 1615, 4651
Cupid and Psyche, 4650
Cantabrian Mountains, northern Spain, 5270
Canterbury, Ecclesiastical capital of England, on the Kentish Stour; St. Augustine visits, 588
arms of the city, in colour, 4990
St. Martin's Church, 1590
St. Thomas's Hospital, 1590
West Gate, 1594
Canterbury bell, flower, 5268
sore-throat remedy made from, 1438
flower, 6379
wild: see Nettle-leaved bellflower
Canterbury Cathedral, Black Prince's tomb, 954
murder of Thomas á Becket, 720
Norman work, 5866, 5874
rebuilding about 1170, by architect of Sens Cathedral, 5871
shrine of Thomas á Becket, 364

Pictures of the Cathedral
aerial view, 1822
archbishop's arms, in colour, 4987
crypt, 5867
massive columns, 719
Norman staircase, 719
St. Augustine's chair, 725, 4860
south porch and west door, 5867
view from south-west, 5875
Canterbury Pilgrims, procession, 368
Canterbury Tales, The, Chaucer's great poem, 363, 5801
Cantharides, blister beetles that eat locusts' eggs: Drake's joke in despatch to Queen Elizabeth I, 6451
Cantilever bridge, first built over the Forth River, Scotland, 548
Canton, John, English electrical pioneer, 5327; portrait, 5323
Canton, William: see Poetry Index
Canton, metropolis of southern China, on Canton river, 6501, 6502, 6509
family on houseboat, 6506
general view, 6506
Great Pagoda, 6505
Honam Pagoda, 5082
Pearl river, 6505
street of boats, 6505
Canute, first Danish Christian king and ruler of Norway and England, 3028, 5146
England wisely ruled, 596
rebuking his courtiers, 3027
Canvas-back duck, bird, in colour, 3261
Caoutchouc, obtained from banyan tree, 3051
plant, in colour, 2685
See also Rubber
Cape Breton Island, Canada, 2194
Cape crowned crane, bird, 3873
Cape girdle-tailed lizard, 4492
Cape hunting dog, 536
Capella, star, 3849
Cape of Good Hope, province of South Africa, 3187
Diaz discovers, 772, 777
arms, in colour, 4985
Caper, plant, what it is like, 2808
in colour, 2686
Capercaillie: see Blackcock
Capernaum, synagogue ruins, 3465
view from north, 3465
Caper spurge, wild fruit, in colour, 3667
Cape St. Vincent, battle of, Nelson wins rank of rear-admiral, 1453
Capet, Hugh, first French king of France, 3918
Cape Town, South Africa, 3187
what is the table-cloth at Cape Town? 5371
British forces' entry, 2081
cottage where Rhodes died, 3195
scene, 3190
Cape Verde Islands, group of Portuguese West African islands, lying off Cape Verde, 5402, 6752

Capillary, derivation of word, 1195
discovery, 1195, 5570
gases pass into blood by means of, 1199
red and white blood cells in the capillaries, 941, 1059
Capital (finance), building up of, 5140
demand and supply affect, 5640
what it is, and its importance, 5139
Capitalist, men who are workers and landlords, too, 5637
rewards of, 5639
who he is, 5140, 5637
Capitol, Washington, U.S.A., Sequoya's statue in Hall of Fame, 5459
Capitulum, in botany, 6495
Cap of Liberty, what is it? 6104
Capped langur monkey, with young, 162
Capping verses, game, 255
Capri, island at the entrance to the Bay of Naples. 4916
Caprifig tree, used in fertilisation of Smyrna figs, 1940
fruit, 1937
Capsicum, cayenne pepper and chillies obtained from, 2804
member of same family as tobacco plant, 2804, 2942
Chinese giant capsicum, 2802
Capsule, fruit, 834, 6495
Captain of Industry, what it means, 5638
Capuchin monkey, 164
Capulet, in Romeo and Juliet, 6159
who were the Capulets? 4387
Capybara, animal, largest rodent, lives in South America, 1036, 1033
Carabus beetle, distribution, 6330
Caracal, member of cat tribe, 419, 424
Caracalla, Roman Emperor, 2881, 2879
Baths of Caracalla, ruins and reconstruction, 1780, 1787
Caracara, South American hawk, habits and food, 3632, 3633
Carácas, capital of Venezuela, 7040
birthplace of Bolivar, 898
house at, 7031
Caractacus, ancient British hero, 2400
captured by the Romans, 590
brought before Roman Emperor, 2397
faces the Romans, 587
portrait, 1667
Caravaggio, Michelangelo da, Italian realist painter, 936
Courbet influenced by, 2923
influence on the Le Nain brothers, 1682
Lastman, Rembrandt's master, influenced by, 1588
Spanish artist Ribera greatly influenced by, 1308
his painting, Lute Player, 3535
Caravan, ancient Egyptians' trade carried on by, 427
Caraway, plant, 2436, 2808
Carbohydrate, digestion of, 2063
what carbohydrates contain, 2183
Carbolic acid, Lister's use of to sterilise wounds in surgery, 2624
Carbon, calcium and magnesium united by acid, 4470
compounds, classified by Dumas, 6313
compounds of, 4348
diamonds made from, 1228
essential to life, 830, 4347
in electric arc, 1097
percentage in coal, 2834
plants feed on through greenstuff in leaves, 202
Carbonate of soda, seaweed used in manufacture of, 3410
Carbon dioxide, action in rainwater, 642
air which contains too much will kill us, 1322
Cave of Dogs has layer on floor, 1323
choke damp of the miner, 2837, 3332
element of atmosphere, 203
how to make it, 6424
living creatures breathe out, 200, 460
making of in human body, and how it is got rid of, 1026, 1063
nature and formation, 3332
on Moon, 3484
plants feed on carbon and reject oxygen, 202

sodium carbonate carries it from the tissues to the lungs, 1063
solidification possible, 5319
what it is composed of, 200
when the body gives off most, 1322
yeast plant turns sugar into carbon dioxide, 699
Carbon filament, in electric lamp, 1098
Carbonic acid, gas, dry ice dropped on clouds to produce rain, 3395
true, 4348
Carboniferous Age, what the Earth was like, 1257
duration, 10
animal life of the period, 10, 1259
fish, 1257
fossil remains, 1259
limestone gorge in Ireland, 5732
vegetation, 1259
map of British Isles, 1258
Carbonisation of coal, 3335
Carbon monoxide, coal gas, 3336
composition, 4346
effect on colour in fire, 4395
Carbuncle, form of garnet, 1301
Carburetter, of petrol engine, how it works, 4322
position on motor-car engine, 4320
position on motor-cycle, 4326
Carcassonne, ancient city of Languedoc, France, 4171, 6358
cathedral architecture, 5990
old cathedral, 6001
Carceres, Spain, dam, 5280
Carchemish, southern capital of Hittite Empire, 6886
identification, 6886
Hittite god at, 6886
Cards, greetings, how to make, 123
puzzling cards, which is larger? 627
robbers and the soldiers, trick, with picture, 5068
various tricks, 999, 2484
games with cards: See Games
Cardiff, capital of Wales, arms, in colour, 4990
City Hall, 4409
Queen Alexandra Dock, 1461
Cardinal beetle, in colour, 6336
Cardinal bird, habits, 2901
in colour, 3143
red-crested, 2893
Cardinal honeysucker, in colour, 3262
Carding, process in cotton making, 175
Cardus, Neville, English writer on cricket, 3830
Carew, Lady Elizabeth: see Poetry Index
Carew, Thomas: see Poetry Index
Carey, Henry, English writer of songs, 1265
inspiration of Sally in our Alley, 1263
See also Poetry Index
Carey, William, missionary, 1137
mending boots, 1139
portrait, 1137
Cargo of Wheat, story, 285
Caribou, migration, 1404, 220
picture, 1398
Carillon, how is it worked? 6231
pictures, 2782–83
Carisbrooke, village in the Isle of Wight, picture, 963
Carlès, Antonin, statue of boy of Gaul, 5133
Carline thistle, member of Composite family, 5022, 6493
flower, 5761
Carlisle, capital of Cumberland, arms, in colour, 4990
street scene, 1834
Carlyle, Thomas, Scottish essayist and historian, 3215
genius defined by, 2602
his words on the Marseillaise, 1261
Life of Oliver Cromwell, 524
on charity, 4337
on Sir Walter Scott, 2720
Ruskin compared with, 3220
Whistler's portrait of, 2930
portrait, with mother, 4135
reading in his room, 3215
receiving his burnt manuscript, 3217
See also Poetry Index

BADGES AWARDED TO BOY SCOUTS

1. AIR SPOTTER. 2. SMALLHOLDER. 3. COOK. 4. STARMAN. 5. AIR APPRENTICE. 6. CAMPER. 7. STALKER.
8. AMBULANCE. 9. ATHLETE. 10. OBSERVER. 11. GUIDE. 12. COXSWAIN. 13. JOBMAN. 14. LIFE-SAVER.
15. FIREFIGHTER. 16. ANGLER. 17. CRAFTSMAN, COLLECTIVE BADGE. 18. SWIMMER. 19. PUBLIC HEALTH.
20 LEADING SIGNALLER. 21. AIR SCOUT BERET BADGE. 22. MARINER, COLLECTIVE BADGE. 23. OPEN
AIR, COLLECTIVE BADGE. 24. ROYAL A.R FORCE RECOGNITION. 25. AIRMAN'S BADGE. 26. SEAMAN'S BADGE
27. ADMIRALTY RECOGNITION.

BADGES AND INSIGNIA OF THE BOY SCOUTS

1. SWIMMER. 2. LEAPING WOLF. 3. ATHLETE. 4. OBSERVER. 5. COLLECTOR. 6. HOMECRAFT 7. TOY-MAKER. 8. ARTIST. 9. HOUSE ORDERLY. 10. GUIDE. 11. CYCLIST. 12. SERVICE STAR (ROVER). 13. TEAM PLAYER. 14. WOLF CUB, TENDERPAD. 15. SCOUT, TENDERFOOT. 16. SCOUT, FIRST CLASS. 17. SCOUT, SECOND CLASS 18. SCOUT, ALL-ROUND CORDS. 19. QUEEN'S SCOUT. 20. BUSHMAN'S THONG.

BADGES OF BROWNIES AND GIRL GUIDES

1. GNOME SIX. 2. FAIRY SIX. 3. BROWNIE, SECOND CLASS. 4. KELPIE SIX. 5. LEPRECHAUN SIX. 6. BROWNIE, JESTER. 7. BROWNIE, FIRST CLASS. 8. BROWNIE, NEEDLEWORKER. 9. BROWNIE, GARDENER. 10. BROWNIE, KNITTER. 11. WORLD BADGE. 12. BROWNIE ENROLMENT. 13. GUIDE, TENDERFOOT. 14. CADETS. 15. RANGER SERVICE STAR. 16. SEA RANGERS. 17. BLUETIT PATROL. 18. GUIDE, SECOND CLASS. 19. GUIDE, LIFE SAVER. 20. ROSE PATROL. 21. KINGFISHER PATROL. 22. PRIMROSE PATROL 23. IRIS PATROL. 24. ROBIN PATROL. 25. CADETS, SHOULDER FLASH

BADGES OF GIRL GUIDES AND RANGERS

1. EMERGENCY HELPER. 2. MUSIC LOVER. 3. FIRST CLASS. 4. GARDENER. 5. MAP READER. 6. DANCER.
7. WELSH FOLK. 8 SPINNER. 9. COUNTRY DANCER. 10. RESCUER. 11. STALKER. 12. QUEEN'S GUIDE.
13. RABBIT KEEPER. 13a. THRIFT. 14. FIRST AID. 15. LAND RANGERS SHOULDER FLASH. 16. SICK NURSE.
17. AIR RANGERS SHOULDER FLASH. 18. WOODCRAFT EMBLEM. 19. SEA RANGERS SHOULDER FLASH
20. ROYAL AIR FORCE RECOGNITION 21. LITTLE HOUSE EMBLEM. 22. ADMIRALTY RECOGNITION.

draughts, **6542**
drawing a pig, **1746**
driving a blindfold team, **3350**
egg cap, **3596**
fan race, **508**
filling the gap, **3724**
fives, **5564**
flags, **3724**
flower-pot race, **3107**
football, **4949**
forfeits and how to pay them, **380**
fox and hounds, **2611**
foxes and bases, **3476**
games to play on the beach, **2729**
game with the atlas, **1120**
garden fives, **3596**
general post, **2118**
gold rush, **1000**
golf, **3843**
guard the block, **6423**
hide and seek in the open country, **3474**
hide and seek on the hearthrug, **1372**
hockey, **4709**
hold fast! let go! **4468**
house paper-chase, **2118**
how, when, and where? **1372**
hunt the ring, **4468**
hunt the slipper, **4468**
I love my love, **1372**
initials, **255**
I spy, **3724**
jingling, **1746**
jolly miller, **3476**
lacrosse, **4218**
lawn tennis, **3103**
leap-frog, **6671**
likes and dislikes, **381**
making palindromes, **870**
making up the donkey, **3472**
marbles, **5562**
musical chairs with a difference, **504**
nature study game, **6544**
netball, **5931**
nine-holes, **3596**
noughts and crosses, **255**
observation game, **2118**
obstacle race, **3108**
old maid, **5687**
outdoor games, **3108**, **3724**
outlines, **255**
passing the plate, **508**
pick-a-back table tennis, **1622**
pictured proverbs, **3848**
post-ball, **2859**
posture, **3596**
proverbs, **3848**
puss in the corner, **4468**
putting on the donkey's tail, **1746**
quoits, **3844**
rackets, with pictures, **5315**
relay race, **508**
rhymes, **1372**
rounders, **6944**
round tag, **3724**
Russian gossip, **1372**
shadow theatre, **869**
Simon says, **1372**
snap, **5687**
snip-snap-snorum, **5687**
Spade the gardener, **5687**
spelling bee, **1372**
spoons, **1746**
spotting the stranger, **2116**
squash, with pictures, **5315**
squeak piggy, **1746**
stick and ring, **3108**
stickerchief, **1863**
table tennis, with picture, **5069**
team race, **3596**
telegrams, **2118**
think of a number, **874**
tit tat toe, **4468**
touch, **3724**
trap ball, **3596**
trying to get to the door, **6302**
up to London, **255**
warning, **3724**
what animals are these? **5934**
what-are-these-things? **6058**
what-is-it? **2116**
where-is-it? **1626**
who-are-these-people? **4216**
why-is-it? **3232**
wolf, **4468**
word game with skittles, **875**
zoo-guess, **755**

Gamopetalae, or Sympetalae, sub-class of plants, **6491**
Gandhi, Mahatma, leader of India Independence movement, **2948**
Gandon, James, architect of the Four Courts, Dublin, **6471**
Ganges, Indian river, **2810**, **2496**
Hardinge Bridge, **555**
state barges, **2499**
Gannet, food, home, and habits, **3750**
alighting on nest, **3748**
pictures, **3022**, **3749**
Gansfleisch, Gutenberg's father, **1512**
Ganymede, cupbearer of gods, **3517**
Gapelet anemone, in colour, **1554**
Garborg, Arne, Norwegian novelist, **4940**
Garcia, message conveyed to him during Spanish-American war, **6965**
Garden, flowers, **6257**
building a rock garden, with pictures, **5311**
how did the father divide his garden? puzzle and pictures, **2859**
how to make a herb garden on a windowsill, **1496**
how to make a submarine garden, with pictures, **2982**
making a garden pool, with pictures, **5683**
pictures of flowers, **6257-59**, **6377-84**
Garden fives, game, **3596**
Garden furniture, how to clean wicker, **256**
Garden of Gethsemane, picture, **3470**
Garden of the Hesperides, what was it? **5246**
Garden saw-fly, in colour, **5714**
Garden snail, picture, **6577**
Garden spider, wonderful web, **5595**
picture, **5593**
spider's web, **5597**
Garden warbler, bird, in colour, **2766**
in nest, **3139**
Gardiner, Allen, English missionary, **1139**, **1141**
Gardiner, Bishop, portrait, **1053**
Gardiner, Samuel Rawson, English historian, **3095**, **3093**
Gareth, Sir, story, **6952**, **6954**
Garfish, in colour, **5100**
Garganey, bird, in colour, **3024**
Gargantua, Rabelais's hero, **4454**, **5490**
Garhaddin Ashurnasirpal II, palace of, discovered by Layard, **6884**
Garibaldi, Giuseppe, Italian soldier and patriot, **896**, **4785**, **4787**, **4795**
looks out from his island home, **892**
meets Victor Emmanuel II, **4787**
portrait, **889**
statue in Rome, **897**
Garlic, broad-leaved, **4780**
Garnet, mineral, **1301**
Garonne, French river, **4169**
Garrick, David, English actor and writer of songs, **1264**; portrait, **1261**
Garrison, William Lloyd, American anti-slavery leader, **3245**, **4203**, **3239**
calling on Wilberforce, **3238**
See also Poetry Index
Garstang, Professor John, discoveries at Jericho, **7006**
Garstin, Norman, British painter, **2546**
Garter snake, American species, **4619**
Gartok, roof of Tibet, **6512**
Gary, Blasco de, Spanish inventor, **3733**
Gas, what gases are and what they can do, **3331**
atomic numbers of gases, **4954**
become liquid when cooled, **140**
Boyle's law, **5201**
gases of the blood, **1062**
Faraday and their liquefaction, **5332**
how a gas meter works, picture-story, **4127-28**
illuminating gas from meteoric stone, **3608**
inert gases, **4345**
in heavenly bodies, **12**, **3850**
in nebulae, **3974**
known as fluid by science, **5197**
law of loss of volume at low temperatures, **5319**

nature of gases, **4100**
rare gases, **4347**
if the gases in water make fire, why does water quench it? **4130**
why do we sometimes say gas and sometimes vapour? **5736**
for Coal gas see Gas, coal
See also Acetylene gas; Oxygen; Water gas; and so on
Gas, coal, its manufacture, **3334**, **3447**
first lighting of a house, **2748**, **3332**
why is the centre of a gas-flame blue and the outside yellow? **6466**
its manufacture, picture series, **3447-53**
Gas-engine, invention led to motor-car, **4319**
See also Gas-turbine engine and Internal Combustion engine
Gas-holder, how it works, part sectioned, **3453**
when nearly full, **3447**
Gaskell, Mrs., English novelist, **3584**, **3579**
Gas meter, how it works, pictures described, **4127-28**
Gaspar, journey to Bethlehem, **3590**
Gaston de Foix, statue, **4900**
Gastropods, single-shelled molluscs, **6583**
Gas-turbine engine, speed of modern engine compared with that of Wright Brothers' engine, **6346**
sectional drawing of aeroplane engine, **4694**
Gas-turbine locomotives, on Western Region, **3950**
Gas works, on the River Thames at Beckton, picture series, **3447-50**
Gatekeeper butterfly, egg, caterpillar, and chrysalis, in colour, **6208**
Gattamelata, Donatello's magnificent equestrian monument, **4523**, **4531**
Gaudier-Brzeska, Henri, French sculptor, **4896**
Gauge, railway, **3944**
Gauguin, Paul, French painter, **3046**
Gaul, conquered by Caesar, **3917**
Caesar receiving surrender of defeated chieftain, **2875**
Gauls, route into Greece, **5156**
Gaur, Indian cattle, **1155**, **1158**
Gauss, definition: see Units of Measurement. **7096**
Gautama, became the Buddha, **5077**
See also Buddha
Gautier, Théophile, French novelist, **4457**
story of cat and parrot, **779**, **3746**
Gavr'inis, Island of, blocks set up by Bronze Age men, **315**
Gawain, Sir, fights Green Knight, **2885**
killed in rebellion, **6954**
story of his marriage, **6827**
Gawsworth, Cheshire, Tudor Hall, **1088**
Gay, John, portrait by Kneller, **1927**
See also Poetry Index
Gayal, animal of India, **1155**, **1158**
Gay callithamnion, seaweed, **3415**
Gay-Lussac, Joseph Louis, French chemist, **5319**, **6312**, **6309**
Gaza, ancient city of Palestine, excavated by Sir W. F. Petrie, **7006**
Samson's feat of strength, **1488**
picture, **3470**
Gazelle, species and habits, **1400**
Cuvier's gazelle, **1401**
Gazette, origin of name as applied to newspapers, **5487**
Gdansk, Poland, formerly Free Territory of Danzig, **5029**, **5035**
St. Mary's Church, **5035**
Gdynia, port of Poland, scenes, **5034**, **5038**
Gean, or Wild cherry: see Cherry
Gear, in mechanics, **6350-52**
Gear-box, how it works, **4324**
assembled in motor factory, **3762**
on motor-car, how it works, diagram, **4321**
position on motor cycle, **4326**
Gear train, in mechanics, **6350**
Gebel Awlia, dam and reservoir on Nile, **6887**
Gecko, distribution and characteristics of 300 species, **4495**
pictures, **4492-93**
Gedding, Suffolk, moated Hall, **1087**

EGGS OF WELL-KNOWN BRITISH BIRDS

1. STARLING. 2. CHAFFINCH. 3. RAVEN. 4. ROBIN. 5. SONG THRUSH. 6. GOLD CREST. 7. NUTHATCH.
8. HOUSE MARTIN. 9. GREAT TIT. 10. SKYLARK. 11. RED-BACKED SHRIKE. 12. MOORHEN. 13. NIGHTJAR.
14. RED GROUSE. 15. BLACKBIRD. 16. JAY. 17. LAPWING. 18. COMMON TERN. 19. KENTISH PLOVER.
20. HAWFINCH. 21. RAZORBILL. 22. YELLOWHAMMER. 23. MISSEL THRUSH.

1. KESTREL.   2. COMMON GUILLEMOT.   3. SPARROWHAWK.   4. BULLFINCH.   5. CUCKOO.   6. HOUSE SPARROW. 7. HEDGE SPARROW. 8. JACKDAW. 9. REED WARBLER. 10. BLACKCAP. 11. BLUE TIT. 12. TREE CREEPER. 13. ROOK. 14. COOT. 15. HERRING GULL. 16. COMMON PARTRIDGE. 17. COMMON CURLEW.

Ice Age: see Glacial Age
Iceberg, depth in water seven times its height above it, **2538**
why does an iceberg float ? **2541**
in North Atlantic, located by International Ice Patrol, 2619
three great icebergs, 2538
Iceland, large North Atlantic island Republic, **5149**
language and literature, **4937**
volcanic eruptions, 518
flags, in colour, 6989
milkmaid, 5168
map, in colour, 7124
map of animal life of the country, 5166
map of industries, physical features, and plant life, 5167
Iceland moss, plant, member of Lichen family, **702**
Iceni, ancient British tribe, **899**
Ices, how to make them without a freezer, **2608**
Ice-sailing, what it is, **3278**
Ichneumon: see Mongoose
Ichneumon fly, or wasp, destroys many insects, 38, 5722, **5842**
life-story, **6453**
picture of, 5843
specimens, in colour, 5714
Ichthyornis, prehistoric bird, characteristics, **2638**
Ichthyosaurus, prehistoric reptile, 644, **1383, 1508**
discovered at Lyme Regis, 1509
fossil remains, 1383
how it became a fossil, 644, 645
Icicle, stalactite, compared with, **6857**
icicles on fountain, 4502
Ictinike the Boaster, story, **4974**
Ictinus, Greek architect of the fifth century B.C., chief designer of the Parthenon at Athens, **4144**
Idaho, American north-western State, logs on St. Maries River, 5358
State flag, in colour, 6987

IDEAS

The following are actual headings of the chapters in this group ; the subjects dealt with will be found in their proper places in the index

Movement, 113
Justice, 243
Courage, 371
Truth, 493
Direction, 617
Distance, 743
Space, 861
Number, 985
Faith, 1109
Eternity, 1235
Vision, 1359
Beauty, 1483
Energy, 1613
Virtue, 1733
Prudence, 1853
Providence, 1981
Hope, 2105
Nature, 2225
Duty, 2351
Peace, 2477
Patience, 2601
Authority, 2723
Success, 2851
Knowledge, 2973
Prayer, 3097
Gratitude, 3221
Patriotism, 3341
Optimism, 3459
Instinct, 3585
Imagination, 3715
Liberalism, 3833
Inspiration, 3957
Immortality, 4085
Liberty, 4207
Charity, 4337

Ides, what they were, **4761**
Idmon, father of Arachne, **6982**
Idocrase, or Vesuvianite, mineral, 1304
Idol and the Whale, story, 410
Idrac, Antonin, his sculpture, Mercury adopts his Wand, 5258
Iduna and the Golden Apples, story and picture, **2887**
Idylls of the King, Tennyson's poem, 368, **3338, 3340**
If no one ever marries me, picture to poem, 479
Igarka, port of Russia, **6024**
Ightham, Kent, example of early English manor house, **6236,** 844
Igloo, what is it ? **5616**
Igneous rocks, what they are, **4639**
Iguana, characteristics, **4495**
various species, 4493
Iguanodon, discovery, 1636
fossil remains, 1635
picture, in colour, facing 1505
I had a little nut-tree, nursery rhyme, picture and music, 969
Ildico, Attila's bride, **2156**
Ilex oak, what it is like, **3785**

Ilfracombe, watering-place in North Devon, view, 1714
Ili, town in Sinkiang, **6511**
Iliad, The, story of Homer's poem, **5303**
Helen on walls of Troy, 5305
Ilion or Ilium, ruins of walls, 7009
See also Troy
Illinois, American State, flag, in colour, 6986
Illness, why are so many people always ill at sea ? **5002**
why are there some illnesses that we cannot get twice ? **4758**
Illumination, the wonderful art that died, when printing was invented, 450, **1051, 1923**
bat and ball game shown on 14th-century manuscript, 1923
David playing the harp, from a Saxon psalter, 1925
fourteenth-century example, 1925
Life of Jesus, in colour, 3961–4
various examples, in colour, 489–92
I love little pussy, nursery rhyme, picture, 356
I love my love, game, **1372**
Il Penseroso, poem by Milton, **1232**
Ilse, German mythical princess, **4422**
Imagination, what it is, **3715**
symbolical picture, 3715
Imitation, part played in life, **4282**
Imitation of Christ, The, book of devotion by Thomas à Kempis, **1389**
Immaculate Conception, The, Murillo's painting at Madrid, 1312
Immortality, greatest of all human ideas, **4085**
Immunisation, what is meant by immunisation? **5492**
Imperial anemone, different kinds, in colour, 1553, 1554
Imperial Chemical Industries, founded by Lord Melchett, **4105**
Imperial Eagle, distribution and characteristics, **3831** ; picture, 3633
Imperial State Crown, worn by Sovereign on State occasions, **7000, 7001**
Impersonal Arms, what it means, **4988**
Imports, what we mean by, **6126**
Impressionism: see French art
Ina, merchant law of, **3382**
Incandescent lamp, Edison invents, **5948**
Incas, American-Indian race of Peru, **1533, 7019**
masonry at Cuzco, 7032
Incense-holder, Florentine, 71
Inch, Loch, Scotland, 1335
Inclined plane, 6349
Income Tax, what it is, **4659**
restrictive effect of high taxes, **5757**
Incorporated Law Society, examination, **4777**
Independent Television Authority, directors of commercial TV, **5109**
broadcasting programmes, 5116
India, Asian republic, 2809
story from ancient times, 2943
Akbar's rule (1542–1605), **4125**
animals that inhabit it, 418, 419, 420
archaeological discoveries, 7013
British rule, **1328, 2076, 2945**
Buddhism, 2032
Calcutta, former capital, 2810
communications, 2947
discovery by Portuguese, 4125
Five-Year Plan after Independence, 2811
Forestry Service, 2947
forests destroyed, 3543, 5350
French influence destroyed, 1328, 2946
languages spoken, 2072
literature, 4206, 5674
part played in two World Wars, **1943,** 2948, 1826
poets, 4206
population, 2041, **6003**
products and exports, 2074
races of ancient origin, 2072, 2282
rainfall, area of heaviest, 2621
religions, 2811, 4091, 5077
self-government, 2948
snakes cause many deaths, **4490**
stories of India: see Stories

Pictures of India

Amritsar, Golden Temple, 2953
Buspa Valley, 2949
carved temple, 76
cement mill worked by oxen, 1153
clouds that bring monsoon, 2743
dancers, 2956
elephants, 2023, 2025
flags, in colour, 6984
Forest Research Institute, Dehra Dun, 2950
girl of western India, 2954
Government buildings, Delhi, 2951, 6614
Gwalior, fort and palace, 2951
Hardinge Bridge, over the Ganges, 555
Hyderabad, street scene, 2950
irrigation methods, 5236–37
Jama Masjid Mosque, Ahmedabad, 2279
Kashmir, river boats, 2955
Lakshmi Narain Temple, New Delhi, 2950
Madura, temples, 2815, 2953
modern flats, Bombay, 2950
moth caterpillars, in colour, 6209–10
Mount Abu, Jain temple, 2952–53
museum at Trivandrum, 2950
native types, 2314, 2954
New Delhi, 2949
Patan, street scene, 2951
Pearl Mosque, Delhi, 2279
postman, 4636
snake charmer, 2954
Srinagar, capital of Kashmir, 2951
state barges on Ganges, 2499
Sukkur Dam on the Indus, 5237
Taj Mahal near Agra, 2815, 2955
temples in different cities, 5081–84
tomb of Hathi Singh, 2952
Udaipur, temple, 2955
Umnabad, temple, 2955

Maps of India

in colour, 7119
physical features, 2820–21
showing historical events, 2822–23
See also names of provinces, cities; and Pakistan
India House, Aldwych, London, 6614
Indiana, American State, flag, in colour, 6986
Indian adjutant, bird, 3868
Indian architecture, its rise out of the varied religions of the people, **5624**
architecture of various buildings, 5625, 5633, 5634, 5636
Indian art, embroidery, **6739**
native carving in wood and ivory, **6732**
Indian black-naped flycatcher, bird, in colour, 3264
Indian brush-tail porcupine, 1032
Indian corn: see Maize
Indian fairy blue bird, in colour, 3262
Indian fig tree: see Banyan tree and Prickly pear
Indian game fowl, bird, 4253
Indian kite, bird, 3627
Indian lantern-fly, 5719
Indian Mutiny, 1858, 2947
defence of Lucknow, poem by Tennyson, with picture, 4797
Indian nightingale, 3017
Indian Ocean, depths, 2413
Indian Python, 4619
Indian rhinoceros, 1771, 1775
India rubber, origin of name, **1165**
tree related to fig, 1936
tree growing in Ceylon, 2565
See also Rubber
Indian runner duck, bird, 3752
Indians, South American tribes, and their habits, **7017, 7019**
what is the Red Indian's pipe of peace ? **5373**
Indian telegraph plant, 586
Indian wolf, 541
Indicated horse power, what it is, **1922**
Indigo, plant, dye from, **2939**
Indigo bunting, plumage, **3904**
Indirect taxes, how levied, **4659–60**

FRUITS FROM MANY COUNTRIES

1. DAMSON.   2. TOMATO.   3. BLACKBERRY.   4. DATE.   5. FIG.   6. MANGOSTEEN.   7. PINEAPPLE.   8. POME-
GRANATE.   9. CORINTH GRAPE (FROM WHICH DRIED CURRANTS ARE MADE).   10. QUINCE.   11. MULBERRY.

1. ALMOND.   2. GUAVA.   3. WALNUT.   4. STRAWBERRY.   5. CHERRY.   6. GREENGAGE.   7. BANANA
8. GOMUTI.   9. PEACH.   10. CRANBERRY.   11. GRANADILLA.   12. DURIAN.   13. MAMMEE.

All the most luscious fruits of the world are found growing somewhere in the British Commonwealth, and the best of them
are shown in colour in these pages.   Many are familiar because they grow or are imported into England ; some of the
others shown here are not so well known.   The mangosteen grows in the tropical East Indies. the guava in the West

1. BLACK CURRANT. 2. PLUM. 3. BARBERRY. 4. APPLE. 5. HUCKLEBERRY. 6. TAMARIND. 7. PEAR. 8. JACK FRUIT. 9. GRAPES. 10. GRAPEFRUIT. 11. ORANGE. 12. MELON. 13. GOOSEBERRY.

Indies, the gomuti in Malaya, the granadilla in the West Indies, the durian in the East Indies, the mammee in the West Indies. The huckleberry is found growing in Canada, the jack fruit in the East Indies, the akee in tropical Africa and the West Indies, the pandanus in Malaya, and the papaw in the West Indies.

1. RED CURRANTS.   2. WHITE CURRANTS.   3. AKEE.   4. RASPBERRY.   5. MANGO.   6. BILBERRY OR WHORTLE-
BERRY.   7. PANDANUS OR PASSION FRUIT.   8. APRICOT.   9. OLIVE.   10. BREAD FRUIT.   11. LEMON.   12. PAPAW.
13. THE RAISIN GRAPE.   14. COCONUT.

Straw, lifting bottle with, **2117**
why we can drink through, **5200**
why did the Egyptians use straw for their bricks? **3649**
why is it sometimes hung under bridges? **4894**
Strawberry, fruit in the seed, **1813**
structure of, **834**
wild strawberry, **4284, 4780**
fruit, 1817, 3668; in colour, **7268**
wild, flower, **4290, 4906**
Strawboard, book covers made of, **3389**
Streaked gurnard, fish, in colour, **5099**
Streak-winged lightning beetle, **6336**
Stream, flowers of the, **6007, 6129**
why does the stream run faster in the middle? **2662**
flowers, 6007, 6009, in colour, **6129–30**
Streamlined Engines, of Britain's railways, in colour, **1041–43**
Streatfeild, Noel, English novelist, **3714**
Street: see Road
Street, Arthur George, English writer, **3829**
Street, George Edmund, English architect, **4230, 6609**
Stresemann, Herr, German statesman, **4302**
Stretcher, bricklayer's term, **2414**
Striata, tapering, seaweed, **3414**
Strike, what is it? **5640**
miners' and General strikes, **1826–27**
Strindberg, Swedish balloonist, **6439**
Strindberg, Johan August, Swedish realistic author, **4942**
String, cut string that does not fall, trick, **3847**
notes found on a vibrating string, **6428**
Stringed instruments, what was the first? **5614**
Striped gopher, animal, **1030**
Striped hyena, animal, **422**
Striped snail, shell, **1177**
Stroboscope, what it is, **1470**
Stromboli, island and volcano in the Lipari Islands, Italy, **2248, 4910**
views, 2132, **4922**
Strong, L. A. G., British poet and writer, **3714, 4084**
Strong Man Who Carried the Poor, story, **6822**
Strontianite, mineral, **1304**
Strontium, metallic element, **3889**
Strowger, Almon B., his automatic telephone system, **1971**
Strudwick, J. M., his paintings, The Golden Thread, **3528**
Parable of the Ten Virgins, **1853**
Struther, Jan, British writer, hymns, **1760**
Strychnine, obtained from nux vomica seeds, **2690**
Stuart, Frances, duchess of Richmond. original of Britannia on penny, **6106**
Stuart, Gilbert, American portrait painter, **3286**
Stuart, John McDouall, Scottish explorer in Australia, **6070**
portrait, **6063**
Stuart, Muriel: see Poetry Index
Stuart Age, **4005**
times that saw a great expansion in trade and shipping, **1205**
coal begins to be used in houses and for smelting iron, **1214**
Stubbs, George, English painter of horses, **2545**
Stubbs, William, English historian, **3095, 3093**
Studies in Contentment, essays by David Grayson, **2970**
Stuffing-box, on steam engine, **3212**
Sturgeon, fish, size and habits, **4976**
in colour, facing 5197
Sturluson, Snorri, Icelandic historian, **4938**
Stursa, Jan, Czechoslovakian sculptor, **4896**
Sturt, Charles, English explorer in Australia, **6066**
life saved by native, **6065**
Stuttgart, capital of Wurtemberg, Germany, **4427, 6371**
castle, **6369**
Stye Head, Cumberland, wettest place in England, **5864**

Styka, Jan, Polish painter, **3398**
Tolstoy, painting by, **3398**
Styrax, or Benjamin tree, **2938**
Styrol, oil contained in benzoin, **2938**
Styx, river of Hell, **3531, 6950**
Submarine, German losses during Second World War, **1944**
German use during First World War, **1710**
unrestricted warfare, **1709**
Submarine cable: see Telegraph cable
Submarine garden, how to make, with picture, **2982**
Submerged repeaters, used in undersea cables, **1603**
Subway, London's subways, **4375**
Success, what it means, **2851**
Succory: see Chicory
Sucker, how to make a leather sucker, **2238**
Sucré, capital of Bolivia, **7037**
Suction dredger, one at work in Suez Canal, **4875**
Suction pump, how it raises water, 923
Sudan, republic of Africa, description and history, **6756, 3318**
revolts from Egypt, **6892**

Pictures of the Sudan

cotton-picking scene, **2561**
flag, in colour, **6991**
gum arabic trees, **2941**
Khartoum railway station, **3320**
Makwar dam on the Blue Nile, **5242**
Omdurman grain market, **3321**
postman, **4636**
people and scenes, **6767–68**
map, in colour, **7122**
Sudan, French, West African colony, **6749**
air view of Timbuctoo, **6751**
mosque at Djenne, **6763**
Negro boy, **6747**
Sudd, what is the Nile's sudd? **5488**
Sudra, Indian caste, **6866**
Suez Canal, ship canal connecting the Mediterranean and Red Seas, **4868**
opening of, **6741**
Napoleon's plan, **1444**
value to international commerce, **6892**
at Lake Timsah, **4875**
blowing up wrecked vessel, **4875**
dredging operations, **4875**
steamship passing through, **4869**
Suffolk, English eastern county, **212**
Pliocene deposits, **1878**
Suffolk ram, **1281**
Sugar, how we get it; its importance and uses, **2311**
alcohol obtained from, **699**
Barbados' production, **3556**
British Guiana's production, **3558**
chemical production, **2312**
conditions for growth, **2621**
Fiji's production, **3426**
food importance, **2183**
formation in human body, **1932**
formation in plants, **460**
Jamaica's exports, **3554**
production in Mauritius, **3422**
saccharin's chemical difference, **1676**
why it absorbs water, **107**
why is sugar sweet? **1676**

Pictures of Sugar

basket of crushed cane, Barbados, **3557**
cane on Queensland plantation, **2454**
cane plantation in West Indies, **2313**
crushed cane arriving at factory, Barbados, **3559**
limits of cultivation on world map, 95
picture story, **2288–94**
sugar-beet crop at Spalding, Lincolnshire, **2313**
See also plant life maps under names of countries
Suger, Abbé, early architect, **5746**
Suggestion, in hypnotism, **4281**
Suir, river of Munster, Ireland, railway bridge, **3071**
Sukkur Dam, on the River Indus, India, irrigation in Sind, **2947**
picture, **5237**
Suleiman I, called the Magnificent, Turkish sultan, **6133**

Süleymaniye, mosque in Istanbul, **6141**
Sulgrave Manor, Northamptonshire, Washington's ancestral home, **1640**
picture of exterior, 1835
Sulla, Lucius Cornelius, Roman general and dictator, **4354**; portrait, 4351
Sullivan, Sir Arthur, English composer, 150, **1266**, 145
Sullivan, Louis, American architect, **6611**
Sully-Prudhomme, René François, French poet, **4458**
Sulphapyridine, drug (M and B 693), used in fighting pneumonia, **2628**
Sulphate of ammonia, as a fertiliser, **856**
Sulphate of iron, ink made from it by ancient Egyptians, **2034**
Sulphides, use of in lighting, **1299**
Sulphonal, coal-tar product, **4472**
Sulphur, volcanic production of, **2033**
an element, **4222**
in an egg, **5615**
in gas manufacture, **3335**
rubber vulcanised with, **1166, 2033**
picture of mineral, **1302**
Sulphur-coloured trefoil, in colour, **4418**
Sulphur-crested cockatoo, 3499
Sulphuric acid, composition, **4346**
Belgian industry, **5650**
specific gravity, **4954**
Sulphur tyrant, bird, **3137**
Sulphur-wort, what it is like, **6012**
picture of flower, 6009
Sultan tit, in colour, **3142**
Sulu, Borneo State ceded to Britain, **3425**
Sumach, plant, in colour, **2685**
Sumatra, island of Indonesian republic, **5532**
map, in colour, **7121**
Sumatran broad-bill, bird, **3147**
Sumbawa, Mount, Dutch East Indies, eruption (in 1815), **2248**
Sumer, ancient kingdom, **6884**
Sumerians, ancient Mesopotamian people, **6884**
tomb of the Sumerian Queen, **6873**
Summer, why it is hot, **269, 2742**
reason for longer days, **2742**
painting by E. A. Hornel, **6197**
Summer Time Act, explained, **4775**
Sun, story of its power, **3109**
angle at which rays fall on Earth, **2618**
distance from Earth, 9, **2618, 2989**
does not rise and set, **266**
Earth's attraction, **4593**
energy radiated from, **2618, 3601, 5443**
facts about, **7085**
gases of the Sun, examination by spectroscope, **3850**
heat of, 12, **2743, 3852**
how to light a match with the Sun, **2485**
in mythology, **3516**
light's effect on life, 14, **201, 333, 4807**
magnetic storms on it, 362
movements, **1678**
origin and formation, 12, 138, **3977**
other suns, **2996, 3974**
speed in space, **2990, 3728**
telegraphing by: see Heliograph
vertical rays at Equator, **2741**

Wonder Questions

does the Sun move? **1678**
does the Sun put out a fire? **6602**
how can we foretell an eclipse of the Sun? **817**
is the heat of the Sun the same as the heat of a fire? **6345**
is there any water in the Sun? **2664**
is there a whiter light than that of the Sun? **1300**
what causes haloes round the Sun? **3166**
what is a day? **5121**
why does the air not stop its light? **4136**
why does the Moon grow brighter as the Sun sets? **5618**
why is the World light when the Sun is behind the dark clouds? **4392**
will the Sun ever grow cold? **4764**

Pictures of the Sun

Earth's tilt to Sun in summer and winter, **5121**

[Continued on page 7320]

STORIES OF THE WORLD TOLD IN THIS BOOK

THE stories in the Encyclopedia are not chosen haphazard ; they are a careful selection from the stories of all lands. Every story is indexed under its title. Here we give a list of the stories in a form which will be helpful to children and teachers.

Stories closely associated with a country are under the heading of the name of that country. Fables, legends, fairy stories, and stories of saints which today may be said to belong to all the world are classified under the headings of Fables, Legends, and so on. The stories of our own land will be found under the headings Legends, Historical Stories, and Miscellaneous Stories.

STORIES, LEGENDS, AND FABLES FROM

MANY LANDS, AND WHERE TO FIND THEM

Taylor, Ann: see Poetry Index
Taylor, Bayard: see Poetry Index
Taylor, Jane: see Poetry Index
Taylor, Jeffreys: see Poetry Index
Taylor, Jeremy: see Poetry Index
Taylor, Samuel, shorthand system, 6856
Tayra, animal, 792, 790
Tchaikovsky, Piotr Ilyich, Russian
  composer, 150
  portrait, 145
Tea, story told with pictures, 2283
Chinese, 6502
colour caused by fermentation, 2286
cultivation methods, 2314
English tax on tea that caused war
  with America, 1637
production in British Commonwealth
  and Empire, 2074
tannin harmful to digestion, 2023
tax explained, 4660
do tea or coffee keep us awake? 2173
why does tea run through a lump of
  sugar? 2418
why is strong tea bad for us? 1679
gardens in Japan, 6626
pictures of industry, 2283–87
plant, in colour, 2688
preparing land for plants, 2314
Teacup, manufacture, 301–02, 303–06
Teak, description and uses, 3789
Teal, wild duck, 3756
in colour, 2767
cinnamon teal, bird, in colour, 3144
Team Race, game, 3596
Teapot, reason for keeping hot a long
  time, 5567
why is there a hole in the lid? 5000
Tear (physiology), what it is, 6603
why are tears salt? 1921
glands in eye which make them, 3664
  See also Crying
Teasel, plant, description, 5021, 205
Fuller's: see Fuller's teasel
flower, in colour, 5143
Tea That Never Came, story, 4854
Teeny-Weeny, picture to poem, 2207
Tees, River, bridges at Middlesbrough,
  556
Teeth, what they are for, and how to
  care for them, 1929, 1929, 1931
what makes our teeth chatter when we
  are cold? 4996
why cannot we grow a third set of
  teeth? 4760
why does a tooth ache? 5980
Tegner, Esaias, Swedish poet, 4942
Teguexin: see Teju lizard
Tegula River, South Africa, riders
  crossing, in Natal National Park, 3182
Tehran, capital of Persia, 6390
wartime conference at, 6390
scenes, 6394–99
Teju lizard, or teguexin, 4496, 4493
Tel Aviv, town of Israel, 6289, 6277
Telea polyphemus of U.S.A., moth,
  caterpillar, in colour, 6210
Telectrograph, what it is, 855
Telegrams, game, 2118
Telegraph, its story, 1469, 1599
five-needle, 1841
Hughes's type-printing telegraphy, 1844
pictures sent by, 1476, 1475
utility of, 854
picture series, 1471–75
  See also Wireless
Telegraph cable, its story, 1600
transatlantic, between Scotland and
  Canada, 1603
picture story, 1604–08
ship that laid Atlantic cable, 1581
Telegraph pole, why has it a little roof
  on the top ? 5493
what are the little white cups on the
  telegraph poles ? 5980
Telegraph printing machine, in newspaper office, 2405
Telegraph wires, why do they hum ?
  4130
why, from a train, do the telegraph
  wires seem to go up and down ? 6866
Tel-el-Amarna, Egypt, Akhnaton builds
  new Egyptian capital, 6813
relics of Egyptian kings found, 6881
steps leading to well, 6878

Tel-el-Kebir, battle of, British victory
  over Arabi Pasha, (1882), 6892
Telemachus, an Asiatic monk who tried
  to stop the gladiatorial shows at Rome,
  1386, 1393
Telemachus, in Greek mythology, story
  in the Odyssey, 5304, 5306
Teleosaurus, fossil, 1507
Telephone, its story, 1725, 1841, 1965
automatic, how it works, 1971
exchange's working, 1965
Bells' invention, 22
cables, 1967
coaxial cable, 1966, 1972
Edison's improvements, 1846
long-distance calls, how made, 1966
manual exchange, how it works, with
  pictures, 1965
microphone first used by Clerac, 1844
range of conversation, 1728
receiver, 1965
Reis's invention the first, 1841
relay system, 1966
selenium used for transmitter, 6854
TIM, clock which gives time, 3168
trunk call, 1971
United States has more than rest of
  world together, 3681

Pictures of Telephones
automatic telephone, diagrams, 1725,
  1974
Bell opening first New York–Chicago
  line, 1843
Bell's first telephone instrument, 1841
diagram of automatic exchange, 1727
Dom Pedro of Brazil astonished, 1847
dynamos and cables at a London
  exchange, 4384
how the exchange works, 1965–70
man working on lines in a tunnel, 4384
operators at overseas exchange, 1973
plastic telephones being made, 4012–13
Reis's invention, 1841
switchboard, 1969
testing line, 1968
  See also Wireless
Teleprinter, what it is, 1470, 1472
room at the Central Telegraph Office,
  1471
Telescope, biggest at Mount Palomar,
  California, 3976
Galileo the first to use it in astronomy,
  1885, 3609
Huygens's twelve-foot telescope, 3613
principle of, accidentally discovered by
  children, 1885
Lord Rosse's, 4861
Mount Palomar dome, California, 3685
telescope of mutiny ship Bounty, 4861
Teleuto spore, what it is, 1578
Television, story of, 108, 1476, 5108
Eurovision network, 5109
experiments at Broadcasting House, 5110
ultra-short waves necessary, 2346
aerial for outdoor events, 2345
Baird's first set, 2339
control room scenes, 2341
Crystal Palace aerial, 2343
inside of set, 2343
televising of programmes, 5113, 5116,
  5119
viewing in the home, 2345
Television City, west London, 5110
Telford, Thomas, Scottish engineer,
  1584, 2157, 4867
Tell, William, Swiss legendary national
  hero, 529
Switzerland's many monuments to, 4670
pictures, 529, 531
Tell-el-Obeid, excavation of temple
  there, 6885
Teilen shell, 6580
Téllez, Gabriel, or Tirso de Molina,
  Spanish writer of plays, 5059
Telloh, site of the Babylonian Lagash,
  6884
Temperature, Centigrade scale best
  form of measurement, 4835
comparative table for various animals,
  7100
conditions affecting, 2618
dew point, 2865

human body's temperature, 1432, 6465
of the upper air and stratosphere, 5372
what it is and how measured, 5444
Tempest, The, story of Shakespeare's
  play, 1108, 6295
Tempestas, demi-goddess, 3519
Temple, Sir William, English statesman
  and essayist, 1730
Temple, in ancient art, 5375, 5495, 5626
oldest in the world, 5376
temple at Jerusalem, 1241, 1988, 2555
ancient Greek and Roman buildings,
  5505–12
Egyptian temples, 5374, 5381–88
reconstruction of Solomon's Temple,
  2355
temples of the East, 5081–84
  See also Apollo; Diana; Greek art;
  Greek architecture; and so on.
Temple, The, London, Gorboduc, the
  first English tragedy, acted in, 857
origin in time of Knights Templars, 720
Wren's work in, 6244
Temple Bar, Jacobites' heads on, 5691
Wren builds, 4227
Daniel Defoe in the pillory, 1481
views, 4862, 6238
Temple Church, the beautiful round
  church the Normans built, 5868
Temptation, Mount of, view, 3466
Tenby, Pembrokeshire, 2002
mass of millstone grit near, 2006
the harbour, 1462
Tench, fish, member of Carp family,
  4979
in colour, facing 5197
Ten Commandments, 1240, 4901
foreshadowed in the Egyptian Book of
  the Dead, 6891
Tendon, in human body, 1809
Tenerife, largest of the Canary Islands,
  6754
fig tree at Orotava, 1937
Tengbom, Swedish architect, 6612
Teniers, David, the younger, Flemish
  painter, 1422
Old Woman Reading, painting, 3778
Players at Tric-Trac, 3775
The Prodigal Son, 1427
Tennant, Edward Wyndham: see
  Poetry Index
Tennessee, American State, cotton-
  picking, 3693
flag, in colour, 6986
Tennessee Valley, electricity from water
  power, 3675
Tennis, how to play lawn tennis, 3103
Tennis ball, how tennis balls are made,
  4259
Tennis Racket, how it is made, 4260
Tennyson, Alfred, Lord, poet, 3337
description of water crowfoot, 6010
his first railway trip, 2752
his Idylls of the King, 3338, 3340
on Nature, 207, 1065
portrait, 4134
Shiplake Rectory, where he wrote, 3337
Somersby Rectory, his birthplace, 3337
walking with nurse by sea, 3339
  See also Poetry Index
Tenrec, small mammal, 294, 293
Tensile strength, what it means, 1183
Tent, simple tent to make, 3104
the way to put up a bell tent, 2731
Tenterden, Kent, probable birthplace
  of Caxton, 1516
Caxton reading in fields, 1510
Tenthredo, girdled, insect, in colour,
  5714
Tenzing, Sherpa, conqueror of Everest,
  6858
Teonge, Henry, diary kept by, 1850
Terborch, Gerard, Dutch painter, 1428
his paintings, Fatherly Advice, 3778
Helena Van der Schalk, 3538
Lady Reading Letter, 1423
Terebra, shells, 1180
Teredo, or ship-worm, mollusc, damage
  done by boring timber, 6582, 6581
Terence, Roman writer of comedies,
  5427; portrait, 5425
Terminus, Roman god of boundaries,
  2877, 3520
Termite, white ant, 5715, 5721

Tern, species and habits, **3995**
Arctic tern's route of migration, 220–21
characteristic pictures, **2637, 2639, 3997**
egg of Common tern, in colour, **7233**
varieties, in colour, 2897–98, 3022–23
See also Arctic tern
Terpsichore, muse of dancing, **3517**
Terra, mythological goddess, **3514**
Terracotta, used by Ancient Greek
sculptors, **4026**
Terra Nova, Scott's Antarctic expedition ship, **6558, 6555**
Terrapin tortoise, characteristics and
distribution, **4498**
Terrier, breeds of the group, **670**
varieties of breeds, 666–68
Terror, Mount, extinct volcano on an
island in Ross Sea, Antarctica, **6550**
Tertiary Period, description, **1877**
animal life, 10
Teschemacher, Edward, British composer, **1269**
Teschen, town of Poland, **5030**
Testament, New and Old: see Bible
Tester, value of: see old English coins,
7094
Tetanus, anti-toxin treatment, **2628**
microbes that cause, 577
Tethys, mythological goddess, **3529**
Tetmajer, Polish painter, **5029**
Teucer, The, Sir Hamo Thornycroft's
fine sculpture in the Tate Gallery,
4768, 4900
Teutoburger Wald, battle of, defeat of
three Roman legions under Varus by
the German hero Arminius, or Hermann,
4310
Teutons, the people of Northern Europe
speaking the Teutonic language, **4291**
Tewkesbury, town in Gloucestershire,
Norman work in Abbey, **5866**
view of Abbey church, 5879
Texas, American State, harvesting
machines, 3693
flag, in colour, 6986
plant from which magnesium is extracted
from sea-water, 3692
Textiles, inventions that founded industry, **5939**
See also Cotton; Linen; and so on
Thackeray, William Makepeace, English
novelist, satirist, and critic, **2850**
seated in his study, 2847
See also Poetry Index
Thaddaeus, apostle, **6803, 6799**
Thailand: see Siam
Thales, Greek philosopher and astronomer, **672, 6860**; portrait, 3487
first star maps made by him, **3487**
men's thoughts directed away from
themselves, 913
Thalia, muse of comedy, **3517**
Thames, English river on which London
stands, 211
Dutch fleet sails up it, 1212
length, **7083**
Rotherhithe tunnel, 4377
view below Tower Bridge, 1219
view at Oxford, 2499
Thames Conservancy, flag, in colour, 6982
Thames House, Millbank, London,
designed by Sir Frank Baines, **4230**
Thames Tunnel, Sir Marc Isambard
Brunel builds, **5946**
how Brunel got idea of tunnelling, 5941,
5947
its construction, 6217
Thanatopsis, by W. C. Bryant, first
American poem to live, **4202**
Thanatos, Greek god of death, **3532**
Thane, Anglo-Saxon title, conferred on
merchants trading overseas, **3382**
Thank God Harbour, Greenland, winter
quarters of explorers, **6433**
Thaulow, Fritz, Norwegian painter and
etcher, his painting, The Halt, 3403
Thaw, does the thaw burst the water-pipes? **2172**
Thaxter, Celia: see Poetry Index
Thayer, Abbott, American figure and
landscape painter, paintings by him,
3289, 3295
Theatre, ancient Greek and Roman
theatres, **5502**
first English one built near London in
Shakespeare's youth, **857**

how to make a shadow theatre, **869**
Shakespearean, **4476**
modern theatres, 6615
Thebes, Ancient Egyptian religious
centre, **6813**
ancient temples and tombs, **5379, 6888**
temple by Queen Hatshepset at, **6890**
wall painting from, 6879
Theine, substance in tea, **2173**
Themis, mythological goddess of justice,
3517, **6950**
Themistocles, Athenian statesman and
admiral, **890, 3123, 889**
Theodosius II, Emperor, peace terms
dictated by Attila, **2154**
Theophrastus, Greek philosopher, **233**
Theotocopuli, Domenico: see El Greco
There was a frog, rhyme and picture,
4186–87
There was a jolly miller, rhyme, music,
and picture, **4061**
There was a little woman, rhyme,
music, and picture, 2830
There was an old woman, rhyme, 232
There were three little kittens, rhyme,
music and picture, 5799
Therm, definition of: see Units of
Measurement, **7096**
Thermionic valve, in wireless, invented
by Sir Ambrose Fleming, **6726, 2091**
Thermo-dynamics, Kelvin's studies, **6314**
meaning of, 5441
Thermometer, Galileo's first thermometer, **5445**
use on barometer, **5200**
Thermopylae, battle of, heroic stand
of small Greek force against the Persians in 480 B.C., **3123, 5126**
painting by J. L. David, 3121
Theseum, Athens, 5510
Theseus, duke of Athens, character in
A Midsummer Night's Dream, **6294**
Thespiae, Ancient Greek town, **4272**
Thessaloniki, port of Greece, **5768**
White Tower, 5777
See also Salonika
Thi, Egyptian architect, **5379**
Thickback, fish, **5105, 5105**
Thick-knee, or Stone curlew, bird,
characteristics and food, **3873**
Thicknesse, Philip, 5698
Thieves and the Cock, fable, **4245**
Thigh-bone, longest and strongest in
body, **1695**
Thimble, why has a tailor's thimble
no top? **5980**
Thimmonier, Barthélemy, sewing-machine inventor, **5946**
Things to Make and Do: the subjects
dealt with will be found in their proper
places in the index
Thirst, why it is so terrible, **2182**
Thirteenth Man, story, 534
Thistle, species and uses, **4414, 4542,
5266**
seed dispersed by wind, **948**
several species, 4412, 4541, 5761
various species, in colour, 4288, 4420,
4664, 5143–44, 5393–96, 6127
Thomas, Dr. Calvin, on Goethe, **4698**
Thomas, Dylan, English poet, 4084
Thomas, Edith M.: see Poetry Index
Thomas, Havard, English sculptor, **4768**
Thomas, Philip, English poet, 4082
Thomas, St., apostle, **6803, 6799**
Thomas, Sidney Gilchrist, his steel discoveries, **4103**; portrait, 4102
Thomas à Kempis, German Augustinian
monk, **1389, 1385**
Thomas de Cantelupe, St., shrine, in
Hereford Cathedral, **5873**
Thompson, Francis, English poet, **4079**
See also Poetry Index
Thomson, Hugh, his painting of Shake-speare's " Whining Schoolboy," 983
Thomson, James, Scottish poet and
writer of plays, **1262, 2102**
portraits, 1261, 2103
See also Poetry Index
Thomson, James: see Poetry Index
Thomson, Sir Joseph John, English
scientist, **4349, 6313**
tube used to discover electron, 2713
Thomson, Robert William, air-filled
tyre patent taken out, **1166**

Thomson, William: see Kelvin, Willia
Thomson, Lord
Thor, god of thunder, **594**
Thursday gets 'ts name from, **2775, 52**
tries to drain horn, 5223
Thordsson, Sturla, Norse saga collect
and historian, **4938**
Thoreau, Henry David, American writ
on natural history subjects, **4332**
Thorgilsson, Ari, Norse saga collect
and historian of 11th century, **4938**
Thorium, an element, **4222**
Thorn, Polish town where Copernic
was born, **3488**
Thorn apple, bursting seed cases, 949
wild fruit, in colour, 3671
Thornback crab, 5477
Thornhill, Sir James, English painte
3860, 5691
Thornycroft, Thomas, his statue
Boadicea, 891
Thornycroft, Sir Walter Hamo, Englis
sculptor, **4768**
his sculptures: Teucer, 4900
The Mower, 4772
Thorpe, John, English architect, **6240**
Thorwaldsen, Bertel, Danish sculpto
Charity, and Cupid and Venus, 52
Greek sculpture restored by him, 40
Jesus Christ, 4655
Thoth, Egyptian deity, 316
Thothmes III, Ancient Egyptian kin
6890, 4899
mummy found at Der-el-Bahari, 687
Thought, brain needs more blood whe
thinking, 1199
can we measure the speed of thought
6227
can we think about things that do n
interest us? 929
can we think without words? 560
do animals think? 1049
freedom of thought essential, 4210
where does a thought come from? 813
as expressed by three artists, 4033
sculpture by Rodin, 4650
Thoughts, Pascal's beautiful book, 445
Thousand and One Nights The, wonder
ful collection of stories, 5676
tomb of the Lady Zobeide still exists a
Baghdad, 5624
Thrale, Mrs., friend of Dr. Johnson, 197
Thrasher, mocking bird, 3025
Thread-like chorda, seaweed, 3416
Thread-like dumontia, seaweed, 3413
Three-bearded rockling, fish, in colour
5098
Three Bears, story, with picture, 661
Three-branched polypody, in colour, 179
Three children sliding on the ice, nurser
rhyme. picture, and music. 4803
Three Cups of Cold Water, story, 6955
Three Dimensional Film, what is it? 241
Three Dimensions, what it means, 340
Three Fishers, fable, 6957
Three Japanese Mirrors, story, 6319
Three Jovial Welshmen, rhyme an
picture, 5548
Three Kings, picture to poem, 3933
Three Little Pigs, story, with picture, 2
Three Musketeers story written b
Alexandre Dumas, 4457
Three Poor Men, story, 1652
Three-spotted wrasse, fish, in colour, 509
Three-toed salamander, amphibian, 474
Three-toed sloth, or Ai, 2271
Three Wise Men of Gotham, rhym
and picture, 5049
Threlkeld, Sir Lancelot, concealed Si
Henry Clifford from vengeance of Hous
of York, 465
Thresher, fox-shark's nickname, 5228
Threshing machine, cutting and thresh-
ing wheat, 1571
Thrift, or Sea-pink, 5518
flower, in colour 5641
Thrincia: see Hawk-bit
Thrips, insect pest, which attacks corn,
5722, 5721
leathery thrips, in colour, 5713
Throat, why does a lump rise in my
throat when I cry? 2665
Throne of Venus, fine Greek sculpture
now in Rome, 4144
sculptured figures from, 4146–47

Trade Winds, effect on climate, **2620**
effect on rainfall, **2744**
what the force behind them is, **2416**
why so called, **5321**
what are the trade winds? **2416**
Trafalgar, battle of, Nelson's great
victory, **1455**
Nelson on the Victory, **1450**
ships of Nelson's fleet, **1450**
signal book used, **4859**
Trafalgar, Cape, Spain, **5412**
Trafalgar Square, London, **4228, 1218**
Traffic, safety rules, **6849**
how traffic-signals work, **6862-64**
model traffic roundabout for children,
6849
Tragacanth, how it is obtained, **2938**
uses of gum, **2690, 2938**
plant, in colour, **2685**
Tragedy, Gorboduc the first English
tragedy, **857**
what it is, **6159**
Tragopan, horned, bird of pheasant
family, **4251**
Traherne, Thomas: see Poetry Index
Trailing azalea, description, **5518**
flower, in colour, **5641**
Trailing rose, what it is like, **4780**
flower, in colour, **4908**
Trailing St. John's wort, flower, in
colour, **4286**
Train, general account of trains and
railways in Britain, **3943**
picture story, **4067, 4191**
wireless conversation from one, **1728**

Wonder Questions

does it take more power to stop a train
than to start it? **1182**
when I walk in a moving train, do I
move faster than the train? **442**
why does a train make a noise in a
tunnel? **6854**
why does a train not run off the lines
when rounding curves? **6729**
why does the whistle change as the
train comes nearer? **2296**

Pictures of Trains

diagram and chart of a Western Region
engine, **3946-47**
development in 19th century, **1583**
early steam coach, **2745**
how it picks up and delivers mail, **4634**
leaving Windsor station in Canada, **3205**
series of pictures, **4067-4076, 4191-4200**
why it keeps on rails, **6729**
See also Railway; Railway engine;
and Underground Railway
Trained bands, leaving London to fight
the King, **4007**
flags of London trained bands, **4007**
Train-ferry, Harwich-Zeebrugge route,
5648
Traitor's Gate, river gate of the Tower
of London, picture, **4860**
Traitor who Became Loyal, story, **3370**
Trajan, Roman emperor and soldier,
2877
his column at Rome, **3284, 4404, 5503**
Arch of Trajan, **1779**
fragment from monument in Forum,
Rome, **1781**
Plotina, his wife, **2878**
portrait, **2878**
Trajan's Column, **1782**
Trajan's Forum, reconstruction, **5501**
Trakl, Georg, Austrian poet, **4700**
Transfiguration, picture by Giovanni
Bellini, **940**
Transformation tables, 7095
Transit Circle, what it is, **5121**
Transmission, in mechanics, **6349**
Transparent trumplet anemone, flower,
in colour, **1555**
Transport, before railways came, **2745**
nation's wealth increased by organised,
5885
reorganisation of transport in Europe
by United Nations, **6483**
rivers as carriers, **2494**
Transporter Bridge, at Middlesbrough,
556
Trans-Siberian Railway, bridge over
Yenisei River, **6028**
Transistor, what it is, **4136**

Transvaal, South Africa, 3188, 5718
arms, in colour, **4985**
City Hall, Johannesburg, **3189**
Hartebeestport Dam, **5238**
lion and motorists in National Park, **3182**
National Park scene, **3182**
Union Buildings at Pretoria, **3189**
See also Rand
Transylvania, province of Rumania,
5770
Trapani, seaport in Sicily, **4915**
Trap ball, game, **3596**
Trap-door spider, nest, **5598, 5593**
Trapezium, how to find area, **7098**
Trapezoid, how to find area, **7098**
Travancore, State of India, Museum at
Trivandrum, **2950**
Traveller and the Heron, story, **4611**
Travellers and the Axe, fable, **4245**
Traveller's dinner, problem, **4467**
Traveller's joy, plant, **948**
flower, in colour, **4288**
Traveller's tree, description, **3052, 3053**
Trawling, deep-sea, **5730-31**
Treacle Bible, what it is, **5734**
Treasure and Where It Lay, story, **6080**
Treasure Island, R. L. Stevenson's
book of adventure, **3711**
Treasure of Rhampsinitus, story, **3622**
Treasury, First Lord of, became leader
of Cabinet in time of George I, **1328**
Trebonianus, Gallus, Roman emperor,
portrait, **2879**
Tree, flowering trees, **4037, 4151**
life-story of one, **3541**
timber-yielding trees, **3785, 3905**
beauty trees, **4037**
coconut palm, its many uses, **2070**
curious way of measuring a tree, **2235**
how to make paper Christmas trees,
6669
how to measure the height of a tree,
and picture, **1246**
in Carboniferous Age, **10**
in Cretaceous Age. **1636**
moss trees in Devonian Age, **1136**
rings of growth, **3544**
signifies garden of Paradise in early
Christian art, **446**
their strength, **84**
uses of, **3542, 5350**

Wonder Questions

how can we tell its age? **4996**
what is the oldest in the world? **6467**
what makes the roots of a tree grow
downward? **2416**
why does a tree grow straight? **4394**
why does a tree grow upward? **64**
why does a tree stop growing? **3652**
why does bark grow on a tree? **5980**
why does lightning strike trees? **2542**
why do branches grow sideways? **1679**
why do some trees flower? **4022**
why do the leaves of the aspen tree
always shake? **3396**
why do trees not die in winter ? **4763**

Pictures of Tress

fine avenue, **3785**
in summer and in winter, **1917**
motor-car in trunk, **456**
power while growing, diagrams, **2417**
root structure, diagram, **459**
timber, picture-story, **5351-62**
timber-yielding trees, **3905-16**
types of root, **456, 2372**
varieties, series, **4151-61**
See also Forest; Timber; and
specific names of trees
Tree Creeper, bird, **3018**
bird, in colour, **3021**
egg, in colour, **7234**
Tree-frog, characteristics, **4744**
Tree kangaroo, picture, **2396**
Tree mallow, what it is like, **5764**
flower, in colour, **5643**
Tree of heaven, winged seeds, **947**
Tree pipit, bird, in colour, **3021**
Tree-shrew, or Tupaia, **296**
Trees in the orchard puzzle, **6300**
Tree sparrow, in colour, **2768**
Tree-wasp, in colour, **5714**
nests, **5834**
Trefoil, grown for food, **2188**
bird's foot, flower, in colour, **4420**
sulphur-coloured, flower, in colour, **4418**

Trefoil, heraldic charge, 928
Trelawny, Edward John, friend of
Shelley, **2599**
Trench, machine used in digging, **3034**
Trench Richard C.: see Poetry Index
Trengganu, Federation of Malaya, **3423**
flag, in colour, **6983**
Trent, Jesse Boot, Lord, founder of
Boots the chemists, **4110, 4102**
Trent, Council of (1545 to 1563), con-
demned the Reformation, **4794**
Trent Affair, American Civil War inci-
dent, **6550**
Trent and Mersey Canal, inland water-
way, **4867**
barge floating into lift, **4880**
Trenton, battle of, Washington on
horseback, **1642**
Treny, Kochanowski's poems, **5027**
Trer Ceiri, ancient camp in North Wales,
7016
Trespass, law as to people and animals,
4904
children looking at trespass board, **4901**
Trevelyan, George Macaulay, British
historian, **3828, 4500**
portrait, **3827**
Treves, or Trier, German city, Lieb-
frauenkirche, **5991**
Roman remains, **4428**
Trevithick, Richard, English inventor,
builder of steam locomotive, **2752,
2836, 3212**
at work on his engine, **2755**
on his locomotive, **2749**
railway set up in Euston Square, **2747**
Triaenodes, insect, in colour, **5713**
Triangle, how to find area, **7098**
Triassic Age, what the world was like
then, **1381**
animal life, **10, 1381, 1383**
fossil remains, **1383**
Tribune of the People, name given to
Mirabeau, **650**
Triceratops, prehistoric monster. **1636**
Trichia fungus, spores exposed to wind,
947
Tricks, balance tricks with pencils, **128**
blowing a brick over on a table, **1867**
card that will not fly away, **1493**
card which somersaults, **2484**
chair that comes to you, **1944**
clever paper catch, **2117**
coin in the handkerchief, **5438**
coin suspended, **5194**
coin that cannot be moved, **1493**
coin tricks, with pictures, **2609**
conjuring trick with nuts, **4951**
cut string that does not fall, **3847**
cutting a pear in two, **6302**
cutting the magic string, **3847**
dumb show tactics, **2484**
feeling the pips, **999**
floating ball and a lively apple, **3232**
for odd half-hours, **2117**
good match, **2235**
guessing a chosen card, **999**
gymnastic exercise, with picture, **253**
how to make a bottle blow out a candle,
1123
how to make a magic knot, **5684**
lifting a bottle with a straw, **2117**
magic touch, **1000**
magic tumbler, **3600**
making a candle that can be eaten, **631**
mysterious bottle of water, **754**
mysterious cricket bat, **3474**
mysterious moving plate, **1123**
mysterious paper purse, **1250**
mystery of the suspended knife, **1991**
pulling a match through another, **3597**
reading the pack, **999**
ring and coin trick, **3600**
robbers and the soldiers, **5068**
simple gymnastic trick, **2112**
simple tricks with a penny, **875**
some hints and tricks to try, **1493**
spotting a touched card, **2484**
stool trick, **5316**
to try on friends, **6671**
trick stick, **1493**
tricks to do with matches, **1624**
tricks with a box of matches, **1496**
tricks with figures, **2114**

Wright, Judith, Australian poet, 4206
Wright, Orville, American inventor with his brother of the first successful engine-driven aeroplane, 24, 21
speed of his biplane's propeller, 6346
with brother in workshop, 23
Wright, Wilbur, American airman, invented the first successful engine-driven plane with his brother Orville, 24, 21
with brother in workshop, 23
Wrinkle, how wrinkles come, 1430, 5370
Wrist, beat of heart usually tested by pulse in, 1196
bones described, 1694
muscles, 1810

WRITING

The following are actual headings of the chapters on Writing in the section of School Lessons
Learning to Write, 130
Keeping a Diary, 259
Without Mother's Help, 386
Making a Cinema, 511
Films and Advertising, 634
Copying the Nursery Rhymes, 759
Questions and Answers, 879
The Twins Give a Party, 1001
Big and Small Letters, 1127
The Poetry Books, 1252
Letters to Granny, 1375
electric transmission of writing, 1470
how to do magic writing, 6671
how to keep a secret in writing, 383
how to write with ink on wood, 2731
methods and mediums in early times, 1292, 2034
sent by wireless, 855
who began writing? 921
why is it hard to write on glass? 6599
why will a pen and ink write on paper better than on a slate? 2921
ancient Egyptian and other kinds, 685
signs on rocks made long ago, 921
stone tablet from Nineveh, 2033
See also Hieroglyphics
Writing and Reading, sculpture by Falconet, 4650
Writing Paper, how are the marks put into writing paper? 1552
Wroclaw, or Breslau, textiles town of Poland, 5030
Wrought iron, melting point: see melting point of metals, 7094
Wrybill, plover of New Zealand, 3874
Wryneck, bird, characteristics, 3256
picture, 3257; in colour, 3024
Wuchang, Chinese town, 6501
Wuchow, Chinese town, 6501
Wulfenite, mineral, 1304
Wurtemberg, German State, an inn, 4436
map, in colour, 7111
Würzburg, city in northern Bavaria, 6372
Neumünster, 6365
Wuthering Heights, Emily Brontë's powerful story, 3583, 4078
Wyant, Alexander H., American landscape painter, 3287
Looking toward the Sea, painting by him, 3291
Wyatt, Sir Thomas: see Poetry Index
Wych elm, how it differs from common elm, 3786
Wycherley, William, English dramatist, 1611
Wycliffe, John, English religious reformer, 118, 956, 1076, 7076
Morning Star of Reformation, 3759
sends out preachers, 119
The trial of Wycliffe, by Ford M. Brown, 119
Wye, river of England and Wales: Chepstow Castle, 961
source near Aberystwyth, 1461
Symond's Yat, 1713
Wykeham, William of, bishop of Winchester; at work on Winchester Cathedral, 950
Wyllie, W. L., modern English painter, Pool of London, painting, 5137
Wyoming, American State, flag, in colour, 6987

X

Xanthos, his Harpy Tomb, 5500
Xanthus, figures from tomb in Acropolis of, in Lycia, 4032
Xavier, St. Francis, Spanish Jesuit missionary, 1390, 5738, 6618
portrait, 1385
Xenarescus, single-horned, beetle, in colour, 6336A
Xenon gas, an element, 4222
Xenophanes, Greek philosopher, 3650, 5182
Xenophon, Athenian soldier and historian, 1889
his army in sight of sea, 1886
Xerxes, Persian king, 4027, 6386, 6816
battle with Leonidas, 3123
fleet defeated at Salamis, 890
crossing Hellespont, 6811
Xiphias, sword-fish's classical name, 5230
X-rays, story of, 2585
electrons in tube, 2713
form of electric waves, 108
use in mass-radiography, 1551
discovery by Rontgen, 6311
Coolidge tube, 2585
pictures of X-ray apparatus, 2585-93
pictures taken by X-rays, 2588-92

Y

Yacht Clubs, flags, in colour, 6992
Yachting: see Sailing
Yak, animal, characteristics, 1155, 1159
Yakutsk, autonomous republic of U.S.S.R., 6010
Yale University, New Haven, Connecticut, 3684
view, 3683
Yallingup Cave, Western Australia, stalactites, 6857
Yalta, Crimea, meeting-place of Churchill, Roosevelt, and Stalin, view, 6028
Yam, food plant, 1436, 2442
plant, 2441; in colour, 2685
Yanbu, small Arabian port, 6264
Yangtse Kiang, Chinese river, 2494, 6501, 6502, 6512
Yapock, water opossum, 2394
Yard, measure, origin, 4834
Yare, Norfolk river, Wherries, painting by Wilson, 2304
Yarkand, trading centre in Chinese Turkestan, 6511
Yarmouth, town and fishing port of Norfolk, 343
Yarrell's blenny, fish, in colour, 5098
Yarrow, flower, 5019
Yates, Peter, British poet, 4084
Yatung, town of Tibet, 6512
Yawning, what makes us yawn? 6604
why is yawning infectious? 5126
Yeames, William Frederick, British artist, his pictures: Dawn of Reformation, 119
Foundation of St. Paul's School, 1080
When did you last see your father? 4207
Year, gradual lengthening of, 6547
how its length is determined, 268
length on other worlds, 3118
Yeast plant, its story, 1440
sugar turned into alcohol and carbon dioxide by it, 699, 1440
cells, 697
Yeats, William Butler, Irish poet and writer of plays, 4080; portrait, 4077
See also Poetry Index
Yellow, why does a thing go yellow with age? 2919
Yellow baboon, 164
Yellow-backed duiker, animal, 1403
Yellow balsam, what it is like, 5520
Yellow bugle: see Ground pine
Yellow bunting: see Yellowhammer
Yellow chamomile: see Ox-eye chamomile
Yellow cress, flower, in colour, 6129
Yellow deadnettle, or archangel, member of Labiate family, 4782
flower, in colour, 4906
Yellow fever, cause and remedy discovered, 2626
Gorgas's successful fight at Panama, 4869

Major Reed saluting men who offered their lives, 370
stegomyia under microscope, 1916
Yellow figwort, flower, in colour, 5143
Yellow fleabane, flower, in colour, 5141
Yellow-fronted manakin, bird, in colour, 3141
Yellowhammer, bird, 2904
feeding habits, 6867
bird, 2892; in colour, 2897
egg, in colour, 7233
nest and eggs, 2903
Yellow-headed broadbill, in colour, 3143
Yellow-horned poppy, 5760
flower, in colour, 5644
Yellow iris, or Corn flag, 2689, 6008
flower, in colour, 6130
Yellow jacket: see Jarrah
Yellow loosestrife, what it is like, 6010
flower, in colour, 6129
Yellow marsh saxifrage, 5892
flower, in colour, 6127
Yellow meadow rue, member of Buttercup family, 5889
flower, in colour, 6127
Yellow monkey-flower, 6011
in colour, 6130
Yellow mountain saxifrage, 5519, 5621
Yellow mountain violet, 5518
Yellow oat grass, 2186, 3308
Yellow ox-eye: see Corn marigold
Yellow pimpernel, what it is like, 4781
flower, in colour, 4906
Yellow-rattle, description, 4416
flower, in colour, 4419
large, flower, in colour, 4663
Yellow River: see Hwangho
Yellow Sea, arm of the China Sea, 6501
Yellow skulpin, fish, in colour, 5100
Yellow spot: see Eye
Yellow Star of Bethlehem, 4780
flower, in colour, 4908
Yellowstone Park, American national park, geyser and hot springs, 3808
Yellow vetchling, what it is like, 4416
flower, in colour, 4417
Yellow wagtail, bird, in colour, 3022
Yellow warbler, bird, in colour, 3262
Yellow water-lily, 6007
flower, in colour, 6129
Yellow-weed: see Dyer's rocket
Yellow woolly opossum, 2389
Yellow-wort, what it is like, 5268, 5267
Yemen, State of Arabia, 6265
flag, in colour, 6991
Yenisei River, Central Siberia, 6014
Yeoman of the Guard, painting by Millais, 2556
Yeomen of the Guard, what are the? 5620
Yeovil, St. John's Church, 1713
Yerba maté, Paraguay tea, 7034
Yew tree, description and uses, 3789
why so many in churchyards? 5491
fruit, in colour, 3667
tree, leaves, and flowers, 3547
Yezo: see Hokkaido
Yokohama, chief port of Japan, 6622
almost destroyed by earthquake, 6622
opened to foreign trade, 6620
Yoritomo, the first of the Japanese Shoguns, 6618
tomb of, at Kamakura, 6622
York, historic capital of Yorkshire, 5872, 6240
Constantine proclaimed emperor, 2883
Mysteries of York, 857
Roman relics, 590, 6732

Pictures of York

arms, in colour, 4991
Guildhall, 6252
Micklegate Bar, 6246
Saint Mary's Abbey, 963
the Shambles, 843
view of the walls, 1833
York Minster, 5875, 5881
Yorkshire, largest English county, 214
description of the moors, 468
Yorkshire terrier, dog, 668
Yosemite National Park, U.S.A., sequoia trees, 3806
Lower Yosemite Fall, 2500
Vernal Falls, 3807

Young, Andrew, British poet, **4084**
Young, Sir Hilton: see Poetry Index
Young, **Dr. Thomas**, British physicist and Egyptologist, **5817, 6874**
Young, **Sir William**, architect who planned the War Office, **4230**
Young Genius, picture to poem, 1719
Young Pretender, attempts to gain throne of England, **1214**
Youth, its optimism, **3460**
Springtide of Life, sculpture by W. R. Colton, 4771
Youth Hostels, what are they? **61**
Youth Listens to Music of Love, painting by J. M. Strudwick, 3528
Youth of Hereward the Wake, story and picture, **4735**
Ypres, Belgian city, **1708, 6371**
Cloth Hall Tower and cathedral, 5657
Menin Gate, 5657
Yser, river of Belgium, **5648**
Yturbide, Augustine de, Mexican patriot, **7022**
Yuan-shih-kai, first president of Chinese Republic, **6504**
Yucatán, State of Mexico, ancient Maya remains, **7025**
Indian mother and child, 7029
Yucca, plant, 1070
Yudhishthira, story of, **660**
Yugoslavia, country in south-east Europe, **4555**
Balkan Alliance with Greece and Turkey, **5768**
formation, **1710**
flags, in colour, **6991**
people and scenes, 89, 4562–63, 4566
map, in colour, 7113
map of physical features, 4557
Yukon, river of Canada and Alaska, **1404**
Yukon Territory, **2196**
arms, in colour, 4985
Yunnan, Chinese province, **6500, 6501, 6502, 6509**

Z

Zadir Shah, King of Afghanistan, **6392**
Zadkine, Ossip, Russian sculptor, **4896**
Zagreb, formerly Agram, Yugoslavia, **4556**, 4562–63
Zama, battle of, between Scipio and Hannibal, **4795**
Zambesi, South African river, **6742**
explored by Livingstone, **3002**
Victoria Falls, **3312**
view above Victoria Falls, 2499
Victoria Falls, 2500, 3313

Zambesi Bridge, great bridge which carries the Cape-to-Cairo railway over the gorge near Victoria Falls, **548**
pictures of its building, 557
Zamosc, Poland, town hall, **5036**
Zanzibar, **British East African protectorate, 3315**
British destroying last strongholds of slavery, 2079
British resident's flag, in colour, 6984
Universities' Mission Cathedral, 3322
Zarco, Joao Gonçalves, Portuguese navigator, **772**
Zarephath, village to which Elijah went, **2481**
Zealand, largest Danish island, **5148**
Zealand, Netherlands, province unites with Holland, **5527**
villagers in church, 529
Zebra, **1899, 1895, 1897**
Zebra shark, of Indian Ocean, **5228**
Zeebrugge, Belgian North Sea port, **5648**
Zebu, Indian humped cattle, **1154**
Zeila, port of British Somaliland, **3318**
Zeno, Greek philosopher, **3124**, 3119
Zephyr, Psyche and Zephyr, sculpture by Harry Bates, 5579
Zephyrus, mythological name for west wind, **3519**
Zeppelin, Count Ferdinand, German inventor, **25, 4448**
Zeppelin airships, raids during First World War, **1710**
pictures, 1710
Zero (absolute), point at which heat ceases to exist, **5318**
Zeromski, Stephen, Polish novelist, **5029**
Zeta Cancri, triple star, in different years, 3851
Zeus, god of Ancient Greece, **3514**
famous statues, 4142, 4272
temple at Olympia, 4028, 5497
figures from temple, 4023, 4031
See also Jupiter
Zhukovsky, Basil, Russian translator of Western poetry, **4816**
Ziggurat, curious pyramidal towers of Babylonians, **5376**
Zimbabwe, Great, Southern Rhodesia, ruins of early African civilisation, **3312**
Zimmerman, Ernst, Come Unto Me, painting, 5435
Zinc, Australia's production, **2570**
British production, **6004**
Canada's production, 2324
conductivity: see melting points of metals, **7094**
tensile strength, **7094**
Zinc-blende, mineral, 1302

Zincite, mineral form of zinc ore, 1303
Zinnia, double, flower, 6383
Zion, Mount, Holy Land, 3465
Zircon, crystal found in granite, 1301
Z M C 2, American metal airship, in hangar, 4447
Zodiac, constellations of, **2993**
what is the Zodiac? **6344**
Zoetrope, Horner's invention, **6703**
Zog, Albanian ruler deposed by Italians, **5776**
Zola, Emile, French writer and humanitarian, **4458**
Zone, of sphere, how to find cubic contents, **7099**
Zoo guess, game and pictures, **755**
Zoo Park, what is it? **3395**
Zoology, Aristotle its founder, **1288**
Zorah, dwelling place of Samson's parents, **1487**
Zorilla, José, Spanish poet, **5059**
Zorille, Cape polecat, **793**, 790
Zorn, **Anders Leonhard**, Swedish landscape and figure painter and etcher, **3398**
his paintings: A Singer, 3401
Fisherfolk of St. Ives, 3403
Zorndorf, battle of, between Russians and Prussians during Seven Years War, **4311**
Zoroaster, ancient Persian philosopher, founder of the Parsee religion, **5675**
Cyrus adheres to his teaching, **6814**
figure, 5077
Zoroastrianism, religion adopted in Persia, **6386**
Zoser, king, Step Pyramid built at Sakkara, Egypt, 3165
Zoutelande, Holland, scene, 5536
Zucchero, Federigo, Italian painter, his portrait of Queen Elizabeth, 1077
Zuloago, Ignacio, Spanish painter, 3400
his painting, The Anchorite, 3404
Zulus, African native race, **3188**, 89
chiefs in leopard skins and feathers, 3193
warriors, practising war dance, 3192
woman having hair dressed, 3193
Zurbaran, **Francisco**, Spanish religious painter of the naturalistic school, **1208**
his pictures: Miracle of St. Hugo, 1311
Saint Bruno and Pope Urban II, 1311
Zürich, Swiss industrial, commercial, and railway centre, **4672**
Zutphen, Holland, battle of, **5535**
Sir Philip Sidney Memorial, 5539
Zuyder Zee, Holland, its reclamation, **5524**
Zwingli, Ulrich, the leader of the Reformation in Switzerland, **4672, 4677**
his teaching, **7077**